Management for Professionals

For further volumes:
http://www.springer.com/series/10101

Gio Wiederhold

Valuing Intellectual Capital

Multinationals and Taxhavens

Springer

Gio Wiederhold
Stanford University
Stanford, CA, USA

ISSN 2192-8096 ISSN 2192-810X (electronic)
ISBN 978-1-4614-6610-9 ISBN 978-1-4614-6611-6 (eBook)
DOI 10.1007/978-1-4614-6611-6
Springer New York Heidelberg Dordrecht London

Library of Congress Control Number: 2013936744

Printed on acid-free paper

Springer is part of Springer Science+Business Media (www.springer.com)

This work is dedicated to the many individuals who have to make sense out of laws, rules, regulations, and conventions covering taxation, and try to generate outcomes that are fair to the enterprises that pay taxes and to the governments that rely on tax revenues.

Preface

Intellectual capital covers the capability of talented employees in modern and innovative enterprises and the intellectual property they generate. Exploitation of these intellectual assets generates the income that businesses need to function and grow. Today, intellectual capital contributes more to modern industry than financial capital does, but its influence on the national economy and global economy is not well understood, and not at all quantified. Rather than discussing intellectual capital in a broad and philosophical way, this book focuses narrowly on its use in multinational corporations.

Valuing intellectual capital properly is a prerequisite for formulating industrial policies, considering how and where jobs may be created, and dealing with issues that are caused when companies shift valuable intangible assets overseas. The invisibility of intellectual capital makes it easy to ignore the driver of modern growth and focus narrowly on financial factors. Once rights to intellectual assets are part of corporate globalization, they are no longer subject to national laws and regulations. Taxhavens have been willing collaborators, enabling multinational corporations to reduce their worldwide taxes greatly, while benefiting from educational and transportation infrastructures paid for by citizens at their home locations. Many offshore countries also provide incentives to grow and create jobs, but are not able to collect taxes subsequently because the earnings wind up in other remote taxhavens.

Tax avoidance is perfectly legal and beneficial for corporations, but when taken to extremes, it has serious consequences for society—both in the USA and in the foreign countries where the companies operate [Johnston:03]. This book explains in clear, understandable terms how legal means for minimizing corporate taxes greatly reduce the government revenue needed for education and public services while they increase the global wealth of corporations and their owners.

Intellectual Capital and Jobs

The public, in the USA and abroad, is affected by the perilous state of the worldwide economy. One concern is the shift of jobs to remote locations [AsprayVM:06]. Politicians take advantage of those concerns by proposing new systems for taxation, which are in turn attacked by their colleagues as hurting the poor, or the middle class, or the rich, or small businesses, or the corporations that are supposed to create jobs. Hosts on TV shows comment on the benefits or faults of the schemes being proposed, but convey little understanding. They invite wise commentators to explain complex alternatives in 5 minute sound bites.

The connection between corporate growth and jobs is a common theme. Helping corporations is supposed to create more jobs. Reducing corporate taxes is supposed to create more jobs. Those workers will buy more goods, causing businesses to prosper. Once these relationship issues are put on a global platform a disconnect becomes clear. Multinationals already enjoy low taxes by using taxhavens. They will create jobs where it is most profitable. Reducing taxes in one locality will help the corporation but not the public in that location. Prices of goods will be low if they are allocated to locations where taxes are low.

Corporate Tax Avoidance

Corporate profits are greatly reduced by paying taxes on their earnings. For multinational corporations taxation is an international issue [Doernberg:08]. Conflicts are created when taxation differs in domestic and global contexts [Sullivan:11]. There will always be some large and small countries that can distort an acceptable economic balance by offering freedom or exemption from taxation as inducements to powerful companies. Waiting for global agreements to be signed and faithfully executed by all parties is not a viable option [JollyK:12].

Tax avoidance by corporations affects nations much more than tax avoidance by rich individuals and celebrities. Multinationals employ more than 14 % of the total US workforce, most in well-paying jobs. Corporate accounts represent the majority of capital sheltered in offshore taxhavens. That capital is not just financial; it includes rights to intellectual capital, the basis for profits and growth in modern technological industries [Sveiby:97].

Although methods used by multinational corporations to avoid taxes are made visible in this book, I offer no recipes for corporate tax avoidance. Plenty of consulting firms provide comprehensive advice and support to corporations wanting to reduce their taxes. Their advice is not broadcast to the general public, and the corporations that follow their consultants' advice are not motivated to inform their shareholders or their employees of any specifics.

Audience

This work is intended to be the source for informed discussions on issues of offshoring, international competitiveness, job creation, and changes to tax policies in the global economy. I will show how offshore investments are distorted by US and international taxation policies. A solid understanding can provide a balance of what is rational and achievable. My intent is not to make the reader mad about what is happening. Instead my focus is on the effects of corporate decisions on governmental tax revenues. Whether those governments spend their income wisely or not is not assessed.

This book contains the background information needed by professionals who want to understand the processes of creating value in modern enterprises and the attendant problems. The focus is on multinational corporations and their intellectual capital because of their importance in the global economy. The flexibility of intellectual capital assignments is poorly understood and ignored by experts using outdated concepts from the past when assets and companies had known locations.

Without being able to assign a value to intellectual capital, reformers have little leverage. Today, intellectual capital generates most corporate profits. Businesses depend on creative workers and smart tools. An emphasis on improving education shows awareness of the need to have a capable workforce that can create and maintain attractive and competitive products. The path from creativity to profits and wealth has not been elucidated. Corporations and their owners manage most of the flows, and their objectives may differ from what the workers and their friends expect. Paying little tax by moving intellectual and financial assets offshore increases the value of corporations, but leaves governments and the services the public expects with inadequate resources.

Today, politicians and the public are subjected to piecemeal discussions of the existing tax code and proposed improvements, interwoven with promises of goodies that taxes will pay for and growth that will follow tax reductions. Articles covering globalization and tax issues in newspapers and business magazines are rarely comprehensive and at times naïve.

Presentation

To describe the process, I have created a model multinational company; I call it MNC. MNC represents structures and features found in actual businesses, but having a model avoids dealing with the excruciating detail and confidential facts of specific cases.

MNC, like many of its high-tech peers, resides in California and moves a basket of operations and financial functions offshore. As it grows, it establishes subsidiary operations in Malaysia and India. Two shell companies, one in Palm Island and the other in The Netherlands, manage and hold rights to financial capital and intellectual capital.

MNC does nothing illegal or explicitly immoral. Still, over a period of a dozen years MNC manages to greatly reduce its taxes and accumulate a trove of capital that is best invested in offshore growth. Because MNC is a US-based company, my computations follow US laws and regulations. Substantially identical methods are used by most US high-technology companies, although their structures will be much more complex than those of MNC [GOA:09]. A few public reports that document specific instances of questionable corporate tax payments are cited. Although I present interactions with other countries, I leave implications for non-US situations to other authors. The in-depth presentation of MNC's growth over 25 years documents the interplay of opportunities enabled by well-intentioned policies that enable extreme corporate tax avoidance. In Chap. 9 I can show that MNC is a valid model for the US corporate economy in general and US multinationals specifically. Although the modeled MNC is realistic, its processes are much easier to follow than the convoluted actions of its real-world peers.

The contents, layout, and style chosen for this book are designed for a broad variety of readers. The essence of the material is presented in ten chapters without distracting detail. The technical alternatives of IP valuation are concentrated in Chap. 5. Throughout, references to material in the appendices allow readers who wish to dig deeper to identify specific items of controversy and assess their relative significance in tax avoidance. If readers feel that changes in policy are needed, the factors and choices that appear throughout this book can help determine what is fair, reasonable, and simple enough to apply in practice.

My final recommendation may be surprising, but should make sense by the time the reader has reached that final chapter. That drastic recommendation, R20, supports recent calls to:

Abolish Corporate Taxation

This recommendation will engender interesting discussions among readers. My support for this change has no ideological basis. It surfaced only as I was writing this book, sorting through the many paths to tax avoidance I have encountered. In the end, tax authorities anywhere are unable to deal effectively with the problems presented. As I dissected the global situation and subsequent problems, it became clear that incremental repairs to the US tax system, by enforcing US laws and regulations globally and patching specific loopholes, will not work.

Chapter Organization

This book covers comprehensively the conditions and methods that multinational corporations employ to avoid taxation. The initial eight chapters provide the foundation to discuss their effect on national economies here and abroad.

Chapter 1 is a brief introduction of the corporate cycle of investing in intellectual capital, creating products, earning income, and using the profits for growth.

Chapter 2 provides a detailed example of how intellectual capital is created and exploited; the specific issues will be dealt with one after another.

Chapter 3 defines precisely the categories of intellectual capital.

Chapter 4 deals with international transfers of corporate assets, as rights to IP.

Chapter 5 details the methods used to assign a monetary value to IP.

Chapter 6 presents the capabilities of a variety of taxhavens.

Chapter 7 applies the technical material of Chaps. 3–6 to MNC's taxes.

Chapter 8 shows why it is difficult for the IRS to deal with the issues raised.

Chapter 9 matches MNC to US corporations and multinationals and allows projection of corporate initiatives in the future.

Chapter 10 lists a score of recommendations, from the obvious to the radical, all intended to make taxation fair and supportive of economic growth. The recommendations I make have been expressed by others, but rarely considered in the setting that modern and global industry presents. Even Recommendation 20, to abolish both corporate taxation and the concessions in the tax code to compensate for double taxation, is still relatively simple.

- Appendix A shows MNC's financial statements.
- Appendix B presents some relevant sections of the tax code. Entries are cited as [B.section.subsection.legal-parapgraphs].
- Appendix C covers payment for intellectual capital by royalties.
- The Glossary, Appendix D, presents extensive definitions to aid readers with diverse backgrounds.
- Appendix E deals with tax expenditures, the credits, exemptions, and deductions that reduce corporate taxes significantly.
- Appendix F presents all substantiating formulas and their justifications. The separation keeps the text easy to read. The formulas are referred to as [F chapter. formula number]. The 14 % fraction of US employment by US multinationals shown in this preface is computed per [F0.1].

An extensive Reference section allows the reader to verify issues and follow-up. The references cover a wide range of related topics, such as corporate economics, technology, globalization, taxation and tax avoidance, and the effects of national laws and regulations on all of those issues.

Stanford, CA, USA Gio Wiederhold

Acknowledgment

I have to thank the dozens of professionals who have interacted with me while consulting and unwittingly contributed to the insights presented in this work. A course directed by Jeremy Dent at the London Business School helped me understand valuation issues in general. Discussions with colleagues and students at Stanford University and the University of Arizona Eller School of Business provided focus. I received constructive feedback from George Bachmann, Avron Barr, Nello Biglegue, Ron Burback, Seamus Grimes, Amar Gupta, Jan Heeramaneck, Bob Herriott, Steve Hoffer, Richard Karpinski, Bipin Lekshmanan, Happy Lust, Kathleen Much, Claudia Newbold, Bill Nowicki, Stanley Peters, John Sauter, Hiner Sierras, Marianne Siroker, Crown Spark, David Waxman, Shirley Wardenclyffe, John Wiederhold, Voy Wiederhold, May Wong, many unnamed experts, reviewers of earlier papers on the topic, and, of course, my students. Kathleen Much, the BookDoctor, edited the writing and May Wong, formerly a technology reporter in Silicon Valley for the Associated Press, added thoroughness and clarity. Voy Wiederhold used her experience in teaching and writing user manuals at Stanford to contribute to the book's final presentation. Marianne Siroker helped in locating the many hundreds of references I perused during the writing process.

Any errors and questionable opinions in this book are, of course, solely my responsibility, but I cannot assume the responsibility for business decisions made based on the use of the presented material.

Contents

Chapter 1
International Corporations and Taxes

International trade has more than doubled over the last 25 years and continues to grow [HinesS:09]. More than 70 % of US international trade is now in the hands of multinational corporations, companies that have operations and legal residences in more than one country [Clausing:06]. More than half of the trade of those multinational corporations, and about half of all US international trade, is shipped among their international divisions [Economist:11M]. Intra-firm trading is not as visible as external sales. Trading among corporate divisions has given multinational companies ample opportunities to minimize taxes by adjusting prices for transfers of their goods [Kopits:76]. What's more, establishing fair transfer prices is especially difficult when dealing with intangible goods and assets [Harrison:03]. Those intangible assets are the principal component of today's knowledge-based industries [Nakamura:99].

Tax avoidance is beneficial to a company competing in world markets. In fact, Wall Street investors applaud companies whenever they achieve a lower tax rate. In the USA and other developed nations, paying taxes at the prescribed rates could reduce the profits of a company by more than one third. The more a firm spends on taxes, the less money it has available for shareholder dividends and investments for future growth.

Companies that manage to pay little or no tax by using tax avoidance methods become more competitive than companies that pay higher taxes. Many of the tax avoidance methods described in this book are based on laws and regulations that are intended to make US companies more competitive abroad [GuptaWS:09]. Once those methods are in place, companies can easily exploit them to cover more than what US legislators originally foresaw. Poor valuation of offshored corporate intellectual capital enables a high share of tax avoidance by modern industry.

As multinationals have become quite competent in avoiding taxes where they operate, companies that remain local—and local citizens—have to bear heavier tax burdens for public services. Raising tax rates is politically unpopular, so balancing national budgets with less tax income means curtailing government services to all residents. Yet the services that governments provide from their tax income do not

G. Wiederhold, *Valuing Intellectual Capital: Multinationals and Taxhavens*, Management for Professionals 23, DOI 10.1007/978-1-4614-6611-6_1,

differentiate among their residents, so that companies engaging in substantial tax avoidance still enjoy the same level of benefits of government investments in infrastructure, national defense, and education.

Our model California-based multinational corporation, MNC, illustrates actual tax avoidance methods. It has a much simpler structure than we find in actual situations, but is not too simple. MNC has just five divisions in five countries, whereas having 50 divisions in a dozen locations is typical for a mature multinational corporation. The offshore operational companies set up by MNC are considered to be Controlled Foreign Corporations (CFCs).

MNC, a typical High-technology manufacturing company, has two offshore operating CFCs, one in Malaysia and one in India. MNC's CFC in Johor Baru, Malaysia, called MNC JB, focuses on manufacturing an electronic gadget, the Maniac, designed by MNC in California. The CFC in India, MNC MY in Mysore, helps develop the software embedded in MNC's Maniacs.

In most multinational companies, product creation and manufacturing are split among local and offshore divisions according to local competencies [WGN:10]. There will also be offshore divisions established primarily for tax avoidance. MNC has two of those, CONCH in Palm Island and CAAS in The Netherlands. (None of these names refer to an actual company.)

Just like most large US corporations, MNC employs a Controlled Foreign Holding company (CFH), where it can park assets and shelter them for the long term. Such holdings are typically located in "taxhavens" [Economist:13]. Section 6.2 describes CFH operations. Our MNC has only one CFH, CONCH. MNC also has established a Controlled Financial Intermediary company (CFI), CAAS, a conduit to move financial assets rapidly and undetected among MNC's locales.

Financial advice and services to MNC are provided by an external consulting firm, Associated Tax Advisers (ATA).

"Taxhaven" is a concept in this exposition

The development of those divisions of MNC is covered in Chap. 2, but their relationships are already sketched in Fig. 1.1.

Fig. 1.1 Business divisions of MNC

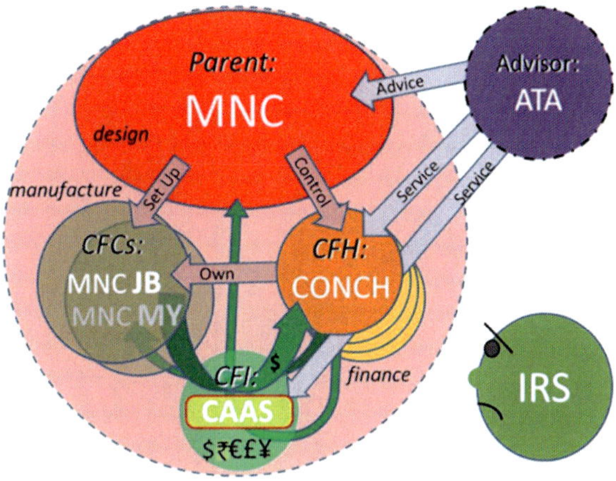

MNC	The parent company in the USA, designs and improves Maniacs
MNC JB	The manufacturer of Maniacs in Malaysia according to MNC's specifications
MNC MY	The software division in India
CONCH	The taxhaven entity that holds financial and intellectual capital and formally controls all offshore sales
CAAS	The conduit company that shuffles funds among MNC's offshore divisions
ATA	The consulting firm that provides advice and services to MNC
IRS	The tax authorities that have to understand what's going on

It is clear that most of the corporate complexity is due to the financial arrangements of MNC.

1.1 Intellectual Capital

High-tech companies depend on intellectual efforts for making valuable products [Sveiby:97]. A business generates income and profits through exploitation of its capital assets by its workforce. Assets can be tangible or intangible. Intangible assets (formally, items we cannot touch) are products of the mind, ranging from inventions to customer lists and trademarks. Intangible assets complement and can dominate a company's tangible assets, such as machines, tools, buildings, and cash [Hulten:06].

Owned assets become property. When ownership can be asserted over intangible assets, they become "intangible property"; an alternate term focusing on the origin of the assets owned is "intellectual property." Both terms are abbreviated as IP, and often the distinction can be ignored. In Chap. 3 the terms and the components of IP are defined in detail.

Table 1.1 Industry sectors that depend on IP

Industry category	Specific issues in international trade	IP characteristic
Electronic consumer products	Manufacturing is mainly assembling parts from Original Equipment Manufacturers (OEMs), often offshore	Assembly know-how is also moving offshore
OEMs making electronic parts and assemblies	Substantial manufacturing is offshore; output is shipped to offshore product manufacturers	Product and IP moves unseen among sites outside the USA
Software product producers	Research and Development is done at multiple sites. R&D is intense, but 80 % of R&D is for improved versions; the manufacturing cost is negligible	Product valuation is arduous, but essential for export as all profits are due to IP
Pharmaceutical companies	Research and Development costs are very high compared to manufacturing costs	There is a long delay before IP generates profits
Financial institutions	Services depend on internal software, employed at worldwide sites, but the contribution of that shared software is ignored in most analyses	Profits are generated by interaction of people and software
Service organizations	Product is not formally protected	Profit is generated indirectly
Consulting firms	The assets are hard to quantify and localize. Know-how is of value	Internal IP is not marketable
Automobile manufacturers	Internal R&D contribution is low per unit sold. OEM suppliers do their own	Costs are visible

The workforce and the IP together make up the "intellectual capital" of a business. In modern businesses they dominate the generation of income. MNC requires little equipment. Rights to intellectual capital can be traded among partners for mutual benefit.

The business scenarios within this book are applicable to industries in any high-tech sector. Whether they specialize in biotechnology or consumer electronics, companies in the real-world benefit from tax avoidance measures. Firms in a wide range of industry sectors practice offshoring. Tax avoidance is easier when the value of their products is based largely on intellectual capital. Consumer product manufacturing companies tend to rely on other companies for components that embody much technical IP, adding valuable integration and marketing competence. In service-oriented companies, the human intellectual capital is crucial. The final entry in Table 1.1, an industry relying much less on IP, provides a contrast.

The common term "IP" is used broadly in this introductory chapter. The focus is on technical IP, but trademarks have valuable IP as well. Chapter 3 categorizes IP into a dozen major types.

1.2 Routine and Nonroutine Earnings

Selling commodity products earns a company what economists refer to as "routine profits." An analysis of nearly 13,000 companies from 1994 to 2000 showed that routine earnings' margins before taxes ranged from 2 to 10 % of sales [HandL:03]. That result comes from formula [F1.1].

Earnings due to IP are referred to as "nonroutine profits." Most earnings in seven of the eight industries shown in Table 1.1 are due to their IP. A company with much IP, a knowledge-based company—if well run—can be very profitable. The average total earnings margin was 25 % of sales for companies that had invested in R&D and advertising [HandL:03]. The earnings margins for successful high-tech firms are much higher than 25 %, but are hard to validate because of poor accounting for expenses associated with generating IP [F1.2].

Nonroutine earnings sustain modern economies through a cycle of public investment in infrastructure and education, and private investment in corporate innovation. MNC's spending on its intellectual capital, namely its staff, R&D, marketing, and their integration, produces the unique product, the Maniac, with a functionality that is highly valued by MNC's customers.

Investing corporate earnings in R&D and advertising creates IP and fosters future corporate growth. The annual growth of companies that can exploit IP averaged 3.4 % versus 0.4 % for the median of S&P companies [Kao:07]. Corporations can grow locally or offshore. Where in the world corporate growth will occur in the future is affected by national and international tax policies. Those issues are addressed in the final chapters of this book.

MNC is an innovative corporation. It is able to earn a high margin on sales of its products because of the intellectual assets it possesses. The two main types of MNC's intellectual assets are the specific competencies of MNC's workforce and its intellectual property (IP), as sketched in Fig. 1.2. The workforce includes MNC's managers, designers, engineers, and marketing staff. MNC's IP are assets that it has legally protected by patents, copyrights, trademark registrations, and by keeping trade secrets. Without specialized competence, a manufacturing company would be able to produce only commodity products. MNC's high-value products earn significantly higher margins, due to nonroutine earnings from its revenues, than commodity products would earn. MNC is characteristic of many successful businesses in the modern world [USCoC:11]. Already in 1998—the dawn of the Information Age—the intangible assets of the S&P 500 made up 85 % of the companies' value [Daum:01].

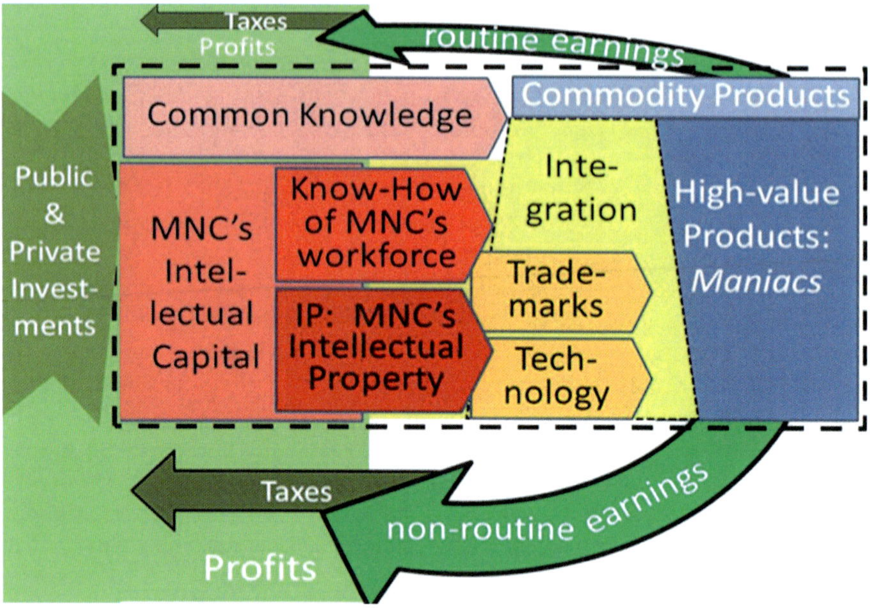

Fig. 1.2 The investment and product cycle of MNC

1.3 Tax Avoidance

Larger companies in the categories shown in Table 1.1 are by nature global and must deal with many taxing jurisdictions. How and where multinationals choose to set up their divisions directly affects their tax rates. IP and the rights to IP are easily moved across international borders, making differences of taxation a consideration. Operating in multiple countries makes tax avoidance harder to understand and detect. Individuals are expected to have one domicile, but businesses can have a legal presence in multiple locales and are more difficult to scrutinize [UScensus:10]. The complexity of international IP transfers makes it easy to move from tax avoidance into tax evasion [Browning:10].

Unless MNC takes advantage of tax-avoidance strategies, it faces taxes on all earnings, both routine and nonroutine. The funds remaining after taxes are paid are available to improve and develop further high-tech products. The taxes collected allow the governments to provide services to the general public and to MNC. A well-functioning public infrastructure keeps MNC effective and operating in a stable environment. A good education system provides the common knowledge MNC's employees need. All of these public contributions help MNC to prosper and grow.

1.4 Summary

Companies that operate internationally can derive many benefits from having distinct, controlled subsidiaries in multiple countries. Such multinational corporations take advantage of differing resources, laws, tax regulations, and enforcement practices in the countries where their divisions establish domicile.

Shifting funds and intangible assets among their divisions is nearly invisible. Most tax avoidance by multinational corporations involves transfers of rights to IP among corporate divisions to benefit from differences in the laws, regulations, and standards of behavior set by a variety of jurisdictions. With ATA's advice, MNC manages to reduce its taxes on its US income from the statutory rate of 35 % to less than 22 % within 10 years, while paying negligible taxes on income from its exports to other countries. The overall tax rate on MNC's worldwide income becomes 11.1 % [F1.3]. Beyond that, MNC can take advantage of tax incentives provided by the US government. Our MNC is still less aggressive than most real-world multinational companies; the average tax rate in 2004 for US multinationals was 2.3 % and is likely much less in 2012, 8 years later [Gibbs:09].

The differences in taxation of US domestic and multinational corporations have a broad impact. Paying 35 % federal tax rather than 2.3 % reduces profits by a third [F1.4]. Companies that remain bound to the USA show lower profits and will pay more for investment capital. US-based companies also accumulate more obligations to their employees.

Let's move on to Chap. 2 to see how our model multinational company, MNC, grew and how it moved into tax avoidance. Observing MNC's history provides the understanding we need to deal with specific issues that enable tax avoidance.

The issues that will be encountered—the scope of intellectual capital, transfer pricing, valuation of IP, the advantages offered by taxhavens, and the governmental inability to deal with taxhavens—need their own chapter. Only then can a responsible summary and recommendations be made.

Chapter 2
Growth of a Multinational Corporation

This chapter covers the life of our model multinational company. It is documented using 25 years of typical corporate records. Although it is simpler than an actual multinational, there is enough detail to support the analyses in the chapters that follow.

2.1 MNC, A US-Based Start-Up Company

MNC is a typical modern company. It produces products and associated services based on its intellectual capital. It was established about a dozen years ago by a combination of developers who had gained experience in their field, had novel ideas, but found that their current employer was no longer willing to take risks. Some recent university graduates ready to work in an exciting setting joined MNC, even though the future of the start-up was not assured. An early prototype showed enough promise to attract funding by a venture capitalist. Within a few years, an initial product, the Maniac 1000, was ready for marketing and sale. Sales of the Maniac grew steadily, and MNC invested its profits in product improvement, new Maniac releases, and marketing to a broader base of consumers. Within 5 years MNC went public, so that its shares were available for trading on the stock exchange. Initially, sales outside of the USA were handled by distributors, who got Maniacs at a 40 % discount and did their own marketing. The distributors used MNC's trademark, so that MNC became globally recognized. On the basis of feedback from its distributors, MNC's staff in California internationalized its product interfaces so that future Maniacs could be easily adapted to worldwide user habits and communication standards. The Maniac 2000, shown in Fig. 2.1, gained wide acceptance.

G. Wiederhold, *Valuing Intellectual Capital: Multinationals and Taxhavens*, Management for Professionals 23, DOI 10.1007/978-1-4614-6611-6_2,

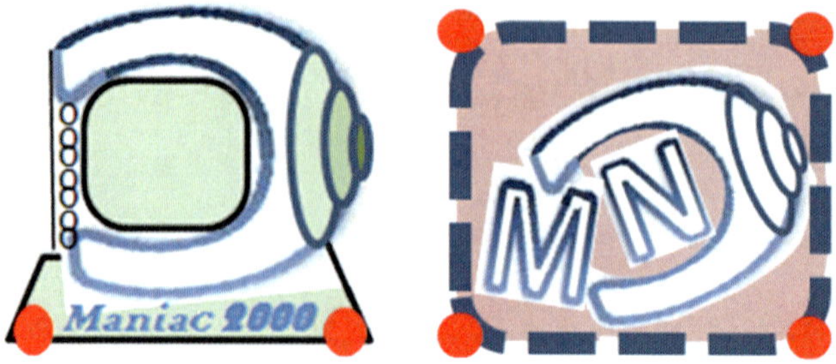

Fig. 2.1 MNC's current product and trademark; both contain MNC's IP

MNC's annual report showed a successful American company poised for further growth based on its valuable intellectual property, as documented in Appendix A.

2.2 MNC Establishes Foreign Sales Divisions

To gain control of sales outside the USA, MNC bought its most effective European distributor, located in Graz, Austria. MNC's management renamed the new division MNC EMEA and transferred all European, Middle East, and Africa distribution of its Maniacs to MNC EMEA, thus establishing MNC's first Controlled Foreign Corporation (CFC).

Soon the EMEA division took on the actual adaptation of Maniacs to standards appropriate to each country in Europe. The costs for those adaptations were charged to MNC in the USA and accounted for about 5 % of the product's prices.

Subsequently MNC established two more CFCs for selling Maniacs offshore. The first CFC was MNC PFE, based in Yokohama, Japan. It sells Maniacs in the Pacific region and the Far East. The PFE division made a special effort to introduce the MNC trademark into Asia. A year later, MNC LSA was set up in Belize to serve Latin-language speakers in Central and South America. After that time, the MNC parent company sold products directly only in the USA and Canada. Figure 2.2 shows the international scope of MNC: a parent MNC US with three distribution divisions, MNC EMEA for Europe, MNC PFE for Asia, and MNC LSA for Latin America.

Design and manufacturing of its Maniacs remained in California. An internal "transfer price" was established for Maniacs shipped from the USA to the three CFC sales divisions. Based on experience with the prior distributors, the transfer price was set at 55 % of the sales price, as computed in Appendix F, formula [F2.1]. That meant that 55 % of the sales revenue from Maniac sales is transmitted from the three "offshore" distributing divisions to the USA as revenue to be booked at MNC US. After deducting the actual cost of manufacturing the Maniacs, MNC books the remainder as gross income. After deducting the expenses MNC incurred for management and financing, MNC paid taxes on the aggregated US earnings, as shown in Table A.1.

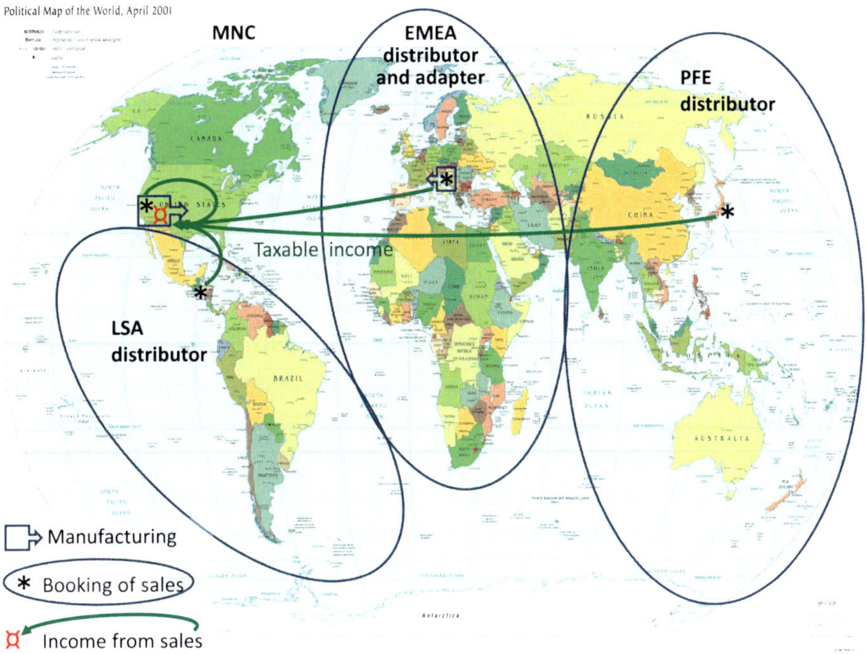

Fig. 2.2 The world of MNC before ATA's proposals: three sales CFCs

Earnings of the three CFC distributing divisions, calculated on their 45 % share minus their costs for sales and distribution of Maniacs, were booked at the CFCs. Those earnings were taxed by the authorities in Austria, Japan, and Belize. Corporate tax rates in those countries are roughly similar to those in the USA, although there are some concessions for products exported to other countries in the region. The after-tax profits were transmitted to MNC in the USA. Although MNC sold its Maniacs worldwide, it still behaved like a US-based company.

MNC's management and its innovators expect continued growth. It will continue to invest in research, but those expenses should not grow as fast as the expected revenues. Figure 2.3 documents those expectations. To achieve that expected growth, MNC will restructure its operations.

2.2.1 *Dealing with Double Taxation and Tax Treaties*

The USA does not have a tax treaty with Belize, so profits of MNC's LSA division are subject to actual "double taxation." Double taxation means that Belize will first collect its 25 % corporate tax on earnings of LSA, and the remaining 75 % of those earnings, when transferred to MNC in the USA, will be subject to the US 35 % tax rate, making the total effective tax rate 51.25 % [F2.2]. Belize is an exception. The US Treasury has tax treaties with 68 other large and small countries [IRS-901:11].

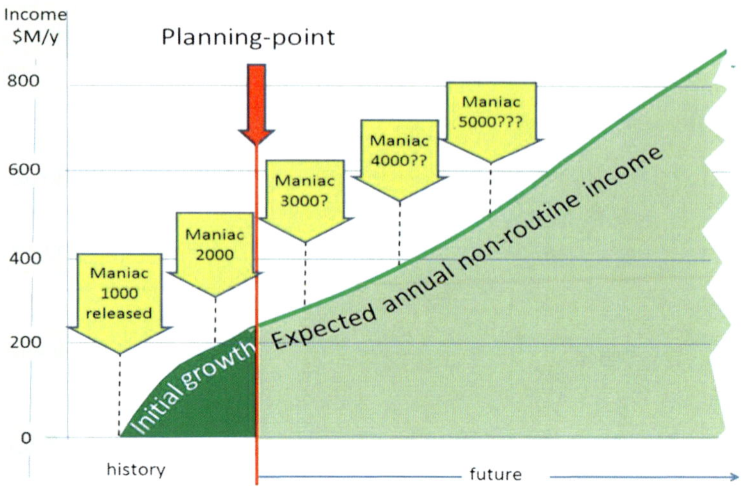

Fig. 2.3 Expected income growth of MNC

Belize, however, does not charge taxes on income from exports to members of the Caribbean Single Market, and the country provides an export allowance for other substantial exports into Latin America. As income attributable to actual sales within Belize was relatively small, MNC ignored the problem of double taxation there, especially because MNC's consulting firm, the Associated Tax Advisors (ATA), was preparing to propose a more comprehensive tax plan to MNC's board of directors.

Double taxation was not a problem for MNC's EMEA and PFE divisions. The US federal government has tax treaties with the two countries, Austria and Japan, where MNC's other foreign divisions are located. Having a tax treaty generally means that taxes that have been paid in those countries will be credited in the USA, reducing US taxes by those amounts.

Taxable earnings at MNC's independent distributor in Austria are based on the revenues it receives from its sales in the EMEA area minus the transfer price for the imported Maniacs and its local expenses. Corporate taxes in Austria are only 25 %. For the Maniacs sold by EMEA, after their import and all expenses in Austria have been accounted for, 9.6 % of their sales price is taxed in Austria, and only the difference between that and the US statutory rate of 35 % is due to the USA [F2.3]. The Austrian government gets $3.2M per year, but the changes being proposed by ATA will reduce foreign taxes as well.

The profit that MNC in the USA makes on those exports of Maniacs to the CFCs is taxed in the USA and in California. Taxes to be paid to the state of California could be reduced by incorporating MNC in a low-tax state in the USA, such as Delaware, but I intend to remain focused on federal tax avoidance.

Table 2.1 Divisions of MNC after offshoring selected sales and manufacturing efforts

Division	Location	Role	Source of IP growth
MNC US	California, USA	Management, R&D, prototyping, and sales	All aspects, main development site
MNC EMEA	Graz, Austria	Interaction with clients, adaptation, and sales	Business intelligence, local adaptation
MNC PFE	Tokyo, Japan	Adaptation and sales	Only trademark and local adaptation
MNC LSA	Belize	Adaptation and sales	Local adaptation only
MNC JB	Johor, Malaysia	Copy manufacturing	No local IP, Copy prototype exactly
MNC MY	Mysore, India	Product test and improvement	Joint software development

2.2.2 *Offshoring of Manufacturing*

In a second phase, MNC moved some of its manufacturing operations offshore. Because MNC realized that the IP within its products was crucial, its management decided not to use contractors for offshore manufacturing, but instead established new, subsidiary corporations.

The existing CFC locations were not deemed suitable for substantial new manufacturing operations. New CFCs were created in jurisdictions that offered both capable labor and inducements to establish operations there: the MNC JB division in Malaysia for its electronic products, and the MNC MY division in India for the associated software development. Both countries offered relatively low-cost, educated personnel and incentives to locate operating divisions there.

Malaysia had established a free-trade zone (FTZ) in Johor Bahru, close to Singapore, providing excellent access and communications. To gain easy access to Indian professional personnel, MNC MY was located in Mysore, an area where many offshore operations from other companies were based, but costs were still modest. Because of its effective interaction with the developments in the growing European Union (EU), the role of the MNC EMEA division in Austria was increased to ensure compatibility with changing European standards.

The IP situation differs in the various CFCs now established by MNC. Table 2.1 lists the parent and its five offshore divisions.

For the MNC JB operations, MNC adopted the "Copy Exactly" technique promulgated by the US chipmaker Intel, to make sure its process and products completely matched those manufactured on prototyping lines in the USA [McDonald:98]. Potential clients for quantity purchases are located mainly in the USA and at MNC EMEA. They are shown current Maniac prototypes and can trust that products delivered from MNC JB will fulfill precisely the same specifications and be reliable and consistent. For the division in India, MNC MY, product incompatibilities are of less concern, as software and software improvements are shipped rapidly over the Internet and loaded into the Maniac hardware just before distribution or sale.

The next step is to establish a foreign holding company, CONCH (Controlled Offshore Nominal Capital Holding), located in the Bermuda triangle, where income, transferred via CAAS, disappears from sight, as sketched in Fig. 2.4.

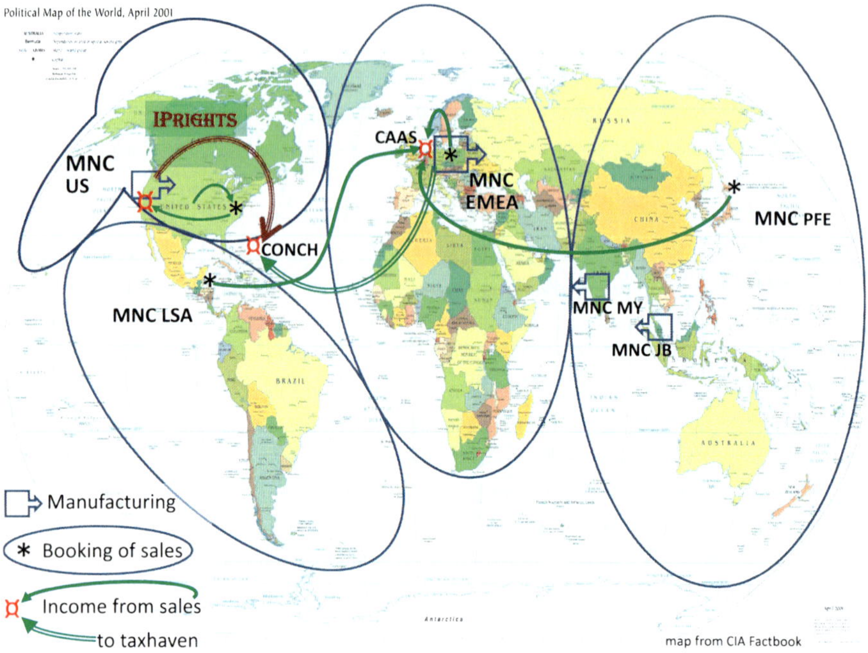

Fig. 2.4 The split world of MNC after the buy-in

2.3 MNC's Controlled Holding Company: CONCH

When MNC started earning more than 40 % of its revenue from foreign sales by its CFCs, the MNC board of directors agreed to set up a controlled foreign holding company (CFH) in a primary taxhaven, following the suggestion of its Associated Tax Advisers (ATA). MNC named that new subsidiary division CONCH. Having a CFH allows income from sales to be sheltered and held there without paying US taxes. The CONCH division was established by ATA in Palm Island, a small Caribbean country, using ATA's existing experience and facilities.

CONCH issued restricted shares, and MNC US purchased those shares, providing an initial $6M capital for CONCH. The directors of CONCH were selected from staff at MNC and ATA.

Palm Island does not levy taxes on income, and once CONCH was established, the annual cost is nominal; only a $3,000 fee is due to the island's registration authorities [Devasabai:09]. ATA's ongoing support charges billed to MNC are low as well, because CONCH shares facilities in Palm Island with many other offshore holding companies. ATA's costs there are mainly keeping some files and ensuring that any mail, e-mail, and faxes sent to CONCH are forwarded to MNC in the USA, where actual control is exercised.

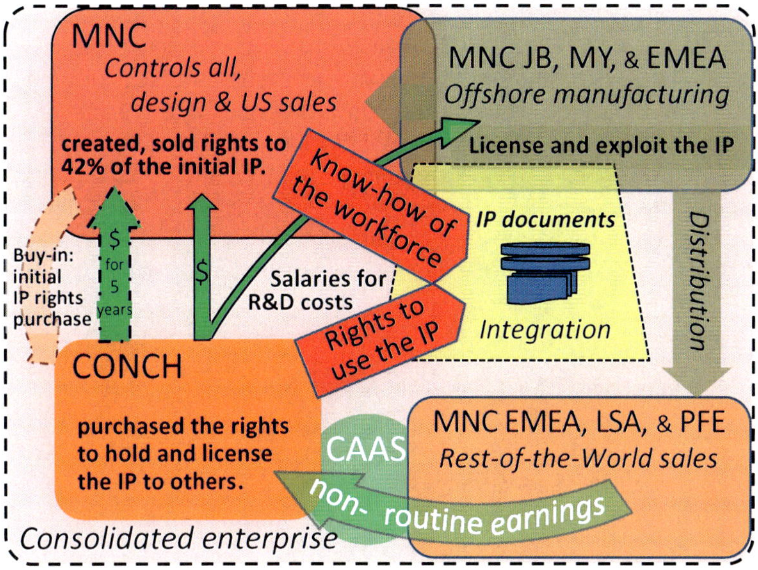

Fig. 2.5 Divisions of MNC and their interaction

CONCH purchased rights to MNC's IP, a fraction or "tranche" sufficient to gain the rights to access all of MNC's intellectual capital, the platform that is the base of MNC's income. It can now collect all of MNC's foreign revenue and hold the derived earnings. MNC in the USA does not pay taxes on any offshore earnings that are not needed to support operations in the USA and are held at CONCH. Figure 2.5 shows the new interplay of the divisions of MNC. The new CAAS division in The Netherlands is set up by ATA to handle the financial transfers.

The fraction of revenue transferred to MNC in the USA was not based on actual cost data but on prior agreements with an independent distributor. When, a few years later, the business relationship changes, these assignments are no longer realistic and should be reevaluated. But the effort to justify new transfer prices and reset existing financial contracts is substantial. MNC had little motivation to change, so it kept the existing rates throughout subsequent events, even though its operations changed greatly.

2.3.1 Buy-In

In order to make CONCH eligible to receive the nonroutine profits, a tranche of ownership rights to the IP was transferred from its current owners, MNC in the USA, to CONCH. In return, CONCH had to make a buy-in payment to reimburse MNC US for the right to use that IP. ATA determined that a fair transfer price for the IP was \$50M, using the percentage of expected sales from distributors outside of North America, which was 42 % [F2.4]. In return, CONCH received the right to collect 42 %, or $105M, of MNC's income. By the end of its first year, CONCH actually could keep $44M of MNC's earnings that year in its local accounts [F2.5].

The loan by MNC for the buy-in payment that enabled CONCH to purchase the IP rights from MNC was to be paid back in installments in equal amounts over 5 years. The low 8 % interest rate for the $50M loan was based on MNC's cost of money. CONCH accounts could easily transfer to MNC the $12.231M repayments due annually from the earnings booked there [F2.6]. Any income received in the USA is subject to income tax, after expenses are deducted. The interest payments for the loan are added to the installment payments for the buy-in and will be taxed. Few new expenses were incurred.

2.3.1.1 Income Shift, Short Range and Long Range

MNC in the USA received the installment income from the buy-in and recorded it on its accounting ledgers as earnings from exports. MNC had to pay taxes on that $3.1M income every quarter for the 5-year term [F2.6]. MNC no longer received the earnings from its foreign operations. The change in the amount of earnings received was initially modest. No shareholder or revenue agent noticed the difference in the type of income. Only in later years does that difference become significant. The independent auditing division of ATA engaged by MNC did not question the transaction and said so in notes attached to MNC's annual reports [Vause:09].

After 5 years, CONCH had paid a total of $61.2M and no longer had to pay quarterly installments. Now MNC no longer received the installment income or any share of the foreign earnings. All net foreign earnings were sheltered at CONCH, free of taxes.

The price to earnings (p/e) multiple of 1.25 for the buy-in, given that CONCH paid $50M to receive $44M that first year and increasing amounts each year thereafter, seems like an over-friendly deal [BodieKM:08]. An IRS analyst checking that p/e multiple against common investment multiples may suspect that the buy-in was not valued fairly. Nevertheless, the risk of any scrutiny is low. MNC's tax returns are convoluted with the interest payments and cost-sharing payments for R&D at MNC, as sketched in Fig. 2.5. The IRS audits only about 25 % of major corporate tax returns [Zerbe:10]. Because MNC delivered all its documentation, including the ATA study justifying the $50M valuation of the CONCH tranche of MNC's IP, the financial reporting was valid. No IRS audit was initiated by the IRS examiner. IP valuations are difficult and require the expertise of economists and other specialists. In fact, detractors will say that fair IP valuations are impossible, but Chap. 5 will show how to reasonably estimate the value of MNC's IP and the buy-in.

2.3.2 Cost-Sharing of Ongoing Development

The buy-in is actually part of a broader cost-sharing agreement between MNC in the USA and CONCH. After the buy-in, research and development continued at MNC in California. Very little changed in the work setting for creative MNC employees. The software group now receives assistance in testing Maniac software from MNC MY in India and gradually turns over the maintenance of prior versions of the software to MNC MY staff.

The IP generated by ongoing development in the USA and software testing at MNC MY will benefit foreign sales of Maniacs as much as the US sales of Maniacs. To reimburse the creators for that benefit, the foreign divisions of MNC contribute to the costs of all such efforts. Through the initial buy-in and the ongoing cost-sharing payments, CONCH shares the ongoing rights to the resulting IP. Only costs incurred for strictly local adaptations will not be shared.

To simplify accounting, all R&D costs incurred by MNC in California and by MNC MY are aggregated in a single account. Because all earnings from foreign selling divisions in MNC's corporate structure flow to CONCH, it pays for its share of the R&D costs. Taxes have to be paid on the funds that CONCH transfers to the USA, so CONCH will actually pay about 135 % of its share of the total R&D cost, or $34M [F2.7]. R&D costs average about 12 % of MNC's revenues; the remaining foreign earnings accumulate at CONCH [F2.8].

2.3.3 Ownership of Rights to Intellectual Capital

CONCH derives an important benefit from the R&D cost-sharing payments; it continues to own a share of the intellectual property generated by those R&D efforts. As the fraction of foreign sales of Maniacs increases, the income at CONCH increases as well, so that it obtains a greater portion of the nonroutine profits from MNC's foreign sales. In recent times MNC's foreign sales have increased by 23 % of the original offshore ratio. CONCH now gets 54 % of MNC's total profits, even though the initial buy-in transfer payment was based on a 44 % share [F2.9]. MNC's portion of taxable earnings shrinks as more income winds up at CONCH.

Because the ongoing development of Maniacs and its successor products takes place in California, CONCH implicitly has access to the workforce and the know-how at MNC US as well. The IP rights hence convey rights to all of MNC's intellectual capital. Chapter 3 defines those rights.

2.3.4 The Financial Intermediary, CAAS

ATA also established a Controlled Financial Intermediary (CFI) for MNC and gave it the name Confidential Asset Accounting Services (CAAS). CAAS collects all foreign income, distributes it to cover all offshore costs, and then transmits what is left to CONCH, MNC's taxhaven subsidiary. The actual services are provided by a division of ATA in Hilversum, close to Amsterdam's airport in The Netherlands. ATA also submitted the required registration to the Dutch authorities and maintains its books. No actual MNC staff is required.

Although the flow of funds through CAAS is substantial, CAAS gets little actual revenue from The Netherlands. As a mere conduit, it has minimal reporting requirements in The Netherlands [Kroon:00]. Because The Netherlands is subject to European Union rules, the assumption is that all receipts and payments follow International Accounting Standards (IAS) promulgated by the IAS Board (IASB) in London. The operations at CAAS are invisible to MNC's shareholders. In 2002, the US Securities and Exchange Commission (SEC) relaxed reporting regulations, so that since then the existence of CAAS no longer needs to be reported in MNC's annual reports. We will encounter CAAS again in Chap. 6, where we deal in more detail with taxhavens.

2.4 Growth of MNC

A company can grow in two ways:

1. "Organic growth" is due to internal technical and marketing innovations created from resources within the company. Technical growth requires spending on R&D.
2. "External growth" is due to mergers and acquisitions. Acquisitions can be supported from excess income, by issuing shares or bonds to investors or by borrowing money.

MNC used both types of growth. The IP growth due to those two approaches overlaps and becomes indistinguishable in the long run. Recognizing the origin of the IP and the nonroutine earnings they generate helps in understanding corporate growth. Quantifying the relative share of the two contributions to growth is impossible.

2.4.1 Organic Growth

Organic growth tends to be steady. Consistent high quality and low prices can keep the rate of growth high for a long time [Sveiby:97]. Once a company is well established in its market sector, it is hard to grow much faster than the general growth of the economy. A company growing only organically also risks being sideswiped by alternative products or technologies.

2.4.2 External Growth by Mergers and Acquisitions

Growth can be accelerated by investing in existing enterprises. Acquiring or merging with other companies provides stepwise growth. Mergers tend to be among equal-sized businesses and help build market share. Acquiring smaller companies

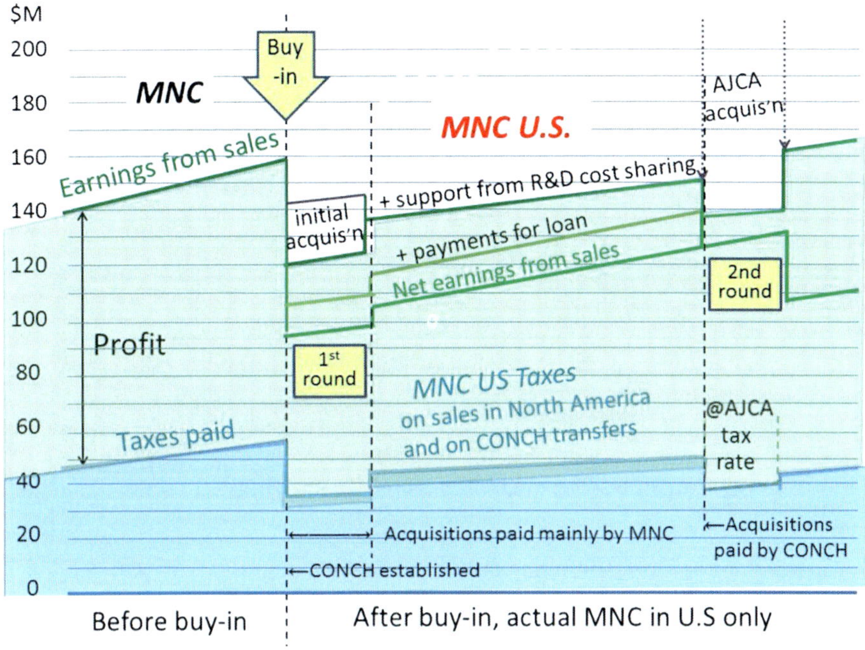

Fig. 2.6 Major income streams at MNC in the USA, and taxes due

tends to complement and advance existing product lines, converting available capital to IP. MNC acquired several smaller companies around the time of the creation of CONCH, expecting to improve its products and to enter new but related markets.

Acquisitions and mergers can be paid for with cash or shares or a mix of both. MNC's shares were valued highly, so half of its early acquisitions were paid for with newly issued shares. The acquisitions made sense to MNC's shareholders, and therefore MNC's share price was not greatly affected.

The first round of acquisitions, made about the time that CONCH was established, incurred a cost of $300M. Sales of MNC shares and a loan paid for the acquisition. The acquisition included IP that also benefits CONCH, so CONCH had to reimburse MNC for its share and taxes on that amount. ATA determined that CONCH had to pay less than $29M for its share of the acquisitions that MNC purchased for $300M [F2.10]. The change in earnings and taxes at MNC in the USA are shown in Fig. 2.6. The documentation for the initial round of acquisitions and the cost sharing by CONCH was provided to the IRS and not challenged.

MNC's management was smart. They invested in companies with technologies and products that match their existing operations. The acquired companies were relatively small, so staff and management could be easily integrated, and no harmful jockeying for senior positions resulted. Such issues crop up in many major mergers, and the resulting disruptions are costly. The companies acquired by MNC all had technology complementary to MNC's existing capabilities, so their integration was effective. MNC's market capitalization soon grew to more than $2,000M while CONCH continued to accumulate cash [F2.11].

2.4.3 Repatriation and Acquisitions

In 2004 the US Congress passed the American Jobs Creation Act (AJCA), giving US-based multinational corporations a one-time tax break. The legislation's objective was to encourage companies to repatriate funds from taxhavens and create jobs in the USA rather than in offshore CFCs [AJCA:04]. AJCA reduced the US tax rate on foreign earnings returned as dividends to the parent corporations in the USA from 35 to 5.25 % [F2.12]. Many US multinational companies participated and spent the funds in a variety of ways [DruckerRM:11].

When AJCA made repatriation of offshore funds attractive, MNC had four choices:

1. Grow by hiring staff. But hiring creative staff for a short term is not feasible.
2. Grow by acquiring companies, gaining instant staff and IP.
3. Buy back stock to increase its value per share, increasing shareholder wealth.
4. Pay dividends to its shareholders, providing shareholder income.

Choices 3 and 4 are inappropriate. MNC is a young company, expected to grow and not to reduce its capital.

MNC focused on the second approach and identified suitable acquisitions amounting to $475M. Following the prior strategy, CONCH would have cost shared those acquisitions as well, and spent $41.2M for the IP share it would obtain, plus the taxes at that low rate [F2.13]. Because MNC had so much capital accumulated offshore, it decided to take maximal advantage of the AJCA tax break and repatriated most of the cash MNC held in CONCH. CONCH paid for nearly $500M in acquisitions and related taxes [F2.13]. The wording of the AJCA specified only foreign income, but any income from MNC's sales of its products in the USA that were sheltered because of the IP rights held in CONCH, qualified as foreign income as well.

AJCA-motivated acquisitions funded by CONCH cost $475M, and the taxes owed for transferring that amount into the USA amounted to only $25M. That kept the repatriated amount just under a $500M limit, so that MNC did not have to open its books at CONCH to the IRS [F2.14]. Without the AJCA tax break, $166M would have been paid in taxes, more than CONCH could afford [F2.15]. The portion of the acquisitions that was identified as IP enabled CONCH to own a larger share of the corporate IP. Figure 2.6 also shows the growth of MNC's US earnings and taxes paid after the second round of acquisitions.

The regulations implementing AJCA could not ensure that the repatriated funds would be used only for job creation. In a traditional economy, planners foresee thousands of workers creating products and infrastructure. A business that relies on creative people to generate IP cannot hire staff rapidly to grow organically at a high rate.

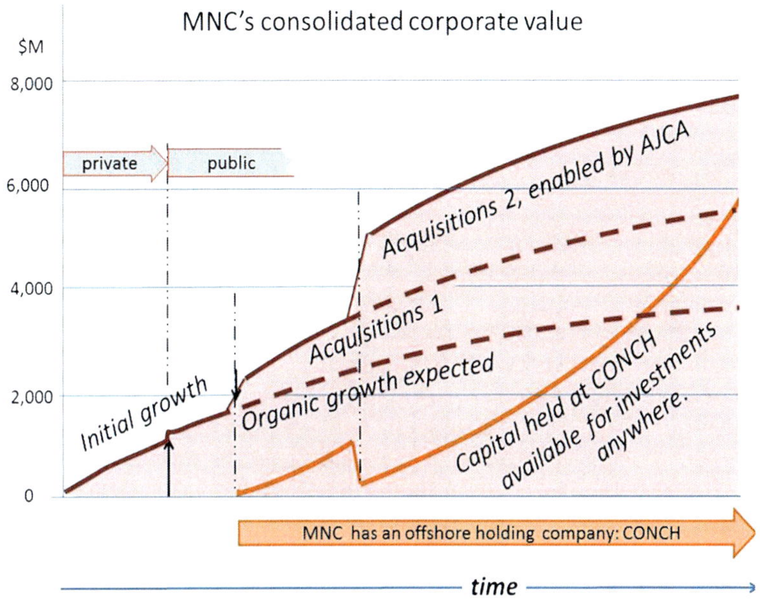

Fig. 2.7 Long-term growth of MNC

The repatriated funds, being fungible, were mainly used in other ways than choice 1, hiring staff [LevinEa:11]. MNC obtained new, valuable employees from those acquisitions, although the support personnel from the acquisitions were redundant and let go, reducing the amount of new staff to 57 % of the acquired personnel, leading to a net job loss in the USA [F2.16].

2.4.4 Combined Growth

By incorporating smaller competitors, MNC was able to grow substantially. It spent a total of $775M on acquisitions, a sum equal to nearly half its market value. Those acquisitions enhanced MNC's value considerably. The capital accumulated in MNC's taxhaven provided the resources. The sketch in Fig. 2.7 conveys a general impression of the growth paths. MNC's early value was determined by its initial investors, but after it went public, its value was set by the shareholders. Shareholders are concerned about future income of MNC as a whole, but have to depend mainly on MNC's consolidated statements that do not report the location of financial and intangible capital.

The consolidated growth of MNC does not show the effect of CONCH directly. Capital keeps accumulating in CONCH. Unless there is motivation for another repatriation, the cash held in CONCH will be used for offshore production capabilities or for acquisition of foreign assets. Attractive are US companies that already have the majority of their value offshore. Such purchases become an untaxed extraterritorial transaction among foreign subsidiaries [Rahn:09].

2.4.4.1 Allocation of IP Obtained from Acquisitions

Rather than initiating new product lines, the two rounds of acquisitions brought new IP value to be integrated into MNC's Maniac products while ensuring that MNC remained at the forefront of innovation. That newly acquired IP is available to all of MNC's worldwide operations, so that it is also subject to the cost-sharing arrangement that was set up when CONCH was established.

We briefly review the studies performed by ATA, MNC's trusted accountants, which allowed CONCH to increase its share of earnings beyond its expected share of foreign sales. Although the financial amounts paid for both sets of acquisitions are known, the appropriate payment for the IP rights conveyed to CONCH has to be estimated. The acquired companies did not yet have sales of their own, the prime basis for IP valuations. Some of the research at the acquired firms might never have a practical application. It was also unclear when and to what extent the acquired IP would contribute to MNC's future sales.

ATA split the initial acquisition amount of $300M as follows: it found $30M of tangibles, considered another $28M to be a control premium that did not add value, wrote off $25M of research in process, assigned $15M as the value of the workforce being integrated into MNC, and valued the useful IP from all those acquisitions at $50M. Acquiring talent was an important motivation for several of the acquisitions, but ignored by ATA. The unaccounted $152M was assigned to goodwill, to be amortized over 15 years [see details in F2.10]. CONCH paid $28M for its share of the IP obtained and the taxes due on that amount. The ATA reports provided for each acquisition included the common term: "ATA believes that the valuation is fair and will not be challenged by the IRS."

For the $475M in acquisitions following AJCA, ATA used a similar valuation process and pegged the total IP value at $106.7M [F 2.17]. Some of those were talent acquisitions as well. MNC had CONCH accounts pay the full acquisition cost and the taxes due at the low AJCA rate, a total just below $500M [F2.12].

Because CONCH funded the entire AJCA-motivated round of acquisitions, all of the additional IP rights and benefits to collect nonroutine earnings were allocated to CONCH. The total amount CONCH paid for the initial buy-in, both rounds of acquisitions, and the taxes for the funds transferred to the USA became $596M [F2.18].

The fraction of IP rights held at CONCH also grew. After the buy-in, CONCH paid for its proportionate share of IP during initial acquisitions, shared ongoing R&D costs, and then paid for all of the IP in the AJCA-motivated acquisitions; CONCH obtained 64 % of the IP-based rights to MNC's nonroutine income [F2.19]. Because of the growth of foreign sales, CONCH's income share grew as well, becoming 69 % [F2.20].

Figure 2.8 shows the effect: substantial US income can now be sheltered at CONCH. By Chap. 7 we will be able to assess to what extent ATA's methods were valid.

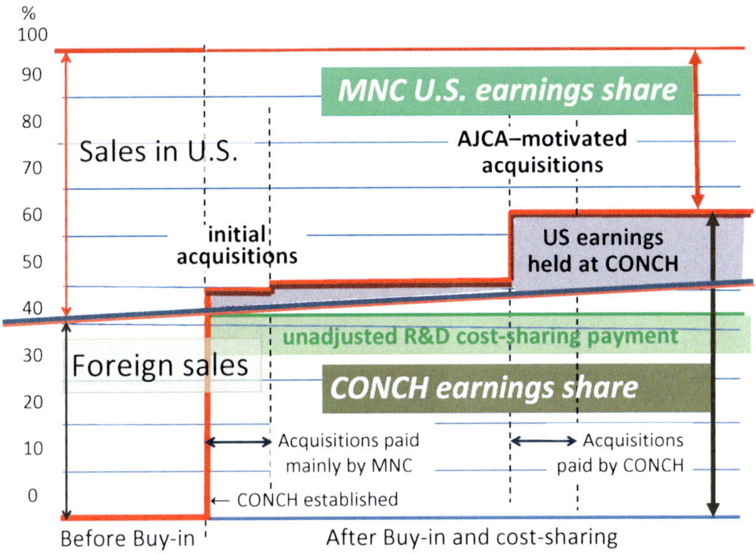

Fig. 2.8 Allocation of non-routine earnings according to relative IP rights

2.5 MNC's Tax Arrangement

With CONCH now controlling more than 2/3 of the IP rights, over 2/3 of MNC's nonroutine earnings will also be booked offshore. The sheltering of US-sourced earnings offshore allows MNC to avoid paying US tax on such earnings. This arrangement has a cumulative effect. As little as possible of the earnings derived from foreign operations is transferred back to the USA, letting US income pay for all routine costs. No US taxes were paid on earnings held at CONCH before AJCA was passed. Then, to pay for the second set of acquisitions, a large amount of capital was transferred at a very low, 5.25 %, tax rate. After that event, no further capital was transferred to the USA

A year after the AJCA acquisitions, MNC in the USA owns only 33 % of the worldwide IP rights to its earnings. The remainder of the earnings from Maniac sales is allocated and held at CONCH. MNC thus pays US taxes only on the 33 % fraction of IP rights it now owns or $28M that year. If it were taxed at the full statutory tax rate, $89M in taxes would be due on its worldwide earnings, or at least $44M on its US-source earnings [F2.21].

Within 10 years after the initial buy-in, all but 26 % of MNC's nonroutine earnings will be sheltered from taxation. MNC's taxes become less than 9 % on its worldwide earnings and less than 14 % on its earnings from sales in the USA [F2.22]. Spending CONCH's untaxed capital on foreign projects and acquisitions will further reduce MNC's US taxable earnings. MNC's capital needs and costs in the USA remain low [F2.23]. Figure 2.9 shows the beginning of the trend.

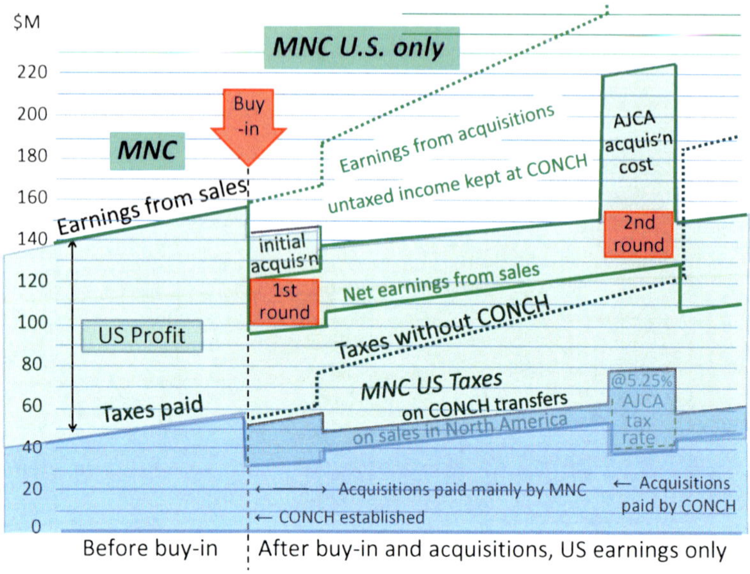

Fig. 2.9 MNC's US earnings and tax effects of the buy-in and acquisitions

MNC is but a small contributor to the sheltering of US corporate income from taxes. For all US corporations, such tax avoidance methods contribute substantially to the approximately $100B annual total of untaxed earnings from US sales, as shown later in Fig. 6.4 [F6.4].

Research Credits

The USA, like many other countries, has adopted tax incentives to encourage innovation. In the USA such incentives are the Research and Experimentation (R&E) credits [B.2.8(4)]. Introduced in 1981, they have been regularly extended and often modified [NAM:04]. Because CONCH's cost-sharing payments overlap with the expenses eligible for the R&E credit, those credits apply to the cost-sharing payments MNC receives. The cost-sharing payments satisfy the prime R&E credit objective, supporting research jobs in the USA, but fail to satisfy the long-term objective of improving US competitiveness. The resulting IP will not generate taxable income for the USA, because the rights to any new IP created by cost sharing will be owned by CONCH, offshore.

Optimizing the benefits from the taxation rules is a balancing act for MNC's accountants. A generous designation of corporate efforts to R&E costs would increase the tax credits earned. Such an allocation would also increase MNC's US income from CONCH and reduce the amount that MNC can shelter in the taxhaven. Because these amounts are documented on different forms submitted to the IRS, any inconsistencies may not be obvious.

2.5.1 Taxes Paid by MNC's Operating Offshore CFCs

When a company is profitable in the country of its residence, it should pay taxes to that country [dAroma:27]. But the nonroutine profits from MNC product sales in India, booked by MNC PFE, will flow via CAAS in The Netherlands to MNC's taxhaven subsidiary, CONCH. Only the profits that remain after paying royalties for the use of IP owned by CONCH will be taxed by India, which has a corporate tax rate of 30 %, similar to that of most industrial countries.

Corporations and their advisors attempt to avoid taxes anywhere. To keep earnings from being taxed, ATA has instituted some further strategies.

Most of the profitable activities of MNC's software division in India, MNC MY, require the use of IP owned by CONCH. By having MNC MY pay substantial royalties for the IP rights that CONCH holds, the earnings in India are greatly reduced, and little tax is paid there. Verifying fair rates for royalty rights is hard. Because the transfer is internal, the rates for the rights can be strategically set so that MNC MY has minimal or no profit in India, and hence pays little in taxes there. The software files and product designs that workers need at MNC MY are actually stored in India, but the rights to use them are owned by CONCH in the taxhaven. ATA has assigned only a file drawer to CONCH in its Palm Island office; there wouldn't be enough physical space to store any actual documents [Contractor:81]. Because MNC MY's software is shipped to the sales locations via the Internet, the value of its exports to the USA and offshore MNC distributors is not documented anywhere [BarlettS:00].

Avoiding taxation for MNC JB in Malaysia is even simpler. Even though the products are tangibles with intangible contents, being in a Free Trade Zone means MNC JB doesn't face import or export duties. No IP is generated at MNC JB. So even though neither India nor Malaysia is a primary taxhaven, their governments receive no significant tax revenues from MNC's business activities. Only the individual income of employees residing there is subject to national income and consumption taxes. Chapter 6 defines more precisely what roles various types of taxhavens play in corporate structures.

MNC does not operate in isolation. It is part of a complex network of enterprises that together produce innovative products that sell well in the market. Many of those companies supply the parts and competence needed for consumer products and services worldwide.

2.5.2 Companies Related to MNC

Maniacs use computer chips designed and supplied by a neighboring company in California, CCC. MNC and CCC worked closely together to make sure that those chips are effective and economical. Their design represents an integration of IP by MNC, CCC, and many other companies, including those that have developed the design software used by MNC and CCC. The actual chips are manufactured for CCC offshore by a chip foundry in Taiwan. CCC assumes only a flash title for its sales, as the foundry delivers the chips directly to MNC JB in Malaysia [GriffithS:09].

More than half of the chips made by CCC wind up back in the USA, as part of products such as Maniacs. It has used an offshore CFH for many years now, accumulating capital in a taxhaven. It now invests most of its earnings in growing its design and engineering capabilities offshore. CCC has acquired small companies in Eastern Europe and hired well-educated staff there. Many of these countries provide attractive incentives. Little growth in California is expected.

2.6 Moving All Income-Generating IP to a Taxhaven

MNC has considered, but not adopted, a further suggestion made by ATA that would allow nearly all US profits to be sheltered from taxation. It would require that all of MNC's IP be transferred offshore to CONCH. Then only routine US earnings, computed as if the Maniac were a commodity product like a light switch, would be booked by MNC US. MNC's taxes would then shrink to <2 % of its earnings [F2.24].

The intent of the US government's cost-sharing regulations was to allow companies to shelter income generated outside of the USA and keep it available for active offshore activities, thus allowing US companies to reinvest foreign earnings to compete effectively with foreign competitors. The rules only require stating that the amounts are held for foreign reinvestment; repatriation of earnings can be indefinitely blocked. Because IP is well-nigh invisible and money is fungible, MNC's tax avoidance approach could be extended to all of its nonroutine profits. To avoid all US taxes would require another buy-in by CONCH, which would pay for all of MNC's remaining US IP rights. A valuation of that IP must then be made; ATA would take on that task.

ATA could even recommend an "inversion," as described in Sect. 2.7. Our model MNC does not engage in any such questionable practices.

2.6.1 An Example Where All IP Rights Reside in a Taxhaven

To assess more extreme strategies, let's look at a documented case of "Globetrotting Profits" [Drucker:10]. A pharmaceutical company, Forest Laboratories (NYSE symbol FRX), has its headquarters in New York and its primary research and testing laboratories (FLR) in St. Louis. The main product of FRX is Lexapro, a medication for anxiety disorders. All IP rights have been shifted to Bermuda, all manufacturing occurs in Ireland, and all sales are in the USA. As shown in Fig. 2.10, the FRX arrangement is simpler than the case of our MNC, as Forest Laboratories sells its products only in the USA

To handle all the shifting of funds, Forest Laboratories uses a CFI in The Netherlands, FFBV. FFBV is registered as a "Besloten Venootschap" (BV) and serves as a conduit of external funds that is exempt from most reporting to the Dutch belastingsdienst (tax authority, NLbd) [deMooijN:08]. FFBV provides services in the Forest Laboratories structure in Amsterdam similar to those CAAS in Hilversum

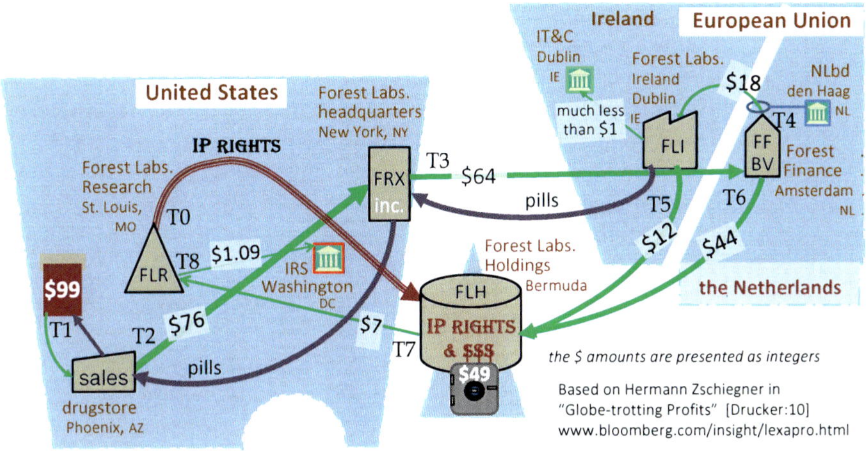

Fig. 2.10 Example of funds and IP flow for Lexapro [F2.25]

provides for MNC (see Fig. 6.6). Indeed, FFBV has no employees to enjoy the conviviality of Amsterdam.

Nothing can be done until the IP is moved offshore, so that becomes the initial transaction:

Transaction 0: At some time in the past, FRX transferred the rights to its IP (specifically the rights to patents that cover Lexapro) from FLR to FLH (Forest Laboratory Holdings), its offshore CFH in Bermuda. We do not know how much FLH paid FRX for the buy-in of those IP rights. If the transfer payment to FRX accounts in the USA occurred when the future sales of Lexapro were hard to estimate, the amount would have been modest.

Following the money paid for a drug purchase, it takes eight transactions to get back to the taxes paid to the US IRS.

Transaction 1: The customer pays $99 for a unit of Lexapro at a Phoenix drugstore.

Transaction 2: The drug store pays $76 for that unit of Lexapro to FRX headquarters in NY. FRX collects $12 for marketing and administrative costs attributed to the sale.

Transaction 3: The remaining $64 flows to Forest Finance BV in Amsterdam (FFBV) to pay for Forest Laboratories' offshore manufacturing operations.

Transaction 4: The expenses incurred in Ireland, $18 in total, are transmitted by FFBV to FLI, the Irish manufacturing subsidiary of FRX. The actual cost of manufacturing a unit of Lexapro is $5. Because FLI has no nonroutine earnings in Ireland—the income is nearly equal to the expenses—the Irish taxes were negligible, only 11 US cents per unit.

Transaction 5: The licensing fees of $12 for the IP used in Ireland are paid by FLI to FLH in Bermuda, the owners of the license.

Transaction 6: Forest Labs's 10-K financial documents imply that all those transfers of funds consume about $2 per unit in administrative costs, leaving about $44 of the drug's sale in the FFBV account. FLH (Forest Laboratory Holdings), which owns all of Forest Labs's IP, has the right to all of that profit. Thus $44 untaxed profit is moved from the FFBV account to Forest Labs's holding company, FLH, in Bermuda, keeping the capital held at FFBV low.

Transaction 7: FLH received $56. In order to maintain its rights to the IP, FLH pays the cost of the research and development employees at FLR in St. Louis, amounting to about 8 % of Forest Labs' net revenues. For that repatriation of earnings to the USA, FLH also pays the US taxes, transferring a total of $7 per unit of Lexapro. The remaining $49 is kept in Bermuda.

Transaction 8: It appears that the IRS is owed about $2.50 in taxes from that payment to FLR, but after credits from a US research incentive and for taxes paid in Europe, only $1.09 is due. The final taxes are 2.4 % on Forest Labs's income, as reported by Business Week [Drucker:10].

After tax credits for Irish taxes and other typical credits and deductions for pharmaceutical companies, Forest Laboratories pays only $1.09 in US taxes, or 2.43 % US tax on its taxable earnings, well below the 35 % US corporate income statutory tax rate [F2.26]. The reduction in taxes paid is not achieved by manipulating the tax rate, but rather by hiding earnings offshore.

The gross profit margin on Lexapro's sales revenue is 71 % [F2.27]. The high margin is possible because the company makes a product based on IP created or acquired in the US operation and pays negligible taxes in all places where Forest Labs operates. The remainder of the amount from a single sale, about $49, after all expenses at the other Forest Laboratories operations, is accumulated by FLH in Bermuda. It can collect interest there, but it is also available for new investments.

If Forest Labs pays dividends to its shareholders, those will also have to be supported by FLH, because all capital is held in Bermuda. Amounts transferred to the USA for dividends will be taxed. Any US resident shareholder will be taxed on the dividend income as well, albeit at a lower rate. Large shareholders are thus motivated to declare their domicile in some taxhaven.

By comparison, generic drug competitors—without the exclusivity afforded by the patents on Lexapro—would be selling an equivalent product for less, earning a 12.5 % routine margin. No taxhaven is needed. If all other costs and tax rates remain similar to Lexapro's, a unit of the generic drug would cost the consumer about $32 [F2.26]. Overall, generic medicines, being commodities, are indeed priced at about 1/3 of their protected predecessors [Levinson:08].

2.7 Inversions

A company willing to be even more drastic about avoiding taxes can elect to move the domicile of its formal headquarters offshore [Shaviro:11]. This arrangement is suitable for multinational corporations that have been adept at moving their IP rights to a taxhaven and sheltering earnings there. Once enough capital has been

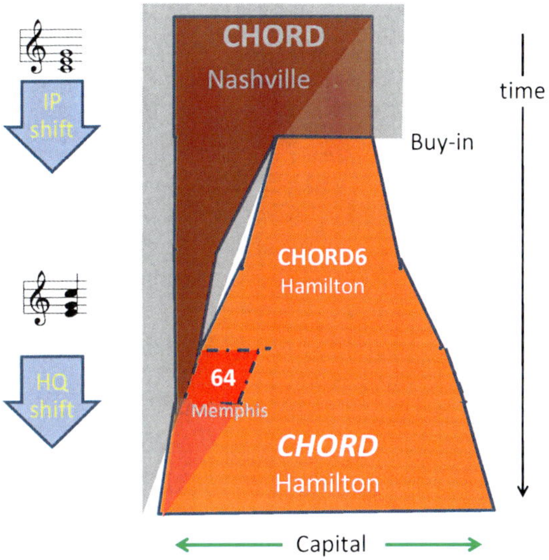

Fig. 2.11 Inversion

accumulated, the funds can be used to buy the parent and move its headquarters out of the USA [AviYonah:02]. Then it no longer has to report its consolidated income to the IRS.

The process of moving the domicile of a company to a foreign jurisdiction is called an "inversion." To illustrate the process I define a fictional company, CHORD, which has its headquarters in Nashville, TN. CHORD's metamorphosis to *CHORD* offshore is sketched in Figure 2.11.

CHORD is a multinational company and has already moved all of its IP to its CFH in a taxhaven, CHORD6. Over a period of about 6 years the IP rights owned by CHORD6 have allowed it to amass much capital offshore, but CHORD's management has not found any attractive investment opportunities [Misey:02]. They are worried that, because all that accumulated capital is not active, it may be taxed under the anti-deferral rules [B.1.2 §1375].

CHORD seeks advice from ATA and agrees to set up a second-level US subsidiary via CHORD6 in Memphis, identified as CHORD64. To capitalize CHORD64, CHORD6 repatriates funds from its taxhaven account and pays US taxes on those funds.

CHORD64 now merges with its grandparent CHORD in Nashville [LonzoOscar:47]. Then the shaded US entity, CHORD, is erased. CHORD64 paid for all the assets that remained, specifically the tangibles and the liabilities that CHORD has accumulated in the USA, including pension and health care obligations to its US staff. US income at CHORD64 can support ongoing costs in the USA.

CHORD6 also purchased the *CHORD* trademark, which had not yet been transferred to Bermuda. US employees in Memphis and Nashville will remain employed. They have become employees of a foreign-owned US business, a CFC as viewed from Bermuda. Royalties for use of the offshore IP by ongoing operations in Nashville are now paid to CHORD6. Their payroll will be covered by US sales.

Some workers may not even notice the shift. Sometimes bonuses and raises have been given to reduce employees' complaints.

The renamed foreign corporation, *CHORD* in Hamilton, is not directly liable for US taxes, although routine markups in its Memphis and Nashville subsidiary, CHORD64, are taxable. Payroll taxes are also due there. In 2003, after this tax avoidance strategy was recognized, direct gains from an inversion company became taxable for 10 years as US income [B.1.2 §7874]. In the long term no taxes on non-routine earnings will be paid by *CHORD* to the USA.

Companies that performed inversions and are now resident in a primary taxhaven can avoid releasing consolidated data, but their registered US divisions are still compelled to do so. The AJCA of 2004 limits inversions, but "adventurous tax planning" will continue [Cantley:03]. Any semi-taxhaven countries that house other CHORD operations will receive less information as well, and they can no longer count on protection that tax treaties with the USA offer.

Some US states allow such a corporate decision to be made without bringing the issue to a vote by its shareholders. Nevertheless, an inversion is drastic enough to be visible to CHORD's shareholders, and likely also to its senior employees and local politicians. Some corporate inversions have incited heated protest and have been abandoned [Lohman:02]. Other inversions have taken place without much public criticism [Baker:07]. There are benefits for the corporation (beyond tax avoidance) to moving companies offshore. Health care and other obligations for US employees of foreign corporations are less. Shareholders lose SEC protection [Brittain:05]. These factors will also be considered in selecting the new jurisdiction. Those reasons are beyond the scope of this exposition; we stay focused on less radical methods of tax avoidance.

MNC has not performed an inversion. It did move its formal headquarters in the USA from California to Delaware, reducing its California tax obligations. If MNC had shifted its headquarters offshore, it would not be possible to compare MNC's tax strategies with typical US corporations.

2.8 Associated Tax Advisers

Creating the complex corporate structures needed for effective and difficult-to-challenge tax avoidance is beyond the competence of the corporate staff in even technically savvy multinational companies. MNC depends greatly on the help of its tax-advising firm, ATA. This dependence grew gradually.

As MNC started earning substantial revenues, the many tax forms required by the IRS became burdensome and distracting [PackmanC:11]. The MNC accountant in charge, later promoted to become MNC's Chief Financial Officer (CFO), started outsourcing the work to a tax preparation firm. By the time tax management required a full-time person, MNC hired the ATA specialist who was serving them as the Director of Taxes in MNC. After all, that person was already familiar with MNC's structure, products, and generation of IP, and was effective in obtaining needed support from ATA staff.

2.8.1 Capabilities

Firms like ATA that provide the advice for setting up tax shelters have developed the required broad competencies needed to deal with the complexity of elaborate tax structuring [AsprayMV:06, p.246]. Most have operational divisions in Palm Island and The Netherlands to serve their customers. Their staff often functions as managers and directors of their customers' CFHs and CFIs. In the case of Forest Labs, the $2.00 overhead on each transaction goes to the various international branches of its tax advising firm for advice and business services.

A value that ATA brings to the table is its experience. For instance, ATA staff in several countries had helped CCC, a chip supplier to MNC, many years earlier in setting up its offshore operations. An executive of CCC is also a member of MNC's board and can testify to the advantages that offshoring offers. ATA's experience was very helpful in discussing with MNC's board and management the usefulness of an offshore financial structure.

ATA was also able to be very responsive once MNC's directors approved the offshore transfer of IP rights. It had already set up a number of corporate shell companies with innocuous names like CoA or CoB in likely taxhaven countries. ATA staff members are named as directors, so that they are authorized to deal on behalf of these shell companies. These companies are available to implement the initial IP transfer transactions without the delays and scrutiny that could be encountered in filing and registering new corporations. In due time the shell companies can be renamed to sound more realistic, as CONCH and CAAS were, without making the link to the parent corporation obvious.

2.8.2 Sharing Information Within ATA

ATA has distinct divisions for its consulting work and for auditing contracts. In this chapter ATA's role vis-à-vis MNC was primarily in consulting. The valuations that ATA performed depend greatly on the financial data, as verified by ATA's auditing division. Sharing the information among ATA's audit and consulting divisions provides efficiencies in dealing with complex corporate structures, but also increases the risk of biased analyses [SullivanZS:09]. Part of the Sarbanes-Oxley Act, which the US Congress passed in 2002, attempted to reduce such conflicts of interest by prompting the issuance of guidelines for independence of auditors versus consultants [SEC:03].

Many consulting firms, and ATA as well, have protected themselves from worldwide legal liability by isolating their operations while still sharing resources. ATA has split itself formally into a bunch of distinct companies, one for each country where ATA operates. Those companies are then bundled by becoming members of an entity set up under a Swiss law that governs clubs (*Vereinsgesetz*). As in any club, the companies that are members of the ATA club do not assume responsibility for each other's work and advice, even if given to the same customer, such as MNC [Fornito:05]. The members of the ATA club can share resources, information, and income with each other. Of course, no outsider can become a member of ATA's exclusive club. The club structure allows ATA's member companies to function as a cohesive firm.

2.9 Summary

MNC grew by investing in internal research effortsand also by acquiring a number of smaller companies. Early in its life it developed an international presence, and it became a multinational corporation when it set up a number of subsidiaries around the world.

Some of these subsidiaries provide manufacturing and distribution, but two are motivated solely by tax avoidance: CONCH in Palm Island and CAAS in The Netherlands. The low valuations presented by ATA for the intellectual capital MNC made available to CONCH enabled CONCH to be very profitable.

A few years later, a law intended to increase US employment, the AJCA of 2004, was advantageous to MNC and many of its peers. MNC used the funds to acquire more companies, but then had to let redundant staff go. The intellectual assets acquired were allocated to CONCH, allowing yet more income, derived from research performed in its California division, to be collected and held offshore.

MNC is now poised to invest offshore for further growth. Figure 2.12 combines the results shown in Figs. 2.8 and 2.9. Sections 2.6 and 2.7 show two arrangements that MNC has not yet adopted: moving all IP rights offshore and an inversion, moving its formal corporate headquarters offshore.

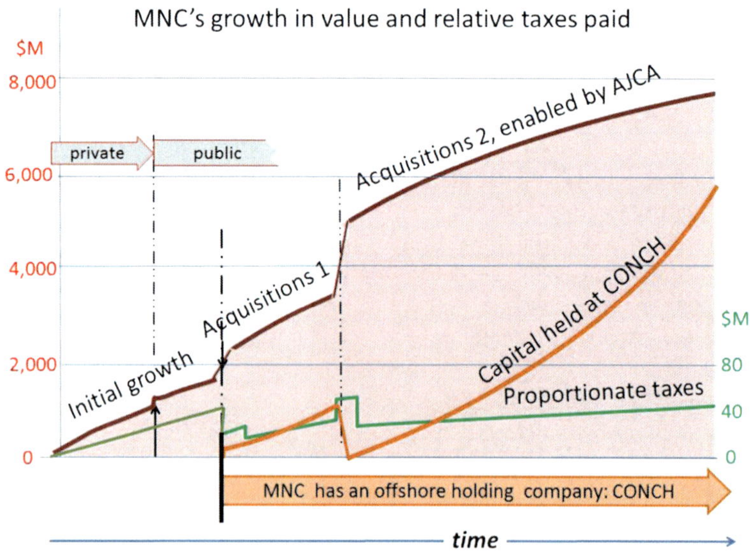

Fig. 2.12 MNC's growth in value, offshore capital held, and taxation

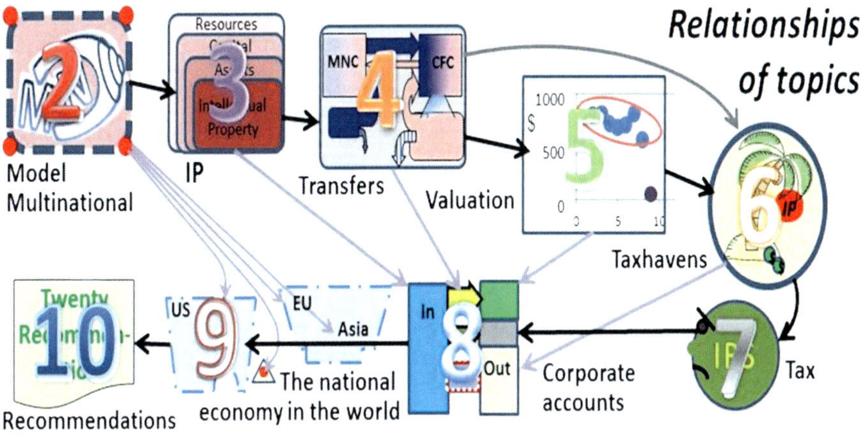

Fig. 2.13 Topics covered in this book and their relationships

Layout of Subsequent Chapters

Chapter 2 provided an example of how intellectual capital is created and exploited, the specific issues can be dealt with one by one. Figure 2.13 shows the dependencies.

Chapter 3 defines precisely the categories of intellectual capital.

Chapter 4 deals with international transfers of corporate assets, including rights to IP.

Chapter 5 details the methods used to assign a monetary value to IP.

Chapter 6 presents the capabilities of a variety of taxhavens.

Chapter 7 applies the technical material of Chaps. 3–6 to MNC. Combining the material from prior chapters explains why the valuations presented by ATA for the intellectual capital shifted offshore are off the mark.

Chapter 8 shows why it is difficult for the IRS to deal adequately with the issues raised.

Chapter 9 matches MNC to US corporations and multinationals and allows projection of corporate initiatives in the future.

Chapter 10 presents 20 recommendations derived from the understanding obtained through this work. Nineteen are detailed and could be rapidly implemented. Recommendation R20, to abolish corporate taxation, is drastic, but still possible without a wholesale revision of the US tax code.

Chapter 3
The Value of Intellectual Capital

Financial capital is easy to measure, being reported in terms of monetary units, say dollars. Other financial units, say Euros, have known conversion rates for any point in time. The essential value of money is what it can purchase in the future. While intellectual capital is diverse it can also be valued according to its future benefits. The shared metric for our purpose is its contribution to future corporate earnings. The concepts introduced in this chapter are a prerequisite to the valuation methods described in Chap. 5.

To earn more than routine competitors, companies must distinguish themselves by having both unique markets and unique competencies. The intellectual capital held by high-tech companies like MNC is responsible for generating such nonroutine earnings. Nonroutine earnings greatly exceed the earnings that can be obtained from commodity products. Those high earnings provide the funds needed for further investment in intellectual capital and corporate growth. Intellectual capital is the intangible "knowledge that can be converted to value" [Carson:08]. The human contributions provide skillful exploitation of corporate assets.

Shareholders in a company are actually interested in the future profits they will receive. Because tax avoidance is a major issue in this work, the focus here is on earnings, the amount available in a business *before* taxes are paid, as accounted in MNC books shown as Table A.1. Some intangibles appear on MNC's balance sheet, Table A.2, but the know-how needed to convert them into earnings is not listed.

While financial capital diminishes when it is spent, intangibles can be exploited without being depleted. Many copies of books, designs, and software can be sold without affecting the master copy. The value of many modern products, say an iPhone, is mainly derived from the intangibles used to create the products. The intangibles embodied in its design, the software, the chip designs, etc. provide functionality and make the product valuable; the tangible raw hardware parts contribute much less [BoultonLS:00].

If products created from intangibles are distributed in high volumes, the earnings margin of the company will be high, since the incremental production costs are low. The creation of value beyond the production cost is due to people and their tools.

G. Wiederhold, *Valuing Intellectual Capital: Multinationals and Taxhavens*, Management for Professionals 23, DOI 10.1007/978-1-4614-6611-6_3,

The company did incur substantial initial costs and risks when it created intangible assets, and those expenses must be amortized over the volume sold. To avoid losing the inherent value of their work, the company will protect the designs, the software, and similar intangibles, which now become intellectual property (IP).

To determine the nonroutine earnings due to intangibles, the routine earnings due to contributions from tangible assets are split off from the total earnings. For many analyses the intellectual assets must be further split into a dozen distinct types, as listed in Table 3.2. Each intangible embodied in a product derives its value from specific intellectual assets and each will have its own life to obsolescence, as discussed later.

Distinguishing among IP asset types is important for valuations that try to determine the proper pricing for specific IP sold, purchased, or shifted among corporate divisions. The categorization of types of intangible assets is the principal topic of this chapter. Because MNC transfers its assets among controlled divisions, it sets the transfer prices internally, but those prices should not distort the economic substance of offshore transactions. Important here is the concept of an "arm's-length comparison," an approach to assess the business value of an asset as if it occurred between independent and willing parties, without coercion [AviYonah:95].

The benchmark for the value of an intellectual asset is the price that an independent buyer is willing to pay to the seller for a similar asset in an open, arm's-length transaction. Because the MNC parent embraces all its divisions, its internal transactions are never at arm's length. When Maniacs made in Johor Baru and exported to the USA for sale by MNC pass through US customs at the border, a valid price has to be given as well. The price shown at customs should be consistent with the prices used elsewhere [B.1.1 §1667(a)].

3.1 Intellectual Capital and Intellectual Property

Intellectual Capital covers all of the intangible resources inherent in the workforce and its output [Sveiby:97]. Intellectual Property is that part of the intellectual capital that can be owned. Asserting ownership entails having definable and protectable rights to the properties—for instance, by asserting patent rights, copyright, or invoking trade secret constraints. Trade secrets can protect both actual records and corporate know-how within the workforce. While no property rights can be asserted over individuals, asserting trade secret can restrict information leaving the company. The know-how of the workforce is needed to make the owned IP productive. A company like MNC could not be successful without both aspects of intellectual capital.

3.1.1 Establishing Property Rights to Intellectual Assets

Intellectual Property (IP) is supported by legal rights that can be asserted and defended. The legal alternatives for protection of intellectual assets are briefly summarized here, as we will need them in assessing IP taxation. Voluminous literature is available if you want to follow up these approaches. Means to protect IP are patents, copyright, trade secret, and employment contracts.

Patents 

Patenting gives the patent holder a 20-year exclusive right to an idea or a process that can be put into practice. A patent is obtained by an application and verification issued by a government office; in the USA patents are granted by the Patent and Trademark Office (USPTO). The matter of the patent should be sufficiently well described that a person with ordinary knowledge of the field could build a copy. Such a description assures that an infringing copy can be recognized.

MNC has patented some innovative mechanisms in its products, as well as the formula of a coating that makes Maniacs resistant to seawater damage. MNC does not patent the innovative methods it uses to develop chips or software. Such patents are hard to file with the USPTO and hard to defend. Patented methods are easily adopted and then used internally, out of sight, by competitors. Software patents are problematical as well [Stobbs:00]. Tracing any misuse is expensive to prosecute.

Trade Secrets 

MNC has developed a process to make its Maniacs exceptionally reliable. This process is considered a trade secret. Patenting would publish the steps of the process, and MNC is not able to monitor whether competitors are copying the process. All of MNC's software is protected by trade secret law as well, because it is fairly easy to escape copyright coverage by writing different software encodings to accomplish the same goals. All employees and contractors of MNC sign Non-Disclosure Agreements (NDAs) to protect its secrets, IRS examiners are also obliged to honor trade secrets [OBrienC:90]. Trade secret protections cover innovations immediately. They are not limited to a statutory lifetime, but are hard to retain over long periods. Trade secrets, by their very nature, are hard to value, but are an essential part of a transfer of IP to an offshore division. Ongoing research and development renews the value of trade secrets.

Copyright 

Asserting copyright provides exclusive right to written or recorded scientific, literary, and artistic expressions and their translations, lasting about a century [HirtleHK:09]. MNC protects the software it creates by citing its copyright, which also extends to the translations into binary form that MNC embeds in its products. Only a segment of software sufficient to identify the program has to be shown.

Copyright also protects the masks for making computer chips designed by MNC. While literary works enjoy automatic copyright protection, masks for making computer chips must be labeled with an M and the company name and registered within 2 years of use.

Trademark

MNC uses its trademark to identify all of its products and literature. The MNC trademark is protected by registering it with the USPTO and similar organizations in other countries. The value of MNC's trademark is continuously enhanced by marketing and advertising efforts, but is also crucially dependent on the quality of its products. MNC can license its trademark to companies making attachments that enhance the Maniac, but to prevent diminishing its value, MNC must be careful not to license it to be used for low-quality products.

Employment Contracts

MNC has made employment contracts or "do-not-compete covenants" with a few crucial employees. Those employees have promised, for some compensation, not to work for significant competitors for a period of 3 years after leaving MNC. Such contracts convert members of the workforce into a valuable asset [ReillyS:98]. Providing stock options that vest after a number of years is a common means to retain employees and the know-how they represent.

Employment contracts do not protect MNC from loss of intellectual capital if the covered employee decides to switch professions and becomes a farmer, but they do reduce competitive risk. We value them in Chap. 5, Sect. M1.1.

3.1.1.1 Defending IP Ownership

Protection of any IP is not automatic. If MNC finds that someone infringes on rights that it holds and values, the company has at least to threaten to sue the infringer and follow up with legal action if the infringer does not stop. Even if MNC decides that some infringement does not matter much, it must follow up if it does not want to risk having its rights become invalidated. A casual, but not directly competing, infringer may well be willing to settle with MNC by paying a modest license fee, which will then protect MNC's future IP rights.

Trade secrets and employment contracts are covered in the USA by state courts and local precedents and attitudes. Trade secrets are appropriate for a fast moving field, while patents and copyrights protect over long and defined terms. Rules and attitudes regarding employee rights differ substantially among the US states. Having good and open employee relationships within a company does more to protect trade secrets than any legal constraint can achieve.

Foreign jurisdictions differ in the application of international patent law and copyright conventions when dealing with multinational corporations. To simplify the issue, MNC asserts legal ownership to all of its IP in California, even after MNC has sold most of the rights to exploit that IP to its subsidiary in a taxhaven, CONCH, but no actual IP resides there.

3.1.1.2 Marketability

Rights to all these intellectual properties can be marketed, licensed to others, sold, and traded. In MNC's transfer of rights to CONCH, all of MNC's intellectual capital was needed by CONCH and included in the transfer contracts. Rights can be sliced and diced and sold as "tranches." In the MNC buy-in CONCH obtained an initial 42 % tranche of all of MNC's rights. The mutual dependency of the IP types makes isolated valuation of the types difficult.

As long as only rights to the IP are sold or licensed, legal ownership can remain with MNC. Keeping the legal rights where the IP originated makes it easier to protect and defend it.

3.1.2 The Value of the Workforce

The value of its staff working together, with shared know-how and common goals, is a major contributor to MNC's success. While staff is an intangible asset, it is not a property. Accountants like to consider a workforce just as a number of individuals in a company. The value of a workforce is then simply the cost of hiring an employee times the number of employees needed. However, any business professional is aware that the value of a cohesive workforce of 20 long-term employees is much more than that of 20 individual hires. The value of an effective workforce cannot be measured by counting people. Having an extant workforce is part of a firm's "Going-concern value," which is worth considerably more than the sum of its parts [SmithP:05]. Members of an MNC's workforce have been motivated to stay by offering stock options. In Chap. 5 the cost and benefits of offering stock options are quantified [F5.3].

Converting a collection of new workers into an effective workforce takes a long time, and it has risks [Glass:03]. Hiring an additional employee initially contributes only the common knowledge consistent with the education, experience, and skill of the new hire. In a supportive setting, that employee will soon learn and adopt the pattern of work seen in the group he is joining. The newcomer may also receive some formal corporate training, but the importance of informal guidance is paramount.

The benefit of having a cohesive workforce limits organic growth. If a large number of new hires are introduced into an organization, they will find it hard to adopt the processes of the workers already there. Assigning to the existing workers the task of training the new hires reduces their productivity. Confusion will ensue. Trying to ramp up development too rapidly has disastrous consequences for intellectual projects. The observation that adding people to a late project makes the project yet later is well accepted in the software industry [Brooks:95].

MNC combined organic growth with investing in acquisitions, allowing it to grow rapidly. Acquiring a company brought to MNC an integrated combination of workforce and IP. Companies considered for acquisitions have to be carefully vetted [MeyerK:04]. They should be complementary and should not create tensions in the existing structure. MNC has focused on modest, early-stage technology acquisitions, and it has been successful in integrating the new workforce and the IP obtained. It moved all the employees retained from its acquisitions to its California locale and makes the rights to the IP available to all of its divisions.

For large acquisitions and mergers to be successful requires that the management styles of the merged companies be similar. It also becomes difficult to co-locate staff. Even if the IP is made available throughout the company, if people remain in distinct divisions, the benefits of the acquired IP for the overall company will be small. Exchange of creative staff among divisions can overcome the problem. In our analyses we assume that sharing of IP throughout the company does occur.

3.1.3 Integration of Workforce and Intellectual Property

MNC has moved most of its manufacturing operations to offshore CFCs. Promoters of offshoring stress the availability of cheap, educated labor. Surveying the components of MNC's intellectual capital makes it clear that MNC's offshore operations could not survive unless all divisions use their assets in concert. We recapitulate the central theme in Fig. 3.1.

If offshoring is to contribute to nonroutine earnings, intellectual capital has to be provided to the offshore sites [W:11]. The initial buy-in made the workforce know-how and the IP available to CONCH, and CONCH licenses it all to the operations at MNC JB and MNC MY.

MNC made the contents of all its IP available to its manufacturing CFCs in the form of documents and CDs containing its development and testing tools and prior versions of the software for the Maniacs. Furthermore, when MNC established MNC MY in India, it did not simply hire local workers and give them access to its IP; MNC also established a training program. Important personnel hired in India spent time at MNC's facilities in California, and MNC sent staff from California to India for training. Some became expatriates and remain in India today. Expatriates were mainly MNC staff who have an Indian background and had come to the USA for their graduate education. Within a year MNC had personnel in India who were well integrated into MNC's workforce. They had become part of MNC's intellectual capital.

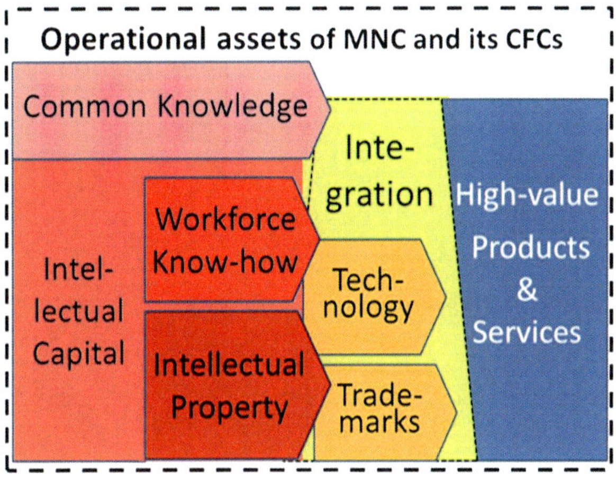

Fig. 3.1 The assets of MNC's operations

For MNC's manufacturing at MNC JB in Malaysia, the transfer of intellectual capital is even more intense. The "copy exactly" method requires tight integration of operations. Sales of Maniacs are driven by major customers' sampling and testing of prototypes. Interaction and feedback from those customers in the USA are essential.

Over time MNC's software operations in California and at MNC MY were coupled even more closely. Day-to-day interaction is now mediated by the Internet, so that software creation can be viewed as a 24-hour distributed factory [GuptaS:07].

The Maniacs are shipped directly from the factory. All the software to be included is transmitted from MNC's business support systems in California via the Internet. The software is loaded just before shipping, as sketched in Fig. 3.2. This process assures that a delivered Maniac will always be distributed to customers with the latest software version installed.

The close interaction among all operational sites continued after the buy-in. Although the workforce is located in the USA and the CFCs in Malaysia and India, the rights to the offshore income generated by its integrated workforce have been transferred to CONCH. Its three sales regions collect the foreign revenue. Some of that income is used to pay for Maniacs received and services provided from MNC. The remaining earnings are held in an account at CONCH. Employees travel among MNC operational sites to share knowledge and plans, but they have no reason ever to visit Palm Island. CONCH has no actual employees. The location and cohesion of the workforce are an important concern in transfer pricing since they represent the know-how that creates the IP.

As shown in Fig. 3.3, little has changed operationally at MNC. Only the flow of offshore earnings has been diverted.

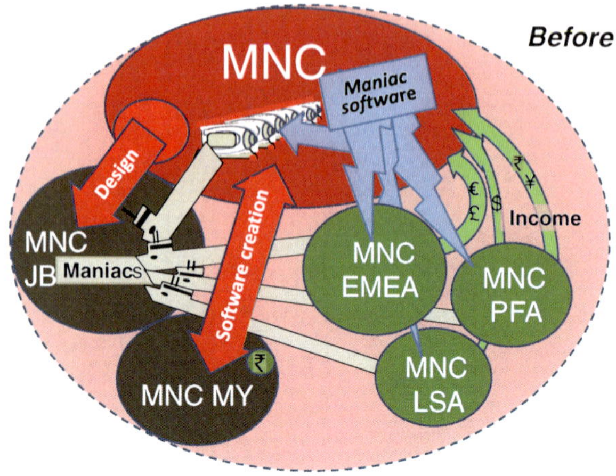

Fig. 3.2 Operational flows among MNC's divisions before the buy-in

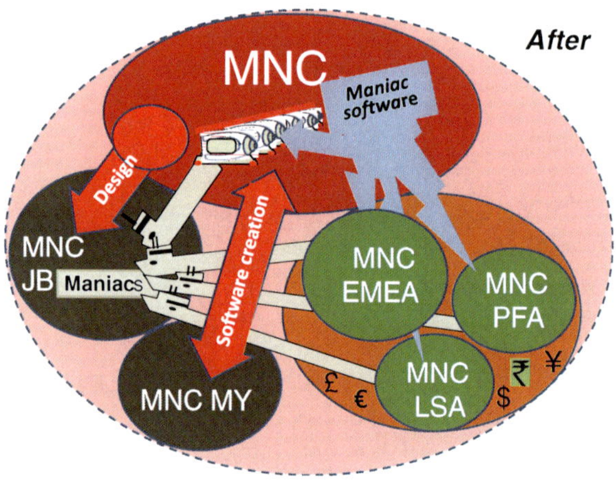

Fig. 3.3 Operational flows among MNC's divisions after the buy-in

3.2 Creation of Intangibles

For intangibles, the benefits of volume production are extreme. Table 3.1 compares some common intangibles and contrasts them with a final tangible product. Many apparent tangibles also contain substantial intangible contents, so the table also lists some of those. The average cost of a year of a creative person is set here at $100,000, considering some overhead.

Table 3.1 Cost components for products containing intangibles

Sample product	Creation effort lag period, employee count, & their average IP effort			Costs			Units to be sold	Unit cost $S + \frac{I+F}{V}$	Sales of product		IP content — used to rank
				Initial	of 1st copy	of next copy	estimate		price	total	
				I	F	*S*	*V*	*U*	*P*	*R*	
metric	y'rs	#	%	$	$	$	no.	$ per unit		$	%
Internet apps	1	5	80	400 K	100	negligible	100K	4.2	8	1M	50%
Consultant report	1	2	75	150 K	1K	100	12	14 K	28 K	336 K	45%
Books	2	1	90	180 K	10K	15	5K	57	114	570 K	31%
Software	3	7	60	1.26 M	1K	10	100K	24	48	4.8 M	26%
CPU chip	3	24	70	5.04 M	15K	50	100K	107	215	21.5 M	24%
Simple chip	2	12	75	1.8 M	5K	10	200K	20	40	8.0 M	23%
Automobile	3	250	80	60 M	90K	12K	100K	12.7 K	25 K	2.5 B	2.4%

K stands for a thousand, 1,000;
M stands for a million, 1,000,000;
B stands for a billion, 1,000,00,000.

3.2.1 Process

The investment in creation of IP precedes sales. That cost is computed as the development period times the average effort spent during that period. During that time interest has been paid on the investments. Investment in new product development is risky and takes time.

Table 3.1 lists the major cost and time factors needed to create intangibles, and the factors needed to estimate product costs and an adequate sales price [F3.1]. All but the last entry are products seen in electronic commerce [ChoiSW:97].

The sales price is intended to be sufficient to recover the investment and production for each product. It is computed as the sum of the costs of the initial creation plus the cost to manufacture the first copy, divided by the expected volume, plus the cost of manufacturing and distributing additional units [F3.1]. The estimated sales price is simply set at twice the cost, enough to cover the expenses in running a business and generate some earnings. That overhead reduces the IP content in the revenue from the product to at most 50 %.

The numbers in the table are merely typical, but they do illustrate the crucial point:

> For intangible products it is not the creation cost that matters, but only the future operating income, i.e., volume × (price − copy cost) − overhead.

The final column of Table 3.1 ranks the products by IP content in each unit sold. Internet applications have the least manufacturing and distribution cost and rank highest. Even though designing an automobile is very costly, the high volume and substantial manufacturing cost reduces the IP content of a car to <3 %.

The impact of IP depends on the volume of the product and the production cost. The Automobile entry in Table 3.1 provides a contrast; while the design effort is huge, it is dwarfed by the manufacturing cost. Alternate estimates for the expected volume change the sales income and IP rank columns.

An Armstrong Siddeley Sapphire automobile, with annual sales of <1,000 cars, would have an IP content of 40 % and rise to rank 3 in Table 3.1. The company could not get an adequate return on its intellectual capital. The manufacture of their Sapphire cars was not a viable business.

Automobile with high IP content because of low production volume

The relative IP content numbers also explain why the earnings margins shown in financial analyses for knowledge-based industries are so high. The expenses of the creative workforce, essential to maintain a competitive position, are not included in the Cost of Goods Sold (CoGS), but rather as R&D. Their efforts enable companies to keep making or manufacturing additional copies of IP-based products at low cost.

The expenses for the required ongoing development to keep products viable are booked as R&D expenses and not deducted from the operating income [Basili:90]. Their work contributes little to the current income, but is essential for a profitable

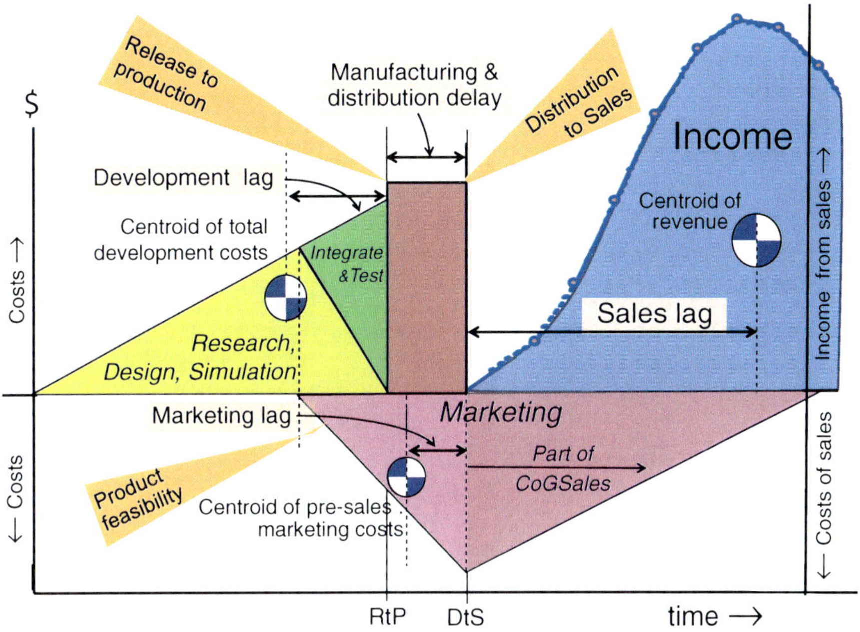

Fig. 3.4 Types of lags and delays

future. When the resulting earnings margin is shown in business analyses, those margins are not a useful metric for assessing the knowledge-based industries shown in Table 3.1. Improvements in accounting treatments of intangible expenses have been proposed, but they have not been accepted by the accounting profession [HandL:03 p.125].

3.2.2 Lag

IP is created over time; it does not just appear magically when needed. Table 3.1 shows that creation of IP, the gestation period, took 1–3 years. During the time of creation and initial development of the product the investment does not create any income. Because the level of effort varies during the development period, a measure "lag" is used, which represents the average effort, weighted by the delays before the product is ready to be manufactured or sold.

The effect of the R&D and testing effort before the first product copy is completed is the development lag. Other lags and delays occur in the business processes that convert an investment into income, deferring income further. A model is sketched in Fig. 3.4; actual data can be obtained from careful accounting. To match scales better, the expected level of net income is shown, rather than revenues that are subject to production (CoGS) and business expenses (SG&A).

The four major types of lag are:

1. Development lag, due to the effort to create the first functionally complete product prototype
2. Marketing lag, defined by the effort made to sell the first product
3. Manufacturing and distribution delays, the time needed to move from having a complete prototype to having sufficient stock to actually sell the product
4. Sales lag, defined as the effective period for product sales or income

The development lag and the delays prior to sales are crucial components in IP valuation.

3.2.2.1 Development Lag

The development used to compute the cost to produce the prototype of products, as shown in Table 3.1, is best computed by taking all the development expenses as incurred and considering how long that cost is incurred before the prototype is ready. The actual effort spent in a business is computed by taking all the development expenses as incurred, primarily the monthly salaries for creative employees. Taking all of those costs and weighting them by the time before sales commence reduces all that information to a single number, the lag [F3.2]. The lag is the effective time from the centroid of the development costs to the time that product can be sold. Such lag estimates were used as a basis for the cost calculation in Table 3.1 with a modest cost-of-money rate of 12 % per year, and become major component of U, the investment before a prototype is ready for production [F3.1].

In different settings the development effort will grow more or less rapidly. Figure 3.5 sketches three possibilities and shows typical values for the average effort percentages and the investment lag. The average effort—less for start-ups, more for mature organizations—tends to be about 50 % of the final expenses times the development period and approaches 100 % for ongoing development [W:06]. The steepness of the curves is limited by the need to have a cohesive workforce. A company cannot add employees at excessive rates without losing effectiveness.

For analysis of the development lag, we may further split the effort types into Research, Design, and Simulation versus Testing. Testing is often carried out by groups outside of development. When some software development is performed offshore, that work will have a significantly lower personnel cost than the $100,000 per person-year assumed for Table 3.1. Testing can commence at the point where product feasibility is established. MNC's MY division in India performs most software testing for the Maniac products.

When detailed information on the effort spent is not available, estimates based on development processes seen in industry, as modeled in Fig. 3.5, can provide an adequate result. Sometimes the lag is simply estimated as half of the development

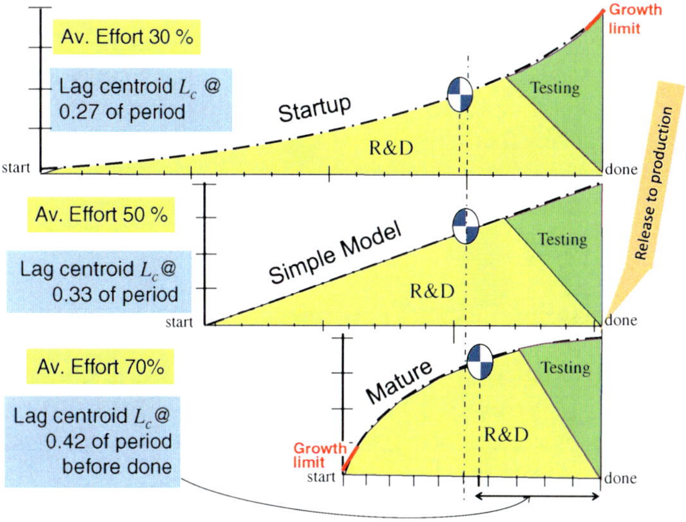

Fig. 3.5 Development periods, effort percentages, and lags in three settings

period. Such a simple estimate implies no changes in the workforce and ignores how companies grow.

A realistic estimate of lag considers the novelty and complexity of the product versus the maturity of the organization. A company starting up will grow more slowly and require a longer time to produce the prototype; whereas a mature organization can ramp up more quickly, as also shown in Fig. 3.5. For a similar product the effective lag may still be similar, because shorter development periods are offset by higher average effort fractions. Many more cases could be considered [W:06]. Chapter 5 compares methods for valuing IP.

Table 3.1 included the investment cost over the lag in the results at a low annual interest rate of 12 %. A venture capitalist would extract a much higher rate from a start-up, likely more than 50 %. The average high risk faced by a venture capitalist increases the IP value for successful ventures.

3.2.2.2 Marketing Lag

The marketing lag represents the effects of the costs expended before the first unit of the product is sold. Marketing efforts also generate IP that will contribute to sales. The magnitude of marketing costs can be similar to or even greater than product development costs, especially if a broad segment of the public must be reached. MNC sells its products primarily to suppliers of larger systems, so its potential customers can be located via trade publications and trade shows, and thus its preproduction marketing costs are modest.

Little marketing is possible before development has reached the testing stage, indicated as "Product Feasibility" in Fig. 3.3. The marketing lag is computed by taking the time from the centroid of the expenses up to the point of distribution to sales. Once products are available for sale, the costs of sales and marketing support together become either part of the Cost of Goods Sold (CoGS) or part of Selling, General, and Administrative costs (SG&A) and are not considered an investment, even though ongoing spending on marketing remains essential to motivate sales.

3.2.2.3 Manufacturing and Distribution Delays

There are often substantial delays to ramp up production and get the products into warehouses and stores so that sales can commence. These costs are part of the initial cost, but they do not generate intellectual property. Manufacturing and distribution delays must be added to the development lag, however, because they further increase the period before the initial development investment contributes to income from sales. These delays differ greatly by product type. Whereas iPhone apps can be instantly available, improved chips for a new iPhone version will be sampled before being incorporated into its design, and the delay before volume sales commence will be about a year.

It takes MNC about 3 months to set up the operation at MNC JB for a new version of Maniacs and validate that they are turning out products that exactly match the functional and reliability specifications of the prototypes created earlier in the USA. The first batches of Maniacs are then shipped by air to MNC's distributors.

The software, developed jointly at MNC in the USA and at MNC MY, can be distributed over the Internet and inserted into MNC's products just before shipment. In fact, MNC's customers expect that delivered Maniacs will always contain the latest versions and all updates of the software. There is no delay to add to the software development lag.

3.2.3 Sales Life and Lag

The sales volume takes time to grow and will eventually diminish [Moore:91]. The resulting sales lag is also computed from a centroid, now based on sales revenues rather than costs. Predicting sales is risky, but having a model documents the prediction and allows corrections to be applied later [W:06]. To estimate the rise and fall of product sales we use Erlang(m) distributions [F3.3], shown in Fig. 3.5.

In Fig. 3.6 the annual sales were modeled using an Erlang(12) distribution [ChatfieldG:73]. If 90 % of sales occur before year 11, the corresponding sales lag for that model of sales growth is 5 years [F3.3]. Products with weaker IP protection have shorter lives. A curve matching an Erlang(8) distribution, giving a sales lag of 1–2 years from start to its sales centroid, is shown for the sale of copyrighted products [SmithP:05, p.408].

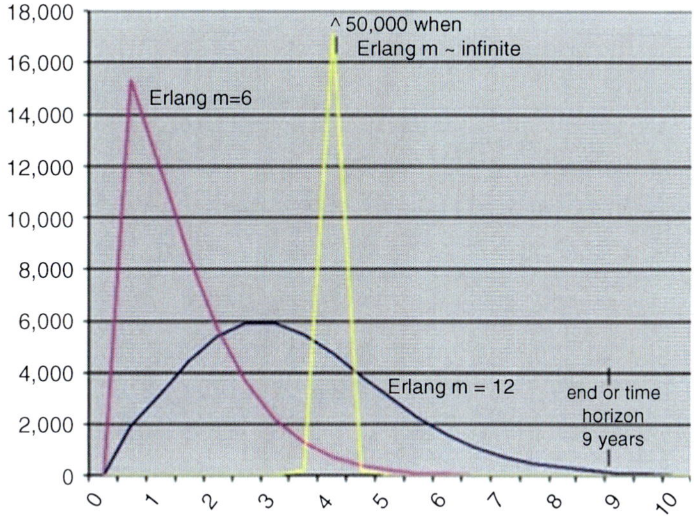

Fig. 3.6 Sales expectations

The expected sales lag is an important number for IP valuation. A long sales lag reduces the Net Present Value (NPV) of its income greatly, here to 53 % of the total actual sales [F3.4]. For MNC the sales lag further depends on the acceptance of Maniacs by its distributors. Distributors will not want to stock large inventories of Maniacs for their end customers, because inventories become obsolete when a new Maniac is released.

For our model company, MNC, we simply assume that income and earnings follow the same sales curve. In practice, over time, production costs should decrease, increasing the operating income. At the same time pressure on prices and increasing business costs reduce the operating income over time. If business records are available, the sales lag can be computed instead of estimated.

3.2.3.1 Stable Sales

The sales curve for an initial product is shown shaded in Fig. 3.7. It is based on the Erlang-model for $m = 12$ shown in Fig. 3.5. MNC, like most high-tech companies, will continue to improve its products and release updated products with new versions of its software, creating a product line. In the long range, that process of continuing improvement allows MNC to achieve profitable sales over many years. Figure 3.5 sketches predicted sales for five product releases, each having an identical sales distribution, given a stable rate of product sales, leading to a product life of ~15 years. Whenever an updated product is announced, sales of the prior product drop. When the new product is released, sales will show a peak [W:06]. For some products the peaks coincide with seasonal variations.

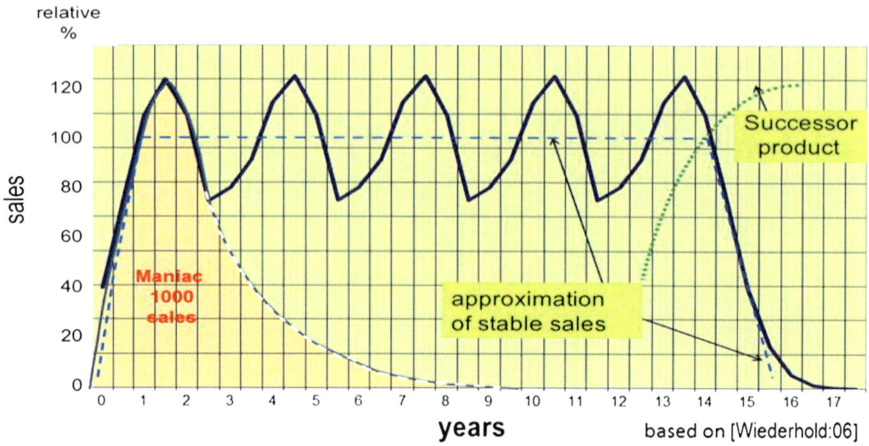

Fig. 3.7 Stable product-line sales due to release of improved products

Superimposed on the flattened long-term curve should be the increase in sales volume of Maniacs due to an increased penetration in the US and foreign markets. The envelope of all product-line sales should follow an Erlang model as well. The annual sales of MNC's Maniac product line actually grew within the years covered by our data, as was seen in Fig. 2.3, indicating that MNC's business is still in the rising part of such a long-term Erlang distribution.

Eventually a product line will become obsolete and its economic life will end. MNC will have devoted a fraction of its intellectual capital to create replacements products. One such replacement product is the ManiMobile, shown in Chap. 5, Sect. M3. If MNC does not invest well, it will be overtaken by competitors. That interaction is sketched in Fig. 5.9.

Within the scope of our analytical model an ongoing income stream is generated by the ongoing productivity of MNC's intangible assets.

3.3 Types of Intangible Assets

Up to this point we have not considered in detail the actual types of the intangible assets that are of concern. Figure 3.8 shows the scope of the intellectual resources we encounter when presenting various activities of MNC. The innermost collection, the intellectual property, is the most visible aspect, as ownership rights to property can be defended. All of the intermediate components within intellectual resources are crucial to having a successful business.

The most important asset is the total intellectual capital of a company. Although it cannot be explicitly transferred, it is the glue that holds a business together and

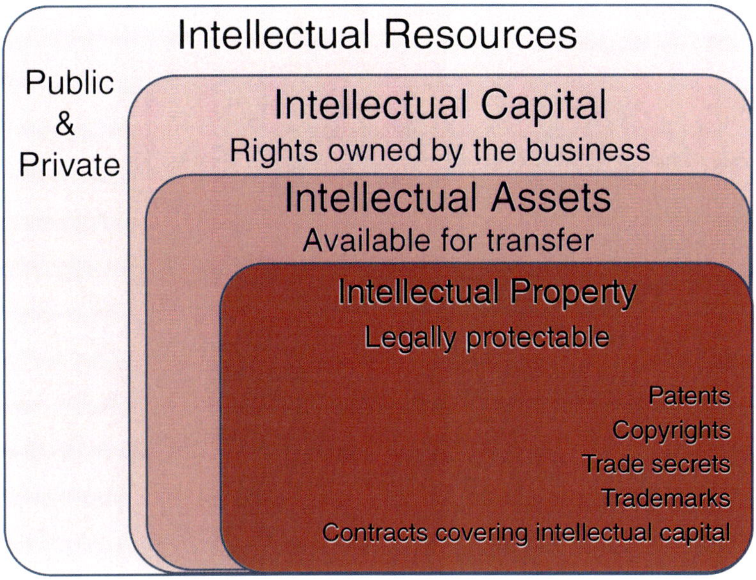

Fig. 3.8 Scope of intellectual resources as used in our exposition

keeps it going, representing the "Going Concern Value" (GCV). The GCV is provided by the leadership and vision of management that drive a company forward. When that leadership is missing or gets distracted, companies will lose value, but the effects of inadequate management can take a long time to affect the GCV, because the visible assets change more slowly.

Although the intellectual capital, including the workforce, cannot be sold, the rights to exploit it can be sold. CONCH appears to have bought a piece of MNC's IP, but it actually purchased a tranche of rights that included the benefits of ongoing services by management and research and development staff.

When a business fails, and is no longer a going concern, only a salvage value is left. Companies based on IP have very low salvage values once the workforce is dispersed.

3.3.1 A Listing of Candidate Intangible Assets

Types of intangible assets that can be protected appear in more detail in Table 3.2; rules for valuation and taxation do differ among those types. Depending on the objectives of a specific analysis, the assets listed will be categorized in various ways. Arguments about the right and best way of categorizing assets have ensued. There is actually no universal best way. It is essential that the objective of a categorization should be stated before it is used.

Table 3.2 Types of intellectual assets

1. Personnel or workforce
   (a) Ongoing creative staff with experience in the income-generating products
      - Employment contracts, such as "noncompete covenants," if any
      - Employees' stock options that are not vested, a disincentive to quit now

   (b) New hires, with adequate education, but no specific experience
      - Stock options, given out as a disincentive to quit early
2. Unique business and technical development and manufacturing processes
   (a) Protected by business patents
   (b) Protected as trade secrets
3. Essential goodwill
   (a) Lists of customers, potential customers, dealers, distributors, and early adopters
   (b) Lists of investors and potential investors (Note that actual investments and shares sold are booked as tangibles.)
4. Trademarks, including Internet domain names
   (a) Registered with the USPTO, state authorities, ICANN, or their delegates
   (b) Used informally
5. Competitive position
   (a) Market share overall or in various regions or market segments
   (b) First-to-market status, with an indication of the time advantage
   (c) Network effects due to position in related market segments
6. Orders
   (a) Orders in hand and not yet produced
      - Omit items already produced and kept in inventory

   (b) Orders expected, with an estimate of probability of order arriving
      - Subtract items already produced and kept in inventory
7. Exclusive contracts
   (a) Licenses to exclusive use of IP owned by others
   (b) Rights to services by others to produce products
   (c) Contracts for parts, supplies, and manufacturing tools
8. Valuable contracts
   (a) Licenses to IP owned by others
   (b) Governmental taxation allowances and future grants and concessions
   (c) Contracts for important services to produce products
   (d) Contracts for important parts, supplies, and manufacturing tools
   (e) Leases and permits for research or manufacturing facilities or equipment
9. Research and development completed or acquired
   (a) Protected by patents or patent filings
   (b) Protected as trade secrets
10. Research and development currently in process, including acquired R&D, with
    - Estimate of time needed to completion
    - Estimated market for the results

    (a) Protected by patents or patent filings
    (b) Protected as trade secrets
11. Design documents
    (a) Protected by copyright
    (b) Protected as trade secrets
12. Software and databases
    (a) Protected by copyright
    (b) Protected as trade secrets

The entries in our table are based on multiple sources, such as [CroninHKLP:11], [Damodaran:99, 00, 02, 05, 06], [DyeGG:07], [Gooch:00], [ParrS:05], [PrattRS:96], [ReillyS:98], [SmithP:05], [vanHiltenEa:10]. The assets were selected, edited, and arranged to suit our focus on issues arising in taxation. The table is arranged with the least tangible asset types first.

Some intellectual assets excluded from the list of intellectual property may well contribute additional income. For instance, services that the workforce can provide and that will be charged to the customer can add considerable income, but unless a contract is in place their expected contribution cannot be valued with certainty. Investors who are familiar with a company will include a rough estimate of potential service income in their valuation.

3.3.2 *Categorization of Types of Intellectual Assets*

Twelve types of intellectual assets are summarized in Table 3.2. Specific asset items, to be treated similarly, are assigned to these types. The list ignores some protected items that do not generate nonroutine income, such as user manuals and marketing literature. Those are provided to technology customers at cost, perhaps with a shipping and handling markup.

The 12 asset types are often grouped into categories for analysis and discussion. A description of common categories follows, focusing on issues raised in transfer pricing. If errors are made in properly identifying IP or assigning it appropriately, the original owner of the IP will be deprived of a fraction of its expected income. The resulting reduction in US earnings is a large component of tax avoidance [LeonardS:05, Ch.22]. Using the definitions shown here with care will allow past errors to be recognized and future errors avoided.

3.3.3 *Results of Research*

For a high-tech company the workforce and results of its research and development efforts are the most crucial assets. Except for any capitalized or acquired research of asset 9, none appear on corporate books [DengL:06]. If assets are documented and protected they are intellectual property (IP); to the extent that they are hidden in the capability of the workforce, they are part of the corporate know-how. Many more detailed asset groupings are possible.

3.3.3.1 Intellectual Property (IP)

IP is limited to property assets that can be legally protected and defended if violated [Woodbury:1845]. Formally protected IP is easier to identify than the other assets, and identification is a prerequisite to valuation and taxation.

Protection is available for

- Patents (for assets 2a, 9a, and 10a)
- Copyrights (for assets 11a and 12a)
- Trade secrets (for assets 2b, 3a & b, 10b, 11b, and 12b)
- Contracts (for assets 1a°, 6a, 7a & b, and 8a, b, c, & d)
- Trademarks (for assets 4a)

Having ownership rights does not provide protection by itself. Defending against violations of IP rights is the owner's responsibility and requires the services of lawyers. Serious fights to defend IP can be very expensive, easily exceeding the value of the protected property.

3.3.3.2 Know-How

Know-how covers many informal assets, such as 1a, 2b, 5c, 9b, 10b, 11b, and 12b. Unique know-how is embodied in the corporate workforce (1a). The workforce provided by the human capital is essential to maintain a successful business [Palmisano:06]. Without management there would be no link from product plans to customer demand. Without engineers who have the know-how to exploit a patent, the patent would be worthless. Contracts that give access to knowledge of others, as 8a and 8c, also contribute to know-how [Contractor:01].

Overall, we cannot even conceive of having a business without people [Sveiby:97]. Granting stock options is a common incentive to keep a staff with much know-how; costs associated with stock options are discussed in Chap. 5, as part of the market cap-based valuation, M1.

3.3.3.3 Intellectual Assets and IP in the Tax Code and Regulations

US laws pertaining to taxes are found in Title 26 of the Internal Revenue Code (IRC), introduced in Appendix B [B.1.1]. Details on their application by the IRS are provided in the corresponding Code of Federal Regulations (CFR) [B.1.2]. Intangible Property is the dominant term used in the tax code for the issues addressed here. The directly relevant material is modest; Table 3.3 provides the text of the two definitions.

The legal definition of IP for transfer pricing issues is a 1976 law establishing tax breaks for US possessions, shown in the first section of Table 3.3 [B.2.1(h)(3)(B)]. In Chap. 6 we will encounter these possessions as nearshore taxhaven.

It was adapted in 1986 for transfer pricing, shown in the second section of Table 3.3. The specific transfer pricing regulations in CFR.1.482 repeat that definition worded slightly differently [B.3.3 4(b)]. Both definitions are broader than the definition of intellectual property used in Table 3.2. Both include the know-how of the workforce needed to support exploitation of the intellectual property, but exclude individual services. The law was less specific about Item vi in its list: "any similar item" than the regulations on transfer pricing, whereas item 6, in the second section of Table 3.3, specifies "other similar items," positively.

Table 3.3 IP definitions in US law and US regulations

IRC§936: The term "intangible property" means any
(i) Patent, invention, formula, process, design, pattern, or know-how
(ii) Copyright, literary, musical, or artistic composition
(iii) Trademark, trade name, or brand name
(iv) Franchise, license, or contract
(v) Method, program, system, procedure, campaign, survey, study, forecast, estimate, customer list, or technical data or
(vi) Any similar item, which has substantial value independent of the services of any individual

CFR.1.482: Definition of intangible. For purposes of section 482, an intangible is an asset that comprises any of the following items and has substantial value independent of the services of any individual
(1) Patent, invention, formulae, process, design, pattern, or know-how
(2) Copyright, literary, musical, or artistic composition
(3) Trademark, trade names, or brand names
(4) Franchises, licenses, or contracts
(5) Methods, programs, systems, procedures, campaigns, surveys, studies, forecasts, estimates, customer lists, or technical data and
(6) Other similar items. For purposes of section 482, an item is considered similar to those listed in paragraph (b) (1) through (5) of this section if it derives its value not from its physical attributes, but from its intellectual content or other intangible properties.

This IRC §936 definition, being a law, takes priority over the CFR1.482 regulations. Both definitions cover all items listed in Table 3.2, as long as the transfer of IP is not performed as individual services. The last line the regulation writers added to the definition of IP has provoked many arguments between taxpayers and IRS staff [Arellano:08].

Both US Treasury definitions in Table 3.2 are somewhat broader than what is covered in economics texts as intellectual or intangible property. Later IRS documents avoid the designation "intangible property" and use the broader term "intellectual assets" instead [IRS-CIP:07]. Having rights to "intellectual capital" covers rights to use all the intangible assets as well as ongoing access to the workforce and its products in a cost-sharing arrangement.

3.3.4 Reimbursement for Services

Individual services, such as visits for training and verification of processes at CFCs, although valuable, are excluded from valuation of IP transfers in the tax code, being excluded in both sections of Table 3.3. Additional agreements are needed to fairly reimburse for individual services provided by the creator of the IP. The rate would be based on costs plus a routine markup [IRS-TS:06]. In practice it is hard to foresee the amount of services that may be required; many IP sellers underestimate the amount of follow-up needed to make the purchaser successful [Contractor:81]. The income from such services becomes part of the taxable earnings of the provider [B.2.3(a)(1)].

That income can be substantial and is the primary source of revenue for companies that support open-source software [LaMonica:05].

Access to services provided by the workforce is implicit where a company splits itself to avoid taxation on foreign sales, as in the case of MNC. In the buy-in by CONCH, only rights to collect income have been ceded; the actual workforce has not been split. No arm's-length service arrangement is possible. An arm's-length assumption does not correspond to the facts. Valuations that assume that the workforce is disjoint lead to false results [McAfee:83].

The alternative to the true situation, shared know-how, requires a rigid separation of engineering efforts, a so-called clean-room setting. Then only formal and public information can be shared. In cases that legally required separated development of IP, clean-room techniques have been used to avoid contamination of rights among IP owners and arm's-length users wishing to improve the provided software [W:08]. Then it is possible to price needed services, and those prices can be high [Jussawalla:92].

Isolation of workforce from the IP is not realistically possible within facilities and divisions of a single company like MNC, whose primary technical staff remains located at a single site in California. In such situations the valuation of the buy-in must include access to the workforce.

3.3.5 Trademark

The MNC trademark is a symbol for all of MNC's intangible assets. As such, its value depends on the overall perceived value of the company. A valuable trademark sustains an existing market position (5a) in Table 3.2, helps in entering new markets (5b), and drives the network effect (5c) [HandL:03]. For products where taste or fashion drives purchases, the value of a trademark can exceed the value of all other types of IP. Coca-Cola is commonly cited as an example of a valuable trademark, although Coca-Cola management will also point to its trade secret-protected formula [Bernasek:10E].

If the same product is sold branded or unbranded, the difference in price can provide a metric for a relative valuation. Companies entering a new business segment may purchase relevant trademarks [HandL:03]. A trademark can even have some value after the owner goes out of business; the name and trademark for Pan American Airlines continues to survive, although its value is now a fraction of what it was when "Pan Am" and its blue world logo stood for innovative service on US overseas air routes.

The value of a trademark diminishes rapidly when the brand is associated with technical failures, say a car that has brake problems or a computer with leaky capacitors [Vance:10]. Overcoming such a product failure requires much marketing effort. Sometimes the trademark has been encumbered to an extent that the company renamed itself, as ValuJet did [Wald:98]. Just having a trademark encumbered by a legal conflict will lower its value [Smith:97].

Trademarks require maintenance. Some of the expenses are considered routine and would be similar for all participants in an industry segment, such as labeling their delivery trucks. Other routine expenses are regular advertising and creating a web presence that matches the competition. Nonroutine expenses for product promotions and similar efforts are considered IP-generating expenses, and those deserve sharing income to the promoter [LeveyW:07]. The boundary between routine and nonroutine marketing expenses is hard to draw.

The value of a trademark can differ greatly from one locale to another, even if the product being sold is identical [TownsendJ:99]. MNC's distributors worked hard to introduce MNC's product in their geographic regions, and they were aided in that effort by MNC's headquarters. When a new version of the Maniac is released, MNC headquarters organizes extensive promotions.

Local sales organizations may decide not to participate in promotions organized by headquarters, as they are more sensitive to local conditions. The 2006 "You are a dinosaur if you still use Windows 2000" campaign was not acceptable to Microsoft's German distributors. The dependence of the trademark on the company's reputation means that a trademark is very difficult to value out of context. A widely cited trademark valuation is actually based on an encumbered trademark [Weiler:95]. MNC has not faced any disasters, so its trademark has a positive value. Because of its own good name, MNC has not retained the trademarks of the less well-established companies that it acquired.

Individuals also have a right to any income that can be derived from using their names and images [SmithP:05]. MNC has no contracts with sports or movie stars who have a publicity value.

3.3.6 Goodwill

The IP category "essential goodwill," listed in Table 3.2 as asset Type 3, covers the opinions of customers and investors about the company. Unfortunately, "goodwill" is also a category used by accountants in the absence of valuations for specific intangible assets. The term "essential goodwill" for assets of Type 3 is used here whenever the distinction is important. It can be valued by estimating the reduction in MNC's sales if that goodwill did not exist.

For the pre-2004 acquisitions, made by MNC for a total cost of $300M, the ATA valuation put many intangible asset types into an accounting basket called "goodwill." Intangible asset types included in the acquisition, but not valued specifically by ATA, were

(1)	Workforce
(2)	Processes that made the acquired company effective
(3)	Essential goodwill
(5 & 6b)	Competitive position and likely orders
(7 & 8)	Contracts
(10 & 11)	Current R&D in process and the associated design documents

All of the asset types listed here were booked into ATA's "goodwill" basket, which then contained 85 % of the accounted assets within MNC's purchase price.

Specifically, the workforce remained in place. Its value remains and cannot be ignored in a fair transfer valuation. For a serious and detailed valuation, only Asset 3: Essential goodwill, should be shown as goodwill, and all the other types that accountants might include in their goodwill category should be assessed independently [IRS-CSA:08].

Booked entries labeled as "goodwill" were easily written off; up to 2004 the default period was 15 years [B.2.9 (a), (b)(2)(D)]. Now annual impairment assessments are needed. Being poorly defined, goodwill is easily considered impaired, and written off anytime [Daum:01]. Such write-offs reduce the value booked from an acquisition. Knowledgeable investors are aware that the value of the acquisition lies somewhere else. All of MNC's divisions profited from the acquired resources of the income-generating IP as a result of those acquisitions.

3.3.6.1 Market Position as an Intangible

The amount of current and future income depends mainly on the sales volume, and a high sales volume depends on a company's market position, the share of sales it captures among similar products in the market. Novelty, especially if protected by patents and supported by having a recognized trademark, helps in entering new markets (Type 5b) [LeonardS:05, Ch.18]. The same factors, and a reputation of quality, sustain an existing market position (Type 5a).

3.3.7 Unrecognized Intangibles

Some types of intangibles listed in Table 3.2, obtained as part of an acquisition, do not appear on the books of the acquired company, such as Type 4: brand names; Types 6, 7, & 8, customer relationships; and Type 10, acquired in-process research and development. While paid for, they are classified as unrecognized intangibles according to General Accepted Accounting Principles (GAAP) [FASB:04]. This lack of recognition makes it hard to assign a proper business value to them. Such assets can be presented in "pro forma" statements provided to shareholders, but they will not be counted into the book value [SlavinK:06]. Assets that are really of no value to the purchaser can be ignored, or if listed, immediately written off. They would have been recognized when the acquisition was planned and not factored in as contributing value when setting an acquisition price.

When a start-up company is acquired, its current "in-progress research and development" (asset type 10 in Table 3.2) is actually the most valuable part of the acquisition. Again, US GAAP rules require acquired current in-process R&D to be written off immediately, although the practice has been questioned [FASB:04]. The reason is that internal R&D expenses are not to be capitalized until a feasible inclusion in a product has been proven [FASB:85]. Capitalization of "internal R&D" can commence at the point marked "product feasibility" in Fig. 3.3. Because acquired current R&D falls into the same category as internal R&D, for consistency of accounting, internal R&D that has not yet been shown to be feasible should disappear from the books. That is accomplished by writing it off. Disregarding significant acquired R&D in valuations because of the accounting requirements grossly distorts an acquisition assessment.

3.3.8 *Aggregating Intellectual Asset Values*

Even though Table 3.2 categorized intellectual assets, they are all crucially intertwined and interdependent. A trademark has no value if there are no products. Without sales personnel no income will be generated. Because of these dependencies, a simple aggregate of parts or identifiable IP types does not adequately represent the total value of an enterprise [SmithP:05, p.20]. On the other hand, it is nearly impossible to create reliable and comprehensive estimates for all 28 asset types listed in Table 3.2. The best solution is to make one pass to determine the actual importance of the IP types in a case. Once the main contributions are well understood, other IP types can be assessed relative to those major types.

The types of IP are not commutative. Combining marketing and product IP works only if there is a decent product. Without a decent product, no amount of marketing will generate sales [LeveyW:07]. Once all specific assets are valued, it is useful to compare the total result with a broad-based estimate, such as the market capitalization for public companies, to see if the result makes sense, as recommended in Chap. 5, method M1.

3.4 Life of Intangibles

IP and rights to IP have a finite life, but possibly a long one. The rights to IP are limited to the life of the IP itself. Further limits can be imposed by law, contracts, or external constraints. Some countries have limited both the royalty percentages and the life of royalty agreements to protect their industries from being exploited. Japan had such constraints when it was trying to grow its industry, and some developing countries do that now. Local earnings become locally taxable. Confidence in a consistent application of tax regulations is increased when tax treaties have been signed among countries. Our MNC was not affected by such constraints.

The life of an asset limits the period over which future income should be aggregated in a valuation. Life differs not only for each asset type but also for specific instances. Software IP can contribute income from a few years to over 15 years [SmithP:00]. Three categories in estimating life are:

Indefinite life means that the life of the asset is unknown, but likely long if routinely maintained as expected. Goodwill, trademarks, corporate reputation, customer lists, and the like are commonly deemed to have an indefinite life. They can be written off or reduced when events occur that impair their value.

Diminishing life means that the value of an initial investment diminishes over time. The contribution of initial core capabilities of a product will diminish as products are modernized and grow in scope. Software, an asset that can live a long time but that is continuously upgraded over successive versions, is a prime example [W:06]. Because some of the core will always remain, life can be considered to have practically ended when <10 % of the original contribution is left. This assumption simplifies later computations.

Statutory life is due to imposed rules. The life of patents is limited by law. The IRS also imposes a 20-year life on assets in many situations, but not on IP in transfer pricing. Contracts can impose limits as well—for instance, a license may lose its exclusivity after 5 years. Accounting rules specify periods for amortization and depreciation, but those are not relevant for IP life.

Unpredictable events can abrogate life. The change may be sudden or slow. Digital recording, for instance, has displaced analog recording. It took a long time for air travel to replace long-distance railroads and steamships. Major surprises are referred to as "black swans" [Taleb:07]. The occurrence and effect of unknowable events are unpredictable, so this aspect of limiting life is best dealt with by choosing a discount rate that represents the long-term historical risks documented in the broader industry [Rosenberg:98].

3.5 Misvaluation

It is easy to make errors when valuing IP and the associated intellectual capital. Because future income is the major determinant of the value of intellectual assets, misjudging the life of those assets is a major cause of errors. In Chap. 5 we show how the use of multiple distinct valuation methods can provide a credible range.

Most modern assets have a substantial value only when they can be counted on to remain functional in the future. An aircraft for which no spare parts are available for maintenance has only a scrap-metal value after a few weeks. Databases, embedded in many products, also require contents maintenance to remain relevant [GardnerR:98]. Software loses its value if it cannot disable new viruses or adapt to new data interchange standards and upgraded operating systems [LientzS:80]. If MNC were to announce that it would stop development of its embedded support software, customers would rapidly abandon the brand. MNC's ManiMobile product is especially at risk, because wireless standards are evolving all over the world.

In a high-tech acquisition, the most valuable part, the intellectual assets obtained, is largely written off the books. Accounting rules encourage errors in valuing acquisitions. In accounting, numbers can be added to create a sum, and interactions are largely ignored. Just listing the assets of a company as stand-alone items, outside the context of an ongoing business, will just yield a salvage value. All these errors may be unintentional, but if errors are corrected only when they increase tax obligations, the effect will be lopsided. The remaining reduced values on the books can greatly shrink the buy-in amount that an offshore operation, as CONCH, has to pay for its share. Financial capital follows intellectual capital rights in moving offshore.

3.6 Summary

A major issue in dealing with intellectual assets is the lack of well-accepted definitions. Since intellectual assets are the major source of corporate income, inconsistencies cause substantial errors. The errors can be exploited to benefit tax avoidance.

Education is lagging behind as well. Few academic courses cover intellectual capital or intangibles beyond the need to protect IP. The educational requirements for the CPAs, who prepare the books that investors and tax authorities must rely on, describe "goodwill" as a category of get book entries to explain mismatches in prices actually paid for acquisitions and items that can be placed on corporate books. US laws, tax treaties, and IRS and SEC regulations provide inadequate guidance. When valuable IP is misclassified, book values become unreliable.

For many modern companies, as MNC, the book value shown is a modest fraction of the value that shareholders assign, namely the number of shares × the price per share. As an example we show in Table 3.4 data from SAP, a major German software firm.

The ratio shown in Table 3.4 is typical of knowledge-based industries. The ratios are yet higher for modern enterprises that mainly lease buildings and computers to preserve resources for creative efforts. Leased tangibles only appear as current costs and future obligations. The largest fraction of tangibles in those firms is the working capital, needed to support operations and bridge the interval from production to receipt of payments for sales.

The educational background of most experts in economics who deal with the problems now faced is similarly unbalanced. While many are aware of the importance of IP, no consistent model of its interaction is shared among them. Failure to consider the significance of intellectual capital to industry leads to meaningless advice.

Table 3.4 Importance of intangible assets

Source of data: SAP AG annual report		2005
Book value from annual report	a	€6.3B
Market capitalization of shares	b	€31.5B
Implied value of intangible assets	$c=b-a$	€25.2B
Ratio of intangible to tangible assets	$q=c/a$	4×

A 52-page report to the president of the USA by a high-level advisory committee on increasing jobs in the USA stresses the need for financial capital 48 times, but cites IP only twice in the context of needing protection [ImmeltEa:11]. The term “innovation” appears 36 times, but either within pleas for more funding or in titles of projects and committees. The authors must have been aware of IP and jobs disappearing into tax-havens, but that issue was ignored.

The preceding chapters have introduced a number of concepts that reappear throughout this exposition.

3.6.1 Concepts Needed to Understand the Role of IP

We list some of the concepts essential to understanding how the flow of rights to intellectual assets, as exemplified by MNC, creates capital that is most effectively used for creating jobs offshore.

- Intellectual capital: the assets of a company beyond its tangibles and financial capital
- Nonroutine earnings: earnings due to exploitation of intellectual capital
- Intellectual property (IP): the portion of intellectual capital that is formally owned
- Controlled Foreign Corporation (CFC): a division of a parent company operating outside of the company’s home country
- Buy-in: the purchase by a CFC of a tranche of the parent company’s intellectual capital
- Transfer price: the price set for products, tangible assets, or intangible assets made available to another company division
- Arm’s-length: the concept of a pricing standard based on transactions with a truly independent partner
- Valuation: assigning an economic value to intellectual capital or a portion of it

The value of intellectual capital and its components is the major component of modern enterprises and yet poorly understood and barely documented. When IP is misvalued in international transactions, as shown in the case of MNC providing access to all of its intellectual capital to CONCH, the long-range effect on the company, its employees, and the country that supports such companies is serious [StolowyJ:01].

Since IP is such a crucial component of modern businesses, insight into IP and how it is created, shifted, and destroyed is essential to follow the growth of multinational companies. Making predictions about government policies and tax revenues that are based on traditional models of capital and labor are likely to be wrong. This issue is revisited in Chap. 10 when we assess recommendations to remove the distortions that tax avoidance generates.

Chapter 4
Transfer Pricing and Rights Transfers

Transfer pricing is a relatively recent topic. In 1996, only US and Australian tax authorities had any rules affecting transfer pricing of intangible assets, but by 2009, a total of 49 countries had developed rules for transfer pricing of intangibles and rights to exploit intangibles [Canale:09]. Understanding transfer pricing of IP is essential to understanding its role in tax avoidance.

4.1 Transfer Pricing

Paying for exchanges of property among divisions of a company is called "transfer pricing" [Feinschreiber:01]. The principle of transfer pricing is that any division of an enterprise that does its own accounting should do asset transfers on a fair basis. If a company sets too high a price for products manufactured in one division and sold by another division, it would report high profits in its manufacturing division but operate its sales division at a loss. Taxes would be lopsided, and the sales division, if set up as a distinct corporation, could even in time declare bankruptcy, wiping out its losses while increasing profits for the company as a whole.

Being fair in transfer pricing means that divisions within a company should not charge each other more or less than they would charge when selling the goods to a company that has no special relationship with them—that is, a company that operates at "arm's length" from the seller. If transfer prices among internal, closely held divisions match arm's-length standards, the divisions do not gain advantages over external competitors in their specific domain.

When goods that are being transferred between divisions are also sold to outside customers, the transfer price is easy to set; it should just be equal to the price that those customers would pay. Some special adjustments may be made, because certain costs, such as sales commissions, will be negligible for internal sales. Volume discounts, if given to external customers, can also be applied. In either case the corporate divisions should still have the same profit margin.

G. Wiederhold, *Valuing Intellectual Capital: Multinationals and Taxhavens*, Management for Professionals 23, DOI 10.1007/978-1-4614-6611-6_4,

When tangible goods that are not available to the public are being transferred, no price is available. Now the issue becomes a bit more difficult [King:10]. An estimate can be based on prices for similar goods that are sold publicly. If tangible goods differ somewhat, an adequate estimate for transfer pricing can be based on adjusted and averaged prices.

Intangibles are not widely sold as such, although products created with IP input are widely marketed. The prices of some intangibles, like patents or the copyright to a book or to a music performance, can be found and used to establish IP values. Prices for other IP are hard to find.

The cost of making an intangible does not give guidance to its value. Estimating the value of an intangible based on the cost, even with a leverage factor, is not reliable. The reason is that intangibles can be copied at negligible cost. Selling a product based on IP does not diminish the IP; actually, a successful sales record can make the IP more valuable [Sveiby:97].

Instead, the value, and hence the transfer price of IP, requires estimating the income it will garner in the future. That income is due to sales of products that are based on that IP, namely the sales price for each unit multiplied by the quantity of products sold. Beyond the IP embedded in the product is the value of the sales acumen and marketing investment employed when distributing the product. Those contributions reduce the fraction of the revenues that are considered when the transfer price is set.

4.1.1 MNC's Pricing of Transferred IP

After setting up CONCH, MNC transferred rights to collect income from sales to CONCH. After paying expenses, CONCH keeps all the earnings. The value of those rights had to be paid for. All of MNC's IP was made available to CONCH in its region. That geographic share was determined by the consultants at ATA to be a 42 % tranche. ATA also determined that the transfer price for the IP made available to CONCH would be $50M. The buy-in amount charged to CONCH is the transfer price for that property.

Without an IP rights transfer, MNC's foreign operations would be treated like any other part of its business. The costs incurred for manufacturing in Malaysia at MNC JB and software testing in India at MNC MY would be costs of doing business and deducted from the parent company's income. Earnings from foreign sales, after their costs have been deducted, would incur the statutory 35 % federal corporate income tax, mitigated by any US incentives.

At first glance it appears that the IP transfer and buy-in is just a shift of assets within MNC, and nobody should care. Nevertheless, a national taxing authority, in this case the IRS, will care, because shifting those assets changes reportable income within its jurisdiction [IRS-TP:94]. The installments that CONCH pays for that buy-in amount become taxable income at MNC in the USA, replacing the taxable income that MNC would have garnered from its foreign operations if it had not transferred rights to receive the income and earnings to CONCH [ChapotonG:88].

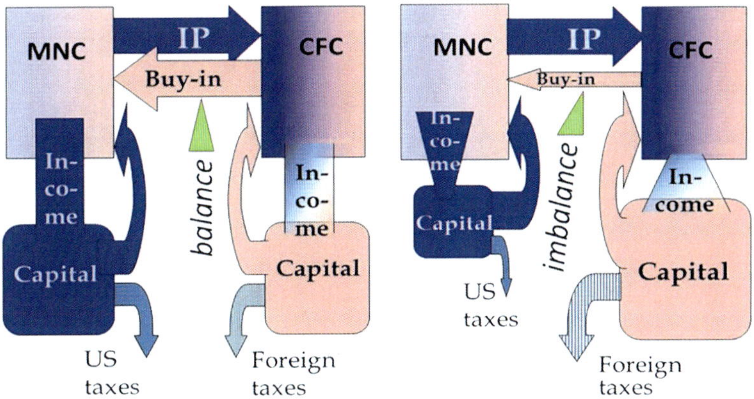

Fig. 4.1 The effects of a fair and an unfair transfer price

Over time the imbalance causes capital to be accumulated in countries where inadequately reimbursed IP has shifted [Caves:07]. The initial imbalance is magnified, because MNC and its CFCs operate in countries that differ greatly in taxation policies and regulations [Markham:05]. The effect is depicted in Fig. 4.1.

4.1.2 Governmental Concerns and Constraints

International transfer pricing is now a concern for many countries [McDonald:08]. Different countries set their tax rates according to their own priorities, so that any mispricing is elevated to an imbalance of payments among countries [LeveyWC:06]. The principle of arm's-length pricing as a basis for fair intracompany trade was recognized as international trade grew [Carroll:32]. With the explosion of trade after the Second World War, international transfer pricing became contentious [Baranson:78]. Transfers within multinational corporations like MNC make up more than 40 % of US international trade [Clausing:06]. Attempts to correct misuse have been made, but have not succeeded [Rossotti:05], [MackEa:05].

International trade organizations have been concerned about trade imbalances [Aujean:01]. Most efforts implicitly addressed tangible exports. The export of intangible assets is of much more recent concern, and most authorities are still quite naïve about it. Much knowledge about the relevant laws, regulations, legal decisions, and their application has been collected by consulting firms like ATA, the advisor serving MNC [LeveyW:07]. ATA's expertise, its own intellectual capital, is not shared with governmental authorities [BorstellH:09].

Under US law, some of this income can be sheltered from US taxes by allocating "extraterritorial income" into a tax-free corporate division (IC-DISC) [DesaiH:00]. When income is transferred from the IC-DISC to the parent, only a 15 % tax is due.

MNC did not take advantage of that scheme, in part because of limits imposed by IRS regulations, but also because ATA showed that MNC could do better by sheltering foreign earnings at a CFH in a taxhaven.

Transfer prices can be limited by governmental constraints. Substantial payments for foreign intellectual assets are easily seen as unfair. Some countries have limited the payment terms for IP transfers to protect their industries from being exploited. Japan imposed such constraints when it was trying to grow its industry, and some developing countries constrain payments for foreign-owned IP [SAT:09].

Payments to taxhaven divisions are even harder to justify than payments to the country where the IP originated. Some countries are starting to investigate the reimbursement practices of CFCs [Houlder:10C]. If limits on IP payments are imposed, some earnings will be retained where products are actually manufactured. The retained earnings are taxed locally and the remainder becomes available for local investment. Such considerations are especially important for emerging economies [KarC:09]. Now the existence of tax treaties, discussed in Chap. 8, becomes a concern. Our MNC was not affected by such constraints.

4.2 Transfers of Rights

It appears to casual observers that the IP transferred is the material information that is needed offshore to make products, but in practice only rights to use the IP are being transferred. These rights can be arbitrarily circumscribed. For instance, CONCH obtained the rights to earnings from MNC's IP only in its geographic region, which amounted to 42 % of MNC's total sales. That obviously does not mean that the actual users of the IP in Malaysia and India received only a 42 % fraction of the hardware and software documentation; they received access to all the information they needed to be effective. The master documents representing the IP remain with the owner, even after a share of the right to exploit the IP is transferred [RICS:04].

A distributor may obtain rights to make products in addition to selling rights. That means the distributor can make product copies, say of a CD containing software. With "make rights" the distributor has better control of product inventory and delivery. The boundary from simple copying to full manufacturing is not clear, and can easily become a controversy, because many regulations specify specific rights for manufacturing [Kennedy:07].

The rights to copy products are not transferred to the purchaser of a product. Just purchasing a disk containing valuable software does not convey the right to market copies of the software to others. The same holds true for the embedded software. A Maniac bought from MNC contains IP in both its hardware and its software. Only a "use license" is given to the customer who buys a Maniac. The embedded software is to be used only within the product.

A purchaser can decide to resell the complete device. The subsequent owner of a Maniac has use of the embedded software. Distinct software on a CD purchased for installation on customer computers is not licensed for use on other computers, not even for subsequent purchasers of the CD, unless there is evidence of its removal from the initial computer.

When a company transfers IP to another company, there is rarely an open competition, and many factors will complicate setting transfer prices [Razgaitis:03]. There is practically no trustworthy public data for IP transfers within divisions of a multinational corporation. Estimating fair transfer prices becomes very difficult. The tax authorities are often mystified [Ault&Bradford in RazinS:90].

The rights that MNC contributed to CONCH are broad in scope, and they cover an entire platform of resources enabling making, maintaining, and selling of products [IRS-TP:12]. The precise scope of this Platform Contribution transaction (PCT) requires locating and matching clauses in license contracts [Pearson:06]. In this case they are limited to a geographic region that covers 42 % of MNC's sales. When actual tangibles are being traded, few purchasers would want 42 % of some good. But rights to tangibles and intangibles can be split into fractional tranches and are then easy to allocate.

4.2.1 *Rights to Tangible Assets*

Selling rights allows sharing of tangibles that are otherwise exclusive. You might be willing to share a washing machine with your neighbor on a 50/50 basis. You'll also split somehow the cost of water, electricity, and space needed to use the machine. Such an arrangement also implies that when a repair is needed, you'll share those costs. Sharing assets easily leads to problems. When important tangibles are to be shared, detailed legal arrangements are needed. By separating the rights to the tangible from the tangible itself, a new intangible is created, which can be conveniently manipulated and split into tranches.

Example 4.1 shows a common business example, where rights to tangible property, USco's building, become an intangible right, available for sale to another party. The purchaser profits from that right, here by collecting rent.

The flexibility of rights becomes useful when less than an entire tangible is to be transferred. A right can be split into fractional tranches. If the building is worth three times the amount of cash needed, then a 33 % share of the rights to the building can be sold. USco will pay taxes only on its income from sale of the 33 % tranche. Maintenance expenses will be shared according to the 66 % to 33 % split. The actual building is not split up, like a condominium; only the rights to it are split into derived tranches. Those derivatives can be bundled and resold.

Example 4.2 shows a situation that is closer to the transaction that MNC performed. In that example a fraction of the rights to its building is sold to a US-controlled overseas corporation. Only a tranche, its size determined by the fraction of the value of the building sold, is transferred.

Example 4.1 A Simple Leaseback Agreement

To obtain cash for growth, a company USco sells the ownership rights to its headquarters to a real estate enterprise, REco, with a provision that REco will lease the building back to USco. The price that REco is willing to pay depends on the value of the future rent USco will pay.

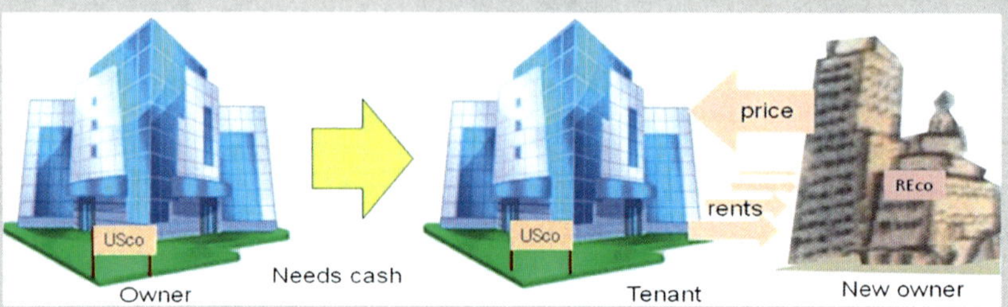

USco receives a fair value in cash for the building, and USco's total tangibles remain unchanged until it starts spending the money it received for the sale. USco now pays an annual rent. REco offers an attractive lease because it takes advantage of depreciation or because it uses a taxhaven as the formal holding domicile [Houlder:11].

Nobody moves, and few employees will notice any change. There may be a new brass plaque on the building and a sign "REco International" on the door to the rooms housing the people who maintain the building.

Example 4.2 An Offshore, Controlled Leaseback Agreement

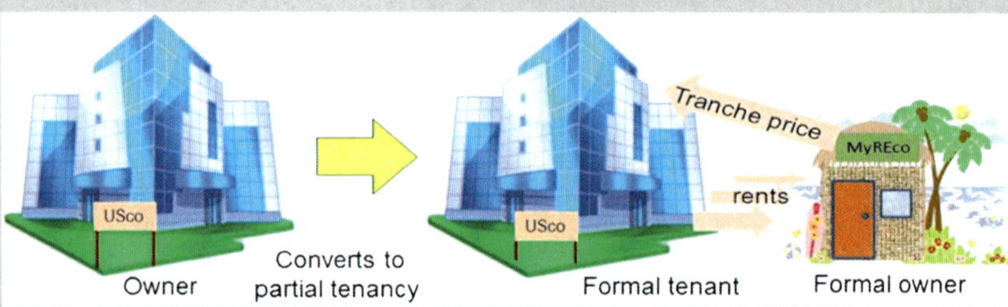

If the actual objective is tax avoidance, USco can set up its own real estate company, MyREco, in a taxhaven. The asset, here the headquarters building, remains under control of USco; all financial transfers are controlled by USco as well. The public consolidated annual report of USco lists only the name and location of the controlled division, the subcorporation MyREco; the assets and incomes are combined. To enable MyREco to get started, only a tranche of the rights to the building is transferred initially. Because the lease receipts and tranche payments cancel each other out, the more complex financial flow is invisible.

The income from the sale does generate taxable income at USco. Because that income comes formally from an offshore business, USco can try to minimize paying taxes on it. A common strategy is to spread out the income and book it in years when losses from other activities can be claimed. Spreading out payments over a long term is akin to USco's providing a mortgage to REco. Income from offshore financial dealings has often led to tax evasion, and since 1966 the US Congress has attempted to constrain such dealings [DesaiH:00]. The resulting regulations, referred to as [B.2.10] have been revised frequently [B.2.10]. Because our MNC has not engaged in pure financial dealings, we ignore that complexity.

4.2.2 Rights to Intangible Assets

MNC's valuable assets are already intangibles. The value of MNC's assets is the nonroutine profit that the intangibles will generate. The company needs to establish a transfer price for the tranche of IP moved offshore. The valuation of IP rights is similar in principle to valuing rights to tangibles. Valuation of intangibles is already hard, and valuing the rights of a tranche of them is yet harder.

All the assets in a tranche are accessible to any rights holder. Having these tranches of rights allows trading and sharing of intangibles without specifying and valuing details of the assets being transferred. For instance, the geographic tranche allocated to CONCH could be further split by customer type, and those rights can be sold to other divisions or to independent resellers. Some specialist resellers may add considerable value and obtain higher prices per unit sold. Transfer prices set for the IP in offshore transactions are hard to track.

Some secondary owners of tranches are quite unaware of the assets they actually own. When tranches are traded and further split and aggregated, the underlying rights, obligations, and risks become less and less visible. As we saw in the case of bank failures due to mortgage derivatives in 2008, a lack of understanding of assets underlying rights to future income can lead to financial disaster. If the transfers lead to taxable profits, the tax authorities will care.

4.2.2.1 Exclusive and Non-exclusive Rights

Rights to intangibles can be shared. MNC could issue nonexclusive contracts to sell Maniacs to two distributors, say in Italy. Having competing distributors may increase sales in Italy and provide better service to customers. On the other hand, in order to compete with each other each of the distributors will spend more money and each would sell less. Although some more Maniacs might be sold in Italy, each nonexclusive contract is worth less.

Even both contracts together bring less income to MNC than one exclusive contract, because of increased expenditures by the competing distributors. In practice, nonexclusive rights can reduce a base license for IP rights by 3 %, reducing a base royalty of say, 7 %, to 4 % for a nonexclusive contract [F7.14].

Nonexclusive licensing is effective for IP that augments noncompeting products, such as bar code technology applied to items for sale [Razgaitis:03]. MNC obtained a nonexclusive license to WiFi technology for its ManiMobile. The licensor benefits from broader use of WiFi.

MNC did not license competing distributors of Maniacs; but when MNC started CONCH, it made the license nonexclusive, increasing its flexibility. CONCH is not an arm's-length entity relative to MNC, so no undue competition would ever be established by MNC. Any worldwide distribution contracts that MNC negotiates, say with Walmart, would still let non-US revenues be credited to CONCH to avoid taxation. In a valuation (Sect. 4.4.2) the IP rights provided to CONCH to distribute Maniacs worldwide are not impaired by omission of exclusive rights.

4.2.3 Allocation by "Reasonably Anticipated Benefits"

When a company transfers valuable rights to another party, it should be properly reimbursed. A simple example, seen in MNC's creation of MNC LSA in Belize, is the right to sell the products in a geographic region, in this case Latin America. Simple selling rights are typically reimbursed by setting a royalty rate on gross sales. Receiving those royalty payments should provide an arm's-length benefit to compensate MNC for the future earnings it loses by ceding the income from the Latin American territory to MNC LSA.

When CONCH was established, it obtained a tranche covering all the rights to all of MNC's intellectual capital outside the USA and Canada. The initial buy-in payment for the IP rights, shown in Fig. 2.5, should compensate MNC in the USA for the lost earnings. The rights allocated to CONCH are not correlated to any particular set of intangible assets of MNC. After the cost-sharing and buy-in transactions, CONCH receives all of the nonroutine income from the three existing sales and distribution CFCs: MNC EMEA, MNC PFA, and MNC LSA.

A convenient way to compute the value of the income forgone by MNC is to split MNC's total income into a tranche for the USA and a tranche for the areas ceded to CONCH. The size of the tranche for CONCH will be based on the "Reasonably Anticipated Benefit" (RAB) that CONCH obtains. The relative value of MNC's offshore IP, now held in CONCH, is then the value of MNC's intellectual property multiplied by the RAB fraction. Criteria for estimating the RAB for CONCH are listed in Table 4.1, with their computed values [F4.1].

Because MNC US loses income by licensing IP rights to CONCH, Criterion 1, the RAB based on their net incomes (i.e., the taxable incomes before R&D investments), is the most appropriate choice at the time of transfer. It measures the actual net benefits forgone by MNC when CONCH purchases a tranche of MNC's IP rights. That choice also follows the law governing the IRS:

> *In the case of any transfer (or license) of intangible property the income with respect to such transfer or license shall be commensurate with the income attributable to the intangible [B.2.1 (h)(3)(B)], based on the taxable incomes [B.2.5(d)(2)(A)(ii)].*

Table 4.1 Criteria for determining the RAB for MNC's foreign operations

1. Net Income in the three CONCH regions versus total MNC Net Income (44 %)
2. Sales in the three CONCH regions versus total MNC sales (42 %)
3. Number of MNC customers in the CONCH regions versus all MNC customers (46 %)
4. Budgets of MNC customers in the CONCH regions versus total customer budgets (54 %)
5. GDP in the CONCH regions versus total global GDP (73 %)
6. Potential customers in the CONCH regions versus worldwide potential customers (95 %)

RAB Criterion 2, sales, is based on data that are easier to obtain than the net income. Normally, with fair accounting, net income should track sales fairly closely. For instance, if a royalty rate of 30 % based on net income is fair, and that income is estimated to be a third of revenue, a 10 % royalty rate on sales should yield a similar income to the licensor. In this case, the costs CONCH incurs in selling Maniacs are a bit lower. The estimated buy-in amount to be received by MNC will be nearly 5 % less when based on sales instead of on net income [F4.2].

Income does not track sales when government or social constraints do not allow a fair income to be extracted [Contractor:81]. Incomes are proportionally less when governmental pricing constraints exist, say in the health-care sector; MNC's products are not affected by such constraints. When there is little competition for a product in a region, sales are easier to achieve, and net income and earnings would be relatively higher, as is the case here for CONCH.

The other four criteria consider future potential. Criterion 3, the size of the customer base, is larger than the income-based RABs, because new customers have not yet purchased as many products from MNC as longer-term customers had bought. Over time purchases by recent customers will increase. All of the first three criteria are likely to change over time as foreign sales grow, so the current RAB does not fully predict the actual income forgone by MNC.

Criterion 4 assesses the future potential benefits forgone by MNC for sales to corporate customers. Although uncertain, the future benefits are what really matters in a transfer of intangibles. A disadvantage of Criterion 4, the financial strength of the customers, is that complete data are unlikely to be available. A RAB based on Criterion 4 is also a likely limit for the foreseeable future.

Criteria 5, GDP, and 6, population, are based on long-range global metrics rather than on the current MNC situation. The likely highest RAB for, say, MNC LSA, covering the Latin American region, would be the fraction of the total Latin American Gross National Product (GNP) relative to the world GNP. If the products are for a specific market, a more accurate terminal limit of potential customers can be estimated. The time to reach that level of penetration must then be estimated as well—10 years seems a reasonable period for many products. The GDP fraction is likely to change little in 10 years, although sales in some regions will grow faster than in other regions. The 95 % for Criterion 6 used in the table was computed by using the entire regional population count. The result can be made more specific to MNC by counting only the customers who are likely to purchase MNC's products in each region. The numbers are useful as limits. Because MNC LSA was just starting, the customer fraction in Latin America should increase.

4.2.3.1 Summary of RAB Choices

To be conservative in our valuations, we consider only the first two RABs, based on net income or sales. Any changes of RAB that may occur in the future are ignored. Because the owner of the IP, here MNC, forgoes the income now collected by the licensee, here CONCH, Criterion 1 is the best choice, but ATA used the more common one, Criterion 2, based on sales.

In true arm's-length business situations, the licensor does not have the ability to control how the licensee computes the cost. The licensor may worry about excessive costs, such as high salaries or unnecessary purchases, being deducted from the licensee's revenues. Inflated costs reduce the reported earnings and the income due to the licensor [deMatteis:99]. Most commercial licensing agreements are hence based on Criterion 2, sales revenues.

CONCH, being owned by MNC, does not have an opportunity to inflate costs in order to reduce reported earnings, so the RAB based on net income can be applied, here 44 % [F4.1]. That RAB should be used for a buy-in case. It can be adjusted when foreign earnings grow.

4.3 Cost Sharing of Asset Maintenance

When rights to an asset are shared, both parties must assume responsibility for the cost of maintaining the underlying asset. The maintenance of tangibles is fairly well understood, and the maintenance costs appear as routine expenses on the books. Intangibles used in business require substantial continuing maintenance to keep their value and avoid obsolescence over their life span. Even routine maintenance expenses of technological intangibles, however, appear as Research & Development (R&D) expenses on corporate books.

4.3.1 Taxation and Cost-Sharing

To maintain rights to shared assets, the costs for maintenance should be shared according to the economic benefits gained by each party [ChapotonG:88]. This rule forms the basis for the laws and subsequent IRS regulations, issued first in 1968, that govern buy-in payments and cost sharing [B.2.1(h)(5)(C)].

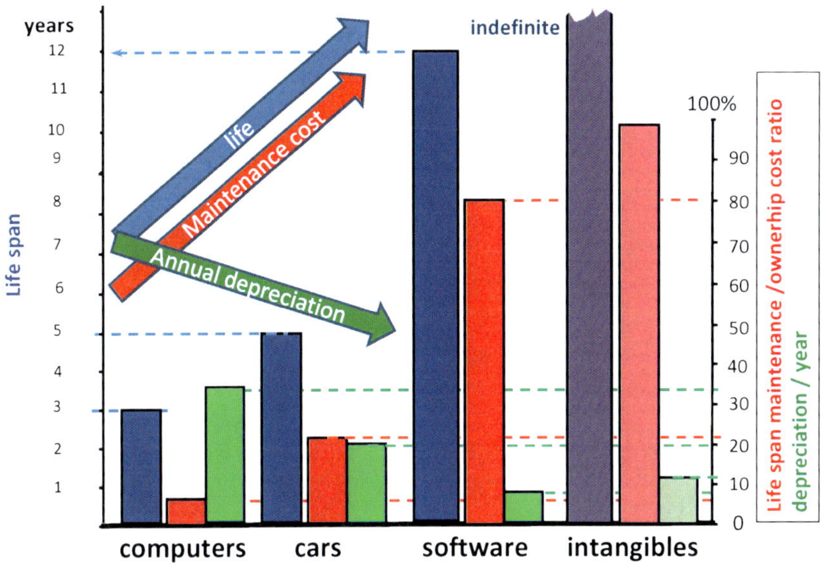

Typical Life, years	3	5	12	18	expected
Maintenance/year	2%	5%	15%	13.75%	compounded
Maintenance costs	6%	21%	80%	most	over asset life
Depreciation/year	33% linear	20% linear	8% linear	12% geometric	of investment

Fig. 4.2 Asset life and maintenance

4.3.2 Asset Maintenance and Life

In general, assets that have a long potential life will require more maintenance over their lifetime, as computed for four product types in Fig. 4.2 [F4.3] to [F4.8]. Most of the total cost of ownership for long-lived intangible assets is due to maintenance.

Tangibles such as cars and computer hardware require limited maintenance, so maintenance is a smaller part of their total cost of ownership. Software must be maintained to remain up-to-date. The quality of software is enhanced by intensive maintenance [Glass:03]. Over its life the fraction spent on maintenance tends to be between 60 and 90 % [McKinsey:03].

CONCH receives substantial benefits from sharing the cost of maintenance of the IP it got in the initial transfer. Most of the development effort takes place at MNC's California location. The maintained assets will generate income and earnings for MNC and CONCH for a long time.

Through the buy-in CONCH received rights to access all of MNC's IP. Through cost sharing it reimburses the costs of IP maintenance, of novel developments, and of acquisitions made by MNC. Maintaining the value of IP embedded in hardware and software has been booked as R&D. The majority of the cost-sharing payments are received by MNC in the USA in order to pay for ongoing R&D efforts.

A fraction of the amount goes to MNC MY in India, to pay for its contribution to software development and testing.

Costs for marketing efforts performed by MNC that have worldwide benefits must also be shared. Current costs can be shared as they are incurred. For some multinational companies marketing costs can be huge, but in MNC's business they are not substantial.

4.3.2.1 Indefinite Life

Having an indefinite life means that life of the IP is constrained by unknown events and cannot be predicted. The results for the last column of Fig. 4.2, pertaining to intangibles in general, are based on a broad historical survey and analysis of the US manufacturing sector [NadiriP:96]. The annual depreciation rate of 12 % computed for intangibles in that analysis assumes a geometric model; for tangible assets it is much less, only 5.9 %.

As the original IP contribution diminishes, some of it remains indefinitely. To enable computation, I consider that IP content in a product becomes irrelevant when it drops to a 10 % level [W:06]. Using that cutoff provides a practical length of life. Applying the 10 % rule to the diminution implied by global manufacturing data gives us a discounted IP life of about 7.5 years, a value used if we cannot determine life precisely [F4.9].

Ongoing maintenance to replace the loss due to depreciation diminishes the contribution of the initial investment. Because software must be well maintained to remain useful, its life is longer, as will be shown when we value the buy-in by the IIP-VM method in Chap. 5 [F5.24]. In practice, the life of software is constrained by ever-increasing maintenance costs [W:06].

4.3.3 *Offshoring Alternatives*

Figure 4.3 indicates the business relationships for the two principal alternatives for offshored operations, independent and controlled. In either case IP will need to be transferred offshore to allow the foreign workers to be effective.

MNC could have engaged Independent Foreign Contractors (IFC) for offshore assembly and software testing. Use of an IFC provides a rapid start of operations, requires little investment, and allows much flexibility in staffing. IFCs make great efforts to protect the IP they will need to access as part of the contracted work, but true isolation is hard to guarantee [WTGS:09].

The risk of loss affects the direct benefits of offshoring [Grove:10]. To assess that risk, management needs to know the value of the IP being transferred to the offshore operation. Results from the valuation methods discussed in Chap. 5 provide the basis for assessing risks.

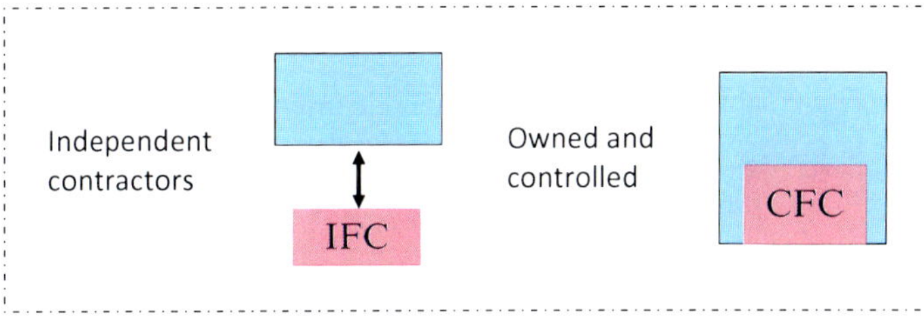

Fig. 4.3 Offshoring alternatives

Because MNC depends so heavily on its intellectual assets, it decided to reduce the risk of loss of its IP and establish instead Captive Foreign Corporations (CFCs) for its operations in both Malaysia and India [AsprayMV:06]. Incentives provided in the two countries reduced the initial investment needed.

An IFC does not expect to benefit from its customer's IP, so issues of correct transfer pricing rarely arise, and when they do, an arm's-length relationship can be assumed.

4.3.3.1 Risk to National Security

When companies are offshoring, there are some risks of loss of IP that are broader than corporate concerns. Direct export limitations extend to offshoring and joint developments of intangibles as well. For instance, in 1972 the White House denied a proposed collaboration by GE with a foreign partner.

> It was felt that … Knowledge of the thermodynamic and management techniques that went into the GE development would be absorbed by the SNECMA technicians and engineers. The transfer of such information would be tantamount to a transfer of technology, that is, design methods, design rationale, and design data. These data would be much more extensive than what might become available by a mere exchange of drawings [Baranson:78].

This case was resolved after a year by an agreement that included a reimbursement by GE to the US government for prior R&D support. Evidently GE felt that cooperation with an offshore partner was worth more than the governmental incentives it had received.

4.3.3.2 Risks in Cost Sharing

Cost sharing implies not only sharing of costs, but also sharing of risks [DurstC:03]. For our model company MNC, that factor is simplified with its CONCH. The company has split itself on a geographic basis, but all the management and operational functions remain joined. In actual arm's-length IP-sharing arrangements, the risks are not equal. Paying for a simple fixed tranche is then not appropriate. In those cases, instead of an initial buy-in and subsequent cost-sharing payments, a royalty-based licensing agreement with explicit reimbursement for exchanged services is more common.

Arranging payment for IP rights by having the receiver pay royalties on future income is a common alternative among arm's-length parties. In the computer and electronics industry annual royalty payments are more than $23 billion [Parr:07]. Appendix C describes setting of royalty rates.

4.4 Sharing the Cost of Acquisitions

MNC grew substantially because of acquisitions made around the buy-in date. The company made more acquisitions during 2004, using funds repatriated from CONCH with the AJCA incentives, as shown in Fig. 2.12. Acquisitions and mergers cover all assets, tangible and intangible, including workforce, know-how, IP, and rights to IP that the acquired company owns.

In a simple case, all assets acquired are useful for the purchaser. The price that MNC paid was a fair, open-market arm's-length price. Acquired tangibles are allocated according to their geographic location; MNC in the USA handles all the cash and debts. CONCH gains access to and obtains benefits from all the acquired intangibles and will pay its current RAB share for them. In an acquisition, the purchaser often obtains items that are of no value, or even items that will cost money to get rid of.

4.4.1 Valuing the Offshore Tranche of Acquisitions

An allocation of the acquisition price needs to be assessed in light of what motivated MNC and the benefits to each of its divisions. Assets that are obtained, but are not the drivers, are easily misvalued. That the motivating assets, being typically relevant to future growth, are often hard to value is no excuse. For most early-stage acquisitions there would be no essential goodwill, so any assignment of acquisition costs to goodwill is suspect.

4.4.1.1 Acquiring In-Progress R&D

A prime reason for MNC's acquisitions was to obtain promising relevant research. When MNC became aware that it had to make the Maniac's capability available on a mobile device, it acquired companies active in that area. Acquisitions allowed it to enter the market much faster than if it had to depend on internal, organic R&D. Being first to market, asset type 5b in Table 3.2 provides considerable benefits.

4.4.1.2 Workforce Acquisition

MNC purchased one company, Wf-inc, solely for its talented workforce. Buying an unsuccessful company can be a good move. In fact, experience with failure is valuable for planning future successes. Especially when expert and competent employees are scarce, obtaining personnel who have worked together is a way to grow rapidly and effectively. Because MNC knew that it could not use Wf-inc's IP, it will soon write off any acquired IP from its books. The acquisition price MNC offered took into account that the IP had no value.

4.4.1.3 Unused Acquired Assets

MNC purchased another company, Pat-inc, merely for the value of the patents that Pat-inc owned. Not having rights to those patents could subject MNC to significant legal risks in the future. Pat-inc had no tangibles. The value of the workforce and all other IP of Pat-inc was not a factor in the discussion to set a price for Pat-inc. Severance costs for the redundant Pat-inc's employees are an additional cost. Because CONCH, as part of the same company, benefits equally from the reduction in risk, CONCH should share all costs.

Example 4.3 clarifies how unjustified cross-border cost accounting reduces total taxes.

Example 4.3 Misallocation of Acquired Assets Among Business Divisions

Miguel and Carlos share a business in the south of Spain, M&C, which uses a delivery van. The van needs some parts that should cost €800, but are not available. They find a matching wreck at a repair shop in Spain and pay €5,000 for the car and the costs incurred by the shop. M&C fixes the van and continues its joint business.

Carlos pays his half share of the expected parts cost, €400, to Miguel. The rest of the wreck remains in the garage in Spain, but has no value on the books of M&C.

At Spanish income tax time, Miguel figures that the repair purchase cost M&C in Spain €5,000 and enters that as a loss against M&C's business profits, reduced by the €400 paid by Carlos. At the Spanish 43 % tax rate, M&C's business taxes on the €4,600 cost are reduced by €1,978. Carlos resides in Gibraltar. M&C pays taxes there at a 10 % rate and reports a cost of €400, reducing his business taxes by €40. M&C's total taxes are €2,018.

Both Miguel and Carlos should have deducted an equal 50 % share of their cost, €2,500. Assignment of the cost of the wreck to Spain made M&C wealthier; if both M&C divisions deducted €2,500, then the total tax deductions would yield only €1,325. Overall, M&C gains €653 by shifting most expenses to Spain while sharing the benefits equally [F4.10].

The accounting that MNC used in allocating the assets it obtained when it purchased Pat-inc encompassed both the patents and the unused assets. The price that MNC paid for Pat-inc was \$4.0M. The severance costs for the redundant employees were \$1.0M. Not relevant to MNC were Pat-inc's research-in-progress and its supply and customer contracts; all those items were classified by ATA as impaired goodwill, amounting to 80 % of the acquisition on the books. Only 20 % of MNC's cost was left after the write-offs. CONCH contributed \$0.8M, and MNC paid for the rest. MNC was left with an after-tax bill of \$2.8M [F4.11]. CONCH shares about half of the benefits of the patents obtained in the acquisition of Pat-inc, but paid only a 27 % share. Assigning unused acquired assets to goodwill and then removing them from asset transfers is a common way to reduce the base on which taxes will be assessed.

4.4.1.4 Mixed Motivation

More typically, the decision to acquire another company is not based on a single type of asset. There will be a variety of tangible and intangible assets to consider, as well as the capability of the workforce. For any substantial acquisition a board of directors' vote is required. The management of MNC relies for guidance on ATA, so MNC contracts with ATA to prepare a "due diligence report" for its board that estimates the effect on the future of MNC. Because of their importance to MNC's competitive position, the due diligence reports and the minutes of the board of directors meetings will be confidential.

The actual acquisitions will be reported in the annual reports sent to the shareholders and in the documents submitted to the SEC. Amounts written off to satisfy accounting rules will also be reported. Reports submitted to external parties need not present the comprehensive motivation that caused MNC to invest in these companies. CONCH must still pay its fractional share of the entire acquisition. Any write-offs of IP and goodwill placed on the books subsequently are irrelevant.

4.4.2 *Scope of Acquired Intellectual Assets*

The values of individual types of IP listed in Table 3.2 can be affected by a number of factors. We consider exclusive rights and various flavors of scope. Many of the factors listed do not apply precisely to all IP categories when internal transfer prices for a buy-in are to be set. Agreements to transfer IP and IP rights often have scope limitations.

4.4.2.1 Exclusivity

A license is more valuable if the licensee is assured that the licensor will not offer the IP to competitors. In internal licensing, as in this case, a nonexclusive license does not cause loss of value, because the MNC parent will not enable competition with its own offshore divisions [IRS-TP:12]. For a valuation, a buy-in transaction, as seen here, can never be considered nonexclusive [B.1.2 #7(c)(2)].

Designating an internal licensing arrangement nonexclusive simplifies negotiating sales with multinational customers, since MNC management is located in the USA, as are most of MNC's customers, while none are located in Palm Island. Revenues can still be channeled offshore, to CONCH.

4.4.2.2 Geographic Scope

Regional limitations, as in the case of MNC, are common. MNC EMEA has the rights to sell MNC's products in Europe, the Middle East, and Africa, and nowhere else. Nevertheless, some categories of IP cross boundaries. IP generated by marketing efforts is effective globally, even though the effect may be smaller outside the primary region. An announcement of a new product by MNC in the USA will generate interest by all MNC customers. An advertisement at an international sports tournament will be seen worldwide.

When the products are purely intangible, regional boundaries become meaningless. The software shipped to update Maniacs is shipped invisibly. That holds both for the software shipped to MNC's distributors before Maniacs are shipped to customers, and subsequently, when Maniacs at the customers' sites are updated. The intangible rights to the IP are held by a shell corporation, CONCH, located in a primary taxhaven. As is typical, MNC actually has no employees at the site where about half of its earnings are booked.

4.4.2.3 Location of Multinational Customers

Scope can also be limited to a specific industry, say aerospace. A specialized distributor of MNC products may have expertise in certifying products for aircraft on-board use. The industry that distributor serves is not bound by national boundaries, and that distributor will not want to have to consider the regional boundaries imposed by MNC for sales in general. All aircraft manufacturers are themselves multinationals, and so are their suppliers. MNC has a tax incentive to consider all sales to that distributor as foreign sales, so that its profits flow to its taxhaven-based division, CONCH. MNC is able to consider the distributor's subsidiary in Toulouse, France, to be the formal purchasing site, even when equipment sold there is used on Airbus aircraft assembled and sold in the USA. The revenues will be distributed via MNC's financial intermediary, CAAS in The Netherlands, validating that it is all offshore income.

In general, MNC's sales to multinational corporations are hard to pin down. Once MNC's products are delivered to a customer location, any cross-border transfer of those products becomes a matter of the customer's transfer pricing approach. Those customers have objectives that differ from MNC's. Using a worldwide approach to compute MNC's income, as practiced by the USA, the UK, and China, is a prerequisite to gather information about possible tax evasion due to questionable booking of revenues. Such controversies are even harder to resolve for revenues from sales of software and other intangibles distributed over the Internet.

4.4.2.4 Temporal Scope

Some licensing contracts have terms that limit the licensee to a certain term. For an arm's-length license, the licensor may provide exclusive rights only for several years. If the licensee fails to produce a salable product, the license would not be renewed. Such limitations are meaningless for MNC, because the Maniacs already existed when the CONCH buy-in took place.

4.4.2.5 Scope of Risk

There is no difference in assumed risk between MNC and CONCH, as there is in arm's-length ventures. There is no staff at CONCH; all the decisions are actually made by MNC's management in the USA, covering all of MNC. CONCH shares equally in MNC's risks. If US management makes poor decisions, all of MNC's divisions lose proportionally, although ATA had put such items as goodwill only on MNC's US books [F2.10]. When intangible assets are written off, CONCH must share those losses according to the RAB ratio used when the acquisitions were paid for, even though the acquisition decisions were made by MNC management. Similarly, CONCH will not have to pay more later if an acquisition delivers larger profits than were projected in the due diligence reports made to justify the acquisitions.

4.4.3 Reimbursing the Cost of IP Transfers

Once the value of the buy-in transfer has been determined, CONCH has to make arrangements to reimburse MNC for the initial transfer of IP. The valuation provided by ATA assessed the total value of the types of IP rights made available to CONCH at $119M. CONCH owed an initial payment of $50M based on the share of revenues from offshore sales [F2.4].

Once a transfer price has been determined, an arrangement for payment must be made. Three choices are available for the CONCH buy-in payment to MNC. Each of those choices should reimburse MNC in the USA equally for the income received at CONCH from its selling subsidiaries, MNC EMEA, MNC LSE, and MNC PFE, but each choice has advantages and disadvantages [RistucciaEa:11].

1. A lump-sum payment: CONCH pays $50M to MNC, but first it has to borrow that amount of money somewhere, and MNC will have to pay taxes on that income.
2. Installment payments: CONCH pays quarterly installments of $3.1M [F2.6]. That amount can be paid out of the income that CONCH receives [F2.5]. Taxes due are spread out. After 5 years the tax-free earnings at CONCH increase by that amount.
3. Royalty payments are a choice for arm's-length parties for unpredictable incomes into the far future [Parr:07]. Common ownership equalizes any risk.

MNC preferred choice 2, installment payments, for its buy-in. CONCH, being a newly established division of MNC, did not have the funds to pay for all the IP rights transferred to it, nor did CONCH have the ability to borrow funds at a reasonable interest rate. The income expected at CONCH is quite predictable, so there is no reason to mitigate risk by using royalties, as described in Appendix C. Because nearly all the IP generating CONCH's nonroutine income was transferred to CONCH, a fair royalty rate would be very high.

The loan was provided at a low interest rate by MNC [F2.6]. If international rights transfers, mergers, or acquisitions transactions require larger loans, multinational companies rely for financing on the Euromarket, but the rates would take risks into account [Argy:06]. We ignore the option of using Eurodollars in MNC's transactions. It further convolutes the available choices and makes offshoring processes yet harder to follow.

Once CONCH was established through the initial buy-in, cost sharing commenced. Now CONCH has to share the costs of ongoing efforts to maintain the IP and any new IP that is covered by the rights it has obtained. CONCH has to contribute to the purchase of any acquisitions. The share of the acquisition costs to be paid by CONCH depends on the tranche of benefits that will accrue to CONCH. Only intangibles will count; both IP and the workforce that will generate future income for all of MNC. On the dates when the acquisitions occur, the current ratio of anticipated benefits (RAB) should be used, rather than the RAB that was valid for the buy-in. The acquisitions are analyzed in Chap. 7, Sect. 7.4.

4.5 Summary of Transfer Pricing

Corporate tax planning must consider the advantages offered by internal transfer pricing and may set up foreign sales or purchasing subsidiaries [vandenDool:12]. Many transactions, like the initial transfer of $6M by MNC to set up CONCH, are tax free [Styron:07].

Figure 4.4 illustrates the similarities and subtle differences of offshore transfer of rights to tangible goods versus transfer of rights to intangibles. In both cases we assume that ownership rights have been transferred to a third party for some price. Physical goods leave the creator's workshop and can no longer be used in the home country. Only information is shipped or transmitted via the Internet to the offshore site. Nothing is gone from the home operation.

Accountants have a choice in placing items on the books, it is tempting to assign costs so that taxes are minimized [Shaxson:11]. In simple cases like our model, funny allocations are obvious. In large multinationals, with hundreds of divisions in dozens of jurisdictions, both unintentional and intentional asset allocations that do not reflect substantive business intentions are hard to recognize.

When transfers among jurisdictions cause revenue losses, tax authorities get concerned [Bell:11]. Mispriced transfers have been a major factor in multinational tax avoidance for a long time [Tang:93]. Governmental attempts to correct the

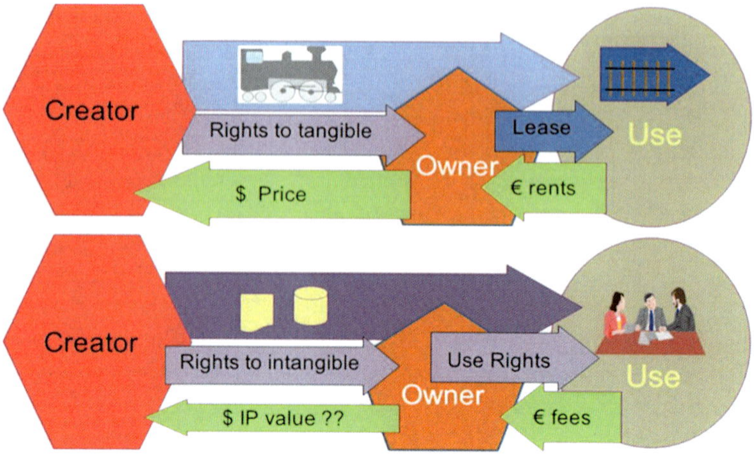

Fig. 4.4 Transferring rights to tangible versus intangible property

processes that allow tax avoidance lead to more regulations and more complexity. Companies can react to changes much more rapidly than any government can.

The information available to the tax authorities is limited. The concept of arm's-length pricing is distorted in practice [DevereuxK:09]. The transfers to a CFC occur over many years. Tracking and assessing fair values for asset transfers is hard, as detailed in a study leading to the current regulations [ChapotonG:88]. Transfer prices that disadvantage one jurisdiction over another, set intentionally or just by not being careful, are common.

- Valuable tangible products are created in some place under some identifiable jurisdiction. Products that depend on IP derive their value from many sources, and the actual point of manufacture may contribute only a small part of their value [Baz:09].
- Modern products, both tangible products in containers and intangible products on the Internet, can now be shipped at very low cost anywhere in the world. That has reduced the cost of moving property and the concepts of a place for manufacturing and a place where sales occur. Being close to the customer now has a social rather than a physical connotation.
- The corporations that produce tangible products used to have an identifiable locality. Today the headquarters, the legal residence, and the operational centers are often in different jurisdictions.
- The source of taxable earnings is still revenue from sales, but an organization just collecting invoiced amounts contributes little when separated from marketing and distribution, and it may not even physically exist.

- Financial capital can flow easily among countries, and is now taxed differently from manufacturing revenues [TuerffEa:08]. Intellectual capital moves just as easily; it is taxed when seen and not taxed when unseen.
- Reliable worldwide reporting of global activities cannot be enforced when there is no motivation to do so.

Still, arm's-length prices for IP rights may have to be determined for offshore transfers among divisions of corporations that do not operate at arm's length. Focusing on the issue at hand, multinational transfer of IP rights, allows this exposition to focus on a specific, but substantive aspect of tax avoidance [Clausing:03].

A principal reason for the difficulties faced in transfer pricing is a dependence on concepts that had their origin in a time when most traded assets were tangible [Ricardo:1817]. Popular textbooks ignore international shifting of intangible property [CowenT:11]. Experience based on tangible examples easily misleads. The transfer of tangibles and intangibles appears to be similar, but their documentation, visibility, and valuation differ greatly. Trading of intangibles, the intangible rights to tangibles, and tranches of those rights in a global economy requires that their value is known.

Being fair has social value. It rewards participants according to their contributions. Fairness encourages social cooperation; society will punish actions that are seen as being unfair [Hochschild:81]. However, fair transfer pricing of rights to intangibles that are shifted worldwide is hard. However, that difficulty is not a reason to do it poorly, and take advantage of the inherent uncertainty of valuing intellectual capital made available across borders. Chapter 5 presents valuation methods and Chap. 7 shows how poor valuations lead to MNC's extreme tax avoidance. Chapter 9 shows that MNC is typical of multinational corporations, and that their effect on the US economy is significant. For transfers within a company, little public information is available. Inadequate information is available today to fully understand the effects of global transfers and the resulting extreme tax avoidance [Swenson:01].

"The intangibles being not reducible to statistics, the food of all bureaucracy, count for nothing"
Book value
Intangibles
IP
[quote in *Here And Now*, 30 Oct 1949]

Chapter 5
Valuation Methods for IP

The objective of this chapter is to show that IP can be valued. Because intellectual capital is the most valuable asset of modern enterprises, it is essential to compute its value. Literature on specific methods to value intellectual property is available, but their applicability varies from case to case [Contractor:01]. Books on intellectual property valuation are frequently updated and now cover intellectual capital as well [SmithP:05]. No consistent assessments of multiple methods seem to exist. By focusing on valuation practices encountered in corporate tax avoidance, it is possible to present multiple methods and compare their suitability and results.

The content of this chapter is technical. Readers looking just for the essential taxation issues may decide to skip this chapter and trust that valuation of IP is possible, although some experts have asserted that IP cannot be valued adequately [Laurie:04]. Opportunities for significant unintentional or intentional misvaluation of IP are indeed rife [LeveyWC:06, p. 52]. For many years the major accounting firms, like our model Associated Tax Advisers (ATA), were trusted to provide a fair result that all parties would accept. As a consequence of the Enron scandal, it has become clear that the results that creative accountants produce may actually be the results that best suit their clients [Dharan:02]. Opening up the field should improve practice.

This chapter introduces eight methods available to value intangibles. Seven are evaluated for the MNC-CONCH buy-in; one is specific to acquisitions. The results of those methods differ, as shown here in a preview of the final Fig. 5.14. The box drawn around them shows that all seven results cluster within a reasonable range. The conclusion is that IP valuations can be fair if the context is clear.

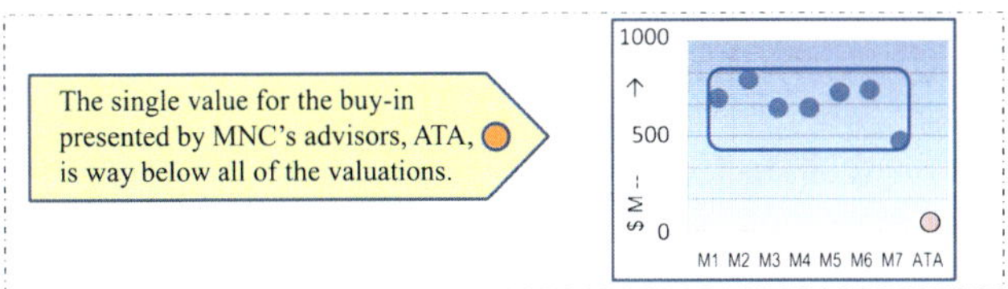

5.1 Assets to be Valued

Incorporating a variety of contributions is infinitely better than a single specific view that can ignore a major contribution to the value of a modern enterprise [FlignorO:06]. Before we tackle the actual valuation methods, let's review some points from Chap. 3 with simple examples.

5.1.1 *Tangibles Are Simple to Value*

Tangible objects require a substantial effort to manufacture. When a product is sold to the public, the price is known. The cost to produce one saleable item is an important component of its price, even when significant IP is embedded in a product. Any purchaser of MNC's product, the Maniac, pays the same amount. Like most manufacturers, MNC sells Maniacs only wholesale, at an established price, to store chains and distributors. The same Independent Factory Price (IFP) is used by all of MNC's selling divisions and is the fair arm's-length transfer price for Maniacs worldwide. The markup to the customers charged by the distributors, 40 %, is similar to the markup for competitive products of similar complexity and novelty [FA.1].

5.1.2 *Intangibles Are Not So Simple to Value*

To value intangibles we establish an equivalent price in terms of a tangible, namely money. Pure intangibles have no manufacturing cost. There is a high cost to make the initial version, but a cost-based valuation is only relevant if no further copies will be made, say, for internal-use software [PrattRS:96]. The cost of making another copy is low and cannot determine the price of all copies. An intangible derives its value, and price when sold, from its projected use. The offshore holder of the IP rights to sell copies uses those rights to generate income and derive earnings and profits. The value of the IP rights to be obtained by the creator must be a fair measure of the expected profits by the seller.

For some intangibles pricing rules have been established. A royalty for the rights to distribute a recorded performance from a Beatles concert is set based on the expected profits from the CD sales. Broadcasting the same music requires another payment [ASCAP:10]. The purchase of a music CD by a fan gives the fan only the right to play it for personal enjoyment.

Indeed, the long-standing practice is that intangibles are to be valued according to the projected future income they generate [Babcock:68]. Even the intangible rights to profit from a tangible, such as an office building, are set on the basis of the sum of the expected rents, as seen in Chap. 4. The rule that IP value is determined by their contribution to future earnings is also encoded in US law [B.2.5(d)(2)(A)(ii)]. The full IP rights stay with MNC or CONCH when a Maniac is sold; only a right to use the embedded IP is conveyed as part of a unit sale.

5.1.3 *Maniac Has Both Tangible and Intangible Components*

MNC's product, Maniac, has both tangible and substantial intangible content. Purchasers and distributors of Maniacs do not gain any rights to copy the IP contents, other than by reselling an entire Maniac unit. The value of a Maniac is still the IFP, or arm's-length price. Some price breaks may be given to MNC's offshore divisions because of shared marketing costs, assumption of liabilities, and so on, but such deals should be scrutinized to assure that the agreed transfer price is fair to IP owners and tax collectors.

5.1.4 *Rights to Anything Are Intangible*

In our example, rights to IP for making and selling Maniacs for the international market are being sold by MNC to its offshore holding company, CONCH. Such "make and sell rights" broadly encompass everything needed to operate a business. Essentially, MNC splits its platform into two major divisions. No set price will be available. To avoid excessive gain or loss to MNC's US division, the transfer price or buy-in amount for the rights to the intangibles transferred by MNC to CONCH must still be set fairly. Fairness is commonly defined as determining an arm's-length value, although this rights transfer is not an arm's-length transaction [B.3.1(1)(b)].

5.2 Financial Value of Intellectual Capital

The eight sections below present a variety of valuation methods that can be applied to arrive at a financial value for MNC's intellectual capital. The first seven are applicable to the buy-in by CONCH; the last one applies only to acquisitions. All can be used to support tax obligations to the IRS, six methods (marked[†]) are currently specifically cited, with examples given. Each method listed in Table 5.1 is applied in this section to the buy-in to illustrate its strengths and weaknesses.

The difficulty in any intellectual capital valuation, and hence of the rights to profit from sales of MNC's Maniacs, is that the future income depends on its price and the future sales volume. This income has to be estimated in some way.

It's tough to make predictions, especially about the future [Bohr:18].

Table 5.1 Methods described in this chapter and their IRS references

#	Code	Meaning—References in CFR Title 26, Chapter 1 §1.482 [B.1.2]
M1	MC-VM†	**M**arket **C**apitalization–based **V**al'n **M**ethod—[B.3.4 7(g)(1)(iv), -(6)]
M2	Inc-VM†	**Inc**ome-based **V**aluation—[B.3.4 7(g)(1)(ii), B.1.2 #7(g)(4)]
M3	IIP-VM	**I**dentified **IP** **V**aluation Method—[B.3.3(a)(4), (d)], [W:06]
M4	CUT-VM†	**C**omparable **U**ncontrolled **T**ransaction **V**al'n.**M**ethod—[B.3.3(a)(1)]
M5	CP-VM†	**C**omparable **P**rofit **V**aluation **M**ethod—[B.3.4 (b)(4)]
M6	PS-M†	**P**rofit **S**plit **M**ethods— [B.3.3 (a)(4)], [B.3.6]
M7	RO-VM	**R**oll-**O**ver **V**aluation **M**ethod—[B.3.3 (a)(4), (d)], [VBM:04]
M8	PP-VM†	**P**urchase **P**rice **V**aluation **M**ethod—[B.3.5 (g)(1)(iii)]

The intellectual property inherent in MNC's products can live and generate income for a long time, so we have to apply discounting to the income garnered in the future to obtain the Net Present Value (NPV) of the IP covered in the buy-in.

Intellectual capital beyond the intellectual property defined in the books is implicit in the buy-in. MNC is a going concern which provides the level of maintenance of its product line that the customers and the distributors of Maniacs expect. Without that ongoing effort, all of MNC's business soon loses value [W:95].

The requirement for a valuation to be submitted for a buy-in to the IRS is that it be "contemporaneous" with the event [IRS-CSA:08]. That statement actually means that it is due when corporate taxes are due, typically some time after the actual buy-in. All current data will be available then. By that time the transfer of the IP offshore has been made and the action is now irreversible. The corporate directors, who approved the decision to go offshore earlier, received information about its value as a due diligence report, but that report may not have had a valuation estimate as thorough as the valuations presented in this chapter.

5.2.1 Approach

All eight methods are analyzed based on the same model data, which represents MNC business over a 25-year interval. Using a sample model distinguishes this work from the mathematical models commonly used by economists [DiamondZ:08]. The simplifications needed for a mathematical model cannot deal with the complexities of IP shifting and taxhavens. Adding temporal factors and events to a mathematical model makes models hard to validate. The dearth of adequate national and corporate data hinders application of the formal models.

We keep MNC's situation simple, to allow understanding, but not so simple that important factors that contribute to MNC's tax avoidance are ignored. Alternatives relevant to other situations are lightly covered. It is impossible to cover alternatives comprehensively because any actual case will differ. A problem in the IRS regulations is that they try to deal with many possibilities without referencing an authoritative source. The solution is to have many examples, taking up about 2/3 of the text of recent tax regulations [F B.1].

5.3 Eight Methods to Value Intellectual Capital

Any valuation method has strengths and weaknesses [ChapotonG:88]. No single method is universally applicable [Andriessen:03]. Crucial to the selection of a method is the availability of data that allow the method to be applied. It's great if multiple methods are suitable and are applied; in that case their results can be compared [B.1.2, #1(c)(2)(iii)]. Some methods may be combined; for instance, a technical evaluation (IIP-VM) can be applied to an acquisition, once the Purchase Price Method (PP-VM) has identified what IP is to be valued. IRS regulations also allow the use of "unspecified methods"; those can be used when the specified methods are determined to be unsuitable. M3 and M7 fall into that unspecified category.

When multiple methods are used, their results will differ. Differences of 25 % are not surprising, because valuing IP attempts to predict the future, and the future is always uncertain. Explaining the reasons for the differences provides additional insights. When, later, the actual results are tallied, those will differ as well. Having to deal with uncertainty should not discourage efforts to value crucial corporate assets. Only when expectations are documented and shared can intelligent planning occur and alternative plans be weighed.

The presentation of methods in this chapter focuses on the MNC-CONCH buy-in, valued by ATA at $21M, although the same methods can be applied in many other contexts. The choice of methods depends on the required scope and on the availability of data. Table 5.2 provides an introductory summary; the meaning of the entries will become clear with the detailed discussions that follow. The final, quantified results appear in Table 5.13.

Table 5.2 Features of valuation methods

#	Method	Scope	Feature	Data source	Reliability issue
M1	MC-VM	All intellectual capital	Available for corporations	Shareholders' wisdom	Volatility of stock
M2	Inc-VM	All intellectual capital	Fairly easy	Projected future income	Growth estimate
M3	IIP-VM	Identified IP only	Technical justification	For each IP type life and lag detail	Selection of IP
M4	CUT-VM	Specific transactions	Need comparable data:	Matching transactions	Comparability
M5	CP-VM	Comparable businesses	Metrics for:	Similar businesses	IP contribution
M6	PS-M	Divisional contributions	Splits income	Investment data	Future allocation
M7	RO-VM	Similar product creation	R&D leverage	Research and sales life	Stability of R&D
M8	PP-VM	Acquisition price	Easy to use	Business records	Motivation

5.3.1 M1: MC-VM, Market Capitalization-Based Valuation Method

The simplest way to assess the value of a public company is to trust the aggregate wisdom of its many shareholders [Surowiecki:04]. The market value, the "market capitalization" of a public company, represents one important metric. That market capitalization is simply the price of a share times the number of shares outstanding. That product provides the basic result when using the Market Capitalization-based Valuation Method (MC-VM).

Shareholders buy and hold shares in a company with the expectation of future gain. Although shareholders have only limited insight into the fundamentals of the company, their aggregate wisdom can be as reliable as that of any quantitative analyst [Fox:09]. Shareholders sense that future benefits will accrue because the company will exploit its intellectual capital effectively. When the earnings are used to grow the company, the share price should increase. Paying dividends, a direct payout of the earnings, is an alternative way to distribute the gains. Companies like MNC, intent on growth, tend to pay no or modest dividends and plow back much of their earnings into research, product line development, and acquisitions.

MNC had 18.5 million ordinary shares outstanding and their price on the stock market was $100, so a simple valuation of MNC, using M1, the MV-VM, is $1,850M [F5.1]. Some complexity arises, since not all shares are created equal.

5.3.1.1 M1.1 Stock Options

Just as most high-tech companies do, MNC motivated its directors and employees by granting them stock options, amounting to an additional five million shares. These additional shares have an intangible value, because they encourage retention of critical personnel with their skill and know-how, but there is a cost. The owners of the outstanding shares will have to share the future income of MNC with those future shareholders, diluting their ownership by 20 %. Overall this was seen as a good move for MNC, and the price of its shares dropped by only 5 %.

When the shares are vested, say, 2 years later, the employees will purchase the shares at the strike price (the price a year earlier when the options were offered), $60. The combined effect of lowering the share price from and having more shares outstanding, and expected stock purchases later at the strike prices, increases the effective market cap of MNC to $1,974M [F5.2].

Under IRS rules for stock options, the recipients pay taxes only when the options are exercised or generate income to the employee. Common, nonqualified, stock options also create deductions for the corporation. Corporate deductions for the liabilities can be taken before they are exercised. Corporate tax deductions for stock options can be huge, often amounting to more than earnings [MackEa:05]. If the options are held more than a year and the shares are not sold for another year, the employees' tax on the spread is based on the capital gains rate, which was 15 % in 2011. Other agencies have been concerned with the actual grant date [FASB:05].

For corporate valuations, stock options not yet exercised have to be considered, and ignoring them makes a substantial difference in the valuation.

Shareholders will assess the costs and benefits of large stock options granted to corporate management. Options are valued differently from shares on the open market. The result increases MNC's market value by $258M and estimates the additional value attributed to the part of the workforce selected to receive options and their intangible contributions [F5.3].

MNC also issued 1.5M shares to pay for acquisitions, and then had 20M shares outstanding, making its basic market capitalization $2,000M. It still held 5M shares for employee options, to be purchased later. Its adjusted market share capitalization had grown to $2,217M [F5.4].

Initial Acquisitions

By the time CONCH was set up, MNC had completed an initial round of acquisitions. MNC spent $300M, half in cash and half in stock. The benefit of the intangibles obtained was seen as positive, even though they are not fully shown on the books seen in Table A.2. MNC's stock price recovered to $100.

5.3.1.2 M1.2 Intangible Contribution within the market price

Because we should value only the intangible part of a company when considering transfer of IP rights offshore, amounts representing tangibles should be subtracted. Corporations will list tangibles in their 10-K reports: land, buildings, machinery, inventory, and cash, as shown in Table A.2. Most high-technology companies own few tangibles compared to their market capitalization, as they lease most of their buildings and equipment. However, MNC had plenty of offshore earnings, took advantage of favorable concessions offered in Malaysia, and actually purchased the manufacturing facilities used by MNC JB. That investment also reduces the risk of having to pay US taxes due on interest earned offshore [B.2.10 (a)(3)(i)]. For MNC the tangibles amounted to $290M. The amount assigned to all intangibles became $1,560M [F5.5].

Subsequently MNC made many changes, as seen in Fig. 5.1. Expecting a rise in stock prices, it gave out stock options to senior personnel [F5.2], it started acquiring small companies [F5.4], and it set up CONCH to shelter offshore income. The companies that MNC acquired had even lower tangible ratios, averaging 10 %, totaling $30M. MNC's cash position (a tangible) was reduced, and it even had to take out a bank loan to keep enough working capital on hand. Only some of the acquired intangibles are shown on MNC's books [LevS:99]. A metric used by investors to assess growth potential, Tobin's Q, increased from 6.4 to 9.6. The shareholders kept the share price high and on that basis the value of MNC's intangibles became $1,786M [F5.5].

Even within a single year, many changes occur and are reported with differing delays. Choosing the appropriate parameters for valuing intangibles in a given interval

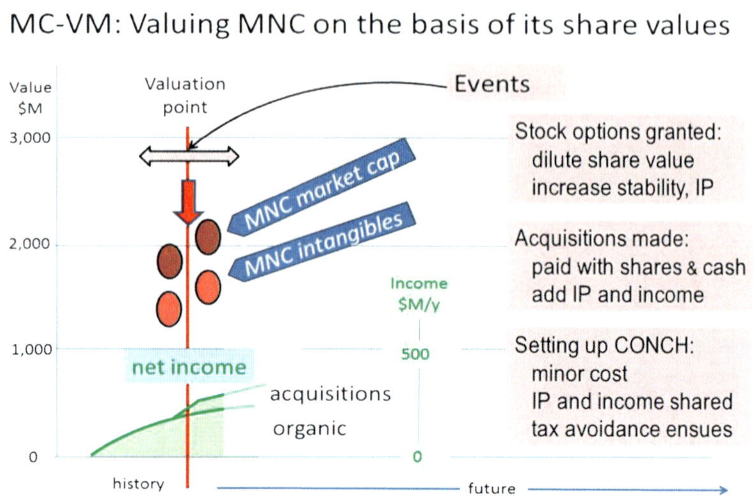

Fig. 5.1 Events around the buy-in time affecting MNC's market value

requires judgment. We just used data before and after the buy-in. All the events, and their effects in the interval before MNC's income tax is due, have their own time line to become effective, even if they appear as point entries on MNC's books.

5.3.1.3 M1.3 Market Volatility

A problem with the market capitalization method as shown is that it uses the value of shares for the company at a single point in time. However, corporate shares also change in value based on an overall perception of the economy and the promise of certain industry sectors, as during the "dot.com bubble." Figure 5.2 shows a particularly extreme case, the annual total market values from 1999 to 2005 in the industry sector "Prepackaged Software" [Compustat:04]. It represents 448 out of 941 public companies. Companies in this sector have very few tangibles, so the curve also represents value changes of corporate intangibles.

We see an obvious market valuation bubble from 2000 to 2003. After that period the market recovered.

> *In the long run future earnings represent present value [although] in the short run the dominant factor is the elusive temper of the crowd*
>
> [Goodman:67].

The total market value bubble shown is magnified by the number of companies reporting, which grew during the bubble by 30 %. During the recovery period, the number of public companies included in the statistic dropped by 18 %, as companies sold out or failed and went out of business [F5.6]. We see that during the recovery period the average share price increased fairly steadily from \$4.80 to \$8.60.

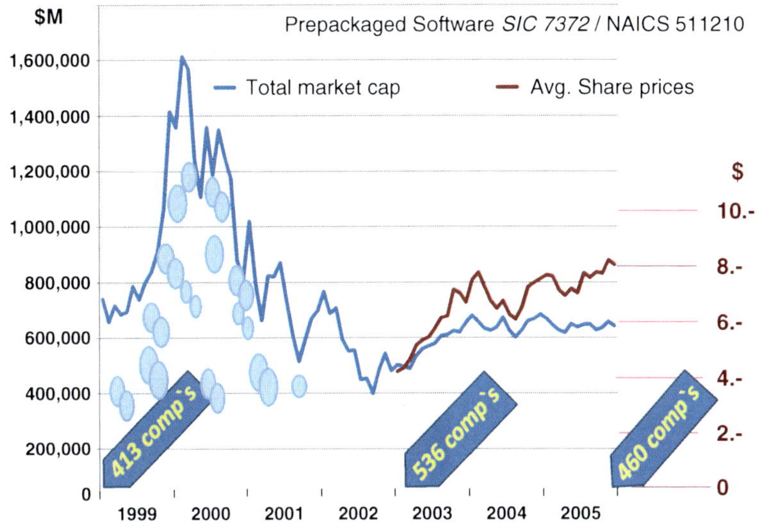

Fig. 5.2 Total market value bubble in 2000

Employees who held on to stock options granted before 1999 and after 2001 received a healthy bonus if their company survived. Many stock options granted in 2000 went "under water," having a value less than the strike price. Such options would not be exercised after 2001. People who exercised their options between 1999 and 2001, but did not sell their shares very soon after, were stuck with actual personal income losses.

Volatility has to be dealt with by taking a longer view [ReinhartR:09]. The other valuation methods in this chapter are not as affected as the market capitalization method by unjustified enthusiasm [Orrel:10]. It is always wise to use more than one method. In the summary section of this chapter we show how to create credible results out of multiple valuations that each can be questioned for different reasons.

Because the value for our company, MNC, was computed outside of the bubble period, we don't adjust the valuation of MNC's intangibles. MNC's stock was quite stable, even as stock options were given out and acquisitions made. The effects of offshoring and tax avoidance were also gradual and raised no concern by MNC's shareholders. We stick with $2,216M for the estimate of MNC's market capitalization after the buy-in events and before deducting tangibles.

5.3.1.4 M1.4 Allocation of the market value

The MC-VM is based on the shareholders' assessment covering all divisions of a company. Using the MC-VM result for specific divisions of the company requires an allocation formula to assign the expected benefits. The initial buy-in payment must compensate MNC in the USA for the lost earnings because the rights to MNC's intellectual capital have been moved to an offshore division, CONCH.

Table 5.3 Relevant market cap-based valuations around the time of the buy-in

MC-VM results	Prior	Afterwards
MNC's intangibles	$1,630M	$1,906M
Rights bought by CONCH	$717M	$839M

The value of the IP held in CONCH will be based on its Ratio of Anticipated Benefits, the RAB fraction, assessed in Chap. 4. Criteria for sharing foreign benefits were enumerated in Table 4.1 [F4.1]. The RAB is often based on sales revenues (42 % at the time of the buy-in), but because CONCH is fully controlled by MNC, CONCH does not have an opportunity to inflate costs to reduce earnings, and so the RAB based on earnings (44 %) can be applied.

5.3.1.5 M1.5 Summary of the Market Cap-Based (MC-VM) Approach

The MC-VM exploits the wisdom of the market. It can be fooled by excessive enthusiasm for a product line or an industry sector. To gain stability, it is wise to look at more than one point in time, say, using values over a multiyear period and correcting for observations about the industry in general. However, a contemporaneous valuation depends on current data. Data from a litigated case showed that a market cap valuation, towards the end of the bubble period, was indeed 32 % higher than an amount based on later evidence, but an income-based method was 11 % below that amount [F5.7].

For public companies, a market cap-based valuation can be rapidly produced using public documents. The simplicity of the method, and the fact that it accounts for everything that the shareholders expect in the future, makes a market cap-based intangible valuation essential as one input into an overall company valuation. Ignoring an available market capitalization in a valuation of a public company is akin to hiding available evidence.

To employ a market cap-based valuation in transfer pricing requires an allocation of how much of the anticipated benefit is due to the company's intangibles. Only the rights to MNC's IP platform are transferred offshore while the tangibles are removed. Of the total MNC IP value, a tranche is being transferred offshore. The size of the tranche is based on the RAB at the time of the valuation, although it is bound to change in the future. If the product penetration outside of the USA is expected to grow, the valuation should be adjusted accordingly. If available, the earnings-based RAB at the time of the buy-in (44 %) should be used.

The results for the various combinations of stock-options, stock prices, and acquisitions for the market capitalization-based method are shown in Table F.4, and summarized here in Table 5.3 [F5.8]. The results to be placed into the final summary Table 5.13 for this chapter shows just the results prior to all the events before CONCH was created and those afterwards.

The most relevant value, given that the buy-in valuation is prepared after the events, and still considered contemporaneous by the IRS, is

M1: MC-VM buy-in: $839M

5.3.2 M2: Inc-VM, Income-Based Valuation Method

The income-based valuation method (Inc-VM) follows established valuation principles most closely [Babcock:68]:

The value of an asset is the income that the asset will generate in the future.

The Inc-VM remains the most widely recognized approach. It can be applied to privately held as well as public companies [Hitchner:06]. Fundamentally, as presented in Chap. 3, the value of an intangible item, the IP, is the nonroutine earnings that it will generate in the future. Obtaining a reliable prediction of future income is the main problem in applying the Inc-VM.

A worked-out example for the online retailer Amazon using historical data is available online [Damodaran:00]. To use the Inc-VM for a buy-in, we need the following information:

1. The amount of annual income due to the transferred asset for a lengthy future period
2. The fraction of the income that is generated from the IP embedded in the asset
3. An allocation of the future income being split among the parent and its foreign subsidiaries
4. The appropriate rate for discounting the generated income to the date of the valuation

Income estimates far into the future are bound to be uncertain. Discounting, however, especially at a high percentage rate, reduces the effect of errors in estimating the future income and future changes in the allocation. For a buy-in, which transfers only IP, a period covering the life of the IP is adequate. Unless the specific income flows can be reliably assigned and allocated, the entire income of MNC is used for the valuation. The allocation from MNC to its offshore CFC, CONCH, is again a tranche according to its Reasonably Anticipated Benefits (RAB) [F4.1]. Because the CONCH buy-in excludes tangible assets, routine income due to tangibles must be excluded. All of the IP is split [IRS-CIP:07]. We will deal with each of these factors in turn.

5.3.2.1 M2.1 Income Growth

While in the market cap method the future profit was based on the shareholders' insights, the income method requires that the amount of the future earnings be projected by the company or its consultants. The relevant base is the operating income generated by the IP, the difference between revenues and all the expenses of doing business, as the CoGS, SG&A, and the cost of capital shown in Table A.1. R&D expenses creating future income are excluded, but costs of IP maintenance should be considered a current expense. Accounting for the distinction is hard, since in the books both types of expenses are called R&D. The amount reported as taxable earnings will be less, because of true R&D expenses and any other investment costs.

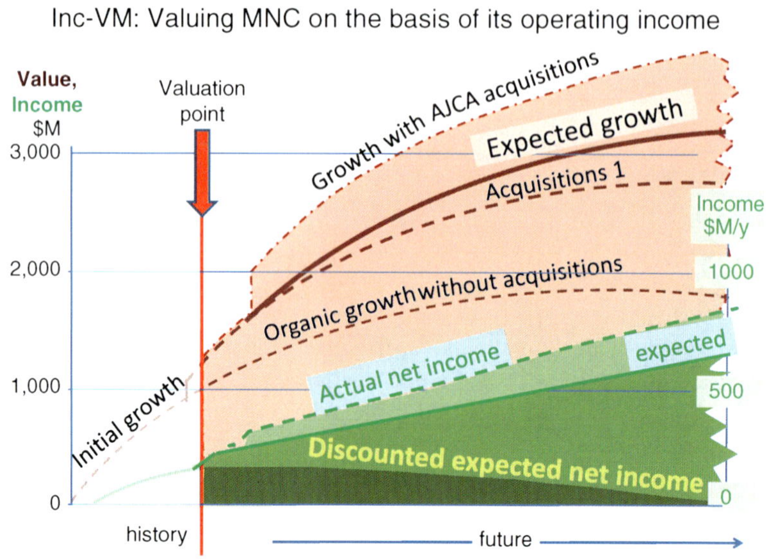

Fig. 5.3 Projected and actual incomes, all due to IP

At the time of the buy-in MNC's earnings margin was 62 % before taxes [F5.9]. After deducting R&D and costs of capital, US corporate income taxes on the remainder are levied at a rate of 35 %. Such high margins are only seen in companies with much intangible property and must be maintained by ongoing exploitation of their intellectual capital. In the case of Forest Labs, operating income amounted to 66 % of its manufacturing revenue, and its tax avoidance strategy enabled Forest Labs to pay only worldwide taxes amounting to about 3 % [F2.27].

Most companies produce estimates of future sales and earnings for internal planning, at least for several years into the future. Because tax avoidance is achieved by sheltering, expected earnings are adequate to make a reasonable projection several years into the future. If the products made by the company have been available for a few years, the current rate of sales growth is known. A current annual growth rate should be leveled off beyond the foreseeable period. A terminal growth rate, reached asymptotically, would be the long-term growth of the market. That growth rate could be estimated by a long-term GNP growth, or even set to zero.

If a company does not continue to innovate, in time its earnings margin becomes equal to that for commodity products, and the nonroutine earnings disappear entirely. Few companies would envisage such a bleak scenario. Because MNC is a young company and has integrated intellectual capital from recent acquisitions, it expects continued growth of income over the next 20 years. Figure 5.3 extends MNC's reported growth 20 years into the future, as shown in Fig. 2.12 [F5.10]. The actual growth, due to later acquisitions made from income sheltered from taxes by profiting from the AJCA incentives, could not be foreseen, so the income and value projections made by MNC management are those shown by the solid lines.

For the income-based method, past historical data are not used directly, but they are important to validate assumptions about the future. MNC cannot control all the parameters that drive future sales growth, but it plans to keep innovating as it did in the past. However, although MNC's sales are increasing, they cannot increase forever. As part of the allocation of foreign sales, MNC has already made estimates for sales growth in the areas covered by its sales divisions, MNC EMEA, MNC PFE, and MNC LSA. The total, when combined with MNC's overall earnings margins, is sufficient to combine to estimate the nonroutine earnings being transferred to MNC's taxhaven subsidiary, CONCH.

Projecting sales is much more difficult when novel products are offered. For enterprise software, projections can be based on a general industry template [Cusumano:04]. Similar approaches, based on IP renewal rates, can be adapted for other industries. If there is a history of a successful product line, reasonable projections can be made. Figure 3.7, assuming stable sales, is a conservative lower bound. In this section we value MNC at a time when it has steady growth, as shown in Fig. 5.3.

Income from known acquisitions is included in the income stream. Early acquisitions by MNC, around the time of the buy-in, were paid for with stock, diluting the shareholders' investment, but preserving capital for internal R&D, promoting ongoing organic growth. Later acquisitions were paid for with capital repatriated from CONCH, due to the reduced tax rate provided by the American Jobs Creation Act (AJCA). These were not foreseen, and their effect is excluded from the expected income. A high rate of acquisitions impacts organic growth. In general, moderate investing in acquisitions reduces the capital available for internal growth, but we assume that MNC's spending on other acquisitions was about as beneficial as spending on internal R&D. The next section shows that errors in long-range expectations affect the current valuation only moderately.

Life of the IP

A valuation of IP requires assessing the benefits it will generate in the future. To actually compute a value for IP, we need to know the length of the period to be considered. For tangibles, depreciation and amortization schedules that imply a limited life are available. Those periods are quite arbitrary and are not applicable to IP assessments.

Conceptually, the life of IP is indefinite, and so practical rules must be imposed on intellectual assets to enable a computation of value [Wills:11]. IP protected by a patent loses its commercial value after 20 years when the patent protection lapses, although the experience in exploiting such IP still contributes to product income. To value IP with lives that are not limited by rules one must consider the diminution of its contribution to income as years pass. In Chap. 4 we saw that some contribution continues indefinitely, but also that the value of IP becomes negligible once less than 10 % of its original value remains. Globally, the need for maintenance of IP reduces initial IP to 10 % in 15.5 years [F4.8]. Well-maintained software has a long life [Glass:03]. Projecting income over such a long time is risky. However, the effect of a long IP life is mitigated by using discounting.

5.3.2.2 M2.2 Discounting Incomes to Net Present Value (NPV)

The projections of income can extend far into the future, as sketched in Fig. 5.3. However, income expected at a far-away date has less value than income received today, so the expected future incomes are discounted before being aggregated into a Net Present Value (NPV) for the valuation date. The NPV is the sum of all future incomes after each annual income has been discounted for the length of time before it is realized [F5.11].

Discounting income each year at 15 %, shown in Table F.5, reduces the value of MNC's estimated organic income over the next 20 years from $12,288M to $2,456M. To get an initial sense, a short-hand formula (Gordon's rule), using a fixed growth rate, gives an estimate of $3,333M, and a mixed approach gives an estimate of $2,667M [F5.12]. Short-hand estimates are useful to get a fast start on a valuation, but have to be presented with care [Veritas:09].

MNC's annual operating income, estimated at the date of valuation to be $600M in year 20, actually became $950M [Table F.6]. The acquisitions, now well integrated, account for about half of that income. Even though the AJCA acquisitions were substantial, the projected results after discounting were only off by about 14 % [F5.13]. Because of discounting, reasonable estimation processes can provide adequate values for an Income-based valuation. This result is as good as any value estimate for sale of a tangible, say, USco's headquarters (Example 4.1).

For the buy-in, the income is projected using the information contemporaneous with the buy-in date. Future events or actions that affect income are unknown. Applying experience with similar enterprises helps set a general trend line. If MNC's management is wise, bad alternatives will be avoided and profitable ones taken. External events are not predictable. Specifically, the low-cost acquisitions due to the 2004 AJCA cannot be foreseen. One can expect that annual growth rates using its intellectual capital will diminish in the future. However, over time research and general costs will grow slower than revenue, so that the net operating income can grow linearly. The effects of offshore tax sheltering have not been included.

Taking such trends into account, aggregating the expected income over 20 years yields a total of $8,341M. After discounting the net expected value of all of MNC, as of the valuation date, becomes $2,295M [Table F.5].

5.3.2.3 M2.3 Allocation of Income When the Inc-VM Is Used

The income-based method (Inc-VM) uses the aggregated net income of all of MNC to estimate its entire intellectual capital. In the prior MC-VM we only had a current market value and used a single current reasonably anticipated benefit (RAB) fraction to estimate the CONCH share for the buy-in. The Inc-VM uses annual projections of future income, so we will also project likely annual changes of the RAB.

RAB Change in the Future

The RAB fraction of MNC's income accruing to CONCH will also change annually. The expected terminal fraction can be estimated by global ratios, such as customers, population, and GNP, as shown in Table 4.1. A linear growth of sales to the terminal limit is the simplest estimate. We start with the 44 % RAB based on earnings. For the terminal limit value we use another, still conservative, RAB metric, the expected spending budget of the existing CONCH customers, 54 % [F4.1]. When we apply this increasing RAB to the values shown in Table F.5, we obtain a total income for CONCH of $4,150M, giving an NPV of $1,089M [F5.14].

Region-Specific Income and Growth

If regional business divisions of the company need to be valued, we can also be more specific with the Inc-VM than with the market cap method (MC-VM). The market cap data provide no information when shareholders expect changes to occur so that the same global RAB allocation ratio was used for all of CONCH.

MNC's management actually projects sales growth in each of its four regions. The regional RAB rates are available and can be applied to MNC's four income streams. Each regional growth rate may be more uncertain than a single estimate, but the sum of the three offshore rates produces a more reliable allocation for CONCH. Comparing the sum of all four regional Inc-VM valuations with an independently produced total valuation for MNC can validate the results. To limit complexity here, we will not attempt to improve our Inc-VM results for CONCH by using region-specific information. ATA will opt for the lowest valuation in its buy-in estimate.

5.3.2.4 M2.4 Computing the Income for the Tranche Transferred

Only the value of the share of the IP rights transferred to the offshore site, CONCH, is to be valued. Excluded from the transfer is the routine income, income not due to intangibles. MNC had an operating income of $250M in the year of the valuation, a margin of 62 % of its manufacturing revenue [F5.9]. The final earnings, after research and capital costs, are $154M, or 41 %. The question is: How much of those earnings is due to MNC's unique IP? Recall that in the MC-VM method the tangibles were taken out to make a similar adjustment to obtain the nonroutine income. Here we must take out the routine income.

Adjusting MNC's Income to Consider Only Income from IP

To distinguish income that is derived from intellectual capital, we must separate it from income streams available to any commodity business. For MNC's foreign operations, while all intangibles are owned by CONCH, its three CFCs, MNC

EMEA, MNC PFE, and MNC LSA, perform all the work, primarily the actual distribution, but do not own any intangibles.

In order to reduce the income to only that due from intangibles, we estimate the income expected in a routine operation and then eliminate such income.

Routine Income

Routine margins in MNC's industrial sector tend to be between 2 and 10 % [HandL:03]. To narrow that estimate we focus on alternative means of distributions of similar products. We also present three approaches that model MNC specifically. The principal routine function that does not involve IP and that could easily be outsourced, domestically or offshore, is distribution of the product. A survey of eight arm's-length distributors determines their average rate of return to be 5 % [F5.15].

We model the business of MNC specifically and create two companies. Then we can compute what the arm's-length return of its hypothetical distribution company would be, and obtain 4.9 % [F5.16].

We can use a published result (2–8 %) for routine returns in MNC's sector companies [Rosenberg:10]. Data based on profits are shown adjusted by 24 % to reflect earnings before US taxes.

An alternative model is a company that sells products similar to MNC's, but without distinguishing IP. That was the approach used to estimate a price for a generic drug in Chap. 2 [F2.28]. Commodity products could not command the same prices, but they have similar costs [F5.17]. This approach yields 4.4 %.

A fifth method considers the types of assets owned. Tangible assets are assumed to be routinely available, whereas only intangible assets create nonroutine income [F5.18].

The five results are summarized in Table 5.4. As is typical in economic analyses, the results vary but generate a credible range. We use 5 % as a reasonable estimate and apply that to the distributor's sales income of $525M [F2.24]. The IRS finds nonroutine incomes of 7 % still acceptable [VidanoT:07]. Higher margins indicate that there is some contribution from proprietary IP. Given the 41 % total earnings margin on MNC's revenues, the nonroutine margin for MNC becomes 36 % [F5.19].

The Income Due to Intangible Assets

Moving to commodity products is not MNC's plan. MNC will continue to spend on R&D as it does currently, so both its management and its investors expect that its 36 % nonroutine earnings margin will continue into the future. We adjust the earnings and their NPVs computed due to the intangible capital held by MNC and CONCH by subtracting the routine income expected of a similar commodity operation from the total income. The results are shown in Table 5.5 [F5.20]. The two final values, $2,012M for MNC overall and $955M for the CONCH buy-in, will be entered into the summary Table 5.13.

Table 5.4 Expected routine earning margins for distributors

Approach	Arm's-length distributors		Commodity producers		Assets
Method	Survey	Model MNC split	Published, adjusted	Model MNC without IP	MNC balance
Earnings margin	5.0 %	4.9 %	2.5–10 %	4.4 %	4.2 %

5.3.2.5 M2.5 Summary of the Income-Based (Inc-VM) Approach

The income-based valuation method (Inc-VM) is based on the fundamental principle for valuing intellectual capital. The value of IP is the benefit it will garner in the future. Instead of relying on the wisdom of the market, it uses estimates of future income. The estimates may be provided by the owners of the company or by external experts. These estimates, by specialists having better access to corporate information, should be more precise than those derived from the shareholders' expectations, as used in the market cap-based approach (M1, the MC-VM). Depending on local data means that bias and motivation to minimize taxes are now a concern.

If applied retrospectively, an income-based method will produce a result consistent with the definition of the value of intangibles. When an income-based method, as the Inc-VM, is applied for a predictive valuation, it depends on uncertain estimates of future income. Estimates used should be cross-checked with the corporate history and with experience of other companies in the same business sector. The income method is suitable for a company that has achieved some measure of maturity, has had a history of sales, and understands its customers' expectations, so that its future is relatively stable. MNC falls into that category.

Because future income for a start-up is uncertain, the Inc-VM approach appears to be unreliable for a valuation of a company just starting up. Alternatives are also difficult. There will be no public shares to provide a market capitalization-based estimate and little data for any of the other methods. For a start-up, the Inc-VM provides the best way to document a business plan. All the data are out in the open, and if they are in a spreadsheet, alternatives can be quickly assessed.

The Inc-VM method is based on estimating the future benefits of all of a corporation's intellectual capital, representing its platform for future growth. It now also makes sense to estimate the split of the expected future benefits ratio (RAB) as the off-shored operation grow. The calculations assume a modest but steady growth in the RAB, increasing the resulting valuation.

In a transfer of IP-rights the Inc-VM is also referred to as the "Foregone Profits Method" [BrooksKW:02]. The name indicates that it estimates the profits that a seller, in our case MNC, has lost by transferring rights in an income-producing asset to another entity, here CONCH. The entire platform of nonroutine income-generating assets was split among the parties, while control remains with the parent. The Inc-VM approach matches the situation in buy-ins that occur in cost-sharing and platform contribution transactions and is central to recently adopted transfer pricing regulations [King:10].

Table 5.5 Earnings due to IP

Expected earnings	MNC overall	CONCH
Total [F5.10, F5.14]	$8,341M	$4,151M
NPV @15 %, applied midyear	$2,295M	$1089M
Remaining nonroutine earnings	$2,012M	$955M

The five assessments shown in Table 5.5 of a reasonable routine income indicate that 5 % is a reasonable estimate in this case. Then the nonroutine income of MNC due to its IP becomes 36 % [F5.18]. The combination yields for Inc-VM an estimate of $955M for the buy-in by CONCH to be paid to MNC. The result of the income-based method (Inc-VM) is 14 % more than the value obtained using the market cap method (MC-VM) ($839M), but still of the same order of magnitude [F5.20]. The shareholders' intuition appears to be a bit less optimistic than the projections of MNC's management of the value of its intellectual capital. Actually our model MNC did quite a bit better in the end. For instance, the benefits MNC and CONCH obtained from the low-taxed AJCA repatriation could not have been foreseen by management or shareholders and are not included in this valuation

M2: Inc-VM buy-in: $955M

5.3.3 M3: IIP-VM, Identified IP Valuation Method

In Chap. 3 we listed the types of assets constituting the intellectual capital of a company like MNC. Methods based on the total income of a company, or a subsidiary, do not indicate the contribution made by the individual assets. The Identified IP Valuation Method (IIP-VM) deals with the details needed when the distribution of assets differs substantially in the parent company and the various CFCs. This will be the case when only selected assets are transferred. An analysis of specific types of IP, as listed in Table 3.2, provides an understanding of the processes that generate value from the intellectual capital in a company.

The nonroutine earnings of a company's assets are based on their IP contents and the actual income over the lifetime of that IP. For each asset the IP-generating and IP-consuming processes can be documented. The life of the asset becomes an important factor in determining the value of the identified IP. In the two prior methods covered, MC-VM and Inc-VM, the life is indefinite, being linked to MNC itself, and all the assets are aggregated. When selected assets are being valued, their interdependence remains, so that a specific valuation cannot assume an isolated, counterfactual setting. Using MNC again as a model of what transpires in the real world, we will first focus on the IP contribution in MNC's products.

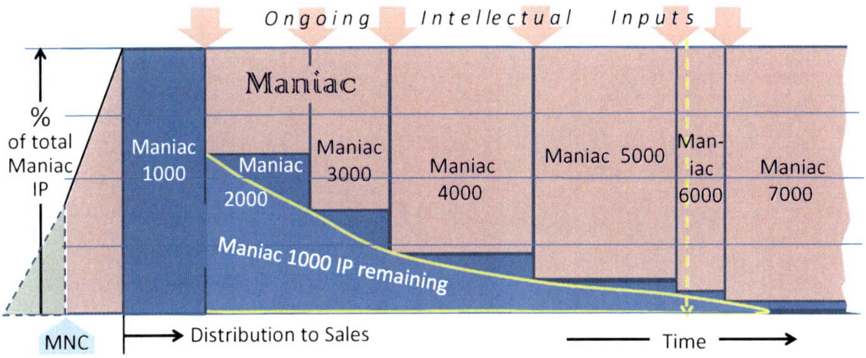

Fig. 5.4 Diminution of initial IP fraction

5.3.3.1 M3.1 IP Diminution

If the IP rights to specific products are to be valued, then the life is limited to the life of products that contain essential, distinguishing IP. MNC's products have all inherited substantial IP from their predecessor products. We will first focus on the Maniac product line, because that is MNC's dominant source of income in the period being analyzed.

Nevertheless, with every improvement, new intellectual input is added into the product line, and that input diminishes the fraction of the original IP introduced. Figure 5.4 depicts how the original IP, created in the Maniac 1000, actually diminishes over time.

MNC's initial product, the Maniac 1000, came out in <2 years after MNC's founding. Selling well, Maniacs became a product line. Six major improved Maniacs appeared over 20 years; the release intervals varied from 1 to 4 years. MNC's average interval up to Maniac 7000 was just under 2½ years [F5.21]. As products mature, Maniac release intervals tend to become longer, unless a release, here the Maniac 6000, has a serious problem and is replaced quickly.

A metric for the IP diminution is the relative effort expended to create new Maniacs. With each new Maniac release the IP remaining from the prior Maniac 1000 diminishes. With data for all the additional efforts spent, we can plot the remaining IP from Maniac 1000 as shown here.

Unless MNC switches to a completely novel product line, some of the IP remains indefinitely. During the development of the Maniac 6000, after 18½ years, <10 % of Maniac 1000's IP was left. In the subsequent paragraphs we refine and quantify the diminution.

IP Life Based on Diminution

Although the life of the IP remaining in successive Maniacs is indefinite, assigning a cutoff date for valuation purposes is reasonable. Just as for the Inc-VM method I consider that IP life effectively ends when its contribution goes below 10 % of the initial level. Although 10 % seems still significant, the discounting applied later to the nonroutine income renders the value of the remaining IP's contribution negligible.

An analysis of the diminution of the IP shows that by the time Maniac 7000 appeared, <10 % of the initial hardware and software IP remained in the product being sold. Although the Maniac hardware now uses mainly commodity chips, the original architecture of the Maniac remains a major and valuable contribution. The software was greatly updated. Using the 10 % IP level as the cutoff for the Maniac IP life, that life is just under 19 years [F5.22].

The effort needed for keeping MNC's product line productive comes from four primary sources:

1. Original work by MNC's R&D staff. The developers benefit from the next three sources.
2. Analysis of product failures and warranty claims, carefully documented and triaged as, say, a user error, a failure due to excessive stress, or a design flaw affecting all copies of a Maniac. Any type of error should be minimized in the future, but the priorities differ.
3. Feedback from MNC's marketing staff, informing the researchers about customers' expectations of future Maniacs in the product line.
4. Interaction with standard-setting organizations to remain aware of and to influence standards that will make a difference in the acceptance of future Maniacs.

Intervals for releasing new Maniacs vary, depending on resources, competitive pressures, and product success. We see that the Maniac 6000 was replaced very soon by the Maniac 7000, with little new input, likely because of a serious problem with product acceptance. Normally it is difficult to market releases of updated product at short intervals.

Predicting IP Diminution

To explain IP replacement, the diminution of the original IP, and the estimate of IP life that can be derived, we need information about the development process.

An accurate quantification of IP diminution in completed projects requires detailed records of time spent and type of work performed for each Maniac release. A Maniac is composed of hardware and embedded software, so that developers' efforts for both aspects must be analyzed and allocated. If no accurate records of efforts invested are available, a valuation analyst can gather approximate information for a fair allocation by interviewing the actual developers.

Note that the IP fraction and its diminution are distinct from sales growth or sales decrease, although significant product improvements should accelerate sales [Larson:11]. Having excellent IP delivers a double punch: the profit margins on each product can be higher and the sales volume can be greater. The IP embodied in Maniac 3000, although only 54 % of the initial fraction, contributes relatively more to the final valuation, because annual sales of the Maniac 3000 are much larger than those of the Maniac 1000, as shown again in Fig. 5.9.

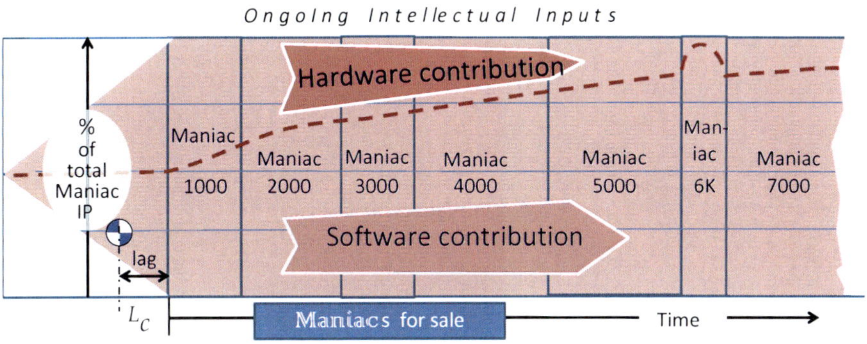

Fig. 5.5 Change in hardware versus software contribution to Maniac line IP

Expected Diminution of Hardware IP

The Maniac, like most high-tech gadgets, relies on hardware components that are controlled and made effective by embedded software. Figure 5.5 indicates that the initial design effort was split equally between hardware and software. Once the initial design of the Maniac was completed, the engineering team continued to work on improvements, but most hardware-based performance enhancements are due to the use of faster, smaller, and more capable components obtained from external vendors, as CCC. The importance of the hardware contribution to the Maniac product line IP diminishes approximately linearly, becoming about 12 % while Maniac 7000 was being sold and the Maniac 8000 was under development [F5.23].

Expected Diminution of Software IP

Software is an intellectual asset type of increasing importance. Software is sold in many forms, as shrink-wrapped products, over the Internet, by enterprise software providers, and by contractors developing specialized software programs for companies. Many companies also develop their own software for internal use. MNC's Maniacs, like most high-tech products, contain substantial embedded software and could not function without the control provided by that software.

MNC has never completely replaced the software embedded in its products, but the company has steadily improved and broadened the functionality of the software. Major software versions have accompanied all new product Maniacs; minor updates occur more frequently, limited only by the quality assurance process needed to avoid disasters. MNC immediately distributes fixes to customers that encounter problems, but it makes the fixes widely available only after testing, and then releases them as part of minor version updates.

Software IP estimation has the advantage that the size of the software code can be used as a surrogate for the effort expended in improving and maintaining the

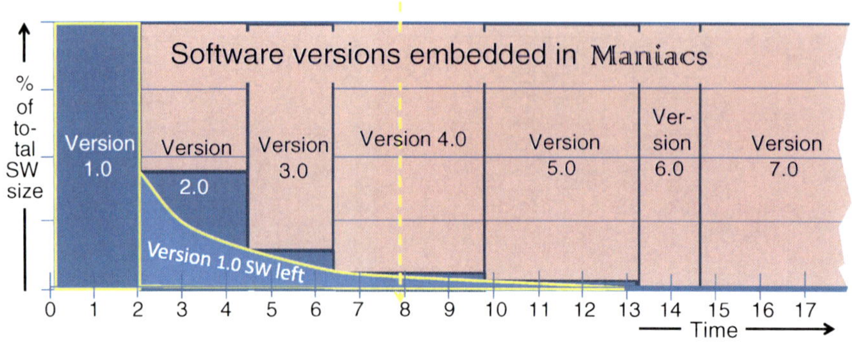

Fig. 5.6 Software growth reduces the initial IP of embedded software in Maniacs

software [Zeidman:11]. Code size has been widely used as a parameter to estimate software development costs [Boehm:00]. The relationships of software size, growth, and development cost have been extensively studied [Jones:96]. Analysis of code changes is needed when one encounters software reorganization—say, a merging of redundant product components or including acquired or free commodity software. An observation called the "Roux rule," which says that software grows in every version by an amount equal to the size of the first working version, gives guidance for a prospective estimation of software IP diminution [Roux:97]. The result is 8 years for the software alone, or just over halfway during version 4.0 development [F5.24].

Because MNC devotes more effort to software than to hardware, the effort share increases, but the embedded software IP component diminishes rapidly and has a shorter life. We see in Fig. 5.6 that by Version 5.0, after 9½ years, the original software IP embedded in a Maniac is down to 7 %.

The effect was considered in the combined data shown in Fig. 5.5 [F5.22]. The software IP component diminishes more rapidly than the aggregate hardware and software IP of the Maniac products. The unique architecture of the Maniac, an important IP component of hardware, lasted a long time [AmdahlBB:64]. Only after 19 years, when the Maniac 7000 was being produced, was the 10 % cutoff level for the combination reached.

Software is also updated for existing hardware. Modern products allow product releases to be upgraded just by reloading software. In addition to numbers designating major release of the Maniac, there will also be software-only update versions, such as Version 3.3 and Version 3.4.2. These software upgrades are made available to MNC's customers free of charge.

When software is sold as a primary product, obtaining a major new software version requires a new purchase, akin to buying a new Maniac release. Minor version updates are typically available for free to purchasers of the major version. In the past, some cost was incurred and charged when customers wanted to receive update disks for minor changes, but today, the low cost and convenience of Internet distribution make frequent and free minor updates feasible. Customers may receive major updates as well by purchasing a subscription.

The interval for issuing major versions of software is constrained by customer patience and by the threat of obsolescence [W:06]. Customers get annoyed when new software versions requiring changes in habits or updates to secondary software arrive too frequently. Software must also remain up-to-date with evolving standards and expectations.

For a prospective analysis, no factual future improvement data are available, so that past experience is the basis for predicting the future. Expected growth rates can be extracted from historical data of prior and similar products. Because in this case the buy-in valuation is being made when the third release of the Maniac is available, some past data are available to help make the needed predictions of future growth due to ongoing development. To make a valid analysis, both hardware and software contributions must be assessed. The IP life, and hence the analyses, can again be terminated at the point where <10 % of the original IP remains.

Common Errors when valuing identified IP

Common errors made when estimating future IP diminution and determining IP life are:

(i) Inaccurate measurement of code growth. Systematic code optimizations between versions can greatly distort the measurement of code that reflects IP growth.
(ii) Dealing correctly with a buy-in that occurs when a product is beyond its initial development; for instance, assuming that a mature product, such as the Maniac 3000, undergoes the same rate of diminution that occurred initially.
(iii) Mixing up multiple product lines, or not recognizing their interaction when the R&D staff is shared.

We will now deal with these three issues in turn.

(i) Measuring Software Size
Getting a good handle on the actual software size is actually quite hard. First there is the issue of using the binary, executable code versus the actual source code used to create the software.

The binary code will include libraries of functions provided by external sources, as the systems vendor, third parties, and likely open-source, free software as well [Spolsky:04]. Such code does not count as contributing IP. Some binary code segments will reappear in multiple places in the distributed code. Only the original code that reflects IP should be measured. Code libraries that contain external code can be identified and omitted. To omit all irrelevant code may be impossible, but including some code that does not contribute IP can offset the intellectual effort developers made in integrating external code bases.

Programmers have different styles of writing source code, so that source lines used for the same functionality can differ greatly. Code can be rearranged, and systematic changes in naming program modules and variables are often introduced in new versions, making simple textual matching risky. Tools for code comparison are in common use for software maintenance. The results of code comparisons should be analyzed by software experts to assess software growth that is associated with IP-generating contributions.

If the volume of code is large, as is the case for significant IP-generating software, measuring tools are needed. A tool for software growth determination checks for exactly matching program names and the text of their source code lines [Zeidman:11]. Anything that does not match is considered to be a deletion. The subsequent analysis considers the efforts spent on deletions to be a value-adding contribution. The combination of deletion and additions will show a more rapid diminution than expected by the Roux rule [F5.24]. Tools that are primarily used to detect software plagiarism focus on structure and can deal with systematic changes of names, but do not focus on metrics useful for IP valuation [Aiken:09].

(ii) IP Diminution in Mature Products

The CONCH buy-in of MNC's IP occurred when the Maniac 3000 was being sold. Now the relative IP diminution has to start as of this release. The rapid diminution from the Maniac 1000 to the 2000 release is not seen any more during ongoing development of successive releases, here at Maniac 3000. The analysis of growth starts at a point during the development of the Maniac 3000, as determined by the date of the buy-in. The horizon for the prediction is extended to the Maniac 8000 and its software, again to a 10 % cutoff.

Because software improvements now dominate, we base all diminution on the Roux rule as adapted for the software embedded in Maniacs. The computation, otherwise identical to the computation as used for Fig. 5.6, yields an IP life to the 10 % level of 16½ years [F5.25].

For our Maniacs we have all the future information. An actual prospective valuation will not have data about the future. A prospective valuation must project data from historical information. As a basis for the future version release times, the average of the first two versions is proposed, just under 26 months for Maniacs 1000 and 2000. To validate that estimate, MNC's engineers are consulted. They find the estimate reasonable and observe that the Maniac 3000 will be released ahead of that schedule. Using 26 months for each release yields estimates as shown in Fig. 5.7, superimposed on the actual known timeline used for the proper computations. Using those estimates, the 10 % IP cutoff level for the software is not reached until the time for the estimated release of the Maniac 9000. The life based on the estimate is now 15½ years [F5.26]. It turns out that the engineers were somewhat optimistic, later versions actually took a bit longer to develop, as is typical when products become more mature.

We see that even for substantial changes in parameters, the results are quite stable; although the actual release intervals varied greatly from the estimates, the IP lifetime difference is only 1 year, 16½ actual versus 15½ years. The closeness of the

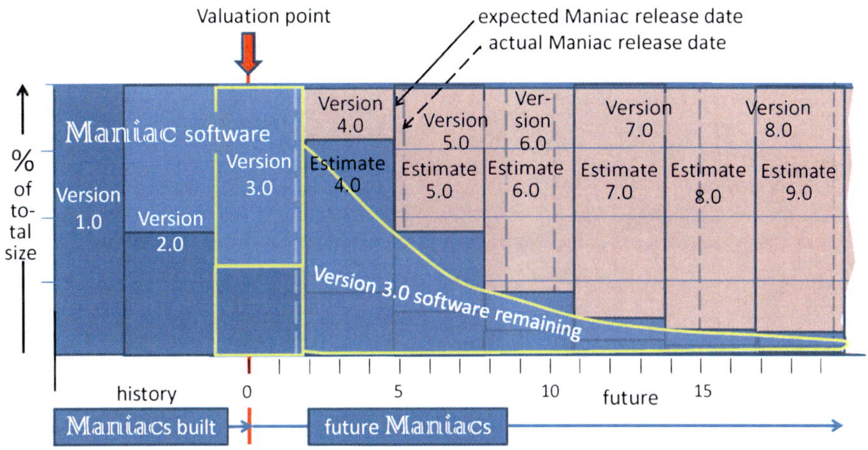

Fig. 5.7 Software IP left from a valuation point, actual and predicted

estimate is achieved because prior experience is available at a more mature stage, improving the quality of the extrapolation. As development proceeds, those estimates can be further verified and improved. The IIP-VM method hence also gives guidance to management, creating a more stable business setting.

Not considering the maturity of product development and applying the initial diminution rate is a significant error. That error shortens the IP life to 8 years, as shown in Fig. 5.6, an unreasonable life for mature products. That error, using the initial rate of diminution at a much later time, when development has settled down, is equivalent to applying the loss of value of a new car when it is driven home from the dealership to a 20-mile trip next year.

(iii) Transfer of IP to Related Products

After the buy-in, MNC decided to produce a complementary product for the mobile market, the ManiMobile. Here the initial IP input came partially from the established Maniac product line, from IP obtained in acquisitions, and also from the four IP sources that contribute to the current Maniac product line: innovative work, analysis of product failures and warranty claims, feedback from MNC's marketing staff, and interaction with standards organizations.

The ManiMobile immediately became popular in Bavaria, but soon sales spread worldwide. ManiMobile development shared much of staff working on Maniacs. Later, the ManiMobile M-Mob m3 also benefited substantially from efforts applied to the Maniac 5000, as shown in Fig. 5.8.

Unfortunately, analyzing each product line distinctly and with its own timeline requires quite detailed data, data that are rarely available when internal R&D is intermingled.

Because ongoing development, marketing, and support of Maniac and ManiMobile are done jointly, it is difficult to disentangle the Maniac and ManiMobile product lines. In our model of MNC, we just consider the Maniac product line

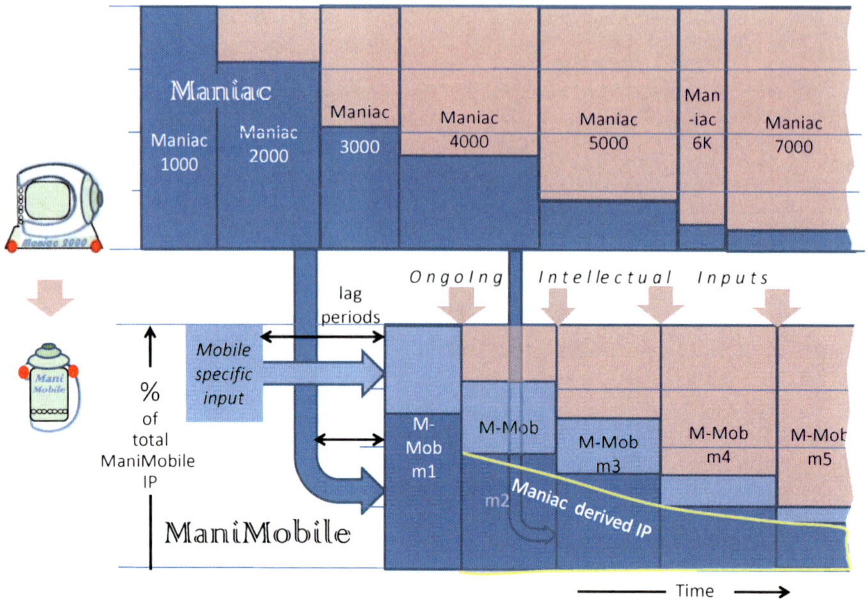

Fig. 5.8 Diminution of IP for derivative products

overall and ignore the complexity that the derived product, ManiMobile, presents. Aggregating costs and benefits is often adequate.

5.3.3.2 M3.2 Lag and Life Applied to Assess Changes in IP

In Chap. 3 the concept of lag was introduced, a metric which accounts for delay between investment spending and deriving income. Figure 5.5 indicated the role of lag in the context of the IIP-VM approach. The lag has to be added to the IP life to match the effects of R&D on income. Detailed effort data are required to precisely compute the lag between R&D spending and product availability. Here we simply estimate the lag, as shown in Chap. 3, using MNC's product release data and obtain 1.2 years for the lag to be applied [F5.27]. We ignore any distribution delay. With a predicted life of 15.5 years the IP generates income for 16.7 years.

The lag precedes the reduction of IP due to the introduction of new IP in successive years. The incomes used are kept undiminished during the lag period, and then reduced following the IP diminution using the forecasts of efforts documented with Fig. 5.7. The subsequent life of the IP remains based on its diminution to 10 % of its original level. Life and lag together for the actual buy-in estimate amounts to 17.5 years. The total income in our model over that period at CONCH is $3,897M. For each year after the lag is passed we have a value for the diminution of the IP. Reducing that income every year of its long actual life by the diminution factor for that year leaves $1,367M [F5.28].

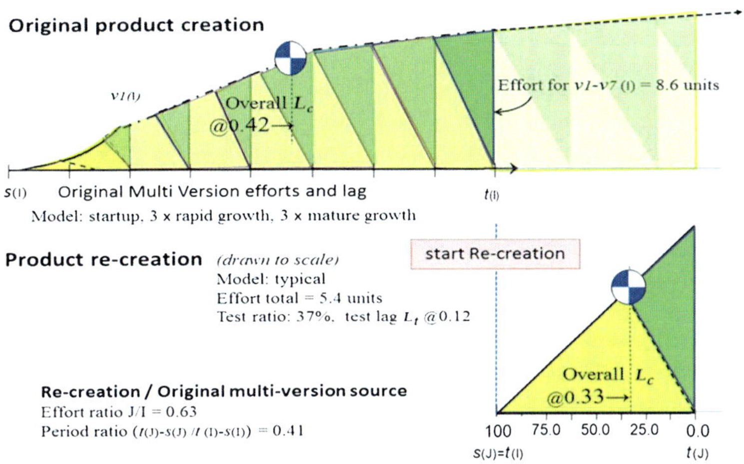

Fig. 5.9 Arm's-length lag estimation

Arm's-Length Life and Lag

We computed up to now the lag experienced by MNC in creating Maniacs. However, when valuing CONCH for a buy-in payment as an independent entity, as expected in an arm's-length setting, using MNC's current lag is not realistic. Going back to first principles, the value of CONCH should be what a willing purchaser would have to pay to an independent and willing seller. MNC is not an independent and willing seller. MNC would not sell the offshore IP rights it provided to CONCH on the open market and deprive itself of nearly half of its revenues at a price that was based on its current lag; it took MNC many versions to get to where it is now.

For a realistic lag we need to consider a realistic arm's-length case. Consider that an independent party, RINCH, wants to build and sell Maniac-like products, Repliacs, worldwide outside North America. There are two options, to buy or to build. Under the first option RINCH must pay MNC for the needed IP rights. The offer forces MNC to decide that the amount is worth more than MNC profits from selling Maniacs in the rest of the world.

The second option is for RINCH to develop, build, and sell its own Repliacs. Now RINCH, operating truly at arm's length, will also experience its own lag. RINCH has to invest in development for some time, an arm's-length lag, sketched in Fig. 5.9. RINCH has access to working Maniacs, but not to their IP. The development period will be shorter, but still substantial. An estimate based on replicating a version 6 of software is 41 % [W:09]. The aggregate the sequence of basic lag estimations as shown in Fig. 3.4 creates a base.

The arm's-length lag is more than the 1.2-year current lag for MNC to create a new version. Our estimate of a fair arm's-length lag is 3.0 years [F5.29].

For a realistic buy-in valuation, an arm's-length lag should be added to the IP life after the buy-in point to obtain an arm's-length life appropriate for a buy-in valuation estimate. The values of lag push the diminution experienced over the IP life to a later time period. On completion, at *t*(J), the re-created product still will not match what the original developer will have available, because MNC will have continued to put effort into the original product over the several years that it takes an arm's-length competitor to re-create a matching product [Contractor:01].

Earnings aggregated over the combined period contribute to the buy-in valuation. During the total period CONCH expected revenues of $3,723M. When we apply the IP life diminution shifted by the lag, the diminished income becomes $1,559M [F5.30].

First-to-Market Advantage

CONCH received ongoing rights to all of MNC's intellectual capital when the buy-in transfer was made. By the time RINCH has the competing Repliac ready, it will not match the MNC Maniac because MNC improves its product during the 3 years RINCH needed to create a matching product [Contractor:01]. CONCH has access to MNC's new, improved Maniacs.

MNC's "first-to-market advantage," listed as IP Type 5.b in Table 3.2, has a high value if competitors could emerge easily. We don't begrudge CONCH sharing that advantage, but it should be included in a valuation that is supposed to be at arm's length. Correcting for the initial effect of that arm's-length lag adds over 21 % to the diminished sales income [F5.31]. That increase is a technical measure of the "first-to-market-advantage," but ignores the additional market visibility advantage that early products enjoy.

5.3.3.3 M3.3 Discounting Future Income from IP

The numbers we have extracted so far are annual results, some projected far into the future. For a valuation as of the buy-in date, they will have to be discounted [F5.10]. The effect on MNC's income as it appears in Fig. 2.3 is recapitulated in Fig. 5.10, computed without the effect of lag.

The analyst creating the expectation of incomes cannot be aware of future acquisitions at MNC, for instance those stimulated by the AJCA. Beyond that time the income is assumed to grow linearly, and the diminution is simply extrapolated on the basis of the average version-release interval of 20 months.

Figure 5.11 shows how the four factors arm's-length lag, IP diminution, CONCH share, and discounting are combined. The graph displays the case for the historical global life with an arm's-length lag, matching the last column of Table 5.6 [F5.32]. Other cases have similar patterns. Sales covered by CONCH are expected to grow at a slightly faster rate than the total sales of MNC, but they increase mainly as a result of MNC's overall growth.

To avoid dealing with indefinite IP life for long-lived but diminishing assets, life is cut off when the original contribution has little value left, given common discount

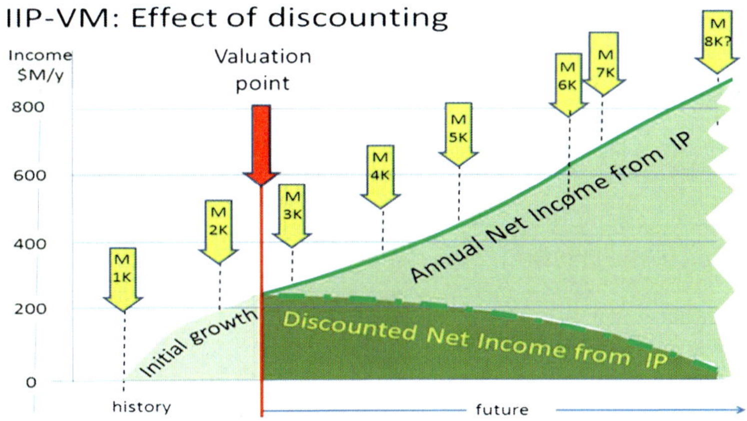

Fig. 5.10 Effect of discounting on significance of income factors

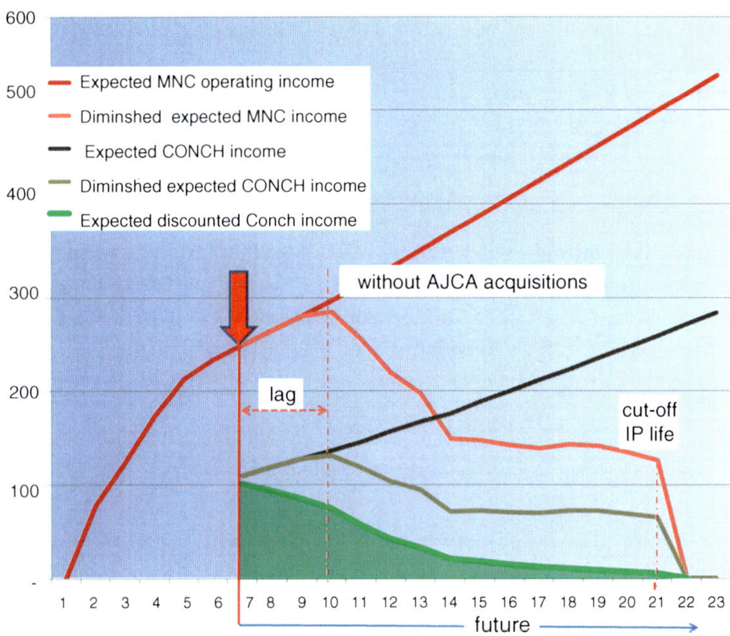

Fig. 5.11 Expectations contributing to an Identified IP valuation

rates. Because IP life was already limited at the 10 % level of the original IP, after discounting any IP contributions to a valuation beyond that point are really negligible. As a result of discounting, the contribution after year 15 (that is, 8 years after the buy-in) is small, although MNC's annual sales and the CONCH share of those sales are nearly double at the IP cutoff point.

Table 5.6 Technical buy-in values for CONCH based on expected life income

Parameters for predictive valuation at buy-in date	Basis for life:	MNC expectations		Global historical data	
	Source:	[F5.26]		[F4.8]	
Expected Life after the buy-in date	Years	15½		7½ discounted life	
Version/arm's-length lags	Source	[F5.27]	[F5.29]	[F5.27]	[F5.29]
	Years	1.2	3.0	1.2	3.0
Total income aggregation period	Years	16.7	18.5	8.6	10.4
Expected MNC income ($M)	$M	6,490	7,482	2,701[a]	3,428[a]
Expected CONCH income	$M	3,161	3,723	1,247[a]	1,617[a]
Expected diminished income	$M	1,207	1,559	742[a]	1,047[a]
Expected Net Present Value (NPV)	$M	548	667	464[a]	591[a]

[a]Based on a discounted life

If insufficient data are available to estimate technical IP life, we can use the calculation based on historical replacement rates for all US manufacturing, with the expenditures discounted, of about 7½ years. This estimate is a lower bound for high-technology industries. The results are shown in combination with other results in Table 5.6.

Table 5.6 shows the computed results for four of the prior expected income computations, with the parameters used to obtain the results and the results after discounting. The expected income for each year is discounted as if it were collected midyear. The global results are based on a life estimate of 7.5 years, which already required discounting [F4.8].

The Table also shows results in both cases for the current version lag and the estimated arm's-length lag. An arm's-length lag is fair and still conservative, but any arm's-length assumption is counterfactual, since MNC would not yield control of its worldwide IP to an independent party. Hypothetical situations should not be used in an appraisal [AF:04].

5.3.3.4 M3.4 Validation of the Identified IP Values

After discounting, the range between the lowest ($464M) and highest ($667M) NPV estimates shown in Table 5.6 is only 36 % about their average; <20 % above and below. That degree of variability is acceptable for estimates into an uncertain future [F5.33].

The true validity of any estimation can only be obtained years later. The actual values in our model of MNC's operations were larger, mainly because of the effect of the acquisitions due to the 2004 AJCA incentives, which allowed the capital accumulated at CONCH to be repatriated at a low tax rate. They are shown in Table 5.7. Those acquisitions provided income that was not expected when the buy-in valuations were made. However, because of the short planning cycle due to a 1-year, one-time tax incentive, those acquisitions also distracted from efficient organic growth. These actual results could not have been foreseen.

Table 5.7 Technical buy-in values for CONCH based on actual income

Parameters for computing the value of MNC		Results	
Life after the buy-in date	Years	16.5	
Version/arm's-length lags	Years	1.2	3.0
Income aggregation period	Years	17.7	19.5
MNC actual model income	$M	7,907	9,476
CONCH income	$M	3,897	4,782
Diminished income	$M	1,367	1,795
Net Present Value at buy-in	$M	567	691

To judge the quality of estimates made by the IIP-VM method, the long-term actual values for our model MNC can be compared with the estimated values [F5.34]. The AJAC motivated acquisition increased the NPV of the actual results by about 3 %. The remaining effect of the 1-year difference between the actual and expected IP lives, shown in Tables 5.6 and 5.7, amounts to <1 % after discounting. The reason for the small differences of the estimates and the actual model is that the estimation errors are mainly in the far-out future.

5.3.3.5 M3.5 Other IP Contributions

Up to now this method was limited to the technical IP that was identified in the products. However, the buy-in by CONCH gives it access all of MNC's intellectual capital, including the workforce, its know-how, the trademark, and all the business contracts of MNC. CONCH must carry its share there as well. Identifiable costs of doing business (SG&A) devoted to CONCH can be identified and directly reimbursed. The costs associated with a specific product, the Costs of Goods Sold (CoGS), are built into the price calculation. The Maniacs that CONCH procures from MNC US or MNC JB have a fair independent factory price (IFP). Missing is the value of access to MNC's research resources.

The technical assessment did not capture important parts of MNC's intellectual capital, such as its workforce and the "going-concern value." MNC's income in all regions is enabled by its work-force and its marketing prowess, as well as its technology. Those contributions differ in each of the regions, with MNC US still supplying the largest part.

We consider just two significant items here.

1. *The workforce that is available to MNC*. CONCH is not in an arm's-length situation, and it can count on ongoing improvements in the Maniac line, and even new products, because all of MNC's capabilities and talents are included in the cost-sharing agreement.
2. *The value of the MNC trademark*. By the time of the buy-in, Maniacs were known to most potential customers. Some of the marketing had been done by its Austrian distributor, but when the company was taken over by MNC, all of its

assets, tangible and intangible, were incorporated into MNC. This takeover took place before the buy-in. If it had been a later acquisition, CONCH would have had to share the purchase cost.

Both of these asset types have an indefinite life. As long as MNC is a going concern they will be maintained, and a share will be available to CONCH.

IP Types with Indefinite Life

When the life of an intangible asset cannot be determined, the concept of an "indefinite life" is used. For instance, trademarks are assumed to have an indefinite life. Having an indefinite life does not mean that trademarks will automatically live in perpetuity and must be valued into eternity [F5.12]. We can use, as shown in Fig. 4.3, the global cost of annual IP maintenance at 13.75 % [NadiriP:96]. Its discounted value reached the 10 % level in <7.5 years [F4.9].

Keeping trademarks effective requires maintenance. Maintaining the value of trademarks is a much more diffuse effort than maintaining technical IP. Companies need to maintain the technical quality of the products that are associated with the product, but they also need marketing, advertising, participation in trade organizations, and the like. While brand names can have an indefinite life, an investment in product-specific advertising supports a much shorter life span than spending on R&D [HirscheyW:85]. The costs, however, of all these efforts are not documented consistently. As indicated in Fig. 3.4, costs associated with product sales are considered to be routine CoGS expenses even when they contribute to long-term sales.

Valuation of Nontechnical IP

As part of the valuation of stock options in the MC-VM approach, we determined that MNC implicitly valued its critical workforce around the time of the buy-in as $258M [F5.3]. Stock options were given to senior technical personnel and management. The selection of individuals as worthy of receiving stock options certainly qualifies their contribution to be nonroutine. Thus, we add that amount as part of the identified IP, though that means CONCH should not pay SG&A costs associated with those stock options. The CONCH share is set proportionally to its current earnings-based RAB, $114M [F5.3].

Trademarks are commonly evaluated using methods that assess values by matching comparable assets, such as M4, the CUT-VM. Their value tends to be reimbursed as royalties on income. We will assume that such royalties are already embodied in the price of the product so that the expenses are part of the CoGS of a Maniac. Ongoing general marketing efforts would be booked as part of the SG&A, so we will ignore their contribution.

The technical valuation of the IIP-VM methods is applied to well-identified assets. To include the value of complementary assets, as the workforce and the trademarks, similar analyses must be performed, but other methods, as the CUT-VM, may be more suitable.

In general, one has to be careful when using a mix of valuation methods for different types of IP and then combine them in a total result. For instance, a market-capitalization method assumes that the shareholders are aware of all factors that bring value to the company. But estimates of development progress used in this method are internal information. When combining valuation results, it is easy either to create overlaps or to leave out crucial items.

5.3.3.6 M3.6 Summary of the Identified IP Valuation Approach

The IIP-VM is based on a more detailed technical and business understanding than the market cap (MC-VM) or the general income (Inc-VM) approaches. It is useful when specific IP has been transferred offshore, but it becomes tedious when many assets are transferred in a broad transaction, such as the enablement of CONCH by MNC. Also, any required product maintenance provided by MNC after the buy-in date is excluded from the IIP-VM valuation, so that subsequent costs, which will be shared between CONCH and MNC, are disregarded.

As the technical basis, we use the expected diminution of IP at the time of the buy-in with the 3-year arm's-length lag, amounting to \$665M [F5.33]. Adding the CONCH share of the value of the critical workforce to the estimated technical IP value makes the result \$781M [F5.35]. For all of MNC the sum is \$1,691M. The amount for CONCH is much lower than the \$955M from M2, the Inc-VM analyzed earlier. That difference is not surprising, because the result of the IIP-VM omits the contribution of the many intangibles that are not specifically identified, such as the value of having an ongoing business and its trademarks.

Valuing and aggregating major assets by the IIP-VM approach provides an understanding that the other methods do not give. When not all contributions are valued, the method provides a lower bound for a buy-in. For instance, in a global transfer the foreign operations are instantly productive, but that will never be true in a real arm's-length setting. The IIP-VM approach provides stable and trustworthy results for IP valuation of product lines that are at least moderately mature

M3: IIP-VM buy-in: \$781M

5.3.4 M4: CUT-VM, Comparable Uncontrolled Transaction Valuation Method

This method estimates unknown values based on comparable transactions. When using the Comparable Uncontrolled Transaction Valuation Method (CUT-VM) a value is estimated based on prices of matching products. It is commonly used in valuing transfers of tangibles, where known current prices paid by purchasers at arm's length can establish a reliable value. Pure intangibles are rarely sold as such; their benefits are embedded in the products sold. Buying a tune on the Internet is the closest approximation of a purchase of an intangible. Intangibles are replicated at a low cost into the products and add much value to the customers; MNC's Maniac products derive most of their value from MNC's IP. The transfer of IP rights from MNC to its controlled division, CONCH, is a very different transaction from a tangible product sale.

However, the CUT-VM approach is mentioned specifically in the IRS regulations for valuing intangibles [B.1.2 #4(c)]. Caveats are that any comparable transactions must have a substantially similar profit potential, so that the future income will also be similar [King:10]. Examples cited in those regulations list a case where the same product was licensed to an arm's-length company in a third region, so that there was a trustworthy comparable transaction. Another example starts with 40 similar industrial licensing agreements and uses the midquartile median of 15 similar ones. The other two examples cited in the IRS regulations show failures to meet the standard of adequate comparability.

The IRS regulations for this method refer to a general rule [B.3.3(a)(1)]:

> §1.482–1(d)(1) In general.—Whether a controlled transaction produces an arm's-length result is generally evaluated by comparing the results of that transaction to results realized by un-controlled taxpayers engaged in comparable transactions under comparable circumstances. For this purpose, the comparability of transactions and circumstances must be evaluated considering all factors that could affect prices or profits in arm's-length dealings (comparability factors).

and then lists important comparability factors.

A strict comparable for the CONCH buy-in would be a transfer of similar IP rights to distribute and sell products in some region. Adjustments to the price obtained can be made by scaling incomes by sales volume, unless the difference in size is so large that the business setting differs materially. Sales volume is a valid metric only if the comparables are of similar maturity; the IP of a start-up will not yet generate stable income.

Even prior acquisitions within a company can be used if the actual transaction was at arm's length. MNC did buy its Austrian distributor a year before the buy-in. However, that was not an arm's-length transaction; there were no other potential purchasers and its main asset of value was the sell rights granted by MNC. It had no IP-based rights to MNC's earnings. Neither can we tell if it was a willing seller. It is rare to have reliable comparables for setting actual prices.

Since it is highly unlikely that comparable buy-in transactions for similar IP could be found, we apply the CUT-VM approach to royalties. The CUT-VM is indeed typically used to compare and set royalties, payments computed as a percentage, the royalty rate, of revenues or earnings.

Using royalties on future income is common in transactions where the potential income is unknown. The seller and the purchaser do not need to agree on an estimate of future income. The royalty arrangement reduces the risk for an arm's-length purchaser that the IP will fail to lead to a marketable product. Reducing the purchaser's risk greatly increases the chance of the seller closing a deal. A seller who values the transferred IP highly can hope that the royalties received will be greater than a purchase price negotiated in the presence of uncertainty. A detailed discussion of the use of royalties appears in Appendix C.

5.3.4.1 M4.1 Comparable Royalties from Uncontrolled Transactions

For an MNC buy-in using royalties, there will be a formal license agreement to document an arrangement similar to the buy-in transaction valued in the three prior methods. CONCH will obtain a complete box of make-sell rights in the region ceded to CONCH. CONCH also obtains full ongoing access to MNC's intellectual capital, which will continuously improve all of MNC's products. In return CONCH will pay MNC a royalty right away on its revenues, at a royalty rate to be determined here. MNC receives an ongoing income stream, starting without delay.

Potential comparable public royalty agreements, negotiated at arm's length, have to be compared to MNC's agreement. Such licensing agreements will document the royalty rates as well as many ancillary conditions. A valid comparable transaction for the CONCH buy-in must also be a transfer of rights to intangible assets used to continue an ongoing distribution operation in a specific region. An issue will be if comparable licensing agreements are for an intracompany transaction, as the CONCH buy-in, or a true arm's-length transaction.

Collecting Comparable Agreements

The CUT valuation method relies on external, arm's-length data. A number of companies provide business data for a fee [IRS-FR:93]. Tax advising companies like ATA will have their own collection of documents. These databases have thousands of entries, and yet trustworthy matches will be rare. The majority of publicly available agreements are for patent licenses, and therefore they are inadequate for platform splits, where broader intellectual capital is shared.

Determining comparability means checking that the type of intangible assets and the circumstances of the transfer are similar [B.3.1 (c)(2)]. If there are modest differences, adjustments should be made. Table 3.2 provided a categorization for all these types of IP. For specific comparisons the IP should be used in similar products or processes within the same general industry sector.

Specific comparability factors are:

(a) Agreement terms, as exclusivity, region, and scope of rights—are the plans to just sell copies, make copies locally, or exploit the IP for further growth?
(b) Stage of development: in progress, prototyped, or mature as MNC's Maniacs?
(c) Rights to updates and maintenance—all implicit in the CONCH transfer.
(d) Uniqueness and protection of IP—as patents.
(e) License duration—assumed to be indefinite here.

(f) Assumption of risk—MNC is still visible and liable, even if CONCH is distinct.
(g) Existence of other relationships—MNC's ownership affects comparability.
(h) Ancillary services—CONCH is just a shell; all R&D and much else comes from MNC.
(i) Availability of data—few public records provide complete data.

All those factors should be substantiated by data to make the comparison reliable. The hardest parameter to assess is the uniqueness and quality of product. Few databases provide such crucial information.

In practice, for a major intracompany transaction such as the MNC-CONCH buy-in, no public comparable data will be found. Transactions like the MNC-CONCH cost sharing and buy-in, where the platform is split, are very unusual for truly arm's-length transactions. Constraints on matching transactions make it hard to find documented comparables for massive transfers of make-sell rights encountered when tax avoidance is an objective [SmithP:05].

The CUT-VM approach is still valid for simpler cases and was used to find royalties for routine distributors [F5.15]. It is also useful to value routine complementary assets, missed in an M3, IIP-VM valuation.

Selecting Comparable Uncontrolled Agreements

There are no standard licensing contracts for intangibles. The detailed terms of any contract for a comparable must be checked to assure comparability. For instance, the basis on which the royalties are computed must be identical. Is the royalty based on the consumer price ($99 for Forest Labs in Fig. 2.6) or on the revenue actually collected ($76)? Who pays for delivery and installation? Who services the warranties? Does the licensor make experienced staff assistance available? Royalty rates found can be adjusted to account for such differences, but each adjustment decreases the reliability of the match [B.3.1 (c)(2)]. Any agreements found will have further conditional clauses expressed in a terminology that only a lawyer could love.

All clauses should be checked, once comparable agreements have been found. Six classes of clauses to watch are listed here, with notes on how they will affect a valuation. Issues specific to the valuation of the MNC-to-CONCH transfer are shown in italics.

(i) Does the licensor receive up-front payments?
If so, add those to the final IP valuation.

All of CONCH's funds come from MNC, all payments in this case are a sham. The licensee would not exist without the licensor's setup

(ii) Does the licensor make substantial experienced staff assistance available?
Having access to the licensor's experience greatly increases the value, especially if the licensor has already produced and marketed the product. The licensor has less risk.

MNC has already produced and marketed its products in the CONCH region. As the situation here is not at arm's length, MNC will certainly make its staff and resulting product improvements available for the foreseeable future.

(iii) Is the license truly exclusive?
With exclusivity the licensor doesn't have to worry about direct competition [FlignorO:06]. The IP is more valuable [F5.36].

Any in-house transfer is in practice exclusive, no matter what any formal agreements may say. MNC won't enable competition with its own operation. By specifying that the rights granted to CONCH are not exclusive, it is easier for MNC to deal with multinational customers for the Maniac product. The actual offshore sales can still be booked at CONCH.

(iv) Are there clauses that terminate the agreement if the licensee fails?
Termination clauses reduce the risk for the licensor. They warrant lower royalty rates.

Because CONCH is fully controlled by MNC, the option to close the division always exists, no matter what their agreements may say.

(v) Can the licensee sublicense others?
The right to sublicense can be valuable to the licensee, for instance, if the product is so successful that additional resources are desirable to cover the market. Being allowed to sublicense the IP warrants a higher royalty rate.

In the MNC-to-CONCH transfer case, because of the control that MNC has, the option to sublicense is always available.

(vi) Is the IP that the licensor is selling encumbered or compromised in some way?
If there are pending lawsuits, if an improved method has been announced, or if technical staff has left—perhaps to start a competitive operation—the value of the IP can be drastically reduced. A company may dispose of valuable goods not central to its core business at a low price in order to survive.

Again, CONCH and MNC would be equally affected.

For royalties set under unequal or unusual conditions, the prices obtained are not a trustworthy base for an arm's-length sale. In the MNC-to-CONCH IP-rights transfer conditions match perfectly.

Each proposed comparable agreement must be diligently checked before it can be accepted as a comparable to be used for a valuation. Not only must the specific transaction to be valued be checked against paper documents, but the facts of the business transaction must be established, before comparability can be asserted. A good understanding is needed to make adjustments when conditions differ.

Computation

For a reliable CUT-VM, an analyst should obtain at least a dozen comparable agreements, each with enough information to make adjustments, before proceeding with a computation. If not enough comparables can be found, one can proceed only if the businesses match and the royalty rates are very similar. Once adequate comparables have been found and the adjusted royalties have been determined, then a trustworthy valuation of the IP can be generated. Such a computation will reject outliers by using an "interquartile mean" computation [F D.3].

Since we cannot search for trustworthy comparables for our model company, in order to produce a CUT-VM valuation, published royalty data for the industry sector that MNC is in were used. An important clause to consider is that, because MNC's products already exist and have been sold, CONCH assumes no distinct development or marketing risk.

The range of reported royalties in MNC's business varies widely from 0 to 70 % [Parr:07]. For electronic products, a royalty rate of 25 % on earnings is appropriate, and for software a royalty rate of 35 % on earnings is appropriate. Combining the product rates yields a typical total rate of 30 % on earnings. Since royalties are typically applied to sales, we use the margin on MNC's Maniacs, omitting R&D and capital cost. For MNC we obtain an adjusted royalty rate on revenues of 20 % [F5.37]. CONCH still has to pay for its share of manufacturing at MNC JB and for any imports of components from MNC and other suppliers in the USA.

In typical licensing cases the licensee is also responsible for distribution. It must set up a distribution network or expand its existing capabilities. CONCH also received a functioning distribution network. That distribution network contains some IP assets as customer lists and sales contracts. Such IP was generated by using MNC's SG&A expenses. For a distribution service, a 5 % royalty rate on its revenue is typical [F5.15]. The total royalty rate then becomes 20 + 5 % = 25 % on revenues, and that rate will be set in the licensing contract.

This is a royalty rate on revenues that is much higher than what is typically seen in arm's-length contracts. The reason is that a buy-in is not a typical situation. An operating business, as MNC, has split its platform into a US and a foreign division, CONCH. CONCH shares all of MNC's intellectual capital and receives nearly half of the earnings that MNC received worldwide. The base, MNC's margins, was high, just as seen in many high-technology companies.

Often much lower royalty rates are proposed in valuations of offshored IP as part of costsharing. Those may be based on comparables that mainly cover IP in patent licensing, whereas splitting an on-going platform with profitable manufacturing and distribution company like MNC presents a very different scenario.

Applicability to the MNC-CONCH Buy-In Transaction

Maniacs are already being manufactured and sold worldwide. There is no need for risk mitigation. Given the current income CONCH derives from the buy-in transaction we can already estimate a fair royalty rate. For CONCH to receive nearly half of MNC's earnings, now and into the future, a royalty rate of 25 % is appropriate given MNC's high earnings margins [F5.38]. The general applicability of royalties is covered in Appendix C.

Equivalent Transfer Value Derived from the Royalty

We have obtained a royalty rate, but not a valuation of the buy-in payment. In order to assess the result of the CUT-VM method we use the available model data for future years. No such data would be available for a contemporaneous valuation.

For a prospective valuation, the royalty rate can be applied to an estimate of future income at CONCH, yielding a valuation estimate based on comparable transactions for the IP rights transferred to CONCH. The derived amount will inherit the uncertainty of the data used in the Inc-VM.

We estimate the equivalent Net Present Value (NPV) of these royalties on CONCH income on the basis of a 10 % discount rate [LeonardS:05, Ch.22]. Such a rate matches MNC's weighted average cost of capital (WACC). A modest discount rate is appropriate here to estimate the value of the future income. The result is $779M [F5.39]. In a valuation made at the time of the buy-in the actual amounts representing the buy-in will be not known. Using the CUT-VM method to obtain a royalty rate does not provide a contemporaneous buy-in amount.

5.3.4.2 M4.2 Summary of the CUT-VM Approach

We have analyzed an IP computation, the CUT-VM that would very rarely be appropriate for a buy-in situation. Because companies differ greatly, the Comparable Uncontrolled Transaction Valuation Method (CUT-VM) approach can yield only a comparable royalty rate. Application of that rate should yield a fair income with little risk. A validation using one of the other methods is essential to judge whether the proposed royalty rate makes business sense. Such an assessment may require, as done here, an estimate of projected income.

MNC would certainly not sell about half of its income potential to an arm's-length party it could not control, and commit at the same time to ongoing services, to be reimbursed at cost plus a modest markup. After the IP rights have been licensed and transferred to CONCH, and CONCH receives all of the earnings, half of MNC appears to be only a commodity supplier of R&D, even if the royalty rate is fair.

The CUT-VM method can be used when more modest transfers of IP are made, and when valid comparables can be located for the type of IP being transferred. Such cases can be found when licensing an offshore manufacturer, say, for a new medication, where the population is known, or a manufacturing technology that has clear benefits and potential customers. The CUT-VM approach is much easier to use for tangibles, and appropriate for setting a transfer price that is a surrogate when no Independent Factory Price (IFP) is available.

When used, the CUT-VM approach becomes more trustworthy when a generous number of comparable transactions are available, and the interquartile range is used. The summary Table 5.13 uses the equivalent transfer value for CONCH only.

M4: CUT-VM buy-in: $779M

5.3.5 M5: CP-VM, Comparable Profits Valuation Method

The Comparable Profits Valuation Methods (CP-VM) compare the earnings of known and valued businesses to earnings of the business that is to be valued. Like M4, CUT-VM, the CP-VM also uses comparisons, but now they are applied to entire companies or divisions of a company rather than to specific transactions. It is unlikely that many companies similar to the one to be valued in both functionality and in earnings can be found. Because of that, the CP-VM approach depends on financial ratios or margins instead of directly on amounts derived from income data [BrealeyMA:06].

Getting corporate income data for the CP-VM approach is easier than getting the licensing agreements needed for the CUT-VM. For comparison with public companies, the data needed to compute the margins are available in the 10-K documents filed with the SEC.

A "functional similarity" of two businesses means that they are similar in how they generate earnings from their assets, and also that the two companies' products should be similar [King:10]. Once comparable uncontrolled businesses are found, data about their business are needed. Data needed to compute margins are revenues, earnings, profits, market capitalizations or, if such businesses have been acquired recently in arm's-length transactions, the purchase prices.

Margins relevant to valuations are "profitability indicators," that then can be applied to the company being assessed. The steps in Table 5.8 will clarify the use of the CP-VM method.

Employing indirection means that the CP-VM approach cannot provide very precise estimates. However, checking these indicators is very useful to determine if proposed valuations and royalties are reasonable at all. They will show when proposed transfer prices and valuations are way out of bounds, not an uncommon situation in corporate tax avoidance.

5.3.5.1 M5.1 Common Indicators

We consider seven indicator types. All of these are described in textbooks oriented towards investors [BodieKM:08]. Values of these ratios, multiples, or margins for public and private companies are found in periodical publications to help investors.

Table 5.8 Steps to determine valuation parameters for CONCH

Step 1. Search for 20 companies that produce gadgets similar to the Maniac
Step 2. From their data and reports determine whether their business is stable, healthy, and representative. Four are not
Step 3. For the remaining 16 companies compute a profitability indicator, say, their P/R ratios, namely their operating incomes P over their revenues R
Step 4. Compute a credible average P/R, removing outliers
Step 5. Applying that P/R to CONCH revenues allows estimating the income

Many investment advisors, based on their experience, use their own variations of these metrics. The majority of common indicators are not appropriate for companies that depend on intangible assets.

The IRS regulations propose only the initial three indicators [B.3.4 (b)(4)]. The IRS also allows the use of other relevant indicators from arm's-length sources [B.3.4 (b)(4)(iii)]. The IRS uses the term ***profit*** for earnings, because they consider all corporate earnings to be profit to be taxed, and refers to the indicator metrics as "profit level indicators"; to help in follow-up, the IRS terms are shown as an alternative to each definition.

RoA: $\frac{\text{Earnings}}{\text{Assets}}$ or Rate of Return on Capital Assets Employed [B.1.2 #5(b)(4)(i)].

The RoA metric works well for traditional financial institutions. However, today's investment bankers depend also on smart people and software. Distributors for costly tangibles use the RoA as well, but modern, just-in-time distribution methods have reduced inventory levels, replacing it with supply-chain software. For a high-technology company, it is the undocumented intellectual capital that counts. Only $230M of intangibles show on MNC's books. MNC's RoA is 34 %, but has little meaning for valuing MNC [F5.40a].

P/R: $\frac{\text{Operating income}}{\text{Product revenue}}$ or Ratio of Operating Profit to Revenue [B.1.2 #5(b)(4)(ii)(A)].

This margin on revenues is the most obvious ratio used to check the well-being of a company. We assume that companies with much IP should have high margins; for MNC the margin is 67 % [F5.40b]. The operations of the comparables should be similar; for instance, the spending fractions on R&D and marketing should match.

Berry: $\frac{\text{Gross income}}{\text{CoGS + SG\&A}}$ or Ratio of Gross Profits to Operating Costs [B.1.2 #5(b)(4)(ii)(B)].

The Berry ratio is a measure of profitability that focuses on costs. Because the gross income also includes nonroutine earnings, companies with similar Berry ratios should have similar profits relative to the costs of producing goods. The Berry ratio for MNC is 2.26 [F5.40c].

NCP: $\frac{\text{Operating income}}{\text{CoGS + SG\&A}}$ or Net Cost Plus [LeveyWC:06].

This margin focuses on the net productivity of an enterprise. The SG&A costs and nonoperating income are excluded from the numerator on top. The NCP has the same issues as the Berry ratio for high-technology companies that have negligible CoGS and important R&D costs. For the NCP the effectiveness of management in controlling selling, general, and administrative (SG&A) expenses dominates even more, because the SG&A does not appear in the numerator. The Net Cost Plus ratio is 1.99 for MNC [F5.40d].

FIPC: $\frac{\text{Operating income}}{\text{Maintenance R\&D + CoGS + SG\&A}}$ or Full IP Cost [W:06].

This margin covers also the fraction of R&D that is essential to maintain the existing IP in high-technology companies, as shown in Fig. 4.3. If the actual maintenance expenses cannot be segregated, a reasonable allocation can be made. If 85 % of total booked R&D at MNC devoted to maintenance is booked as R&D, this indicator for MNC is 1.26 [F5.40e]. Because beneficial effects of R&D appear later than the expenses due to development and sales lags, this margin is appropriate for enterprises that have a stable structure.

p/e: $\frac{\text{Price}}{\text{Earnings}}$ or share market Price/Earnings per share multiple.

The price/earnings multiple is commonly used by investors to decide if corporate shares are worth buying, but can also be used to assess an entire company or division. MNC's p/e multiple before the buy-in was 12, MNC was still relatively new to the market [F5.40f].

Tobin's Q: $\frac{\text{Market cap - Debt}}{\text{Total assets}}$ or excess market value.

A Tobin's Q greater than one shows that there are assets valued by the market not shown on the books [Tobin:69]. MNC's Q is 8.0, typical for companies with many unbooked intangible assets [F5.40g]. It provides a quick identifier for high-technology companies.

5.3.5.2 M5.2 Use of the Ratios

The most problematic task in any method based on comparables is finding comparable companies that match adequately. Mature companies will have public records, but if a start-up has to be valued, getting adequate data about early-stage companies is nearly impossible. Investors face that problem when considering startups. It is less of a problem when dealing with tax avoidance. Companies concerned about taxes tend to be mature so that comparables can be found.

For each company found to be an adequate match, the selected indicator is computed. To get rid of outliers, the results should be reduced to be in the interquartile range [F D.3]. Some analysts, and the OECD, object to that procedure, saying that it just indicates that selection criteria were inadequate [OECD:06]. Realistically, it is hard to recognize all possible unusual conditions in complex business settings. The indicator for the company or division being assessed should fall into that range of matching companies.

Multiple indicators, listed here or found in textbooks, can be used for validation. General business margins cover all assets of a company, as MNC. Being largely dependent on book values reported by public companies, most indicators are not very satisfactory for high-technology businesses and service-oriented companies. Those businesses will have a high Tobin's Q indicator.

Table 5.9 Computation of a Berry ratio for uncontrolled comparables

		Company ID:					
Parameter		C1	C2	C3	C4	C5	C6
Gross income	g	180	27	85	260	75	300
SG&A + CoGS	s	34	7	32	180	53	290
Berry ratio g/s for selection	b	5.29	3.86	2.69	1.44	1.42	1.03
Interquartile mean (C2…C5)	im				2.35		

We consider only two indicators further, although all of them can play a role in valuations.

1. The Berry ratio, which had its origin in assessing an early transfer pricing case [DuPont:79]. It cannot provide a valuation as such, but can determine if the reported operation of a corporate division is imbalanced.
2. In order to obtain a valuation using the CP-VM approach, we will use the p/e multiple.

Testing the Balance of Income versus Expenses

The Berry ratio, using revenues/operating expenses, is the best for routine functions of high-technology industries, such as distribution [LeveyW:07]. For high-technology companies that produce mainly intangible goods, the CoGS is negligible, and the Berry ratio becomes mainly a measure of business overhead, although a large fraction of R&D is actually needed to keep on producing the goods [PrzysuskiL:05]. Nonoperating income and operating expenses (selling, general, and administrative expenses, or SG&A) or overhead costs should be looked at with care, as unrelated costs from the past and investments for the future can be hidden there.

Table 5.9 shows the computational steps of estimating the operational balance of CONCH using six functionally comparable uncontrolled companies [F5.41]. Even MNC itself is a candidate to be used, being functionally perfectly similar to CONCH.

We see that the expected Berry ratio for CONCH is 2.35, just a bit over the Berry ratio for MNC, 2.26 (F 5.4c), and well within the interquartile range.

The Full IP-Cost

The Full IP Cost (FIPC) provides a metric that accounts for the costs needed by knowledge-based companies to stay in business. A large fraction of booked R&D is needed to maintain the ongoing business and much less R&D actually goes to developing new products [W:06]. Profitability indicators that ignore R&D do not reflect business reality. A correct cost allocation will provide better guidance to investors and management [F5.40e]. Since we do not have data to compute the FIPC for comparable companies, we cannot value MNC based on this indicator.

Table 5.10 Valuation using the p/e multiple of uncontrolled comparables

Parameter		Company ID: C2	C1	C5	C3	C6	C4
Market cap of uncontrolled co's $M	*p*	400	2,000	800	1,700	1,100	3,600
Tangibles shown in 10-Ks	*t*	100	250	100	500	100	300
Intangibles left $p - t$	in	300	1,750	700	1,200	1,000	3,300
Earnings	er	50	200	75	100	90	250
ip/e multiple *in/er*	ie	6.0	8.8	9.3	12.0	11.1	13.2
Interquartile mean ip/e	im				10.3		

Valuation by the CP-VM Approach

We use the p/e multiple here, because it uses the market capitalization as a factor. The typical range of p/e observed is 5–50, where a p/e 5–15 indicates a good buy and 30–50 means investors should avoid it, unless they know that something very nice may happen that nobody else knows about [BodieKM:08]. The p/e indicator is often used by independent investors. Corporate stocks that are neither rated as a buy or a sell by investment advisors usually have p/e multiples around 20.

Since we just wish to value the intangibles at CONCH, we use a market cap reduced by the tangibles shown on the books or corporate 10-K statements. For MNC's intangibles the ip/e multiple becomes 10.6 [F5.42].

Table 5.10 shows the computational steps of estimating the value of CONCH using six functionally comparable uncontrolled companies [F5.43]. They are arranged by their ip/e multiples.

The interquartile mean of the comparable companies is 10.3, again somewhat more than the value for MNC itself. In the buy-in, CONCH received 42 % of MNC's IP, and at the 10.3 ip/e multiple should be valued at $667M [F5.44].

5.3.5.3 M5.3 Summary for the Comparable Profit (CP-VM) Approach

The CP-VM approach uses common business metrics to check if a company performs as expected relatively to its peers. The comparable profit approach does not provide by itself a very trustworthy valuation of intangible capital transfers, since the records on corporate books are inconsistent and incomplete, and even removing outliers only provides a general impression of expectations in a business sector.

The result is still useful to check if information about a controlled subsidiary, as CONCH, makes sense. Even though the CP-VM approach is imprecise because of its indirection, checking these indicators allows judging the validity of other results [OBrienO:02].

M5: CP-VM buy-in: $677M

5.3.6 M6: PS-M, Profit-Split Methods

The Profit-Split Methods (PS-M) are not valuation methods by themselves. Profit-split methods provide a way to determine an allocation of profits or earnings among divisions of a company, such as MNC in the USA and CONCH, based on their contribution to the joint earnings. In profit-split methods, the parties are known, while in M4, the CUT-VM method, it is hard to find comparable transactions.

For valuing a buy-in, without having an amount of profit to be split, profit-split methods are still suitable when there is a contingent payment arrangement, such as payment by royalties. Those royalties can be split, giving each division a share of a yet undetermined future benefit. We encountered use of royalties in M4, the CUT-VM method. Computing royalties means that an equivalent valuation must again be estimated using future income projections.

MNC chose not to use royalties for reimbursement by CONCH, because the buy-in did not match the typical licensing situation, where risks differ for the two parties. MNC just split its existing operation into a US and a foreign part in order to book its income into different taxing jurisdictions, so that the use of royalties is not appropriate. Appendix C discusses in depth when reimbursement by royalties makes fair business sense.

Current IRS regulations do not specify when royalties should or should not be used, so that reimbursement by royalties has been used in tax avoidance situations similar to MNC's buy-in. Since royalties are an indirect reimbursement method payments are uncertain (Appendix C). IRS regulations issued in 2011 constrained the use of the PS-M approach to situations where both participants actually contribute valuable intangibles [B.1.2 #7(g)(7)].

Indeed, CONCH contributes no value; it did not even exist before the buy-in, and remains a shell. Its distribution subsidiaries existed prior to the buy-in and are routine. MNC EMEA has done some specific adaptations for the Maniacs it distributes in Europe and the Middle-East, as allowing right-to-left data entry. For those services it receives Maniacs at a slight discount. MNC's offshore manufacturing operations were never independent operations and depend on MNC's US platform. In summary, CONCH had no assets of its own when the IP licensing and cost-sharing arrangement was set up by MNC, and should be valued as a PCT [B.1.2 #7(i)].

It is only MNC that splits itself. The relative value of CONCH is just the value of the IP rights obtained in the buy-in. For the sake of demonstrating the use of profit-split methods, in the remainder of this analysis CONCH is treated as if it were a valid and contributing entity.

The profit-split method allocates shares of earnings among participants in a transfer transaction, using a formula based on the participants' contributions.

5.3.6.1 M6.1 Contributions to the Split

In cases where all contributions to profit, tangible assets and intangibles assets are proportionally split among the parties, earnings could just be allocated in the same proportion. We first consider the MNC platform split, where one participant contributes all intellectual capital. Such a case is no longer considered a buy-in [IRS-TP:12]. In Sect. 5.2.6.3 (M6.3) we consider the case where the two parties contribute their own IP.

Such "formulary allocations" are now used to split US multistate business incomes, such as income of interstate trucking companies, according to a formula based on parameters as shipper, receiver, and active business locations and their contributions. If simple totals cannot be determined, specific contributions or residuals specific to the transfer transaction have to be extracted. Our focus is on earnings due to intangibles, as listed in Table 3.2.

5.3.6.2 M6.2 Residual Profit-Split

To assess the relative value of the shared intangibles, we must determine the contributions that create IP. Those are called the "residual contributions," and they are computed by removing all the routine contributions that contribute to earnings. For a high-technology company the residual contributions that create IP will greatly outweigh the total of the routine contributions.

Potential contributions to MNC's earnings include:

1. *The creation of the intangibles*. Most of the R&D effort that generated the IP is performed in California. In order to simplify the accounting and assure ownership rights, the payroll costs incurred by MNC's Mysore software operation are reimbursed from the US R&D budget. Now all R&D costs are allocated to the US division [F D.2].
2. *Manufacturing costs*. At the time of the buy-in MNC had shifted all of its manufacturing to Malaysia. The US distribution arm of the company pays a fair IFP for the Maniacs that are shipped and sold in the USA [F5.45].
3. *Management and capital costs*. Both MNC in the USA and the operations that fall under CONCH incur management costs. The majority of management is located in the USA, so CONCH will have to reimburse MNC for the cost for those services.
4. *The routine distribution function*. Together with local sales and marketing support, a royalty appropriate for the distribution part of a business can be determined by searching for comparable distribution-only businesses. Many smaller companies employ independent distributors and reimburse them by granting them a royalty on their revenues. Using such comparables, we find a fair royalty of 7 % [F5.19].

To find the residual contribution of the intangibles, the routine contributions (Items 2, 3, 4) are subtracted. The CP-VM, M5, is commonly used for estimating those routine contributions.

For Item 2, a search for comparable manufacturing companies that do not have substantial IP is performed. The approach mirrors the one performed to assess the routine distribution royalty used in the income-based method, M2. Such companies produce goods under contract that are designed by others, but remain independent. Those companies also have management and capital costs. Contract manufacturers do invest in their manufacturing processes, but just like MNC's manufacturing operation in Johor Baru, they depend greatly on guidance from the designers to assure the quality of products. Management and capital costs would be higher for a company investing in IP creation, but that difference is allocable to intangible creation as well.

Item 3 is dealt with by direct reimbursement in the CONCH and MNC arrangement. All costs reimbursed directly by CONCH are excluded from the royalty estimation. CONCH has no employees, but some work is performed by ATA staff in Palm Island and at CAAS in The Netherlands. The allocation for relevant personnel at MNC headquarters in the USA can be based on the relative sales, using the established RAB ratio [F5.46]. All capital was provided by MNC, but CONCH pays interest to MNC on the funds provided. MNC will have larger actual SG&A expenses, to be reimbursed by CONCH, beyond payments from offshore revenues based on the royalty rate that is being established here.

For Item 4, we again subtract the royalty appropriate for the distribution function. Instead of doing an actual comparable analysis, we just use general information for the three routine contributions. The distribution royalty was 5 % [F5.19]. There is also the cost of manufacturing the Maniacs, the CoGS. Contract manufacturers have margins of 7–10 % [Jayson:10]. Larger margins would render them noncompetitive versus their peers, but they should earn enough to be attractive to investors. Manufacturing, not supported by CONCH, was valued at a 9 % rate.

What is left is due to the intangibles, item 1, and can now be estimated. MNC had a 41 % margin. The final royalty, after manufacturing and distribution, is what is left for CONCH, namely a 27 % share for the intangibles it can contribute after the buy-in [F5.47].

5.3.6.3 M6.3 Intangible Property Contributions by Two Parties

In the MNC transfer of IP rights to CONCH, all the IP creation was supported by MNC in the USA, including the modest fraction generated at MNC MY in Mysore. If there would be an independent IP generation by other offshore divisions, or by multiple other divisions, their generated IP contributions will affect the allocations. The royalty must be split according to each division's contribution to the residual income.

To show the process, assume that the foreign distribution was not set up by MNC before the buy-in, but by an independent organization, Independent World-Wide Internet Distributors (IWWID). IWWID developed novel and unique marketing approaches, creating software for Internet-driven distribution. This approach to distribution is not used by MNC in the USA.

Both parties invested in IP over several years. The relative value of the investments will determine the profit split. To determine those values at the time of the profit split each party's past expenses must be capitalized so that they reflect the commercial value of the prior investments. Given the risk of R&D investments we use again a capitalization rate of 22 % [F5.23].

MNC's contribution is the IP from its research. They are relevant to Maniac sales in the USA and offshore. Because the effect of IP is the aggregate of many years of work, we must capitalize its R&D expenditures over the past years and also consider two other factors:

1. The investment in research occurs before its benefits, so all of those costs should be capitalized at an appropriate interest rate.
2. Not all research remains valuable, so some of the capitalized amount should be written off each year.

At the time of the buy-in, MNC's capitalized R&D investment amounts to $340M [F5.48]. The acquisitions made at the time of the buy-in have to be capitalized and added. The total obtained is $473M. IWWID's RAB share at 44 % is $215M.

IWWID itself had spent $50M over 2 years on development of its Internet technology, amounting to a capitalized value of $53M [F5.49]. In order to allocate royalties for the two parties, we now consider the R&D investments made by the two parties, MNC for its products and IWWID for its marketing approach. MNC did not adopt IWWID's Internet-based approach. Those investments occurred in the past, and both were capitalized before they became comparable.

The royalty to be paid, after excluding distribution and SG&A, was 27 %. The investments of IWWID contribute 26 % to sales, reducing its base royalty from 27 to 22 % for the nonroutine income or a total of 27 % after the 5 % markup [F5.50]. This royalty reimburses MNC for the R&D costs of ongoing Maniac development. MNC still pays for the software support provided to both parties by MNC MY, because those are outside of IWWID's scope. Separately IWWID has to reimburse MNC for any management services it receives [VidanoT:07]. In this sample case, those costs will be less than the 9 % because IWWID is more independent than CONCH.

This example, demonstrating the use of profit-split methods with two contributing parties, can be generalized to more than two IP contributors as well.

5.3.6.4 M6.4 Equivalent Valuation

We return to the simple case of our model, where all of the initial IP was contributed by MNC in the USA. That led to a royalty rate on the nonroutine income it collects of 27 % [F5.47]. Some of the routine income CONCH receives will be needed to reimburse MNC for services it receives, described as Item 3 in the list of contributions presented in Sect. 5.2.6.2 (M6.2).

When a buy-in is reimbursed by using a royalty scheme, there is no need for cost sharing of future R&D expenses. Past and future R&D costs can be included in the ongoing royalty rate.

To assess the reasonableness of the royalty rate, we apply it to the expected annual income used for the Inc-VM. Because payments based on a royalty rate eliminate the risks, we now discount the income only by an interest rate that reflects MNC's cost of capital, 8 %. The discounted amount for the total expected royalty-based income becomes $890M [F5.51].

In any case, a royalty rate has to be fair, and to the extent that it is used to allocate future income, setting a rate into the future assumes that the relative contributions and benefits are stable. If at some point in the future the division's relative contributions change, the royalty rates should be recomputed and reset. For instance, the contributions of MNC MY in India may grow to a level that this division is best recognized as an independent IP-generating party.

5.3.6.5 M6.5 Summary of the Profit-Split (PS-M) Approach

Using a profit-split method (PS-M) for benefit allocation is based on a thorough and fair allocation of contributions by all participating divisions. Only contributions that generate IP are to be considered. For valuations motivated by joint offshore operations, the corporate divisions can simply be assigned into two groups, a US group and an offshore group in a Cost-Sharing Transaction (CST). As shown in Sect. 5.2.6.3 (M6.3) some contributions may create IP used by only one division; other contributions benefit both divisions. When there is only one contributing participant, as in a Platform Contribution Transaction (PCT), there is no basis for a contribution allocation, only the market is split [B.1.2 #7(c)(3)].

If MNC uses funds held in offshore accounts at CONCH to fund new projects, then those funds will be considered not to be of US origin, and a profit-split method application must consider CONCH as the source of contributions to the split, although the actual intellectual capital resources still reside at MNC in California. CONCH will license the IP rights it holds already to the new venture. With increasing globalization and cooperative development methods, additional IP contributions will be made offshore as well [SeshasaiG:09]. The rights to them will go to the funder, likely CONCH. Overall, the flows of financial and intellectual capital will become more difficult to trace, making it nearly impossible to allocate earnings fairly. The resulting complexity can only help corporations to avoid taxes.

For our case MNC supplies all the residual IP and CONCH owes MNC a 27 % royalty on its income. That royalty rate is much higher than that seen in arm's-length situations where an inventor garners a royalty from a developer–manufacturer–distributor. Here CONCH assumed no risk greater than what is assumed by MNC, because it obtained rights to products that were already being sold and took over an existing distribution network.

The actual amount that CONCH will pay, given that royalty rate, will depend on the actual future income in the region ceded to CONCH after the buy-in. Using a royalty gives actually no assurance what the amount will be.

M6: PS-M equivalent buy-in: $890M

5.3.7 *M7: RO-VM, Roll-Over Valuation Method*

The Roll-over Valuation Method (RO-VM) is based on considering IP Generating Expenses (IGE), such as spending on R&D, as an investment and then predicting what the resulting nonroutine income will be [KaplanN:04]. Roll-over valuations

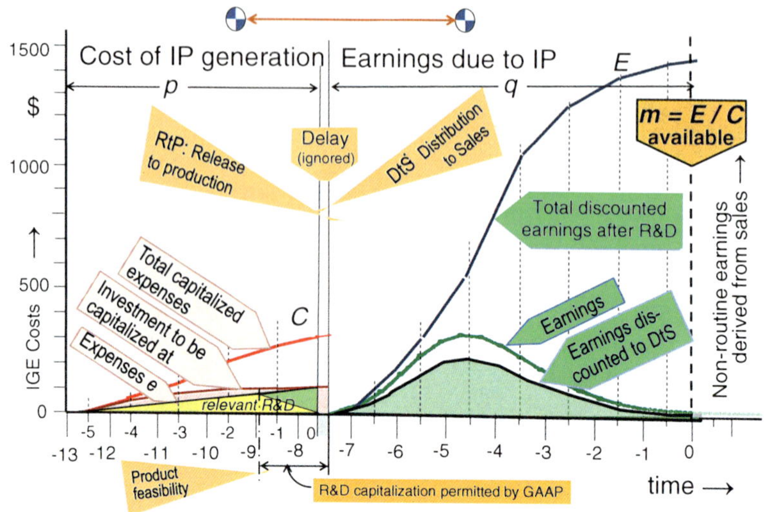

Fig. 5.12 Computing the roll-over leverage factor ***m***

violate the principle that costs should be immaterial to the value of intangibles, but the method does present an alternative that can be useful at times. Roll-over estimation is relevant to investors because it quantifies investment decisions that management must make [Contractor:01].

Broad-based research has shown that investment in R&D generates rates of return of about 20–35 % annually [VBM:04]. The leverage of an R&D investment then averages about a factor 2 over a 7½ year period [F5.52]. A study of about 500 US corporations also gave a leverage factor 2 for earnings and 5 for market value over a 7-year period [Sougiannis:94]. Moving from such a general guideline to a specific case valuation requires good data over extended periods. Such data are rarely available.

Application of the RO-VM proceeds in four steps:

1. Capitalize IGE incurred during research and development in an early period *C*.
2. Assess the value of the income from the products due to the IGE *E*.
3. Use the two results to compute the leverage factor *m* of the IGE *E/C*.
4. Multiply ongoing research and development expenses by that leverage factor *m* to obtain an estimate of expected benefits.

The leverage factor *m* can relate R&D to any income measure. This exposition uses earnings, the amount left after all costs have been deducted, including also the R&D costs themselves.

Figure 5.12 sketches the data used in Steps 1–3, the computation of the leverage factor, following the cost and income shown in Fig. 3.4. The shaded area on the left in Fig. 5.12 represents the result of Step 1, aggregating and capitalizing the 5-year R&D effort prior to the product's Release to Production (RtP). The shaded area on the right in Fig. 5.12 represents the resulting income, Step 2. The income is discounted and aggregated to the start of Distribution to Sales (DtS); here we need 7.5 years before we have enough data. Step 3, at time zero, combines those results to provide the historical leverage factor $\boldsymbol{m}$. That leverage factor is applied in Step 4 to value subsequent investment in R&D.

Relevant IGE expenses to create the intellectual property are incurred before the IP becomes available to create income. During Step 1, the annual expenses are capitalized and aggregated to the date of completion, RtP. Capitalization can be viewed as the inverse of discounting; early IGE expenses contribute relatively more than recent costs. Applying the capitalization rate increases the value of early R&D expenses. Since early R&D expenses tend to be small, as shown in Fig. 3.5, the effect of capitalization is less pronounced than the effect of discounting. R&D investments had to be capitalized also in Sect. 5.2.6.3 (M6.3), the PS-M Profit-split approach, where both MNC and IWWID contributed initial IP [F5.50]. When setting a capitalization rate one must again consider that R&D investments have a high risk.

5.3.7.1 M7.1 Applicability of the RO-VM

Within a particular company, RO-VM can be used to justify R&D expenditures in light of future earnings. For truly innovative R&D, the initial risk becomes less as progress can be documented, so that the risk-premium portion of the capitalization rate can be reduced over time. Nevertheless, compensating for a high level of uncertainty with high and changing capitalization rates will not produce a reliable valuation, making the RO-VM unreliable for innovative R&D.

The roll-over method is justified only where there is a stable pipeline from ongoing R&D to products. That situation exists for ongoing maintenance-level developments, the situation at MNC soon after the CONCH buy-in. In those situations, information allowing a projection of income from the products should be available as well, and the income method M2, the Inc-VM, can also be used, a much more reliable approach than RO-VM. For management a roll-over estimation still provides an important validation of corporate planning decisions.

The historical leverage factor m is computed as the ratio of discounted earnings E over capitalized costs C. The R&D capitalization of relevant R&D provides C. The discounted earnings attributed to the products derived from IP created by relevant R&D provides E. The related earnings appear over a long period after the IGE investments are completed, so the computation needs data spanning the R&D life of the investments p plus the life of the sales q shown in Fig. 5.12. The total period of data needed, $p+q$, to compute a leverage factor is likely well over 10 years. Very few high-technology enterprises have had a sufficiently long stable history to be able to estimate their leverage factor m, although R&D leverage is clearly a useful metric for management and planners.

Other IP generating expenses (IGE), as spending on advertising and promotions, are also justified by expectations of subsequent sales growth. If the company, as most, also depends on advertising, those costs can be capitalized as well. Such data are harder to extract out of most public reports than R&D information. The life of advertising IP tends to be only 1–3 years.

Because the initiation and effect of marketing promotions and campaigns occur over smaller intervals than technology, roll-over methods have been used to assess the value of marketing IGE. Here the spending period p may just be a month and any resulting increases of sales, q, would occur within a year. Some leverage factor data are available for such investments, but the associated variables (media, timing, demographics, etc.) vary so much that the leverage factor estimation is rarely trustworthy [Wilson:07]. On-line advertising promises better collection of relevant data to link expense to sales benefits [OPA:10].

5.3.7.2 M7.2 Computation of a Roll-Over Valuation

Let's look at a computation of the RO-VM for MNC's technology. To compute the leverage factor m for MNC, we have to combine two factors, C and E, from different time periods.

No adequate R&D capitalization giving a value of C will appear in MNC's current books. GAAP accounting rules permit capitalized R&D to appear on the books only after product feasibility has been established [F5.53]. To determine a true investment, we need in Step 1 to aggregate all of the relevant IGE spending. The four parameters are the R&D period p needed to create productive IP, the annual expenses incurred e_i, the rate at which research results become obsolete $1/p$, and a capitalization rate r appropriate for high-risk investments.

The known and planned R&D investments provide the basis for computing e_i, the annual contributions to IGE costs. Not all past expenditures remain relevant. In earlier valuation methods we diminished the availability of prior IP due to maintenance in specific cases [F5.24], [F5.48]. Here there is no prior beneficial IP as such. Instead, we use a loss rate based on a 3-year validity of newly created IP. Given that interval, each year only 67 % of the prior year's total R&D investment survives. Applying that loss rate, <10 % of earlier R&D survives after 6 years, so we limit the aggregation of costs to cover 6 years of R&D expenses.

For the capitalization rate we include a high-risk premium. MNC's current cost of money [F5.51] is not relevant now. The capitalization rate must also be substantially higher than the annual reduction in value of completed IP embedded in products being sold, 15 % [F5.23]. The expenses include risky early R&D; leading to a capitalization rate, $r = 22$ % [F5.54]. That rate is still lower than what a venture capitalist expects. The capitalization of MNC's R&D before the buy-in is $187.7M [F5.55]. Basing the result on a single series of data is always questionable, so we repeat the calculation for the next 2 years as well, using the planned R&D expenditures. The sum of all three is $710M, as shown in Table 5.11 [F5.56].

Now Step 2 is to be performed. To compute the benefits of the R&D expenses, again historical corporate information is used. We need to know the MNC earnings data over a period equal to the IP benefits; we had earlier estimated a discounted life

Table 5.11 Capitalization of MNC R&D costs over R&D life

Mid year	−7	−6	−5	−4	−3	−2	−1	0	Totals
R&D spending e_i	13.8	17.3	34.6	51.8	69.1	86.4	96.8	108.4	\$273M
Survival at 67 %	11 %	16 %	24 %	36 %	54 %	82 %			to 100 %
Surviving R&D	1.5	2.8	8.4	18.8	37.6	70.6			\$140M
Capitalized R&D	4.4	6.8	16.8	31.0	50.7	77.9	[F5.55]→		\$188M
at 22 %		For next 6-year span							\$236M
			For next 6-year span						\$286M
	Three-period total								\$710M

Table 5.12 Earnings obtained due to R&D spending

Mid year	1	2	3	4	5	6	7	8	9	10	Totals
Organic revenue	376	620	867	1,060	1,162	1,163	1,076	933	764	595	\$6,792M
Organic earnings	154	254	356	435	477	476	441	191			\$2,785M
E Discounted	142	199	237	246	229	185	154	57			\$1,462M
earnings					Next 7.5 year span						\$1,664M
at 15 %					Next 7.5 year span						\$1,771M
					Three-period total T						\$4,898M

of 7.5 years [F4.9]. The research capitalization precedes the sales life, making the total interval for which data are needed 13 years, as shown in Fig. 5.12. Our model has a problem here, MNC has not been in existence that long, and it certainly was not stable in its early years. We hence greatly simplify the computation for our example. The R&D interval ends at the buy-in date, and the actual initial organic earnings are used as a surrogate for the earnings due to the R&D investment. The corresponding earnings estimates are shown in Table 5.12 [F5.57].

Now the risk appropriate to innovative research is not a factor and the standard discount rate on income of 15 % is used. The small delay between completion of research and product availability is ignored. To gain confidence in the stability of the leverage factor $\boldsymbol{m}$ to be computed later, the computation is repeated for two prior periods. The sum of the three corresponding income estimates is \$4,898M.

Computing the Leverage Factor

We now have an estimate for the R&D investments over 3 periods, namely \$710M and earnings over the corresponding 3 periods of \$4,898M. The effect is that MNC's investments in R&D have a leverage factor m of 6.9 [F5.58].

MNC experiences a higher leverage factor m than the factor 2 derived from studies that cover industry in general [VBM:04]. For innovative computer companies a leverage of 4.5 has been reported [Audretsch:95]. The leverage factor m can range from 1 to 20, and even 1.2 is still considered satisfactory in highly competitive industries [HsiehMG:03].

The lack of long-term high-quality public data makes refinement to specific industry sectors less trustworthy [Sougiannis:94]. Within a company insiders can obtain data to project an expense-to-earnings ratio m from internal experience. The variability in products, setting, markets, and management capability to realize benefits from R&D investments cripples comparability of specific enterprises using the RO-VM approach. Stories of companies that have not been able to convert promising research to earnings are rife [Gladwell:11].

Being in a high-tech industry, and having low capital requirements for R&D, contributes to the high effectiveness of MNC's research and its favorable 6.9 leverage factor, compared to US industry overall. Leverage factors for successful high-technology companies have not been widely published. A venture capitalist has reported that the top third of his deals had an $m = 10.2$, the next fifth came in at $m = 2.6$, and the rest failed or were unrealized [Wilson:07]. The willingness of venture capitalists to keep investing in start-ups makes those ratios credible.

Leverage ratios can also be computed from business plans presented for proposed projects and start-up ventures. Given alternate proposals with equal risks, a venture investor would select the proposal with the highest leverage. Those leverage ratios can also be compared with those of similar past enterprises.

5.3.7.3 M7.3 Valuation Based on the Leverage Factor

The leverage factor m is now applied to the current, capitalized R&D investment of \$188M. The result gives the expected earnings for MNC, \$1,295M. To obtain the result for CONCH it is multiplied by the RAB, and the resulting RO-VM valuation for CONCH, where taxes can be ignored, is \$570M [F5.59].

If the operations are stable, a leverage factor can also be used for single-year estimates, but both the lag for ongoing research and development (here 1.2 years [F5.24]) and the sales lag (here 5 years [F3.2]) have to be taken into account. For such a computation around the buy-in date, we find that the RO-VM leverage factor m predicts earnings of \$596M at a date 5 years out into the future. The annual expected and booked nonroutine earnings vary greatly in our model so far into the future, but their average at that time is quite close at \$593M [F5.60]. MNC has shown steady organic growth and earnings from its R&D investments.

5.3.7.4 M7.4 Summary of the Roll-Over Valuation (RO-VM) Approach

The roll-over method extrapolates the experience from past research or marketing investments to yield expected benefits of current investments. It is applicable only if an adequate historical record of past investments and related benefits exists. We had investment data for our model MNC corporation, but the income data needed were well beyond the buy-in date. No reliable contemporaneous valuation could have been made.

Counting on the result of an RO-VM valuation remains risky.

(a) The benefits of R&D investment are uncertain, and trying to capture that risk in a capitalization rate is an oversimplified approach. Technological advances are rarely stable over the long interval needed to estimate the leverage factor reliably.
(b) The RO-VM approach does not distinguish the types and life of IP value generated by multiple sources, such as R&D costs combined with marketing efforts. The lags for such investment types differ. For MNC that is a minor factor, but for many enterprises the marketing contribution tends to be roughly equal to the technical IP contribution.
(c) The R&D expenses do not consider the R&D that was obtained as part of the acquisitions made by MNC. We ignored in our analysis the cost and the income from acquisitions. In business practice, acquisitions are enabled by accumulated earnings and are an alternative to R&D spending.

The RO-VM provides another data point in an overall assessment of the value for CONCH [F5.59]. This result is relatively low when compared to other estimates. Because MNC is a young company, its substantial research investments, including its recent acquisitions, did not yet pay off as much in the past as they should in the future. A prediction based on its own past history is not reliable.

M7: RO-VM buy-in estimate: $570M

The seven methods covered so far are appropriate for valuing the buy-in that allowed CONCH to collect earnings from offshore sales of Maniacs, products built with IP created earlier by MNC. The next method addresses valuation of the acquisitions made by MNC.

5.3.8 M8: PP-VM, Purchase Price Valuation Method

Valuing a business purchase is quite simple in principle, and even in practice. The result of a Purchase-Price Valuation method (PP-VM) is simply based on the amount that an independent buyer is willing to pay for it. During two periods in its history MNC was a willing buyer of independent companies with related expertise, and those acquisitions contributed to the growth of MNC. The value of those companies for MNC is the price that MNC paid. To trust the price we just have to be sure that the purchaser and seller are truly at arm's length [B.1.2 #7(g)(7)(5)].

If a public company is acquired, the market capitalization will provide alternative guidance, as computed using M1, the MC-VM approach.

5.3.8.1 M8.1 Validating the Price

In every acquisition MNC obtained valuable intellectual capital, including intangible property, and also some tangible property, perhaps including some debt. The amounts reported as part of the price for the transaction should be checked with care to assure that everything is indeed included and that any deductions taken are reasonable. The amounts placed on the MNC's books will never match the actual purchase price. For instance, obsolete tangibles are excluded, and a trademark of value to the seller, but not to the buyer, can be abandoned. To make books balance, the portion of the price that cannot be explicitly accounted for is placed on books as goodwill, seen in Table A.2 and enumerated in Chap. 4.

Why care? In general, outsiders should not care if acquisitions are fairly priced and whether the acquired assets have been placed properly on the books. However, MNC's offshore divisions, especially CONCH, will share the benefits of the intellectual capital being acquired. If MNC's or its CFC's books underestimate its value, CONCH will pay less than a fair share, creating an imbalance as shown in Fig. 4.1.

The numbers that accountants put on the books are influenced by regulations having little to do with the motivation that led MNC to purchase the company. Specifically, the books of the acquired company will only show capitalized IP. If the company is acquired at the time that a product is ready (RtP), at most 63 % of the IP investment will be booked [F5.61]. What is booked never includes a leverage factor, as presented with M7, the RO-VM.

Some purchases can have conditional clauses. There may be additional, but deferred, payments if the purchase leads to sales for MNC that exceed basic expectations. There might even be "clawbacks," required refunds of part of the price, if some expected benefits, such as orders previously signed with the seller, are cancelled after the acquisition.

Arm's-Length Considerations of Prices Paid

Some investigation is needed to assure that the purchase transaction is truly at arm's length. A transaction is not at arm's length if the purchaser, at an earlier time, invested in the company being acquired, has been involved in its growth, and has provided access to its technology. In such cases, the company would not be fully available to a competitor because of IP constraints. A special case are controlled subsidiaries or Special Purpose Entities (SPE) that have been set up to segregate some activities, such as a risky research venture. Now a price paid to reintegrate successful research is meaningless.

Once the arm's-length situation has been established and the price has been adjusted for conditional payments and refunds, that price gives the best measure of the total value. If the price is not trustworthy, more work is needed.

MNC acquired both a few public companies, called here PubC, and some companies that were privately held, called PrivC. In either case, payment can be made by cash or by shares. Shares embody some risk, so the price that the seller will consider is likely to be higher. Combinations of cash and shares, as well as conditional payments, are also possible.

Pricing of Public Companies

PubC's market value establishes a value that can be used for MC-VM calculations. MNC gains ownership by purchasing PubC's shares for cash or by offering MNC shares in exchange. If the actual cash price is not known, the price of the acquisition is simply PubC's market capitalization, the price per share of PubC times the number of PubC shares on the market [F5.1].

MNC can also offer its own shares in exchange for PubC's shares, at a ratio based on the two companies' share market prices. To motivate PubC's shareholders to sell, some bonus increment may be offered to them. Such a bonus then becomes part of a "control premium."

In major acquisitions and mergers, share prices can become volatile. If MNC's shareholders sense that the number of shares being handed out by MNC for PubC is excessive, reducing the value of their investment, the price of MNC shares can drop. Such volatility affects the setting of a precise acquisition price for major transactions. It's best to wait a bit to make a valuation based on the market price. There should be enough time available before a contemporaneous valuation for the amounts of cost sharing to be paid by CONCH has to be delivered to the IRS.

Pricing of Privately Held Companies

MNC's payment for PrivC may also be made in cash or using MNC shares. The owners of PrivC will also be concerned about the value of the reimbursement if they receive shares. There are no market capitalization data for PrivC that can be checked to see if the price is reasonable. Although some private stock may have been sold, few reliable data are reported [Protalinski:12].

MNC's books will show the price paid in cash or according to its share prices. Volatility induced in its share price from the dilution will be small for modest acquisitions. Sometimes the sale of the shares provided is restricted for some time, lowering their value to the level of stock options [F5.2].

Using Acquisitions as Comparables

If the price paid for an acquisition is suspect because it was not an arm's-length setting, surrogate prices may be used. Prior arm's-length acquisitions of similar companies can provide comparable data, so that the valuation can switch to M4, the CUT-VM approach. MNC made a number of acquisitions before the buy-in, as shown in Fig. 2.9. These acquisitions match MNC well in terms of the IP acquired. Since these acquisitions were to be integrated into MNC's operation, they will also have been valued by MNC using the same business model and corporate structure. Although the information is based on internal data, not strictly at arm's length, they will be acceptable if adequately documented.

The chance of finding multiple matching acquisitions by unrelated companies is small.

Using Indicator Ratios to Validate Purchase Prices

For a merger or an acquisition of a mature company, the profitability indicators of comparable companies, as presented in the CP-VM approach, can help in validating the reasonableness of a purchase price. All of them can be computed from public records of incorporated companies. Such ratios allow a rapid comparison of alternate investments and should already have been part of a due-diligence report, as provided to corporate directors before spending on a major acquisition can be approved. Any inconsistencies should be a trigger for further investigations.

5.3.8.2 M8.2 Acquisitions within Cost-Sharing Transfers

MNC made a number of acquisitions, starting at the time of the buy-in, and they increased MNC's value accordingly. All the intangible capital acquired is also available to CONCH. That asset should be cost shared, so that a proportion of the acquisition paid for by MNC becomes, in effect, an export. Some asset types acquired in the purchase are only useful to MNC in the USA and should be excluded from the cost-sharing reimbursement. The value of all other assets must be allocated to CONCH according to the current RAB.

(a) Real estate holdings, equipment, and other such tangible items located in the USA are not transferred to CONCH.
(b) Cash and other financial credits and debits that remain in the control of MNC's management in the USA are excluded as well.
(c) The workforce that provides business services, charged by MNC and paid directly out of CONCH accounts, such as management and accounting services, is excluded.
(d) Sales staff that is exclusively dedicated to US sales should be excluded, but sales staff operating outside the USA should be charged to CONCH. Using the Ratio of Anticipated Benefits (RAB) is convenient if it is hard to allocate specific worldwide sales staff to MNC's regions.
(e) The workforce that creates intellectual property (IP) by research and marketing efforts for MNC in the USA and for CONCH is to be shared according to the current RAB fraction. Talent acquisition is an important component of the valuation. After the initial cost-share payment for the acquisition this workforce will continue to be supported by periodic cost-share transfers to MNC.
(f) Any capitalized intangibles on the books will be shared as well, as they will benefit MNC in the USA as well as CONCH. Any shared IP assets are again allocated according to the current RAB fraction.

The books of the acquired company will record only the tangible items, (a) and (b), and perhaps some capitalized IP, item (f) [DengL:06]. The value of the administrative workforce, item (c), is not relevant for IP generation and nonroutine profits, so that it can be ignored in a cost-sharing valuation. For acquisitions of small, growing technical companies and start-ups that benefit MNC, the value of the engineering workforce, item (e), is paramount. In practice, costs incurred for R&D, item (f), are often not fully booked as such. R&D applied to feasible projects should be capitalized. Other expenses can be deducted from current income [Musher:00].

All the categories of IP that might be considered were listed in Table 3.2. Accounting practice often delegates much of that IP to goodwill, making the amount to be cost shared easy to misvalue. Especially when acquiring an early-stage company, talent acquisition is easily undervalued. No IP is likely to be shown on its books, and without a proper analysis, much of the value of the workforce and research in progress is just entered on the books as goodwill [SlavinK:06]. If there were a large number of similar acquisitions, a regression would provide insight into how the offered price is composed, but such opportunities are rare [LeonardS:05, Ch.9]. Goodwill is an easy asset category to reduce. It cannot be revalued upward [Vause:09].

Once booked as goodwill, the benefits obtained are easy to write off by labeling them as being unavailable or impaired. Accountants tend to ignore the technical motivation that convinced MNC's management to set the acquisition price.

It does not matter if an acquisition does not work out [Contractor:01]. CONCH participates in the same benefits and the same risks as all of MNC, and must cost share all acquisitions.

Control Premium

MNC may be willing to overbid current minority shareholders of a company that it wants to acquire to gain control of a competitor or obtain strategic synergy. In those cases an excess price or "control premium" of up to 30 % has been cited [Razgaitis:03]. It becomes hard to judge what part of an offering price is a true valuation, based on expected income of the current assets, and what is a pure control premium due to an expectation that the acquirer will be able to exploit the acquired assets better than the current owner can [Damodaran:05].

A common assumption is that any amount paid in excess of market capitalization is a "control premium," but MNC management may consider other factors that provide real value, such as eliminating competition or acquiring options for subsequent initiatives. Any control premium benefits CONCH as much as MNC, so CONCH should share its cost as well. It is then irrelevant if an acquisition price includes a control premium. On the books, the cost of a control premium will show as a debit, and the offsetting credit will likely be booked as more goodwill.

When a company is not public, no control premium can be computed. The price alone is the best guide. It might include an increment, designating assets that the acquired company can offer MNC, but not relevant to other potential purchasers. For instance, some acquisitions allowed MNC to create its ManiMobile products by providing IP specific to the mobile aspects, technologies where MNC had little prior experience. CONCH also benefited proportionally from that investment.

5.3.8.3 M8.3 Option Values within Acquisitions

An acquisition can be motivated by new markets it enables. An option defines such a potential benefit, but one that may never be realized [Damodaran:02]. Say that MNC acquired a company, MobiIP, which had created IP that would enable creation of a mobile version of MNC's Maniac. However, the decision to proceed with the development of a ManiMobile was deferred until it was clear that there would be a market for ManiMobiles [McNair:03].

Little benefit appears on the books from the MobiIP acquisition because the decision to proceed, or not, has been deferred to a time when enough information is available. Only after the decision is made to exploit the acquired assets will the acquisition participate in the normal business of MNC. The two alternatives are sketched in Fig. 5.13.

In estimating MobiIP's value, MNC considered two specific alternatives:

1. The probability that it would decide to build ManiMobile, its development costs, and the eventual income that the IP would generate in ManiMobile sales.
2. The complementary probability of abandoning the idea and selling MobiIP to any willing purchaser at a salvage value.

Both alternatives are translated to the net present values (NPVs) at the time of acquisition. The option value is the sum of the two alternatives. The delay reduces the $360M benefit expected from building and selling ManiMobiles to $297M [F5.62].

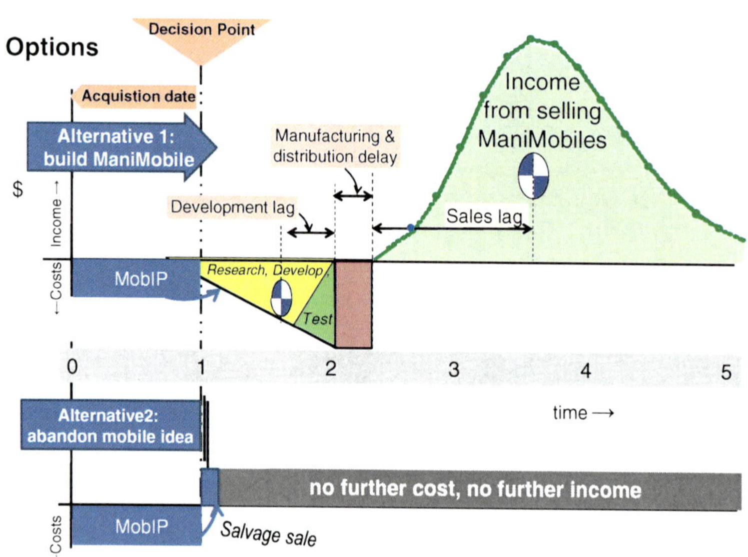

Fig. 5.13 Estimating an option value

An interesting aspect of options is that they reduce the effect of uncertainty in making decisions. If the probability p of choosing alternatives is hard to assess at acquisition time, because the future is volatile and uncertain, the option becomes more valuable [BrealeyMA:06].

Once the option value has been determined, it becomes part of the cost-share amount to be reimbursed by CONCH. Options can apply to any valuation, but they are particularly relevant in acquisitions. MNC's reasoning may not be made public. In valuations based on the MC-VM or the Inc-VM, the value of known options may already be included.

Sometimes an acquisition is made to waylay a competitor. For instance, an acquisition may provide nothing of value other than some patent applications. An acquisition with the purpose of denying a resource, say, a patent or an expert, to a competitor is also a form of option. Now, instead of computing an income, we calculate the value of the acquisition as the avoidance of lost income that would have occurred had a competitor obtained those resources.

When there is no income, there are no taxes to be paid. But not generating income is not an excuse to ignore an acquisition. When acquisitions include options, their value and costs must be shared with the subsidiaries that will share in any possible benefits. In our case, both MNC and CONCH will profit from the acquisitions, and because MNC in the USA acquired the options, it should be reimbursed by CONCH as part of a cost-sharing arrangement.

5.3.8.4 M8.4 Summary of the Purchase Price (PP-VM) Approach

The PP-VM method is applicable only to MNC's acquisitions. We assume in our model that all of them were at arm's length, that the prices paid were fair, and that no special provisions were invoked that would make the price paid different from the value that MNC obtained.

At times the valuation of acquisitions is not that simple. If the acquisition transaction was not at arm's length, if payment was by volatile stock, if there were conditions that led to deferred payments or restrictions on stock sales, a PP-VM valuation becomes more complex than discussed here. However, the purchase price remains the prime determinant.

During the year of the buy-in, MNC spent \$300M on acquisitions. All of the acquired companies were relatively young and did not have significant sales. They leased most of their facilities and equipment, and they had negligible cash and liquid assets. An analysis showed that only 10 % of their assets were tangibles. The value of the acquired IP is then \$270M and the CONCH share at the average RAB becomes \$121M [F5.63].

M8: PP-VM valuation of the initial MNC acquisitions: \$121M

5.4 Choosing and Combining Valuation Methods

An initial description of the IP valuation methods appeared in Table 5.1. After much work, the results of the methods are appended in Table 5.13. The purchase price method (PP-VM) applies only to the cost sharing of acquisitions. We also show the valuations that MNC's advisor, ATA, proposed for the buy-in and the initial acquisitions.

These results are based on the many assumptions made when the model company, MNC, was created. The assumed values were based on numbers seen in practice, but any actual company will differ.

Only the second, the post buy-in approach, of the two MC-VM results will be used beyond this point. For other assumptions, and for any actual company, the values and the relative rank of the results of the seven methods may differ as well.

The results from the seven methods used for the buy-in valuation differ moderately, as shown in Fig. 5.14. The statistical average of all seven methods is \$783M. Their standard deviation (SD) is \$121M. All but two of the results are within one SD. The range from the largest to the smallest result is 49 % of their average [F5.64]. The outliers are 7 % over and 27 % under the mean of all methods, a range acceptable for economic predictions [Black:96].

Table 5.13 Valuation methods and results

Method	Scope	Expertise	Uncertainty in	IP result	
Buy-in valuations				*MNC*	*Buy-in*
M1 MC-VM	All nontangible capital	Public wisdom	Volatility	\$1,630M	\$717M
	And stock options	+ Expectation	And growth	\$1,906M	\$839M
M2 Inc-VM	All intellectual capital	Internal expect's	Growth	\$2,012M	\$955M
M3 IIP-VM	Identified IP @ CONCH	Technical IP diminution	IP selection and coverage	Skipped	\$781M
M4 CUT-VM	Specific transactions and a distribution network	Public comparables	Matching IP licenses	CONCH royalty	\$779M
M5 CP-VM	Comparable businesses	Business metrics	Similarity	Sample	\$677M
M6 PS-M	Royalty profit split	Relative contribution	Future actual income	Not assessed	\$890M
M7 RO-VM	Stable product creation	Long-term R&D data and effects	Stability of enterprise	\$1,185M	\$570M
ATA	Selected IP	Contracted	Trusting ATA	\$119M	\$50M
Initial acquisitions				*MNC*	*Cost share*
M8 PP-VM	Acquisitions only	Price-based	Motivation	\$270M	\$121M
ATA	Acquired business	Contracted	Trusting ATA	\$50M	\$21.0M

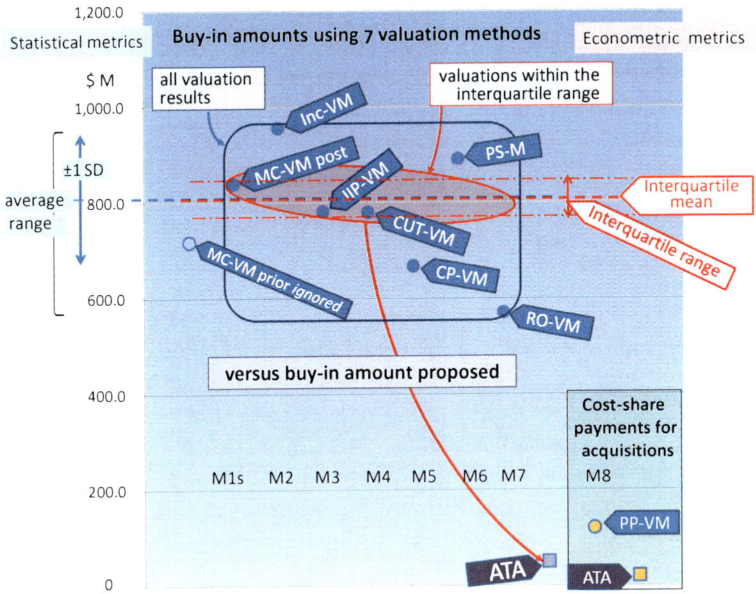

Fig. 5.14 Variability in buy-in valuation results for CONCH

The differences among the results can be explained once the methods are understood. For instance, the income method (Inc-VM) gives the highest valuation; it depends on management projections, which can be overly optimistic. The roll-over method (RO-VM) gives the lowest estimate; the RO-VM, relying on the leverage of organic R&D, was based on too little experience and also did not include the effect of acquisitions [F5.60].

When methods are compared, all assumptions should match to avoid conflicts and errors. For instance, assumptions regarding IP life should be matched. Factors that reduce IP into the future should not be combined arbitrarily, as that will lead to an unwarranted reduction of IP life and generate misleading valuations. Having inconsistent discount rates is common.

Figure 5.14 shows the range of buy-in valuations as big dots. When there are sufficient samples, economists improve the reliability of the result by focusing on the interquartile range, removing the outliers. Here the interquartile range is only 7.5 % about its mean. Four of the seven methods are either inside or within 100 % of the interquartile range. Such an outcome is a nice and tight result for any economic analysis. Instead of deciding which method is best, the interquartile mean, \$800M, is a trustworthy result [F5.65]. Using the IRS definition of the interquartile computation the mean becomes \$790M.

The value that ATA presented to MNC is considerably less, only about 6 % of the interquartile mean of the seven buy-in valuations covered and about 9 % of the lowest valuation made, shown as squares in Fig. 5.13 [F5.66]. Chapter 7 explains how ATA arrived at its unexpectedly low buy-in valuations.

We must always be suspicious of results created by abstract models [Derman:11]. Using a quantitative, multiyear model allows validation of details. Results of models built on equations are quite sensitive to assumptions [AltshulerHT:10]. Applying intuition, understanding and checking alternative methods greatly increases confidence in the result.

5.5 Valuation of Cost-Shared Acquisitions

MNC purchased a number of companies that it soon integrated into its own business, and that integration provided synergies in further developing and broadening its Maniac product line. Table 5.4 also shows the valuation of the cost-share contribution CONCH should make for the initial acquisitions, \$121M. The ATA presentation is about 20 % of that estimate [F5.67].

The motivation for an acquisition affects the choice and parameterization of valuations. The primary approach is the PP-VM, detailed in Sect. 5.2.8 (M8). We briefly review the applicability of the other methods that were introduced for the buy-in valuations in valuing acquisitions.

M1, MC-VM for Acquisitions:

The Purchase Price Valuation Method, PP-VM, is already a version of the market cap valuation method (MC-VM). The price MNC paid for the acquisition is essentially a market cap valuation, even for private companies. If the company is public, the price should be close to the public market cap. Any difference will be ascribed to the benefits expected by MNC now exercising control and assessed as the control premium.

M2, Inc-VM for Acquisitions:

The income from acquisitions that are integrated cannot be distinguished from income that MNC generates organically. Here, an acquisition is best seen as a replacement for internal R&D investment. A motivation for MNC's investment was that acquisitions allowed it to grow its capabilities more rapidly than it could have done internally, allowing it to move rapidly into new market sectors.

M3, IIP-VM for Acquisitions:

If an acquisition provides well-identified IP, then establishing its IP life and R&D lag is needed. However, that information must still be combined with a specific dependent income stream, a difficult task. The talented workforce that comes on board with an acquisition will also generate long-term, indefinite benefits. The IIP-VM will provide a reasonable valuation only if the acquisition remains a distinct division, as may be the case of a merger.

M4, CUT-VM & M5, CP-VM for Acquisitions:

The comparable-valuation methods are normally based on a comprehensive set of transactions. Before MNC spends substantial amounts to acquire a company, it has already surveyed the field and weeded out unpromising candidates. Therefore, a simple mean or an interquartile mean of all actual transactions reflects the selection made by MNC [F D.4]. Using the mean of the upper half of the comparables, in essence the 75th percentile point, has been advocated [Razgaitis:03]. Such a simple calculation should still not be used without vetting the selected comparable transactions.

If the CUT-VM approach uses royalties as a base, and prior arm's-length acquisitions have established a royalty rate that is appropriate for the type of IP being acquired, then the best comparable can be drawn from internal information. Similar technologies to be integrated into the technology and business model of a parent deserve similar royalties.

Comparable-profits methods might help for mergers and acquisitions of mature companies, as discussed in the closing summary of method M8, the PP-VM.

M6, PS-M for Acquisitions:

The profit-split method is risky for most acquisitions, since data for capitalization of early-stage acquisitions needed to match the purchaser's prior investments are rare.

M7, RO-VM for Acquisitions:

Estimating leverage factors by the roll-over method always helps management, even if the results are only trustworthy for valuing stable businesses.

Acquisitions are an important part of corporate growth, and we will encounter acquisition issues throughout the remaining chapters. Consider also, as discussed in Sect. 5.2.8 (M8), PP-VM valuation, that not all acquisitions are truly at arm's length.

5.6 Summary of Valuation Methods

Although valuation of intangibles is hard and necessarily imprecise, as any prediction into the future will be, valuations can be done and are worth the effort. This chapter presented eight methods. Each method depends on different data and different assumptions and will give a different result. Those differences can be understood when the sources and the assumptions made are exposed. A variety of methods for valuing IP have been published in the literature, but they all seem to be variations or combinations of the eight approaches presented here.

The argument for not placing intangibles on the books of corporations is that IP valuations are not reliable [Laurie:04]. That reasoning is flawed. Tangibles, as buildings, are placed on the books with valuations down to the penny, when it is known that future real-estate prices will vary due to unforeseeable economic conditions. Derivatives of tangibles have been placed on corporate books based on assessments by accounting firms using methods that were quite obscure [Anderson:09]. Showing the primary contribution to the value of high-technology businesses on the books can only help shareholders and the public. Bringing the values into the open will justify actions of corporate management, creating shareholder trust [PrattRS:96]. As recording the value of IP becomes more common, the approaches will become more standardized and reliable [Sveiby:97].

Business is always subject to risk. In businesses that rely on intangibles, their value must be known to assess the magnitude of the risk [RileyV:12]. Offshoring increases the risk of loss. Valuation of IP transferred becomes essential. Management should not wait with valuing of their enterprise until the IRS requires IP valuations to examine tax avoidance.

It is rare to have sufficient data available to allow all seven primary methods to be used for a buy-in valuation. For our model company, MNC, adequate data could be assembled in a simple and usable form. However, two of the methods, M4, CUT-VM, and M5, CP-VM, depend on comparable data, requiring a match of public data to MNC. In practice, a search through databases containing business data in a matching industry sector is needed for valid matches to MNC. Instead, our analyses used data that matched general business expectations.

Having results from more than one approach increases confidence in the results. Specifically, having seven different applicable methods allows computation of trustworthy mean and median values. However, using the same method with slightly differing parameters does not provide greater confidence, so that the M1, MC-VM, using data prior to the buy-in was ignored in favor of the MC-VM that accounted for the later effect of stock options and acquisitions.

As shown in Table 5.13, the valuation proposed by ATA is way below the range of the results produced using methods in this chapter. As such it appears to be out of line. The estimate using the same method (M2, Inc-VM) used by ATA gives a much higher result, just above the interquartile range. The problem is hence not in the method chosen, but rather in its application. Using ATA's valuation, MNC receives a much lower reimbursement for the IP rights moved offshore than we would expect, as shown later in Chap. 7. The difference winds up in MNC's offshore taxhaven and grows there.

Such controversies are common. In a taxhaven case that went to court, the taxpayer's consultants proposed only 8 % of the valuation provided by external experts hired by the IRS [Veritas:09]. Serious errors were made on both sides, but the judicial setting did not allow a reasonable compromise to be made [F5.68]. The next chapter presents the taxhaven jurisdictions and their exploitation that enables corporate tax avoidance.

Chapter 6
Taxhavens

A country that facilitates tax avoidance is considered a "taxhaven." The use of taxhavens by corporations is relatively recent and often derided [Folbre:11]. A simple definition has been offered by Geoffrey Colin Powell (former economic advisor to the Island of Jersey):

> What ... identifies an area as a tax haven is the existence of a composite tax structure established deliberately to take advantage of, and exploit, a worldwide demand for opportunities to engage in tax avoidance. [Doggart:02]

A more detailed definition by the Organisation for Economic Co-operation and Development (OECD), shown already here as Table 6.1, focuses on primary taxhavens, small countries that support tax avoidance. In 2000 the OECD created a list of 38 uncooperative taxhavens [Makhlouf:02]. Refinement of OECD criteria allowed all those taxhavens to comply, and by 2000 a few were left [Almeida:04]. Subsequently the OECD list was emptied and deleted [Sharman:06]. The requirements for being removed from the list are easy to satisfy [Rittel:10].

Changing the definition of taxhavens does not change their activities. Many advertise their existence [LowTax:11]. Some organizations maintain and publish their own lists of taxhavens [PalanMC:10]. When political pressures on a recognized taxhaven actually causes change, other countries are encouraged to take over its role.

This chapter presents the wide variety of options and interactions exploited by creative tax advisors and ingenious corporations. It does not discuss the societal or political benefits or harms caused by differential taxation of corporate divisions. Tax avoidance becomes a game in which taxable earnings mysteriously appear and disappear, to benefit the companies and escape taxation.

G. Wiederhold, *Valuing Intellectual Capital: Multinationals and Taxhavens*, Management for Professionals 23, DOI 10.1007/978-1-4614-6611-6_6,

Table 6.1 OECD definition of taxhavens

Key factors in identifying and assessing harmful preferential tax regimes for the purposes of this report
(a) No or low effective tax rates
A low or zero effective tax rate on the relevant income is a necessary starting point for an examination of whether a preferential tax regime is harmful. A zero or low effective tax rate may arise because the schedule rate itself is very low or because of the way in which a country defines the tax base to which the rate is applied. A harmful preferential tax regime will be characterized by a combination of a low or zero effective tax rate and one or more other factors set out in this Box and, where relevant, in this section
(b) "Ring fencing" of regimes
Some preferential tax regimes are partly or fully insulated from the domestic markets of the country providing the regime. The fact that a country feels the need to protect its own economy from the regime by ring fencing provides a strong indication that a regime has the potential to create harmful spillover effects. Ring fencing may take a number of forms, including the following: a regime may explicitly or implicitly exclude resident taxpayers from taking advantage of its benefits and enterprises which benefit from the regime may be explicitly or implicitly prohibited from operating in the domestic market
(c) Lack of transparency
The lack of transparency in the operation of a regime will make it harder for the home country to take defensive measures. Non-transparency may arise from the way in which a regime is designed and administered. Non-transparency is a broad concept that includes, among others, favorable application of laws and regulations, negotiable tax provisions, and a failure to make widely available administrative practices
(d) Lack of effective exchange of information
Lack of effective exchange of information in relation to taxpayers benefiting from the operation of a preferential tax regime is a strong indication that a country is engaging in harmful tax competition

6.1 Functions of Taxhavens

A common misconception assigns any taxhaven an identical role. Four categories of taxhavens, primary taxhavens, conduit taxhavens, semi-taxhavens, and nearshore taxhavens, are defined in this chapter. Each category has its specific function. Three of these categories, in combination, enable MNC, our model of a multinational company, to avoid much taxation in the USA and worldwide.

6.1.1 Categories

1. *Primary taxhavens* host shell corporations that hold financial capital and rights to intellectual capital. Much of MNC's worldwide assets are assigned to its captive foreign holding company (CFH), CONCH, located in Palm Island. Actual activities there are performed for MNC by a local branch of MNC's financial consultants, ATA.

2. *Conduit taxhavens* facilitate opaque transfer of funds. MNC's captive financial intermediary (CFI), the Dutch subsidiary CAAS, receives and allocates its foreign revenues. CAAS is operated by a branch of ATA in The Netherlands.
3. *Semi-taxhavens* provide incentives that will encourage businesses to establish manufacturing. MNC's actual offshore manufacturing operations, performed by MNC JB and MNC MY, are located in semi-taxhavens. MNC has actual staff in these two CFCs. Having MNC located in these emerging economies provides significant direct and indirect employment.

Nearshore taxhavens are jurisdictions with independent legislatures that enable tax avoidance within boundaries of other countries. This category serves only minor functions for MNC, but is important to enable tax avoidance by some businesses.

Laws enabling a taxhaven may cover all businesses in a country, but conduit and semi-taxhaven countries are typically fairly selective about the type of corporate clients and activities they will support. Such taxhavens have "ring-fencing" laws and regulations in place that prevent its own citizens and businesses from securing the incentives that encourage foreign activities. Many have tax treaties with the USA assuring predictable allocation of taxable income [Doernberg:08]. A company's controlled foreign corporate (CFC) divisions may also benefit from local incentives, as credits, exemptions, regulations, and conventions offered in smaller jurisdictions within a country, such as by a Swiss canton or a free-trade zone in Malaysia [PalanMC:10].

Although taxhavens are primarily seen as being offshore, several US states treat businesses exceptionally nicely. Those states become domestic taxhavens, available to US and foreign businesses. Special rules for US possessions have created a class of US "nearshore taxhavens," covered in Sect. 6.5. The various jurisdictions vary greatly in their rules, and large multinationals, helped by their advisors, adroitly exploit the concessions of dozens of taxhavens [AviJonah:12].

As MNC became technologically successful, it located its divisions in four distinct taxhavens, each contributing its own benefits, shown in Fig. 3.3. The Dutch CAAS financial intermediary receives all payments from customers and is directly controlled by MNC, assuring close control [vanDijkWM:06]. Structurally, CONCH is the primary captive foreign company (CFC) of MNC; nominally all other MNC's offshore divisions are its subsidiaries. However, CONCH itself is just a shell, a captive holding company (CFH); it has no employees. MNC, in addition to manufacturing operations in Malaysia and India, uses its Austrian subsidiary, MNC EMEA, for installing up-to-date software in Maniacs just prior to shipping.

The common combination of a manufacturing operation in Ireland and a CFH like CONCH in a primary taxhaven is known as a "Double Irish" strategy [DarbyL:07]. The three-layer structure of a CFH, a CFI, and operating CFCs, sketched in Fig. 6.1, is now referred to as a "Dutch Sandwich" [Drucker:10B]. Many other organizational structures are feasible.

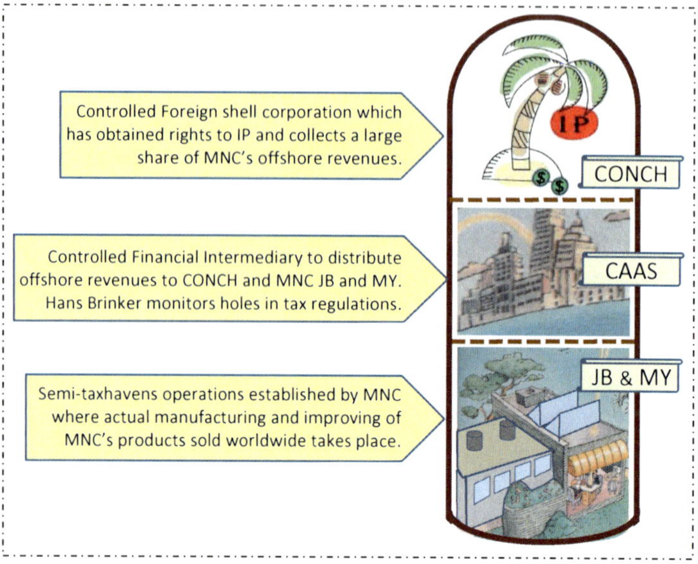

Fig. 6.1 MNC's Dutch sandwich of taxhavens

6.2 Primary Taxhavens

Primary taxhavens are countries with small populations that focus on features that attract CFHs. A CFH will not engage in productive activities. No local personnel will be hired. Services needed for a CFH, as an address, an initial registration with the local government, payment of annual fees, mail forwarding, and the arrangement of board-of-directors meetings, are offered efficiently by consultant firms like ATA and their local branches.

A well-publicized example, a single 5-story building in the Cayman Islands, Ugland House, is the address for more than 18,000 holding companies [Collins:11D]. The entire country has less than 50,000 inhabitants, but more than 90,000 companies and banks are registered there. The Cayman Islands protects its privileges. Immigration is strictly controlled. Without a prior work permit, you must provide evidence of independent means and an investment of $180,000 to reside there and share the benefits [HFR:09].

Ugland House
Getty Images/Bloomberg 2011

Fig. 6.2 Location of some important primary taxhavens (*open circle*) and ports (*filled triangle*)

The income from registration fees (in 2009 only $3,000 per year) for each of the thousands of companies allows the Cayman Islands to forego the collection of income or capital taxes. A US Treasury report estimates that by 2007 about 63,000 companies owned by US corporations or wealthy US individuals were located in taxhavens [Shropshire:09]. To be attractive to businesses outright tax evasion and money laundering are discouraged. Because of limited reporting requirements, protection of corporate privacy, and relationships that are many levels deep, that count is hard to verify [Deloitte:11]. Enron, in the year 2000 alone, established 441 interrelated special-purpose entities (SPEs) in the Cayman Islands [Cornford:04].

A primary taxhaven will always offer negligible taxation and little transparency. Often no reporting of income and assets is required, and the IP held in the CFHs is never assessed. At the same time, companies like MNC will look for government stability, low risk of expropriation, and a functioning court system to settle conflicts. Given that US law and British law are closely related, it is not surprising then that many taxhavens are in British Crown Colonies and former British territories (BOTs). Many primary taxhaven jurisdictions retain links to Great Britain and use English as their primary language. Figure 6.2 shows the location of some primary taxhavens; several are listed in Table 6.2. For non-US companies, several US states can be their primary taxhavens [Shaxson:11].

Obligations that primary taxhavens impose are modest. Cayman-based corporations must have one annual meeting in the Cayman Islands; all other board meetings can be held anywhere. That requirement is waived if the nominal headquarters of the CFH are in another British territory, a service that ATA can provide as well. Cayman companies need not have external directors on their boards, and having staff provided by ATA can satisfy most requirements; a CFH that is fully controlled

Table 6.2 Some prominent taxhavens

<table>
<tr><th>Taxhaven locale</th><th>Relationship / Approach / tax rate *non-resident</th><th>Tax-haven</th><th>Focus</th><th colspan="2">Metrics A/C/D/E/F/G [F 6.10]</th></tr>
<tr><td>Andorra</td><td>France&Spain, ~~EU~~ // 0%</td><td>Prime</td><td>Banks</td><td colspan="2">C=16.7, E=27, G=2.9</td></tr>
<tr><td>Bermuda</td><td>BOT // 0-2%nr</td><td>Prime</td><td>Finance, Ins</td><td colspan="2">A:8%, D=5.4, E=2088, G=5.9</td></tr>
<tr><td>British Virgin</td><td>BOT, UKCI // 0%*</td><td>Prime</td><td>HT, Ins</td><td>C=37, G=1.1</td><td rowspan="4">UKC Islands overall: A:3%, E=673, high F</td></tr>
<tr><td>Cayman</td><td>BOT, UKCI // 0-5%</td><td>Prime</td><td>HF, HT</td><td>C=2, D=1.1, G=2.3</td></tr>
<tr><td>Trinidad&Tbg.</td><td>Ex- BOT, UKCI // 0%*</td><td>Prime</td><td>Oil</td><td>G=26.3</td></tr>
<tr><td>Turks&Caicos</td><td>UKCI // 0%*</td><td>Prime</td><td>Banks</td><td>C=0.013, G=0.2</td></tr>
<tr><td>Jersey & Guernsey</td><td>BCD, ~~EU~~ // 0%</td><td>Near-shore</td><td>Banks, HNWI</td><td colspan="2">C=0.3, G=7.9</td></tr>
<tr><td>City of London</td><td>UK / control / 28%</td><td>Cndt</td><td>Banks, Ins</td><td colspan="2">C=2 [F 6.11], G=58.0</td></tr>
<tr><td>Gibraltar</td><td>BOT, EU // 1-10%</td><td>Prime, Cndt</td><td>Finance, e-gaming</td><td colspan="2">C=1, G=1.3</td></tr>
<tr><td>India</td><td>/FTZ 0%-18.5% / 30%</td><td>Semi-</td><td>SW, services</td><td colspan="2">G=1,508.0</td></tr>
<tr><td>Isle of Man</td><td>BCD, ~~EU~~ // 0% now</td><td>Prime</td><td>Banks, HNWI</td><td colspan="2">C=0.4, G=2.7</td></tr>
<tr><td>Ireland</td><td>EU/ incentives /8-12.5%</td><td>Semi-</td><td>Pharm, HT</td><td colspan="2">A: 7%, D=.5, G=204.3</td></tr>
<tr><td>Liechtenstein</td><td>Swiss // 7.5–15%</td><td>Prime</td><td>Shipping, HNWI</td><td colspan="2">C=0.7, E=100, G=5.1</td></tr>
<tr><td>Luxembourg</td><td>EU / SOPARFI / 1-22%</td><td>Cndt</td><td>Banks, dictators</td><td colspan="2">A: 8%, E=900, G=54</td></tr>
<tr><td>Malaysia</td><td>/ FTZs & incentives</td><td>Semi-</td><td>HT</td><td colspan="2">G=238.0</td></tr>
<tr><td>Mauritius</td><td>ex-BOT, France, India</td><td>Cndt, Prime</td><td>Finance</td><td colspan="2">C=0.03, E=350, G=9.7</td></tr>
<tr><td>Singapore</td><td>UK, China</td><td>Semi-</td><td>HT, SW, Pharm</td><td colspan="2">A: 4%, D=0.1, G=222.7</td></tr>
<tr><td>Switzerland</td><td>~~EU~~ /cantonal incentives</td><td>Semi-, Cndt</td><td>HT, HNWI</td><td colspan="2">A:6%, D=0.2, G =523.8</td></tr>
<tr><td>ex.: Zug</td><td>Swiss // 8.5% total</td><td>Prime</td><td>Traders</td><td colspan="2">C=1.15, G=6.4</td></tr>
<tr><td>The Netherlands</td><td>EU / BVs / 5-34.5%</td><td>Cndt Semi-</td><td>Finance, SW</td><td colspan="2">A:13%, F:20, G = 723.3</td></tr>
<tr><td>United States</td><td>/ state incentives / 35%</td><td>Semi-</td><td>Non-US Corp's</td><td colspan="2">C=0.02 (all businesses) G = 14,430</td></tr>
<tr><td>ex.: Nevada</td><td>US / no reporting / +0%</td><td>Cndt</td><td>Warehousing</td><td colspan="2">C=0.1, G=125.7</td></tr>
<tr><td>Vanuatu</td><td>France, HK, Australia</td><td>Prime</td><td>Finance, Ship</td><td colspan="2">F=0.5 [Sharman:06], G=0.7</td></tr>
</table>

Legend: BCD=British Crown Dependency; BOT=British Overseas Territory; EU=European Union; ~~EU~~ =Europe, but not in EU; FTZ=Free Trade Zones, UKC=UK Caribbean Islands.
Taxhaven categories Prime=Primary taxhaven; Cndt=Conduit taxhaven, Semi-=Semi-taxhaven.
Focus of services: HF= hedge funds; HNWI=high net worth individuals; HT=high-tech. manufacturing.; Ins=insurance; Pharm=pharmaceutical mfs's; Ship= shipping; SW=software
Metrics to identify taxhavens: A=US CFC income excessive; C=#corporations / population; D= $M profit per employee; E=assets / employee spending; F=funds flow / GDP; G=GDP.

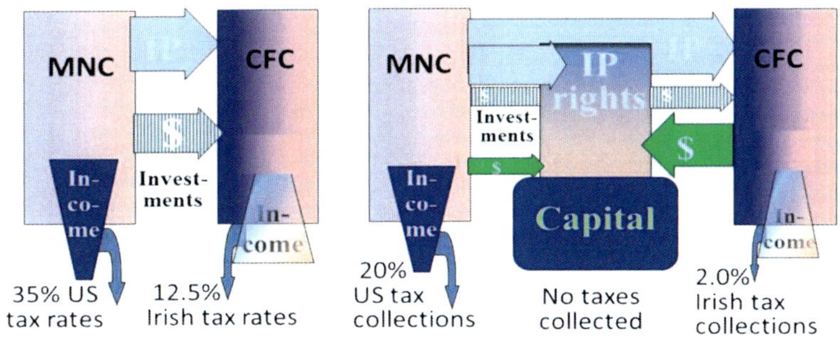

Fig. 6.3 Taxation and taxhavens, simplistic and actual

by another corporation has only one stockholder anyway. Neither audits nor annual reports are required. To comply with recent OECD rules, records will be made available for criminal cases. However, without open access to corporate records to begin with, it is difficult to even make a case that illegal activities have taken place.

Figure 6.3 expands the effect of transfer pricing, seen in Fig. 4.1, to show what happens when a primary taxhaven is interposed. Popular arguments about taxhavens focus on simple offshore operations, for instance, US companies that establish manufacturing in Ireland or Swiss cantons, as shown on the left-hand side [Stahl:11]. The low Irish statutory corporate tax rate is advertised by Irish officials as an incentive to relocate manufacturing there. For people worried about US job losses, a simplistic presentation becomes an argument for lowering US corporate taxes as well. The IP shift is invisible. How the money escapes from US worldwide taxation is a mystery to casual observers.

The right-hand side of Fig. 6.3 illustrates what actually happens once the primary taxhaven is interposed. The taxable income in the foreign manufacturing corporation is drastically reduced, because it does not own any rights to the IP which is responsible for the majority of the profits. Some US income can also escape US taxes when rights to US income are shifted to the taxhaven. Most of the accumulated financial capital is kept in accounts of banks in The City of London, using nearshore taxhavens, described in Sect. 6.5.

Figure 6.4 illustrates the annual effect of taxhavens on US corporate earnings during 2005–2010, skipping the recession years 2008–2009 [F6.1]. "Net earnings from foreign sources" includes all businesses, financial and industrial, and any buy-in payments from foreign sources that represent foreign operations [BlumenthalS:06]. Amounts repatriated are taxed, but the remainder is held offshore, untaxed, for future investments. The $400 billion (B) US-sourced income is from sales in the USA, but credited to the taxhaven because the rights to book those US earnings have been accumulated or moved offshore [DavisRKM:11]. Forest Laboratories provided an extreme example [F2.25]. The overall results for 2010 and 2011, after the major dip due to the worldwide recession, appear to be similar, except that taxhaven use has grown, as seen in Table F.14, which shows annual data from 2005 to 2010.

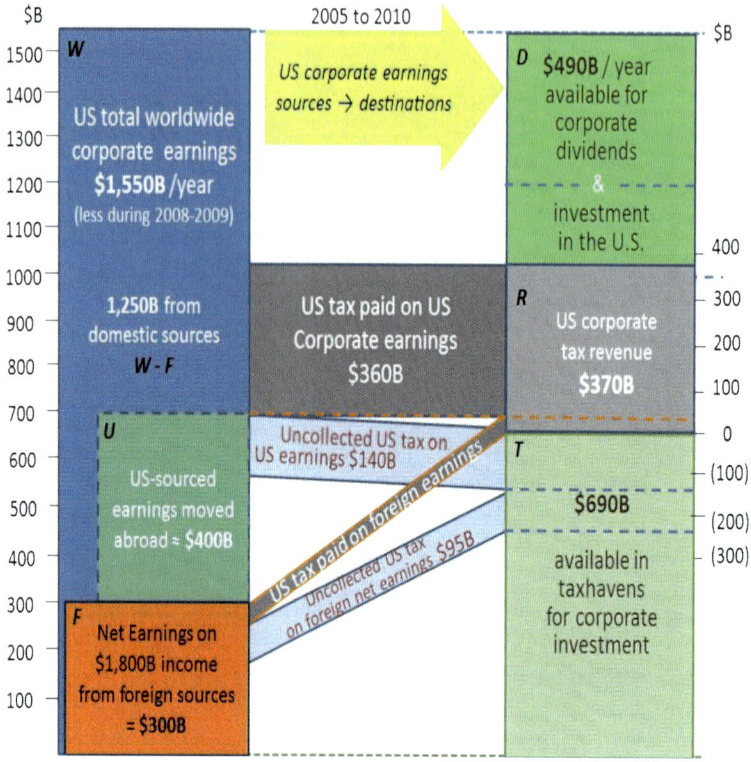

Fig. 6.4 Worldwide flow of earnings from US resident corporations

The use of primary taxhavens by US companies means that after taxes and moving domestic earnings offshore, only \$490B, or 39 % of domestic corporate earnings, was available for investment and paying dividends to US shareholders [F6.2]. A larger amount, \$690B, or 45 % of the total corporate earnings, wound up in primary taxhavens. If covered by a "blocker" statement offshore funds will not be taxed, unless repatriated to the USA [F6.3]. Those funds are available for investments outside the USA and for paying shareholders who have established foreign domiciles [Palan:06]. The amount of uncollected potential taxes can only be estimated, but it appears to be about \$235B annually [F6.4]. An IRS analysis cites estimates for the US tax loss from evasion using taxhavens for 2001 of \$40B to \$123B annually [Shropshire:09].

The estimates shown in Fig. 6.4 are rough and based on inconsistent sources, but they do convey the magnitude of the issues exposed in this book [F6.5]. In order to shift nearly \$700B of annual earnings to primary taxhavens, conduit taxhavens and semi-taxhavens participate in corporate tax avoidance [CBO:05].

An investigation of a specific company showed 42 % of foreign sales (*F*), but 73 % of foreign low tax income (*F* + *U*) [Browning:11]. Estimates of capital shifted to taxhavens have to be inferred from public records or specific investigations [Levin:12]. Financial authorities in taxhavens collect minimal data. To protect their own privacy as well as that of their resident corporations, taxhavens do not provide summary statistics. Any physical corporate records are actually filed in offices in their home country or at their advisors' locations. Electronic documents may well be located on servers in the clouds.

The use of taxhavens is not exclusive to American companies. For instance, Greek-owned shipping companies avoid taxation by registering their ships in semi-taxhavens such as Panama and establishing a domicile in trusted primary taxhavens, often in Liechtenstein, far away from any port. The amount of taxes lost annually, nearly $28B for its shipping industry, is more than half of the 2011 Greek government deficit of about $50B, contributing to a debt load that is driving Greece toward bankruptcy [F6.6].

6.2.1 IP in Taxhavens

The movement of IP right to taxhavens is a major contributor to the growth of capital from earnings that have not been repatriated. Without having data on the IP rights owned by taxhaven entities, only the effects on financial capital are visible. These effects are not well documented, since corporations do not have to segregate their financial holdings by country. Without audits, the US Treasury only obtains indirect information about the financial amounts held in CFHs [GAO:09]. One estimate is that by 2009 the Cayman Islands alone held $1,900B, more than twice the total US corporate income that year [Morgenthau:09]. The total for the dozen or so other active primary taxhavens is likely to be at least that much. That amount includes capital moved offshore in purely financial transactions, bypassing US Treasury rules that make the accumulation of such passive income subject to immediate taxation [EdenK:05].

The amount of corporate IP rights held offshore is yet harder to identify. Only their effect is visible, as corporate earnings are being collected in corporate taxhaven accounts. Earnings from active offshore operations are only taxed when repatriated. Funds not needed by the parent corporation in the USA for expenses, such as production, administration, R&D, or dividends, stay in the taxhaven. The capital remains available in the taxhaven for future investment and benefits.

Initiatives to repatriate financial capital to the USA by offering temporary tax exemptions ignored the role of offshore ownership of IP, understandably so since no information is available about the IP held in CFHs [AJCA:04]. The stated intent of the legislation was to increase financial investments and jobs in the USA. However, without the complementary intellectual capital, namely creative people and worked-out plans, financial capital cannot be effectively absorbed. Since

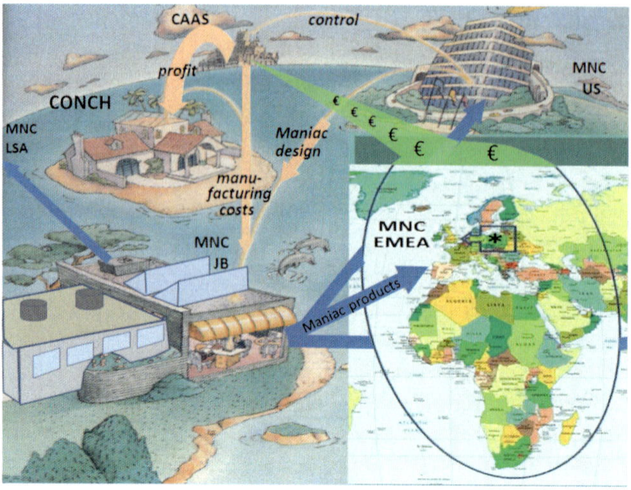

Fig. 6.5 Flow among MNC's divisions

dollars are fungible, 92 % of the funds repatriated due to the AJCA in 2004 appears to have gone to shareholders at all levels [DharmapalaFF:09].

Without a corresponding repatriation of IP, the capital held in CFHs was reduced only temporarily and subsequently accumulated faster than financial experts expected [Henchman:11].

6.2.2 *MNC's Taxhavens*

As MNC started selling its products overseas and established offshore manufacturing operations, it sought advice from its financial advisors, ATA. With ATA's help, it established CONCH to shelter from US taxation the income it received from the rest of the world. Only a modest direct investment (FDI) was needed. CONCH will share costs and be used to manage income from offshore operations, as recognized in US law [B.2.4 §936(h)(5)(C)(i)].

Keeping some working capital offshore for ongoing foreign operations is necessary to grow export capabilities [FeldsteinHH:95]. Having offshore operations, such as MNC JB and MNC MY in semi-taxhavens, creates opportunities for tax avoidance [B.2.2, 2004 amendment].

Figure 6.5 illustrates the flows of IP, product, and payments related to MNC in Europe, the Middle East, and Africa. MNC's service node, MNC CAAS, in a conduit taxhaven, shares data in a cloud. For the US tax authorities, all these divisions appear under the umbrella of CONCH. All actual control remains with MNC US management; CONCH has no actual employees.

In later years, some of MNC's US income was sheltered as well, because the IP rights held in CONCH, its CFH, also covered IP embedded in products sold by MNC in the US proper.

6.3 Conduit Taxhavens

The focus throughout is on the role of intellectual capital when corporations try to avoid taxes, but it is actually the financial flow that follows the IP that is taxed. To track what is going on in taxation, one has to "follow the money" [Felt:76]. Money has to flow from the revenue sources to the holding companies in the primary taxhavens. A Controlled Financial Intermediary (CFI), will be established in a jurisdiction that encourages conduit activities by offering suitable tax treaties, laws, and incentives [OECD:86]. The CFI becomes the formal location or "nexus" for the receipt of sales revenues. Countries that support conduit taxhavens are well connected to financial centers. Advising companies in such conduit taxhaven countries will provide the necessary financial services to their customers [Miles:05].

ATA created a corporate division, CAAS, to be the CFI for MNC, located in their Dutch associate's offices. No presence of MNC staff is needed. CAAS allows MNC to control the flow of money from offshore revenues to CONCH. The income pays for expenses and the excess is held in CONCH's capital accounts.

Since a conduit taxhaven division merely passes funds among other corporate divisions, it does not hold financial capital for a long time. Its operation does not replace jobs in the country where a CFI is located and remains quite invisible. Only when capital flows through a country become disproportionate is there a hint of something being out of kilter [Hines:10H].

CFIs located in conduit taxhavens have an essential role in managing the financial arrangements among offshore corporate divisions [DarbyL:07]. CFIs are trusted to reliably handle large amounts of funds and provide a variety of intermediate services confidentially, including services that enable tax avoidance. Conduit taxhaven jurisdictions differ in regulations and overhead costs. It is not unusual for a single company to be supported by multiple CFIs located in several conduit taxhavens.

6.3.1 Reporting Requirements in Conduit Taxhavens

Countries that support conduit taxhavens allow businesses with a low level of activity within the country to submit no or minimal annual reports to the tax authorities [Hampton:96]. In The Netherlands, the cutoff level for a local business to avoid reporting and taxes is 5 % of gross income [LowTax:11]. Exemptions are common for income beyond that level [Pollock:12]. Such ring fencing distinguishes foreign from local businesses. Advising firms can service many external customers. Multiple

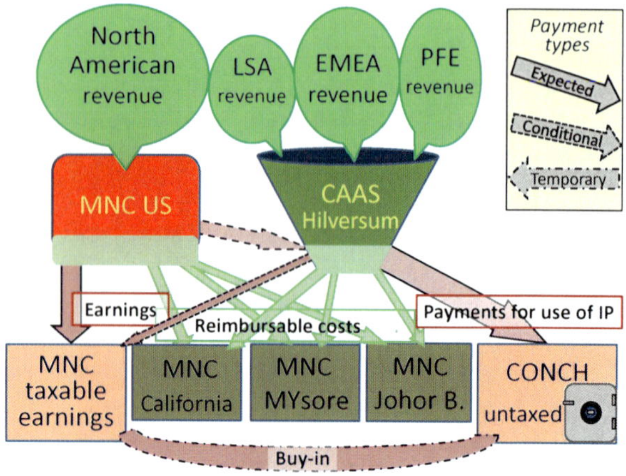

Fig. 6.6 Financial nodes and flows among MNC and its controlled divisions

divisions of a company with extensive holdings can share administrative and accounting services so that intracompany extraterritorial transfers remain within the host country's boundaries, reducing global visibility. US rules designed to assure that capital cannot be accumulated without being taxed cannot be enforced if nothing is reported [EdenK:05].

6.3.2 *Functions of Operations in Conduit Taxhavens*

Operations in conduit taxhavens may include actual services, as issuing and tracking invoices, collecting the receipts, processing claims, and keeping books for financial and tax authorities. MNC does not require much help, since it has already three divisions that distribute its Maniacs and account for their operations, but having a centralized conduit operation assures that its money flows integrate invisibly [Hines:05D].

MNC's offshore financial services are provided by CAAS, its CFI located in The Netherlands. Because MNC's CAAS has no staff and no operational role, CAAS could be ignored when valuation and IP are discussed. CAAS is organized as a Besloten Vennootschap (BV), a corporate form subject to specific Dutch governance and taxation rules [Weyzig:12]. CAAS is a shell organization, established and managed by a division of MNC's tax advisor, ATA, located in Hilversum, near Schiphol airport. The interposition of CAAS allows MNC to avoid most taxes in the jurisdictions where it has offshore operations [Kroon:00].

CAAS only collects, aggregates, and allocates MNC's offshore revenues, as sketched in Fig. 6.6 [KesslerE:06]. CAAS is the funnel that nominally receives all income from MNC's three offshore distribution companies (MNC EMEA in Europe, MNC LSA in Latin America, and MNC PFE in Asia).

CAAS distributes funds for expenses incurred to the three sites where production takes place (MNC in California, MNC JB in Johor Baru, Malaysia, and MNC MY in Mysore, India). All remaining funds are transferred and parked at CONCH, which is MNC's primary taxhaven.

Over time some IP rights for US sales also move to CONCH, allowing MNC to transfer some US earnings to accumulate at CONCH. The fraction of untaxed US-sourced earnings amounts now to about 25 % of overall US corporate earnings, but is 50 % for the sector of pharmaceutical companies [Sullivan:11]. It is hard for US authorities to track the actual source of that income.

6.3.2.1 Relabeling of Investment Sources

A financial intermediary provides flexibility in managing financial flows. Many countries provide incentives for foreign investments to stimulate their economies. When MNC is ready to make investments, it can transfer funds held in CONCH to locations where they have the most leverage. A country that supports growth as a semi-taxhaven, such as Malaysia and India, considers any funds that MNC transfers as foreign investments and will make concessions to MNC, even though the funds came from earnings derived from manufacturing in Malaysia or India [RauG:12]. Concessions enabled by "round tripping" are not available to investments made by a local company, even though the local company has actually paid taxes on its income.

6.3.2.2 Terminating Audit Trails

Moving revenues via an intermediate CFI in a conduit taxhaven, a country with minimal or no reporting, makes it difficult to track sources of funds to their true nexus. An audit, initiated by tax authorities of a country that suspects income not being reported properly, will get as far as the CFI. The results reported by a conduit operation located in a trusted jurisdiction, such as a country in the European Union (EU), are assumed to satisfy the reporting standards of the jurisdiction they reside in [KesslerE:06]. The audit needs to go no further.

Income from countries where the reporting and auditing standards are not trusted will be transferred into a country in a region that is trusted, such as The Netherlands. When extracted, funds transferred from a trustworthy jurisdiction appear to satisfy EU standards. EU membership has been useful to other conduit taxhavens as well, including Luxembourg and Malta [Ogley:00].

One reason why a company might want to limit its auditability is exposure of expenses that are ethically questionable, such as payments to officials to facilitate business arrangements [Baker:05]. For instance, costs associated with compliance to specific US laws are to be charged only to the US parent, but can raise objections there [B.1.2 #9(I)(5) Example 9]. That issue is outside of this book's direct taxation concerns, but it can affect a company's choice of taxhavens.

6.3.2.3 Intermediaries for Distinct Product Lines

More clarity in a business is achieved when distinct product lines are represented by distinct corporate divisions. For instance, the ManiMobile product of MNC has a life, market, and growth pattern different from MNC's original products. Having another CFI dedicated as the nexus for the ManiMobile revenues, instead of CAAS, allows a separation of financial flows for the Maniacs to match the distinct Manimobile IP being covered.

When companies grow by acquiring mature businesses that are not directly integrated, assessing the success of the investment is easier when the acquisitions continue to have distinct books. In any case, IP, in the form of technical and marketing prowess, is bound to flow across the divisional boundaries. If the divisions operate in differing jurisdictions, the IP flows should also be documented and values assigned to complement the interdivisional payments. If divestments of divisions occur, it is necessary for correct taxation to determine whether the sale amounts to a loss or a gain, and IP transfers cannot be disregarded.

Under current US accounting rules, subsidiaries that manage less than 10 % of a company's assets need not be listed in annual consolidated corporate reports [Deloitte:11]. Splitting a business into multiple subsidiary divisions makes it unlikely that they will be visible to the public, although a 10 % slice of a large multinational company is still a significant enterprise. Having many such entities, with different but overlapping roles, will further confuse external observers [MoskRC:12].

6.3.3 Identifying Conduit Taxhavens

Without records, the tax authorities in the USA and the EU cannot discern the flow of potentially taxable earnings. Many conduit taxhavens also shelter accounts of "high net worth individuals" (HNWIs), making their function in corporate tax avoidance less obvious. Corporate CFIs, as CAAS, operate primarily in countries that also have substantial domestic business activities. To enable low reporting requirements for businesses owned by foreigners, conduit taxhavens have implemented "ring fencing," laws and regulations that allow segregation of services and taxation of external businesses from services and taxes applicable to their own population for the purpose of reporting and oversight [Hampton:96].

Dutch residents pay high taxes on their local, territorial, income, but none on any external income, so that an exempt Dutch BV (a BFI) is an attractive financial intermediary for truly multinational companies [vanDijkWM:06]. By booking royalties as dividend income, taxation is avoided. Most worldwide companies have a division in The Netherlands [EikelenboomDG:11].

Other countries in the EU have objected to Dutch support of tax avoidance [Browning: 07]. The Dutch government did respond, but new constraints imposed were easy to circumvent by multinationals. If The Netherlands were to cease offering those benefits to BVs held by nonresidents, the Dutch government and its population could lose about €2B government income and accounting jobs, because a CFI could rapidly move to another jurisdiction willing to oblige the needs of multinationals [Blessing:09]. Putting pressure on taxhavens to reform conflicts with national sovereignty [Christians:09]. The OECD has been the organization identifying harmful tax practices. The USA and Switzerland are both OECD members. Since the US states and Swiss cantons also serve as conduit taxhavens for foreign companies, the OECD has focused primarily on primary taxhavens.

Opportunities as provided by Dutch BVs are also available for an entity organized as a "SàRL" in Luxembourg, another country in the EU. Luxembourg, with a population of about half a million, has been a favored locale for financial conduits for a long time [DuhiggK:12]. However, Luxembourg augments its fee income by charging an annual tax on capital held, and requiring a modest amount of capital to be kept in Luxembourgeois banks. Financial enterprises made up 43 % of the Luxembourgeois GDP there in 2001 [Statec:10]. Rules in other conduit taxhavens are unique as well; ATA can provide the needed advice.

Ireland is moving towards providing conduit services as well as offshore manufacturing [GrimesC:09]. The UK government considers that conduit operations enable tax avoidance strategies previously associated with primary taxhavens. Court cases on that issue have been lost and won [O'Gara:10]. Controversies based on assigning domicile for income collection and taxation are likely to continue, for instance when a Dutch BV becomes a UK resident for tax purposes [Clark:10].

Conduit taxhavens appear to be more trustworthy than primary taxhavens [Shaxson:11]. A CFI that has a role as a nexus must be trusted by customers when paying for products they receive. They are best located in countries with stable governments and legal institutions. A country that collects much income in relation to its size or its GDP (metric A in Table 6.2) is likely to support conduit functions. For instance, the Dutch GDP is about 2 % of the EU GDP, but US companies in The Netherlands collect 8 % of their aggregate income there [MarkleS:09]. Because that income merely passes through among external entities, it is not reported there, and accounts do not provide reliable data.

6.3.3.1 Conduit Financial Intermediary Services Provided for Forest Labs

As described in Chap. 2, Forest Laboratories also uses a BV located in The Netherlands, FFN, as its CFI. Figure 6.7 summarizes the offshore activities shown in Fig. 2.10. Forest Laboratories books its income from the USA at FFN, while its pharmaceutical products are manufactured at its Irish manufacturing operation, FLI, following recipes developed at its US research labs.

Following an IP rights transfer from the USA to FLH in Bermuda, FFN transfers most earnings to FLH, the holding company paired with FLI. The capital accumulated there is safely controlled by FRX in the US. The Irish tax authorities, IT&C, never see the records of actual earnings from the drugs produced in Ireland. By interposing FFN, Forest Labs avoids most taxation by the USA and Ireland.

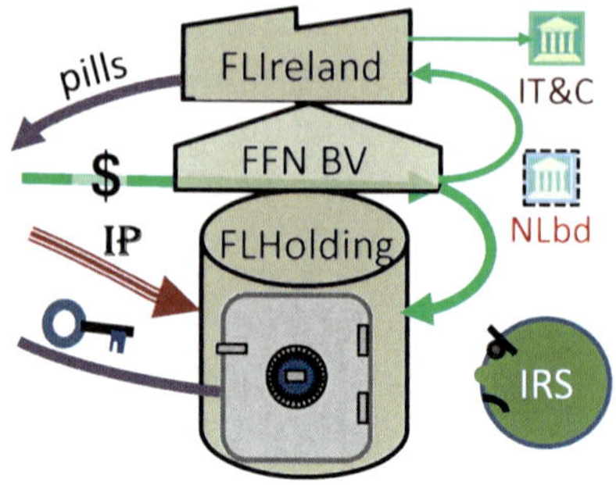

Fig. 6.7 Offshore financial flows among Forest Labs affiliates

Metaphorically, FFN supplies the cheese for Forest Laboratories' "Dutch Sandwich" tax structure [Drucker:10]. The actual flow is unclear from formal documents, since banks provide reliable services worldwide, without having to state where funds are actually assigned. A conduit taxhaven that operates as a nexus for sales in a region may be found by checking where customers send the payments for their purchases [DuhiggK:12].

Only manufacturing and licensing expenses are incurred in Ireland. In the example illustrated in Fig. 6.7, 17 % of the retail cost for the Lexapro pills was transferred to FLI in Ireland, along with a routine markup, say 5 %. Only that increment represents taxable earnings in Ireland. It is then taxed at Ireland's low 12.5 % corporate tax rate, yielding about $5.7M total. Without the Dutch Sandwich, Ireland's tax revenues from Forest Laboratories would be $21.6M [F6.7].

Multinationals will deduct licensing fees paid into their primary taxhavens from local earnings. Most semi-taxhavens will not question those charges. Countries with much experience and competence in hosting offshore operations can impose constraints. For instance, China limits royalty payments, to ensure that as the new operation becomes productive, its earnings remain in the country, both for ongoing investment and as a basis for taxation [SAT:09].

Ireland, as a member of the EU, must assume that taxes on income collected in The Netherlands have already been paid and should not be taxed again, avoiding double taxation within the European Monetary Union. Because FFN is not a Dutch operating entity, it has few obligations to the Dutch Tax Administration (NLbd). FFN transmits the bulk of Forest Labs revenues to Bermuda, where the IP rights for Lexapro reside, out of Ireland's territorial reach. No further tax is paid unless the profit is repatriated to the USA.

Theoretically the US government levies taxes on worldwide income. The exception that allows offshore income not to be taxed is to encourage US companies to invest and compete abroad. When the US Congress in 1968 passed legislation intended to make US companies more competitive worldwide, it was not the intent that revenues from US-generated IP and sales within the USA would avoid US taxation [Levy in LeveyEa:01]. Cost-sharing regulations were defined in 1984 [ChapotonG:88]. A requirement was that the foreign subsidiary had to be an active participant was removed by Congress in 1986 [RostenkowskiEa:86, Section 8670]. This requirement has been reinstituted in the 2012 update of the regulations [IRS-TP:12].

If Forest Laboratories would actually be taxed based on the jurisdiction where the revenues occur, its taxes would be substantial. That simple solution does not deal with MNC's actual worldwide income, nor does it solve the problem of sales over the Internet.

6.4 Semi-taxhavens

Countries or jurisdictions that look for the jobs, growth, and opportunities that foreign investment can bring will provide incentives to attract manufacturing and service operations [Sullivan:09]. Those countries become semi-taxhavens [Sullivan:06]. Success in attracting basic manufacturing leads eventually to establishment of research and development laboratories as well [GrimesC:09]. Important factors in attracting foreign capital are capable employees, favorable taxation, and high-quality services. Because semi-taxhavens also have a substantial internal economy, they also establish ring-fencing rules that allow the local economy to be taxed as before, while foreign investment is encouraged and jobs for its population are gained. Often the benefits are limited to specific geographical areas. The jurisdictions where MNC actually manufactures its Maniac products, Johor Baru in Malaysia, and where it tests and maintains Maniac software, India, have regional semi-taxhaven jurisdictions.

6.4.1 Incentives

Typical benefits that semi-taxhavens offer to encourage new ventures are no taxation on initial investments, multiyear tax holidays on earnings, support for training staff, and low-cost real estate leases. Often these benefits are associated with free-trade zones, where no import or export duties are levied unless the products are imported into the host country. The concessions and protections differ among semi-taxhavens [Shaxson:11]. Expert advice is provided by companies such as ATA to select the best combination for particular objectives.

Countries intent on growth, such as Israel and Ireland, have offered tax holidays to enterprises setting up activities there. The ascendance of Ireland as a semi-taxhaven was devised and promoted by the government of Ireland and led to the emergence of the "Celtic Tiger" economy [Finfacts:10]. India provides incentives for companies that export software. Slovenia recently established a 0 % tax rate for investments [CMSR:11]; in any of its economic zones the corporate tax rate is 10 %. Other Eastern European countries are considering similar initiatives. Still, for a company to set up an operation in a semi-taxhaven requires contributing financial and intellectual capital, so that the workers can become productive in a short time [W:11].

Local jurisdictions supplement national incentives. Local real estate taxes may be forgiven, infrastructure improvements may be provided, and housing for employees may be erected. In Switzerland, where income taxes are collected by regional authorities, dispensation from local taxes makes a substantial difference [Vaud:09].

There is much more diversity in semi-taxhaven structures than in primary taxhavens. Three aspects are important: jurisdictional scope, the type of incentives, and the length of incentives.

6.4.1.1 Jurisdictional Scope

First, the scope of a semi-taxhaven's jurisdiction varies. Incentives can cover an entire country, a province or state in the country, or a municipality; they can even be limited to an industrial park or a specific building.

- In the Swiss federation, financial incentives vary among its 26 cantons. Cantons have considerable autonomy and compete with each other for foreign investment.
- Free-trade zones started out as warehousing areas in seaports, and later at airports, to facilitate trans-shipping, but now cover manufacturing as well. In India the central government has established free-trade zones in cooperation with its states to simplify the complexity of multilevel bureaucratic hurdles. Free-trade zones will not levy import duties on raw materials used in making products for export.
- The government of Malaysia supports investment initiatives in its free-trade zones. MNC's JB operations in Malaysia are within Johor Baru, a developing area in southern Malaysia, taking advantage of the supply of educated labor and proximity to Singapore.
- Local areas may also waive real estate fees and taxes. Slovenia has more than 100 economic zones where state and local incentives are combined.
- In the Philippines, specific buildings can be designated for a call center.

6.4.1.2 Type of Incentives

The second distinction is the type of incentives provided.

- Countries often provide direct infrastructure support in underdeveloped areas, such as buildings, power lines, roads, and other utility services.
- Authorities may help arrange low-cost loans for the initial investments and set up training for the workforce to be hired. Cash incentives may be available for job creation. Ireland's Industrial Development Agency (IDA) provides a subsidy of about $25,000 for each new job [Stapleton:12].

- Ireland also spends $750M annually on job training, much of it benefiting the multinationals settled there [F6.8].
- Research support can be provided via institutes supported by the taxhaven government. Countries that face underemployment of their university graduates find research support to be an effective means to attract foreign investment. The institutes are encouraged to spend resources on projects that benefit companies operating locally. Generated IP may be assigned exclusively to cooperating companies.
- Some jurisdictions encourage expatriates to settle there. An active community transfers knowledge and broadens the local industrial culture. The services provided may include relocation support, housing, schools, and sometimes confidentiality of records pertaining to nonresidents. Tax concessions are common as well. Capital imported to start operations will not be taxed. Manufacturing equipment can be imported, updated, and exchanged tax free. Importation of IP, if its role is recognized, will certainly be encouraged. There can be reductions of income taxes.
- Taxes on earnings from exports can be reduced. Earnings in India's free-trade zones—Special Economic Zones (SEZ) and Software Technology Parks of India (STPI)—will be taxed at 18.5 % starting in 2012 [KonvisserS:11].

6.4.1.3 Length of Incentives

For a single new facility, local, state, and central government concessions all have their own rules and periods.

- Tax incentives are often only for a limited period. Semi-taxhavens expect that after some time their incentives should return benefits. They tend to serve old and new multinational operations alike. The periods initially announced are often extended.
- Many incentives are intended just for attracting new businesses, so that the periods for all incentives have to be specifically negotiated. ATA and its colleagues are very capable in extracting good terms for their clients. Many high-tech operations are mobile and can use the threat of moving to another semi-taxhaven to encourage continuation of tax benefits [Alderman:10].

The negotiations about incentives can be long and tedious. Companies considering substantial offshore investments may well play one jurisdiction against another. The rules, facilities, and incentives offered by semi-taxhavens change frequently. Still the benefits that multinationals can obtain from effective exploitation of taxhavens will be substantial.

Example 6.1 documents a US company. The tax structure of such an actual company is too complex to be analyzed by any single author. Even a simplified intra-European Dutch Sandwich example shows 17 divisions [KesslerE:06].

Example 6.1 Effect of Taxhaven Use

As [General Electric] expanded abroad, the portion of its profits booked in low-tax countries such as Ireland and Singapore grew far faster. From 1996 through 1998, its profits and revenue in the USA were in sync—73 % of the company's total. Over the last 3 years, though, 46 % of the company's [reported] revenue was in the USA, but just 18 % of its profits.

Since 2002, the company has eliminated a fifth of its work force in the USA while increasing overseas employment. In that time, G.E.'s accumulated offshore profits have risen from $15B to $92B.

Minimizing taxes is so important at G.E. that [the leader of its tax department] has placed tax strategists in decision-making positions in many major manufacturing facilities and businesses around the globe. ... Company officials acknowledged that the tax department had expanded since he joined the company in 1988, and said it now had 975 employees.

At a tax symposium in 2007, a G.E. tax official said the department's "mission statement" consisted of 19 rules and urged employees to divide their time evenly between ensuring compliance with the law and "looking to exploit opportunities to reduce tax."

The company spent $4.1 million on outside lobbyists last year. In 2010 G.E. actually received a tax refund of $3.2 billion. [Kocieniewski:11G]

6.4.2 Trade-offs

Incentives can conflict. Low corporate tax rates reduce the effect of R&D tax incentives and are counterproductive to local IP growth [GrimesC:09]. For semi-taxhavens direct subsidies and services are more effective. However, those will increase earnings and taxes, and US tax credits.

High-technology companies have to rely on their financial and tax advisors when dealing with semi-taxhavens. They can then combine the benefits of offshore financial intermediaries with those of actual primary taxhavens. Just comparing the corporate tax rates in various countries does not provide adequate information for location decisions. The costs of effective offshoring can be high, but the increase in corporate profitability can be huge [WGM:06]. A recent report provides an example [Nakaso:12].

Not all taxhavens are in remote offshore jurisdictions. Larger countries may allow internal regional jurisdictions to provide concessions and incentives to businesses settling there [DesaiFH:04R]. The reason may be historic or legislated to encourage growth of underdeveloped regions.

6.5 Nearshore Taxhavens

Countries that operate as a federation allow states within their boundaries to differentiate themselves in taxation, creating internal or nearshore taxhavens. Nearshore taxhavens vary greatly.

US States

In the USA, the state of Delaware has become a favorite domicile for corporations. Delaware has no state corporate tax, allows simple corporate structures, permits legal adjudication without juries, and provides much privacy protection. Nevada does not require the actual corporate residence and management names to be given [DuhiggK:12]. Nevada does not collect corporate tax and shares no information with the federal government [NDT:11].

Possession Taxhavens

A category of nearshore semi-taxhaven was created by the US Congress in 1960 and broadened in 1976 to provide incentives to businesses operating in overseas possessions of the USA [B.2.7 (a)(2)(A)]. The territory of Puerto Rico is the prime beneficiary [Levin:12]. The US Virgin Islands, Guam, American Samoa, and the Northern Mariana Islands are covered as well [Drucker:11P]. Divisions of companies established to benefit from concessions there are referred to as "possession corporations." *Unusual* tax credits are available [Browning:11]. Some credits provided were phased out between 1995 and 2005 [Arellano:08]. The phaseout motivated companies to set up new controlled foreign corporations with headquarters in a primary taxhavens such as the Cayman Islands or Bermuda [Sullivan:06].

European Union

Member countries of the EU have inconsistent tax rates and regulations. The differences are in part historic, but also due to widely differing economic resources. Their harmonization is difficult [BettendorfEa:09]. The differences are being vigorously exploited [Vigueras:08].

Switzerland

Switzerland leaves taxation entirely to its constituent cantons. Cantons collect the federal share of taxes and transmit them to the federal Swiss government for defense, international representation, and large-scale infrastructure [LocherB:02].

The City

The most important nearshore taxhaven is within the UK. The City of London Corporation, covering about a square mile within Greater London, is a largely independent jurisdiction. Banks and other financial institutions located in "The City" provide a large fraction of the world's financial services. The City's institutions manage the Eurodollar funds, money not backed by any government. Starting in the year 1067 the City has obtained amazing and singular privileges [Roberts:08]. For instance, in addition to its 9,000 residents, the City's 32,000 businesses have voting rights in its governance, if they are members of one of its guilds. A recent guild is the "Worshipful Company of Tax Advisers" [Woolf:10]. ATA would be a member. A representative of the City, the "Remembrancer," sits in the UK parliament behind the Speaker of the House, assuring that City's concerns are considered [Shaxson:11].

British Crown Dependencies

The banks of The City actually register most accounts in British Crown Dependencies (BCDs), as the Islands of Jersey or Man, second-level nearshore taxhavens.

The availability of nearshore taxhavens creates additional complexity when they can be combined with benefits from other locales. At one point it was possible for US companies to establish joint residency in Delaware and the underprivileged Canadian province of Nova Scotia. Because Canada is part of the British Commonwealth, assets can be transferred freely to other Commonwealth members, such as Bermuda, that are considered primary taxhavens. An agreement between the IRS and Revenue Canada now disallows that option.

6.6 Prominent Taxhavens

The total amount of US-source earnings that are booked in taxhavens and thus avoid taxation appears to be about $300B annually. This shift of income from US sales to taxhavens, enabled by IP transfers, is not the intent of the cost-sharing regulations devised to make US companies more competitive worldwide. The amount is sufficiently large now to create inconsistencies in advice given to the US Congress by experts in tax legislation [Jackson:10].

Corporate filings of multinational corporations reported on the average a dozen offshore entities [F6.9]. Forest Laboratories has 11 subsidiaries offshore [Drucker:10]. Since 2005 SEC reporting requirements have been relaxed, so that it has become easy to omit taxhavens [Deloitte:11]. Even when they are listed, their roles, their holdings of capital and IP, and the relationships among them are not provided, following international (IASB) guidance.

Table 6.2 lists a few prominent taxhavens and their focus. Some taxhaven jurisdictions actively solicit and lobby for business, citing their advantages for; several have Web sites to promote their capabilities [LowTax:11].

At least 70 distinct countries have appeared on lists of taxhavens at one time or another [Ogley:00]. Business rules in taxhavens vary greatly [Ogley:00]. The actual roles of a taxhavens can change over time. Transactions among taxhavens are opaque. The interposition of multiple taxhaven entities makes roundtrip transfers of earnings very hard to track. Similar questions are arising within European countries [Castle:11].

Although there is quite a variety of taxhavens, published analyses tend to focus on one specific category, depending on the author's focus [DharmapalaH:06]. Their interaction is rarely addressed. Others intermingle data from different categories, weakening the conclusions [DesaiFH:05D]. The four categories used in these analyses are based on their corporate roles.

6.7 Formal Definitions of Taxhavens

The most commonly cited definition, shown in Table 6.1, of harmful taxhavens was provided by the Organisation for Economic Co-operation and Development (OECD) [OECD:98].

The development of OECD document led to guidance spelled out in the *EU's Code of Conduct for business taxation* of 1997.

The criteria for identifying potentially harmful measures include:

- An effective level of taxation which is significantly lower than the general level of taxation in the country concerned
- Tax benefits reserved for nonresidents
- Tax incentives for activities which are isolated from the domestic economy and therefore have no impact on the national tax base
- Granting of tax advantages even in the absence of any real economic activity
- The basis of profit determination for companies in a multinational group departs from internationally accepted rules, in particular those approved by the OECD
- Lack of transparency

Some countries, as South Korea and France, maintain their own lists of taxhavens. A recent proposal is to label any jurisdiction that has tax rate lower than 10 % as a taxhaven [RubinZ:11].

6.8 Shifting Ownership of Assets Held in a Taxhaven

The role of a taxhaven does not need to end when its parent dies. Consider a US company, POOF, that received few earnings from its offshore CFCs since most of the earnings went to its taxhaven subsidiary POOCH.

If POOF declares bankruptcy, its remaining assets are sold to satisfy outstanding liabilities to POOF's creditors and employees. As part of the bankruptcy settlement

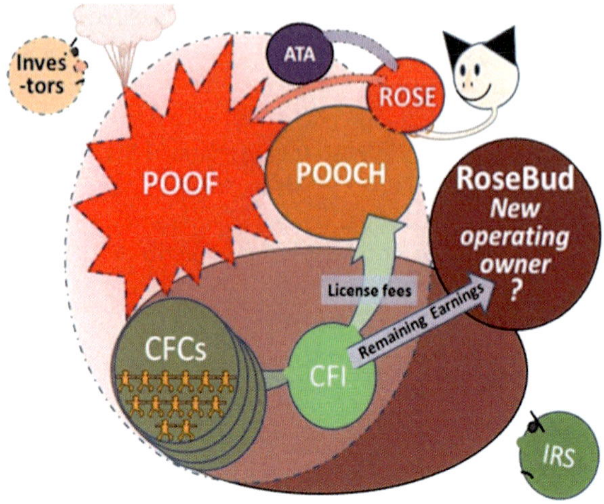

Fig. 6.8 Shifting IP in taxhaven during bankruptcy

foreign divisions of recognized value will be sold. A sale of those foreign assets to a new operating owner, RoseBud, does not bring in much money. POOCH had invested its capital for its operations, only IP is left, and any salvage value is small, so that little can be recovered from POOCH to settle POOF's obligations.

Little IP is shown on the books of POOF, so that IP rights available to POOCH seem to have no value. There are few assets in its CFI, since that is just a shell conduit intermediary. The relationships are sketched in Fig. 6.8.

After the bankruptcy any liabilities POOF had that are not covered by its documented assets are canceled. But substantial IP is still available in POOF's offshore taxhaven subsidiary POOCH. Since that IP does not appear on the books, no creditor or bankruptcy judge requested that the IP at POOCH be valued. After the bankruptcy POOCH continues to exist and collect funds from any ongoing offshore operations at the CFCs, even though the interposing CFI has new owners. The CFI distributes the remaining earnings to the new owner. Those new owners accepted the license obligations for the IP rights that POOCH owns.

After the bankruptcy the ownership of POOCH is unclear. Since ownership of POOCH was vested in the board of directors of POOCH, who would be former directors of POOF and its CFI, and their financial consultants, a revised, independent ownership structure, ROSE, can be established and salvage assets of POOF at a little cost. ROSE can collect income due to licenses that POOF arranged with its offshore CFCs before its bankruptcy. Copies of the documents that represent the IP had remained at the manufacturing CFCs, so there is no interruption in actually producing products. Some former POOF employees are available for consulting as needed.

The lack of awareness of the role of IP, combined with the misvaluations common in dealing with IP, contributes to distorted assessments of corporate value located in a variety of corporate divisions. In case of a bankruptcy, when the value of having an ongoing business is lost, lack of clarity of ownership of IP disables honest allocations. The confusion can easily cause unwarranted losses to investors and employees, and gains for people who are close to the action.

POOF has effectively committed suicide. If POOCH were a person who executes such a suicidal action he'd be considered a terrorist. All of its offshore assets are now held by ROSE for the new operating owners, its former handlers, and kept in a far-off place. Those handlers have much to cheer about. They have received valuable assets, located in a taxhaven and out of sight, for a modest investment. The IRS regulations that try to control inversions do not apply.

6.9 MNC's Use of Taxhavens

When MNC started offshoring its manufacturing operations, it naturally chose jurisdictions that were in attractive locations. MNC JB and MNC MY were established in semi-taxhavens that had facilities, potential employees, and a transportation infrastructure that could contribute to success. ATA helped by gathering information to help MNC establish operational CFCs in Malaysia and India. It also proposed gaining tax advantages through additional CFCs. A CFH, CONCH, was established in a primary taxhaven, Palm Island, a British Overseas Territory in the Caribbean. The variety of flows of IP and payments is sketched in Fig. 6.9.

ATA also created the controlled financial intermediary (CFI) for MNC called CAAS. MNC uses CAAS to shift funds so that they are invisible to countries that might want to tax them. CAAS has only a switching function and does not hold

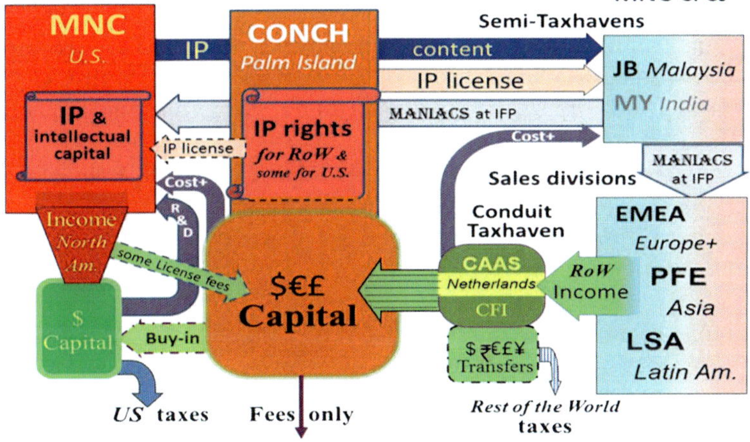

Fig. 6.9 The flow of IP and money among MNC's divisions

intellectual or financial IP capital. Because MNC does not have substantial manufacturing operations in Europe, the role of CAAS, MNC's CFI in The Netherlands, is not as broad as that of Forest Labs' FFN.

The parent corporation and the operational CFCs have costs and need working capital. CAAS, controlled by the MNC parent, will distribute such funds as needed, including some for repatriation to the US parent company. The amounts that must be repatriated to cover costs are a small fraction of the income that CONCH can retain.

6.9.1 Selection of a Jurisdiction for Growth

Companies have a broad choice in choosing taxhavens. For a primary or conduit taxhaven, the main factors behind the decision are minimal financial and oversight provisions. For semi-taxhavens the availability of personnel, the cost of shipping, and inventory logistics are the main issues [Hummels:07]. For intangibles, location is not a concern, since the Internet reaches anywhere [Cairncross:97]. The existence of tax treaties is also a factor [Doernberg:08].

Logistics have undergone radical changes in the last 50 years. Manufactured products are shipped in containers moved by ships, rail, and trucks. Shipping by containers between modern ports is extremely cheap. The containers are put on trucks for shipment to operations centers. Ports of interest to MNC for Austria and Ireland are marked with a ▲ in Fig. 6.2.

Table 6.3 shows the factors that MNC management and ATA will consider. We will look only at locations used so far by MNC and Forest Labs. The centroid of MNC's current EMEA customers is close to Austria. Forest Labs manufactured in Ireland. Both European countries primarily tax territorial revenues, so that the "Double Irish" strategy, where income attributed to IP is booked into an affiliated taxhaven—CONCH for MNC—can be exploited in both locales.

MNC initially used air freight, but as its product volume grows, the company considers container shipment to its distribution centers, such as to MNC EMEA in southeastern Austria. Ireland, the location used by Forest Labs, was an alternative contender.

The shipping cost from MNC JB in Malaysia to MNC EMEA in Graz is only \$2.00 per Maniac [F6.12]. Out-of-stock products and spare parts can be shipped by air within a day. Recent software updates are sent over the Internet from MNC US or MNC MY, to be loaded by MNC EMEA into the Maniacs shipped to Austria before delivery to customers.

The routine redistribution of MNC's products from Austria to the rest of Europe should bring some profits into MNC EMEA in Austria. However, any nonroutine income will remain invisible to Austria because it is collected and distributed by CAAS in The Netherlands. Because CONCH paid for acquisitions obtained with low-taxed AJCA transfers, gaining IP rights, an increasing fraction of earnings from

Table 6.3 Factors for deciding a site for future MNC EMEA operations

Factor	Candidate EMEA sites: Graz, Austria	Coolock, Ireland	Assessment considerations
Ease of doing business	Fair	High	Bureaucracy vs. flexibility
Incentives provided	Increasing	Established	Similar value
Serving existing customers	High	Very good	Both improve on MNC JB or US support
EMEA shipping to Munich	450 km	1,800 km, ferries	
Access to new markets	High	Modest	Growth in the East
Local corporate tax	25 %	12.5 %	MNC's CAAS can be used to avoid most local taxes
EU member	Yes	Yes	
Tax levied	Territorial	Territorial	MNC local sales are low
Tax treaty with US	Yes	Yes	Local taxes are credited
Capable workforce	Yes, pop. 8.2 M	Yes, pop. 4.6 M	Any EU national can work
Labor cost vs. US @ 51	36.5/h	46.7/h	OECD 2009 metric
Language capabilities	Adequate, many	Excellent, English	Growth favors Austria
Seaport for containers ▲	Trieste	Dublin	Risk of strikes in Italy
Backup seaport ▲	Gioia Tauro	Southampton	Additional trucking cost
Johor Baru ▲ to seaports	3 weeks	4 weeks	Less to backup seaports
Cost per 20' container	$1,750	$2,250	Much less than air freight
Port capability	Excellent	Excellent	Trieste handles more
Trucking port to EMEA ops	300 km	15 km	Graz takes another day

US sales will also go to CONCH. MNC accomplishes its tax avoidance with just two taxhaven entities covering the three rest-of-the-world areas out of its four product distribution areas.

6.10 Trends Enabled by Taxhavens

Initially, MNC's US vs. offshore earnings are proportional to regional sales. Figure 6.10 sketches the trend enabled by the offshoring of its IP over time. The offshore earnings are derived from MNC's IP shift to CONCH after the buy-in. The initial buy-in by CONCH was based on proportional IP rights for sales external to the USA, more in keeping with the intent of transfer pricing legislation. Over time the IP rights held offshore grew, as capital accumulated at CONCH was used to acquire more IP. That in turn causes the fraction of earnings booked offshore, at CONCH, to increase.

Developments similar to those seen at MNC occur in any company that shifts IP offshore to avoid taxation [Srinidhi in Contractor:01]. Since 2000, pharmaceutical companies have managed to book about 80 % of their income in taxhavens, although their foreign sales are 52 % of the total [Sullivan:10P]. In general, the rate of the shift to offshore earnings is unpredictable, but the trend is clear [W:11]. Some

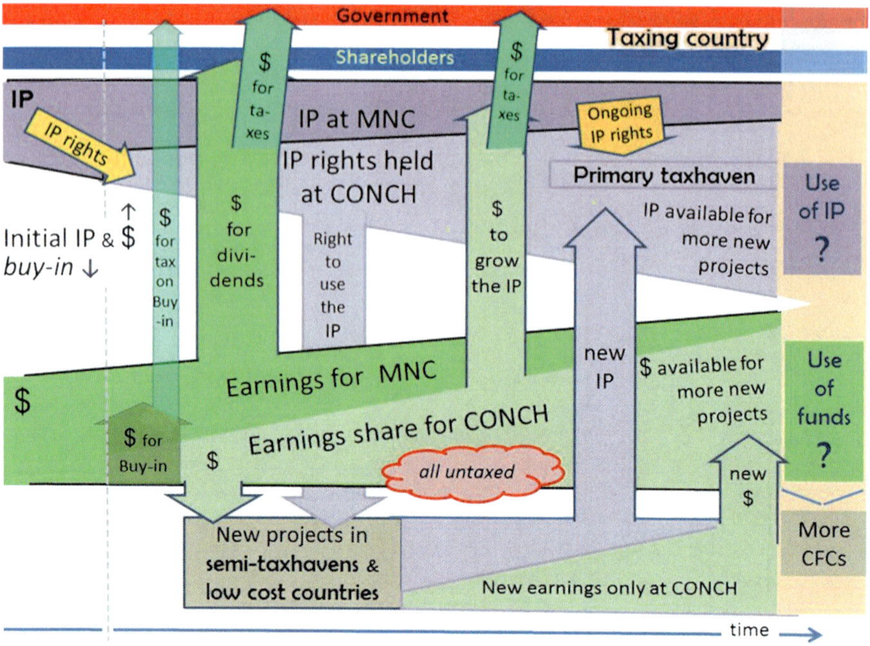

Fig. 6.10 Time sequence for IP flow and payments among MNC's divisions

analyses downplay the effects of the use of taxhavens on US jobs [Lohr:06]. Labor unions do observe trends, are puzzled about the flows, and get upset [Rasmus:06]. An effect on US wages has been documented [HassettM:10].

Having divisions in multiple distinct taxhavens allows companies to take advantage of the distinct incentives provided by each jurisdiction and category. With that many intermediaries, it is difficult to track the movement of IP and the revenues that are generated. Interposing CFIs based in conduit taxhavens allows the capital flow to be further obscured. Trying to track the flows and recover tax losses to the home economy could well cost the government more in expert and legal fees than the eventual benefit from settlements [Schwarcz:04].

6.11 Summary

The availability of rapid communication and economical worldwide shipping allows high-tech companies to move their operations to any location in the world [Kahn:12]. A knowledgeable advisor, as ATA, with a presence in all locales, will suggest a combination of a variety of primary, conduit, nearshore, and semi-taxhavens to their customers, and make it all work.

Revenues are booked into accounts of a CFI located in the conduit taxhaven. Actual costs and routine profits are reimbursed by the CFI to operating divisions worldwide that produce or sell the product. The balance goes to the holding CFH in a primary taxhaven. Nothing of value stays at the CFI, allowing it to maintain a low profile. In the end, the sum of all taxes paid by multinational companies to the many jurisdictions where they set up shop will certainly be less than 10 % of their earnings.

The untaxed earnings accumulate in primary taxhavens. The consolidated worldwide corporate profits reported by MNC and its peers are independent of where the funds are held, where the operations are located, and where the workers are employed. Shareholders are happy with the great global earnings reported on the consolidated balance sheets. High net worth individuals and corporate shareholders may have moved their domicile to taxhavens as well, saving taxes on repatriation for the company and dividend taxes for themselves.

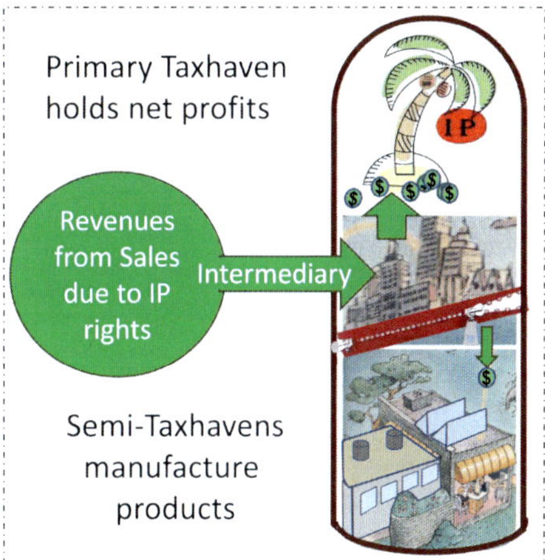

All three principal categories of taxhavens interact to avoid worldwide corporate taxes. A failure to distinguish their roles allows each category to claim innocence. A taxhaven can shelter many thousands of businesses. US multinational companies had 26,342 offshore subsidiaries, 11.6 average per company, greatly reducing taxes paid for most of them [F6.9].

The amount held by US corporations in taxhavens in 2010 was estimated to be about $1,375B [Davidoff:11]. Funds that are repatriated for investments or dividends will incur US corporate taxes. Shareholders in corporations that repatriate funds will also be taxed on their income from current dividends or later capital gains as well, albeit at a low rate.

Deferring repatriation and just keeping accumulated funds in a taxhaven is not a good business strategy. Available money is best invested in further growth of the business. Coming from a foreign country those funds will be eligible for investment concessions provided by semi-taxhavens. The IP stays in the primary taxhaven and soon causes capital to grow again. The role of IP is not recognized even when taxhavens are discussed in depth [PalanMC:10].

Actual business growth is associated with manufacturing or productive services. Primary and conduit taxhavens do not provide facilities for actual production and have no or few employees. Some conduit taxhavens also provide financial services, but those do not add value to high-tech industries, especially when acting primarily as a nexus for collecting sales revenue. Most growth will occur in semi-taxhavens that compete to attract productive investment, while the earnings flow to primary taxhavens [DesaiH:04] [Sullivan:11].

The traditional assumption that job creation occurs where innovative companies originated, where innovation is promoted, and where management makes operational decisions is not valid for multinational corporations [Summers:08]. Hiring will occur globally, in jurisdictions where the combination of competent staff and incentives exists and the perceived costs are low.

Chapter 7
Taxation of MNC

Prior chapters have provided the background of the structures that enable tax avoidance. Moving operations offshore alone does not reduce taxes. Transferring rights to exploit MNC's intellectual capital in a buy-in allowed MNC's taxhaven, CONCH, to collect earnings from foreign sales. Those earnings are held offshore, and while shown on MNC's consolidated books, they are not subject to US taxes. The value that MNC's tax advisors, ATA, assigned to the rights to share MNC's intellectual capital buy-in by CONCH was \$50M, whereas a simple average of the seven valuations performed in Chap. 5 was about \$783M. ATA's valuation for that initial offshoring transaction is 6.4 % of that average [F7.1]. The resulting imbalance has the effect that MNC pays much less tax than we expect for a successful public US company. The financial and intellectual capital held at CONCH is available for subsequent investments, which will not be subjected to taxation if made offshore.

7.1 Misvaluation

Results of valuations using different methods will vary, but should converge to a cluster around a credible result. Because of uncertain data and incomplete coverage of assets, economists accept a wide range above and below the mean in the results of valuations using different methods [Black:96]. The total range of our seven valuations is acceptable, at less than 50 % about their mean [F7.2]. The assessment by MNC's tax advisors was far below the cluster, as shown next in the simplified view of Fig. 5.14.

G. Wiederhold, *Valuing Intellectual Capital: Multinationals and Taxhavens*, Management for Professionals 23, DOI 10.1007/978-1-4614-6611-6_7,

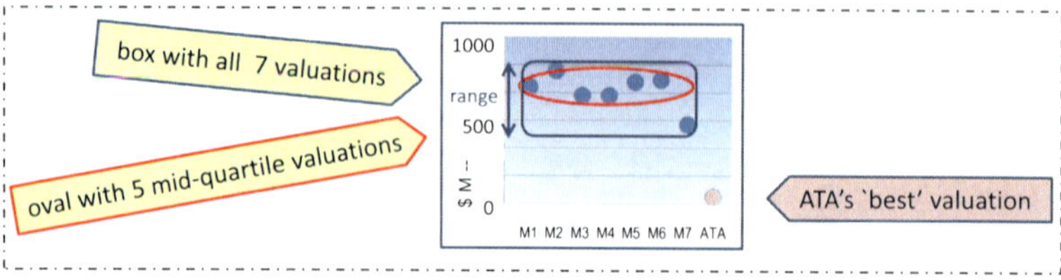

As argued in Chap. 4, transfer prices must be fair to the seller and the buyer, but CONCH was able to pay only $50M for an asset that earned $110M in the first year and increasing amounts in successive years [F7.3]. The implied price/earnings (*p*/*e*) multiple is only a tenth of what an investor would already consider to be a desirable investment [BrealeyMA:06]. Nobody complains that such a misvaluation violates common sense [Shay:12].

As described in Chap. 2, a low valuation of the rights that allow CONCH, a controlled taxhaven entity, to access MNC's intellectual capital initiated the process of tax avoidance. Subsequently MNC could avoid substantial US taxes using various taxhaven entities created for MNC by ATA, Untaxed earnings accumulated in CONCH. Employing MNC's intellectual capital and the financial capital held at CONCH begets ever more IP rights. Taxes are due if any such funds are ever repatriated to the USA, but both capital and IP rights are available for investment and growth outside the USA without paying US taxes.

7.1.1 Acceptance of Tax Avoidance Approaches

Taxes on corporate earnings substantially impact profits. Multinational corporations can easily benefit from tax incentives in the many locales where they operate. It was natural for MNC's director of taxes to ask an outside consultancy like ATA for advice. ATA already had experience in devising corporate structures to take advantage of various taxhavens. After some staff interviews, ATA prepared a report on what could be done. The report included the common phrase that it was "more likely than not" that the proposed structure would not be challenged by the IRS examiners [PSoI:03].

ATA's report was reviewed by MNC's board of directors. To what extent MNC's management can simply rely on external consultant's advice is a legal question. When a proposed valuation and the resulting payment by CONCH is far out of line with the company's market value, a number well known to corporate management, MNC's directors should ask how ATA justified such a low value, being aware that MNC is giving up its rights to nearly half of its IP. The fact that the IP was assigned to taxhavens could also raise concerns. MNC's directors, being technically oriented, trusted the ATA valuations; there is little motivation to critique a good financial deal that is well packaged.

Board members at MNC are chosen for their technical and business competence and not for the arcane knowledge this book covers. ATA pointed out the effective tax rates at competing companies that had established taxhavens, making the board's choice obvious. Exploiting rules that differ in various jurisdictions is the essence of the game that leads to effective tax avoidance. When outside experts like ATA present complex financial transactions with a specific objective such as reduction of taxes, possible long-term effects are unclear [HoggEa:08]. Even when ATA lists ancillary issues, such as risk of loss of IP, it is hard for the board members to consider all possible outcomes. They will not question the proposals [Cornford:04].

ATA also offered the services of its associated companies in several countries. The board of directors of a public company like MNC has to approve any major change in business strategy [Steele:10]. That includes setting up offshore corporations, issuing stock options, and so forth. It is the directors' responsibility to represent the aggregate interests of the stockholders, as well as to ensure that the company remains a good "corporate citizen" wherever it operates. Obvious ethical conflicts have to be balanced; in the UK these are now made explicit [AlcockBG:09].

Executives of a corporation should be aware of major asset transfers. A contemporaneous valuation of tangible and intangible assets being moved abroad is not only a requirement for the IRS [B.2.5(c)(2)]. A valuation is also essential to assess the costs and risks of moving assets offshore and should be made available to the board of directors [WTGS:09]. We know that the board considered MNC's IP important; to reduce the risk of loss, it decided to set up controlled foreign corporations (CFCs) for offshore work, rather than depend on independent foreign contractors (IFCs) [WGN:10].

The effort to produce a thorough valuation may take more time than the planning cycle for implementing a business decision, so it is common for actions to be initiated before such a valuation is available. Chapter 5 showed that adequate estimates are possible with a modest effort. Once a decision is made, there is a benefit in having a low value assigned to the IP being transferred offshore, for both tax avoidance and apparent reduction of risk.

7.2 Range of Valuations

In Chap. 5 we applied seven different valuation methods to the assets MNC transferred to CONCH. The interquartile range, based on the three boldface amounts shown in Table 7.1, was less than 8 % [F7.4]. Three results, M1, M3, and M4, are close to the interquartile mean; why the two outliers, M2 and M7, differ is easily explained from the data used in the analyses.

Any proposed valuations that differ greatly are likely to have fundamental errors. The ATA valuation at $50M is just 6 % of the interquartile mean of the alternatives—and even less than 9 % of the low M7, RO-VM valuation [F7.5]. With the background we have developed, that valuation is clearly unacceptable, but MNC's directors never considered any alternatives.

Table 7.1 CONCH buy-in payment valuation results and ATA proposal

#	Method	Source of information	Feature/uncertainty in	Buy-in
M1	MC-VM	Shareholders' insights	Visible/volatility and growth	**$839M**
M2	Inc-VM	Management expectation	Opaque/growth	$955M
M3	IIP-VM	Identified existing IP	Technical/IP selection	**$781M**
M4	CUT-VM	Comparable transactions	Using IP licenses/coverage	**$779M**
M5	CP-VM	Comparable businesses	Using metrics/similarity	$677M
M6	PS-M	Royalty profit split	Relative contribution/actual income	$890M
M7	RO-VM	Stable product creation	Long-term data/maturity and stability	$570M
M1 through M7		Mean of interquartiles (M1, M3, M4)/overlap of sources		**$800M**
ATA		Selected IP	Contracted/trusting ATA	$ 50M

The immediate effect of the poor valuation is that MNC pays $235M less in US taxes than would be due on a credible buy-in payment by CONCH. The long-range effect is that due to this transaction alone CONCH accumulates in 20 years $8,300M of unjustified capital for future offshore investments [F7.6].

The next section deals with the question, how did such a large misjudgment occur? Section 7.3 assesses the effects of such a difference in valuation on the future of MNC and its offshore holding company, CONCH, in more detail.

7.2.1 The "Best" Method Rule

The IRS regulations specify that, in general, a "best method" should be chosen to reach a valuation [B.3.1 1(c)]. Using only one method means that no inconsistency will ever be seen and have to be explained. There is a loss of information when results of any other applicable methods are ignored. At least simple cross-checks, as using the market cap M1, MC-VM, or margin analyses, as described in M5, CP-VM, should always be made. When multiple methods produce inconsistent results beyond a reasonable range, then other methods that produce consistent results can be taken into account. ATA used just one method, an M3, IIP-VM approach for technical IP only, omitting know-how. Even if an IIP-VM calculation is limited just to the technical IP, ATA's result is still only 7.5 % of the result computed in Chap. 5 [F7.7].

It seems that the method proposed by ATA as being "best" does not produce a great result. However, it is not the fault of the method. The low value presented by ATA for the buy-in by CONCH was not due to one egregious error, but rather due to many misestimations, which, in the aggregate, produced a result that makes no economic sense [F7.3].

The ATA valuation is provided to the IRS as a supporting document when MNC's income taxes are filed. Initiating a cost-sharing arrangement with a new offshore subsidiary is recognized by the IRS as an important transaction [Chaback:08]. It is assigned to a local IRS auditor, who we will call "Matthew," for investigation.

Table 7.2 Differences in buy-in computation parameters and their isolated effect

Discrepancy			Expected value	ATA value	Reduction and effect (%)		Ref [F *x*]
D1 a, b	Ignores nontechnical IP		$813M	$600M	30	70	*x* = 7.8
	IP list ignores senior manpower		$114M	0	15	**85**	
D2	Research in progress ignored		$140M	0	22	**78**	7.9
D3	IP diminution type over life years		HW&Roux/15	Linear/4	35	65	7.10
	Wrong start point for diminution		During mod. 3	At mod.1	19	**81**	5.25
D4 a, b, c	Lag	On total CONCH income	3 years	1.2 years	11	**89**	7.11
		NPV of CONCH income			17	83	
		Centroid position in a, b	0.41	0.50	−22	**122**	7.12
D5	Discount rate for high-risk R&D		15.00 %	20.47 %	20	**80**	7.13
D6	Rate for nonexclusive license		7 %	4 %	43	**57**	7.14
D7	Base for RAB, earnings vs. sales		44 %	42 %	5	**95**	7.15
D8	Keeping RAB fixed over time		44 % → 54 %	44 %	14	**86**	7.16
D9	Interest on full buy-in payment		$159M	$11M	17	**83**	7.17
D10 a, b	Interest rate on buy-in payments		18 %	8 %	2	**98**	7.18
	Interest rate combined with full buy-in payment of D9 (*ignored*)				51	49	
Combined effect $\prod$ (D1:D10)					4–10		7.19

7.2.2 The Valuation of the Buy-in for CONCH

ATA estimated the value of the IP transferred by MNC to CONCH at only $50M, a small fraction of the income that CONCH will earn from the IP over the foreseeable future. This low estimate is due to a combination of many factors. Table 7.2 presents ten factors that combine to yield the final serious misvaluation. For each factor we show the reduction in the valuation caused by the discrepancy. For some factors there is choice for its computation. The choices made by ATA and its cumulative effect on a final result are shown in boldface. All computations are elaborated in Appendix F.

If MNC is selected for an audit, many documents will be required [Pearson:06]. Matthew, the IRS auditor, is provided with detailed guidelines [IRS-CSA:08]. A single drastic discrepancy would stand out and be questioned. The ten smaller misestimations, each leading to modest changes in taxable amounts, are harder to spot. Discrepancies in factors leading to a valuation multiply, whereas common errors in tax returns are additive.

The combined product (Π) of the 11 boldface definite, but isolated reductions in Table 7.1, is already 10 %, and accounts for a large fraction of the low ATA valuation. Combining the higher estimates would reduce the valuation to 4 % of its full amount [F7.19]. In the actual valuation, the parameters interact in much more complex ways and combine to generate the $50M or 6 % valuation presented by ATA [F7.20].

Most of the discrepancies shown in Table 7.2 reduce the final valuation. Each is just as much work to analyze as one egregious fault. Most discrepancies do not, by

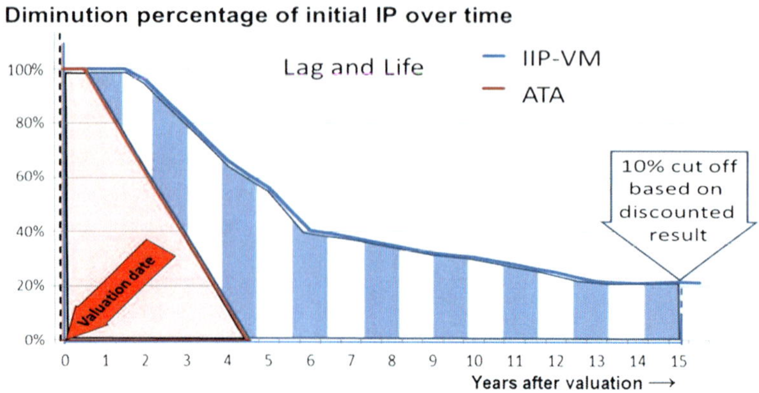

Fig. 7.1 Lag and diminution used by ATA vs. real data

themselves, make a crucial difference, but because most lower the valuation, their effect is one sided and major.

The excessive discount rate, discrepancy D5, is an issue in many valuation controversies [Veritas:09]. Making that correction increases the ATA valuation by 20 % and looks like a good result when no other valuations are available. The large discrepancy, D6, for the royalty rate for a nonexclusive license, is no longer acceptable [IRS-TP:12].

Correcting more obscure factors may require help from an economist [LeveyW:07]. For Mathew to adjust any discrepancies found requires getting data from the taxpayer, entering them into IRS computers, recreating the taxpayers' computation, and recomputing the result.

Figure 7.1 shows the combined effect of just two of the ten factors, the rate of diminution, D3, and the lag, D4. The shaded area represents ATA's data; the striped area should have been included to produce a proper result. All other factors interact as well, disabling incremental repairs of a valuation.

Observe that ATA has not taken advantage of any single, simple loophole in arriving at its low buy-in valuation. Each discrepancy can be rationalized and justified with some precedent or citation. When an alternative assessment is legally challenged, inducing doubt on even one correction can cause the entire IRS position to be questioned [OatesO:11].

7.2.3 Correcting a Misvaluation

Dealing with so many factors makes adjusting the valuation to a reasonable estimate very difficult. Each factor must be considered thoroughly by Mathew and IRS economists to achieve an adequate correction.

Perhaps each discrepancy shown in Table 7.1 can be corrected. But for all factors we are dealing with projections into the future, rather than accurate accounting. None except D10b, the loan interest rate applied to the full valuation, has enough of an effect by itself to explain the unexpectedly low total valuation. MNC borrowed concurrently $50M, but that loan was not specifically tied to CONCH. Adjusting an interest rate to a rate appropriate for an arm's-length setting is only significant if all other discrepancies are corrected first, because it applies to a corrected amount needed to establish CONCH, which in turn is based on the valuation. The taxpayer may argue that the chosen interest rate falls within the safe harbor range of the federal rate as in the regulations, motivated by concerns about financial deposit manipulation [ChapotonG:88].

Piecemeal repair is infeasible. Only by starting over, and applying and averaging several alternative methods, can a trustworthy result be obtained.

7.2.3.1 Foreign Investments as Business Expenses

MNC provided the funds needed to start CONCH, an investment of $6M and a $50M loan, to be repaid by CONCH over 5 years at MNC's base interest rate [F2.4]. It provided implicitly a valuable financial guarantee [Ramelli:12]. MNC can claim that expense as a foreign direct investment (FDI) and deduct the amount from its current taxable income. It is not a productive investment however; MNC sales will not grow because of it. It is not a profitable financial investment either, because CONCH repaid the loan over 5 years at the same interest rate that MNC was charged by its lender. The sole benefit is that income that CONCH now gathers from sales in its territories is sheltered from taxation and MNC will pay less tax.

MNC did not defer repayment of the $50M start-up loan to set up CONCH. It received quarterly repayments from CONCH for the loan and paid taxes on that income. Those payments evened out MNC's income, compensating in part for the income lost from earnings on foreign sales. The payments evened out the changes in annual US taxes being paid, as seen in Fig. 7.2. The buy-in transaction became less visible to MNC's stockholders and to IRS examiners. MNC was not audited.

7.2.3.2 The Immediate Effect of the Buy-in on MNC's Taxes

The effect of MNC's moving its IP to CONCH caused an immediate reduction in taxable income from its revenues. Observing such a change could raise suspicions. Repayments to MNC of the $50M loan, with interest, which enabled the move offshore, offset some of that reduction, as seen in Fig. 7.2. Instead of an expected payment of $87.5M, only $39.7M in taxes is due to the IRS that year [F7.21]. The contemporaneous acquisitions make Matthew's task more difficult [LeveyW:07].

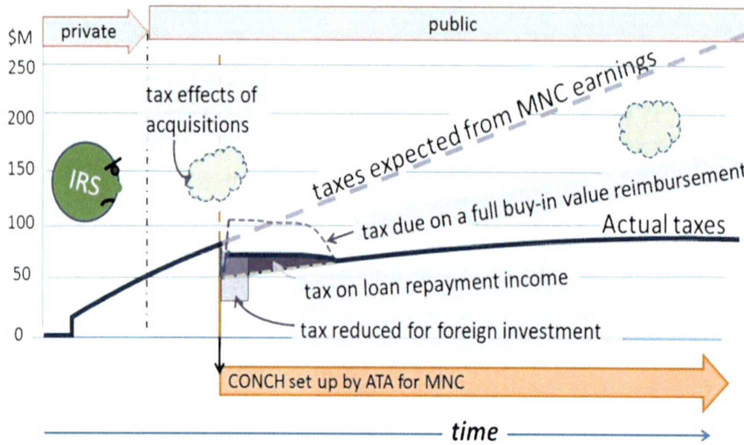

Fig. 7.2 US taxes to be paid by MNC

In these estimates the R&D expenses at MNC in California that benefit CONCH are ignored [DesaiFH:04F]. The cost-sharing arrangement specifies that, after the buy-in, CONCH reimburses its share of R&D costs. MNC will also receive federal research and experimentation (R&E) credits, reducing CONCH's share of R&D payments further [Kocieniewski:11V].

The IRS will receive reports on transactions that export capital and IP [B.2.5 (d) (2)]. There are no accounting entries that allow Matthew, the IRS auditor, to check to see if the reported IP values make business sense. Matching IP values to R&D expenses cannot automatically trigger an investigation. Analyzing the financial effects of IP transfers requires access to inconsistent offshore records [StolowyJ:01]. If a buy-in is poorly valued, as shown here, it will only have a modest impact initially. With all the other events that occurred during the buy-in period, seen in Fig. 5.1, the misvaluation of the IP export is easy to miss.

The taxes on the repayment of the loan for the full IIP-VM buy-in value would be $61M in each of the first 5 years, as indicated by the dashed line of Fig. 7.2, but the payments are actually reduced because of a deduction for the investment during the first year [F7.22]. Ignored are other items that can affect taxes due, such as write-offs of goodwill from the acquisitions, so that the change in taxes being paid can be even less obvious.

7.3 A Corrected Valuation Cannot Be Accommodated

A buy-in amount closer to its true value, $800M, would substantially increase the repayments due, becoming $193M annually, even at a low 8 % interest rate [F7.23]. In a true arm's-length situation CONCH would be seen as a risky start-up business, having to pay an 18 % interest or $255M annually for its loan. CONCH does not generate enough income to pay either amount in 5 years. Over a longer time, CONCH could pay off the true amount, since CONCH will generate income for a long time. Paying the full $800M for the buy-in instead of $50M requires that the loan period would have to be stretched out. At an 8 % interest rate it will take 14 years to pay off such a large loan, using all of CONCH's income [F7.24]. No funds would be accumulated for further acquisitions. At an 18 % rate, the loan cannot ever be written off.

Say that Mathew determines in an audit that the buy-in valuation submitted by MNC is unacceptable. If the IRS now insists on a payment for the full value from CONCH, the business strategy created by ATA becomes infeasible. However, by the time the audit is completed the IP rights for foreign sales are held offshore and foreign earnings are transmitted to Palm Island. The situation cannot be rationally reversed. Forcing MNC to change its structure can lead to claims that the IRS is ruining MNC's export business.

The untenable situation was created because the strategy pretended that CONCH operates independently and at arm's length, when that assumption does not match the facts. There was no reason to transfer nearly half of MNC's successful ongoing business to an offshore shell company in Palm Island if there were no significant tax advantages. Setting an unreasonable low buy-in price made the strategy feasible. MNC could have continued selling its Maniacs overseas without creating CONCH and transferring IP rights for foreign sales there.

If ATA would have presented a valid buy-in valuation for the offshoring strategy to MNC's board of directors, the board would not have approved the proposal to start CONCH as an IP holding company. First of all, MNC could not obtain a loan for the $800M needed to allow CONCH to start up; the loan amount would be more than 32 % of MNC's market capitalization at the time [F7.25]. Taking on so much long-term debt just to lower taxes, without actually generating any new revenues, makes no business sense for MNC and its investors.

The essential problem is that an arm's-length equivalent to the entire MNC buy-in is no longer a valid business model. A valuation that is based on what actually should happen in an arm's-length setting cannot be accommodated in practice, so that piecewise hypothetical settings are constructed. For instance, the shell entity CONCH is considered a true contributor. Another hypothetical assumption is that MNC may stop maintaining the IP, leaving CONCH with short-lived IP rights. Such hypotheticals easily mislead and should be avoided [AF:04]. The entire arm's-length argument is counterfactual; it ignores the fact that the arrangements made between the parent MNC and its taxhaven division, CONCH, would never be undertaken between companies that truly operate at arm's length. Example 7.1 shows another situation where a misvaluation led to inconsistent outcomes.

Example 7.1 Outcome of a Failure to Analyze a Poor Valuation

A US software company, Veritas, in 2002 transferred rights to its IP in Europe to a new Irish subsidiary. The buy-in was valued by its advisors at $166M—later reduced to $118M. In 2006 the IRS challenged the buy-in valuation all the way to court [Veritas:09]. The IRS hired two experts that valued the buy-in amount due at $2,500M and $1,675M. The 40 % difference made the results suspect. The IRS proposed the lower amount. As expected in any complex case, neither report was perfect, and issues with the experts' analyses were presented to the judge handling the case. Why the taxpayer's proposed valuation was only 8.0 % of the mean of the values presented by the experts was not analyzed.

Instead of considering all of the information, problems identified in the IRS' experts' valuations results caused the court to accept the taxpayer's single valuation with minor adjustments [Veritas:09].

While the case was in court, in 2005, all of Veritas was acquired by another US software company for $13.2B [Johnson:05V]. Based on that acquisition, a purchase price (M8: PP-VM) valuation of the taxpayer's buy-in yields $1,870M, within the estimates of the IRS' experts [F7.26].

Using that valuation, not available in 2002, means that the proposed buy-in payment amounted to 8.9 % of its value. Based on the difference of acquisition price and the valuation, the new owner of Veritas saved $537M in US taxes [Davis:09].

7.4 Subsequent Growth of MNC and CONCH

CONCH now collects the earnings from the sales of Maniacs to the rest of the world outside North America (RoW). It pays its share of MNC's R&D expenses and some of MNC's corporate overhead. For the first 5 years, it also pays amortization and interest on the loan that got it started. CONCH accounts are credited for 20 % of overall SG&A expenses. That amount pays for ATA's charges at CAAS and CONCH, as well as for the reporting costs incurred by the sales divisions. Most selling and administration expenses continue to be borne by MNC in the U.S.

CONCH books the operating income of its three regional sales divisions, MNC EMEA, MNC PFA, and MNC LSA. Over the first 5 years, CONCH booked $752M in operating income. Out of those funds CONCH reimbursed MNC for its share of the R&D costs the parent company incurred, according to the current Ratio of Anticipated Benefits (RAB). CONCH also paid for its share of the acquisitions that closed after the buy-in. The reimbursements are added to MNC's taxable income and appear to increase its earnings. MNC is obliged to spend all that income on the R&D. Compensating MNC for the US taxes due on the transfer of funds increases the share that will be transferred from CONCH accounts to $55.5M [F7.27].

Because CONCH's RoW income grows faster than MNC's overall earnings, CONCH's ownership of MNC's IP grows slightly over the 5-year period. Research at MNC MY in India is paid directly by MNC, and the actual Maniacs built by MNC JB in Malaysia are billed to distributors worldwide at their established Independent Factory Price (IFP).

The earnings accumulating at CONCH during those 5 years amount to \$327M. The growing capital held is invested in secure 3.75 % interest-bearing bonds, adding another \$34M, so the final accumulated capital available is \$373M [F7.28].

Just holding excess capital in an offshore account is not wise. Low-risk, passive investments earn little and don't exploit MNC's intellectual capital. Treasury rules disallow keeping passive income, as bank interest, untaxed offshore [Misey:02]. Offshore capital accumulation has grown manifold; the IRS plans are to focus on high-risk cases [George:11]. MNC interest income, \$23M, is small. MNC's exposure grows, but recovers 5 years later when it can move about \$500M out of the CONCH accounts at low tax rate. MNC did nothing illegal and passed the 3-year statute of limitations [LeveyW:07]. MNC also protected itself by repatriating less than \$500M; companies repatriating more were required to open their books to the IRS [AJCA:04].

MNC did not engage in more complex schemes available to multinational corporations. A US multinational corporation can deduct expenses incurred on offshore projects, while leaving the earnings that are generated offshore and not pay taxes on them. Disallowing most tax incentives until taxes are paid on offshore earnings would increase US tax revenues by over \$60B from 2011 to 2019 [Gibbs:09].

7.4.1 Acquisitions

Acquisitions allow MNC to grow significantly faster than it could have from ongoing internal research and development alone. Options for growth are:

(a) Initiate new R&D efforts to expand its intellectual capital for broad-based growth.
(b) License IP from external sources for further development within MNC.
(c) Acquire companies to grow staff and bring in experience as well as new concepts.
(d) Acquire companies with novel IP to gain a first-mover advantage.
(e) Acquire operational companies that will contribute rapidly to income generation.

The last three choices, acquiring a complementary company, involve selecting successful start-up businesses, but reduce the substantial risk of trying to coax existing R&D staff to be innovative. However, integration of an acquisition into an existing setting requires careful management and substantial efforts.

To summarize the 20 acquisitions made by MNC, they are arranged into two distinct rounds, shown in Fig. 2.8, based on the period when they took place. The

Table 7.3 Acquisition cost-share valuations and results

# Method For cost share		Source of information	Feature	Uncertainty in	Result for CONCH First round	Second round
M8	PP-VM	Purchase price, RAB share	Public	Motivation	$121M	$202M
ATA		Purchase price less selected IP	Contracted	Trusting ATA	$21.0M	$49.7M

initial round took place during the time of the buy-in. A second round was driven by the opportunity created by the reduced taxation rate for repatriated funds provided by the American Jobs Creation Act (AJCA) of 2004 [AJCA:04]. Both rounds are shown in Table 7.3.

7.4.1.1 Initial Round of Acquisitions

About the time of the buy-in, MNC made a number of acquisitions. MNC paid for them with $150M cash and $150M of newly issued shares. MNC's spending on acquisitions was a successful business decision, even as the company continued to spend substantial amounts on internal R&D. After a few years the acquisitions were fully integrated into MNC's business. The acquisition never generated significant independent income. Once operations were integrated the income streams could not be segregated.

The acquisitions will be as valuable to CONCH as to MNC. Because the first round of acquisitions closed after the buy-in valuation was completed, they were excluded from ATA's buy-in valuation. ATA made separate valuations for all acquisitions obtained in the first round. ATA used a purchase price method (PP-VM), omitting tangibles and much intellectual capital, to arrive at a total share for CONCH of $21.0M [F7.29]. Using the same method M8 in Chap. 5 produced an estimate of $121M [F5.52]. The difference is mainly due to ATA assigning 85 % of the acquisition price to "goodwill." A market capitalization, M1, MC-VM, omitting the tangibles, but keeping the control premium, valued the acquisitions at $113M [F7.30].

CONCH actually has an obligation to reimburse MNC for the stock it issued for the other half of the acquisitions. MNC issued new stock for those acquisitions at the time of the buyin. Those obligations were missed and ATA did not include those payments in its assessments, which would have doubled the cost to $42M [F7.31].

The low valuations of the buy-in and the initial acquisitions initiated amazing growth of available capital at CONCH. Without aggressive cost-shared research spending, the offshore capital accumulation would grow to $659M over the subsequent 8 years [F7.32]. MNC's substantial total spending on its internal R&D over that 8-year period amounts already to $1,058M [F7.33]. MNC's research plans cannot effectively accommodate the funds accumulated in CONCH to grow internal research. MNC had no motivation to have CONCH repatriate more than the required R&D cost share and pay full US taxes on repatriated funds it did not need.

7.4.1.2 The Second, AJCA, Round of Acquisitions

As MNC management had hoped, Congress passed the AJCA legislation in 2004. It allowed MNC to repatriate the capital held in CONCH to its US accounts at a low 5.25 % tax rate. During the short window provided by the AJCA incentive, MNC used funds that had been sheltered at CONCH for a second round of purchases of a number of US companies, paying the $475M cost. An additional sum of $26M was transferred to MNC to reimburse MNC for the low taxes due, so that the capital held at CONCH was reduced by $501M [F7.34]. At the end of the AJCA round, only $23M was left in the CONCH accounts [F7.35]. Being the source of funds, CONCH acquired the right to benefit from all the IP obtained in the AJCA round of acquisitions.

ATA performed a valuation for this second round, using the same method it had used for the first round, submitting a result of $107M [F7.36]. Based on that valuation, the share CONCH had to pay became $49.7M. Paying that amount would already have preserved the right of CONCH to collect all foreign earnings. That valuation is much less than the $202M calculated under a simple PP-VM valuation, based on the purchase total of $475M [F5.63]. Those results are also shown in Table 7.3.

7.4.2 The ATA Acquisition Valuations

We analyze now why ATA's acquisition valuations are so low. Because the operations do not remain distinct, income due to prior IP and acquired IP cannot be distinguished and a valuation based on future income is not possible. Valuation methods that depend on comparisons with other operations or on splitting internal benefits fail as well because the operations of the acquiring company, MNC, are so much more mature than those of the acquisitions. The purchase price (M8, PP-VM) must be the primary basis for the valuations.

For the cost-share estimate any assets that are not transferred to CONCH must be subtracted from the purchase price. Tangibles, as real estate, stay in the U.S. or are disposed there. The discrepancies in the valuations are entirely due to ATA's looking at the accounting books and trying to segregate only the explicit IP being made available to CONCH. The discrepancies in the ATA acquisition valuations are listed in Table 7.4. The major discrepancy is that ATA accepted the accountants' booking of goodwill, shown in line E1. As discussed in Chap. 3, any amount that is not explained is just booked as goodwill. There are two major problems with grouping dissimilar types of assets as goodwill:

1. Some types of intellectual assets that would not be available in an arm's-length setting, such as access to ongoing operations, have a high value at CONCH.
2. Some types, such as the value of the trademark or customer lists, can differ in quality and hence value, but any such differences need to be explained.

Table 7.4 Elements omitted in valuations of acquisitions and their effect

Valuation elements	Initial acquisition round			AJCA acquisition round		
Purchase price	\$300M			\$475M		
Acquired US tangibles	\$30M (deduct)			\$41M (deduct)		
Deduct from remainder	ATA reduction and effect			ATA reduction and effect		
E1 Goodwill	\$150M	57 %	43 %	\$210M	48 %	52 %
E2 Control premium	\$30M	11 %	89 %	\$50M	11 %	89 %
E3 Manpower acquired	\$15M	6 %	94 %	\$27M	6 %	94 %
E4 Research in progress	\$25M	9 %	91 %	\$40M	9 %	91 %
E5 Discontinued products	None	0	100 %	\$20M	5 %	95 %
E6 RAB based on sales vs. current earnings	44.8 % → 42 %	6 %	94 %	46.6 % → 42 %	10 %	90 %
Effect of deductions	$1-\prod$ (E1:E6)		Actual	$1-\prod$ (E1:E6)		Actual
Reductions	12 %		17 %	10 %		53 %

Most items that are labeled as "goodwill" in conventional accounting are as beneficial to CONCH as they are to MNC. Many are listed in Table 3.2. Goodwill should be limited to asset types that reflect the corporate reputation, customer lists, and so on. Those are minimal for the acquisitions, all young companies that have not yet brought products to market.

Misclassified IP is easy to write off. Accounting rules requiring the write-off of early stage R&D does not mean that in-progress R&D is irrelevant to the value of the acquisition [SlavinK:06]. In fact, tracing the motivations for MNC's acquisitions, in-progress R&D dominates. Omitting talented manpower, because it remains in the U.S., is inappropriate as well, because the creative workforce of the companies that were acquired provide the know-how to exploit MNC's IP, creating innovations that allow MNC and CONCH to go forward. Some nonroutine income is created by local labor, but most of the actual manufacturing work is already offshore at MNC JB in Malaysia.

For the acquisitions of public companies ATA also deducted a "control premium," based on the amount that the purchase price paid exceeded the market capitalization. Paying a control premium is justified if the acquisition enables new business opportunities for MNC. Those opportunities have an equal value for CONCH.

A computational issue is that ATA continued to use the benefits ratio (RAB) it had used in its earlier valuation reports [F7.29]. In fact, the entire second set of valuation reports were an edit of its initial consulting reports [F7.36]. Because those reports had been accepted by Matthew, the IRS auditor, ATA updated its prior analysis with the new information. That decision allowed ATA to profit greatly as well, reusing its own IP in subsequent consulting reports; those were listed and assessed in Table 3.1as their product type based on IP.

In the AJCA-motivated acquisitions, MNC also obtained some products that were available for sale but that were discontinued. Their effect is shown on line E5 of Table 7.4. The fraction was small, because MNC focused on young companies, just starting up.

Each specific reduction has only a modest effect. Because the deductions are taken successively, the product of the isolated reductions differs from the total effect. Because of the computational interaction, the actual reduction tends to be less than their product.

The funds to pay for the second round of acquisitions were spent and transferred over a 3-year period. CONCH paid $62.7M in each of the eight quarters covered by the AJCA 85 % tax reduction benefit [F7.35]. By the end of that period, CONCH had only $41M left in its offshore accounts, but all the IP remained at CONCH, ensuring that offshore working capital needed by MNC was replenished in a short time and its holdings would grow further.

Even though both rounds of valuations used very similar parameters, their actual results differ greatly. ATA had little incentive to drive down the valuation for the AJCA acquisition, because CONCH was paying the entire cost. All acquired IP rights from these acquisitions are now allocated to CONCH, even while most creative work remains at MNC in California.

We see again that corrections to individual items will require much analysis, and if IP is involved, competence needed for such a task is scarce [AmirLS:03]. Dealing with goodwill requires considering about a dozen of the intellectual asset types listed in Table 3.2. A transfer of specific identified IP to CONCH makes it appear that the IP is beneficial and of value in isolation. Although many IP items can be valued one by one, the totality of the IP and the knowledgeable workforce has much greater value than the sum of the items.

MNC acquired these companies as integrated units, and it paid the price needed to obtain them, with the items it wanted and some items that it did not plan to keep. Even if the price included product lines that are irrelevant to MNC, that issue was investigated and known beforehand. Irrelevant items cannot be valued distinctly and then omitted from CONCH's cost-sharing obligations.

7.4.3 MNC's Motivation for Acquisitions

When we analyze acquisitions in depth, it is important to understand the motivation of management. Some acquisitions may be seen just as an attractive investment, a better place to park excess capital than a bank. Some acquisitions are motivated by access to a distribution channel—for instance, to gain access to military organizations, which tend to rely on trusted suppliers. Yet others provide options for future initiatives, as considered in Fig. 5.12.

Acquiring talented engineers and their research in-progress was the motivation for MNC's acquisitions. Using nineteenth century accounting concepts for industries and ignoring assets that comprise intellectual capital are bound to lead to misvaluations [Lev:01]. We revisit this problem in the recommendations presented in Chap. 10.

For MNC and its peers in the high-technology industry, the value of acquiring a small and young company is in the potentially attractive products they will generate.

An important asset type is a workforce that has the capability to create new and innovative products. There are no sales records yet to allow an income-based valuation. These items are indeed hard for accountants to value.

MNC issued press releases to convince its shareholders that the expenditures, substantial compared to MNC's income, were worthwhile. The motivation given, including terms like "synergies," "rounding out the product line," and "establishing MNC as a leader in its field," indicates the benefits management expected from the acquisitions. MNC's shareholders reacted positively, so the MNC share price stayed high even while the shareholders' equity was diluted by more than 8 % in the first round of acquisitions [F7.37].

For the AJCA round of acquisitions, MNC did not have to dilute its stock. There was, of course, a great reduction in MNC's excessive financial capital holdings, as reported in its consolidated reports over the 24 months of the AJCA low-tax window. Using the same intangible deductions used by ATA in the cost-sharing valuation for CONCH, MNC will put 77 % of the acquisition costs on its books as assets [F7.38]. The offset reduced the shareholders' equity on the books by less than 7 % [F7.39]. Because US accounting does not follow the congruency principle, the company is not obligated to have identical numbers on the corporate books shown to shareholders and the books submitted to the IRS.

7.5 Further Financial Capital Accumulation Offshore

The initial buy-in cost for CONCH was $50M [F7.1]. For that payment CONCH received rights to an income stream valued at $817M [F5.64]. Although not immediately accessible, it amounted to an initial capital gift of $780M [F7.40]. The short-range benefit is sufficient to pay back the loan from MNC that was used to start this offshore financial process.

CONCH also did not have to pay its full share of costs in the first round of acquisitions. Following the ATA valuation, it paid $21M for its share of incremental income due from the acquisitions. This share was valued using the PP-VM at $121M [F5.24]. CONCH can expect to receive $106M additional income if the control premium is not exploited by MNC [F7.41]. If the acquisitions benefit MNC as much as management expects, CONCH expects to gain $119M due to its participation in the cost-sharing arrangement [F7.42].

No loan was required for the second round of acquisitions. By the time the cost-share payment for CONCH's cash share of those acquisitions was due, sufficient offshore earnings had accumulated at CONCH to pay its share.

CONCH paid annually an average of nearly $100M in R&D support to MNC [F7.43]. Those funds were offset by actual R&D expenses at MNC in California and allowed CONCH to continue to collect all offshore earnings. While those are taxable income, they are fully offset by R&D costs, which MNC would be incurring in any case.

About 5 years later MNC participated in lobbying for repatriation of offshore funds at a low tax rate. When the resulting AJCA legislation passed, MNC had

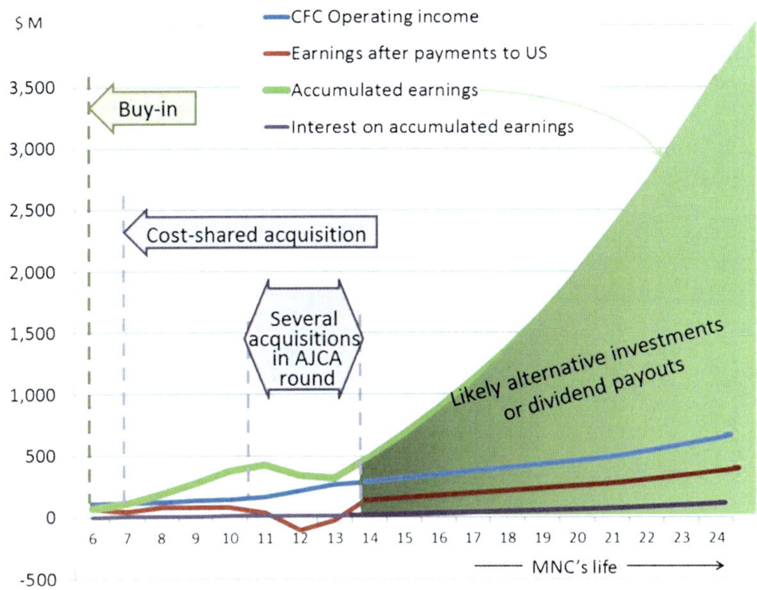

Fig. 7.3 Income leading to offshore capital accumulation at CONCH

CONCH transfer more than \$500M to MNC's US accounts [F7.34]. That much money is not easy to use for a company of the size of MNC. A high-tech company cannot hire qualified employees effectively at a high rate [Brooks:95]. The \$500M exceeds by a factor of 3 the annual cost of MNC's R&D staff in the U.S. and in India [F7.44]. It makes no sense to add much creative staff other than tax experts. By 2004 all manufacturing employees were working in Malaysia. The facilities there can easily keep up with sales.

MNC could have paid large dividends to its shareholders, as some companies did after the AJCA passed [DharmapalaFF:09]. Repatriated funds were not supposed to be used for that purpose, but because money is fungible, repatriated funds could be used to free up other obligations.

Paying dividends is unexpected for growing high-tech companies, and it signals stasis. So MNC used repatriated funds to grow by acquiring a number of start-up companies. The capital growth at CONCH and some of the contribution to financial flows are shown in Fig. 7.3.

Making long-range projections about growth and capital accumulation for further years based on the current window is risky. Certainly MNC will not want to accumulate capital to the extent that it can. It will invest wherever its capital can be profitably employed [Studt:07].

The total value of the excess capital that the low ATA valuation provided to CONCH for the buy-in and the subsequent acquisitions is \$961M [F7.45]. The actual amounts are realized over time, but they keep growing beyond the scope of the valuation analyses performed during the transactions. Unrealistic buy-ins cause companies to accumulate much capital offshore, and that capital wants to be employed. Whenever funds are transferred to the U.S., taxes will be due at current tax rates. Investments outside of the U.S. and dividends paid to shareholders who establish a domicile outside the U.S. will not be taxed. It all can be viewed as gift from US taxpayers.

7.6 Intellectual Capital Rights Accumulation Offshore

The obvious choice to use the available capital was to acquire companies in the same line of business. MNC had to compete with other companies that had also taken advantage of the AJCA tax break. MNC obtained $434M in intangible assets with the acquisitions [F7.46].

The companies acquired in the second round were not as carefully selected. MNC gained 200 employees and some product lines that were soon written off at $20M [F7.47]. The long-range benefit was relatively less than the benefit gained from the first round of acquisitions. Several of the acquired businesses were closed, and only a few of their creative staff were retained. The new acquisitions did provide the workforce and IP to create the novel Manimobile.

Most remaining operations were merged, allowing MNC to reduce redundant selling and administrative staff. Even though sales did not increase proportionally to the investment, MNC was soon back to its level of 12 % SG&A based on its gross income [F7.48]. Judging from R&D expenses 5 years later, when all integration was complete, MNC's R&D employment has grown only moderately. At least half of the acquired employees quit or were let go, reducing MNC's overhead costs, but an unintended consequence of the AJCA act [F7.49].

From the acquisitions enabled by the AJCA, CONCH obtained the rights to a larger share of MNC's nonroutine income. Once all of the acquisitions in the AJCA round are paid for, CONCH has the right to book over 70 % of MNC's total nonroutine earnings, even though the sales in the CONCH RoW region are still less than 50 % [F7.50].

CONCH continued its cost-sharing payments to MNC based on the current, nearly 50 % RAB. The benefits have increased, so CONCH has to pay a bit more. The investment in R&D at MNC in California is very profitable, so those increased costs are offset by the large share of MNC income that is booked offshore at CONCH.

MNC's offshore capital holdings continue to grow. Without further investments they would reach well over $1,350M in the 5 years beyond the AJCA acquisitions [F7.51]. MNC's directors and their peers are again ready to lobby for another opportunity to repatriate capital to the U.S. at a low tax rate [Drucker:10C]. The fact that the IP rights stay offshore is ignored by proponents of repatriation of financial capital [Huntsman:11].

7.7 Summary

We see in this chapter how advantageous to MNC's finances and growth ATA's low valuations of transferred and acquired intellectual capital are. They allow the establishment and growth of a profitable taxhaven assignment that diverts about half of MNC's income in the first 7 years and more than 70 % forever after. To add insult to injury, the funds that MNC transfers overseas, so that CONCH can buy access to MNC's intellectual capital, are regarded as a foreign direct investment and get a favorable tax treatment from recipient countries.

After all the shifting MNC taxable income is only $110M from sales in the US and another $100M for the R&D it performed for CONCH, about 2/3 % of its worldwide earnings [F7.50]. We assume that MNC pays corporate taxes on US income at the average corporate 2008 tax rate of 21.0 % [IRS-ST:09]. The combined effect of an average US corporate rate and no taxes on earnings retained offshore is that MNC paid less than 16 % taxes on its worldwide earnings.

After the second round of acquisitions, the annual tax paid to the IRS becomes $26M plus $24M on the cost-sharing payments repatriated from CONCH that support R&D at MNC in California and India, or a 5.8 % effective rate [F7.52]. The final Fig. 7.4 shows where MNC's earnings are generated and where the money winds up. On the left side is the offshore contribution. The center bar shows the earnings booked in the U.S. after all costs have been subtracted. Part of the US earnings is also sheltered from US taxation after the AJCA acquisitions. The right-hand bar shows where the earnings are collected. After taxes, those are US corporate profits. Over 70 % of MNC's earnings wind up in its offshore taxhaven for further investments [F7.53]. In the end, more than twice the capital is accumulated offshore vs. profits booked for MNC US while the offshore sales revenues are now 50 % of total sales. MNC US does pay taxes on its third of total earnings.

The imbalance of profits booked in the U.S. vs. untaxed earnings booked offshore was created because ATA selected and computed the valuation according to a single "best method" which neglected much of the intellectual capital being made available to MNC's offshore subsidiary, CONCH. No cross-checks, using other methods, as shown in Chap. 5, were made by MNC's management or by Mathew, the IRS auditor. Shareholders were not clear about the actions, and would in any case find it hard to understand long-term effects of offshore initiatives. Not using all the information reduces the likelihood of a fair valuation. The majority of the effort that created and marketed MNC's innovative products occurred in its California facilities. Just getting reimbursed for R&D costs is inadequate. If MNC were to pay

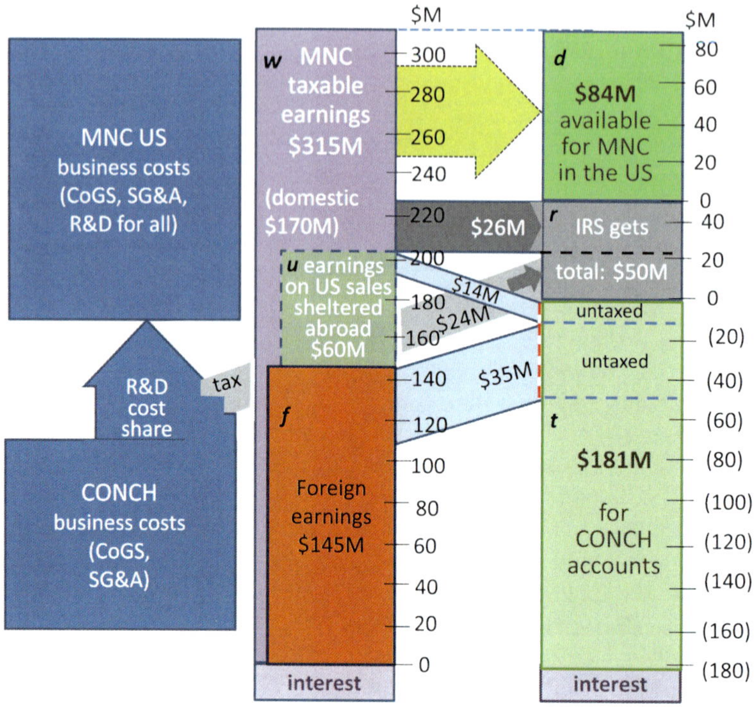

Fig. 7.4 MNC income and tax flow

dividends to its shareholders those payments would come out of the earnings collected in the USA. Currently the shareholders are happy with capital gains due to the increasing share prices of MNC. If MNC's management invests wisely, MNC's share prices will continue to rise.

Once a business model is based on exploiting a misvaluation, it cannot be reversed. The government, including the IRS, cannot force a business to change its structure to correct the effect of a past misvaluation. Chapter 8 reviews the capabilities of the IRS to deal with poor valuations.

What is best for the taxpayer is unlikely to be seen as the fair choice by an IRS economist. Conflicts ensue, both in specific cases and in national policies that attempt to assure fair taxation [deMooij:05].

The advantages created by offshore investments are not available to US companies that invest at home. Obtaining the tax benefits from becoming a multinational takes many years.

Saint Mathew is the patron saint of accountants and tax collectors.

St. Mathew the Accountant Tenders his Accounts (2009).
Courtesy of Tobias Stanislas Haller, BSG

Chapter 8
US Taxation

Every country needs money to run its government. A government can collect fees for the services it provides, but countries other than taxhavens spend much more than fees alone can provide. In particular, services such as national defense and welfare cannot be supported by user fees. It is also impractical to use fees to support all of a country's infrastructure. Roads, education, and fundamental research provide benefits to all residents. To be able to spend the money needed for such benefits, governments collect taxes from individuals, businesses, and transactions among them. This chapter describes the US system; many countries have a similar structure.

8.1 Authority and Means to Collect Tax

In the USA the authority to levy taxes derives from the Constitution.

The Congress shall have power

> *To lay and collect Taxes, Duties, Imposts and Excises, to pay the Debts and provide for the common Defence and general Welfare of the United States; but all Duties, Imposts and Excises shall be uniform throughout the United States [U.S. Const:1787, Art.1, §8.1].*

The US Congress makes the laws that determine taxation.

The execution of tax laws is assigned to the US Department of the Treasury. Taxes are collected by a unit of the Treasury, the Internal Revenue Service (IRS). Its Large Business and International (LB&I) division is responsible for collecting taxes from companies like MNC. LB&I employs a variety of personnel, including

1. Revenue officers, responsible for the actual collection of money.
2. Revenue agents, responsible for reviewing and auditing tax returns.
3. Economists, responsible for valuations when questions arise about a tax return.
4. Engineers, specialists in technical domains, to provide data for economists.
5. Lawyers, to resolve disputes when taxpayers disagree with tax assessments.

For major controversies the IRS also engages external consultants.

G. Wiederhold, *Valuing Intellectual Capital: Multinationals and Taxhavens*, Management for Professionals 23, DOI 10.1007/978-1-4614-6611-6_8,

Table 8.1 Main categories of US government revenues [F8.3]

Source of federal tax revenue	1978 Amount $M	1978 % of US spending	1993 Amount $M	1993 % of US spending	2008 Amount $M	2008 % of US spending
Individuals	181,000	39 %	495,000	35 %	1,146,000	39 %
Payroll	123,400	27 %	418,000	30 %	900,000	31 %
Large businesses	60,000	13 %	99,000	7 %	304,000	10 %
Other	37,600	8 %	88,000	6 %	174,000	6 %
Total revenues	402,000	88 %	1,100,000	78 %	2,155,000	86 %
Total US spending	459,000	100 %	1,410,000	100 %	2,931,000	100 %
US nominal GDP	2,217,000	1/21 %	6,667,400	1/21 %	14,369,100	1/20 %

To sketch the scope of the task the IRS faces, Table 8.1 shows major annual revenues collected by the US Treasury by category, relative to US government spending at 15-year intervals. The amounts are not inflation-adjusted, but that doesn't matter when looking at the percentages. The percentages shown are based on the actual total spending by the federal government; after all, that's what the taxes are for. The spending amounts include expenses that were not anticipated in the president's budget, recently close to 20 % [OMB:11A]. The deficit varies from 12 % to 26 % in those 30 years. The total government spending relative to the nominal US Gross Domestic Product (GDP) is presented in inverted form to show the fraction of the US GDP that is being spent by the federal government.

Payroll taxes to support Social Security and Medicare benefits are collected as contributions from employers and by withholding from employee wages, or by taxing self-employed individuals directly. Minor sources of federal revenues include gift, estate, and excise taxes.

In 2006 the IRS spent just over 0.5 % of the total tax revenues to collect those revenues [F8.1]. A sample study that did not consider taxhavens estimated that at least 15 % more total revenue could have been collected if all tax returns were audited and the missing taxes paid [F8.2].

8.1.1 History

Funds for the US government came initially from import duties or tariffs, even though such taxes levied by the British Government in 1773 on imports of tea had sparked the US Revolution. Other early sources were excise taxes on specific goods considered to be luxuries and stamp taxes on documents, eventually including even photographs. Some such taxes remain; they provide about $15B annually to the federal government [TTB:11]. The IRS was established in 1862 with the right to collect federal taxes.

Income taxes were first levied by the federal government during the American Civil War, but they were allowed to lapse in 1872. In 1886 the US Supreme Court

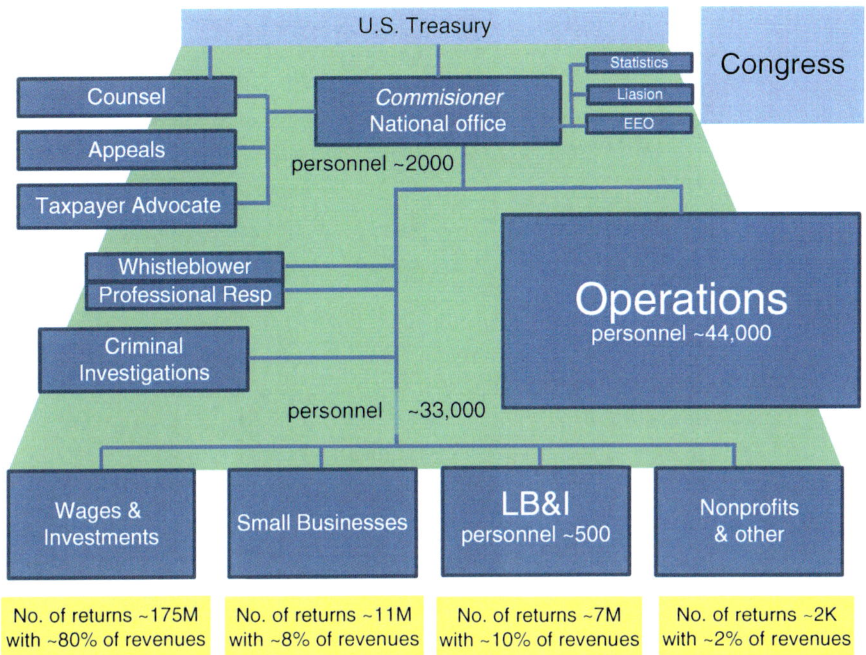

Fig. 8.1 Functional organization of the IRS [Daily:02]

assigned to corporations the concept of legal "personhood," giving them the right to free speech and implicitly making them subject to taxation on their income [Harlan:1886]. A corporate income tax was enacted in 1894, but was held unconstitutional in 1895. Federal direct income taxes were again enabled by the 16th Amendment in 1909 and eventually ratified in 1913, with corporations paying an excise tax on sales. Corporations were taxed in the lowest taxable bracket for individuals, 1 %.

World events affected tax rates. During World War I tax rates increased. Corporations paid 12 % and were also subject to a "war profits tax" of up to 60 % of excess profits or 9 % on invested capital. During the depression, President Herbert Hoover had to raise the rate for major corporations to 15 %, and individuals paid a top rate of 63 % to compensate for loss of revenues.

Payroll taxes started in 1937, when the Social Security system was initiated, 2 years after the enabling law was passed [SSA:11]. Taxes to support distinct Social Security trust funds are collected according to the Federal Insurance Contributions Act (FICA). Between 1968 and 1986 trust funds were integrated into a unified federal budget. Table 8.1 shows the amounts within the overall federal budget. Figure 8.1 shows the flow through the IRS to the Treasury.

During World War II the corporate tax rate went up to 40 %, and the individual top rate was raised to 94 %. Rates were reduced slightly after the war, but were raised again to 52 % and 91 % during the Korean War. President John F. Kennedy reduced the top rates to 46 % and 70 %. In 1986 President Ronald Reagan reduced the marginal rate to 39 %, making the overall rate for large corporations 34 % and the top rate for individuals 50 % [HallR:07]. At the time this book is being written, the rate for medium-sized and large corporations (ones with more than $18.3M taxable earnings) is 35 %. Unless stated specifically, all calculations shown in this book are based on that statutory 35 % federal corporate rate. The marginal rate at that level is now 38 % [IRS-1120:11]. The majority of the business taxes listed in Table 8.1 are corporate taxes.

8.1.2 Organization of the IRS

The staff of the IRS is substantial; there are about 95,000 employees at all levels, of whom about a half process more than 125 million tax documents received each year [IRS-ED:10]. A third focus on the contents of the returns [F8.4]. Others deal with Congress [JCT-18:12]. The IRS has four divisions which actually collect taxes [HedemannSP:10].

1. Individual returns ~175M with ~80 % of revenues
2. Small business returns ~11M with ~8 % of revenues
3. Large and international business returns ~7M with ~10 % of revenues
4. Other returns ~2K with ~2 % of revenues

Congress has assigned to the IRS substantial responsibilities to administer disbursements. While originally IRS disbursements were limited to refunding overpaid taxes, since 1975 other legislated initiatives require the IRS to issue checks to persons who are not required to pay taxes. The initial benefit handled by the IRS was the Earned Income Tax Credit (EITC), now supplemented by many other benefits and rebates [SanJuan:11]. Those disbursements add much to the IRS workload [Olson:11]. We will continue to focus on corporate taxation.

8.2 Current Corporate Taxation

Taxes for corporations with assets greater than $10M are handled by a distinct division of the IRS. It was created as part of the IRS reforms initiated after 2000 and at the time was called the Large and Mid-Size Business (LMSB) Division [RothEa:98]. It has since been renamed the Large Business and International Division (LB&I) [LB&I:10]. Before 2000 all tax returns were examined within one of the 33 local districts [SanJuan:11]. The reorganization improved services needed to deal with large corporations in specific industries [Rossotti:05].

Within LB&I there is a further specialization by industry. About 20 major industry sectors are now grouped into five subdivisions. MNC was in the sector "Manufacturers," those sectors are being realigned [Trivedi:12]. Manufacturers, Data Processing, Technology, and Pharmaceutical companies depend greatly on their intellectual capital. Many businesses in those sectors operate globally and benefit from differences in taxation and incentives. Within LB&I national specialists focus on transfer pricing. There is also a "Global High Wealth" taxpayers industry subdivision.

The industry specialization within LB&I helps IRS staff to understand the technical business aspects of those taxpayers. As these industries become more knowledge- and IP-based, the most valuable assets are not on the books [BarlettS:00]. Because reported tax amounts due to taxhaven strategies change gradually, as seen in Fig. 2.6, it is hard to recognize when tax avoidance becomes extreme. A stronger focus on international transfer pricing cases in 2011 is intended to address that issue [Schuster:11]. Increased workloads and reduced budgets place stress on IRS operations, but more funding is requested for 2013 [GAO:12].

8.2.1 Dealing with Large Enterprises

Very large businesses, with revenues in the billions and hence tax obligations of commensurate size, have IRS examiners and revenue agents on site all year. For other large companies, IRS staff is shared among multiple taxpayers in a region. International examiners will be assigned to companies like MNC that have a substantial international profile. Over time the local IRS staff develops a deep insight into the workings of a particular company. Such business-specific knowledge is essential for understanding the many documents that support tax returns. When questions arise, more documents will be requested [Deloitte:10]. All those documents fill numerous file cabinets and many CDs. They are gathered from a variety of internal sources, contain much irrelevant material, and are often in formats that are inconvenient for IRS use [GAO:07]. Valuations of IP exports and acquisitions may need to be reviewed by an IRS economist. An IRS expert engineer will help the economist understand technical arguments made by the taxpayer about products, processes, and IP creation and life [Stewart:11]. The quantity of data is often vast and complex [Johnson:05S].

To reduce the possibility of collusion of IRS staff with the taxpayer, IRS staff at a local corporate taxpayer site rotates regularly. For a business, a change of staff reduces intellectual capital. When IRS staff auditing MNC rotated in 2003, valuable knowledge about MNC's operations disappeared, and the new assignees had to start over.

Organizational complexity is another hurdle. In 1899 the state of New Jersey first permitted a corporation to own another corporation. That privilege spread rapidly [PalanMC:10]. Our MNC owns seven offshore divisions, one for research support in India, one for production in Malaysia, three for worldwide distribution, and two shell entities supporting international tax avoidance. An actual multinational corporation may have well over 50 offshore subsidiaries serving the various functions of its international operations. In many jurisdictions the actual owners do not need to be identified [Shulman:10D].

The flow of corporate responsibility is tortuous as well [ResslerM:11]. MNC's office in California controls MNC's research and production divisions, as well as the intermediary conduit division in The Netherlands, CAAS [vanDijkWM:06]. MNC's CFH in Palm Island, CONCH, forms a distinct group with its three offshore distribution divisions. We ignore throughout MNC's divisions in the USA, its nominal corporate headquarters in Delaware and MNC's licensing division in Nevada. Actual multinationals are assembled into much more complex structures, often many levels deep. Their organization charts extend over many pages. Subsidiary divisions have amazing interlocking ownerships [Collins:11I].

As we saw in Chap. 6, several types of corporate divisions, located in jurisdictions that provide specific advantages, interplay in tax avoidance. The actual reason for their existence is not explained to the public.

8.2.2 Corporate Costs of Taxation

A study commissioned by the IRS more than 25 years ago estimated that all businesses spent 3,614 million hours that year on record keeping, data processing, learning the rules, and filling in and submitting tax forms [ADLittle:85]. Corporate compliance costs were twice as much in total as individual compliance costs, and amounted to over 15 % of the tax corporate tax revenue [Payne:93]. These amounts did not include costs for tax planning and taxhaven operations. The costs would have increased greatly since then. The overhead percentage will have increased even more as tax avoidance efforts grew while collection of corporate taxes diminished.

The cost of dealing with foreign-source income has been assessed at 8.5 % of the tax paid on foreign income, but that ratio does not consider how much potentially taxable revenue was sheltered by this effort [BlumenthalS:06]. It makes sense for MNC to let ATA spend substantial amounts to reduce its tax liabilities [CBO:12].

A proponent of the flat tax counts a total 500,000 people involved in all forms of tax activities, including 70,000 lobbyists. The cost is about $35B annually [HallR:07].

8.2.3 Corporate Privacy

Corporations rightly worry about having their trade secrets leaked to competitors [Scheier:11]. Public corporations must supply selected data to the Securities and Exchange Commission (SEC). Any information that a company has to deliver by law or regulations to the IRS must be kept private, although the Freedom of Information Act (FoIA) allows access in certain cases [Roberts:11]. While shareholders are considered to be the owners of public corporations, they don't gain any access privileges to corporate information.

The IRS protects tax returns and related data carefully. IRS staff, working already under strict rules of confidentiality versus external entities, have additional internal restrictions imposed on them. To protect corporate privacy, specific findings can be presented only in formally organized and scripted meetings. IRS staff members are not allowed to discuss cases with other IRS staff who are not assigned to the case [B.1.1 §6103(h)(1)]. IRS staff are even prohibited from making abstract opinions public [Kennedy:06]. Those constraints make it nearly impossible to discern novel patterns of questionable tax avoidance by taxpayers.

Legal advice provided to a taxpayer is protected by the lawyer's attorney–client privilege rules [Terr:10]. The privilege does not extend to documents used to prepare a tax return [LeveyW:07]. Banking secrecy laws in several jurisdictions provide additional protection. Banks threatened with disclosure requirements at home are now establishing subsidiaries where oversight is less [Daly:11].

No legal restrictions are imposed on corporations or their advising firms that would constrain their sharing of information. Even competing companies share tax avoidance approaches that have passed IRS scrutiny through shared staff and directors. ATA is one of about a dozen advising companies sufficiently competent to structure corporate international tax avoidance strategies; it has many customers. ATA will reapply its experience about methods that work when helping other customers. Taxpayer and advisor interactions are protected by the ability to ship and store the advice and the taxpayer's documents in encrypted form [BarlettS:00]. The IRS cannot request documents when it has no evidence of their existence or relevance.

8.3 Worldwide and Territorial Taxation

Under a worldwide taxation regime, a corporation is taxed on a residence basis—that is, in the jurisdiction where the company declares its domicile to be. All of its global income and expenses are to be reported there, and its taxes are then adjusted there for concurrent taxation elsewhere. The assumption is that control over all its finances is vested at its domicile. The alternative is territorial taxation, taxing the company in each jurisdiction only on local revenue [JCT:06].

8.3.1 Worldwide Taxation

The USA, China, Japan, Korea, the UK, and some other countries tax their residents, in principle, on their worldwide income. Japan and the UK allow an increasing percentage of qualified foreign earnings to be deducted from corporate taxable earnings [GaukeEa:10]. To avoid deducting earnings that are transferred from primary taxhavens, Japan does not qualify deductions of dividends transferred from countries that have a tax rate of less than 25 % and, in the absence of a tax treaty, levies full taxation on them [Miyatake:09]. The rule caused The Netherlands to keep their corporate tax rate just above 25 % [vanDijkWM:06]. Countries, such as the USA, with worldwide taxation, allow foreign taxes paid to be credited.

Countries that have invested much in generating intellectual capital desire that the nonroutine earnings generated anywhere should benefit the creators [LevN:04]. Worldwide taxation requires collecting worldwide information from the corporation. Taxes to be paid must then be allocated according to clear criteria and mutual agreements in tax treaties [LeveyW:07]. The complexity to do so fairly can be overwhelming [GaukeEa:10]. The IRS has to rely on the completeness and correctness of worldwide information provided by its taxpayers [Terr:10].

Suggestions have been made to share information needed for the application of regulations and taxation among governments worldwide [RazinS:90]. Getting every country to agree to share information needed for taxation is unlikely. Some information desired globally is not collected, for instance where no local taxes are levied by some jurisdiction [NDT:11]. When pressure has been exerted, unwilling jurisdictions have found ways to satisfy the rules formally, but not in any meaningful way [Sharman:06]. Under these conditions it is tempting for multinational corporations not to report details of offshore operations that would increase their taxes. Because of these circumstances, it seems "administratively not feasible to tax on a residence basis" [Slemrod:95].

The rules about where a person can establish domicile differ greatly among countries, and in jurisdictions where corporations are accorded personhood, corporations inherit privileges initially granted to individuals. While natural persons are not allowed to own other persons, a corporation can own subsidiary corporations, assign their domicile, and control their actions.

8.3.2 Territorial Taxation

The alternative to worldwide taxation is territorial taxation. With territorial tax, taxes are only imposed on revenue collected in a country. It is a widely used traditional standard and is easy to administer [Carroll:32]. The problem is that the tax base can disappear when taxable earnings for goods produced and sold locally are collected elsewhere, perhaps in a taxhaven.

Territorial taxation assumes that distribution and sales outside of the country that produced them are booked just as merchanting income and costs, and that the net earnings are remitted to the country that produced the goods. Those exports would be documented in customs and the earnings can then be taxed. For nonroutine earnings derived from products with substantial IP such accounting fails. Even if customs office documents an export of a CD, it cannot reliably determine its value. Is it a 10 cent blank, is it a $10 music performance, a $1000 software system, or a master for a product to be duplicated which will earn $100,000? Under territorial rules, the fact that those earnings wind up in a taxhaven jurisdiction, and will not be taxed at all, is immaterial.

The ability to move IP rights nearly invisibly into a taxhaven linked to a territorial jurisdiction causes that jurisdiction to lose tax revenues. Even if transfer prices for goods sold there are reported, they are often unrealistic [deMooij:05]. Mispricing is hard to notice when the scope of tax authorities is limited to territorial constraints, as shown in Example 8.1.

Example 8.1 Recognizing Worldwide Territorial Imbalances

A global company, Happy Bytes, with a branch in Tanna, sells half-pound hamburgers made with meat shipped from its main plant in Kansas City, KS. If Happy Bytes sells the meat for 20 cents/pound to its branch in Tanna, its profits in Tanna will be large, but the US division will lose income on that part of its business, allowing it to deduct the losses from its income from sales in the USA and pay lower US taxes. Happy Bytes' global corporate earnings will be greater, because taxes on food production in Vanuatu are minimal. Matt, the tax inspector in Kansas City, might notice a mismatch of incoming and outgoing shipping records, suspect that something is not right, and follow up.

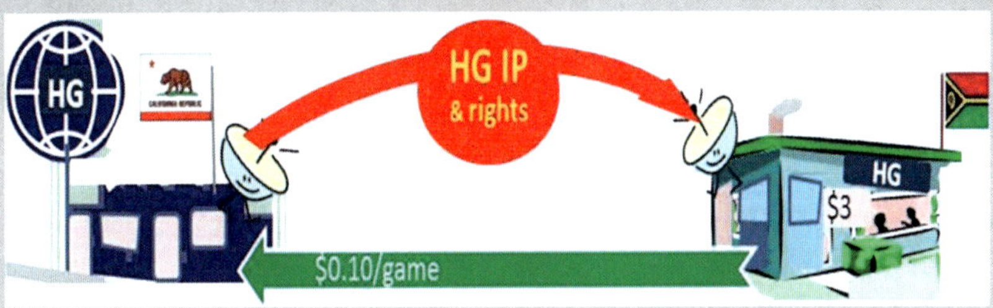

Another global company, Happy Games, with a branch in Tanna, sells game CDs made by copying a master file transmitted from its development studio in Culver City, CA. The blanks are supplied from the Philippines. If Happy Games licenses the right to make a copy for sale for 10 cents/CD to its branch in Tanna, the profits in Tanna will be large, but the US division loses income on that part of its business and pays less in US taxes. Happy Games' global corporate earnings will be greater, because taxes on manufacturing in Vanuatu are minimal. Mateo, the tax inspector in Culver City, must access worldwide business data for Happy Games [LeveyW:07].

8.3.2.1 State Taxation as an Example

Determining the jurisdiction where products are actively sold, the "nexus," has been an issue among US states for a long time, but now the concerns are global [Rashkin:07]. The US states of Delaware and Nevada provide an example of exploiting territorial boundaries. Any activity that is not physically bound to a "nexus" in a US state can be assigned to a domestic subsidiary located in any state [GriffithS:09]. For instance, most Internet sales are booked and untaxed in Nevada [DuhiggK:12]. Within the USA, public businesses are still under purview of the SEC. Worldwide, the prime institution concerned with taxation, the OECD, has no enforceable authority [Christians:09].

8.3.2.2 Financial Transactions

Pure territorial taxation allows income from financial capital to escape taxation by moving it to a taxhaven and collecting interest there from investments anywhere in the world [Hampton:96]. Capital can move very rapidly among jurisdictions [GrubertA:08]. Foreign inbound investments are rarely taxed, hoping that they will spur economic activities [Lewis:11].

If investments are actively used for growing companies, benefits will accrue to the investor, and should generate taxable earnings after some time [WilliamsF:06]. That expectation motivates tax incentives allowing foreign earnings and interest to be held offshore for ongoing operations (Appendix E).

Capital shifted just to avoid paying taxes will only garner passive income, primarily as interest payments or arm's-length dividends. Most countries view moving capital to avoid their taxes on interest income as tax evasion. To patch that loophole, even countries that use a fundamentally territorial approach to taxation still attempt to tax passive income worldwide.

It is hard to discern if a transfer or retention of financial capital is motivated by making active investment or by passive tax avoidance. Formulating a clear distinction between passive use and active use is impossible. A "blocker" statement can be filed with the SEC asserting that funds are intended for active offshore use [Wunder:09]. The large amounts of capital being held in taxhavens by corporations are invariably labeled as "active" and being "subject to management's decision to indefinitely reinvest those earnings" [Immelt:11, p. 35]. This book ignores misuse of transfers of financial capital, an issue that has already been widely lambasted [Shaxson:11].

8.3.2.3 Shifting Intellectual Capital

The fact that intellectual capital is even easier to move around than financial capital is generally ignored in discussions of worldwide versus territorial taxation. The failure to understand the role of IP leads to ineffective policy recommendations.

It is the use of IP in taxhavens that allows financial capital to grow tremendously. As sketched in Fig. 8.2, repatriating financial capital, as MNC did in 2005 under the AJCA, does not return the IP rights back to the USA [DavisRKM:11].

Having those rights allows holding companies located in taxhaven jurisdictions to continue to accumulate earnings [CoyD:11]. A large multinational company with stable overall revenue and earnings had a 5.5-fold growth of offshore corporate capital in 5 years, giving it an amount that is not justifiable by needs of working capital for foreign operations [F8.5].

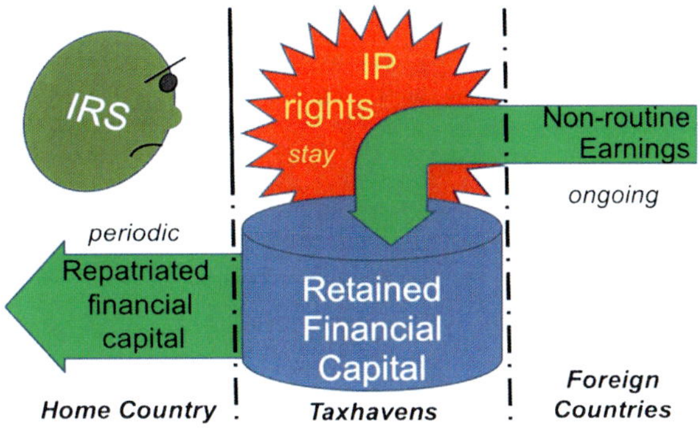

Fig. 8.2 Intellectual capital rights stay offshore while it begets financial capital

8.3.3 Worldwide Versus Territorial Taxation

Presentation of the two alternatives, residence-based worldwide taxation or source-of-revenue-based territorial taxation, illustrates a conundrum—both alternatives fail, but for different reasons.

Basing taxes on worldwide income is often chided as being double taxation, because both foreign governments and the USA can levy taxes [PalettaMcK:11]. That issue is best dealt with independently, and is covered in Sect. 8.6.1. The prime motivation for worldwide taxation is to gain visibility into the effects of international financial and perhaps even intellectual capital flow [Shulman:08]. Being fair is a secondary issue.

From a top-level view, an advantage of the worldwide system is that a US company would pay the same amount of tax whether its earnings are domestic or foreign, so there should be no bias toward foreign investment. An advantage of the territorial system is that the US company investing offshore is taxed the same as other investors in that foreign country.

Corporate tax avoidance in either system is enabled by transfer of rights to non-routine earnings to a taxhaven [TuerffEa:08]. Tax avoidance using taxhavens is easier when a company is operating in countries with territorial taxation, as we saw in the Double Irish strategy in Chap. 6, where IP rights and the nonroutine profits that follow are in a Caribbean taxhaven out of Irish reach. To avoid taxation in the worldwide approach, the Dutch Sandwich strategy has to be used to assure that revenues are not visible to tax authorities. In both cases, misvaluation of intellectual assets assigned to a taxhaven increases the leverage [Shay:12]. Even worldwide taxation does not provide visibility into holdings and effects of intellectual capital.

Although the UK, like the USA, taxes on a worldwide basis, since 1957 UK-based businesses owned by non-UK residents are no longer subject to UK financial controls [Palan:06]. This rule greatly benefits the prominence of the City of London as a financial center [Roberts:08].

Some US politicians advocate switching to territorial taxation [Huntsman:11]. The scope of such a move is hard to assess for outsiders, since after 1996 income from foreign entities can be consolidated, making worldwide operations less obvious [IRS-PS:96]. The European Union (EU) is modifying its Savings Tax Directive to extend its members' current territorial approach to cover all of the EU, and levy taxes by actual residence of the beneficial owner [PalanMC:10].

8.4 The Taxpayer Chooses the Methods for Its Business

The IRS cannot tell a taxpayer how to run or value its business. For instance, it is not illegal for a company to pay large salaries and bonuses to reduce its taxable income. Investing in overseas operations is also a business decision beyond the concern of the IRS. Only when it appears that decisions are motivated solely by tax avoidance can questions be raised. Moving activities offshore has many motivations and involves multiple phases. As shown in, Sect. 7.3, any use of questionable practices is seen mainly in the outcomes, many years later.

For a transfer of substantial intellectual assets a valuation is required. A taxpayer can use any of the methods spelled out in the regulations to value a buy-in or an acquisition. Even unspecified methods can be used if the taxpayer presents a good argument that the alternative methods are not reliable [B.3.3(d)]. ATA will choose a method that is most advantageous to the taxpayer. Not choosing the most favorable method for the business violates the shareholders' expectation of maximizing profits in the business they own. Then the taxpayer can sit back and see if the valuation will be challenged.

A taxpayer who sets up a business strategy counting on substantial tax benefits would not use the same strategy if those benefits did not exist. Taxes, if significant, always distort actions versus what would be done in their absence [AltshulerHT:10]. An expectation that a firm will be able to avoid a portion of its taxes will affect its business plans [LeveyWC:06].

MNC would not have been able to set up CONCH without the very low buy-in valuation of the IP. CONCH could not have raised the amount required to pay for the valuation estimated in Sect. 5.2. Without being able to accumulate capital in CONCH and to later use those funds to make acquisitions, MNC might not have been able to develop and sell ManiMobiles.

It takes the IRS many years, eight in one actual case, to complete a complex audit, try to settle with the taxpayer, go through appeals, and obtain a court judgment [Veritas:09]. During that time the taxpayer has made and executed business decisions based in part on the expected profits after taxes in the USA and offshore. The IRS has up to 3 years to find fault with a tax return, unless it is outright fraudulent [LII:92, §6501].

Even if the IRS shows that the valuation method applied was faulty, and the valuation needs to be redone, yielding higher payments, the path that the company has taken cannot be undone. Having to change a business as it is constituted will hurt the existing competitive position of a taxpayer [AlmDM:04].

The final recommendation in Chap. 10, R20, to abolish corporate taxation entirely, is in part based on the observation that past actions, based on opportunities made available to make US businesses more competitive in the worldwide market place, cannot be undone. A large fraction of US worldwide businesses operate globally, and keeps financial and rights to intellectual capital in places where it is sheltered and available for effective deployment [GAO:09]. Stopping future flows, as envisaged in updated regulations, will not alter the current situation.

8.5 Controversies

Controversies in taxation imply conflicting interpretations of regulations. We avoid legal issues here, but in Chap. 7 it was shown that valuation results can differ greatly using the same regulations and methods. The valuation that ATA produced for the buy-in was an order of magnitude less than those produced by other valuations: \$50M versus \$800M. The difference was due not to any single drastic misestimation, but to a combination of ten factors, which all combined to greatly reduce the expected share of earnings due to the IP transferred to CONCH [F7.19]. If the IRS selects MNC for an audit, a controversy will ensue.

8.5.1 Controversial Valuations

Observing that the MNC buy-in valuation appears to be low, the IRS examiner, Mateo, has to determine why the valuation does not match business expectations. If a simple adjustment is adequate and the taxpayer agrees, the case can be closed.

Dealing with a controversy requires much effort by the taxpayer and IRS staff, and joint planning and cooperation are recommended [LeveyW:07]. In a transfer pricing situation more data about the taxhaven entities can be requested [OConnor:08]. If MNC were audited, the IRS examiner will notice that there is no actual MNC staff at CONCH and CAAS and that the Hilversum address in The Netherlands is shared with dozens of unrelated corporations. It is unlikely that CONCH and CAAS contributed valuable IP.

To produce an alternate valuation the IRS has to redo much of the work that was previously performed by the taxpayer. Mateo will have access to the taxpayer's income data. The taxpayer had a much larger staff, instant access to the all the data, and a number of years to accumulate the information. The IRS gives preference to the "best method" selected by the taxpayer, so that alternative valuations as shown in Table 7.1 may not be considered [B.3.1 (1)(c)]. In that case, the data supporting the taxpayer's results become the focus.

For an alternative valuation the income method, M2, Inc-VM in Chap. 5, is a principled choice. Estimates of future offshore income, as needed for the income method, will have to be requested or projected. Projections must be based on information available at the time the taxpayer's valuation was created. Presenting an alternative valuation easily leads to controversies [LeveyW:07]. Arguing about faults in valuation methods is not very hard, because any method that has to predict future income will have weaknesses. It is difficult to get close to perfection in complex valuations. The taxpayer may claim that an alternative approach used by the IRS was "arbitrary, capricious, or unreasonable" [Kroll:06]. In general it is wise to avoid controversies and seek a settlement [DyeGG:07].

If the controversy reaches the courts, any inconsistencies will be used by lawyers to support their position [Morgan:10]. Even the regulations may be attacked as not being consistent with the laws that they implement [Clausing:05]. Now the IRS also has to defend the complexity introduced by the US Congress. Such challenges have become harder to mount [Bennett:11].

8.5.2 Penalties

Penalties can be imposed on proven tax evasion, but the penalties are modest compared to the potential benefits and the low risk of actual prosecution [B1.1 §6662-§7201]. The penalty for a corporation not providing required documentation to the IRS is \$50,000, or \$200,000 for specified "listed" transactions. The largest penalties for tax evasion are a doubling of the tax due and a \$0.5M penalty for a corporation [B1.1 §6672].

In 1998, in response to perceived taxpayer abuse by IRS staff, penalties and authority to seize property were greatly reduced [BarlettS:00]. The statute of limitations for enforcement is typically 3 years [LeveyW:07]. There are no requirements that American taxpayers or their agents report offshore, extraterritorial transfers among their foreign accounts, limiting the ability of the IRS to determine whether taxpayers are paying what they owe [Gibbs:09].

Those penalties do not stop corporate taxpayers or their advisors. A standard clause in advisors' reports is that the proposals are "more likely than not" acceptable to the IRS [Shaw:06]. That clause allows a taxpayer to avoid a 20 % accuracy-related penalty, forgiven if the taxpayer believes that the tax strategy was more likely than not proper [MauldinA:08]. Even a risky proposition can be quantified. One advisor report stated that "the penalties would not be greater than \$14,000 per \$100,000 in . . . fees," and that risk is even less when few tax returns are audited [PSoI:03].

The intent of penalties is to set an example for others. In the period from 1996 to 2000 taxpayers paid \$16M in penalties, but multinationals paid none for the use of taxhavens [Rossotti:05]. Even with the penalties, due to the modest risk, aggressive tax avoidance is typically a beneficial option for a corporation [F8.6].

Penalties, although significant, will never be of a size to disable a business. That is not the intent of government. Even when successful tax avoidance has driven a less aggressive competitor out of business, penalizing the offender will not make the sunk party whole, especially after its going-concern value has been lost. Any follow-up becomes a matter for the courts, not for the IRS.

8.5.3 *Rollback and Settlements*

More rational than a penalty would be instituting a rollback. MNC's tax avoidance started when CONCH was established. A misvaluation can be corrected, but not its effects. The excessive capital that CONCH accumulated allowed MNC to acquire the resources to develop and market the ManiMobile. However, rolling back years of history is impossible for any business. All multinationals practice tax avoidance, although some have been more aggressive than others. Trying to roll back some businesses and not others would be even more unfair.

Because issues affecting any form of intellectual capital are difficult to bring to court, achieving a reasonable settlement is the best solution when there has been substantial tax avoidance or even presumed tax evasion. Settlements may be a great relief to the taxpayer. Corporations allocate contingency reserve funds for uncertain tax positions [Deloitte:10]. Since 2007 such information, as provided to SEC, must also be made available to IRS audits [IRS-TI:11]. A settlement allows them to return the excess into their working capital [AP:11]. For instance, in 2011 pharmaceutical company AstraZeneca was able to return \$2.3B from reserves for uncertain tax positions to its income lines after settling with the IRS for \$1.1B [F8.7].

The details of any settlements typically remain under seal. Even though much information may have been gathered, the information is not available for future guidance. A settlement does provide useful information to the advisors and lawyers that participated about limits for tax avoidance strategies.

If no settlement is achieved, information disclosed as part of the settlement process cannot be used in subsequent litigation. A careful taxpayer will identify all such documents specifically so that the IRS has to start over [OatesO:03].

8.6 Double Taxation

One motivation for MNC to set up CONCH, its CFH, was to avoid double taxation. Double taxation occurs when profits after taxes are transferred to another taxing jurisdiction or entity, booked there as contributing to earnings, and taxed again. Issues involve both the allocation of income and the tax rates levied by both jurisdictions [OatesO:09]. The issue of double taxation has been recognized for a long time [Churchill:26]. Guidelines to avoid onerous double taxation have been available for a long time [dAroma:27].

Table 8.2 Various flavors of double taxation among countries

Flavor of double corporate taxation		Tax rates: *Home*	*Foreign*	Final total	Comment
Full double taxation		35 %	10 %	45 %	Rare, only if ***H*** does not trust ***F***
Sequential taxation		35 %	25 %	51.25 %	Foreign taxes are only deducted
US tax credits	Rate@ ***H*** > ***F***	35 %	33 %	**35 %**	Only 2 % tax remains due in ***H***
	Rate@ ***H*** < ***F***	35 %	45 %	45 %	A tax loss of 10 % rolls forward in ***H***
	$F_{nom} > F_{act}$	35 %	[25 %]	15 %	***F*** provides 20 % hidden incentives
	H defers	deferred	25 %	(25 %)	Tax credit on deferred income
Repatriation holiday		5.25 %	0 %	5.25 %	Capital was held in a taxhaven
Selectable taxation		Member		Select	Only one country in a tax union (***G***, ***I***, . .), such as the European Union, levies taxes on a taxpayer
		I	***G***		
Tax exempted within a monetary union		12.5 %	24 %	I_{tax}:12.5 %	
		12.5 %	0 %	G_{tax}: 0 %	

There is also a double taxation of corporate payouts; those are covered in the subsequent Sect. 8.6.2. Both kinds come in a variety of flavors. When people argue about issues, they rarely distinguish what kind and flavor is involved.

8.6.1 *Flavors of Double Taxation*

Table 8.2 summarizes the various flavors of double taxation among independent countries [F8.8]. Details differ depending on their tax treaties.

Full Double Taxation

This is a rare case, occurring when a company formally resides in two jurisdictions and each jurisdiction collects taxes on the same earnings. It happen only if one country, say ***H***, does not recognize the taxing authority of another country ***F***, and does not recognize tax documents of ***F*** to be valid. Perhaps ***F*** is indeed a taxhaven. If country ***F*** actually levies 10 % taxes and country ***H*** levies 35 %, the total tax becomes 45 % of earnings [Miyatake:09].

Sequential Double Taxation

Earnings are accumulated in the foreign country ***F*** and taxed there at a 25 % rate. The profits left after those expenses are transferred to country ***H*** and taxed there at 35 %. The effective tax rate on foreign earnings is 51.25 %, as is the case for MNC in Belize [F2.2]. But that tax rate is only for sales within Belize; Belize levies no taxes on income from external sources. Since sales in Belize itself amounted to only

4 % of MNC LSA sales, MNC's effective tax rate for sales from its LSA operation is 36.65 % [F8.9]. When complaining about double taxation, a tax rate exceeding 50 % will be quoted. If that rate were actually due on all LSA earnings, MNC LSA would move its domicile somewhere else.

Foreign Taxes Credited

The country receiving worldwide income, ***H***, credits actual income taxes paid in a foreign country up to its own tax rate. Granting foreign tax credits (FTC) is routine and formally enabled by bilateral tax treaties among countries or trading zones [DesaiH:00]. The USA credits only income taxes, not other types of taxes paid in foreign countries [DesaiFH:06A]. Those just become deductible expenses of doing business.

For instance, the initial US-made ManiMobiles were sold in Austria (***F***) which had a 33.6 % tax rate; the USA (***H***) levied only the remaining 1.4 %. A manufacturer in Japan would be subject to yet a higher tax rate, say 45 %. No taxes would be due in ***H*** and the 10 % difference becomes a credit, which the company can roll over to other tax years. The immediate tax being paid is, however, equal to the highest rate of the two jurisdictions. To extract a benefit from such tax credit rollovers, a company may engage in loss-making activities in the foreign country, such as investing in new facilities in ***F*** or in an alternate offshore jurisdiction.

Problems arise with US tax credits when the foreign country posts an income tax rate that is reduced through hidden incentives [Pollock:12]. Say that country ***H*** credits taxes paid in country ***F*** nominally at $\mathbf{F}_{\mathrm{nom}}=25$ % up to its own tax rate, 35 %. To attract business, country ***F*** actually levies only $\mathbf{F}_{\mathrm{act}}=5$ % under certain conditions. If ***H*** recognizes the formal 25 % base rate and levies only the remaining 10 %, the combined tax rate is just 15 %. At times the foreign tax credit exceeds all taxes paid, forcing the IRS to issue substantial refunds.

Repatriation

A one-time dividend tax reduction of 85 % was enabled by the 2004 AJCA legislation. That holiday is included in Table 8.2 for comparison. The benefit that MNC gained from the AJCA legislation was demonstrated in Chap. 2. It prompted MNC to use nearly $500M accumulated earnings at CONCH to acquire smaller US companies. The effects on MNC and its peers are assessed in Sect. 7.4.

A "blocker" statement allows earnings to be deferred to support foreign investment, but a foreign tax credit can be claimed even though the earnings are not repatriated and taxed at all in the USA [Gibbs:09]. Now the company can receive a credit, although it pays no actual taxes [HoulderMG:11].

Selectable Taxation

Countries that have formed trade or monetary unions may tax income only in one country. When their tax rates have not been harmonized, as in the European Union,

Table 8.3 Double taxation of corporate payouts

Dividend taxation income		Source	Recipient	Total tax on distributed earnings	
Shares owned by individuals	>$69,000	25.3 %	20 %	40.3 %	Received by a couple from a typical corporation source
	<$69,000	25.3 %	0 %	25.3 %	
Shares owned by a corporation		25.3 %	25.3 %	44.3 %	Arm's length to a corporation

tax rates are used to compete for business among countries [Kovacs:05]. Enterprises not bound to a locality can take advantage of their flexibility and move their domicile within the union [Ogley:00]. Using member country ***I*** as its base means paying 12.5 % instead of 24 %, even if most activities are in member country ***G***. Tensions arise when tax rates within a union differ greatly [Alderman:10].

Taxhavens can take further advantages of being members of an economic union. Tax concessions and exemptions encourage individuals to report income in the most favorable jurisdiction, For instance, Cyprus and Malta do not levy a capital gains tax on nonresidents, allowing investors in other union countries to avoid that tax altogether [LowTax:11]. A pan-European registry does keep track of where taxpayers claim residence so that taxes are paid at least once.

8.6.2 Double Taxation of Corporate Payouts

A part of corporate profits, after taxes have been paid, can be paid to the shareholders as dividends. Those will then be added to the shareholders income. The complementary way for shareholders to benefit from corporate earnings is by selling their shares at a higher price than the price paid. Now the shareholders gain from invested corporate earnings. On income from profitable sales capital gains taxes are due.

We cover both alternatives for US taxation below. Some countries have low or zero tax rates for income from dividends or capital gains versus ordinary income. High taxes have motivated "High Net Worth Individuals" to leave their high-taxing home country and formally settle where dividends or capital gains are taxed less, often in a nearshore taxhaven.

8.6.2.1 Dividend Taxation

Here the double taxation issue is about taxes being applied to earnings reported by two parties in sequence. Table 8.3 covers taxation of dividends paid out to shareholders [F8.10]. The source is active arm's-length corporation that has similar paid taxes on its earnings, and the recipient is a passive corporate shareholder who receives dividend income from the corporation's after-tax profits and pays taxes on those dividends. Actual US corporate tax rates, after a variety of tax credits (but not deduction), are about 25.3 % [F8.11]. Lower rates (20 % as of 2013) on qualified dividends reduce the effect of double taxation on individual investors. The rates have been frequently adjusted and differ for dividends received by individuals versus corporations. Transfers among domestic corporate divisions are just pretax internal transfers.

Tax rates applied to dividends vary greatly among countries, from none to more than 50 %, and everywhere rates and rules have been subject to frequent changes. US resident individuals pay at rates of 23.8 %, 20 %, 18.6 %, 15 %, or 0 %, depending on their income [Henchman:13]. However, dividends from offshore subsidiaries of US businesses can be paid directly into offshore accounts. When a company sells shares of one of its subsidiaries, it amounts to a divestiture, the opposite of an acquisition, and taxation differs there as well, depending on the recipient's domicile.

8.6.2.2 Taxation of Capital Gains

Capital gains are the profits made when individual investors or unrelated corporations sell property at a price greater than the purchase price. MNC's shares have become more valuable over time, and when they are sold, the income from the increase is subject to capital gains taxation. The issues of taxation of capital gains are diverse and open to challenge. A strong argument has been made that deferral creates an imbalance in tax revenues [LafferM:10]. Reduced tax rates for capital gains are motivated by:

1. Similarity to profiting from dividends [ATRA:13]. But, since corporate investments are deducted from earnings before corporate taxes are paid, invoking double taxation is not valid.
2. Compensating investors for the risks they take. But corporate profit margins already reflect risk. Riskier investments are expected to yield higher returns, not lower taxes.
3. Compensation for monetary loss due to inflation for long-term investments [Paschall:00]. This argument ignores the fact that corporate earnings, and hence capital gains, also increase with inflation, so that the effect of inflation will approximately cancel out.

None of these motivations for reduced tax rates on capital gains appear to be valid. Still, the issues have caused controversies and frequent changes to capital gains tax rates and the holding periods required to qualify for them [Reich:11].

Most individuals will be taxed after 2012 on US capital gains at the 20 % basic rate for stocks held for more than 1 year; in 2003 the Bush tax cuts had lowered it to 15 % [Bush:05]. The rate was 28 % from 1986 to 1992. Since capital gains taxes can stymie ongoing operation of inherited assets, such as farms, held for the long term, no capital gains tax is levied on transfer of assets to inheritors after death.

Inflation is still perceived as a disincentive for long-term investments. Adjusting capital gains taxes over the holding period has been proposed [FeldsteinS:78]. A major issue is that the capital gains tax rate is independent of the holding period from purchase to sale of stock. Having one fixed reduced rate independent of the actual holding period encourages short-term investments. The conflicts arising have led to a labyrinth of regulations [Burman:99].

Increasing capital gains tax rates, as foreseen in Recommendation R20 in Chap. 10, will increase pressures on reducing capital gains rates to incentivize investors, even though corporations will have more capital available after their taxes are abolished. The alternatives listed here would allow a more rational way for individuals to deal with inflation in the context of capital gains.

1. Provide a deduction for inflation when capital gains are realized based on the aggregate inflation over the years that an investment was held [Walsh:11]. This rule requires careful record keeping of investments [IRS-550:12].
2. Record keeping can be simplified by allowing aggregation and averaging of assets, a current option in some cases. A combination with the prior alternative gives taxpayers a choice.
3. Adjust all investments every year by the inflation rate (CPI) or a similar factor. Allow an annual deduction from taxes based on the current inflation increment, or aggregate the credits and defer crediting the sum to the time of the actual sale of stock [Slemrod:95].
4. Tie distinct deduction percentages to typical holding periods in order to qualify for various types of investments. Currently there are four types: collectibles, real estate, business assets, and small business stock. Lobbyists will have fun increasing the number of types.

8.6.3 *Tax Treaties*

The USA has established tax treaties with 66 countries [IRS-WT:06]. An important feature of many tax treaties is that they allow tax credits to compensate for double taxation [IRS-MTC:06]. Each country has different methods of taxation. Treaties are negotiated with each country, so that opportunities for tax avoidance due to specific local settings can be minimized. Those differences open up new opportunities for tax avoidance for corporations that can establish residence in multiple countries, even if taxhavens are not used [Dagan:00]. Individuals who try to use the same approach must physically move around at a high cost to their lifestyle [Stewart:12]. Tax treaties that are written to solve problems encountered by individuals convey unintended benefits to corporations with multiple parallel domiciles.

As corporations learn to take advantage of laws, rules, conventions, and ongoing changes in each country, tax treaties must be updated [UStreasury:07]. The IRS must expend substantial effort to try to maintain these arrangements and prepare them for Congressional approval [Rossotti:05].

Tax treaties do not handle triangular transfers, as occur in a Dutch Sandwich [SwensonS:11]. Extraterritorial transfers to a primary taxhaven are invisible. In the case of Forest Laboratories, described in Sect. 2.6, it was assumed in our sketch that it paid 35 % on repatriated earnings, but the actual rate on its earnings, all derived from US sales, was less than 2.5 % after taking advantage of the US tax credit for research and experimentation [F2.26].

Advocates of particular economic issues may illustrate their point with examples of double taxation that are unrealistic for the situation at hand. Most people already abhor taxes; all want to be free of double taxation. The simple argument that the USA should not tax foreign income because tax has already been paid somewhere ignores the facts. Income taxes are intended to support the creators. Sales taxes are, of course, another matter; they tax the local buying public.

8.7 The IRS

In the 1970s the IRS was broadly vilified as an agency out of control, in part because some agents abused the power they had over taxpayers [Rossotti:05]. An agency that collects 20 % of the national income is an easy target for criticism. Any faults can be exploited for political objectives. The 1999 reorganization of IRS operations, in response to taxpayer complaints received by Congress, imposed strict working conditions. The improvements also imposed constraints on IRS operations [BarlettS:00].

All work at the IRS has to be performed under strict controls that protect the taxpayers [GAO:03]. Much effort has to be expended to assure that examinations and audits of corporations are adequate. The congressional mandates, while understandable by people who don't like to pay taxes, are increasing the effort needed for fair tax collection, especially for complex corporate tax returns.

8.7.1 Documentation

To understand the veracity of a proposed valuation, many corporate documents that are not a routine part of a corporate tax return have to be obtained and analyzed [LeveyW:07]. Statements in a valuation about contributions to IP by US and foreign divisions of multinationals must be supportable.

The IRS requests supplemental documents using a formal Information Document Request (IDR). The taxpayer typically has 30 days to respond, but can ask for extensions. The documents delivered may refer to other documents, triggering further requests. Domestic records of income transferred, as W-2 and 1,099 forms for individuals can be matched. No such standardized corroborating information is available for intracompany extraterritorial transactions [Simpson:02]. The IRS cannot obtain complete data from multinationals that have taxhaven subsidiaries in countries that have secrecy laws or do not register the names of the beneficial owners [Shulman:08]. Unless an illegal action can be demonstrated, IRS responses are constrained [LeveyWC:06]. The system as constituted now is considered inherently unfair to the broader community of taxpayers [AlmDM:04].

Only documents that already exist, or that should have been created according to the regulations, can be requested [LeveyW:07]. An opinion voiced by a global accounting firm has stated that the tax authorities should not even request documents to support valuations that use a different method from that proposed by the taxpayer; after all, the taxpayer knew what data were available and might have rejected an alternate valuation for lack of such data [OECD:06]. Information regarding the intellectual capital and IP shared with an offshore operation may be impossible to obtain, since no record keeping regarding intangibles for agencies as the IRS or SEC has been authorized.

As we saw in Chap. 5, the data used by alternate valuation methods differ, making it difficult to obtain a comprehensive view on a case where excessive tax avoidance is suspected. Without access to facts, an alternate reason cannot be discerned.

8.7.1.1 Interviews

Where documentation is inadequate, interviews with corporate staff may be needed to determine how estimates used in the taxpayer's valuation were obtained. Any visits to corporate sites have to be coordinated with the taxpayer. Detailed rules cover and limit travel by IRS personnel [IRS-TG:12].

8.7.2 Adapting to Modern Business Processes

When a case is audited, the source and disposition of earnings have to be determined, because taxes are assessed on earnings. As described in Sect. 4.2, nonroutine profits, the earnings due to innovation, are allocated according to ownership of the IP [B.2.2]. Since IP does not appear on the corporate books, documentation of appropriate allocations requires information that is not readily available. Financial examiners, often educated as CPAs, must look for IP beyond goodwill, which was the focus of their CPA exams [WhittingtonD:12]. It is the broader intellectual capital that generates corporate profits for MNC. The methods listed explicitly in IRS regulations to assess IP have their strengths and weaknesses; their reliability depends on having adequate data available [B.3.1 (c)(2)(ii)]. Crucial data are easy to miss.

Part of the 2004 tax legislation ordered the Treasury to study how to improve the handling of Cost-sharing arrangements (CSAs) [IRS-TP:04]. The resulting paper (CIP) defined a distinct category of buy-ins for corporate splits as Platform Contribution Transactions (PCT) [IRS-CIP:07]. In 2009 platform-based methods, intended to simplify valuations of the initial transfer of all intellectual capital to a CFC, were introduced as temporary regulations; now [B.1.2 #7]. Interaction with prior CSA regulations made their application complex and contentious [King:10]. Problems with subsequent court cases caused the motivating CIP to be withdrawn [Gregory:12]. In early 2012 the temporary regulations, slightly revised, were finalized [IRS-TP:12]. Use of PCTs provides an alternative to CSAs for dealing with proposed transfers of intellectual capital. The IP transfer used by our model MNC would have to be valued as a PCT [B.1.2 #7(b)(1)]. Unfortunately, by 2009 the majority of US corporations had already transferred much of their IP offshore, so that only recent corporate splits and acquisitions will be affected [Levin:12].

8.7.3 Resources at the IRS

Critics of the IRS tend to assume that the IRS has massive resources to combat tax avoidance and tax evasion. The public also assumes that, if more resources are needed, that they will be provided, because increased tax revenues will help reduce US budget deficits. The actual situation is different [Wilson:89]. Strict operational and staffing constraints are imposed on the IRS by the US Congress [RothEa:98].

The division that deals now with the returns of corporations, reorganized as LB&I in 2010, had at that time about 1,500 staff in total, including about 120 economists [Shulman:10R]. Many others are CPAs. Their work is supported by about 300 engineers, as well as by lawyers assigned out of a Treasury pool of 1,500 attorneys [IRS-ED:10]. In complex cases, temporary external experts may be engaged to help the IRS [JefferySO:88]. LB&I has started to establish a specialists' information base [Elliott:12]. The IRS staff also supports many other tasks mandated by Congress [Shulman:10C].

In 2009 there were plans to increase the number of specialists in international taxation by more than 50 %. Instead, the 2012 Congressional budgets reduced the funding of the IRS, saving the US budget \$300M [Cohn:12]. The average amount of tax "underreporting" IRS auditors found for each hour spent examining corporations was \$9,354 [Zerbe:10]. Having fewer audits is expected to reduce tax collections by perhaps \$4,000M [RubinZ:11]. However, more experts are being hired in 2012 for transfer pricing cases [TempleWest:12]. Many bring in experience from accounting firms [Shiner:12]. That should overcome shortages that professional tax advisors have noticed [LeveyW:07].

Legal assistance from the Department of Justice (DoJ) is also constrained by Congress. In 2011 the position of Assistant Attorney General in DoJ's tax division had been vacant for about a year [Romano:11].

Rules are in place to assure treating small and large taxpayers equally [McKenney:12]. Staff workloads, assignments, and promotions at the IRS are independent of the amount of money involved [GoreR:98]. Instead, qualitative and quantitative metrics are specified [B.1.2 §801.6(b),(c)].

8.7.4 Imbalance of Resources

Taxpayers, as MNC, have some in-house staff, but also depend on engaging advising firms like ATA to prepare tax documentation [LeveyWC:06]. Large companies invest substantially in their tax departments. General Electric has nearly 1,000 employees in its tax department, which is headed by a former IRS official

[Kocieniewski:11G]. Corporations also spend about a third of their tax department budgets on external advisors.

The three major tax-advising companies employ more than 500,000 professionals worldwide [Gleeson:94]. About a dozen other firms are quite substantial; the firm engaged by MNC, ATA, is one of them. The firms can marshal the needed support staff easily. Some of their staff gained experience at the IRS [ByrnesL:03]. Specialized legal firms also provide expert backup [OBrienO:99]. These firms gain competence by sharing information about taxpayer cases they handle, even while segregating private data. Any time that a weakness or inconsistency in the tax regulations is discovered, that vulnerability is shared, so that it can be exploited in many other corporate tax strategies [Rossotti:05].

Most major accounting firms have now structured their divisions in each country as Limited Liability Partnerships (LLPs). An LLP is a relatively recent structure, initiated originally in the Bailiwick of Jersey, a British Crown Dependency in the English Channel, a jurisdiction with its own government [Shaxson:11]. An LLP combines the advantages of a partnership, not having to reveal business data, with those of a corporation, which absolves the owning shareholders from being liable for debts and any incurred legal obligations.

The major firms have independent company divisions in many countries. Those divisions are in turn associated by being members of a "club" organized under the Swiss Vereinsgesetz. As club members they can share resources and information, without having any liability for a challenged action or advice by a member company [Fornito:05]. Now advice given by, say an offshore associate company of a firm, cannot be used to prosecute another member company in a home country.

8.7.5 *Fixing Imbalances in Taxation*

When problems of fair taxation rise to the level that Congress cares, the natural solution is to pass new laws. Each year over a dozen laws involving taxation are passed; many of them employ taxation to deal with social issues, as a law to encourage hiring of veterans [PearS:11]. New laws, good or bad, induce costs at the IRS and if not well implemented, will be counterproductive, as analyzed Sect. E.3.

All new laws have to be converted to regulations. That effort requires interactions with all parties that might be involved. Other government departments have to be consulted. If corporations are affected, their lobbyists will likely present suggestions on their wording [Economist:11L]. In the case of a law to help veterans, privacy regulations have to be expanded to allow sharing of certain tax information with officials at the Veteran's Administration [B.1.2 §6103(h)(1)]. Officials in other governmental departments will have to be vetted to assure that tax information stays secure. Delays of over a year are common [Rossotti:05]. Tax forms and processing software have to be updated. Once the regulations are issued, IRS examination and operational staff have to be trained in their application. The IRS provides many unreimbursed services for other government agencies [Burman:11].

Tax regulations deal with tax evasion and legitimate business objectives at the same time. For instance, the regulations to assure taxation of passive income in taxhavens also interact with regulations on interest rates, domicile, shipping, emissions, insurance companies, etc. All have had to be cross-checked and revised as well, every time any tax regulation changes [RazinS:90].

When tax returns are received, they will be checked. New regulations may be unclear to taxpayers. Especially returns of multinationals are affected [Pearson:06]. Questions raised about the taxpayer's interpretation of the new regulations have to be answered. In order to resolve discrepancies that arise, the IRS has to have resources at a scope and level that is commensurate with the resources that taxpayers will muster [vanHiltenEa:10].

8.7.6 *Governmental Resources*

Many corporations invest in aggressive tax avoidance [Shulman:08]. The savings that US corporations would obtain by just reducing their effective tax rate by 1 % is of the same order of magnitude as the entire budget for the US Treasury [F8.13].

That budget is less than 3 % of US discretionary spending, a segment of the US budget under intense pressure [F8.14]. The IRS is looking for an increase of its budget for fiscal year 2013 of about 4 %, but any increases are currently capped at 1.8 % [OMB:12B]. Some funds for Treasury international operations are budgeted with the Department of State.

Efforts are in place to encourage repatriation of funds accumulated offshore [Barthold:11]. It seems unlikely that they will have much success unless it can be done without paying taxes [Drucker:10B]. Purchasing offshore assets is a legal way to reduce excess offshore controlled holdings of capital [Sullivan:11]. The extraterritorial transfers needed are invisible [BarlettS:00]. Tax advisors are aware of the limitations of government budgets and resources [LeveyW:07].

8.8 Other Taxes

We have focused throughout on corporate income taxes. Income taxes are not the only alternative a government has for collecting revenues [Lynch:11].

Tax on Capital

Taxes can also be collected annually on assets held. Taxation of real property is common now. Many countries do levy taxes on capital held, typically at quite modest rates. States in the US states refer to that type of tax as a Franchise tax; the rate in Delaware is 0.035 % on gross assets, with a maximum of $180,000. Many US states also have an inventory tax.

The US federal government has not taxed capital holdings except in times of war, even though such taxes have been proposed [Johnson:07]. Taxing intellectual asset holdings would be harder still. An "intangibles tax" on corporate shares in North Carolina was enacted in 1937, at a rate of 0.25 % of their market value. It was struck down by the US Supreme Court in 1996.

Consumption Taxes

Taxes on sales of goods and services are a major source of income for many states and localities in the USA. The Internet has disabled taxation on many intangibles, and efforts not to tax any "digital goods" are opposed by US State authorities [Mazarov:12]. Here double taxation, sales taxes at an offshore seller and the US buyer, is an argument as well.

Federal sales taxes are now applied to some products, such as gasoline. Imposing them more broadly will require political will and rebalancing of priorities [Sullivan:11]. Interactions with corporate taxes now are modest.

A proposal for US taxation to move to sales taxes is the "Fair tax," which would abolish individual and corporate income taxes and replace it with a broad-based sales tax paid by the final consumer [BoortzL:06]. All taxes would be collected by the states and the majority of proceeds forwarded to the federal government; that aspect is close to the current Swiss system. To reduce the effect on low-income families all individuals would receive monthly "prebates" from the federal government to cover sales taxes on essential items.

Value-Added Taxes

In Europe, a variant of sales taxes, Value-Added Taxes (VAT), is common. Here sales taxes are collected at every intermediate level, subject to credits for VAT taxes paid on purchases at that level. Because they are imposed on more, smaller transactions, the overhead in administering them is greater [GregoryS:11]. All businesses become involved. VAT taxes are credited for foreign sales, providing a tax incentive. VAT taxes provide a large fraction of tax revenues in Europe, as shown in Fig. 9.7.

Transaction Taxes

A form of sales tax have been stamp taxes, levied on business transactions. The UK HMRC levies a 0.5 % Universal Transaction Tax (UTT) as a fee on certain share transactions; other EU countries are following. Rates of 0.1 % to 0.01 % have been proposed. A transaction tax or fee has also been proposed by US tax activists [Bingham:12]. One motivation of taxing stock and similar financial transactions is to discourage excess volatility in trading [Rosenthal:12]. Speculators will need margins in excess of that tax rate to be profitable. A transaction tax could have a major effect on some financial strategies. There is, not surprisingly, intense pushback by some traders, with threats to move their business to places without such taxation, as Switzerland. Since the financial markets are all electronic and globalized, it is unclear how such taxation could be comprehensively enforced [Martin:11].

Tariffs

Traditionally businesses involved in international trade paid substantial import duties and tariffs. A hundred years ago those taxes produced a major part of US government revenues. Now import duties and tariffs bring in only about 0.7 % of US revenues and have little effect on the US economy [FeenstraMRS:09]. Being based on old laws, intangible exports and imports are ignored. The imposition of tariffs is also affected by free-trade considerations [ChoiH:04].

Gift and Estate Taxes

Gifts and inheritances are taxed following rules specific to individuals [BradfordS:77]. The rules have been fluid. Limits before taxes are due are high, so that they mainly affect wealthy individuals [Friedman:86]. Since corporations don't die, they can only merge, be acquired, or go bankrupt, estate taxes do not apply to corporations. Tax-deductible donations to worthy causes do reduce corporate taxable earnings. Wealthy persons often set up corporations, partnerships, and foundations to channel capital transfers beyond the limits imposed in the tax code on individuals [Collins:11I]. This aspect is not covered here, but is a major topic of many treatises that complain about the US tax system [BarlettS:00].

All Federal Taxes

All federal taxes are imposed by Congress, although the president must sign the final bills. The IRS collects all taxes levied by the US federal government. Although many specific issues have arisen, tax avoidance in those areas has not had the effect that avoidance of corporate income taxes has had.

8.9 Summary

Most issues that the IRS faces are in its dealings with several hundred million individual taxpayers, nearly the entire US population. But the IRS also has to deal with complex laws, advancing technology of IP generation, and the intricate corporate structures of large multinational corporations [Sullivan:11]. Numerous changes in tax laws have to be implemented every year "while attempts by taxpayers and tax practitioners to evade compliance with the tax laws become more sophisticated" [George:11]. The use of taxhavens has few economic risks and great potential gains [Rossotti:05]. Weak enforcement creates disrespect for the law [Kaplow:99].

Corporate tax avoidance is achieved primarily by keeping income from being taxed. Checking that all deductions are proper is the task of IRS computers and staff. Complexity and lack of documentation regarding intellectual capital combine to disable automation and increase the effort needed for examinations by IRS staff. The gains from aggressive tax avoidance can be significant [F5.51].

IRS management has recognized that just adding staff at the IRS will not be effective for dealing with international cases, where many of the taxpayers purposely avoid detection [Shropshire:09]. Threats of vigorous enforcement don't scare corporate taxpayers [Schapiro:09] [McDonald in TuerffEa:08]. More transparency of corporate accounts will make abuses more obvious and could increase the number of cases being investigated.

It is easy to criticize the IRS for being unfair, but that does not solve the problem [Zerbe:10]. As long as demonizing the IRS by politicians pleases voters, it is hard for Congress to increase resources needed by the IRS [Khimm:11]. The interaction of political objectives and corporate welfare is hard to break [Friedman:86].

The IRS has a good defense. Its budget has been cut in recent years, and with the most aggressive tax shelters structured to involve many layers of transactions and dozens of tax returns, the workload is up. Even without the cutbacks, the rising complexity of the tax code has made enforcement harder than ever, and strategies for skirting the rules become ever more plentiful. [ByrnesL:03].

Although the USA imposes worldwide taxation, the mechanisms used by corporations to shift IP rights and reallocate earnings offshore appear to be out of the reach of the regulatory reform [Shulman:08]. Without broadly accepted norms of corporate behavior it is impossible to formulate rules and regulations that will make a significant difference if they conflict with the primary objective of corporations: to increase profits [Brittain:05]. Simplifying regulations, as often proposed, and part of the recommendations in Chap. 10, will reduce the effort that now has to be expended to understand corporate structures and processes. Simplifying allocation of extraterritorial taxable incomes by a formulary allocation, based on relative investments, has been suggested [Clausing:09]. Such investments must include investments in intellectual capital. Any recommendation should reduce the load now placed on the IRS.

Chapter 9
Effect on the National Economy

Now it is time to look at multinational corporations at a level that transcends specific companies. The tax avoidance methods used by a single company, MNC, can be fully understood and modeled. Extrapolating the effects to the 80 % of US companies listed on the NYSE that have offshore operations will not give precise results, but the principles are similar.

This chapter recapitulates briefly issues raised in early chapters, but with a focus on the entire US economy. The comparison focuses on what happens with corporate incomes and ignores details of how the incomes are obtained. After costs are deducted, corporate earnings are available for investments and, after taxes are paid, for dividends to shareholders, at home and offshore.

First, I establish that MNC is a valid model for US multinationals. That model was built based on common business experience, without using data about the US national economy. Next, I assess the trustworthiness of data used to provide advice to the public and to policy makers. Using that information, we can chart the growth of foreign activities by US corporations, considering opportunities offshore and at home. We can also estimate their effect on jobs in the USA and offshore. The summary tries to resolve what globalization of access to intellectual capital means for the US economy. The breadth of the result provides the basis for the recommendations in Chap. 10 and data for people motivated to institute reforms.

9.1 MNC as a Model

MNC is a model of a typical multinational corporation, although it is not one of the large ones that attract a lot of attention. MNC has a limited range of products and it has offshore divisions in only six countries. MNC's earnings are just 0.2 % of the total earnings of all US corporations [F9.1]. Figure 9.1 contrasts Fig. 7.4 for MNC and Fig. 6.4 covering all US corporations. The pattern we see for MNC is similar to the entire US corporate economy. Being multinational, MNC is more successful at tax avoidance than the average US business.

G. Wiederhold, *Valuing Intellectual Capital: Multinationals and Taxhavens*, Management for Professionals 23, DOI 10.1007/978-1-4614-6611-6_9,

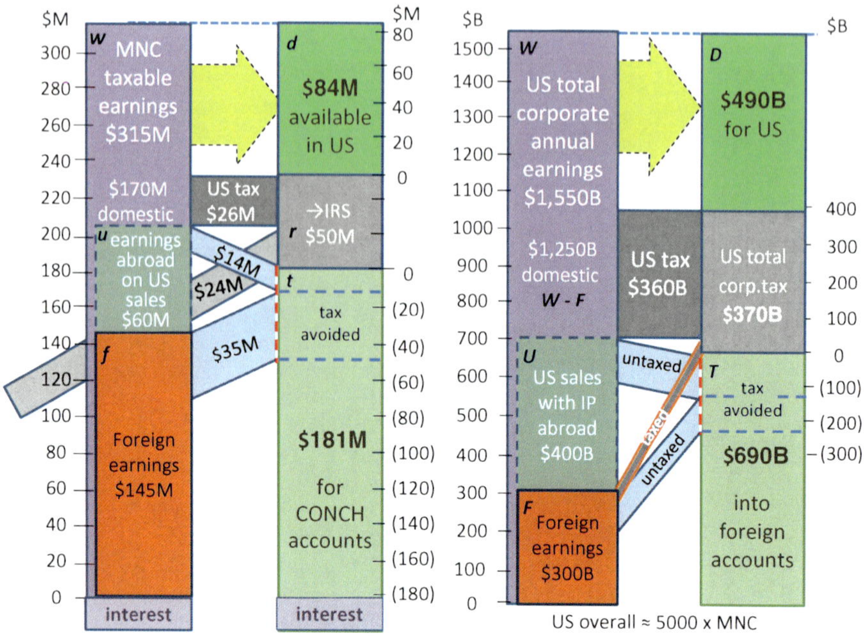

Fig. 9.1 MNC models the US corporate economy

In Fig. 9.1 MNC is compared with all other US corporations. To construct the national side of the summary graph a variety of data sources had to be used. Unfortunately, different sources will use inconsistent metrics and mismatching time intervals, so the information depicted and used throughout this chapter, relating what we observed from MNC to the overall situation of US corporations, is based on a careful integration of estimates rather than fully consistent facts [F9.2]. Section 9.4 addresses the issue of trustworthiness further.

The remainder of this section uses parameters such as assets, employment, sales, earnings, and taxes paid to compare MNC with US businesses, US corporations, and US-based multinationals.

9.2 MNC Versus Other US Businesses

MNC differs in size from the great majority of US businesses. Only about 6,000 US employers have more than 1,000 employees, the number that MNC had when it started CONCH, its offshore holding company. Companies with more than 1,000 employees together employ more than 40 % of the US workforce [F9.3].

Few small businesses are structured as corporations, and their influence on the US job market is amazingly small. In total small businesses employ fewer than

15 % of US employees other than their owners [HurstP:11]. Single persons in full- or part-time business by themselves comprise 77 % of US businesses, and another 19 % have fewer than 20 employees [F9.4]. We will focus our comparison on US corporations.

9.2.1 Similarities of MNC and Other US Corporations

MNC has taxation characteristics that mirror large corporations, defined for tax purposes as businesses that pay more than $1M in taxes annually [F9.5].

Using a definition based on taxes paid excludes corporations with large revenues that report negligible earnings, either because of operational losses or because of successful tax avoidance. A sample study showed that 61 % of large corporations by revenue or asset metrics paid less than $1M in taxes, and 37 % paid less than $100,000 in 2005 [Drucker:08]. Some of those low payers found in the study had been using extreme tax avoidance methods.

Looking at revenues as a base instead, we find that MNC paid 6.4 % in taxes on its gross receipts, close to the average 7.9 % paid by its peers [F9.6].

9.2.2 Differences Between MNC and Other US Corporations

Many US corporations are purely domestic. The average foreign sales proportion for all US corporations is about 20 % versus about 50 % for MNC [F9.7]. MNC, as a growing high-technology, high margin company, spends much more than US corporations overall on research. Overall US corporate R&D spending is about 1 % of earnings, but expenditures vary greatly by sector. MNC spends about 13 %, similar to its high-technology peers [F9.8]. Estimates by industrial sector using IRS data are distorted because of tax credits for domestic production, research credits, and specific deductions, referred to as "tax expenditures" [AltshulerACK:08].

Because MNC is in the high-technology manufacturing sector, which depends little on tangible assets, its assets-to-gross-income ratio is just 1.1. The assets-to-gross-income ratio is 3.1 for all US industries and 1.4 for US manufacturers [F9.9]. That low ratio makes MNC and its peers less dependent on external financing and also contributes to their high margins.

Its sector and its individual performance make MNC attractive to its shareholders. MNC enjoys a multiple of its market capitalization price to its annual earnings (*p*/*e*) of 5.3 [F5.51]. For all US companies the *p*/*e* multiple is about 3.3 [F9.10]. The market capitalization of all corporations' worldwide stock, converted to US dollars, was about $50,000B [Anderson:09]. These numbers fluctuate with market conditions. US-based corporations make up about $15,000B of the current total [Guru:12]. Some of that US market cap is due to foreign companies that obtain capital in the US stock market. Major corporations anywhere also obtain capital in foreign markets, in particular the Euromarket based in the City of London.

9.2.3 MNC Versus Other Multinationals

About 2,270 US corporations are multinationals, but those are important to the US economy [Jackson:10]. They pay about half of US corporate taxes [DauchyN:09]. Smaller businesses may have Foreign Personal Holding Companies (FPHCs) to hold funds offshore. Not having actual foreign operations they are best ignored in these summaries [RhoadesL:12]. The large US-based corporations employed more than 18 % of US workers in 2007, and because they pay higher salaries in general, they contributed more than 27 % to the total US payroll [USCoC:11].

By 2007 MNC's offshore sales revenues were growing to about half of its total sales; that fraction was about a third for all US multinationals [F9.11]. Adjusting the 20 % foreign sales fraction by the employee ratio of US corporations and their multinational subset, we expect offshore sales of multinationals to be about 36 % of their total sales [F9.12]. A sample of 30 US high-tech companies showed a fraction of 40 % [F9.13]. When MNC started CONCH, it had already a higher fraction, 42 %, of income from sales outside of North America.

US multinationals spend about 10.4 % of their gross income worldwide on R&D [F9.14]. MNC, as a growing high-technology corporation, spends more of its earnings on R&D and acquisitions that contribute intellectual capital than the typical US corporation, 12.5 % of revenues, a fraction less than Forest Labs' average of 19 % [F9.15]. MNC's Maniacs are priced the same worldwide, but medicines benefit from higher US prices.

The major part of MNC's research remained in California. Because MNC is growing rapidly, it has an unusually high research budget (23 % of gross revenues), and its taxable cost-sharing payments are much higher than the US average [F9.16]. Its offshore division, CONCH, paid annually about 11 % of MNC's total revenues in R&D cost-sharing support to MNC, an amount certainly much greater than typical [F9.17]. Nevertheless, Forest Labs' captive foreign holding company (CFH) had to pay even more, nearly 16 %, because there were no offshore sales [F9.18].

Because many multinationals operate in the high-technology sector, their tangible assets on the average are less than 11 % of their gross income, matching MNC [F9.19]. These modern businesses depend mainly on intellectual capital, supported by R&D spending.

Overall, multinational corporations repatriate as little as they can. In the end, they paid only 2.3 % tax on their foreign earnings in 2004 [Gibbs:09]. After having CONCH accounts pay for the 2004 AJCA acquisitions, MNC had no need for repatriation of its offshore capital to pay dividends or make further US investments. Because of large cost-sharing payments, MNC still paid about 4 % in taxes on its offshore income. Forest Labs paid 3.3 % [F9.20].

Today, tax codes actually provide a competitive advantage to multinational companies that invest and create jobs offshore, compared to companies that invest and create those same jobs domestically [Gibbs:09]. It should not be necessary for a country to promote tax avoidance for its multinational companies when operating out of their home country to the extent that its domestic companies are placed

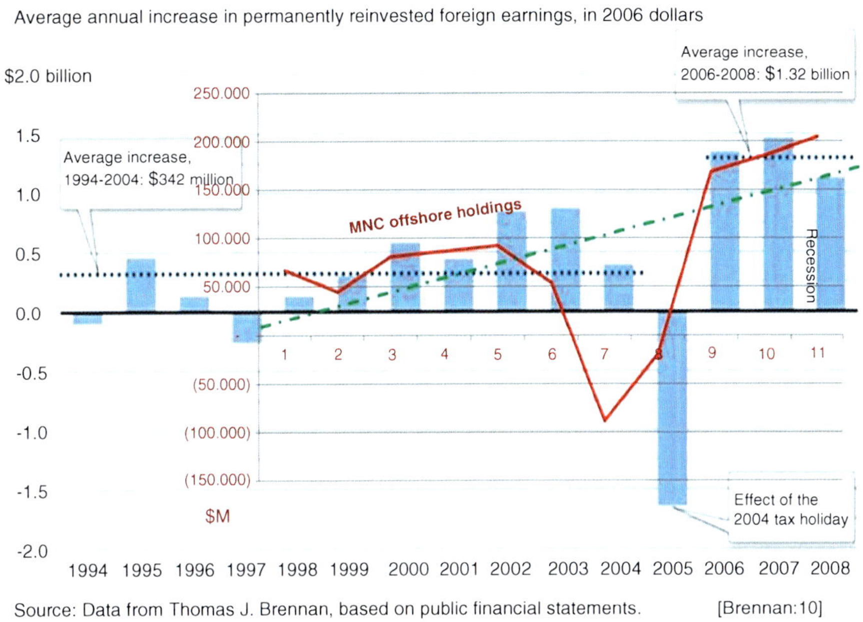

Fig. 9.2 MNC's offshore capital increase versus all US multinationals

at a disadvantage [GAO:04]. We will revisit that concept when I present my recommendations in Chap. 10.

Total foreign earnings of about $300 billion annually show the strength of US exports [BlumenthalS:06]. Because the majority of foreign sales are by multinational corporations, using their offshore subsidiaries, the data likely ignore most offshore transfers of IP rights.

The majority of foreign earnings continue to wind up in taxhavens. They can be invested offshore or held for new opportunities. The American Jobs Creation Act of 2004 (AJCA) provided an incentive for repatriation of offshore funds. Figure 9.2 shows the annual increase of capital held in MNC's offshore operation, CONCH, superimposed on the growth of capital held offshore by all US corporations [F9.21]. MNC was a bit faster than most in taking advantage of the AJCA repatriation incentive, but the trend is amazingly similar.

9.2.4 *Summarizing the Match*

Although US businesses show great variability, MNC, the model company used throughout this book, matches US multinational corporations quite well. The differences seen are explained by its business sector and its maturity. Specifically, MNC matches companies in the manufacturing sector for electronic devices.

MNC's divisional structure, while simpler, also matches the organization of most multinational manufacturers [Gladwell:07]. To protect its IP, MNC still controls its offshore manufacturing by owning its IP in the USA and only sharing rights to its IP via a controlled foreign holding company (CFH) with the operating CFCs in Malaysia and India [WTGS:09]. Many other manufacturers of electronic gadgets are willing to delegate all manufacturing to independent foreign contractors (IFCs) and just control the supply chain [SaterianoB:11]. Companies that produce software do not need offshore facilities at all, although some will copy and package disks at offshore sites, taking advantage of offshore manufacturing incentives by calling such operations "manufacturing" [B.1.2 #7(c)(4)(ii)].

9.3 National and Multinational Trends

Having been able to match MNC to US corporations in general, as well as to US-based multinationals in particular, we can now assess the image that multinationals present to the tax authorities. Extrapolations from the much more sparse corporate data that are available to the general public can be assessed using our detailed understanding of the processes MNC used.

9.3.1 *Offshore Finances*

MNC, as a multinational corporation, can reduce its taxes more easily than businesses whose assets and customers are mainly within the USA [Hines:10H]. Figure 9.1 compares MNC with all US corporations. US corporations are taxed worldwide, with credits given for foreign taxes.

The territorial view is that offshore sales determine offshore earnings. Two factors invalidate that simple relationship. The formal location of a sales division, the "nexus," can be located anywhere, and delivery and payments over the Internet can be anywhere. MNC receives its revenues at CAAS in The Netherlands. The location of taxable earnings no longer depends on the location where sales take place or where products are used. Having intellectual capital allocated offshore means that proportional earnings will be collected offshore as well. Some companies do even better in avoiding taxes. For instance, pharmaceutical companies, with products that depend greatly on IP, report that 80 % of their earnings are attributed to offshore sources, even if their US sales are typically greater than 50 % [Sullivan:06].

9.3.1.1 Offshore Income

Keeping income from being taxed is the primary means of tax avoidance [ChristensenCN:01]. MNC is able to avoid paying taxes on 62 % of its worldwide earnings [F2.22]. The tax rate on what is left, about 25 %, is typical for US corporations that invest in research [Sullivan:11]. MNC's effective tax rate on its worldwide earnings is now just 5.8 % [F7.52].

A large fraction of MNC's ongoing US taxable income represents funds repatriated to support US R&D expenses. Those are in addition to the initial payments, the buy-in, when the offshore controlled subsidiary purchased rights to sell and collect earnings in its region from the parent company. As we saw throughout Chap. 5, the appropriate transfer price for a buy-in is hard to validate, because MNC and its peers do not sell rights to their R&D capabilities to independent buyers.

Additional funds may be needed for US investments or dividend payments to shareholders. When such funds are repatriated from offshore accounts to the US parent company, they will be subject to US corporate income tax as well, but those can sometimes be avoided [Levin:12]. Domestic shareholders who expect tax rates to be reduced in the future may prefer to own more capital offshore rather than receive a reduced amount at home [Wamoff:12]. They have good reasons for such hopes. In 2003 the legislation that included the "Bush tax cuts" (JGTRRA) also reduced rates and gave preferences to income derived from holdings in countries that had signed tax treaties [Sheppard:04]. The AJCA in 2004 led to unexpected dividend payouts [DesaiD:07].

9.3.1.2 Offshore Costs

Just as reporting low transfer prices on exports reduces US taxable income, maximizing the prices paid on imported material and products for sale in the USA reduces income. The low visibility, increasing importance, and difficulty of valuing intangibles exacerbate the problem of both intracompany IP exports and imports [Nakamura:08].

Even though the USA practices worldwide taxation, the amount it collects on foreign earnings is modest, about 2.5 % of total tax revenues, because most earnings contribute to funds held in taxhaven accounts [F9.22]. The effect is that companies that depend on tangible US assets have an average tax burden that is much higher than that of MNC and its peers. Unfairness abounds. Similar issues have arisen throughout the world's history [Basse:11].

9.3.1.3 Paying for Rights to Intellectual Property

Initially the income at the controlled foreign holding company (CFH) has to be used to reimburse the US parent company for the assumed value of the IP rights transferred [LeveyWC:06]. That amount is typically paid over several years. Moving the IP rights early in the life of a company, when there is little IP to be valued, and the risk of failure is high, increases the leverage of the approach [B.1.2 #7(g)(2)(vii)(B)].

The income collected offshore in the CFH will also be used to share the cost of ongoing R&D creation—that is, to pay designers, engineers, and programmers [BrooksKW:02]. While the value of the initial IP purchased diminishes over time, the total IP held offshore in the CFH increases as the product is improved. Talented workers are based not only at the parent company but also at offshore locations. Staff hired offshore may be temporarily relocated to work in US facilities, but depending on the type of visa, they remain assigned to an offshore division [AsprayMV:06]. The payments by the CFH for creative work assure that the rights to the resulting IP will belong to the CFH.

9.3.1.4 Untaxed Offshore Funds

Earnings not needed to support US R&D and acquisitions remain in the offshore taxhaven CFH, untaxed. A substantial fraction of earnings tends to remain offshore, about $690 billion annually for US multinationals in the period 2005–2010, as shown in Fig. 9.1. In each yearly cycle yet more funds will flow to their CFHs. The growth rate is shown in Fig. 9.8.

Funds held in an offshore division earn a modest interest while invested in low-risk offshore bonds, as in the Euromarket. When a US company shows losses, transferring offshore funds to the USA can balance payments of corporate income tax. Then the books shown to the shareholders look better. A block of the accumulated capital may be repatriated whenever the USA offers tax amnesties for capital repatriation [Clausing:04].

9.3.2 *Trends in Corporate Taxation*

The summary of corporate information shown in Fig. 6.4 provides an aggregated summary covering the 6 years 2005–2010, omitting the effect of the 2008–2009 deep recession. Business results vary greatly from year to year, and the taxable earnings vary even more. It is useful to inspect some trends over a longer period, as shown in Fig. 9.3.

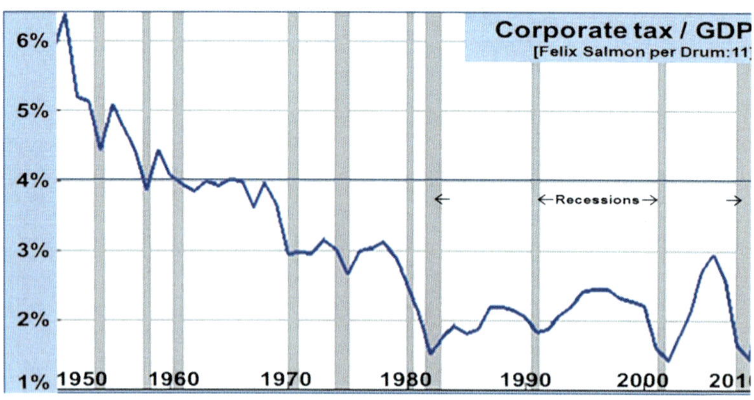

Fig. 9.3 Federal corporate tax collected as a share of US GDP

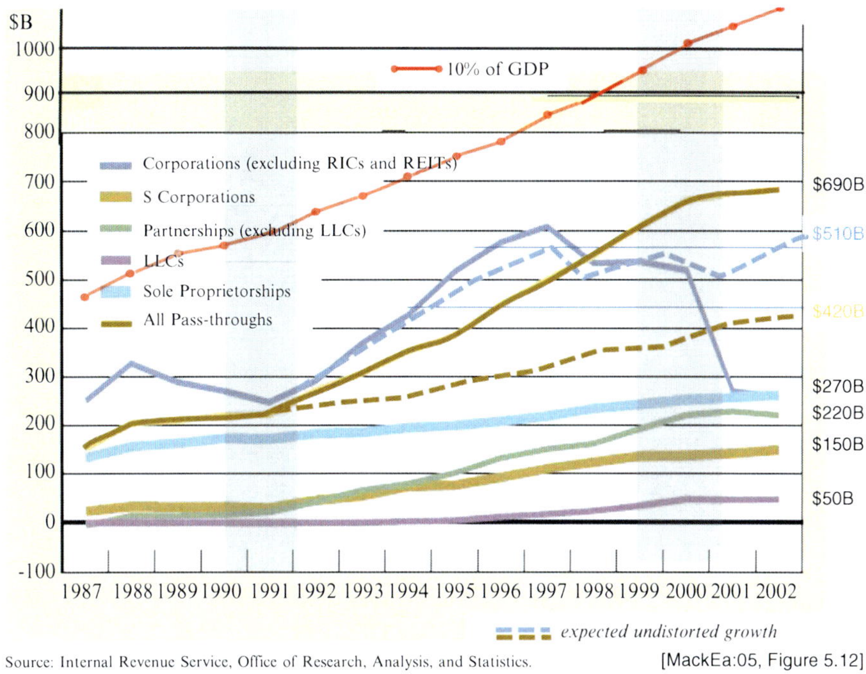

Fig. 9.4 Business net income by legal entity, 1987–2002

Recessions reduce taxes received, and for corporations the losses extend into subsequent years. Economic problems also motivate legislative reductions in corporate tax rates. Since the reductions due to the 1986 tax reform, corporate taxation has again increased from slightly over 2 % of total treasury revenues to 3 % at recent economic peaks. The trend over a longer term actually shows a steady decline in corporate taxation, shown later in Fig. 10.6.

Data supplied by the IRS for the 2005 tax reform study show that the net income reported to the IRS for C-corporations decreased drastically starting in 1995, from 57 % of the total business revenues to 28 % in 2002. The net income of other business entities in the USA, totaled and shown as "All Pass-throughs" in Fig. 9.4, continued to grow, to 72 % of US tax receipts. The graph has been augmented by GDP growth and expected trends in the absence of tax avoidance.

Several factors can explain the amazing reduction in corporate taxation:

1. Change in business activity due to recessions, as marked in Fig. 9.3.
2. Changes in taxation rates and increases in incentives provided to businesses.
3. Changes in corporate financing that reduce taxes.
4. Businesses changing their structure from C-corporations to LLPs and S-corporations.
5. Increased use of taxhavens by corporations.
6. US corporations performing inversions and moving out of the country.

Tax avoidance as such cannot be measured [Walker:06].

Fig. 9.5 MNC income

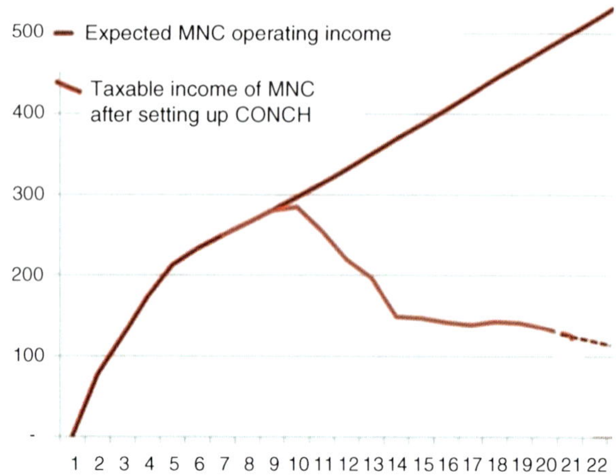

Figure 9.5 shows income data from Fig. 5.11 for MNC, our model corporation. The expected and the actual MNC income diverge sharply after CONCH was established. Comparing the national and MNC data, we perceive a similar trend, but matching trends do not establish causality. More information is needed if the significance of shifting IP and capital to taxhavens is to be proven.

All but about 4 % of the shift in Fig. 9.4 seems to be caused by smaller C-corporations switching to partnerships (LLCs) or becoming S-corporations [F9.23]. That avoids double taxation, and became even more attractive when, in 2003, dividends, instead of being taxed as ordinary income, were taxed at 15 % for individuals [ClevengerP:04]. As of 2013 the tax rate is 20 % for high-income individuals [ATRA:13]. The reorganized entities create new complexities for taxation. For instance, S-corporations submit income tax forms, deducting all their costs, and then distribute their earnings to their owners as salaries or as dividends, subject to different tax rates [F9.24]. Undistributed earnings held in accounts at an S-corporation are not taxed, leading to further regulations to minimize that path to tax avoidance. Partnerships lead to similar opportunities to avoid taxes [DickinsNW:05]. Since partnerships are established under state rules that differ among states, coordination with federal taxes is a nightmare.

9.3.2.1 Effects of Taxhavens

No definite effect of the increasing use of taxhavens is seen in Fig. 9.4, but capital accumulated in taxhavens does not show up in GDP data, nor as income, and certainly not as tax revenues. Without information on intangibles on the books, the effect shifting intangibles offshore on US corporate tax revenue is unclear. Efforts increase access to CFC data have failed [BrownEa:12].

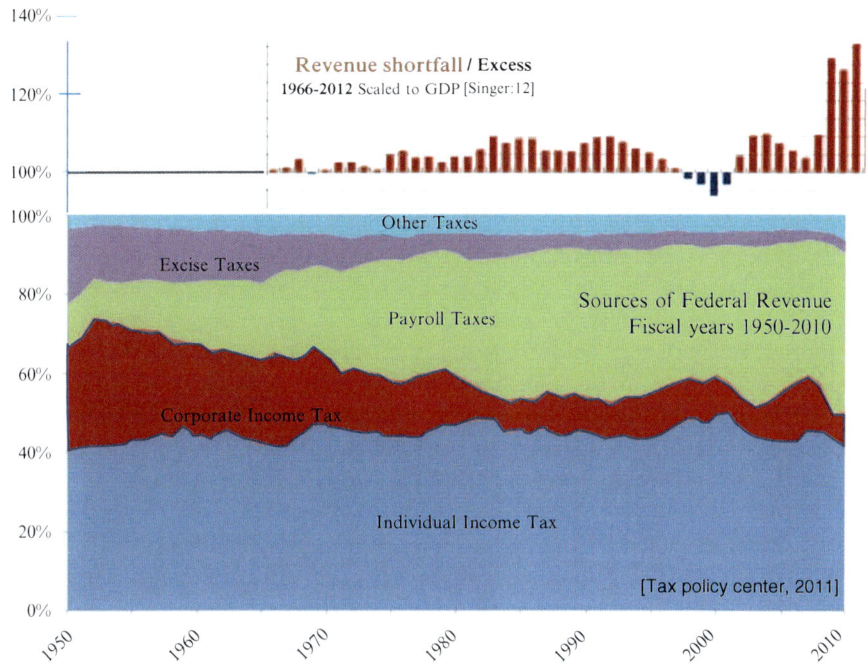

Fig. 9.6 Share of US tax receipts, and US deficits [Thompson:12]

The MNC model elucidates the mechanism, but IRS economic analyses cannot quantify the effect. Even for a single corporation the IRS does not get trustworthy data about export of IP, and it gets no information about derived earnings allocated to taxhavens, unless a specific and costly audit is initiated.

9.3.2.2 Actual Corporate Taxes Paid

Actual corporate tax payments are affected by tax credits and the reduced taxable base due to deductions. Figure 9.6 shows the contribution of corporate taxes relative to all tax revenues and the US Gross National Product (GNP).

The corporate tax contribution changed from 30 % of all federal revenue in the mid-1950s to \$221B or 8.8 % in 2010 [F9.25]. After 1984, it appears relatively steady, due in part to corporate income rising until 1996, as was seen in Fig. 9.4. Payroll taxes, collected to support Social Security, Medicare, and similar social benefits, are actually split between individuals and employers, raising the cost of hiring. Not obvious in the original graph was the effect of deficits, included in Table 8.1. Above the revenues in Fig. 9.6 I show the relative shortfall due to federal spending, for instance 135 % of tax receipts in 2010. The differences are deficits that contribute to the US national debt.

9.4 Trustworthiness

The data used to present issues about the national economy and national taxation that I and other commentators have to rely on vary greatly in scope of coverage, timeliness, and data sources. Some sources cover all businesses assigned to the IRS' LB&I division, others just cover C-corporations. Lack of data about intangible transfers is a complementary problem [Daum:01]. Even when recognized, little can be done to get adequate data. Some accounting initiatives to improve reporting of intangibles have been withdrawn [FASB:04]. Inconsistency abounds [StolowyJ:01]. For instance, when US exports are measured using data of goods shipped through customs, the exports mediated by the Internet are ignored [BernardJS:06].

Any numbers used for analyses should be corroborated with alternate sources if possible. If data differ substantially, the discrepancies should be explained. For instance, the sum of worldwide exports reported is $311 billion greater than the sum of worldwide imports. Substantial purchases by "Martians" are unlikely [Economist:11M].

Internet commerce, too recent to be captured in long-term government analyses, creates even more uncertainty about business growth and taxation. Now very small businesses can sell internationally and provide many services worldwide [HurstP:11]. Small entrepreneurs can sell anything to anybody, from specialized tools and parts to trinkets, directly or on eBay. Intangible goods, such as music and apps for iPhones, are already sold mainly over the Internet. Without records, such US sales and exports are likely to escape most taxation.

There are many motivations for hiding imports. Avoiding payment of customs duties is just one of them. Corporate tax avoidance tends to lower transfer prices of exports and raise transfer prices on imports [Swenson:01]. For governments, exports are a source of national pride; imports of essential goods can be embarrassing and hence poorly reported. With a good general understanding and adequate information, most data differences can be clarified.

Analyses of territorial versus worldwide taxation make sense only if the actual source jurisdictions of the revenues and costs that generate the income are known. No adequate data are available now to allow a quantitative comparison.

9.4.1 Distortion Due to Taxes

Insidious are data that are correct, but have been affected by actions that distort behavior. Taxes, unless negligible, always distort behavior [ChapotonG:88]. Low gasoline taxes, combined with high annual license fees on cars, encourage driving [Austin:08]. Sometimes behavior change is the intent of taxation, as consumption taxes on tobacco and alcohol, or excise taxes on imported luxury goods [MS:11].

Taxes also change corporate behavior. Corporate responses to changes in taxation can be rapid [Chamberlain:06]. In 1986, a new requirement that US shipping companies report all global income for taxation reduced the US-registered shipping fleet from 25 % of ships registered worldwide to 5 % by 1999 [Edwards:03].

9.4.2 *Bias*

Not all authors who deal with tax reform seek a balanced understanding. Numbers selected by proponents of a predefined position are chosen to make a point. The support for their positions leads to bias in the selection of simple facts. The lack of trustworthy data makes it easy to come to surprising conclusions [Wolf:05]. A common simplistic argument to reduce US corporate taxes uses the statutory tax rate: 35 % federal in the USA and only 12.5 % in Ireland, as shown earlier in Fig. 6.3. No multinational corporation pays US taxes on US income at the US statutory rate, nor would it pay taxes on offshore income at the Irish statutory rate [Drucker:10B].

9.4.3 *Effective Tax Rates*

Getting to the actual tax rates paid by corporations on operational income is not that simple. This section covers how alternative tax rates arise. Corporate taxes are reduced first by taking deductions to lower the taxable income base, and then reducing the computed tax amount by applying credits. When looking at the taxes actually collected, it soon becomes obvious that few corporations pay the statutory rate on their operational earnings [IRS-SC:12]. Presenting the actual or effective tax rate paid in corporate income is an obvious solution.

Unfortunately, there are as many computations of the effective tax rate as there are advocates for changing the tax system [Ditmer:11]. Values quoted for US corporate tax rates range from 28 % to 16 % and sometimes yet less [Kocieniewski:11B].

The process to obtain an effective tax rate must be presented at two levels, first considering credits applied to the taxes otherwise due on corporate income, and then, at a second level, the reduction of corporate taxable income by taking deductions from operating income. Those deductions and credits that lower taxes for some businesses, but not for all equally, are considered to be tax expenditures, but also often derided as "loopholes." Appendix E describes tax expenditures relevant to corporations. Optimistic estimates of "loophole" removal would increase US corporate tax revenues by about $85 billion per year [F9.26].

9.4.3.1 Level 1: The Corporate Tax Rate on Taxable Income

Taxes due by US corporations are reduced by a variety of tax credits. Summaries over all US businesses are made available annually by the IRS, reporting corporate revenues, taxable income, and tax credits, categorized by size and business sectors. The IRS reports also provide an effective tax rate by comparing the taxes that would be paid on taxable earnings before those credits have been taken. The reported numbers differ annually a fair amount, because they are affected by the economic health in each industrial sector as well as the waxing and waning of tax incentives. For all US manufacturers, the rate paid was less than 18 % in 2007, but in 2008 it was 21 % [IRS-ST:09].

The effects of credits differ greatly in specific industrial sectors [DevereuxL:11]. The range of tax rates experienced by major industry sectors varied in 2008 from 34.1 % to 18.2 % [F9.27]. Subsectors are especially affected by focused incentives, as for domestic manufacturing and growth of R&D activities. The computer industry paid 9.0 % and pharmaceuticals 6.7 %. The lighting equipment manufacturers, where GE dominates, came in lowest, at 5.9 %.

Effective rates for selected high-tech companies ranged from 21.6 % to 28.5 % [CohnC:11]. Because we focus on offshore activities, our MNC model did not include the advantages that MNC could have obtained from US tax credits. Applicable tax credits could have reduced MNC's taxes over 5 years by another $6.6M [F9.28]. The actual amount of US tax being paid by a specific corporation can be obtained from corporate reports submitted to the SEC.

Effective tax rates for multinationals are further reduced by foreign tax credits, offsetting tax costs incurred overseas. US taxes on earnings are deferred until the earnings are repatriated. Foreign taxes paid can be credited to US taxes as incurred offshore in deferred earnings.

Within the IRS more focused analyses can be performed, such as the rate of tax paid by US multinational corporations on offshore earnings, 2.3 % [Gibbs:09]. Some of that low rate is due to credits for foreign taxes paid, but because most multinationals employ taxhavens, it is difficult to get insights into extraterritorial transfers that warrant tax credits [GAO:09].

9.4.3.2 Level 2: The Corporate Tax Rate on Business Income

Deductions reduce the taxable income before taxes due are computed. Expenses of doing business must be deducted from corporate revenues to arrive at a taxable income. We encountered those throughout as selling, general, and administrative (SG&A) expenses. However, not all deductions that can be taken are obviously essential business expenses. Any deductions and reporting exemptions that are specific to corporations or specific industrial activities should also be classified as tax expenditures [ChristensenCN:01].

Rules for deductions differ for businesses versus individuals. An important corporate deduction is interest paid on loans, a deduction only available to individuals for home mortgages. For corporations the cost of interest on bonds and loans taken out is deductible.

Tax expenditures and their cost in terms of federal tax revenues have been produced for the US Congress since 1972 [HallS:99]. If we read the summary of the 1986 tax law, most of the roughly 400 deductions individually seem reasonable [RostenkowskiEa:86]. In totality, however, those deductions, and the thousands that have been introduced by Congress since then, reduce taxable income greatly. The largest amount benefits individuals, while the largest number of deductions applies to industry and has more modest effects. Many deductions are being challenged, some as not being effective in achieving promised benefits to the national welfare, some as supporting obsolete industries, and some as being narrowly focused loopholes. Removing unwarranted deductions will increase the taxable income of corporations.

Deciding which deductions beyond SG&A are a reasonable part of doing business and which should be classified as tax expenditures is still left to the beholder. Realistic estimates for effective tax rates after incentives are always subject to opinions on what can or should be removed and what deductions should be kept. Published IRS data provide little guidance for making changes, because the IRS must follow the laws and regulations that define exemptions and deductions.

Removing deductions beyond the fair cost of doing business would broaden the taxable base substantially and is part of most proposals to change taxation. Unfortunately, such proposals rarely provide specific lists. The proposers don't want to upset any constituency.

9.4.4 A Better Basis to Compare Tax Rates

To avoid the effect of questionable taxable incomes, comparisons of taxation levels are best based on gross income or operating income [Helman:10]. For public companies the 10-K data submitted to SEC are the appropriate source. The basis would be the operating income, since the net income can include deductions other than R&D expenses. Income shown to tax authorities need not conform to the income reported to shareholders, but should differ less than other sources [HanlonM:09]. Using IRS data the effective tax rate in 2008, without any deductions but all credits, was 14.7 % for all corporations and 17.5 % for manufacturers [F9.26]. An OECD estimate for the effective US corporate tax rate from 2000 to 2005 was 13.4 % [DoT:07].

For estimation of effective territorial rates of a multinational corporation, US revenues versus foreign revenues need to be identified and expenses split accordingly [Drucker:10]. Because rights to intellectual capital can be held anywhere, tax avoidance has encouraged booking income derived from intangible assets in locations inaccessible to analyses. Those financial intermediaries provide investment flexibility. However, they also hinder reporting and taxation [MurphyCK:05].

9.4.5 A Choice of Effective Tax Rates

When corporations or politicians complain about high tax rates in the USA, they have choices. They can cite the marginal tax rate that is applied to US earnings, 35 %. They can show the tax rate on their worldwide earnings before credits, 24 %. They can give the actual tax rate for the part of their business that is domiciled in the USA, averaging 21 % [F9.29]. All those percentages vary greatly by year, by industrial sector, and by extent of offshore activities and use of taxhavens [IRS-SC:12]. Removing all corporate tax expenditures to recompute a new taxable base yields an effective corporate tax rate for 2008 of 15.3 % [F9.30]. This tax rate is similar to the result based on IRS data [F9.26]. Being able to select from a wide range of numbers makes discussions on taxation and tax rates confusing. Understanding the motivation of the presenter often clarifies the reason for choices made.

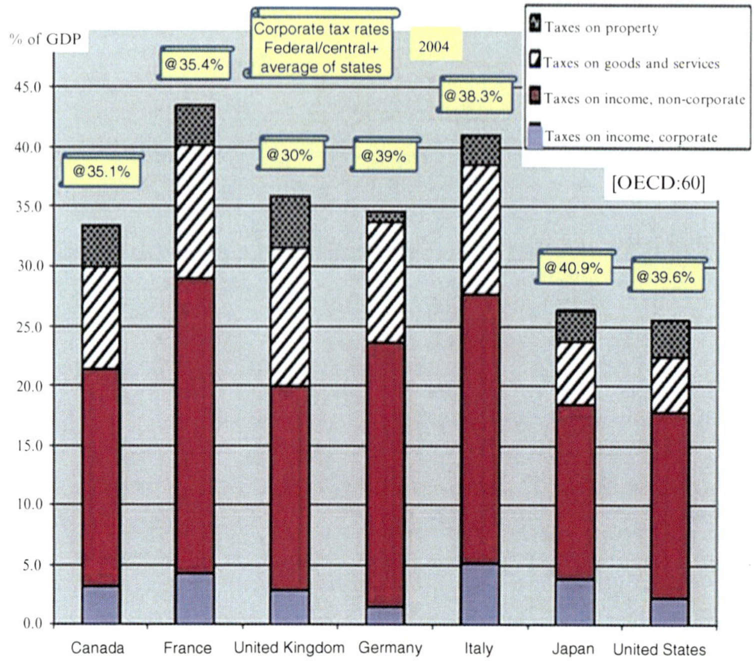

Fig. 9.7 Tax revenues in seven industrial countries relative to their GDP

9.4.6 International Effective Tax Rates

US statutory tax rates on earnings are at the high end, although quite close to major EU nations and Japan, but US effective rates are low [CollinsS:99]. Figure 9.7 shows the actual tax revenue distribution for seven industrialized nations (G7) and their statutory tax rates in 2005. The proportion of corporate taxes is lowest in Germany, but greater in Japan, France, and Italy.

Figure 9.7 shows a different picture from the data commonly cited in proposals to change taxation. Corporate taxes cannot be considered in isolation. Taxes on goods and services include sales taxes (collected locally in the USA) and Value-Added Taxes (VAT) in Europe. Use of VAT has been proposed for the USA as well, but such a comprehensive alternative will upset many "apple carts" and expectations of the "apple vendors" [Bartlett:12B]. Experiences in changing tax policies have been mixed [TanziS:00].

As shown in Fig. 9.6, corporate contributions vary greatly with the state of the economy and changing incentives, more than any other revenue component. Providing tax credits and deductions as incentives to businesses is not unique to the USA; effective tax rates are less than statutory tax rates throughout the world.

The variety and relative emphasis of revenue sources internationally make comparative arguments to change corporate taxation even less trustworthy [MarkleS:09]. Multinational corporations everywhere manage to further reduce their taxable earnings reported to tax authorities for worldwide taxation relative to domestic corporations in their countries by transferring substantial earnings to primary taxhavens.

It is important to remain aware that worldwide growth is not a zero-sum game. It should be possible to increase employment all over, as argued by proponents of globalization [Stiglitz:06]. The world can grow enough food to keep us all from starvation [Sachs:05]. We can also produce enough iPhones to let everyone communicate as much as they want. How population growth limits growth of individual income remains a question [AbramitzkyB:04]. These high-level arguments are important, but they do not address tax avoidance and the use of taxhavens, the issues that this work tries to illuminate.

9.4.6.1 Developing Nations

Checking whether transfers of intangible capital are fair is hard for countries with stable economies; it is nearly impossible for developing countries [Wydick:08]. Reports state that losses due to taxhaven use in 2006 caused a $125 billion loss to developing nations [Rittel:10]. The weak governance in most developing countries makes it easy to assign domestic earnings to foreign taxhavens. The issue motivated publication of a list of about 30 uncooperative taxhavens by the OECD. Government officials in the affected taxhavens protested.

In response, the OECD set a rule that any country that cooperates with several other countries would no longer be considered an uncooperative taxhaven. It was easy for taxhaven countries to make agreements with related countries, ignoring countries that demand true transparency [Houlder:10B]. Some countries consider those agreements inadequate and are still following up [JollyK:12]. For instance, France still publishes its own list of taxhavens [Mitchell:11]. The original OECD listing has now disappeared from its website. In all the uproar, little concern has been shown for the effects on developing countries [KarC:09].

China presents a unique situation. It is at the same time a developing nation and a world economic power [Grimes:11]. Its tax authorities have recognized the imbalances that occur when intellectual capital rights cause earnings to be transferred out of the country, rather than kept available for internal growth [SAT:09]. Being able to avoid lobbying pressures from China-based corporations and multinationals allows effective government enforcement, even while the local bureaucracy, auditing companies, and legal assistance are still coming up to speed.

Hong Kong provides useful nearshore taxhaven services. Those capabilities are also becoming attractive to Swiss and EU clients, as public and political demands to limit corporate tax avoidance by European multinationals become more vocal [CremerG:00].

9.5 Growth of US Offshore Activities

The tremendous growth in international activity by US enterprises is relatively recent. Figure 9.8 shows that US-offshore activities grew rapidly. Both outgoing foreign direct investment (FDI) by US businesses and incoming FDI grew much faster than the US Gross Domestic Product (GDP) [Shropshire:09]. Both FDI flows became similar in magnitude to the US GDP by 2007. The offshore holdings of US multinationals are scaled by a factor 10 for the graph, but they are significant. By 2008 those holdings represented 7 % of the US GDP, and they are growing much faster than the GDP itself [F9.32]. For comparison, that amount exceeds the total 2008 GDP of the seven US Great Plains states, 6.5 % of GDP [F9.33]. Offshore holdings keep growing because of the untaxed contributions made each year by the CFCs. JPMorgan Chase estimated that by 2010 US multinationals had $1,375B in cash sitting overseas [Davidoff:11].

Figure 9.8 illustrates those trends. Because the data are derived from multiple sources, the beginning and end points differ in time, and intermediate fluctuations are ignored. In order to show trends in a consistent manner the trend lines have been adjusted to account for the relative GDP growth to the end year of each trend line [F9.31]. That adjustment also accounts for the factor 4 inflation from 1975 to 2010. The counts of individual and corporate taxpayers have been adjusted to compensate for a mix of GDP and corporate growth. The numeric values attached to the trend lines are not inflation adjusted.

Since about 1980, the legal and technological barriers to the movement of capital, goods, and services have declined dramatically. These advances have provided

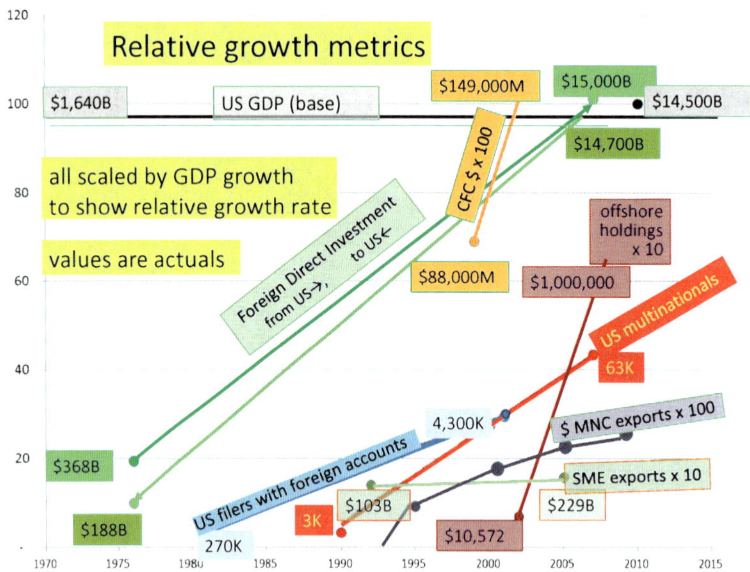

Fig. 9.8 Some US-offshore growth parameters

opportunities for offshore investments that were once possible only for large corporations and wealthy individuals. Individuals and Small- to Medium-sized Enterprises (SMEs) now participate in international trade as well, but still to a modest extent. To make them visible in Fig. 9.8 their numbers are scaled up by a factor ten. For comparison, MNC's growth is also plotted in Fig. 9.8, scaled by a factor 100. MNC started small, but grew internationally, taking advantage of taxhavens once it had substantial offshore revenues.

Corporate and individual use of taxhavens started in the 1950s but remained limited until the hosting countries and tax advising companies learned how to market their advantages without creating excessive suspicion by the public and the IRS.

It is clear that the USA can no longer be seen in isolation. National policies have to account for international interactions. Information used for political decision making tends to ignore international effects. Throughout my work I have been concerned about the poor recognition of intellectual capital. Trustworthy decision making, even for US-centered policies, is unreliable without solid data about global trends in trade.

9.5.1 *Operating a Taxhaven*

Taxhavens have become an important component of the global economy, more than their sizes warrant [Hines:10H]. A total of 51 primary and semi-taxhavens received 6.06 % of the foreign employee compensation of US firms in 2004. Taxhavens similarly accounted for 6.5 % of the foreign property, plant, and equipment of US firms in 2004.

This pattern reflects the attractiveness of putting income-earning activities in taxhavens and investments where earnings are taxed lightly or not at all. The data used did not include information on the location of intangible assets, such as intellectual property, but if they did, they would surely show that ownership of IP is also strongly concentrated in taxhavens.

Combinations of primary, conduit, and semi-taxhaven functions occur in larger jurisdictions, such as Hong Kong, Ireland, Singapore, and Switzerland. American multinational firms locate 27 % of their foreign gross assets in taxhavens, despite the relatively small sizes of these economies, and report that 42 % of their foreign incomes are earned in taxhavens. International transactions that could be ignored 25 years ago now control much of the US economy [DesaFH:06E].

9.5.1.1 Choosing a US Jurisdiction to Prepare for Offshore Transfers

For US companies, there is typically a two-stage process in getting ready to transfer rights to intellectual capital offshore. First, rights to the assets are consolidated into a US division, typically incorporated in a US state that provides favorable conditions for further actions. The taxation rights of states are defined by the concept

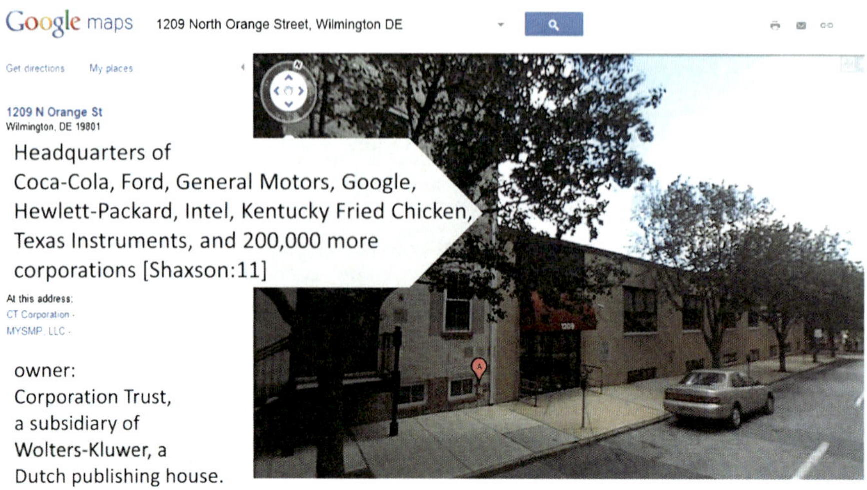

Fig. 9.9 Corporate headquarters of MNC [image from Google *Streetview*]

referred to as the "nexus" or the location of business activities, such as an active sales entity. The distinction has existed for a long time.

> Section I, Article 4. Income from shares or similar interests shall be taxable in the State in which the real centre of management of the undertaking is situated.
>
> Article 5. Income from any industrial, commercial or agricultural undertaking and from any other trades or professions shall be taxable in the State in which the persons controlling the undertaking or engaged in the trade or profession possess permanent establishments.
>
> The real centres of management, affiliated companies, branches, factories, agencies, warehouses, offices, depots, shall be regarded as permanent establishments. . . . Should the undertaking possess permanent establishments in both Contracting States, each of the two States shall tax the portion of the income produced in its territory [dAroma:27].

Restrictions are hard to enforce among states of a federation that places no restriction on commerce. In the USA, Delaware and Nevada provide attractive conditions. In Europe the City of London dominates, but Luxembourg and Malta, also members of the European Monetary Union (EMU), are other favored choices. If the formal domicile of a corporate division, or an entire company, is moved out of state, the state where the "permanent establishment" is actually located loses control of taxation.

MNC's formal US domicile is shown in Fig. 9.9. That location is shared by many other corporations. No MNC employees are located in that dismal office. More than 90 % of California corporations with out-of-state headquarters are based in Delaware; next is Nevada [Bishop:08]. ATA creates a distinct subdivision of MNC there to hold the IP rights to be moved offshore.

MNC also has a formal presence in Reno, Nevada, used for collecting license fees it receives from CONCH and other licensees that use MNC's patents. MNC US keeps ownership of all its patents. Nevada collects no corporate income tax and hence provides no information on corporate activities and income to the federal or any foreign government [NDT:11]. The ability to *liberate* parts of corporate records using territorial state regulations makes Nevada attractive to many corporations [Quinlan:02].

On the average, the 46 US states that tax corporations or general businesses collect less than 5 % of taxable income [Sullivan:11]. In 1986 the average was as high as 10 %, but corporate relocations to low-tax states and reductions in state tax rates have had a drastic effect. Currently New Hampshire (8.7 %) and California (8.4 %) garner the highest fraction of corporate taxes.

9.5.2 Use of Assets Held in Foreign Taxhavens

Once the assets to be moved offshore are assembled in the Delaware subdivision, the second step to shelter income from taxes is to move the rights to those assets to an offshore taxhaven. Such a shift is essentially an export, and taxes have to be paid on the income received for the sale of those assets. Having moved the rights to Delaware keeps the IP export invisible from California, which also asserts a right to worldwide taxation. Prior chapters covered and valued export of IP rights and the required buy-in payment. Once the transaction is completed, and the IP rights are offshore, foreign earnings are sheltered and will accumulate offshore.

The amount that has accumulated and is ready to be invested is large. During 2008, just 30 US high-tech companies increased their offshore capital by nearly $430 billion, an amount close to the total US federal deficit in that year [F9.34]. Cisco alone reported that it had $30 billion available, even though it had earlier spent substantially on foreign acquisitions. In the first 8 months of 2010, offshore acquisitions by US multinationals were reported to amount to $7.6 billion, a 168 % increase from the same period in 2009 [Saitto:10].

9.5.2.1 Use of Funds in Taxhavens

Those funds can be invested anywhere in the world. If wisely invested, complementing intellectual capital, they will create attractive products, and their sales will generate nonroutine profits. How the accumulated capital will be used is a corporate decision. Investments must make sense over a time frame that makes sense to shareholders. To achieve growth a business will make rational investment decisions.

Funds that are not actively invested earn only routine interest. If the owners cannot claim that they are holding them for future investment, they are considered to be passive holdings and derived income is taxed by the IRS [SlemrodW:09]. However, the rules to identify passive holdings are complex [B.2.10 (a)(3)(i)]. A company which is not primarily a financial holding company, and can claim its own capital needs, can easily circumvent those rules [DesaiH:00].

The offshore funds and IP rights can be used effectively in various ways to

(a) Increase offshore manufacturing, given sufficient demand for the product.
(b) Acquire offshore businesses to broaden product offerings.
(c) Establish research laboratories offshore, to improve one's products.
(d) Repatriate capital, using the IP to continue accumulating capital offshore.
(e) Repatriate IP rights through a buy-out and create capital growth at home.

Valuation of repatriated IP rights raises new issues. IP imports are not taxed, but reduce the value of assets held offshore. That reduction is then a tax-free repatriation of capital gains of the IP rights that were exported previously. Without accounting for owned IP appropriate allocation of gains from such a buy-out versus earnings derived from sales becomes a mystery.

Creating and funding subsidiaries in semi-taxhavens that have a lower tax rate than the parent company's are more broadly beneficial than investing in the parent country [Saitto:10]. Investments that grow product sales will create jobs.

9.5.2.2 Growing Offshore

Some capital will be used to grow the existing multinational operations overseas [Wolverson:11]. Improving products is essential to maintain the corporate position. A new project to broaden the existing product line can be located anywhere in the world. The choice of location considers labor costs and availability, access, and incentives offered, as described for MNC in Table 6.2. Future investments made by MNC, using funds accumulated at CONCH, favor semi-taxhavens that provide tax advantages and other incentives.

New projects require financial capital, personnel, infrastructure, and intellectual property. CONCH can provide both financial capital and rights to intellectual property. The assets that the semi-taxhaven has to provide are personnel and facilities. Many US companies have invested in semi-taxhavens and are continuing to do so [Kao:07]. Having funded the project allows the existing holding company, CONCH, to collect all nonroutine earnings.

9.5.2.3 Acquire Companies for Growth Offshore

Organic growth has limits, and R&D results take time to come to fruition. To grow companies in breadth, there have to be "great" new products for new customers. Acquiring new assets, such as complementary companies, broadens talent and IP. Offshore investment capital can be used to buy companies offshore without paying US taxes.

Relative to the large amount of capital held by US companies offshore, the opportunities are limited for high-technology companies. Israel has been a prime source for US multinationals [IATI:12]. The opportunities will grow as more countries, including current semi-taxhavens, successfully nurture start-ups. Many countries do put limits on foreign ownership, but if a US company has already established a CFC, deals may well be negotiated.

When an existing company is acquired with taxhaven funds, all the assets belong to the taxhaven entity, including all existing IP. If the acquired entity is already offshore, no capital repatriation is needed. The purchase is paid for by offshore funds, and the right to collect earnings offshore increases. The parent company now has to pay for use of the IP rights held in its taxhaven. To purchase the initial IP rights requires a transaction called a "buy-out," which mirrors a buy-in. Now there is a motivation to set the price of the acquired IP high, so that more funds will be transferred offshore and avoid being taxed.

9.5.2.4 Starting Offshore Research Ventures

Investing offshore capital in R&D offshore to develop new products is worthwhile. Offshore talent can bring needs and new concepts into a business. Offshore R&D can start small, as did MNC's tailoring of its products for the European market at its EMEA distribution center in Graz, Austria. The ManiMobile was a result of global joint efforts, each contributing local advantages, a concept sketched in Fig. 10.6.

Graduates of foreign universities bring new talents and competencies into a business. For MNC, growing the software operation at MNC's subsidiary in Mysore, India, makes good business sense.

Management has to carefully balance independence of acquired ventures to ensure that the R&D opens up new markets and remains relevant to the corporate goals and direction. Payoff from research investments always takes time.

Tax considerations will be only a minor issue in decision making for R&D investment. To ensure that IP rights are retained in the taxhaven, however, all research will be supported by CONCH, while patent ownership is assigned to the US parent. The value of new patents, if encumbered by offshore rights, is low.

9.5.2.5 Employing Taxhaven Capital in the USA

If MNC acquires a US company, its existing IP becomes available to CONCH. Funds held in CONCH accounts have to be transferred to MNC to pay for the value received. A valuation is required as discussed in Chap. 5, M8. If excellent investment opportunities arise in the USA, funds can be repatriated at any time, but they will be subject to the 35 % marginal US corporate tax. MNC may have CONCH transfer enough funds to cover the taxes due. Removing that disincentive is proposed in Chap. 10, Recommendation 20.

Repatriation of the large amounts held offshore at the regular US corporate tax rate will increase US tax revenue. Given that more than 7 % of the US GDP is now held offshore, substantial repatriations could reduce the deficit and the national debt. If Cisco's available sheltered funds would be repatriated and invested in the USA, the taxes due on that amount would exceed the total of NSF's and DARPA's 2009 funding [F9.35]. Similarly, repatriating General Electric's holdings would pay for all Pell grants to US students by the US Department of Education. But such moves are unlikely without substantial motivation.

Devising incentives for repatriation of offshore investments requires understanding of the process that creates value. The 2004 bill, the American Jobs Creation Act (AJCA), encouraged repatriation taxhavens funds to improve US business activities [AJCA:04]. The repatriation was at a tax rate reduced to 5.25 % [F2.12]. As shown in Fig. 9.2, about $300 billion was repatriated in 2005, five times the typical annual rate [DharmapalaFF:09]. Most companies cannot invest such a one-time stimulus effectively. Hiring workers is a long-term commitment, and any new hires will be effective only after they have acquired the needed know-how through training and participation. The AJCA included some constraints on how the repatriated capital could be spent, but money is fungible, and many choices remained. Many mergers and acquisitions occurred that year due to the availability of capital at the low tax rate [Schaefer:04]. Acquisitions became attractive that would not have been considered otherwise [Jackson:10].

Encouraged by the provisions of the AJCA, MNC in 2004 used all of the funds it had amassed in its taxhaven subsidiary, CONCH, to acquire several innovative smaller US companies. MNC paid a one-time tax bill of $26M in order to repatriate the needed $500M. Although the acquisitions caused MNC to grow by about 40 %, this investment did not create any new jobs at MNC in the USA. Our model estimates that about 40 % of the acquired staff were redundant and let go [F2.16].

MNC was typical of the many multinational companies that took advantage of the AJCA [MarrH:11]. Looking at 10-K reports for that period, we find a rash of acquisitions. In most of the acquired companies, positions that overlapped were eliminated [Clausing:04]. The unintended alternative was to pay bonuses to owners and larger dividends to shareholders [DharmapalaFF:09]. Any job creation from those choices would be quite indirect. The funding of US acquisitions from accounts at CONCH increased the share of rights to US-sourced corporate earnings held by CONCH.

9.5.3 *The Missing Piece: Where Goes the IP?*

Repatriation as reported excludes IP and rights to IP. Having IP rights continues to drive the collection of earnings in the taxhaven. Just repatriating financial capital is akin to trying to bail out a leaky boat without fixing the hole that lets the water in. Multinational corporations can and will exploit opportunities anywhere in the world. The associated flow of intellectual capital is much less visible than the flow of financial capital. This flexibility seriously distorts expected outcomes by legislators and tax authorities.

MNC will invest in the USA if such an investment will be truly effective; even paying the taxes on repatriated financial funds makes sense. It may even increase its US workforce relative to its offshore workforce, making people concerned about job loss happy. But the IP rights stay offshore. If IP held offshore is needed by employees in the USA, rights to use it will have to be obtained through a buy-out or by licensing it from the offshore corporation. That means that even a fully taxed repatriation of offshore capital does not provide long-term tax revenue where the research is performed. The offshore earnings will increase if the US workers are more productive, the opposite of what the public expects.

The lawmakers sponsoring the AJCA never tried to learn why the companies collected so much capital in their taxhavens; rights to intellectual property were never considered when writing the bill. The corporate IP remained offshore and offshore collection of earnings continued, as sketched in Fig. 8.2 [Sullivan:04]. The fraction of earnings retained offshore grew even more rapidly after repatriated funds were used to increase the offshore ownership of the IP rights. That was the case for MNC. The IP rights to MNC's nonroutine income held offshore increased to 62 %, covering US sales as well [F2.22]. More repatriations for US R&D investment will further increase offshore IP rights, increase earnings sheltered offshore, and further reduce the taxes paid to the US government. Calls for repatriations of Cisco's and General Electric's capital ignore that their IP rights will remain offshore and rapidly refill their coffers there [Chambers:10].

There is never a motivation to move IP rights from a low-tax jurisdiction upwards to a higher tax jurisdiction, no matter how small the tax rate difference is. Intellectual capital is not consumed by use, it can be used offshore and in the USA, and no matter where it is used, rights to its exploitation collect licensing fees at the place where it is formally held [BlouinKR:12]. With rights to IP of multinational corporations being largely held in zero-tax jurisdictions, and well-nigh invisible, quite drastic measures would be needed to get IP rights to flow uphill to the creators.

9.6 Allocation of Jobs

Outsourcing of work, including offshore outsourcing, is initially motivated by removing aspects of a business that do not involve corporate IP and do not contribute to nonroutine profits [BronfenbrennerL:04]. The staff remaining in the core corporation can then concentrate on the essentials of the business and be better recompensed for its contribution [Sakey:12]. For instance, outsourcing is routine for shipping goods to distributors [Desai:09]. In fact, the shipping companies develop their own expertise, which is valuable IP for them, and then are able to deliver better services at favorable prices to their clients [HendelMT:08]. Outsourcing its financial and taxation work makes a lot of sense for a high-technology corporation.

9.6.1 Outsourcing Services

Modern society spends an increasing fraction of its income on services rather than on manufactured goods. Manufacturing has followed agriculture in becoming so efficient that the number of jobs it generates is becoming a smaller fraction of the population [Stern:11]. In the USA the percentage of workers in manufacturing decreased from 30.8 % in 1980 to 16.7 % in 2010, while employment in services increased from 65.7 % to 81.2 % in that interval [ILO:11]. Within manufacturing the number of researchers, designers, and developers is increasing relative to actual production staff. The imbalance is even greater when the comparison is based on dollars spent on salaries and wages.

The business models differ for manufacturing and services. In financial services, the value is generated solely by people and the computing they need to select and carry out their actions. Banking services require substantial working capital, but few other tangibles. Understanding the mix of tangibles versus intangibles in a large corporation is relevant to discussions of taxation because of the way regulations are imposed and taxes are collected from businesses in those sectors.

The reliability and broad accessibility that the Internet has achieved now enable further shifting of income generation while employing similar intellectual capital. Consumers can now make a choice between buying software, say a word-processing program, or using cloud services to edit and store their documents. Music and movies can be purchased or enjoyed online. MNC has to decide how to deliver the unique benefits its Maniacs and ManiMobiles provide without forcing its customers to purchase a physical device with embedded intangible property. If it succeeds MNC will be able to close its manufacturing and distribution sites.

9.6.2 Outsourcing Core Competencies

Multinational corporations were initially focused on manufacturing, but customers require and are willing to pay for related services as well. Intellectual efforts are even harder to track than intellectual property. Ignoring the shift to services when formulating policies distorts any predictions [NorwoodEa:06].

Offshore employment by US multinationals is increasing; during the 10 years from 1999 to 2008 it grew by about three million, to ten million. Manufacturing employment in the USA decreased by about 1.7 million in the same period, to 21 million [F9.36]. The offshore growth of workers is likely much greater, because much work is outsourced to independent foreign contractors (IFCs). The effect will be substantially greater when local suppliers and contractors are included [FreemanAB:09]. Wages and salaries are still low in many countries where work is offshored, so that the financial imbalance is less. Well-educated professionals and scientists will feel the effects of offshoring more slowly [AsprayMV:06]. The imbalances of capabilities provided offshore at CFCs versus at the parent corporations are becoming less.

Opportunities in developing countries are increasing, and higher paying jobs are growing offshore as well.

Figure 9.10 sketches the trend. We cannot yet predict the rate and final magnitude of the effects [TambeH:10]. Offshoring of manufacturing jobs creates far-reaching issues [Wessel:11]. Many advances in product development derive from insights made on the manufacturing floor [Grove:10].

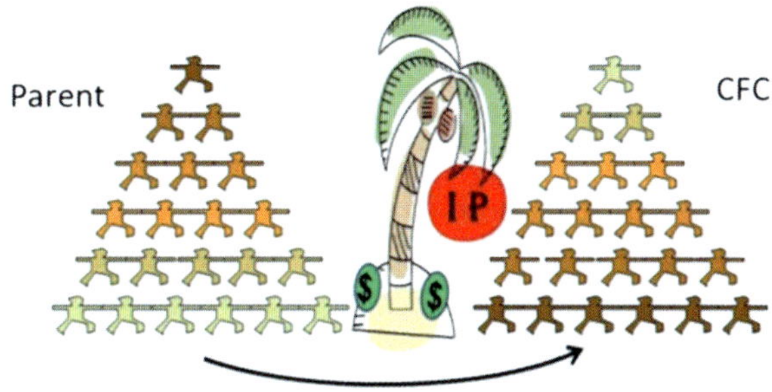

Fig. 9.10 Job allocation when offshoring

Transferring insights gained at remote sites back into new product development requires an ability to share competencies and motivation [Sveiby:97]. Losing that internal input to corporate IP hollows out the corporation [Simms:11]. Over time the staff composition changes, and the offshore entity will gain staff at all levels [BeckerEM:09]. Eventually it becomes effective to move the research organization offshore as well [Simpson:02]. However, investing to make creators and workers more productive at home can counteract that trend [Philips:12].

9.6.3 A Global Disconnect: Growth and Job Creation

In 2010 the USA experienced the start of a "jobless recovery." A recovery implies that corporations are becoming healthy, growing, and increasing revenues, and that their market capitalization will increase. The expectation is that more hiring will soon follow. The problem is that what is true globally does not need to happen locally [Pearlstein:11]. Our large corporations report consolidated earnings from their global operations. They may even report their global hiring trends. The assumption that substantial hiring will occur in the USA is just a hope. Given the payroll and tax advantages for growing projects offshore, much of the job creation will occur away from home.

We do not have enough data for any quantification. Data provided by the US Department of Labor on US job losses due to offshore movements (4,663 losses in the first quarter of 2004) versus reported growth of the Indian IT and development service industry alone (50,000 average growth per quarter in 2004) are so grossly out of line that no reliable analysis is possible [BronfenbrennerL:04], [FarrellKS:05].

Crucial job growth occurs in the smaller businesses, although not in the mom-and-pop shops. Those enterprises may do little offshoring directly, although their suppliers may. Even small- and medium-sized enterprises showed little export growth, as seen in Fig. 9.8. Their growth is not captured by stock market indexes, so we really don't know what the relationship of corporate growth is to job creation. There is certainly no direct connection.

9.6.4 *Incentives Offered by Foreign Countries*

When we think of taxhavens, an ability to attract shell companies and hide income seems paramount. Many other countries that actually want to develop their industrial infrastructure will offer considerable incentives. Those countries become semi-taxhavens for foreign enterprises, as discussed in Chap. 6. Financial structures adopted by modern corporations allow multinationals to take advantage of those incentives, without returning the expected benefits there. Countries that have territorial taxation are easily deprived of any nonroutine earnings that are generated by locally provided IP. They mainly benefit from increased employment, local purchases of supplies and services, and spillover of know-how to local industry.

When semi-taxhaven countries attract investments in tangibles—say, a car factory—benefits are retained after the incentives are spent. Many of the effects of incentives to attract high-technology businesses that depend largely on intellectual capital are volatile. Such businesses are not bound to any locality. Contracted work can be rapidly redeployed. Only a few senior people may have to move physically when a corporation decides to move production to another semi-taxhaven. Governments setting up semi-taxhaven incentives rarely realize how rapidly corporations can close facilities that depend primarily on IP. Their incentives do not provide the long-term benefits these countries expected in return for the tax losses [Alderman:10].

The tax avoidance enabled by accumulating IP and money in any taxhaven reduces the ability of governments of the countries where the actual work is performed to support the infrastructure needed for a healthy economy [Sachs:05]. That infrastructure includes public roads and transportation, health services, and education for the next generation. Such scarcities can be seen in Silicon Valley, Silicon Gulch, Silicon Fen, and Electronics City, Bangalore. Not everyone in these jurisdictions is happy about the balance of corporate demands, taxes, and the level of jobs being created [Hirst:02].

MNC exploited the incentives offered by taxhavens only modestly. And yet, the corporate structure chosen allowed MNC to avoid much of USA taxes. MNC used incremental tactics to reduce its buy-in payments to 7 % of independent valuations. Making estimates of parameters used in valuations is by its very nature uncertain. The fact that these estimates were consistently off in the direction that will reduce taxes to be paid is not surprising. Our model shows that the results are akin to tax evasion [Martin:11]. The incremental tactics used by MNC cannot be simply classified as being legal or illegal.

9.7 Tax Avoidance or Tax Evasion?

I now have to ask some crucial questions:

- Is what we have seen about the structure of business activities by multinationals just legal tax avoidance or is it illegal tax evasion?
- If it is a systemic aberration then another question can be raised: is it harmful? [OECD:98].

Every action that MNC undertook was legal. Misvaluation of its IP allowed MNC to be more profitable than its domestic peers. That pattern has been seen in broader studies using corporate tax filings [AltshulerACK:08]. If the effect appears harmful, should laws be changed to mitigate the harm?

Once extreme tax avoidance is perceived as a broad, systemic issue, two more questions arise:

1. Are the financial effects on government revenue so serious that extreme tax avoidance must be squelched? This question must consider not only the countries that corporations deal with directly, but all of the world's countries, rich and poor.
2. Does an impression that taxation is imbalanced lead to an attitude that if some corporations get away with objectionable behavior then individuals should try it as well?

If any of these answers indicate that extreme tax avoidance is harmful, then systemic changes are required.

Multinational companies are not new. The Vereenigde Oost-Indische Compagnie (VOC), founded in 1602 in Amsterdam, is commonly regarded as the first multinational enterprise. The VOC fought for—and achieved—independence from governmental controls [delaVega:1668].

In the past only wealthy individuals and large corporations took advantage of tax avoidance schemes. These days, tax avoidance is widely used and publicized and its use is broadening. The effect on the nation can be measured by economists [HinesS:09]. Companies like ATA have the experience, the resources, and the motivation to spread their competence to a broader audience [OBrienEa:98]. The effect is that more and smaller companies are now taking advantage of taxhaven strategies. It is hard to tell to what extent extreme practices will become common, but once tax avoidance is established, it is hard to reverse direction.

When assessing the effects for a national economy, it does not matter if loss of governmental revenue is due to the incremental tactics versus one large loophole that allows a similar level of evading taxes. The effect is the same: financial and intellectual capital is accumulated outside of the jurisdiction where the public and private investments and efforts originated.

9.7.1 Tax Avoidance Is Legal

It is perfectly legal to avoid taxes using existing laws and regulations [Hand:35]. US corporations operate in a competitive world, and they naturally desire not to be at a disadvantage versus their international competitors. Public sentiment and Congress are sympathetic to this issue. Nevertheless, it seems impossible to define laws and regulations in the USA to ensure global fairness. Many parties participate in setting laws and regulations, and they differ in their objectives and their understanding of the effects. The magnitude of intended effects is hard to predict. Unintended consequences are, by definition, not assessed beforehand.

Avoidance of double taxation is a frequent motivation of taxation proposals. We defined a dozen flavors in Tables 8.2 and 8.3. The issues affect not only divisions within a company, but the payments to its shareholders as well. A multinational business will find that the rules differ in each of the jurisdiction where it operates. It is natural to take advantage of the differences.

When we are dealing with IP in international transactions, the complexity of the arrangements makes it easy for corporations to push the boundaries of legality when they are trying to be competitive. Once a few multinationals find a way to use aggressive tax avoidance to compete more effectively, all others will follow soon. One metric is the gap between income reported to shareholders and to the IRS; it was already 30 % in 1996 [F9.37].

The tax expertise in modestly sized high-technology companies is insufficient to engage in extreme tax avoidance. Their directors would certainly not approve of illegal tax evasion schemes. But the proposal from their advisors is always worded carefully, so that no intimation of dishonesty is made obvious. As seen in Chap. 7, it is just the pattern of always taking one side where choices are to be made, which leads MNC into extreme tax avoidance.

Aggressive methods are promulgated by some corporate tax advisors. Some contracts even specify that they will obtain a percentage of the tax savings their methods generate [Rossotti:05]. They will not be concerned about the effects on the communities where the companies they advise operate. Many state and local taxes are based on the same reduced earnings reported to the federal government; state and local income will be reduced as well. That means that avoiding federal taxes affects local communities and the services they provide as well.

9.7.2 Extreme Tax Avoidance Versus Tax Evasion

Tactics of tax avoidance can be employed moderately, as MNC does, or aggressively. A more aggressive company will present more extreme positions, such as stating that the majority of its IP is generated offshore. Such a position is hard to check by IRS accountants, who never see intellectual capital on any books and can only make inferences from reported export valuations [IRS form 926]. Although the IRS has software to track reported financial calculations down to the last dollar or euro, no such software exists for intellectual property, so that experts are required [IRS-TG:07]. An alternate valuation may be prepared, leading to a reassessment of taxes due [LeveyW:07]. If a revised assessment is appealed, the firm can, after several lengthy cycles, engage lawyers who will negotiate a settlement [OatesO:03]. A settlement may look impressive, but typically it still represents a modest fraction of what independent experts would consider fair, if they had access to all of the information [Wright:11].

Tax evasion becomes even more tempting when a company has less favorable results than expected. By shifting or deferring expenses, it can manipulate operational business results to make results look better than they are. Reporting good results may imply higher taxes than actually need to be paid. Keeping distinct, nonconforming books for the shareholders and the tax authorities becomes necessary to match the taxes to the poor results. In most countries keeping multiple sets of books is legal.

Once a company has tax avoidance structures in place, many rearrangements of postings on the books can be done in offshore accounts, invisible to scrutiny by both shareholders and tax authorities. The consolidated books report only aggregated assets, so that the jurisdictions where financial assets are held are not reported [LeuzTW:06]. Nobody is told where the intellectual assets are, although annual reports tend to brag about them [Palmisano:06].

Without specific data, discussions of corporate tax evasion are elevated to the national level, and all corporations, their advisors, and the lobbyists they employ are blamed equally. At that level, tax avoidance and tax evasion become indistinguishable. The lack of a clear distinction makes discussions of corporate taxation contentious and further discourages transparency [Baker:05]. A relatively open and very public company gets lambasted in the press for successful tax avoidance [Drucker:10B]. Other companies that manage to operate under the radar succeed with much more extreme tax avoidance tactics [Drucker:10A].

9.8 Summary

Hundreds of books and periodicals deal with the complexities of national taxation. The discussion in this chapter is limited in scope. My analyses dealt only with federal corporate taxes levied on multinational corporations. Figure 9.6 showed that individuals in total pay a much larger amount. Payroll taxes for social security and old-age medical care, paid jointly by employers and employers, are similar in magnitude. The social issues in deciding who should pay for what are more complex for individuals as well.

Closely related to corporate taxation are the taxes that individuals pay on corporate dividends and capital gains, sales taxes levied by states and local authorities on sales of products developed and marketed by corporations, and excise taxes on imported products and raw materials. Throughout, we find interactions with taxation of small, unincorporated businesses. As they grow, some will become C-corporations. Overall the amount of taxes paid by C-corporations has declined, while their importance in the global economy keeps increasing.

The focus on corporate taxation allowed coverage in depth on one specific issue rarely raised in discussions about taxes and proposals to change them: the use of transfer of rights to intellectual capital to taxhavens. Modern industrial processes and products make income from tangibles less and less important.

Given the lack of public data on intellectual capital, I modeled a company, MNC, in detail and over its lifetime. Having a model allows going beyond abstractions. Integrating business knowledge obtained over a long time enabled creation and populating the model with typical data. I was glad to find that when I looked for data to match MNC to the US economy, the model's results matched general corporate data. The national numbers used in this chapter are estimates, likely accurate to about 10 %. Such numbers are good enough to convey a quantitative understanding of the processes and trends.

9.8.1 Who Should Care About Intellectual Capital Held in Taxhavens?

The detailed model of MNC presented in this book reflects US corporations in general. How does it affect you, the readers? Most of you are not corporate tax advisors, or major owners of corporations who can benefit personally from corporate tax avoidance. However, most of you work in institutions and enterprises that are affected by imbalances in worldwide taxation.

Many of us are proud to be part of the knowledge-based society, having brought forth a new revolution of human productivity in the last 50 years. We have moved well beyond the industrial revolution that started more than a century earlier. Globalization is held forth as a means to distribute its benefits widely. Unfortunately, the growth of assets in taxhavens deprives workers worldwide of benefits they could reasonably expect. Those hidden assets have grown to be greater than annual industry revenues, and they may already exceed the assets held in the countries where the IP is being created. Determining and publicizing the magnitude will require transparency regarding IP and financial assets held globally. The next and final chapter presents my recommendations.

Chapter 10
Recommendations

In this final chapter I present a score of recommendations to reduce "harmful tax avoidance" and assess their benefits and liabilities. Until some changes are made, taxpayers, their advisors, and the IRS will have to deal with the situation described in the preceding chapters. In the meantime, more and more will be written about problems of investment, taxation, and growth from many points of view [Stossel:12]. My recommendations here are feasible steps to get out of the mess that stymies fair corporate taxation. Most of the steps are small and one is drastic, but all of the recommendations are straightforward.

Although the earlier chapters are based on objective and verifiable information, any recommendations are, by nature, subjective. These recommendations are based on quantified observations, rather than on opinions. Readers who disagree with any recommendation can refer back to the material in earlier chapters, the background references, and develop and validate alternative conclusions. Readers who start here, at the end of the book, can find definitions for a broad selection of relevant terms in the Glossary, Appendix D.

Just the fact that recommendations are called for implies that something is not right with the current tax system [LynchEa:11]. Reformers focus on the complexity of the tax code and its failure to deal fairly with modern businesses [AngusNSW:10]. Proposed solutions are simple to state: scrap the tax code, reduce tax rates, and eliminate loopholes. But once such broad concepts are submitted to analysis, their complexity becomes overwhelming. Even expert economists can no longer understand the US tax code and its effects [Friedman:86]. The code and its regulations have certainly become a mystery for ordinary people [Kocieniewski:10]. After agreeing that something is seriously wrong, the reformers diverge rapidly [Mankiw:12].

Discussions are often driven by ideological opinions, such as "the rich should pay more" or "taxes should be reduced to encourage investment and growth" [DavisRKM:11]. My recommendations are intended to resolve problems in executing the stated intent of the tax code fairly, not to solve social ills or redistribute money via public spending [TanziS:00].

G. Wiederhold, *Valuing Intellectual Capital: Multinationals and Taxhavens*, Management for Professionals 23, DOI 10.1007/978-1-4614-6611-6_10,

10.1 Scope of the Recommendations

The scope of this book is limited to corporate taxation, and specifically to the effects of transfers across national borders of financial and intellectual capital needed to manufacture, distribute, and sell high-technology products. These limits enable in-depth coverage of an important issue: tax avoidance by multinational corporations. I ignore explicit tax evasion.

As such, my recommendations deal only with corporations, specifically multinational corporations. While they only contribute about 7 % of US tax revenues, their impact on the US economy is very significant [Bartlett:12T]. Revenues of US corporations amount to about 60 % of the US gross domestic product (GDP), of which about 1/3 is attributed to US multinationals [F10.1]. Multinational corporations benefit greatly from current US tax policies and are able to also exert considerable leverage on Congress and regulators [Kaiser:09].

My recommendations are organized into five main areas:

R1–R4 Top-level recommendations about changes to the tax code and regulations.
R5–R14 Specific recommendations to increase transparency. Without transparency, motivating and assessing changes to corporate taxation are impossible.
R15–R17 Changes to increase fairness in the way taxes are collected.
R18–R19 Specific changes to corporate incentives now provided via taxation.
R20 Abolish corporate income taxes altogether and exploit the consequences.

That final and overarching recommendation, R20, to do away with corporate income taxes altogether, is as drastic as the context of the work allows. Although it will be politically difficult to realize, it is conceptually the most effective way to deal with the complex issues of multinational tax avoidance and the resulting imbalances. A crucial consequence is that it eliminates double taxation of corporate income received by individuals. Trying to compensate for double taxation by integrating income tax concessions is the reason behind many objectionable distortions in individual taxation [Byrne:12].

10.1.1 The Complexity of Change

My recommendations are specific and implementable. Effective change is more likely by making modest steps in directions that can be understood by the variety of people involved. Broad recommendations by others are burdened by excessive context. Proposals considered by the US Congress mix general objectives with local specifics, and then leave the details to regulators. The results become complex as regulations are written to fix many interactions with prior regulations while balancing objectives. As of 2011, ten major tax proposals and numerous minor bills had been submitted to the 113th session of Congress [Bickley:11]. Even the more focused bills cover much ground and affect many regulations, such as a bill to increase American competitiveness worldwide [Camp:11]. The major bills, not analyzed here, will affect the social fabric of the USA [Sullivan:11].

10.1.1.1 Incremental Changes

Politicians and their constituents rally around specific tax issues, but rational solutions have been few and some are simplistic. For instance, requiring that an old regulation be removed for every new regulation is a cute idea, but infeasible if we study the actual texts [Howard:01]. The skeletal summaries of offshore transfer tax regulations shown in Appendix B can provide some insights.

Since 1986 an average of two changes per day to the tax code have been initiated by Congress, many embedded in broader bills [MackEa:05]. All of them increased the complexity of the tax code. Each change requires creating corresponding regulations. Draft regulations are available for analysis and comments by the public and corporate lobbyists [Alter:11].

Incremental changes to repair abuses of tax laws initially seem attractive, until their secondary effects are analyzed. Closing loopholes always sounds desirable, but removing misused incentives is upsetting for people who have built legitimate businesses that depend on them. To stop interlopers who are exploiting the incentive as a loophole, new laws and complex regulations are promulgated that try to distinguish the good guys from the bad guys. All the aggrieved parties will form a noisy coalition and prevent rational solutions [TuerffEa:08]. It is easy to find fault in any proposal and magnify the faults to prevent any serious reform.

The failure to deal with multinational tax avoidance by encouraging repatriation is well recognized [Clausing:09]. Dealing with the underlying problem is harder. That IP rights that have been shifted offshore will continue to accumulate capital there is overlooked. The common and erroneous excuse that IP cannot be valued discourages people from trying to understand the global flow of funds and IP [Johnston:12]. I hope my explanations and model computations help to remedy this deficiency.

10.1.1.2 Comprehensive Changes

It is nearly impossible to garner support for changes in taxation that affect many stakeholders. Impressive initiatives are viewed with suspicion by the public. Such suspicions are justified.

> *One way would be real tax reform—scrapping the Internal Revenue Code and replacing it with something simpler and flatter. Forget targeted tax cuts, which simply create more opportunities for gaming and more business for lobbyists. Just think how much more productive businesses would be if they spent the same time and money on their products and services, that they do on influence peddlers and lawyers.* [Baum:10]

This statement sounds perfectly easy to agree with, until it becomes clear that a flat tax is being promoted [LafferM:10]. Like any new tax collection system, the flat tax has opponents as well as proponents [Bartlett:12B]. Opponents of the flat tax have already marshaled a panoply of real and imaginary issues, most dealing with effects on low-income earners.

Any fixes proposed to make the effects less onerous again increase complexity; in fact, the Tax Reform Act of 1986 was based on earlier flat tax analyses

[Chamberlain:06]. It changed over 400 provisions of the tax code. Opposing a flat tax is not the same as not wanting a simpler tax system [Gladstone:1898].

Twice in recent years, comprehensive tax revisions have come under scrutiny. In 2005 a high-level study identified many problems with the current US tax structure and proposed two alternative plans [MackEa:05]. Their effects were carefully analyzed [DesaiFH:07]. The plans were detailed and led to a Senate bill [Dorgan:07]. However, the US Congress largely ignored the proposals. In 2010 major changes in taxation were part of a set of recommendations to deal with our troubling national deficit [BowlesS:10]. The proposed recommendations were ignored by all parties and never even reached the floor of the US Congress [Cusack:11]. In both cases, interest groups found unacceptable items in the recommendations, such as cuts in services to deserving populations or increased taxes. Subsequent debt negotiations led to a political stalemate and failed [Trumbull:11].

A problem with any comprehensive plan is that it requires widespread support from US individuals and corporations. If people and businesses cannot be confident that they understand the effect on their future, no reform can garner support [Bartlett:12B].

10.1.1.3 Who is to Blame?

There is broad agreement that the US tax system is broken. When the public or the media sees inequities, its first reaction is to find somebody to blame. That makes a good story, but does little to restore balance. Letting lawyers resolve conflicts produces little insight. Let's look at four constituencies: corporations, economists, politicians, and the IRS.

Corporations are easily vilified as being "evil" [CavanaughEaM:04]. Their financial advisors and lawyers who help to minimize corporate taxes are just doing their job. The managers of the corporations have been told that the prime role of a corporation is to maximize return for its owners [Damodaran:02]. They would be violating their professional obligations if they did not engage in legal tax avoidance. Competition among companies and their advisors means they will push the boundaries of legality.

Economists in academia have presented many theories about taxation, while ignoring many of the practical issues of implementation [Frisch in RazinS:95]. Because effects of economic theories are hard to measure, academic recognition cannot depend on relevance. Many issues debated in depth make little difference in corporate or governmental budgets and are based on examples irrelevant to actual tax avoidance accomplished through the shifting of intangibles [Wolf:05].

Politicians have to listen to their constituents and juggle their interests. Providing a tax benefit for some cause or group is seen as a positive action, while providing an equal amount of cash for that cause is called wasteful spending and derided as an earmark. Past incentives, such as program grants and tax expenditures, cannot be abandoned, so we get gridlock or "demosclerosis" [Rauch:94]. Support by lobbyists, encouraging churning, is more effective now than ever [Kaiser:09].

The IRS gets directions and advice from everyone, but primarily from Congress. Yet the feedback its employees can provide to Congress is severely constrained

[Kennedy:06]. The IRS does have the responsibility for creating the regulations that taxpayers must follow, and each bill passed leads to hundreds of new and revised lines in the regulations. Being the executor, the IRS brings the bad news to the public and suffers the blame [Rossotti:05]. As a result, we even see congressional proposals to repeal the 16th amendment to the US constitution [KingEa:07].

This book, while documenting inequities, has no ideological basis and does not apportion blame. It presents a technical and business point of view, so that it can provide a basis for quantification of decisions now made by businesses and people interested in change. My recommendations follow in the same spirit.

10.2 New Laws and Regulations: R1–R4

Making taxes simple is a goal that is easy to believe in. Studies initiated by the AJCA recommended a simplified valuation of IP transferred in a common form of buy-in [DesaiH:04]. A new concept, a Platform Contribution Transaction (PCT), was introduced [IRS-CIP:07]. Following regulations that became final early in 2012, the case of a company splitting itself is to be considered a PCT, rather than a cost-sharing transaction [IRS-TP:12]. In a PCT there is no valid offshore participant and most of the intellectual capital contributed by the parent can be valued. In that case, the valuation of buy-in IP transfers will be primarily income-based and easy to administer. However, the additional rules made the regulations more complex [B.1.2 #7(g)].

If a change in the global flow of corporate funds and IP is called for, implementation will not be easy. We will need greater transparency before any substantial political effort can be motivated. Creating a tax structure that encourages innovation at home has been advocated, but the benefits should not be lost to offshore jurisdictions [AsprayMV:06].

10.2.1 Implementation Costs of Changing Tax Laws

US businesses and households devoted at least 2.5 billion hours in 2010 to comply with tax laws [Keating:10]. That cost estimate does not include the time that the IRS spends to define and administer them [George:11]. Congress continues to pass more laws, increasing everyone's efforts [Friedman: 86]. The IRS staff is already overloaded [JCT:03]. My first recommendation therefore is:

R1: Changes in the tax code must commit resources at the IRS.

This recommendation is based on a venerable rule of warfare: Don't attack without having adequate troops to win [Tzu:340BCE]. Most changes in the tax code legislated by Congress require resources to assure thorough processing by the IRS. Initially, the IRS must create and publish regulations that represent the intent of new laws subsequently. In many cases, considerable long-term resources are needed for adequate enforcement [Olson:11].

10.2.2 Overloaded Bills

Recommendation R2 is related to the first one. Most bills passed by Congress are the result of political compromises. Those bills pile many related and unrelated changes onto the original single bill, greatly increasing its complexity. The bill enabling a year of low-taxed repatriation of offshore funds, the American Jobs Creation Act of 2004, is 423 pages long—but 88 % of those pages deal neither with tax topics nor with jobs [F10.2].

R2: Bills passed by Congress should deal with only the topic in the title.

A pragmatic definition of a topic is that any section of a bill must fall within one of the 51 Titles in the US Code. For tax laws, that would be Title 26. That title already has 11 subtitles. Trade-offs made to pass a law will become more explicit if this recommendation is adopted. If the trade-offs involve distinct titles, they should at least be clearly segregated. Narrowing the scope of each bill will make it easier to understand and will avoid complexities when financial and social objectives are combined.

Interaction of Objectives

The tax code is often used by well-meaning lawmakers to solve local or temporary social or structural problems [SalantG:11], though the fundamental purpose of taxes is to support the operation of the federal government. Anytime the tax code is amended to address peripheral issues, it provides opportunities for unintended exploitation [Posner:77]. Trying to deal with non-tax issues through the tax code makes each subsequent tax bill and its related regulations more complex, because more and more related regulations have to be dealt with. The regulations that must be issued become more convoluted and intrusive. On average, regulations are ten times the size of the law that was passed. A recent example is the section on not taxing rum from Puerto Rico within the Sandy hurricane relief bill [Toombs:13].

The complexity of the tax code is now so great that the effects of a change and its interactions cannot be predicted or monitored. Regulations that appear to have valid intentions are easy to insert but easily misused. For instance, the ongoing debate about farm subsidies exposes unresolvable conflicts; benefits important to family farms are also used by huge agricultural corporations [Anderson:10].

A complementary benefit, supporting Recommendation R1, is that new laws that do not primarily deal with taxation, but add requirements on IRS operations, must do so explicitly.

10.2.3 Global Consistency

Countries of differing size and resources will also differ in taxation methods, chosen to be suitable for their communal values and capabilities [HinesS:09]. Most laws treat their country's finances as a closed system. It is natural for multinationals to take advantage of differences in taxation just as they already benefit from differences in natural resources and labor costs.

That issue arises in arguments of territorial versus worldwide taxation, presented in Chap. 8. In principle, the USA taxes worldwide income, giving credits for taxes paid to other jurisdictions. Multinationals operate in dozens of jurisdictions. That complexity leads to many frustrations and repeated calls for the USA to move to the apparent simplicity of territorial taxation [Huntsman:11]. Superficially it appears that US companies will become more competitive if they can operate freely offshore and never worry about US taxes. With territorial taxation, any income from US products and innovations that is not bound to a definite US source can be booked offshore and out of sight. As long as corporations are to be taxed, I advocate:

R3: Don't move to territorial taxation.

Only countries that derive most of their income from tangible products can benefit from the simplicity of territorial taxation. Any country that hosts businesses that derive much of their income from worldwide sales of products with a high IP content should favor worldwide coverage, even with the complexity it entails [Thomson:12]. Ignoring how businesses operate worldwide just strengthens the capabilities of taxhavens. Countries that now have territorially limited taxation can observe that tax revenue on domestic production is modest because corporations adopt a "Double Irish" strategy, shifting rights to their earnings to jurisdictions in territorially inaccessible taxhavens, as described in Chap. 6.

Nobody who favors territorial taxation in principle would agree that the sales income of CD players shipped from country H to country G to be sold there should go to a billing service F in a third country, without the producer in H and the seller in G receiving any profits. But that is easily done with rights to intellectual assets, so that countries H and G, with territorial taxation, won't see what's going on. The transfer of IP rights offshore from MNC to CONCH was at least reported to the US IRS, even if valued at a fraction of its potential income.

Countries with territorial taxation that are moving towards IP-based exports may want to rethink their approach, and several are doing that now. Because IP rights are easily transferred out of territorial boundaries into taxhavens, their investments in incentives may not yield the expected benefits at home, as was sketched in Fig. 6.3 [CBO:05]. Governments that limit their view because of territorial taxation are not able to assess extraterritorial shifts of capital.

If the USA were to adopt territorial taxation, any other foreign country could become a taxhaven for US sales of products based on US intellectual capital. Multinational corporations will gain yet greater advantages over domestic businesses [Kleinbard:12]. Companies that now just operate domestically will be driven to set up taxhaven operations as well.

10.2.4 Overly Specific Regulations

Expanding the intent of laws with explicit regulations is necessary but easily overdone. Devising bureaucratic regulations that try to resolve every possible business situation that might occur in the future is fool's work [Economist:12A]. Yet, under the "precautionary principle," the IRS is expected to be able to write regulations to deal with all possible corporate behavior in the next 20 years [ChapotonG:88]. Conditions in those regulations may appear reasonable, but often lead to unreasonable consequences. Subsequently, escape clauses for current situations are easily misused by careful wording of business contracts.

The resulting labyrinth of regulations invites locating loopholes [Posner:77]. It gives large businesses a foothold to minimize their taxes by legalistic tactics. Excessive specificity also prevents reasonable judges from making fair decisions when they are faced with reams of regulations that attempt to define detailed corporate behavior rather than stress the outcome that the legislation intended.

R4: Write regulations that focus on principles, rather than trying to resolve every possibility of future tax avoidance.

For instance, the top-level principle in valuation of intellectual property (IP) is straightforward and understandable: The value of IP is to be commensurate with the income to be derived from that IP.

Current US regulations state that principle, but also specify multiple methods to apply that principle of IP valuation and add the apparently reasonable directive that a "best method" be chosen [B.3.1(c)]. Exceptions are allowed if problems are identified in a method, but corporations may not have shown the IRS any data beyond those that support their assertion of a best valuation. As shown in earlier chapters, depending on only one view of an innovative buy-in transaction is unreliable.

Limiting the scope of valuations to a single method limits the analysis. Presenting just one method leads to suppression of data and information. Checking multiple methods requires more data, but might show that the chosen method fails to give a credible result, as sketched in Fig. 10.1, based on Fig. 5.14.

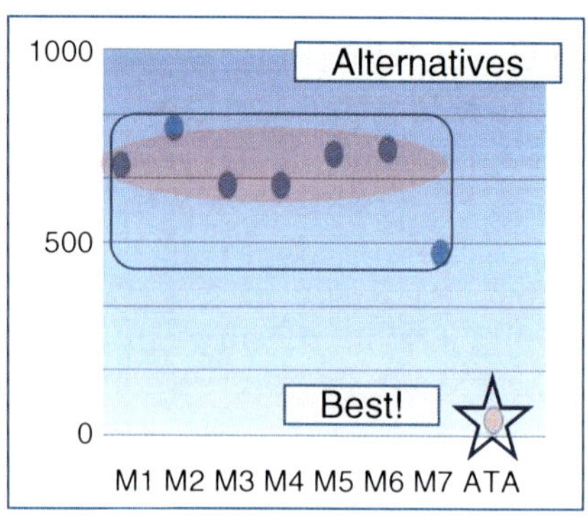

Fig. 10.1 Alternative valuations, ignored when the focus is on single proposed method, stated to be best

Writers of regulations cannot be expected to be familiar with all technical issues that new regulations will touch upon. That forces the authors to rely on input from corporate experts, interest groups, and concerned advisors [Dwoskin:12I]. Lobbyists can help, but they do not have to reveal the full scope of the effects they have considered [Kaiser:09].

Excessive detail invites legalistic controversy. It's easy to criticize any method that attempts to predict future income from IP. Allowing the taxpayer to just present and argue for one best method allows corporate executives and their advisors to hide information and select the one method that maximizes tax avoidance.

An additional complication is that in most cases the same set of income tax regulations has to treat "natural persons" as well as "corporate persons." Regulations that try to avoid unfair treatment of natural persons, such as rules regarding residence, are then applied to corporations that can have legal domiciles in any number of jurisdictions.

10.3 Transparency: R5–R14

Transparency into the processes that allow tax avoidance will be needed before any substantial informed political effort to change taxation can begin [HackerP:10]. Quantifying the effect of applying the processes requires more disclosure of corporate business data [McIntyreGWP:11]. The recommendations presented in this section are specific to corporate offshore operations. Recommendations R5–R8 are intended to increase visibility into offshore operations. Recommendations R9–R12 are intended to give visibility into corporate intellectual property. Recommendation R14 is intended to open up information about settlements.

Corporate reporting requirements are set by the US Securities and Exchange Commission (SEC) and intended to combat fraud. Nonetheless, multinational businesses, as illustrated by our model company MNC, are able to keep information about their tax structure hidden from shareholders, employees, and the public at large. Some companies are so complex that they cannot be understood at any level of effort [Schwarcz:04]. In MNC's case, the IRS chose not to do an audit, so that the IRS did not see detailed information that explained why MNC's US taxes were nearly flat while its earnings increased steadily. Few US companies are audited to the depth needed to detect unusual long-term trends [GAO:09].

10.3.1 Visibility into Offshore Operations

Structures of multinational corporations are complex. In this book, MNC was designed to be simple by having only seven offshore divisions, but actual companies may have hundreds of them [Schwarcz:04]. Offshore business activities are hard to validate and often obscure [Gleckman:02].

Starting in 2005, the SEC waived its requirement that all corporate subsidiaries be listed in annual 10-K reports. The current rule is that divisions that contribute less than 10 % to the total income need not be listed. It is easy for any company to structure itself so it does not need to list any divisions. Corporate divisions in tax-havens are the first to disappear from sight.

The waiver was justified by the Paperwork Reduction Act of 1995 [PRA:95]. Its application here is ludicrous. If a company finds it worthwhile to establish a subsidiary, even just a shell corporation, the added cost of one printed line in an annual report is negligible. The actual motivation for the waiver can only be to hide information from the public. Many other SEC requirements, such as detailed stock holdings by directors, consume many times that amount of paper.

R5: Each subsidiary division of a corporation should be listed in corporate annual reports, with its place of business.

Recommendation R5 is a minimal requirement to reinstate a simple listing. The location should be the actual place of business, not just the place of incorporation. The SEC requires both locations to be given in the primary corporate documents.

If it is worthwhile for a company to establish a subsidiary and pay at least several thousand dollars in annual registration fees, its existence can be shared with its shareholders [Ogley:00]. This recommendation just restores earlier conventions, but it's not enough [OsterB:02]. Listing the name of a shell corporation with a mailbox address in a building owned by a service division of an advising company still leaves the public and the tax authorities with a mystery.

The next recommendation is an extension to the disclosure rule as it existed before the SEC waiver. Any primary report submitted to the SEC already must list the responsible directors, as well as the financial interests they have in the business [Houlder:11]. This practice must be extended to all corporate divisions. Anonymity in financial affairs simplifies mischief [Palmer:10].

R6: The responsible executives and directors of all subsidiary divisions of a corporation should be shown in the corporation's consolidated annual report.

Recommendation R6 refines Recommendation R5, making it possible to assign corporate actions to a responsible individual. Companies often have a great deal of pride in their managers and feature them prominently in their annual reports. However, controversies ensue when executives of a parent company claim they did not know or understand what was going on within their subsidiaries. Because the senior executives of the subsidiary divisions are responsible in the end for the proper operation of the subsidiary companies, their names and addresses should be listed as well. Having full data on their location is important to establish the applicable legal authority for local laws and regulations.

In most jurisdictions the name of the actual person in charge is recorded when a corporation is being registered. The interpretation of this rule should not depend on conventions in some secrecy jurisdictions. Listing another corporation as the owner, allowable in such taxhavens, is not adequate. Often the directors and CEOs of subsidiaries to be named are the same executives who are in charge of the parent company; at other times responsibilities are delegated to lawyers or staff of advisory firms. The decisions made in their name affect the well-being of the overall company. Identifying responsible individuals inspires trust [Bernasek:10E].

Recommendation R7 goes further. Consolidated tax returns currently combine domestic and offshore activities and aggregated financial results. Accounts of subsidiaries can be merged by "checking a box" on the form 1120 used for corporate tax returns [IRS-PS:96]. Not reporting details of corporate divisions, including offshore operations, obscures intracompany transfers [GerthMH:11]. Because domestic and foreign incomes are treated differently for taxation, their information should certainly not be comingled [Shay:12]. The total financial assets held offshore must already be reported to the IRS for the allocation of any interest deductions [B1.1 §6038]. Because knowing the amount of IP rights held in subsidiary divisions is required to allocate taxable income, the criteria used for allocation of earnings should be disclosed as well.

R7: For each subsidiary, list the financial capital, the size of the workforce and the aggregate payroll, and the fraction of corporate IP rights held.

All these data are already available inside the corporation. Information on subsidiaries is now accessible to IRS auditors [B.1.1 §6038]. The reason given for not making them public is to preserve corporate privacy and not to give useful information to competitors. Any serious competitor could obtain adequate estimates at a modest cost. The real worry appears to be that revealing such facts could raise questions of balance among divisions by shareholders and employees. For instance, information on the distribution of the workforce would reveal the actual extent of offshore operations [PalanMC:10]. Having information on the workforce will also unmask any fictitious claim about actual offshore operations.

With that information, buy-in and cost-sharing arrangements of international controlled entities can be reviewed. Intracompany licenses are set not at arm's length and many standard legal contractual terms are meaningless. It is easy to impose an unfair arrangement on the controlled licensee. To avoid US taxes, however, the cost-sharing licenses tend to do the opposite: they give the licensee excessive rights relative to the license payments, allowing capital to shift offshore.

In the past, much tax information was publicly available, but gradually, to avoid misuse of information, restrictions were imposed [Bernasek:10T]. Applying expectations of personal privacy protection to public corporations makes little sense. Considering how owners of a corporation can avoid liability, while burdening others with the cost of failures, should motivate rules that allow public inspection of corporate tax return information [LenterSS:03].

Recommendation R8 is a logical follow-up to Recommendation R7. It requests information regarding the actual transactions that led to the results to be documented according to Recommendation R7. Annual results alone do not reveal the intermediate actions among the multiple subsidiaries that are involved in tax avoidance.

R8: Show transfers of assets, financial and IP, among subsidiary divisions, including those involving Eurodollars and similar debt instruments.

This recommendation addresses the conflict that underlies the debate over territorial versus worldwide taxation. The validity of the simple view that a country should tax only income from sales in its own jurisdiction is undermined when international divisions of a corporation can shift assets invisibly across borders. The intellectual assets that generate income are now shipped invisibly all over the world, while the revenues and profits go to yet other jurisdictions.

Keeping or adopting worldwide taxation, advocated by Recommendation R3, also requires that sufficient data are available to assess the transfers that lead to holdings in corporate subsidiaries, as reported if Recommendation R7 is implemented. Many transfers can occur within a year, as shown during the period the CONCH buy-in occurred (Fig. 5.1). Transfers similar in kind might be aggregated, but distinguishing major tangible, intangible, and financial transactions will show the actual role of the subsidiary divisions. Making such information public can identify imbalances. Some of MNC's shareholders may wonder why CONCH got such a bargain.

The USA now has some rules on reporting extraterritorial transfers to combat money laundering [Wayne:12]. But, as emphasized throughout, financial assets are just one component of worldwide trade. Some asset transfer information may warrant temporary privacy protection; in that case, public release may be deferred, but the tax authorities certainly need access to valid information.

Having asset and transfer data available for aggregation will allow worldwide economic trends to be spotted earlier without loss of privacy [FeenstraEa:10]. At present, understanding corporate growth and development as shown in Fig. 6.10 requires much guessing and extrapolation, mystifying shareholders and potential investors [Kornhauser:05]. Some of our nation's trading partners already require exchange of such information [SAT:09].

Intracompany transparency increases innovation and productivity [Heymann:10]. If employees understand what is going on, they will work more efficiently. The reason given for corporate privacy is to hide useful information from competitors. Another reason may well be that some of the complex tax avoidance approaches would raise questions by concerned employees, even if they make the company more profitable.

10.3.2 Reporting of Intellectual Capital

Intellectual capital is the main value driver of modern enterprises. Corporate management needs to understand generation and consumption of intellectual property (IP) for internal decision making [Sveiby:97]. Denmark has instituted a requirement to show IP on corporate reports [Daum:01]. IP information is already used in corporate accounts to allocate profits, so the reason given that it is not available because it is too hard to value does not hold water. Analysts will recognize the uncertainty of IP amounts placed on the books, just as they deal now with uncertainty in goodwill and real estate valuations.

However, an indication of IP obtained in an acquisition is routine, since nearly always the IP is the motivation. Some independent publications present information on specific categories of IP already, relying on secondary, external sources [Interbrand:07]. A few companies report their assessment of IP now [Murthy:11].

It is essential for business analyses to have comprehensive and relevant data; it is time to change accounting requirements to reflect how the modern world operates [Damodaran:02]. Being uncertain about the value of intangibles is not an excuse. Any valuations of tangible holdings other than cash are also uncertain, even when reported to the penny.

R9: Annual reports should provide a corporate estimate of the value of their intellectual assets.

Recommendation R9 currently just asks for an estimate, recognizing that corporate IP has not been measured as consistently as tangible property. The reported value of inventories depends greatly on rules that have little basis in fact [Gu:01]. Similar problems exist in assessments of real estate held, which are further complicated by depreciation [ShimSD:10].

How the reported IP asset values should be aggregated into the corporate books remains an open question. Some IP now appears on the books subsequent to acquisitions, creating confusion. During any transition period, IP estimates are best kept distinct in a complementary "pro forma" listing. Then it can be left to analysts to combine estimates of IP values with commonly reported assets as they see fit for specific purposes.

Once valuations of IP assets become as trustworthy as values assigned to other corporate assets, they should appear in corporate balance sheets as well. Analysts can always ignore doubtful entries.

Recommendation R10 addresses the complementary component of intellectual capital, the creative workers and management, which indeed cannot be accurately quantified in financial terms. Nevertheless, providing information on this essential component of corporate value in the same context as other corporate assets will help investors understand the business model.

R10: Report and discuss the value of the creative workforce in annual reports.

People are the major contributors to corporate growth, but receive too little attention relative to financial and tangible assets. Distinguishing the creative workforce, with metrics of education and experience, will add to insight and trust by investors. Consistent reporting will help the public understand modern enterprises much better. Having such information helps in following the flow of investments from IP generation to revenue generation and earnings aggregation.

Most annual reports already proclaim the importance of their workforce and its capabilities. Some Scandinavian countries have taken the lead in quantifying those assets [Sveiby:97]. In many annual reports the size of the workforce is already being reported, but without consistency of categorization. Now, if needed, information can be extracted from the amount of payroll taxes being paid. Extraordinary payments to management and directors are shown. From other public information, the composition of the workforce can be deduced. Having this information in a consistent form will avoid misunderstandings by investors and tax authorities.

10.3.3 Capitalization of IP Creation

Inconsistent reporting of corporate assets created through investments in intellectual capital misleads investors and analysts. In high-tech manufacturing, the staff costs of creating IP exceed the costs of making the actual products. Each segment creates value, but only the actual product going out the door can be reliably measured. Early creative work—research—is indeed hard to assess. Recommendation R11 supports Recommendation R9 by advising that once development commences, investments should definitely be capitalized [Damodaran:99].

Capitalization means placing expenses on the books and increasing prior amounts by the cost of money during the development intervals. Recommendation R12 deals specifically with the costs of ongoing development needed to maintain IP.

R11: Investment in development of intellectual property should be capitalized.

Although there is always a risk that an investment will not succeed, the accumulated value of IP-Generating Expenses (IGE) should be reported. Failures can be written off against those amounts, whereas now write-offs are taken without a corresponding basis.

Accounting rules state that R&D expenses are expensed up to the point when product feasibility is established; after that point the costs should be capitalized on the books [FASB:85]. Corporate accountants currently apply that rule with little consistency depending on what looks better in the company's annual report [Lev:01]. No conformance with tax documents is required [Rossotti:05]. Corporate tax professionals can either expense R&D costs or capitalize them. When acquisitions are booked, large amounts of in-progress R&D, which often motivates the acquisitions, are routinely written off because they do not match the accounting that was performed on internal R&D [SlavinK:06].

In time, analysts will realize that having reasonable IP assets on the books will improve stock valuation, and companies may be motivated to make an effort to value and report it more accurately. Providing IP estimates will allow companies to counteract excessive swings in corporate market value, induced by trends in shareholder sentiment.

Because research is seen to be a risky investment, R&D expenses are not considered part of the cost of doing business, but only capitalized when feasibility of resulting products is established. That rule fails to deal with the fact that for products based on IP, substantial ongoing maintenance and development efforts are needed for the products to keep their value in the marketplace.

Recommendation R12 addresses the substantial expenses incurred in maintaining such long-lived product lines as software-based products. The ongoing costs to maintain a viable product line should be distinguished and not presented as innovative R&D as they are now. Costs of ongoing maintenance of IP are an ongoing expense. They should not be booked as if they were R&D generating uncertain income in a distant future.

R12: Book ongoing maintenance expenses as CoGS or SG&A.

Costs incurred for plant and equipment maintenance used to manufacture products are accepted as routine expenses. Maintaining the IP for products in the market is necessary and routine for businesses that derive their value from IP. All costs needed to keep products in the market, including IP maintenance, should be accounted as such [W:06].

Costs incurred after first product release can easily amount to 80 % of total costs [Pigoski:97]. MNC spent about 75 % of its engineering costs on IP maintenance out of the total expenses that are now booked as R&D [F10.3]. Current practice, bundling all technological efforts as R&D on the books, is inconsistent and open to interpretation by investment analysts [LevS:96]. I recommend that only expenses that create new products or add identifiable and marketable improvements be booked as R&D.

To qualify costs for R&E credits the taxpayer must already provide information to support the allocation of costs of personnel performing innovative R&D versus product maintenance. If Recommendation R12 is adopted, summaries of such information will also be delivered to the SEC and the public. Costs identifiable with a unit product are to be allocated as Cost of Goods Sold (CoGS). Costs incurred for general IP maintenance would be booked as a line under Selling, General, and Administrative (SG&A) costs. Profitability estimates, as well as transfer prices for IP, can then be based on current and capitalized expenditures and the expected income from those assets. This change in reporting also simplifies the elaborate rules that try to assure that the R&E credit (see Recommendation R18) is not applied to routine work.

10.3.4 Settlements

Most taxation and valuation controversies are settled by negotiation. Only the most contentious cases wind up in court and establish precedents for subsequent practice [Baxandall:12]. Settlements made out of court are typically sealed and not available for inspection. Only the lawyers in the case gain any new insights. Normally, in law, precedents provide guidance for future behavior, avoiding the need to bring similar situations for repeated legal scrutiny. The fact that the IRS or SEC settles a disputed assessment in a contested case does not mean that the settlement terms should not be reported [Economist:11S].

R14: Do not make settlements confidential.*

At present, public information about legal precedents is based on the few extreme cases that wound up in court and not on the bulk of cases where some degree of agreement was achieved. Public disclosure of facts and considerations that lead to settlements will encourage conformance with acceptable practice. Now precedents are based on a fairly small number of litigated cases [OBrienEa:98]. Litigated cases represent extreme positions that could not be settled. Observing very favorable settlements achieved by corporate lawyers encourages aggressive litigation.

Fewer conflicts will arise if settlement information were available [OBrienO:02]. Hiding information also raises suspicion of unfairness. Concern by outsiders about being treated unfairly destroys trust. Lack of trust encourages attempts at extreme tax avoidance.

All the information obtained in Recommendations R5–R14 should be electronically reported and available online. Keeping records in databases seems obvious today, but the tax authorities in Nevis, a Caribbean island, are proud that they keep all corporate records on paper [Brooks:12]. *Recommendation 13 is intentionally omitted.

10.4 Tax Collection: R15–R17

All of my recommendations up to now dealt indirectly with the fair allocation of taxes due. We must also confront tax collection specifically. If the process of tax collection is not perceived as being fair, trust in the system disappears [Kornhauser:07]. Issues of unfairness encourage legal challenges, increasing the workload of the IRS even more. Tax avoidance will increase.

10.4.1 Realistic Treatment of Anticipated Benefits

Allocation of costs and earnings among international partners is based on the reasonably anticipated benefits of their shared intellectual capital, the RAB. Taxes are based on earnings, but the earnings are only realized in the future. In Chap. 5 the focus was on future earnings, but in Chap. 4, Sect. 4.2.3, various choices of RAB ratios were presented [F4.1]. Alternatives 3–6 there provide projections into future ratios. While current RAB are relatively easy to determine, projections of future divisional earnings in the partner countries present the same issues as any projections into the future. However, as part of projecting overall earnings, country differences will have been considered, providing a basis for RAB projections. RAB ratios should be based on current and future earnings. However, sales are commonly used as a proxy for earnings. Use of Sales data as the basis for setting the RAB ratio was promulgated already in 1927 within the League of Nations' proposals on taxation, although the rule also allowed for bilateral renegotiations [dAroma:27]. It was recognized that the types of investments and costs can differ, so that sales cannot always be the determinant. As a remedy, rules just distinguished "manufacturing" and "merchanting" profits. Having only an agent on commission or a merchant in another country to support promotion and distribution was not to be taken as evidence of residence for income purposes.

The difficulty of identifying costs of manufacturing from merchanting has increased in the modern world, where corporate functions and ownership rights can be shifted freely [DuhiggB:12]. A corporation's choices of how and where to carry out aspects of its business have been multiplied. Is copying papers or CDs manufacturing? Corporations split phases of manufacturing as well as support functions among many jurisdictions. Valuable components, intangibles, and services can be shipped across borders at negligible cost.

In modern commerce, basing the RAB ratio on sales income rarely reflects the effort expended on making, distributing, and selling products by multiple worldwide divisions, so that sales are no longer a valid proxy for fair divisional earnings [F10.4]. A minimal presence in a taxhaven can justify a sales-based RAB ratio unrelated to local value creation. Countries that ignore actual contributions to income or allocate them differently allow reporting of corporate income to be unbalanced and escape taxation.

In simplistic valuations a single Reasonably Anticipated Benefit (RAB) ratio, set initially and based on a nexus, a shell entity where revenue from sales is booked, may be used to unfairly determine long-term allocation of benefits.

R15: Base the divisional allocation of net income on the costs incurred in IP creation and its benefits into the future.

Cost and earnings in many jurisdictions must be assessed and balanced. In each jurisdiction expenses to sales revenues in other jurisdictions are incurred. The allocation of net income in all jurisdictions is to be based on relative product costs in each operating division. At the final sales' nexus, the contribution may just be the local distribution costs. The costs would be those documented by the unit costs (CoGS) and a share of the overhead costs (SG&A) according to sales volumes.

Major investments must be allocated over a reasonable lifetime. Since investments to generate intellectual capital are transferred among jurisdiction in buy-ins, cost sharing, and buyouts, the RABs used must reflect the earnings ratios over the future life of the intellectual capital. Since, as analyzed as part of rollover valuations (Method M7 in Chap. 5), the leverage of that investment is expected to be major, a failure to be careful can lead to significant errors.

When sales are truly global and mediated over the Internet, basing the allocation on a reported sales' location is meaningless. Sales of software and entertainment products are not bound to localities. Since the locations of the actual purchasers are invisible to governments, there is no verifiable base of sales data to compute the intended benefit allocations. Trying to assign all income to one nexus leads to misvaluations.

While difficult, options to fairly assess costs and estimate income exist. Determinations of production costs incurred during each of the many phases from raw materials to a final product are made already today by businesses in jurisdictions that levy value-added taxes. Assigning cost fairly removes an inducement to manipulate transfer prices. The estimate of residual income due to routine costs cannot be manipulated easily, because routine margins are known to always be less than 10 % [HandL:03]. The use of royalties can remove uncertainties of future income, although they open up new opportunities for tax avoidance.

A fair allocation provides an appropriate flow of revenue from earnings to tax authorities worldwide. If adopted in productive semi-taxhavens, it would increase their revenues as well.

10.4.2 Avoid Inappropriate Use of Royalties

IRS regulations allow buy-in payments for the transfers of IP rights to be made by three methods:

1. A single payment, a lump sum based on a valuation.
2. A lump sum paid in installments—as used by MNC.
3. Royalties based on the actual future income.

Royalties have an important role in arm's-length transactions, as described in Appendix C. Royalty payments accrue to a licensor as a percentage of future sales by the licensee. Their use is appropriate in true arm's-length transactions where an inventor has some IP, but does not have the means to exploit it, as sketched at the top of Fig. 10.2.

In such a conventional setting situation the inventor will license the rights to exploit that IP to an independent manufacturer. The licensee develops the actual product, assesses the market, manufactures the product, and then starts selling it. A portion of the revenues, determined by the royalty rate set in the license agreement, goes to the licensor, the inventor [Parr:07]. The arms-length licensee, planning to manufacture a product, assumes most risks:

1. Can the IP be reduced to practice?
2. Can it be produced in volume?
3. Is it really unique?
4. Is it competitive with alternative products?
5. Is there a market?
6. Will it be ready in time?
7. Can the market be convinced?

If no sales ensue, the inventor receives nothing, but the manufacturer has lost the investments made to get the product to market, which may well be a much greater amount.

Fig. 10.2 Licensing settings

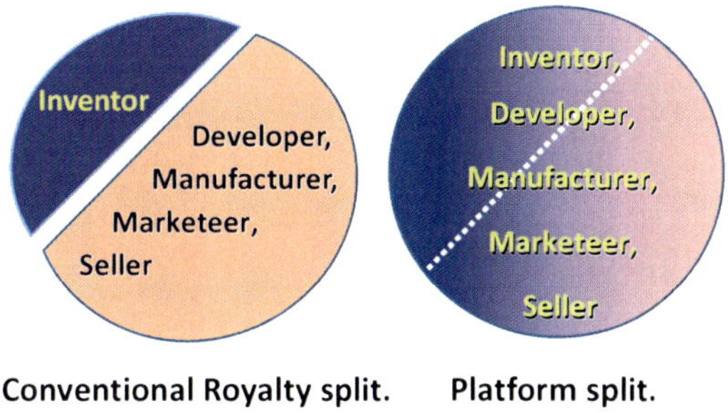

The situation differs radically when an extant enterprise splits its platform into two parts, a domestic and an offshore part, taking advantage of incentives intended to make US businesses more competitive. No distinct risks exist when a company licenses its capabilities to a participant who is an owned and controlled offshore operation, as shown at the bottom.

In a platform split transaction the foreign entity is just a shell, it contributes no IP, and its function is indistinguishable from the parent's offshore operations as they existed prior to the split.

R16: Do not allow royalties to pay for low-risk transactions.

All the prerequisites for product sales have already been met [Morgan:10]. The valuation has merely to assess the amount of expected offshore income from the entire box of intellectual capital made available [B.1.2 #7(b)(1)(ii)]. That income would be similar if the company did not split itself, and the margin of revenues would be similar as well.

Using a counterfactual business model distorts the intellectual contributions of the two parties. Arm's-length inventor's royalties on revenues tend to range from 3 % to 15 %, whereas the actual margins for offshore operations of most existing companies that are split are 25 %–80 %. The tax consequences are huge and cannot be reasonably adjusted after the fact [Mihaly:93]. The US licensor will receive royalties amounting to perhaps 20 % of what could be earned if the income were allocated according to a fair RAB, as defined in Recommendation R15 [F10.5]. The remainder of the offshore earnings winds up in the licensee's taxhaven.

10.4.3 Repatriation of Assets From Taxhavens

We saw in Chap. 2 how MNC was able to take advantage of the 2004 Jobs Creation Act [AJCA:04]. Like most participants, MNC used the transferred funds to acquire smaller companies, resulting in job losses [Sullivan:04]. As a side effect, the repatriated funds from MNC's taxhaven, CONCH, actually increased CONCH's right to receive MNC's nonroutine profits from 45 % to 68 %. This had the effect of

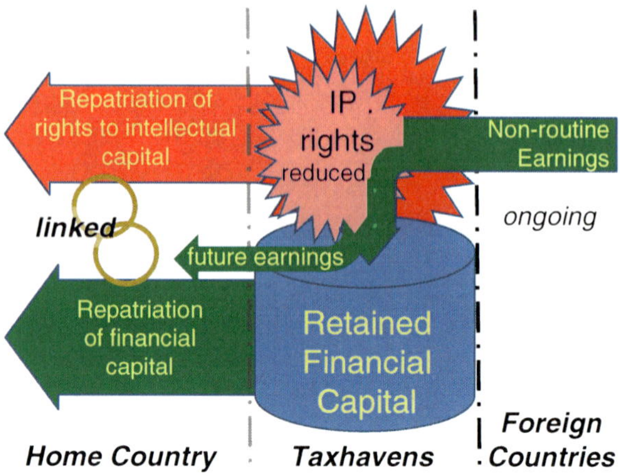

Fig. 10.3 Joint repatriation

increasing the rate of capital accumulation in CONCH and decreasing the taxes paid to the US Treasury from MNC's worldwide operations.

A short-term repatriation window cannot produce organic growth, as documented after the AJCA 2004 attempt [LevinEa:11]. Repatriation of excess financial capital ignores the intellectual capital that created those funds. The rights to exploit intellectual assets are left behind allowing offshore funds to grow again [KangN:12].

R17: Link any repatriation incentive for financial capital to a commensurate repatriation of IP, so that future earnings are received in the USA as well.

Laws designed to give incentives for repatriation are already questionable. But, if enacted, to be effective, such laws and the derived regulations must address the fundamentals that create and maintain capital imbalances.

Any repatriation of capital, whether under the full tax rate or at reduced (or zero) rates, should be accompanied by repatriation of the IP that creates the capital in the first place. Not doing so is equivalent to trying to empty a lake without stemming the spring that feeds it. The intent is sketched in Fig. 10.3, derived from Fig. 8.2. Implementation requires records of IP held in taxhavens, as advocated in Recommendation R7.

Analyses of the relationships between tax rates and economic activity have ignored the effect of retention of IP rights, as seen subsequent to the 2004 AJCA-motivated capital repatriation, shown in Fig. 9.2 [Auerbach:06].

The failure to link financial profits with intellectual efforts and ownership of IP rights causes much expert advice on changes to taxation to be irrelevant [Atkinson:11]. The data are also easily manipulated to make simplistic arguments about the effects of changes in corporate taxation [Milsted:12].

10.5 Role of Tax Expenditures: R18–R19

In this section I present two recommendations regarding incentives given by the US Congress that directly affect corporate taxation. They are just two examples of incentives now implemented through tax expenditures, concessions as tax credits and deductions that are best replaced by focused financial subsidies.

Governments establish policies to encourage activities or behaviors considered to be beneficial to the national interest. An example is a tax credit available to purchasers of heavy hybrid trucks [IRS-QV:11]. This law gives tax concessions to a few profitable businesses and has cost the US government about $200M annually for several years [CBO:08]. The costs incurred by the IRS of drafting the regulations, considering the interaction with other regulations like the Clean Air Act, assuring consistency with the Department of Transportation, designing forms, and administering and auditing the credits—and the cost to the taxpayer to comply—are not accounted for when the incentives are legislated.

Tax credits and deductions, as covered in more detail in Appendix E, are a popular alternative for legislators to provide incentives. Direct support of a worthy cause increases the federal budget, whereas tax reductions do not change the spending; they just reduce the revenues available [Toder:00]. Except for the overhead, the economic effects are similar for the country and for corporate taxpayers [Bartlett:12B]. But the numbers—and the politics—look better.

However, the cost of tax expenditures varies with the level of economic activity. The effect is that tax expenditures provide less benefit in years when economic activities and corporate tax obligations are already at a low level, the opposite of the desired objective [Hungerford:11].

Tax expenditures differ administratively from subsidies. They place administrative responsibility on the Treasury and the IRS to achieve objectives that are the intrinsic responsibilities of other governmental departments, such as the Department of Commerce (DoC) or the Department of Defense (DoD). The IRS has to interact with those departments on rule making and implementation. However, all those US government departments have already the means to provide grants and subsidies to deserving recipients.

We describe one example in Appendix E, namely veterans' employment legislation, where tax incentives are provided to help the clients of the Veteran's Administration of the DoD. Now DoD obligations are offloaded onto all taxpayers and the administrative work onto the IRS.

Many tax expenditures aim to benefit some businesses without incurring a visible line-item cost in the federal budget. Recommendations R18 and R19 focus on two of the many incentives intended to make US manufacturers more competitive.

10.5.1 Supporting Research

To encourage innovation, many countries give concessions to companies that engage in research [Hall:01]. Deducting R&D costs from taxable income is a simple approach [Damodaran:99]. The current US approach is the Research and Experimentation (R&E) tax credit provided for increasing domestic corporate research [Sullivan:11]. Following fairly complex rules, up to 20 % of qualified research expenses can be credited to taxes instead of expensed [Dumagan:95]. They are to be extended permanently in the 2012 budget, although the supporting report cannot provide more than a factor 1 leverage [UStreasury:11]. Government tax credits support mature companies that a venture capitalist would never consider, who expect leverage factors from 2.5 to 10 [F5.58].

No test is required to determine who will own the IP resulting from the supported research. Given that corporate funding paths are complex and that money is fungible, finding out who will benefit from that research is impossible [Clausing:04]. US-based research supported by foreign funds is eligible for these R&E credits, even if the rights to its exploitation and its profits end up offshore [Rashkin:07]. R&E credits are one of the government's largest corporate tax expenditures, and they reduce the taxes of US manufacturers by more than 10 % [F10.6].

In practice, large businesses benefit much more from these R&E credits than smaller enterprises, even though small enterprises are thought to be the main drivers of innovation and job growth [Green:12]. Tax credits are irrelevant to the many research activities carried out by entrepreneurs who do not yet earn revenues. An enterprise just starting up rarely has any profits that could benefit from R&E credits [BierceEa:11]. Tax concessions that have been proposed as incentives for start-up companies are equally questionable [Obama:12].

R18: Do not use tax credits to support research.

The $8.3B annual tax revenue reduction due to the R&E credit would be better spent on direct support of research [Bartlett:12B]. A direct mechanism already exists in the Small Business Administration (SBA). Government agencies now allocate 2.5 % of their annual expenses to their Small Business Innovation Research (SBIR) programs, a total of $2.3B in 2008. Employees at these agencies that specifically oversee matters such as communication, the environment, or health are familiar with the research being performed. Already now SBIR funding is to be increased to $4.0B annually [Obama:12]. Improving its management and making the SBA administrative process less risk adverse could help a lot [Wessner:08].

To be eligible for R&E credits requires keeping records of employee activities. At the same time the availability of the R&E credit encourages companies to book R&D costs differently for the IRS from what they report to their funders and owners [JCT:11]. Examining tax returns using R&E credits puts a heavy burden on the IRS examination teams [Chaback:07].

Recommendation R19 addresses another incentive provided as a tax expenditure: benefits that are given to software producers and filmmakers. Auditing them requires a level of expertise that is a challenge even for experts. The 200 pages of those tax regulations are hard to read and understand for software experts [B.1.2 §199-0 to -9]. Any decision may well be delegated to corporate tax departments. It is hard to envision how a taxpayer can be confident that all of the incentive has been obtained and that the boundary into tax evasion has not been crossed.

R19: Do not attempt to support specific categories of research.

For example, MNC's product, the Maniac, depends on innovative software that is loaded onto the chips that MNC JB in Malaysia purchases from its suppliers in Taiwan. The embedded software code was designed and tested by MNC engineers in California.

Requiring IRS staff to decide whether the chips are primarily hardware or simply a way to package stable software makes no sense. Hardware, after all, is petrified software [Lentz:89]. Many pages of regulations are written to help nonexperts decide technical issues in an industry that changes rapidly. Not all software is eligible [IRS-199:12]. Because the rules are complex, MNC will engage legal help if it wants to benefit from the tax regulation §199 incentive for the embedded software it loads into its Maniacs before sale to its customers.

10.6 Abolish Corporate Taxation: R20

A drastic solution for many of the issues raised in this book is to stop taxing corporations at all. Abolishing taxation of corporate income strikes at the root of the issues I have presented [Crowell:37].

Our challenge is to do no less than pull the current income tax code out by its roots [Rosenbaum:95].

Complete abolition of the frustrating taxation of corporations gets rid of a noxious weed—a better approach than being wounded when trying to prune its thorny branches by trying to plug holes in the fence one at a time [Lessig:11].

Abolishing corporate income taxes was part of a carefully analyzed model tax proposal devised by the Secretary of the Treasury in 1977 [BradfordS:77]. R20 provides a full integration of corporate and individual income taxation. Today's globalization and the growing use of taxhavens make the arguments stronger [OTP:07]. Being focused, it is simple to implement.

This book has shown that multinational tax avoidance, as practiced by MNC and the majority of its real-world peers, is unfair to other US businesses. No resources could ever be marshaled to make enforcement in the USA evenhanded. Furthermore, the issues are too complex to be adequately solved by more laws and regulations.

The radical, but clean, solution is to abolish taxation of corporate income. An immediate effect is that double taxation of corporate earnings is gone. Dividend and capital gains distributions can now be fully taxed when received by the shareholders according to their income tax rate [Burman:11]. Increasing taxes on those corporate distributions substantially reduces the effect of abolishing corporate taxes on total federal tax revenues [CohanA:12].

This recommendation is not based on preexisting or political principles. Neither is it derived from any of the many macroeconomic theories that are bandied about [Economist:11T]. Instead this recommendation stems from the frustration felt by anyone having to deal with the myriad of interwoven regulations that govern corporate taxation. This issue is not limited to US taxpayers and tax authorities; it threatens corporate taxation in the EU as well [deMooij:05]. The head of UK revenues stated that taxpayers are fending in a tax jungle [Nolan:10].

R20: Abolish corporate taxation entirely.

To be fair, abolishing corporate taxation has to apply equally to all businesses, not just to multinational corporations or any specific industry subset [Economist:11F]. It must be applied to any corporation and to all its corporate divisions domiciled in the USA. The loss of government income is compensated substantially by levying standard tax rates on income from dividends and capital gains, as was independently proposed earlier [BowlesS:10]. Double taxation of corporate earnings is gone; all taxation of corporate earnings is deferred until the earnings benefit the individual owners, following the existing approach used by S-corporations and partnerships [BradfordS:77].

Much tax legislation and complex regulations exist now to reduce the effect of double taxation of corporate earnings, once at the source and subsequently when corporate profits are passed on to the shareholders. They all become irrelevant once corporate taxation is abolished. Business can be structured independent of tax concerns. C-corporations become similar to S-corporations that pay dividends in addition to wages, salaries, and profits to their owners. Corporate profits after investments for growth are dividend payouts [BradfordS:77]. All corporate payouts received by individuals are taxed at the rate set by the recipients' income brackets.

Proposals that only reduce corporate taxation still justify lower tax rates on dividends and capital gains received by individuals to offset effects of the remaining double taxation. Proposals to significantly lower the corporate income tax rate are common, but they do not reduce tax complexity and ignore the offsets given to individuals [HassettB:07]. Novel proposals, such as a zero tax rate to be applied only to manufacturing companies, are too complex to regulate, because manufacturing and financing are strongly integrated [Gleckmann:11]. As long as corporate income is taxed, double taxation remains an issue, and the controversy on how to tax dividends and capital gains will continue while evermore complex regulations ensue.

Recommendation R20 increases the taxes of the recipients of corporate earnings. That trade-off is simple and easy to understand and has been advocated recently by some expert economists for less pragmatic reasons [AltshulerHT:10]. The change does not directly affect most individuals, so the pushback should be much milder [Rauch:94]. But the change needs to be clearly explained. When President Reagan informally mentioned doing away with corporate taxation, his remark had to be squelched to avoid backlash. Most reformers still feel that just substantially lowering corporate tax rates is politically not feasible [Sullivan:11].

The next four sections discuss the effects for businesses, individuals, and government when abolishing corporate taxation and full individual taxation:

10.7 Financial effects on businesses, individuals, and government.
10.8 Operational, administrative, and social effects.
10.9 Objections and rejoinders to the shift from corporate taxation.
10.10 Likely international effects and responses.

These sections aim to establish feasibility and support for this recommendation.

10.7 Financial Effects of Abolishing Corporate Income Taxes

An immediate question arises when reduced or zero corporate taxation is proposed: Will it bankrupt the US government? The short answer is "No." This section analyzes how the absence of double taxation can compensate for much of the revenue loss.

I do not trust the Laffer Curve cited by many proponents of lower corporate tax rates [Gabriel:11]. The curve is based on an apex beyond which taxpayers will work less or evade taxes more. Reducing taxes below that point promises greater tax revenue due to increased corporate activities [MankiwW:05]. Not everyone agrees [Bartlett:12B]. In any case, Recommendation R20 will have less effect on such growth because it also increases taxation of individuals' dividends and capital gains. Taxes on investors' income reduce their spending power, although those reductions should be offset by higher corporate payouts. The effect of these basic expectations is quantified in the final part of this section.

This subsection covers the financial effects of Recommendation 20 on

1. Corporate income in Sect. 10.7.1.
2. Small business income in Sect. 10.7.2.
3. Individual income in Sect. 10.7.3.
4. US government tax revenue in Sect. 10.7.4.

While the effect on government tax revenues will be the major concern of many readers, changes in taxpayers' incomes must be covered first.

10.7.1 Change in Corporate Activity and Payments

In broad-based proposals, the effects of changes in corporate taxation nearly disappear [Sullivan:11]. The total corporate tax collected during 2008–2010 was less than 10 % of total US tax revenues and the percentage is decreasing [F10.7]. Corporate tax revenues fluctuate more than total tax revenues because businesses are more affected by changes in the state of the US economy, changes in tax deductions and credits, and effects of globalization.

Nearly 5.6 million businesses filed US corporate tax returns in recent years. For 2007 they reported a total of about $80,000B in assets, $27,000B in revenues, and $1,100B in earnings. After tax credits, they paid about 26.5 % of those earnings in tax [F10.8]. For estimating the effects of abolishing corporate taxes, I use averages over multiple years.

10.7.1.1 All Corporations

The immediate benefit to corporations is a substantial gain in potential profits. Without adding new investments the amounts of profits becomes equal to earnings. The availability of the money saved by not paying taxes can flow to three destinations:

1. Corporate capital. Multinationals are already holding much capital offshore which collects interest free of tax. However, just having capital is not very profitable.
2. Investment in corporate operations and growth. That is the expectation of economists and the hope of politicians. To be able to do that effectively they also have to grow their intellectual capital by hiring and training their workforce. In Sect. 10.7.3, I will quantify expected effects based on past experience.
3. Dividend payments to corporate shareholders. Some dividend increases will be demanded to offset the full taxation of dividends by US resident shareholders. That amount will be estimated in Sect. 10.7.3 as well. There may be some higher payouts, as occurred after the 2004 tax holiday due to AJCA [DharmapalaFF:09]. But now, when shareholders no longer have low tax rates for dividends received, more benefits will accrue from wise corporate investments than from payouts.

Corporations also gain considerable administrative and operational efficiencies. An important effect of abolishing corporate taxation entirely is that it equalizes treatment of corporations bound to domestic assets and corporations with assets in many locations worldwide.

10.7.1.2 Multinational Corporations

In 2004, the most recent year for which I have data available, US multinational corporations paid only about $16B of US tax on approximately $700B of foreign active earnings, or an effective US tax rate of about 2.3 % on that income [Helman:10]. US companies, not being able to use foreign tax credits and hold earnings in taxhavens, paid 27.5 % taxes on domestic revenues [F10.9]. Being a multinational corporation engaged in tax avoidance, MNC's profits would increase only by about 11 % without corporate taxation [F10.10].

The vast difference in effective tax rates of foreign-source income and US-source income is a convincing argument that the current tax laws and regulations are unfair [Hines:05C]. Abolishing all corporate taxes removes the distortion.

Once US corporate taxation is abolished, dividends by all controlled subsidiary corporations are also untaxed by the US treasury. The parent corporation can decide to move any and all funds now held in its offshore accounts home, as needed for investment or for shareholder dividend payouts. Equalizing taxation removes the advantage that multinationals have in acquiring businesses worldwide, often leading to job losses.

10.7.1.3 Repatriation of Offshore Capital

With adoption of Recommendation R20, all multinational corporations will be able to repatriate capital held offshore as needed, without paying taxes. Permanence of tax levies or, in this case, their absence, allows for long-term planning. The benefits of spending on investments versus dividend payout to shareholders can be rationally assessed.

One-time repatriations in the past have encouraged ad hoc expenditures rather than long-term investment for a litany of reasons:

1. Low-tax repatriation applied only to multinational companies, giving them an advantage over US investors in acquiring domestic businesses and start-ups.
2. The acquisitions are poorly vetted for compatibility, and often abandoned.
3. IP remains in the taxhavens, so that future earnings again wind up offshore.
4. Low tax rates for dividends remain and add to the imbalance.
5. Maintaining a taxhaven remains useful to shelter subsequent earnings.
6. No efficiency in the tax regime is gained [DesaiH:04].
7. Complex regulations to deal with corporate taxation remain in force.

Permanent abolition of corporate taxation will have a fundamental, long-term effect on repatriation of offshore capital. Abolishing corporate taxes nullifies having to credit foreign taxes; they become business expenses. Repatriation and reinvestment in the USA will occur as needed, although repatriation might take longer than expected by proponents of radical plans to abolish all income taxes [BoortzL:06]. Once corporate tax avoidance is no longer an issue, rights to intellectual capital can revert to their creators. No tax advantage accrues to offshore investments, so that corporate growth patterns will differ drastically [Barthold:11].

10.7.1.4 Corporate Income and Spending

The primary sources of corporate revenue will not be directly affected, but without taxation of income, more funds will be available for investment in R&D and marketing. Investment in the USA will not be disadvantaged by tax differentials. With successful corporate investments, economic activity will increase, further raising corporate revenues and promoting growth. The extent of these developments will depend on many other factors.

10.7.1.5 Dividend Receipts

Domestic financial transfers will change little. Corporations can also receive dividend income from arm's-length domestic companies. In general, a 30 % tax rate is now applied to dividends from such sources. The total amount is minuscule, less than 0.15 % of operational corporate income. Dividends received from controlled domestic corporations are not taxed now.

Abolishing corporate taxation removes the difference between controlled domestic and foreign corporations, and the resulting distortions. Currently any dividends received from controlled foreign corporations are taxed at the full corporate income tax rate, 35 %. Because of that high rate, income received by the parents of foreign corporations amounts to less than 0.5 % of corporate income. The reason for different distribution of offshore earnings is gone. However, like many high-tech industries, MNC does not pay dividends now, so its shareholders will still not expect dividend distributions. If MNC's management invests the additional funds wisely, MNC's market value will increase more rapidly, leading to increased capital gains for its shareholders in the future.

10.7.1.6 Corporate Financing

The balance of costs for obtaining capital changes when corporate taxes are abolished [Boskin:10]. Without a corporate income tax, there is no longer a tax benefit from paying deductible interest on loans, so that a prime motivation to borrow rather than to sell stock to finance corporate growth is gone [Gideon:05]. Funding for investment will shift away from financial institutions to shareholders. More profits can be paid out as dividends, when interest payments to financial institutions are reduced. The reduced importance of financing by banks may diminish the effort made by banks to supply investment advice to businesses [deMooij:05]. Financial institutions that invest in corporate shares will become more important. The extent of such a shift by investors warrants further analysis [GordonL:00].

10.7.1.7 Corporate Earnings Distribution

Dividend and capital gains tax rates must be considered jointly in any analysis dealing with corporate earnings, because dividends and capital gains are alternative ways for the shareholders to receive benefits. Corporate decisions to pay dividends to shareholders versus investing to grow capital should not be excessively affected by taxation, but rather by business considerations [BradfordEa:91]. Without taxation more funds are available for investment. Dividends should increase as well.

10.7.2 Effect on Small Businesses

Well over 30 million small businesses pass their tax obligations through to their owners. About eight million of those are formally incorporated, gaining liability protection, either as S-corporations or as Limited Liability Corporations (LLCs) [MackEa:05]. LLCs can have offshore divisions.

Small businesses vary greatly in size. More than 90 % had fewer than five employees; many have none. About 2.2 million had 5–100 employees, and only 108,000 businesses were larger [IRS-SC:12]. The simple management and simpler paperwork associated with partnership arrangements (LP, LLP, or LLC) and S-corporations are attractive to these businesses, and larger businesses have joined them [Green:12].

Under partnership structures and in S-corporations, earnings are passed through to the owners, who then pay tax at their individual rates [HurstP:11]. Hence, those businesses are not directly affected by abolishing corporate taxation, but any income their owners receive as dividends or capital gains will now be taxed fully. They may still be eligible for tax credits and deductions. However, a motivation for distorted reporting of income has gone away.

For a growing small business, converting to a C-corporation and gaining easier access to capital becomes more attractive. Aggregate taxation will no longer differ, now an important consideration in choosing the legal form of a business [Goolsbee:04].

10.7.3 Effects on Individual Incomes

Jobs are a primary concern for corporate employees, and income is an issue for shareholders. Models of economic activity must consider the secondary effects on all citizens as well.

10.7.3.1 Effect on Jobs

If corporate taxes are abolished, more funds are available for investment, which should increase corporate activities and encourage growth of corporate employment. Investment can make US workers more productive [HackerL:12]. The taxation-based inducement to hire workers abroad will disappear, though global wage differences remain. We return to this topic in Sect. 10.11.

Investment spending can also be directed towards acquisitions. Long-term assurance of no taxes will avoid the acquisition stampede seen during the 1-year AJCA tax holiday. Workers in smaller corporations, now paying higher taxes, are less threatened by job losses after acquisitions by lower taxed multinationals.

Other countries, unless they also abolish corporate taxation, will have less of a cost advantage in attracting jobs. Countries can still offer other incentives to attract jobs, such as education, training, infrastructure, and real estate benefits. Most countries that now do not levy any corporate income taxes are small and do not have resources for job growth.

10.7.3.2 Dividend Tax Rate Effects

For individuals relying on substantial income from investments, the effects are major. Adoption of Recommendation R20 means that corporate profits distributed as dividends to the owners of the corporations are not taxed at the corporate level. Shareholders will be taxed at full individual tax rates, according to their individual tax brackets, on their dividend income.

Taxes due by high-income individuals who derive much of their income from corporate dividends and capital gains on that portion of their income will nearly double, from 20 % to up to 39.6 %. The current two brackets for dividend taxation will in effect be replaced by the tax brackets for individuals [IRS-1040:12]. For individuals earning above $250,000, the tax rate on that dividend income will increase by 84 % [F10.11]. Couples earning under $72,500 annually are not affected.

Investors who now pay higher taxes on their dividends will demand compensation for the reduction in their after-tax income. There is flexibility. The 2003 reduction in the dividend tax rate from 38 % to 15 % more than doubled corporate dividend payouts [AmrominHLS:05]. Bigger corporate dividend payouts are feasible now because the corporations will have saved more on their taxes [Johnston:12]. The increase in dividend payouts needed for full compensation of investors in the top bracket is 32.5 % and 26.6 % for high earners overall [F10.12]. Increased dividend payouts at that level give an income a boost to all other shareholders. The increased income from corporate dividends and capital gains may push individuals that receive dividend income into higher tax brackets.

Investors like Warren Buffett will see a substantial tax increase [Fifield:11]. A large fraction of Buffett's income comes in the form of dividends from Burlington Northern (BN). At a 26.6 % increase for compensation, BN's total dividend payout would increase by $333M. BN, because it is a domestic company, had an effective tax rate of 38 % in 2010; it would save $1,529M in taxes and still benefit after the offset [F10.13]. However, General Electric (GE) will have to spend $1,388M in order to compensate its shareholders. Because GE had no US income taxes due in 2010, it has no tax savings to offset such costs [Kocieniewski:11G]. To pay its US investors the amount needed for the tax offset, GE could repatriate, now without paying taxes, just 1.5 % of its current offshore holdings [F10.14]. That amount will not make a dent in its business prospects.

10.7.3.3 Capital Gains Rate Effects

Corporations will have substantial savings left after compensating their shareholders for increased dividend taxation. If companies effectively invest the remaining savings from the abolition of their taxes, their market value will increase. Over time, it will benefit shareholders waiting to collect capital gains. Of course, a company should invest only if it sees actual business opportunities, say an unmet demand for its products or for derived products [LynchEa:11]. An alternative way to increase the value of its shares is to buy back its stock.

If a company had been valued by any of the methods sketched in Chap. 5, the parameters used can now be adjusted, and the corporate valuation can be revised. It will always increase, but differ among companies. Overall, long-term investors will gain substantially by increased corporate valuation because Recommendation R20 does not affect inflation. Many other proposals to encourage economic growth are likely to increase inflation, reducing the benefits of capital gains. I return to that issue when enumerating objections in Sect. 10.9.

Currently there are important exemptions to capital gains taxation, such as real estate transfers and estate taxes. These will not be affected directly by fully taxing corporate capital gains.

10.7.3.4 Effect on Retirement Incomes

Dividends are important to retirees who have made investments, such as IRAs, with pretax income. Although the Bush tax cut rates of 15 % and 0 % were scheduled to expire by 2013, it is unclear to what extent retirees and retirement funds were prepared for a dividend tax increase to full rates [Auerbach:99]. For FY2013 a 20 % rate was added for high-income taxpayers [ATRA:13]. Being knowledgeable and concerned about retirement funds, these organizations have considerable clout with corporations [Farrell:12]. Retirement funds and life insurance companies own 23 % of US corporations [F10.15]. Retirement accounts, as Roth IRA plans, funded from post-taxation income are not affected, since they do not have to pay taxes when benefits are taken out [McIntyre:08].

To compensate individuals in typical tax brackets, an increase in dividend payouts of about 6.25 % will compensate for the increased dividend taxes [F10.16]. The organizations that manage such funds should be able to argue strongly for such a minimal adjustment in corporate earnings allocation. Major investors will argue for greater increases in dividend payout, and if they succeed, retirees might benefit greatly. While there may well be corporate resistance, the issues should unify shareholders sufficiently to convince corporate governance.

Retirement investments that have been made with income already taxed will not be affected; they can still distribute benefits tax free [RothEa:98]. Individual income tax forms still have to segregate that income. Fewer individuals will have to deal with AMT calculations, since shifting excess amounts of ordinary income to low-taxed dividend and capital gains has been a favorite tax avoidance strategy by "high net worth" individuals.

10.7.4 The Effects on US Government Tax Revenues

While removing a component of US tax revenues is an obvious and worrisome concern, it just accelerates the trend. As shown in Fig. 10.4. corporate tax revenues as a fraction of US GDP have been decreasing steadily. It shows a linear extrapolation of the corresponding trend in effective corporate tax rates using economic data from a Federal Reserve Bank. US tax revenues from corporations become zero by the year 2050!

The contribution of Corporate Income Tax (CIT) to the US economy in 1994 was already less than 2.5 % of GDP [Slemrod:99]. The 2008 recession and reactions to it lowered the amount of corporate income tax shown in Table 10.1 significantly. There is no indication that the trend will change.

I limit the remainder of this section's analyses to the major components of expected effects that can be quantified with some confidence, extrapolating earlier data to 2010 for consistency. The results are as uncertain as any prediction.

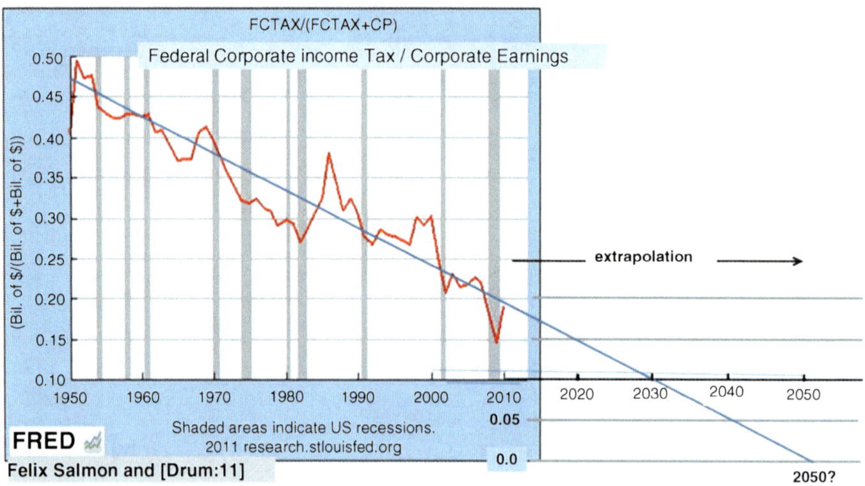

Fig. 10.4 Extrapolating corporate tax rates shown in Fig. 9.3

Table 10.1 Annual US revenue effects of abolishing the corporate income tax

Taxed item	Action	Change	[F _]	Motivation
Corporate income tax, after-tax incentives	Abolish	($143.3B)	10.17	Cannot be fairly administered
Dividends to individuals	Tax as any income	$30.4B	10.18	Treat all sources of individual income identically
Capital gains cashed in by individuals		$69.0B	10.19	
Compensation of share-holders for tax increase	Corporate	$9.6B	10.21	Tax on greater dividend payouts
Effect of new investment		$20.4B	10.22	Tax on increased purchases
Tax credits and deductions for research, manufacturing, etc.		No effect, no tax cancels credits, etc. Any incentives to become explicit		
Total estimated effect		($13.8B)	10.23	0.5 % loss of US tax revenues

10.7.4.1 Tax Revenue Decrease From Abolishing Corporate Taxation

Actual business tax revenues, including those from pass-through entities, were steadily decreasing to $191B by 2010 [F9.25]. In 2009 pass-through entities comprised 71 % of US business tax returns and represented 48% of business net incomes [IRS-ST:12]. The immediate loss to the treasury from abolishing taxation of C-corporations appears then to be about half, but is likely more because the larger corporations will have profited from a much larger share of tax expenditures, such as deductions and tax credits. Pass-through entities do not benefit by reverting to C-corporations. We will assume that 75 % of business tax revenues are lost when taxation of C-corporations is abolished, while 25 % are passed through to S-corporations and LLCs. The expected loss in government revenue becomes $143.3B in 2010 [F10.17].

10.7.4.2 Tax Revenue From Fully Taxing Dividends and Capital Gains

In 2009, 18.5 % of individual taxpayers received dividend income. Most of the income received will go to taxpayers in the top brackets. The marginal top tax brackets are 33 % for incomes above $174,400 and 35 % for incomes above $379,150 [ATRA:13]. Using scaled averages, I estimated that the increase in taxation from 15 % or 20 % to a 35 % or 39.6 % rate yields $30.4B [F10.18].

Net capital gains income varies much more; it was $231.5B in 2009, but approximately $500B outside of recession years. About 16.7 % of individuals reported capital gains or losses. Individuals can choose when to cash in, and their behavior will change in response to changes in taxation, as seen when rates changed in 1986 [DowdMM:12]. An estimate based on 2007–2009 scaled data, but reduced to 70 % to account for behavior change, yields $69.0B per year [F10.19]. Taxing capital gains fully, but in isolation, has been estimated to yield at least $533B over 10 years, again depending on behavioral effects [Wamoff:12].

Offsets by raising taxes on dividends at individual rates and capital gains by up to 28 % are expected to yield already \$87.2B [AltshulerHT:10]. My estimated yield for both taxes on dividends and capital gains at the full individual rate (up to 35 %) is \$99.5B total [F10.19].

10.7.4.3 Second-Level Increase from Greater Corporate Dividend Payouts

As presented in Sect. 10.7.3, corporations will be pushed to share their windfall with shareholders to make them whole. Those dividend payouts will cost about 19 % of the savings corporations gain from not being taxed [F10.20]. The shareholders will be taxed at the full individual rate, yielding \$9.6B in tax revenues [F10.21].

10.7.4.4 Second-Level Increase from Stimulus Effect of Corporate Spending

Corporations, even after making payouts to shareholders, still gain substantial income for spending and investment. A study of regional growth induced by military contracts to private industry indicates the likely effects of increased business activity [NakamuraS:11]. Each dollar spent led to \$1.50 in local benefits as local employment and spending increased. Taking the USA as a single region leads to an estimated effect of investments of \$20.4B annually [F10.21].

This effect is not based on the indirect effect of corporate growth due to those contracts, but merely on increased spending by corporations that have funds to grow. Effects of tax-free repatriation are still ignored.

10.7.4.5 Tax Expenditures

All government tax expenditures related to corporations are gone once corporate taxes are abolished. That means that revenue loss estimates cannot be based on a reduction from the statutory rate of 35 %, but must be based on actual corporate tax revenues, which equate to a rate of less than 28 % [F10.8].

10.7.4.6 Total Effects

With all of those adjustments, the expected changes to US Treasury revenue are shown and totaled in the summary Table 10.1, all extrapolated to 2010 [F10.22]. Although the loss of even 0.5 % of US tax revenues is significant, it is not overwhelming. The main point is that from a governmental revenue point of view, abolishing US corporate taxation entirely is feasible and only advances an existing trend.

More than 90 % of the loss in tax revenues collected from all businesses due to abolition of corporate income tax is compensated by adjustments for elimination of double taxation and direct spending, making it nearly revenue neutral, extrapolating past data with 2013 taxation updates [F10.23]. Ongoing changes in the tax laws will further affect these estimates.

Individual tax returns are easier to check and match automatically than corporate returns, so that revenue losses due to aggressive tax avoidance and tax evasion should decrease. Other sources of federal revenue, enumerated in Chap. 8, Sect. 8.8, are left untouched.

Some transition time will be needed for the effects to be realized. The timing of capital gains effects is especially hard to estimate, because income from sales of shares is taxed only when shares are sold. There is likely to be a short-term bump in revenues, as holders try to cash in before their capital gains tax rates rise [AltshulerHT:10]. The available amounts will vary with the state of the economy [CBO:08]. Sales prices of shares reflect both the actual increase in corporate value and inflation [Walsh:11].

10.7.4.7 Uncertain Effects of Corporate Growth on Government Income

Lowering corporate taxes and encouraging repatriation of capital is widely expected to increase corporate activities and innovation. In turn, increased activity should result in growth of individual tax and other tax revenues. Such predictions vary greatly, and it is risky to count on any of their quantifications [Bartlett:12B]. The least careful guesses have the highest benefits. Figure 9.4 showed the mix of contributions to government revenues, hampering predictions.

Our Table 10.1 only adds taxes from increased spending, or a 14 % compensating effect from corporate tax reductions [F10.22]. Models by various prognosticators have been much more optimistic. Extreme views predict a factor of 20 increase of economic growth with a reduction in corporate taxation, leading to 4 × tax revenue increase [Conard:12]. Experience in Europe with reduced corporate tax rates did show economic growth, but tax revenues remained stable, showing that the effect was fully offset [PiotrowskaV:08]. Formal analyses of past changes assign a 50 % tax revenue recovery to the growth effect from reduced corporate taxation [GravelleS:06]. Longitudinal studies have not verified the effect sufficiently [Reich:11].

Recommendation R20 does not have the same effect as a negligible or zero corporate tax rate, because it is combined with increased taxation of dividends and capital gains. Taxing such income reduces the spending power of investors unless it is fully compensated by higher dividend payouts. If corporations fully recompense investors for increased taxes on their dividends, 81 % of the tax benefits will remain for internal investments [F10.23]. Based on the average rate US corporations pay, about 26.5 % [F10.8], the combined effect is equivalent to a 23 % reduction of the statutory corporate tax rate to 12 %, well below proposals being made during the 2012 election cycle [ReinhartR:10].

Changes in corporate financing should increase investor participation versus bank financing. Interest costs paid by corporations were already eligible for deduction, so there will be no change in earnings, and no effect on corporate profits due to interest costs. Reduced corporate business by banks may reduce their income and hence the taxes they would have paid. But if the activity is taken up by individual shareholders, who are still subject to taxation, tax revenues from financing corporations will increase.

Not having a corporate income tax simplifies the incredible complexity of documenting, computing, and administering corporate taxation by businesses and the IRS. That cost was estimated in the past to be $50B for businesses, equivalent to 25 % of the actual corporate payments to the US government [F10.24]. IRS audits add at least another 2 % [F10.25]. Only part of this cost will be eliminated, as accounting of revenues and costs will continue. Corporations will still have to file tax returns to document other taxes. Their annual 10-K reports to the SEC will also document the dividend payouts to shareholders. Nevertheless, businesses should see substantial savings in tax preparation.

In my analysis, I do not dare add the benefits of increased activities and reduced costs to my estimates, since models by most prognosticators ignore modern business structures. The result is not based on the reasoning behind the Laffer curve [Slemrod:94]. However, an undetermined increase in government revenue beyond those shown in Table 10.1 is likely.

10.7.4.8 Modeling the Effects of Changes in Taxation

Making a more detailed prediction of how US Treasury income would be affected by simply abolishing the corporate income tax (CIT) is beyond the scope of this book. It seems also to be beyond most current economic models, which all ignore intellectual capital and global transfers.

The US Treasury, the Congressional Budget Office, and consulting organizations have data that could provide more detailed predictions [CBO:08]. The effects of two, much more complex, taxation proposals were analyzed in 2005, and much of that framework should still be valid [MackEa:05]. To deal with transition effects, they typically use 5- or 10-year projections. Assessing the effect of Recommendation R20, abolishing corporate taxation and taxing individuals income consistently, will be relatively simpler. The motivation to keep assets inaccessible in taxhavens is gone, and allocation of income to individuals becomes less complex.

Broad predictions have been notoriously wrong. At the onset of the Economic Growth and Tax Relief Act (EGTRA) tax plan instituted in 2001, a prediction was made that the entire federal debt could be retired by 2012 [WilsonB:01]. There were, of course, major unforeseeable events, such as the 9/11 terrorist attack, subsequent wars, a new drug entitlement, and a recession. Now the federal debt is greater than ever.

Current US as well as European studies ignore the effects of IP transfers and taxhavens, which make them inherently inaccurate. Any predictions specific to corporate tax revenues, which are based on data before intellectual capital became the main driver of corporate income, are now obsolete. Financial data and information from locales where actual production takes place are nearly irrelevant, but commonly relied upon [DesaiH:04]. Consolidated corporate data on financial assets are meaningless when it is held in taxhavens and not made available. The US Congress still relies on analyses that use obsolete models and irrelevant data when it has to assess the effect of current proposals to change taxation [Barthold:11]. There is likely some additional information or factors built into models used by for-profit institutions [Dalio:09].

To validly represent the current situation, existing economic models will have to be updated to consider intellectual assets and taxhavens—not an easy task while so little data is available. Implementing Recommendations R5–R14 will make such data available. However, existing models also suffer from many other questionable assumptions, as symmetric reactions to change, which is unrealistic when economic distortions are major [Orrel:10].

10.8 Operational, Administrative, and Social Effects of R20

Making a drastic change in taxation is bound to have more than financial effects. Much effort goes into dealing with taxes. In the end, taxes affect the whole social fabric [SlemrodB:08].

10.8.1 Corporate Business Operations

A primary benefit of the recommendation to abolish corporate taxation is that corporations will be able to make investment decisions that are not distorted by tax effects [HinesS:09]. All businesses, LLCs, C- and S-corporations, are now treated equal.

1. No offshore subsidiaries in taxhavens are needed to shelter taxes from the IRS.
2. Repatriation of capital from taxhavens can occur without loss due to taxation.
3. No reason to move rights to IP offshore so that nonroutine profits go offshore.
4. IP and IP rights can be kept together where created, avoiding a legal disconnect.
5. No need to book earnings in jurisdictions that exempt non-territorial earnings.
6. There should be no need to keep separate books for the SEC and the IRS.
7. The corporate alternative minimum tax (AMT) and related bookkeeping disappears.

On the other hand, corporations will no longer have some of the advantages that were not available to small businesses. The need for a start-up to be acquired by a large corporation to extract profit from its own accumulated intellectual capital will be reduced.

Organizations that now promote tax benefits for corporations will have to lobby for explicit subsidies. Direct and visible incentives may be harder to obtain from Congress than tax expenditures. Some current tax expenditures are so narrow that they fall into the category of "earmarks" [Tanzi:11].

The flow of financial and intellectual capital will not change instantly. Corporations will be able to assess benefits of offshoring by primary business criteria: labor productivity, available infrastructure, and stability. Some firms will move resources now devoted to tax avoidance to increase quantified assessments of corporate intellectual property. Many loose ends will have to be cleaned up in corporate governance once the distortions engendered by corporate tax avoidance are no longer beneficial. If that information reaches their shareholders, the public will gain a better understanding of the role and scope of intellectual capital in modern business.

10.8.2 Administrative Effects on Individuals and Small Businesses

There will be no changes for the 80 % of individual US taxpayers who do not currently declare dividend or capital gains income [F10.26]. The income from dividends and capital gains for the remaining 20 % will be taxed as regular income, using the same brackets and rates and thus slightly simplifying their tax preparation.

1. No separate computation will be needed for dividends or qualified capital gains received directly or indirectly from investments as mutual funds.
2. A major component of the AMT adjustments is eliminated. When less revenue comes from the AMT, the costs of calculating and collecting it may lead to its disappearance.

For individuals, the tax forms needed are unchanged under this proposal. There will be some simplification, but without reforms in individual taxation, the reduction of effort in preparing tax returns will be modest.

10.8.2.1 Effects on Small Businesses

The eight million small businesses that are organized as partnerships or S-corporations will see no differences in the effort needed to file taxes, unless they have engaged in tax avoidance. Payouts for wages and salaries remain unchanged. Untaxed profits from earnings distributions passed through to their owners are considered dividends and now do not qualify for a reduced tax rate.

Some small businesses may wish to restructure themselves as C-corporations and pay their owners through dividends rather than through a mix of distributions. Most large pass-through entities, as shown in Fig. 9.4, appear to be motivated solely by tax avoidance [Sullivan:11]. The current tax motivation to choose a pass-through entity will disappear [GordonG:97].

Some of the capital these businesses accumulate can still be held in abeyance as "carried interest," to be distributed later as capital gains to their managers [Schmidt:12]. Carried interest can still be distributed flexibly, sometimes into family accounts and sometimes as offshore investments [ToderB:07]. But now, carried interest, when finally distributed, will also be taxed at individual rates.

Regulation and enforcement of many tax avoidance tactics become simpler, because the current inconsistency of C-corporations versus pass-through entities such as S-corporations and partnerships disappears [Tyson:11]. Where pass-through entities were used for tax avoidance, by replacing wages and salaries with low-taxed dividend payouts and "carried interest," the effects will be greatest. The allocation of income to carried interest is also common in modern financial institutions and funds, and many of those are not small at all [Orszag:07]. Owners of private tax shelter funds may decide to move offshore.

10.8.2.2 Tax-Exempt Organizations

Charitable organizations that are now exempt from taxation would continue to be tax exempt. Deductions for giving to social, cultural, and educational charities amount to about $50B per year [Reich:12]. But now tax deductions will only be advantageous to individuals.

Corporations will no longer have tax benefits to motivate giving. "Gifts in kind" that allow deducting higher amounts from taxable earnings than the actual value to the business will no longer convey that advantage. However, increased profits can motivate larger donations. Currently, gifts containing a high fraction of intangibles, such as software and computers, are highly valued and cheap to produce. If corporations do not compensate high-income taxpayers fully for increased dividend taxes, charitable donations by individuals may decrease as well.

Investments by charitable organizations amount to over 4 % of US corporate shareholdings [F10.27]. When corporations compensate for higher recipient taxes, they also will benefit from increased payouts, but still not pay taxes on that income. However, interposing charitable organizations is already a major means for high net worth individuals to evade taxes [Collins:11I]. There is already an argument that charitable organization should be taxed on their investment income [Halperin:11].

10.8.2.3 Employment Effects on Individuals

Making any changes in the tax code over time involves nearly everybody. Some specific groups will be specifically affected by abolishing corporate taxation.

On Employees

Workers at all levels suffer from corporate taxes that discourage investment in the USA, reducing their productivity. Analytical models indicate that workers suffer from high corporate taxes in proportion to the contribution of labor and capital [Gordon:86]. The relationship of the ease of international capital flow versus locality-bound jobs has been argued, and there is evidence that lower corporate taxes help the local workforce as well as the shareholders [JensenM:11].

Investments in corporate growth should benefit employees overall. However, many investments in productivity tools allow fewer but better trained workers to replace an existing larger number of workers with less training. The balance varies by type of industry. The high-technology sector, where many multinationals operate, depends greatly on a well-trained workforce to create its IP. Well-educated employees anywhere in the world should benefit the most from abolishing corporate taxes.

Employees in secondary industries and service occupations will benefit indirectly from local increased business activities. They constitute a larger fraction of the workforce than the employees in manufacturing industries. Studies disagree about the effect of corporate taxes on jobs, but distortions are clear [Auerbach:05]. Most data used in the analyses were collected in periods before IP played a significant role, and their predictions are unreliable.

On Tax Consultants

The community most obviously affected is the cottage industry of experts now involved with corporate income taxation (see Chap. 6). They may number well over 100,000, although many deal with other taxes as well [HallR:07]. The leaders among them are among our brightest people. Reforms can reduce that waste of talent [GrubertA:08]. Those experts may then apply their intellectual skills instead to devising projects using the funds that will become available when corporations pay no tax and can repatriate offshore holdings to grow US corporations directly. New initiatives will benefit the economy [Schlunk:00].

On the General Population

Everyone agrees that US taxes are excessively complex, but implementing broad proposals will have wide ranging effects. These effects will lead to behavioral changes by most of the country's population, so that the long-term result cannot be predicted [Lindsay:09]. The specific recommendation to abolish corporate taxes will, in the end, affect most individuals as well, but to a much more limited extent than for corporations. Once the shift is accepted, voter complaints that corporations profit from preferential loopholes in the tax code become irrelevant.

On High Net Worth Individuals

Higher tax rates on dividends and capital gains following Recommendation R20 can motivate high-income individuals to move offshore [FishmanW:01].

10.8.3 Governmental Changes Without Corporate Taxes

We have already estimated a modest, but still significant loss of revenue, even when offset by full taxation of corporate payouts. The transition has to be managed well. The limited scope of Recommendation R20 makes the needed effort more manageable than other proposals to change taxation [Sullivan:11].

A simple overview of expected transitions includes seven items:

1. Requests for subsidies will be made to compensate for loss of specific tax expenditures.
2. Tax collection will be simplified. Corporate taxes currently require a disproportional effort, and their complexity reduces applicability of automation.
3. The complex arguments and ongoing adjustments to try to be fair regarding double taxation of corporate payouts are eliminated.
4. Corporations are no longer subject to international double taxation; any foreign taxes paid just become deductible business expenses.
5. For US corporations, the distinction between territorial and worldwide taxation will disappear. Abolishing corporate taxation is a relatively simple solution to the difficulties addressed in Recommendation R3.
6. There will be no distinction between passive and active income held offshore.
7. Thousands of tax regulations affecting corporations will become meaningless and can be simply ignored, because they tend to deal with tax incentives and their interactions.

State taxes, sales tax, and such alternatives as value-added taxes are not addressed specifically by Recommendation R20, the abolition of federal corporate taxation.

While corporate income taxes levied by states are significant, the ability of large corporations to move their headquarters or specific operations within the US to no-tax states is already a major concern for other US states. Abolishing federal corporate income taxes could motivate other states to abolish their corporate income tax as well. Some US states then need other sources of revenue. For instance, consumption taxes provide fewer opportunities for tax avoidance and may allow states to regain control over local business operations. Section 10.9, on likely objections, addresses some of the expected concerns related to other taxes.

10.8.3.1 Disabled Regulations

By not just lowering the tax rate for corporations, but abolishing taxation altogether, application of tax regulations is greatly simplified. Probably half of the thousands of pages in the tax regulations would no longer be needed. Initially little if any rewriting of those regulations would be required; regulations dealing with corporate taxes would just no longer be invoked. Over time they should be removed. This task will keep busy some of the people who have been spending their time trying to interpret tax laws passed by Congress and transform them into fair and applicable regulations. Tax laws will be similarly affected by an overriding law.

10.9 Objections to Abolishing Corporate Taxation

Although my Recommendation R20 is not as broad as some other proposals to change US taxation, abolishing taxation of corporations is still a serious change. Many objections will be raised. If proponents of abolishing corporate taxation cannot deal with objections, any change will be unlikely. Not having facts at hand makes objections and gripes seem more credible. The earlier chapters in this book elucidated many details.

10.9.1 Twenty Likely Gripes and Rejoinders

I will discuss 20 expected gripes and objections here (G1–G20); many are familiar, because they arose when other corporate tax reforms were proposed [Cray:09]. With each gripe I present matching counterarguments. Readers can decide the relative validity of the rejoinder I present.

G1: Corporations get all the benefits individuals get and should pay for them.

Critics observe that a corporation benefits from government-provided services, paid for by taxes, just as individuals benefit from those services. Corporations benefit from a country's physical infrastructure, from the security it provides, and from its support of the general welfare [Amadi:02]. So why should we treat corporations differently?

C1: A rejoinder is that in the end it is the shareholders, employees, and customers who benefit from corporate activities. A corporation is only a shell enabling an effective organizational structure [Quiggin:98].

Furthermore, much of the important infrastructure is provided by local and state governments. Recommendation R20 only addresses the federal corporate tax; Objection G18 addresses US state taxation.

G2: Corporations count on government to offload their problems.

The government deals with many problems incurred by businesses. So why should companies not reimburse the government for the costs incurred? I list just three balancing initiatives here:

1. *Corporations take risks that affect their workers.*

C2.1: True. However, all businesses are already required to participate in insurance schemes that compensate workers who are hurt in the workplace. Other taxes, specifically payroll taxes, pay the corporate share of retirement, disability, and old-age health benefits.

2. *When a business goes bankrupt, the PBGC, a federal corporation, protects retirement obligations incurred by the business.*

C2.2: True. Businesses pay into the PBGC funds. To the extent that those funds promote the general welfare in a country, all tax revenues are equally relevant.

3. *Corporations affect the environment and should pay for that*

C2.3: True. The pollution created by many industrial processes, for instance, needs attention [BovenbergdM:94]. A general corporate income tax only addresses one segment of polluters. An LLC can pollute as much. It is better to strengthen controls for specific pollution emissions that affect the public.

Each of these cases applies to businesses in general, not only to C-corporations. Obviously, many of these insurance protections could be strengthened. Levies and fees to support the funds should consider costs based on specific businesses' activities and risks. Corporate taxation is a very crude tool for solving these problems. Once corporations do not pay taxes, they have no reason to argue against paying fees or obtaining insurance relevant to the specific problems they cause.

G3: Corporate owners gain the valuable liability protection

The corporate setting relieves its owners of personal liability. Serious errors or faults can only bankrupt the corporation, but the directors and owners have no obligations to the creditors of the corporation. Even for criminal actions only the executives can be held responsible. Risky behavior has little cost. The added value that corporations obtain should be paid for.

C3: The dispensation from liabilities used to be valid consideration. However, C-corporations are no longer unique in that respect. Limited liability partnerships (LLPs, LLCs) and S-corporations also convey such protection to their owners [Thomas:12]. The benefit is already available without income tax obligations. It is a moot argument for taxing C-corporations differently; if anything, it is an argument for taxing all business structures that convey liability protection identically.

To what extent businesses and their owners should be free of responsibility for actions is an open question, but a legal issue. It is external to consideration of fair taxation, If Recommendation R7 is implemented, the increased transparency will make it easier to locate the responsible management.

G4: Corporations have legal rights, similar to individuals.

The courts have upheld the corporation's "right to due process and equal protection of the laws under the Fifth and Fourteenth Amendments" [Gowri:98]. More recently, a corporation's right of free speech and political expression under the First Amendment has been upheld. With such corporate "personhood" come equal obligations, such as paying taxes. Abolishing taxes for corporations breaks the equivalence of a corporate person with a natural person.

C4: The rejoinder is that current laws and tax codes already treat corporate persons differently from natural persons. Laws, regulations, tax incentives, deductibility of interest, and IRS forms are all different for individuals versus corporations

[IRS-1120:11]. Corporations can own other corporations. Having corporations pay income taxes similar to those paid by individuals conveys on them a legitimacy that may not be in the overall national interest [Elliott:12].

There is also a substantial distinction in the public perception. The fact that some current laws equate a corporation with a person, when people have such different morals, motivations, loyalties, and obligations, is considered a philosophical mistake by many observers [Gore:08].

The right that an individual citizen has to return home has no corporate counterpart. A key differentiator that arises when discussing this objection is the concept of loyalty, which should be a symmetric obligation. The difference between how corporations are managed versus the management of an individual's property was already a concern of Adam Smith [Smith:1759].

Loyalty

We talk about US companies, but the concept of national loyalty is meaningless for multinational corporations with worldwide divisions. Those divisions do research, manufacturing, and selling wherever it is advantageous for them [PackmanC:11].

An individual who is or becomes a citizen of the USA declares loyalty to the USA and its institutions. However, a corporation never declares any such loyalty, nor do its directors in their official capacity. For the last 30 years at least, the accepted view has been that corporations are primarily beholden to their shareholders, wherever they are [Martin:11].

In that sense a corporation's structure is more like that of a tribe. The Kurds have a primary fealty to their tribe and its assets, whether they live in Turkey, Iraq, or Iran. Imposing national boundaries and rules on them created conflicts. Once a tribe observes that rules for the general welfare of one country hurt them, all kinds of escapist behaviors become justified [Quiggin:98].

Imposing national rules on multinational companies likewise creates conflicts. Moving to a narrow nation-state based approach, as in territorial taxation, encourages the use of taxhavens. Only a multinational corporation can create a "Double Irish" structure or enjoy a "Dutch Sandwich." Most individuals find such strategies objectionable [TaylorFC:06].

G5: Corporations should pay more taxes because they have fewer operational constraints.

Corporations should compensate the nation for the additional moral and operational freedoms they enjoy. Taxing corporations compensates the public for the costs incurred due to the extra privileges afforded to corporations, freedoms that enable them to gather income from actions that an individual cannot engage in.

A US corporation does not have the same moral constraints as those that are imposed on a US citizen. It doesn't have to profess loyalty to the US Constitution—in fact, a multinational corporation could not do so. A corporation can select tactics for growth that would be criticized if the same tactics were employed by a citizen [CavenaughEa:04]. Does a corporation have to stop when it accidentally hurts a pedestrian?

C5: This may be the most valid argument for taxing corporations. However, it implicitly condones behavior that would not be acceptable for natural persons. Paying for unacceptable behavior seems to legitimize such actions. Furthermore, other, untaxed, business structures have fewer constraints imposed on them as well.

This objection is a generalization of the issues raised in objections G2, G3, and G4. Emphasizing that corporations are different from natural persons does not mean they should be taxed more heavily.

G6: Natural persons have residency constraints imposed, so should pay less taxes.

Perhaps natural persons should pay less if they are subject to constraints that do not apply to corporations. Individuals, for tax purposes, are constrained to have a single domicile. While a corporate person can have its parts in many locales, an individual is a single unit. An individual person can move to a taxhaven, but then all of that person is domiciled there, and protections that the person's prior domicile offered are no longer available.

C6: Taxing corporations does not address the issue of allowing multiple domiciles for multinational corporations. Taxation only motivates misuse of unnatural privileges.

A corporation can split itself, having active hands in multiple jurisdictions, as sketched in Fig. 10.5. MNC derived substantial benefits from that capability.

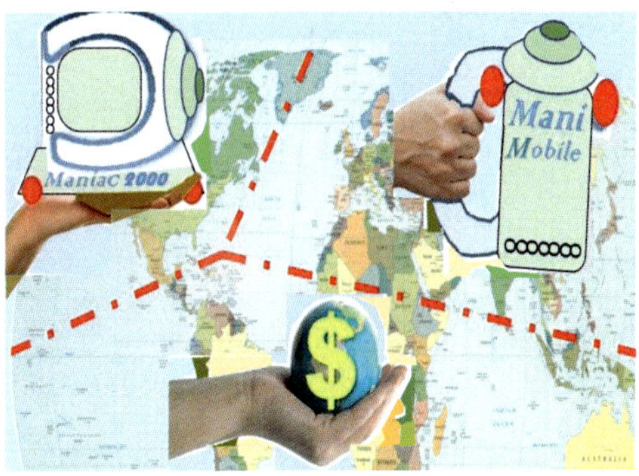

Fig. 10.5 A corporate person

In an extreme case, when a division of a corporation feels threatened by taxation, its parent can rapidly and invisibly transfer the subsidiary division's intangible assets to a safer taxhaven and effectively have it commit suicide in one location, as the advice given POOF, described in Chap. 6.

For a natural person, suicide is fatal.

G7: Closing loopholes will solve the problems of corporate tax avoidance.

Appendix E lists relevant tax expenditures—the various benefits and incentives provided to corporations by targeted tax deductions and tax credits. Many proposals to change the US tax system view tax expenditures as loopholes and propose to do away with all or many of them.

C7: The effect of closing corporate loopholes is less than might be expected. US domestic corporations still pay an average of 28 % [F10.9]. If corporate taxation is abolished, all corporate incentives enabled by tax deductions or credits become meaningless. The effect of Recommendation R20 would be minor, unless incentives now provided to corporations are converted to explicit subsidies.

By far the largest amounts of tax expenditures are for the benefit of individuals. Taxpayers who derive much of their income from dividends will be pushed into different brackets and may lose eligibility of some of those benefits. More individuals than the current fraction, 2.7 %, may become subject to a simpler AMT [IRS-SI:12]. Those affected may well demand some adjustments.

G8: Abolishing all corporate taxation is too extreme to deal with multinationals.

If the problem is just with multinational corporations, why abolish taxes for all corporations?

C8: Just abolishing taxes for multinationals will further disadvantage domestic corporations. A rational reaction for domestic corporations would be to establish an offshore subsidiary, likely in a taxhaven. The argument of double taxation would remain for domestic corporations and become even harder to administer.

G9: Not taxing corporations enables more personal tax evasion.

A serious objection to the abolition of corporate tax is that it encourages individuals to incorporate, opening loopholes to shift income, and escape taxation of earnings [FeldsteinHH:95].

C9: Those loopholes already exist in other business structures and are a major means of tax evasion now [Sullivan:11]. Partnerships and S-corporations do not pay taxes as such, can spend money in ways that benefit their owners, and pay out a share of their income as dividends and capital gains [PSoI:03]. While S-corporations are restricted to operate domestically, LLP's can own C-corporations and collect dividend income for low-taxed distribution to their owners. Not taxing C-corporations only opens another window in a building where all the glass is already shattered.

The simplest means for entrepreneurs and high-income individuals to reduce their taxes is converting income to low-taxed dividends. That option disappears if Recommendation R20 is accepted. When incomes are credited to a partnership, the earnings can be paid to partners and owners as either salaries or dividends. Taking a small salary and high dividends now reduces total taxes due. Many regulations in the tax code were devised to constrain that loophole; they will no longer be needed once salaries and dividends are taxed equally. The communities that can no longer can shift income to lower taxed dividends will complain loudly [Sullivan:11].

G10: Individuals can use corporations to shelter earnings in taxhavens.

If dividend payouts and taxes increase, more US taxpayers will want to shelter income offshore. If they do not want to actually live in palm islands they can set up a corporation there [Frank:11].

C10: Keeping capital offshore is a strategy already available to LLPs at a lower cost than setting up a C-corporation. US laws and regulations, which tax interest earned offshore on passive holdings in any business structure, already provide the basis to deal with such tax shelters.

The IRS relies on voluntary compliance, but explicit offshore underreporting of income requires specialized resources and cooperation with third parties [IRS-TG:07]. Congress has not funded the IRS adequately [Olson:11]. Limited enforcement encourages more tax evasion [Yablon:10]. One need is a focus on outright tax evasion by individuals [Shropshire:09]. If Recommendation R6 is implemented some individuals are easier to locate.

High-income earners can still move themselves completely out of the USA to profit from lower dividend tax rates on funds transferred offshore. US law allows US taxation to continue 10 years after giving up citizenship, although that law has also been hard to enforce [Stahl:11]. Moving to a nearby country has been a common ploy for wealthy UK citizens [Krouse:12]. When top income tax rates became 50 %, more citizens left, reducing UK tax revenues [Browne:12].

Individuals from those countries already see some US states as an attractive tax-haven. Such individuals, just like US citizen sheltering income in palm islands, would use partnership entities and not public corporations that have to report incomes to the SEC. An offshore entity can pay dividends directly to offshore shareholders. How to deal with all these issues of individual tax evasion is beyond the scope of this analysis; it is certainly not new.

G11: Not taxing corporations enables indefinite deferral of paying taxes.

Another path now open to wealthy individuals is tax deferral, by investing their earnings and capital in privately held corporations. Then they can defer paying taxes on them indefinitely.

C11: Holding capital is already a strategy already available to any business entity or foundation. If the capital is gainfully employed, that seems fine. If the funds receive only routine interest, their deferral is equal to having tax-deferred savings. The amounts sheltered in corporations are not subject to the limit imposed on Individual Retirement Accounts (IRAs). Accumulating savings without paying taxes remains a good strategy if the funds are held to retirement, when one's income tax rates are expected to be less. When the gains made are finally paid out they become capital gains income, and income taxes have to be paid by those investors. That issue leads to objection G13.

G12: Current tax deductions already take care of double taxation.

Table 10.1 shows that about half of the double taxation of corporate payouts is compensated now by the reduced tax rates on dividends and capital gains. Why make any changes?

C12: The motivation for Recommendation R20 is not trying to solve the problem of double taxation of individual income derived from corporate earnings, although it is an important component. It is to deal with inability to deal equitably with corporate taxation in a global setting.

G13: Increasing capital gains tax rates: why hurt investors and savers?

Collecting capital gains at some suitable time in the future is important for many investors and differentiates capital gains from dividends. Companies decide between those two alternatives for business reasons, trading growth for stability. Today's lower tax rates, namely 20 % versus 35 % to 39.6 % on capital gains received by individual investors, are motivated by two reasons:

1. *Double taxation of long-term corporate earnings seems unfair.*

C13.1: This common objection is false. Capital gains are not a case of double taxation, since corporate values increase due to untaxed investments taken out of earnings [Sullivan:11].

2. *Lower capital gains rates reduce the effects of loss from inflation.*

C13.2: Using a single deduction, as is done today, encourages speculation over investment.

During 1922 to 2003 capital gains were taxed at a lower rate than dividends, but holding periods to qualify for the lower rate were longer. If the 2003 "Bush tax cuts" expire, the rate will be 28 %. Recommendation R20 just raises capital gains tax rates to the rate prior to 1978, and does not alter the basics.

Taxation of corporate gains is still deferred. Without paying annual taxes a company that uses its net income for growth will grow faster, and the investors' capital gains will also rise. For instance, because MNC does not pay dividends, it will be able to invest the 10.8 % US tax it still pays on earnings into growth [F10.11]. A domestic corporation that does not distribute dividends will be able to invest all of its former tax payments, up to 35 % of earnings, into increasing its market value.

The investors gain effectively by the deferral of corporate taxation, even if the profits, when taken, are taxed at personal tax rates.

The effect of loss due to inflation is not well dealt by tax rates. Capital gains increase as investments are held for longer periods. Inflation further increases the value of corporate assets. Investors should be encouraged by corporate growth to hold on to their shares until their investment pays off. Investment in MNC took over 6 years to pay off [F10.28]. Investments to create infrastructure take dozens of years to mature, but then have log payout periods. Some alternatives that address inflation are given in Chap. 8, Sect. 6.2.

G14: Investors take risks, so they should pay lower taxes.

A frequent argument for lower tax rates on dividends and capital gains, complementing the argument of double taxation, is that because investors take risks with their money, they should pay lower taxes [Burns:12].

C14: This argument defends attempts to double the benefits of investing. Income from risky investments has always been higher than income from risk-free investments, as bank savings or treasury bonds [Sharpe:85]. Income margins from risky investments, as start-up companies and junk bonds, are naturally higher.

There is no reason why returns on risky investments should yet be made greater by applying lower tax rates on investment income versus ordinary income. Taxing all income equally, an essential part of Recommendation R20, disables common tax schemes to avoid or evade taxes by high earners. No "Buffet Rule" is needed to capture dividend income for high earners [Garofalo:12].

G15: The role and value added by banks is reduced.

Because the deduction for interest costs will no longer affect corporate taxes, the huge tax advantage of taking out loans versus selling shares is gone [BurnhamO:05]. If more capital is needed, corporations are more likely to look to shareholders. If banks lose corporate customers, they will spend less effort on analyzing corporations. Bank depositors will only be protected by FDIC insurance.

C15: Investment and retirement funds that invest in shares will continue to vet companies, and they have done at least as good a job in the past as banks have done.

G16: The USA should just fix its international taxation.

The USA already has worldwide taxation and just has to implement it properly to assure thorough taxation of multinational corporations. Then the U.S, will collect more taxes from multinationals to balance national revenues.

C16: We have shown throughout this book that commensurate enforcement is not feasible, given available IRS resources [Trivedi:12]. The UK and

Japan are moving towards full deduction of offshore earnings, while trying to still exclude taxhaven earnings [Miyatake:09]. A comprehensive change of US corporate taxation is needed [AngusNSW:10].

International tax cooperation has been limited to major industrial nations, as the OECD and the JITSIC information sharing initiatives. We cannot wait for global harmony. Taxhavens are sovereign entities [Christians:09].

G17: There will be no US taxes to offset foreign taxes.

Corporations lose the ability to offset foreign taxes. Without US corporate taxation the credits to offset foreign income taxes become meaningless [GrubertA:08]. Those credits were substantial. Now all foreign tax costs just become expenses incurred by doing business offshore, as done in the UK and Japan. Tax treaties will not help US corporations any more.

C17: The rebuttal is that paying no taxes, and deducting foreign taxes as expenses, is better for corporations than paying the excess of US taxes over foreign taxes. Omitting credits for foreign taxes also removes excess benefits claimed when foreign countries levy substantial income taxes, but then reduce costs by offering hidden direct incentives [F8.9]. Cases that upset the public, as when companies claim tax losses while having substantial offshore earnings, go away as well [Chittum:11].

G18: If corporate taxation is changed, all other taxes need updating as well.

Taxing corporate income at the individual level does not alter the many other taxes imposed by the federal government. State income tax will be affected. Some states depend substantially on corporate and individual income taxes and their revenues will change similarly, as their rules tend to follow the federal model. California collects more income tax than any other US state, although the base for corporate taxation has an option which exempts out-of-state property [Yamamura:12].

C18: Major corporations have already moved their domicile for national income accounting to low tax states, such as Nevada and Delaware, causing other US states to lose much local income, mirroring offshore shifting and inversions. Individuals are unlikely to move domicile for taxation [YoungV:11].

Taxing dividends fully in the locations where the recipients live versus where businesses declare their domicile will increase the tax base for many US states. Larger dividend payouts will help even more.

Sales taxes, a primary means for collecting revenues for local governments, will not be directly affected. Those states will be positively affected to a lesser extent by any increase of corporate activities and spending.

Other federal taxes are minimally affected by this change. Excise taxes on imports and luxury goods can remain unchanged. Taxation of imports is an international political issue, best left untouched because of their sensitivity to open global commerce.

Federal sales taxes or value-added taxes (VAT) are attractive to economists and derided by politicians.

G19: Making a transition out of the current system is impossible.

There are two aspects here: emotional and financial. Recommendations R5–R14 are needed so that a broader public understands what is going on, and that the current systems cannot be fixed by simple slogans such as "closing loopholes." The financial issues are substantial. There are many forms of corporations now that have accumulated capital. A transfer to a system where corporations do not pay tax, but their owners do, will require a transition.

C19: The problems of transition must be faced by any change. The relatively simple change proposed here, which does not directly affect individual taxpayers, should be easier than most alternatives.

Many types of transitions have been proposed [Sullivan:11]. The primary proposal, to replace all or most of income taxes by a Value-Added Tax (VAT), requires a much more drastic change. Some countries, especially taxhavens, that do not collect income tax instead charge an annual tax on capital held. Taxation of capital has rarely been considered in the USA.

G20: Why concede such an important issue and let corporations win?

Abolishing corporate taxation does mean that the USA gives up on trying to tax corporate income fairly. The USA would become a de facto corporate taxhaven [BoortzL:06].

C20: It makes little sense to continue fighting a battle that we are bound to lose, as Congressman Lloyd Doggett already observed [Stahl:11].

Although multinational corporations seem to win if this recommendation is adopted, the concession primarily deals with the reality of globalization. It removes a major advantage from those countries that provide the means for harmful tax competition [SlemrodW:09]. Their rates and secrecy allow the creation of corporate structures that enable exploitation of extreme tax avoidance. These global opportunities are beyond any government's control.

Most US multinationals have already established offshore taxhavens [Ciesielski:12]. When most horses are out of the barn, it's best to open the doors wide, hoping to get some back.

The media trust the corporate statements: everything we do is *perfectly legal* [Nakaso:12]. That attitude encourages smaller companies to join the race to tax havens, increasing the business for the advising companies, who have by now have covered most of the high-end corporate market. Their experience allows them to be more efficient, and assure that it will become ever harder for the IRS to issue challenges. All are confident that complex buy-in valuations and royalty schemes will rarely be challenged, no matter how misleading they are.

10.9.2 Misuse of Taxation to Compensate for Corporate Costs

Objections G2–G6, if accepted, raise an important issue. They focus on the benefits that corporate status provides, the costs that are incurred, and the concept that paying taxes is a valid compensation.

If corporations are to be taxed on their special status, taxing corporations is actually fair. The revenue obtained by the government compensates the public for the extra privileges afforded to corporations, which enable them to gather income from actions that an individual cannot engage in. If corporate taxes are to be levied akin to penalties for such purposes, an appropriate tax rate that reimburses the public for those privileges should be set. That rate is unrelated to any income tax. A tax for corporate privileges is distinct. There is no issue of double taxation, and shareholders should still be fully taxed on their dividend income.

A US corporate income tax is not the way to address corporate privileges. The majority of the costs are felt worldwide. Punishing US corporations selectively is not a reasonable approach.

10.10 International Effects and Responses to a US Abolition of Corporate Taxation

Deciding to abolish corporate taxation will have financial, organizational, and social effects in US relations with other countries. It is unclear to what extent the USA should react to feedback. When other countries have changed tax rates or preferences, the US government has never reacted strongly. Calls for action have arisen only when the effect on the US economy of many changes by many countries over many years became evident [ImmeltEa:11]. Any changes initiated by the USA, which represents nearly 25 % of the world's economy, may nevertheless engender reactions from its partners [NicolaidisH:01].

10.10.1 International Capital Flows

A strong motivation for abolishing corporate taxation is removal of inducements to shift intellectual and financial capital offshore. Tax-free repatriation of passive capital now held offshore is now enabled permanently. Little changed internationally as a result of the one-time capital repatriations following the 2004 AJCA. Eurodollars will become less important for US offshore investors.

I assume that once corporate taxation is abolished, it cannot be reinstated. During planning for such change, it will become widely known. Confidence in its persistence allows businesses to adjust. The change will then not cause a sudden, destabilizing shift, as when sudden and temporary changes are proposed. Foolish expenditures, such as excessive acquisitions leading in the end to job losses, to take advantage of a temporary tax holiday are not needed.

Without considering the effect of income taxes on their profits, companies will be able to decide where their investments will do best. They will select jurisdictions according to the availability of a suitable, educated workforce, attractive infrastructure, and a stable environment. Competing in that realm, rather than being driven by tax incentives, allows a return to fundamentals [ChapotonG:88].

Movement of rights to intellectual property will also no longer be motivated by relative tax advantages. Valuation of IP no longer needs to be influenced by differential taxation. IP licensing will continue and should provide a fair income to the creators of intellectual property.

Not all issues surrounding valuation and exploitation of intellectual capital are resolved by abolishing corporate taxation. For instance, it will not stem misappropriation and outright theft of IP. Removing a prime motivation for misvaluation of IP will make it easier to quantify the risks and settle conflicts [WTGS:09]. Furthermore, the locations where corporate taxes are levied differ from where the shareholders are now taxed, leading to an imbalance in tax collection, which is avoided when there is a primary taxation of generated intangible values [Schlunk:06].

10.10.2 Effect on Taxation in Other Countries

If the US government decides to abolish corporate taxation, its trading partners will accuse it of having joined the "race to the bottom," a race that many other countries are engaged in already [Summers:08]. The worldwide trend is clear. In 2006 the nominal weighted corporate tax rate outside the USA was still nearly 34 %, but by 2011 it had gone down to 26.4 % [F10.29]. Countries that levy high taxes on corporations will become less attractive, because the US government will no longer offer tax credits. Countries that collect VAT revenues already credit those taxes to their exporters, leaving little tax to be credited on imports [Jovanovich:02].

The race to lower corporate taxes was led by taxhavens, countries that had few corporate businesses of their own to tax in the first place. Lowered US rates due to the 1986 reform led the other OECD countries. All industrial countries followed, reducing their corporate tax rates. Ireland went furthest, reducing their corporate taxes to 12.5 %. In 2011 the UK lowered its rates from 28 % to 24 % [HMT:10]. Japan is reducing its rate as well; it is now less than the US combined federal and states rate [Hodge:12]. Both countries provide a high level of deduction for qualified foreign earnings, following a trend towards territorial taxation [AngusNSW:10]. Figure 10.6 shows the trend for industrial countries.

Effective corporate rates are lower than the posted statutory rates because of incentives [KellerY:09]. Incentives offered to corporations worldwide go well beyond tax deductions and credits [RicuperoEa:00]. As we saw in Chap. 6, the type and leverage of incentives offered differ so much that comparing effective tax rates among countries appears to be impossible.

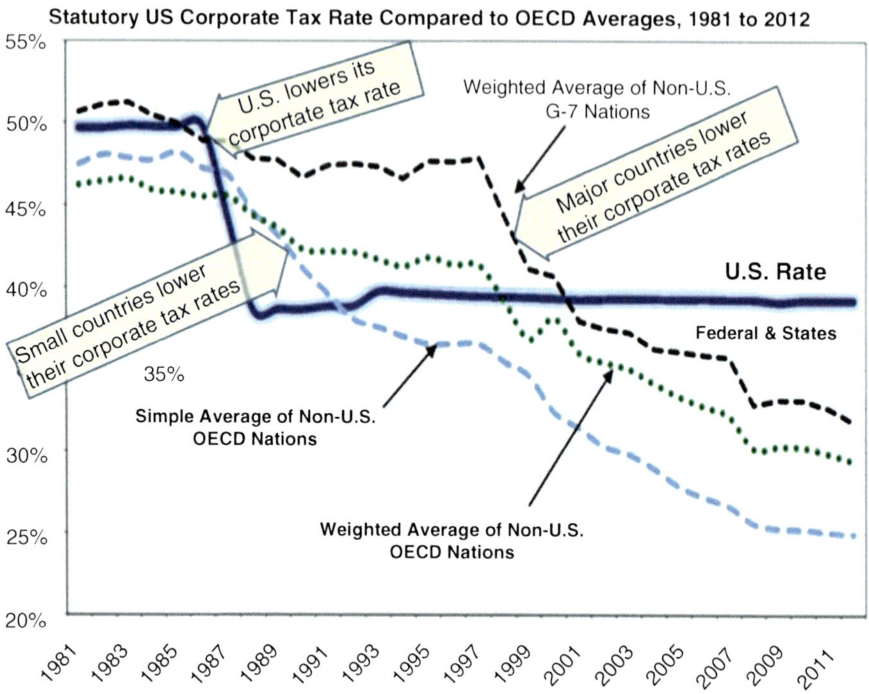

Fig. 10.6 Statutory tax rates in OECD countries, simple and weighted

Abolishing corporate taxation by the USA will accelerate the global trend towards lower corporate tax rates. In most countries the trade-off of lower corporate tax rates and economic growth is being discussed. Analyses in Europe also expect growth when corporate taxes are reduced, but those analyses did not consider raising taxes on corporate payouts and ignored taxhavens [deMooij:05]. The experience in Ireland has been mixed [Alderman:10].

Many countries already suffer from low receipts from corporate taxation, being subject to the same tax avoidance methods described here [Dohmen:09]. Countries with poor methods of tax collection from individuals will incur larger relative losses from eliminating corporate taxation. Tax evaders have many choices to escape taxation beyond moving to palm islands. Several states in the USA are already a taxhaven for wealthy foreigners [Shaxson:11].

Over time, other countries will follow US leadership in abolishing corporate taxation. Exempting foreign companies from taxation by ring fencing, as is now done by conduit and some semi-taxhavens, would be an initial response.

Countries have a variety of tax streams, so that no general approach to rebalancing government revenues can be foreseen [SlemrodB:08]. Industrialized countries, where a large fraction of the population is employed by enterprises that keep payroll records, have revenue profiles similar to the US profile. However, they all deal differently with the issue of double taxation of corporate earnings vis-à-vis individuals. Some countries allow direct credits, requiring no changes. In other countries lower corporate tax revenues cannot easily be offset without increasing deficits.

Countries that depend on corporate taxes to a large extent, as in the OECD, will have the most difficulty in adjusting. Countries where individual tax evasion is rampant, such as Russia and Brazil, will have the hardest time [DonadioP:11]. Alternative taxes like the VAT provide a valid alternative to taxation of income, as they lead the movement towards consumption taxes. Countries—as well as some US states—that rely largely on sales, VAT, or property taxes will be less affected by an abolition of corporate taxation.

10.10.3 International Trade

Arguments promoting unfettered international trade are based on traditional arguments that countries selectively manufacture what they do best. Profitable trade will achieve an optimum balance, like wine in Portugal and woolen cloth in England [Ricardo:1817, cited by LafferM:10]. Taxhavens have been left out of the equation or denigrated by promoters of globalization [Wolf:05]. Measurements are difficult, in part because of privacy-protecting fences between US agencies [HousemanR:09].

The fundamental argument for globalization remains valid, but the assumption that a product creates income where the workers live has been subverted. Today's intangible products can collect income in places where they are not created.

As sketched in Fig. 10.5, Adam Smith's invisible hand has been circumvented. Although connected to the same corporate body, the hand collecting the revenue is located where taxes are avoided, and not where the hands create the products.

On the other hand, people and their employment choices are still tied to locality. Even though the USA prides itself as an immigrant nation, legal and illegal immigrants in the US represent just over 10 % of the population [F10.30]. Together with US citizens they represent valuable intellectual capital in the USA. The same situation holds for countries the world over. But rights to any capital can be transferred internationally rapidly and nearly invisibly. Abolishing corporate taxation removes the factor of unequal taxation that motivates shifting jobs internationally, following transfers of IP rights that flow to the lowest taxed jurisdictions. Routine manufacturing can still move to where labor costs and the needed infrastructures are attractive. Taxhavens that provide actual services will be judged on the quality of their work [Hawkes:08].

10.10.3.1 Tax Treaties

Tax treaties with US trading partners will be affected by abolishing corporate taxation. Any specific rates and arrangements for corporations in those treaties will be largely invalidated. Trying to make distinctions in tax treaties between arm's-length corporate transactions and controlled foreign corporations is especially awkward. Not all countries provide the protection that corporate "personhood" gives to US corporations. The inherent conflict in formulating US tax treaties to deal fairly with individuals working outside of their home country, while trying to avoid excessive concessions for multinational corporations, will be greatly mitigated.

10.10.4 International Responses

Responses from some international trading partners to an abolition of US corporate taxation may be harsh. However, most of them are already moving to lower corporate taxation and increasing taxation of individual income from dividends and capital gains [AltshulerHT:10]. Currently there is great variability in their application [Paschall:00]. Given the lengthy discussion that will occur before the US Congress adopts any change, US trading partners will have had a lot of warning. Primary taxhavens may complain the loudest, but they deserve to be ignored, given their responses in the past to international complaints about their operations. Some taxhavens will retain real income from financial services, but may have to begin levying payroll, transaction, or capital taxes [MurphyCK:05].

Abolishing corporate taxation internationally is bound to affect the trend towards globalization of trade. Abolishing corporate taxation in the USA will not stop businesses from investing overseas if market and labor conditions encourage such decisions. Foreign countries will likely still try to match their rivals by providing incentives. The USA has to deal already with incremental changes in Europe [DevereuxL:11].

Worldwide, the cost to corporations in complying with current tax laws is large [GregoryS:11]. If other countries abolish corporate taxation, all businesses would benefit similarly. Because Recommendation R20 does not alter payroll, excise, capital, transaction, nor any sales or VAT taxes that are levied, businesses will still worry about taxation. But the effort to deal with corporate income taxation, the most noxious of them all, will be eliminated.

10.11 Employment by Multinationals

Figure 10.7 provides a long-term view on the growth of employment by US-based multinational corporations. There was a major dip in employment starting in 2000. Some of that downturn can be attributed to the recession at that time, but the reduction in employment continued to 2003, when offshoring became common. After 2004 the change in US employment by multinational corporations kept at least pace

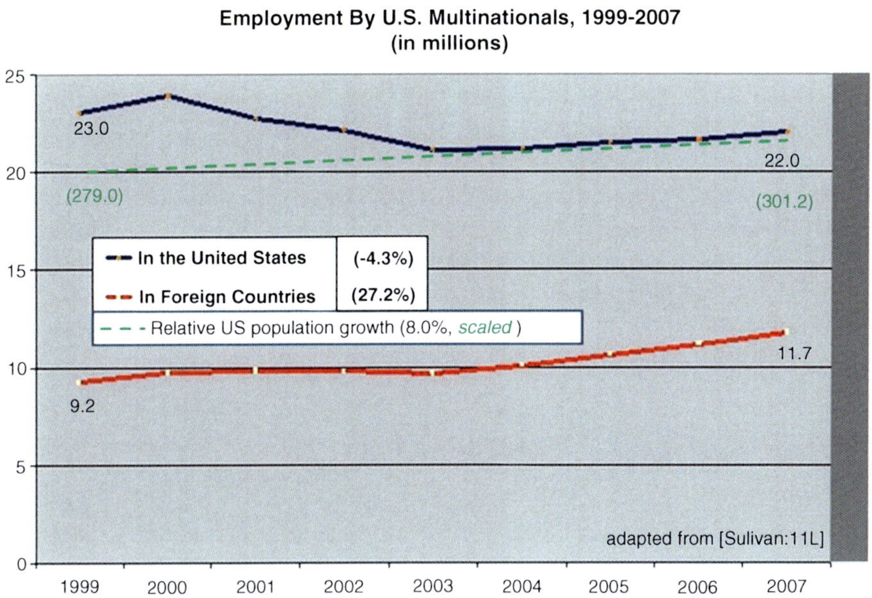

Fig. 10.7 Multinational employment trends prior to the 2008 recession

with the growth of the US population. There is a similar break in growth in the hiring by US multinationals offshore. After 2004 offshore hiring grows more rapidly. The growth of offshore hiring is even greater in absolute terms than US hiring, and on a percentage base, after 2004, more than 3 × more rapidly.

The big question is, of course, what has happened during the much more serious recession that started around 2008. Even if the numbers were known now, the relative causes of any changes are always up for debate. The model that MNC provides, with sketches of its growth as seen in Fig. 6.10, will at least provide concepts for further discussion and analyses.

10.12 Summary: Ending Unbalanced Taxation

This book investigated a narrow but problematic aspect of economic well-being and governance: the imbalances in taxation of corporations that are as large as some countries [Haass:13]. These corporations act fully rationally, but violate our sense of fairness. Without an understanding of the processes, initiating change is hard [MackEa:05]. Governments cannot deal effectively with global markets [Tanzi:11]. Observing unfairness without being able to make changes leads to frustration.

10.12.1 Origin of the Lack of Balance

The issues raised derive from a variety of business, technical, and economical situations that have undergone rapid change in the last 50 years. Business has become a worldwide enterprise, and technology has reduced the cost of global access drastically. For most tangible goods, the costs of shipping are a fraction of their price. Moving intangibles is nearly free and invisibly [Cairncross:97]. Intellectual capital, anywhere, drives economic growth [Idris:03]. People, the jobs they perform, and their know-how are now the remaining critical asset bound to locality. The shifting of intangible assets, enabled by current laws, invalidates the assumptions underlying traditional economic models.

10.12.2 Exploitation of Opportunities

It is only natural for people, including those responsible for managing and advising corporations, to take advantage offered by inadequate understanding of profit generation. Misvaluation of intellectual capital, being poorly understood seems to be not much more of a sin than donating an old car to a charity and writing off more than it could have been sold for at arm's length. As shown in Chap. 7, the aggregate of many misvaluations provides enormous opportunities for transferring rights to income overseas, abetted by laws and regulations intended to make the USA more competitive worldwide.

10.12.3 Repairing the Damage

In retrospect many misvaluation can be repaired. Actual income data become available as the years pass, so that applying the principle for valuation, namely the net income discounted to the transfer date, can easily be applied. But even a retrospective fair payment, with or without penalties, cannot change a business model that is based on having moved essential assets overseas at an initial low cost. Repair of past errors and replay of consequences is impossible. Such reasoning leads to the recommendation made here to abolish corporate taxation. That one change in taxation can initiate bringing the assets back to their creators.

10.12.4 The Future

Globalization of innovation, development, production, and trade should not be a zero-sum game [Clinton:11]. The interposition of taxhavens makes it a negative game for the trading partners. Fixing any system is hard. As I studied the shifting of resources and taxation of multinational corporations, many problems became evident. In the end, my final recommendation, abolishing corporate taxation and its consequences, specifically getting rid of the concessions for double taxation, emerged as the most feasible alternative.

Without public understanding, a proposal that seems to benefit corporations is unlikely to be accepted [Cray:09]. The attractive side effect, disabling thousands of lines of unenforceable regulations, benefits mainly administrators and bureaucrats.

10.12.5 Initial Recommendations

My initial recommendations, R1–R19, can be adopted without any major direct financial effects to businesses, individuals, or the government. They will add considerable clarity and potential fairness into the current processes for corporate taxation. The important intellectual property transfers in modern society will become visible and measurable. As the reasons for the imbalance in taxation of multinationals versus domestic businesses become clear, more drastic changes can be proposed. Opponents are disorganized and will have few good arguments against my initial recommendations. We could start on these changes immediately.

Dealing with the question—*is extreme tax avoidance harmful?*—requires an understanding that requires transparency as advocated here.

10.12.6 The Final Recommendation

My final recommendation, R20, abolishing taxation of corporations and eliminating the compensation for double taxation of shareholders, is considerably simpler than any of the many broad proposals being advocated elsewhere. Its adoption requires minimal changes to the current laws and regulations; many just become irrelevant. The thorny issue of territorial versus worldwide taxation disappears. Not taxing corporate income also puts the USA in a leading position on an issue that now frustrates industrial and emerging nations.

Recommendation R20 avoids also the thorny issue to what extent current corporate tax avoidance practices are legal. That their extreme international tax avoidance is legal is common claim by corporations, repeated in the media [Nakaso:12]. To what extent misvaluation of rights to intellectual capital which enables extreme tax avoidance is legal, remains an open question. Abolishing corporate taxation does not answer that question, but removes the motivation.

10.13 Call to Action: What's Next?

If extreme tax avoidance is seen to be harmful, then it becomes essential to move beyond complaints to action. Observing the results, and hearing that it is all perfectly legal is frustrating. It is as if we are seeing a child suffering because its parents are exercising their legal right to withhold medications that might help.

Action requires an educated population, one that is not fooled by proponents who base their advice on ideological preconception, bolstered by economic theories that are obsolete. Focusing on legal, but extreme tax avoidance, enabled by inadequate valuation practices, rather than on illegal tax evasion, makes it clear that any changes have to address the system, rather than punish individuals.

Understanding the role of intellectual capital in today's world is crucial to initiate actions, but one cannot expect every citizen to understand the issues to the same level of depth.

The general public will accept that the value of modern enterprises is no longer due to having massive machinery and large pools of labor as shown in Chap. 1.

Entrepreneurs who now sense where value is generated in businesses can be helped by models of corporate growth as sketched in the example given in Chap. 2.

Investors and workers in specific industries need to understand the types of intellectual resources needed and available in the businesses they participate in, as listed and structured in Chap. 3.

Investors in the global market will need to understand the options for transferring resources throughout the world, as specified in Chap. 4.

Analysts must become comfortable with intellectual property valuation methods, as laid out in Chap. 5. If the value of what one is agitating about cannot be determined, the leverage of any argument is gone.

Policy makers need to understand the capabilities of taxhavens shown in Chap. 6, and how they can be combined to foil good intentions.

Tax authorities can use the example worked out in Chap. 7 to identify the complex factors that lead to extreme tax avoidance.

The capabilities of tax authorities shown in Chap. 8, must be considered if any proposals require their participation.

Predicting national and international effects, shown in Chap. 9, requires modeling of the flows of financial and intellectual capital.

Implementing the initial recommendations of this chapter provides the information needed by communities that wish to effectively press for reform. Such knowledge provides a basis for moving on to Recommendation R20 or other substantial changes in taxation that are warranted.

If we are concerned we cannot afford inaction!

———— the end of this book, but not of taxes ————

Appendix A: MNC's Annual Report

This appendix presents the essential accounting information for MNC, as given in an annual report to shareholders and also in the 10-K report submitted to the SEC. These data are frequently referred to in this work. Informally this information is referred to as MNC's books, maintained by the bookkeepers in MNC's accounting department. During the time covered, more than 20 such annual reports will be created. Reporting to the SEC started when MNC became a public company. Table A.1 shows data from the time of the buy-in. Quarterly reports delivered to the SEC, 10-Qs, carry less information.

The SEC requires that corporate books be audited annually. MNC's auditor is a division of ATA. Other divisions of ATA also provide business and tax advice to MNC.

The table uses the terms as found throughout this work. In the literature some terms, such as "income" and "profit," are often used inconsistently depending on their context; they and many alternative terms are defined in the glossary, Appendix D. For comparison we also show the data for Forest Laboratories, an actual pharmaceutical company introduced in Chap. 2. The Forest Labs data were provided per unit of the medication sold [Drucker:10].

The most important number here is the operating income, the difference between what MNC sold and how much it costs to make the products it sold and run its business, its CoGS, and SG&A. Those costs reduce MNC's operating income to about 2/3 of revenues. MNC spends a very large amount on research, 23 % of its revenues. Such spending leads to an expectation of rapid growth in future revenues. Stable companies, even those that depend on IP created through research, will spend much less. Forest Laboratories is more typical; it spends 6 % of its revenues on research.

Like most high-tech companies MNC does not require a great deal of capital investment beyond what its shareholders contributed; 3 % of revenues suffices to pay interest on its loans.

Taxes, at the current US statutory tax rate, take away 14 % of the revenues, leaving MNC with profits of 27 % of revenues. Most high-tech companies have learned to avoid high taxes. Forest Laboratories pays <3 % on its revenues. Chapter 2 shows

G. Wiederhold, *Valuing Intellectual Capital: Multinationals and Taxhavens*,
Management for Professionals 23, DOI 10.1007/978-1-4614-6611-6,

Table A.1 Income statement items for MNC and Forest Labs [FA.1]

Income allocation	MNC	ForestLabs
Sales revenue = units sold x unit price	525M 140%	$99/unit 130%
Corporate revenue (after Distributor markup)	375M 100%	$76/unit 100%
Gross income (after Production cost, CoGS)	284M 76%	$56/unit 74%
Operating income (after Business overhead, SG&A)	250M 67%	$45/unit 59%
Net income (after Research, R&D)	164M 44%	$40/unit 53%
Earnings (after Capital cost, $$)	154M 41%	$35/unit 47%
Profit (after Taxes)	100M 27%	$33/unit 44%

how over the next dozen years MNC is able to lower its taxes, although its tax avoidance never becomes as effective as the extreme tactics used by Forest Laboratories.

A.1 MNC's Income Statement

The income statement shows how well MNC did that year. It allows investors to assess the performance of MNC's management. A company is not obliged to show the sales revenue from products actually delivered to its customers; it may even be unknown. It is a useful number, however. A high markup, here 40 %, shows that there is some flexibility in pricing, but can also show that selling costs are high. Having an efficient supply chain lowers the cost of delivering products to the customers. Having to stock a large variety of products increases the cost. MNC has an efficient supply chain. The ability to load the needed software at the distributing site allows MNC to deal effectively with product variants and updates.

MNC currently earns 41 % on its revenues, high, but not atypical in its high-technology sector. A major concern for investors, a major topic of this book, is valuation. To profit from MNC's intellectual capital, investors must buy its shares at the current market price. Experienced investors will first check the price/earnings (p/e) multiple. A company with a p/e <10 is considered a very good buy. MNC's current p/e multiple is already 12. Potential earnings due to its intellectual capital and ongoing research are becoming recognized [F5.40f].

Investors, observing the income statement, will decide that MNC is a healthy and mature company, typical of the businesses this book deals with. The balance statement shows the results of MNC's operations.

A.2 MNC's Balance Statement

The balance sheet Table A.2, showing the corporate book value, lists the assets of a business. Only few intangible assets will be shown, as discussed in Chap. 3. The effect is that the value shown here, the book value mainly, shows tangible assets; note that money is a tangible asset.

Since MNC had acquired a number of other businesses, and paid more for them than their book value, MNC's accountants placed $140M in a poorly defined category, goodwill. Goodwill is often written down rapidly, because it is so meaningless without a value of all the other substantial intellectual capital created by MNC's R&D and acquisitions. Writing off intangibles obtained in an acquisition, while reducing the cash held and adding loans on the books, makes it appear that acquisitions are unwise.

A knowledgeable investor cares little about goodwill that is posted. The estimated corporate value estimated by the market, given the current share price and the numbers of shares outstanding, is already $1,500M [FA.2]. With that estimate MNC's market/book ratio is nearly 5, showing that other investors believed that MNC had good prospects [FA.3]. Such a ratio is not uncommon; it was also 5 for SAP, a German software firm, in 2005 [W:06]. The excess is a measure of the value of a company's intellectual capital, the capability of the workforce and the intangible property already available.

If MNC would not be public, share price information would be sparse. Using a common expected p/e multiple of 10 allows an investor to guess that the market price of MNC, if its stock were issued in an initial public offering (IPO), to be also about $1,500M [FA.2].

The market/book ratio of Forest Laboratories was less than that of MNC, just 2.5. That number indicates that its investors were likely worried about its patents expiring and competition from generic drugs reduced the significance of its intellectual property [FA.5].

For modern, high-technology businesses the values shown in corporate books are inadequate [Damodaran:02]. Smart shareholders will be aware of this artifice, which represents neither true intangibles nor a tangible value. The shareholder's book equity is just $330M. Since IP has no salvage value, in a bankruptcy the shareholders can only be assured of the tangibles, a net of $100M. An ongoing high-technology business has a much higher value, here $1,500M, so that in practice the shareholder's equity is only a mechanism to balance the books.

The valuations in Chap. 5 provide more insightful assessments than corporate books.

Table A.2 Consolidated balance sheet for MNC [FA.4]

Assets	MNC	$	Liabilities	MNC	$
Plant	Factories in the USA and Malaysia	40M	Mortgages	Factories and land in the US and Malaysia	35M
Property	Land in Malaysia. Unsold inventory	30M	Rents on leases due	US land, offices all over the world	15M
Equipment	Manufacturing tools & Office equipment	50M	Obligations to employees	Retirement, health care & employment contracts	11M
Cash & equivalents	Bank, notes, receivables due	100M	Debts and interest due	Loans for acquisitions & to start CONCH	50M
subtotal	tangible assets	220M	Reserve for taxes due	Accumulated each quarter before paid	9M
Capitalized R&D	Mainly from acquisitions	90M	subtotal	tangible liabilities	120M
Goodwill	Left from the $300M initial acquisitions after write offs	140M	Shareholders' equity	$100M in excess tangible assets plus $230M in intangibles.	330M
total	book assets	450M =	total	book liabilities	450M

Appendix B: Tax Laws and Regulations

This appendix provides an introduction to the laws and regulations that govern US taxation. Only a few specific laws and regulations that are directly relevant to international IP transfer are referenced. The extracts presented are isolated from their context and only intended to simplify checking citations used in the body of the book. Having the extracts will help readers locate the full publications if they want to research a topic in detail. An excellent summary to the tax laws for international transaction is provided by [Doernberg:08]. The authoritative sources are always the laws and regulations as published by the government as of a specific date [Thomas:11]. We use the consolidated publications shown in Fig. B.1.

The printed version of the Internal Revenue Code is 5,700 pages long [CCH:09], and the corresponding Code of Federal Regulations on taxes takes 93,500 pages of dense print, all on thin paper [CCH:10]. It is quite understandable that many tax reformers want to start over fresh [Economist:11F].

All these documents are updated as laws are amended or repealed and as regulations are expanded or invalidated, or as situations arising in specific cases require clarification. When trying to understand the background of some of these laws, checking when amendments came about is useful. At times it is wise to even go back to the congressional record to see what the intent of a law was. Tracing back the motivations for updates to regulations is harder. For the 2012 changes it requires going back to departmental papers [IRS-CIP:07].

The complexity of regulations discourages analyzing their contents and implications [Coglianese:12]. It is even harder to propose fixes. Making regulations available online while they are being developed is a first step [Coglianese:11]. It is essential that automated software for search, cross-referencing, and integration be available to the public and the regulators. Tools are essential to manage complex regulations [LauLW:05].

G. Wiederhold, *Valuing Intellectual Capital: Multinationals and Taxhavens*, Management for Professionals 23, DOI 10.1007/978-1-4614-6611-6,

Fig. B.1 Leonardo da Vinci's and Johann Wolfgang Goethe's collected works versus US tax laws and regulations

B.1 Overview

There are many types of government publications that provide tax information. We deal here only with US federal government issues. All the documents needed are in the public domain. A well-formatted and maintained online source is provided by Cornell University [LII:92]. US tax documents are grouped into Title 26. Three levels of information are relevant:

1. Laws passed by the Congress of the USA.
2. Regulations developed by the US Treasury that expand on those Laws.
3. Guidance documents issued by the IRS to clarify application of the regulations.

Some guidance and related government documents cited are listed in the references.

We introduce laws and regulations before moving on to the actual citations. The remainder of this chapter cites skeletal extracts of important sections.

B.1.1 Laws

Laws passed by the US Congress that deal with income taxes make up the Internal Revenue Code (IRC) Title 26, Subtitle A of the federal laws. Title 26 has 100 Chapters, of greatly varying size and depth of subchapters, parts, and subparts.

Luckily the paragraphs are numbered throughout, up to §9834. To obtain the full text for a specific IRC paragraph "§" of Title 26 in the archive of the Cornell University Legal Information Institute [LII:92] use

<http://www.law.cornell.edu/uscode/text/26/§>

The paragraphs of primary concern to our exposition are all in Title 26, Chap. 1, namely, IRC §936, §367, and §482. Those paragraphs make references to some other paragraphs and we will show some relevant subparagraphs as well. For instance, the definition of intangibles for §1.482, updated in 1985, is actually in §936. That paragraph was created earlier, in 1975, to provide tax incentives for US overseas possessions, as presented in Chap. 6. Occasional experts will refer to a sequence of paragraphs by a group name. In our case, a grouping used at times is "subpart F," deferred repatriation of offshore funds, which covers the 55 pages comprising §951–§965, located in subchapter N of Title 26, Chapter 1.

B.1.2 Regulations

Regulations greatly expand the laws and provide information on how the objectives of the laws are to be achieved. They are documented as the Code of Federal Regulations (CFR). While the length of IRC §482 and its amendments is only 548 words, the Treasury Title 26 of CFR §1.482 to implement IRC §482 requires over 60,000 words. Proposed, temporary, and final regulations are published in the Federal Register, and referred to as Treasury Decisions (TD).

To locate the first section (always §-0) for a specific CFR paragraph "§" in Part 1 of Title 26 of the regulations in the archive of the Cornell University Legal Information Institute [LII:92] use

<http://www.law.cornell.edu/cfr/text/26/1.§-0> and then click to get to successive sections, or

<http://www.law.cornell.edu/cfr/text/26/1.482-#> for a specific transfer pricing numbered section.

The laws and regulations are numbered many levels down, for instance the definition of intangible property appears in IRC Title 26 as §936(h)(3)(B)(i–vi) and is repeated in the IRS regulations as 26 CFR §1.482-4(b). In printed and online government publications higher level numbers are not repeated, and require tedious searching up in the hierarchy. To help readers, the extracts shown here use indents to indicate the hierarchical relationships. To focus on the essentials, most of the text has been elided, marked by ellipses (…) and brackets to indicate [text that is paraphrased]. Some [*clarifications have been inserted*] as well. These extracts are not adequate for making any decisions about actual taxes. *been inserted*] as well. These extracts are not adequate for making any decisions about actual taxes.

B.2 Relevant Laws of the United States

B.2.1 Definitions of Intangible Income, Property, and Cost Sharing

This section of the law was created in 1976 when, in the context of nearshore tax-havens, valuation of intangible property first became an issue in taxation.

26 USC §936. Puerto Rico and possession tax credit

(h) Tax treatment of intangible property income
  (3) Intangible property income
    (A) … The term "intangible property income" means the gross income of a corporation attributable to any intangible property other than intangible property which has been licensed to such corporation since prior to 1948 …
    (B) … The term "intangible property" means any—
      (i) patent, invention, formula, process, design, pattern, or know-how
      (ii) copyright, literary, musical, or artistic composition
      (iii) trademark, trade name, or brand name
      (iv) franchise, license, or contract
      (v) method, program, system, procedure, campaign, survey, study, forecast, estimate, customer list, or technical data
      (vi) any similar item, which has substantial value independent of the services of any individual
    (C) Exclusion of reasonable profit [routine earnings]
    The term "intangible property income" shall not include any portion of the income from the sale, exchange or other disposition of any product, or from the rendering of services, by a corporation … which is … a reasonable profit on the direct and indirect costs incurred … which are attributable to such income.
  (5) (C) Methods of computation of taxable income
    [A CFC] shall compute its income derived from the active conduct of a trade or business in a possession with respect to such product or type of service …
      (i) Cost sharing (I) Payment … [The CFC] must make a payment for its share of the cost … research which is paid or accrued by the affiliated group during that taxable year. … In the case of intangible property described in subsection (h)(3)(B)(i) which the [CFC] … own[s]… in no event … less than … required under §367(d)(2)(A)(ii) or §482 if the [CFC] were a[n arm's-length] foreign corporation. [More in §482–7(b). see B.3.3.7(b)]

26 USC §936. (h)(5)(C)(i) (continued)

(a) Product area research … includes nine…) the research, development and experimental costs, losses, expenses and other related deductions—including amounts paid… expenses within the meaning of section §41(b); …
(b) Amounts paid or accrued for the use of … research or any of the items … in subsection (h)(3)(B)(i); and a proper allowance for amounts incurred for the acquisition of any of the items specified in subsection (h)(3)(B)(i)—… apportioned … to the same product area as [of the CFC], and a ratable part of any such costs, losses, expenses and other deductions which cannot definitely be allocated to a particular product area. ……..
(e) Product area [is] defined by … the three-digit classification of the [SIC]. …

B.2.2 Transfer Pricing

26 USC §482. Allocation of income and deductions among taxpayers

In any case of two or more organizations, trades, or business (whether or not incorporated, whether or not organized in the United States, and whether or not affiliated) owned or controlled directly or indirectly by the same interest, the Secretary may distribute, apportion, or allocate gross income, deductions, credits, or allowances between or among such organizations, trades, or businesses, if he determines that such distribution, apportionment, or allocation is necessary in order to prevent evasion of taxes or clearly to reflect the income of any of such organizations, trades, or businesses. In the case of any transfer (or license) of intangible property (within the meaning of paragraph 936(h)(3)(B)), the income with respect to such transfer, or license shall be commensurate with the income attributable to the intangible [1945]. [*Complete*]

B.2.3 Definition of Taxable Corporate Income

26 USC §61. Gross income defined

(a) General definition

Except as otherwise provided in this subtitle, gross income means all income from whatever source derived, including (but not limited to) the following items;

(1) Compensation for services, including fees, …, and similar items;
(2) Gross income derived from business;
(3) Gains derived from dealings in property; (4) Interest; (5) Rents;
(6) Royalties; (7) Dividends;…

B.2.4 *Corporate Tax Rates*

26 USC §11. Tax imposed

(a) Corporations in general A tax is hereby imposed for each taxable year on the taxable income of every corporation.
(b) (1) in general The amount of the tax imposed by subsection (a) shall be …—
(D) 35 percent of so much of the taxable income as exceeds $10,000,000.

B.2.5 *Transfers to Yield Commensurate Income*

26 USC §367. Foreign corporations

(a) (1) … gain shall be recognized on such [corporate] transfers …
(2) … (A)… not … (B) … not (A) … [*what remains is*] (iv) intangible property …
(c) (2) Contribution of capital to controlled corporations
…, any transfer of property to a foreign corporation as a contribution to the capital of such corporation by … persons who, immediately after the transfer, own (…) stock … least 80 percent of the … stock of such corporation … shall be treated as an exchange of such property for stock of the foreign corporation equal in value to the fair market value of the property transferred.
(d) Special rules relating to transfers of intangibles
(1) In general [it applies to] transfers … intangible property (within the meaning of section 936 (h)(3)(B)) to a foreign corporation in an exchange …
(2) Transfer of intangibles treated as transfer pursuant to sale of contingent payments
(A) In general ... If paragraph (1) applies to any transfer, the United States person transferring such property shall be treated as—
(i) having sold such property in exchange for payments which are contingent upon the productivity, use, or disposition of such property, and
(ii) receiving amounts [matching] the amounts which would have been received—
(I) annually in the form of such payments over the useful life of such property,
The amounts taken into account under clause (ii) shall be commensurate with the income attributable to the intangible.
(B) Effect on earnings and profits
…, the earnings and profits of a foreign corporation to which the intangible property was transferred shall be reduced by the amount required to be included in the income of the transferor of the intangible property under subparagraph (A)(ii).

26 USC §367. (a)(2)(C) (continued)

(C) Amounts received treated as ordinary income
…, any amount included in gross income by reason of this subsection shall be treated as ordinary income. For purposes of applying section 904 (d), any such amount shall be treated in the same manner as if such amount were a royalty.

B.2.6 Foreign Tax Credit

26 USC §901. Taxes of foreign countries and of [us] possessions …

(a) Allowance of credit
…, the tax imposed by this chapter shall, subject to the limitation of section 904, be credited with the amounts … of subsection (b) plus, in the case of a corporation, the taxes deemed to have been paid already [on dividends and deducted from income]
(b) Amount allowed Subject to the limitation of section 904, the following amounts shall be allowed as the credit under subsection (a):
  (1) Citizens and domestic corporations. —In the case of a citizen of the United States and of a domestic corporation, the amount of any income, war profits, and excess profits taxes paid or accrued during the taxable year to any foreign country or to any possession of the United States; and
  (2) Resident of the United States or … a bona fide resident of Puerto Rico … .

26 USC §904. Limitation on credit

(h) Source rules in case of United States-owned foreign corporations
  (2) Subpart F and passive foreign investment company inclusions
  … shall be treated as derived from sources within the United States to the extent such amount is attributable to income of the United States-owned foreign corporation from sources within the United States.
  (4) Dividends (B) United States source ratio [RAB]
  …, the term "United States source ratio" means, with respect to any dividend paid out of the earnings and profits …, a fraction—[B.2.6 (a)(2)(A)]
    (i) the numerator … is . the earnings and profits … from … within the United States, and
    (ii) the denominator … is the total amount of earnings and profits … .
  (6) United States-owned foreign corporation
  For purposes of this subsection, the term "United States-owned foreign corporation" means any foreign corporation if 50 % or more of— … (*the stock of such corporation*), is held directly (or indirectly …) by United States persons (…).

26 USC §904. (h)(7) (continued)

(7) Dividend
For purposes of this subsection, the term "dividend" includes any gain treated as ordinary income … or as a dividend … .
(10) Coordination with treaties
(A) In general If— … this subsection shall not apply to such amount to the extent attributable to such item of income (but …).

B.2.7 Possession Tax Credit

26 USC §936. Puerto Rico and possession tax credit

(a) (2) …, there shall be allowed as a credit against the tax imposed by this chapter an amount equal to the portion of the tax which is attributable to the sum of—
(A) the taxable income, from sources without the United States, from—
(i) the active conduct of a trade or business within a possession of the US, or …
(4) Limitations on credit for active business income
(A) in general The amount of the credit … shall [be balanced]. The … percentage is: …[for] 1998 and thereafter 40.

B.2.8 Research Credits

26 USC §41. Credit for increasing research activities

(a) General rule … the research credit … shall be an amount equal to the sum of—
(1) 20 % of the excess (if any) of—
(A) the qualified research expenses for the taxable year, over (B) the base amount,
(2) 20 % of the basic research payments determined under subsection (e)(1) (A), and …
(b) Qualified research expenses
(1) … [are] the sum of …
(A) in-house research expenses, and
(B) contract research expenses.
(2) In-house research expenses … (A) [are] …
(i) … Wages paid for qualified services …
(ii) … supplies …, and
(iii) … amount paid … to use computers … .

26 USC §41. (b)(3) (continued)

- (3) Contract research expenses (A) … 65 % …
  - (C) … to certain research consortia (i) … 75 % …
  - (D) … to … small businesses, universities, and Federal laboratories (i) … 100 % … .
- (4) Activities for which credit not allowed …
  - (E) Computer software … for internal use by the taxpayer,
  - (F) Foreign research.

(e) Credit [for] payments to qualified organizations for basic research …
- (1) (A) the amount … shall be equal to [100 % of] the excess of—
  - (i) such basic research payments, over
  - (ii) the … organization base period amount, …
- (6) Qualified organization[s] are
  - (A) Educational institutions …
  - (B) … scientific research organizations …
  - (C) Scientific tax-exempt organizations

26 USC §1298. special rules

(e) Special rules for certain intangibles …
- (1) Research expenditures The adjusted basis of the total assets of a [CFC] shall be increased by the [R&E] … paid or incurred by [a CFC] … [reducing the credit.]

B.2.9 Goodwill, Amortization and Definition

26 USC §197. Amortization of goodwill and … other intangibles

(a) General rule A taxpayer shall be entitled to an amortization deduction with respect to any amortizable section 197 intangible. The … deduction [amortizes] the adjusted basis over the 15-year period [since the] intangible was acquired.

(b) No other depreciation or amortization deduction allowable
- (1) … the … intangible— … (B) … is held in connection with the conduct of a trade or business … .
- (2) Exclusion of self-created intangibles. (A) not … in (D), (E), or (F) of subsection (d)(1), and (B) which is created by the taxpayer.

(d) Section 197 intangible (1) …
- (A) goodwill,
- (B) going concern value,
- (C) any of ….
  - (i) workforce … its composition and terms and conditions (…) of its employment,

26 USC §197. (d)(C) (continued)

- (ii) business books and records, operating systems, or any other information base (including lists [of] current or prospective customers),
- (iii) any patent, copyright, formula, process, design, pattern, know-how, format, or other similar item,
- (iv) any customer-based intangible,
- (v) any supplier-based intangible, and
- (vi) any other similar item,

(D) any license, permit, or other right granted by a governmental unit …
(E) any covenant not to compete (…) … in connection with an acquisition …
(F) any franchise, trademark, or trade name.

B.2.10 Passive Income "Subpart F"

26 USC §952. Subpart F income defined

(a) In general For purposes of this subpart, the term "subpart F income" means, in the case of any controlled foreign corporation, the sum of—…
   (2) the foreign base company income (as determined under section 954),
   (3) an amount equal to the product of—
      the income of such corporation other than [active] income which—
      (i) is attributable to earnings and profits of the foreign corporation included in the gross income of a United States person
   (4) the sum of the amounts of any illegal bribes, kickbacks, or … be unlawful under the Foreign Corrupt Practices Act of 1977 …
(b) Exclusion of United States income … subpart F income does not include any income from sources within the United States …
(c) Limitation (1) In general
   (A) Subpart F income [is] limited to current earnings and profits … .

B.3 Regulations to Implement Laws of the USA

Regulations have the force, if not quite the authority, of law. They specify many situations to excruciating detail, but still leave many issues open for debate. We have seen that transfer pricing and IP valuation are complex. There is much reliance on examples. Although short and dense, in the regulations proposed in 2007 examples comprised about 2/3 of the text [F B.1], Many regulations and examples still situations that are based tangibles rather than on tangibles.

It is impossible to write regulations that cover all cases that can occur in the future, and since rule-making takes many years, regulations remains vague for fast-moving high-tech situations. Relying on examples introduces yet more complexity.

First one has to locate the most relevant example, and then the example itself has to be matched the facts of the situations. Opportunities for controversy are rife.

B.3.1 Income Allocation Among Controlled Corporations

The CFR Title 26 Chapter 1 §1.482 regulations, first issued in 1968, specify in detail how the law, specified in Title 26 IRC §482, should be applied. Substantial revisions were made in 1992–1993 and in 1995–1996 to deal specifically with intangibles. Temporary revisions for platform contribution transactions (PCTs) made in 2007 were revised and finalized in December 2011 [IRS-TP:12]. There are many other laws and regulations that interact with transfer pricing, as regulations pertaining to taxhavens, tax treaties, preferential treatment for certain countries, possessions [B.2.1], and industries, protection of IP, methods of accounting, penalties, etc.

26 CFR §1.482-1. Allocation of income and deductions among taxpayers

(1) Purpose and scope. … ensure that taxpayers clearly reflect income attributable to controlled transactions, and to prevent the avoidance of taxes with respect to such transactions. [Put] a controlled taxpayer on a tax parity with an uncontrolled taxpayer by determining the true taxable income of the controlled taxpayer. …
   (b) Arm's length standard. … (1) … determining the true taxable income of a controlled taxpayer, the standard … in every case is that of a taxpayer dealing at arm's length with an uncontrolled taxpayer. A controlled transaction meets the arm's length standard if the results of the transaction are consistent with the results that would have been realized if uncontrolled taxpayers had engaged in the same transaction under the same circumstances (arm's length result). However, because identical transactions can rarely be located, whether a transaction produces an arm's length result generally will be determined by reference to the results of comparable transactions under comparable circumstances. See … §1.482-1(d)(2) (Standard of comparability). Evaluation of whether a controlled transaction produces an arm's length result is made pursuant to a method selected under the best method rule described in §1.482-1(c).
   (c) Best method rule. …
      (1) … The arm's length result … must be determined under the method that .. provides the most reliable measure of an arm's length result. Thus, there is no strict priority of methods, and no method will invariably be considered to be more reliable than others. A … result may be determined .. without establishing the inapplicability of another method, but if another method subsequently is shown to produce a more reliable measure …, such other method must be used. Similarly, if two or more applications of a single method provide inconsistent results, the … result must be … that, under the facts and circumstances, provides the most reliable measure of an arm's length result. ….

26 CFR §1.482-1. (1) (c) (continued)

(2) … . Data based on the results of transactions between unrelated parties provides the most objective basis … . …, it also may be relevant to consider whether the results of an analysis are consistent with the results of an analysis under another method. These factors are explained in … (c)(2)(i), (ii), and (iii)…

(i) Comparability. The … reliability … depends on the degree of comparability … after making adjustments … in (d)(2) … if adjustments are made to increase the degree of comparability, … the reliability of the results of the analysis [is less].

(ii) [Reliability] depends upon the …

(A) Completeness and accuracy of data. …

(B) Reliability of assumptions. … selection of the appropriate interest rate [for computing the] capitalized intangible development expenses …

(C) Sensitivity of results [to] differences in management … product characteristics …

(iii) Confirmation of results by another method. If two or more methods produce inconsistent results, the best method rule will be applied [to] provide the most reliable measure of an arm's length result. If the best method rule does not clearly indicate which method should be selected, and additional factor … in selecting a method is whether any of the competing methods produce results that are consistent … . Further, … different applications of the same method, the fact that a second method (or another … method) produces results that are consistent with one of the competing applications may be taken into account.

(d) Comparability. ….

(3) Factors for determining comparability.

(i) Functional analysis.

(ii) Contractual terms. …

(B) (1) Written agreement.

(2) No written agreement. …

(iii) Risk. …

(B) Identification of party that bears risk. …

(C) Examples. …

(iv) Economic conditions. …

(v) Property or services.

(4) Special circumstances. …

(i) Market share strategy. …

(ii) … geographic markets. …

(e) Arm's length range.

(1) … application of method may produce a number of results from which a range of reliable results may be derived… . A taxpayer will not be subject to adjustment if its results fall within such [an] arm's length range.

26 CFR §1.482-1. (1)(e) (continued)

(2) Determination of arm's length range—
  (i) [*May be*] determined by … a single … best method rule to [multiple similar] uncontrolled transactions. Use of more than one method may be appropriate … (c)(2)(iii) ….
  (ii) … Uncontrolled comparables must … be sufficiently similar to the controlled transaction [for] an arm's length result. If material differences exist … adjustments must be made to the results of the uncontrolled transaction … . The arm's length range will be derived only from those uncontrolled comparables that have, or through adjustments … can be [made] similar [in] comparability and reliability …
  (iii) … (A) In general. The arm's length range will consist of the results [where] the information ,,, is sufficiently complete … .
    (B) … If [not, then] statistical methods are used to establish a range … .
    (C) Interquartile range … is the range from the 25th to the 75th percentile of the results derived from the uncontrolled comparables. …

(3) … if taxpayer's results are outside arm's length range [*the IRS*] may make allocations that adjust the controlled taxpayer's result to any point within the arm's length range. … ordinarily be to the median of all the results. …

(4) Arm's length range not prerequisite to allocation. The rules … do not require that the [IRS] establish an arm's length range prior to making an allocation … .

(f) Multiple year data. (iii) … It may be appropriate… to consider … for one or more years before or after the year under review.

B.3.2 Embedded Intangibles

26 CFR §1.482-3 (f) Coordination with [IP] rules

The value of an item of tangible property may be affected by the value of intangible property, such as a trademark affixed to the tangible property (embedded intangible). … the transfer of tangible property with an embedded intangible will not be considered a transfer of such intangible if the controlled purchaser does not acquire any rights to exploit the intangible property other than rights relating to the resale of the tangible property … . …

If the transfer of tangible property conveys to the recipient a right to exploit an embedded intangible (…), it [*is*] necessary to determine the arm's length consideration for such intangible separately from the tangible property, applying methods … under §1.482-4. [*See §1.482-7(b)(5)(iii), (c)(4)(ii), and (c)(5) for examples of combinations with software.*]

B.3.3 Methods for Valuing Transfers of Intangible Property

Part 4 of the CFR Title 26 §1.482 regulations includes a definition of intangibles. They received updates in 2007, which were on hold up to 2012. Table 5.1 provides the match of the methods specified by the IRS to the methods described and assessed in Chap. 5. The new material on Platform Contribution Transactions (PCTs) replaced a section §1.482-7(g) and refers frequently to the earlier methods in section §1.482-4. It includes many new examples, but does not stand on its own. For that reason it is not copied here.

26 CFR §1.482-4 & -7 Methods to determine taxable income

(a) In general. The arm's-length amount charged in a controlled transfer of intangible property must be determined under one of the four methods listed in this paragraph (a). Each of the methods must be applied in accordance with §1.482-1, …. The arm's-length consideration for the transfer of an intangible determined under this section must be commensurate with the income attributable to the intangible. … . The … methods are—
   (1) The comparable uncontrolled transaction method,… [§1.482-4(c), which refers back to a method for tangibles, §1.482-1(d)(1)] [*for PCTs see §1.482-7(g)(3)*];
   (2) The comparable profits method, described in §1.482-5;
   (3) The profit-split method, described in §1.482-6; [*for PCTs§1.482-7(g)(7)*]; and
   (4) Unspecified methods described in … (d) [*for PCTs §1.482-7(g)(8)*].
   [Many examples are given in the regulations with each of these methods.]

(b) … an intangible is an asset that comprises any of the following items and has substantial value independent of the services of any individual—
   (1) Patents, inventions, formulae, processes, designs, patterns, or know-how;
   (2) Copyrights and literary, musical, or artistic compositions;
   (3) Trademarks, trade names, or brand names;
   (4) Franchises, licenses, or contracts;
   (5) Methods, programs, systems, procedures, campaigns, surveys, studies, forecasts, estimates, customer lists, or technical data; and
   (6) Other similar items. For purposes of section 482, an item is considered similar to those listed in paragraph (b)(1) through (5) … if it derives its value not from its physical attributes but from its intellectual content or other intangible properties.

   …

(d) Unspecified methods—(1) … . Methods not specified in (a) … may be used to evaluate whether the amount charged in a controlled transaction is arm's length. Any method used under this paragraph (d) …must be applied according to … §1.482-1. … an unspecified method should provide information on the prices or profits that the controlled taxpayer could have realized by choosing a realistic alternative [… as—7(g)(8)] …

26 CFR §1.482-7(g) Revisions to deal with pCTs

§1.482-7 (g) Supplemental guidance on methods applicable to PCTs—

(1) In general. This paragraph (g) provides supplemental guidance on applying the methods listed in this paragraph (g)(1) for purposes of evaluating the arm's length amount charged in a PCT.

...

(8) Unspecified methods—Methods not specified in (g)(3) through (g)(7) ... may be used to evaluate whether the amount charged in a PCT is arm's length. Consistent with the specified methods, an unspecified method should take into account the general principle that uncontrolled taxpayers evaluate the terms of a transaction by considering the realistic alternatives to that transaction, and only enter into a particular transaction if none of the alternatives is preferable to it. Therefore, in establishing whether a PCT achieved an arm's length result, and unspecified method should provide information on the prices or profits that the controlled participant could have realized by choosing a realistic alternative ... [It] will not be applied unless it provides the most reliable measure of an arm's length result under the principles of the best method rule. See § 1.482-1(c). Therefore, in accordance with § 1.482-1(d)(Comparability), to the extent that a method relies on internal data rather than uncontrolled comparables, its reliability will be reduced. Similarly, the reliability of a method will be affected by the reliability of the data and assumptions used to apply the method, including any projections used.

B.3.4 Profit Level Metrics

26 CFR §1.482-5 Comparable profits method

(b)(4) Profit level indicators ...Profit level indicators are ratios that measure relationships between profits and costs incurred or resources employed. A variety of profit level indicators can be calculated in any given case. Whether use of a particular profit level indicator is appropriate depends upon a number of factors, including the nature of the activities of the tested party, the reliability of the available data with respect to uncontrolled comparables, and the extent to which the profit level indicator is likely to produce a reliable measure of the income that the tested party would have earned had it dealt with controlled taxpayers at arm's length, taking into account all of the facts and circumstances. The profit level indicators should be derived from a sufficient number of years of data to reasonably measure returns that accrue to uncontrolled comparables. Generally, such a period should encompass at least the taxable year under review and the preceding two taxable years.

26 CFR §1.482-5 (b)(4) (continued)

(i) Rate of return on capital employed. …
(ii) Financial ratios.—(A) Ratio of operating profit to sales; and
(B) Ratio of gross profit to operating expenses. …
(iii) Other profit level indicators … . [Any] based solely on internal data may not be used.

B.3.5 Methods to Determine Taxable Income when Cost-Sharing

26 CFR §1.482-7 Methods to determine taxable income in connection with a cost sharing arrangement [CSA]

(a) … The arm's length amount charged in a … cost sharing arrangement (CSA), as described in … (b) … must be determined under a method described in this section. …
  (1) RAB share method for cost sharing transactions (CSTs) [as R&D and acquisitions].
  (2) Methods for [*PCTs* used for *buy-in transactions*]. …
(b) … [*In*] A cost sharing arrangement … controlled participants share the costs and risks of developing cost shared intangibles in proportion to their RAB shares. …
  (1) Substantive requirements—
    (i) CSTs. All controlled participants must commit to, and in fact, engage in cost sharing in each taxable year … is in proportion to [*their*] RAB share.
    (ii) PCTs. All controlled participants must commit to, and in fact, engage in platform contributions … and must … make arm's length payments [*PCT Payments*] to [*any*] [PCT Payee] that provides a platform contribution. …
(c) Platform contributions (1) In general. A platform contribution is any resource, capability, or right that a controlled participant has developed, maintained, or acquired externally to the intangible development activity (whether prior to or during the course of the CSA) that is reasonably anticipated to contribute to developing cost shared intangibles. … .
(d) [Costs] …—7(e) [RAB] …—7(f) [Change]…—7(g) [Methods] …
  (1) … for … a PCT.
  (i) The comparable uncontrolled transaction method described in … (g)(3), [based on [§1.482-(c)], or the comparable uncontrolled services price methods (CUSP);
  (ii) The income method, described in … (g)(4) [*added*]
  (iii) The acquisition price method, described in (g)(5) of this section; [*added*]

26 CFR §1.482-7 (d) (continued)

- (iv) The market capitalization method, … in paragraph §1.482-7(g)(6) [*added*]
- (v) The residual profit-split method, described in paragraph §1.482-7(g)(7); and
- (vi) Unspecified methods, described in paragraph §1.482-7(g)(8) [, *but similar to §1.482-4(d)]….*

(h) … -7(i) [Examples are given in the regulations with each specified method. See §1.482-7 (b)(iv)2, (b)(5)(iii)1–4,(c)(5)1, (e)(2)(ii)9, (g)(2)(ii), (g)(2)(vii)(B)1–3, (g)(4)(viii)1–4, (g)(vi)1–3 and (h) for examples of transfers of software and similar high technology.]

B.3.6 Profit Split Methods

26 CFR §1.482-6 Profit split methods

The original (1994) paragraph, 482-6, was revised in 2007 as CFR § 1.482.6T [B.1.2 #6], with new examples and many references to the original paragraph. For PCT's see -7(g)(7)

(a) … . The profit split method evaluates whether the allocation of the combined operating profit [by] controlled transactions is arm's length [using] the relative value of each … contribution to that combined operating profit or loss. The combined operating profit [is to be] from the most narrowly identifiable business activity … for which data is available… . …

(c) (1)… the profit split method [uses] one of the following allocation methods—

- (2) Comparable profit split …
  - (i) is derived from the combined operating profit of uncontrolled taxpayers whose transactions and activities are similar to those of the controlled taxpayers in the relevant business activity.
- (3) Residual profit split …
  - (i) … the combined operating profit or loss from the relevant business activity is allocated … following the two-step process … .
    - (A) Allocate income to routine contributions. The first step allocates operating income … to provide a market return for its routine contributions … . Routine contributions are contributions … similar … those made by uncontrolled taxpayers involved in similar business activities [and] include contributions of tangible property, services and intangibles … .

(B) Allocate residual profit … (2) Nonroutine contributions of intangible property. … the relative value of nonroutine intangible property contributed by taxpayers may be measured by … the fair market value of such intangible property. [or] estimated by the capitalized cost of developing the intangible property and [maintaining], less … amortization … . Finally, if the intangible development expenditures of the parties are relatively constant over time and the useful life of the intangible property contributed by all parties is approximately the same, [*as in the case where a company splits itself into a parent and an offshore division*] the amount of actual expenditures in recent years may be used to estimate the relative value of nonroutine intangible property contributions. [*in the case of a platform split of an existing enterprise, as in the MNC to CONCH mode, they are equal.*]

Appendix C: Royalties

C.1 Paying for Transferred Intellectual Assets

The methods in Chap. 5 estimated a value for intellectual assets being transferred. Specifically, the methods set a price for a buy-in transaction where a controlled offshore entity, CONCH, was acquiring make-sell rights to intellectual property created by its parent corporation, MNC in California, as part of a cost-sharing agreement. The assets also included ongoing access to MNC's workforce, and the products and product improvements they were generating. A tranche of rights to all of MNC's intellectual capital was being sold [IRS-CIP:07].

Once a price has been determined, the payments can be made in several ways. Our model company considered four choices, or a combination of them, to receive the payment due:

C1. A lump sum payment in cash, due immediately from CONCH.
C2. Shares of CONCH stock equivalent to the lump-sum value.
C3. Installment payments, drawing largely on the income to be received by CONCH from the sales subsidiaries, MNC EMEA, LSE, and PFE.
C4. Royalty payments, set as a fraction of the income received by those selling subsidiaries, paid out from the monies received at CONCH.

Each of those choices should fairly reimburse the parent in the USA, MNC, and yield about the same amount. The choice is made by MNC's management; CONCH, being a controlled division, has no voice. MNC, with ATA's help, will choose the reimbursement depending on its convenience. That convenience will depend in part on the amount being due; larger amounts are harder to handle. CONCH accounts have not yet accumulated any capital and CONCH has no publicly traded shares to offer. MNC chose payments in installments.

G. Wiederhold, *Valuing Intellectual Capital: Multinationals and Taxhavens*, Management for Professionals 23, DOI 10.1007/978-1-4614-6611-6,

Two of the methods encountered in Chap. 5 are deemed to be more suitable for valuing transactions are based on royalties. Those were M4, based on comparable transactions, and M6, the profit-split method. In those methods royalties were determined and then the equivalent valuations were computed by applying those royalties to estimated future income. In practice, royalties are used when future income is too uncertain to allow a valuation that would allow the use of payment methods C1, C2, or C3 listed above [ChapotonG:88]. If no valuation is possible that provides a credible lump sum result, then payment using royalties becomes mandatory [B T.4].

In the remainder of this appendix only royalties applicable to reimbursement for intellectual assets are considered, focusing on intracompany transfers of intellectual capital. A wealth of references on the topic of royalties is available [Parr:07].

C.1.1 Contingent Payments Using Royalties

In a royalty license contract, a licensor grants rights to use IP to a licensee who will pay a percentage royalty applied to the future income that the licensee will earn by exploiting that IP [Parr:07]. The reason a licensor is willing to convey valuable IP to another party tends to be that the licensor, say an inventor, does not have adequate resources for development and marketing. If a trustworthy valuation of the invention were available, the licensor could obtain the same income immediately by simpler means, as by receiving a lump sum payment for that amount.

The value of an invention, or any other IP, is determined by the income it brings in. If the investments and risks of the licensor and the licensee were identical, a 50/50 split of the earnings seems reasonable. However, inventing something may cost relatively little, while the development needed in order to have a saleable product and then marketing it may be costly. The licensor and the licensee also function on different time scales, making a simple allocation of income impossible.

Typically the licensee incurs much higher costs. In software, the ratio of moving from a working prototype to a product ranges from a factor 5 to a factor 20 or more.

C.2 Applicability of Royalties

Royalties are commonly used to reimburse for the investments made by parties that are complementary, say an inventor and a company able to design, develop, market, and sell a product based on the invention. There are no standard rates [Smith:11]. The licensor and licensee differ in function; each party brings their valuable competency to the table, as one party having unique IP and the other party having manufacturing prowess. The relative risks are a crucial aspect of determining a fair royalty rate. Risks, being uncertain by nature, are also the hardest aspect to quantify.

C.2.1 Relative Risk in Arm's-Length Contracts

The licensor assumes the risk that the licensee will fail to convert the IP into a saleable product, and no income will ensue.

The licensee of the IP, planning to manufacture a product, assumes much greater risks.

- Can the IP be reduced to practice? Only a small fraction of ideas are practical at any point in time. Storing and searching all the world's books was not feasible in 1983 [W:83].
- Can it be produced in volume? Scanning books for computer entry required much manual labor until recently. Without enough data the promised capability cannot be reached.
- Is it really unique? For many readers, having original works available online may not offer much more than having only recent literature available online.
- Is it economical compared with alternative products? If costly data entry requires high subscription rates, alternate information sources will be preferred.
- Is there a market? Uniqueness, broad availability, and price define the size of a market segment. Those factors are uncertain until some time into development.
- Will it be ready in time? Much information loses its value if delayed. If embedded software is delayed, a product depending on it may never make it to market.
- Can the market be convinced? Keeping personal health records available online for rapid access has not become acceptable because of privacy and reliability concerns.

By the time a licensing contract is negotiated, some of these issues will have been resolved. The licensee is convinced that there is a good chance that the IP will be the basis for a product. At times, IP will be licensed just to prevent it from becoming available to a competitor.

C.2.2 Mature IP

If the licensor already possesses experience in developing the IP into a product, sharing that experience with the licensee is very valuable. That experience could include, in order of increasing value:

1. Having built a prototype.
2. Having built a product based on that IP, and licensing that IP for reuse.
3. Having previously built a product similar to what the licensee envisages.
4. Having built the same product, but only sold it in home markets.
5. Having already marketed and sold the same products world-wide.

The latter case is unlikely in arm's-length arrangements, but arises in buy-in arrangements, such as the platform contribution transaction of the CONCH buy-in of MNC's resources. The life of such IP is indefinite.

An example of IP reuse would be if MNC, instead of developing, building, and marketing the mobile version of the Maniac itself, licenses a set of specified assets. Instead MNC would make available a "box" of IP to an arms-length licensee, adequate for making a product akin to the ManiMobile. Devising a fair license contract involving services will take much effort.

If the IP is mature, the licensor and the licensee will profit from having an ongoing relationship. The licensor has experienced staff, and that experience can prevent the licensee from making errors. Product and income will be realized much more rapidly. The value of obtaining ongoing services is immense, since now the risks to licensee are greatly reduced [Contractor:81]. Reimbursements for such services can be a combination of a higher royalty rate and paying high fees for consulting contracts. If the services are only needed initially, paying for consulting is the preferred choice, since a lower royalty rate remains fixed over the long term. However, it is not unusual that the licensee underestimates the amount of help needed, and incurs higher consulting costs than expected.

In the CONCH buy-in ongoing services are implied. CONCH does not have any distinct development staff. The R&D staff at MNC in California does all the work already.

C.2.3 Risk Mitigation in Arm's-Length Contracts

Since the licensee is only liable for payment if sales materialize, the licensee's risk is mitigated. If the licensee finds that the licensed IP is not useful, nothing is paid to the licensor. In case of failure the licensee's loss is limited to the funds the licensee spent up to that time. If the products based on that IP generates less income than hoped for, the licensee pays less.

A confident licensor hopes to earn more than could be obtained by a lump-sum payment upfront, because the licensee is protected from all risks related to the IP rights purchase. If the products based on that IP generate more income than expected, the licensor receives more.

Given a cost ratio of the licensor to the licensee of 1:5 the license rate would be 17 % of earnings from the product. However, the licensor's expenses occurred earlier, and their capitalization would increase their value, as presented in the M7, the roll-over method, and the rate becomes 21 % [FC.1]. That capitalization could continue until actual sales are made and the licensee pays licensing fees. However, in setting a contract, use of known information is preferred. At the same time, the factor 5 development and marketing cost is a lower bound. Negotiations to obtain a reasonable license rate can be lengthy.

Using a royalty arrangement may be the only way the owner of the intangible can motivate a purchaser and have a chance to obtain a substantial income. If the licensor has few alternatives for realizing income from the IP it holds, the licensee will have a strong negotiation position [Contractor:01].

C.2.4 Payment Base

Royalties are payments based on a percentage, the royalty rate, of income or earnings by the licensee. Conceptually, the earnings, after the licensee's costs are deducted, should be shared.

However, an arms-length licensor rarely wants to base a royalty payment rate on the earnings that a licensee posts. Earnings of a business are affected by many factors not under control of the licensor [Razgaitis:03]. For instance, a licensee could pay very high bonuses to everyone involved once the product is on the market, significantly reducing earnings and hence royalty payments. For that reason, royalty rates are typically based on revenues; revenues collected are easier to check.

If a company has a margin of earnings on royalties of 25 %, the 21 % royalty rate on earnings becomes about 5 % royalty on revenue, a figure that is not uncommon and often used as a basis for negotiations [FC.2].

C.2.5 Royalty Rate for Intracompany Transactions

The situation in a transaction among corporate division differs completely from the common arm's-length situation. The risks are joint; any loss in one division due to a poor setting of a royalty rate will be compensated by increased profits in another division. Setting of intracompany royalty rates cannot be trusted [Parr:07]. However, differences in tax rates among jurisdictions for various divisions will make a difference to the consolidated corporate income. Being controlled by the same management, there is no meaningful negotiation. The division that has the role of licensor, often the parent, has a wide choice of business paths to develop the product; it does not depend on a single or a few candidate licensees to realize income from its IP.

Furthermore, a royalty mechanism makes no sense when acquiring rights to a mature product-line in a cost-sharing arrangement, as is the case with MNC and CONCH. CONCH brings no expertise to the table that MNC did not have already. Ongoing services, as R&D, can be arranged contractually in an arm's-length setting, but would not be based on a share of revenues, since the licensee would not have any revenues until actual sales commence. Being inherently unsuitable, arranging payments using royalties in a buy-in and cost-sharing situation is one of the most contentious elements in offshore taxation [Becker:02].

In the case of a buy-in, as the transfer of IP rights from MNC to CONCH, the situation is even more extreme. The new CFC, CONCH, assumed no risks whatsoever. Maniacs were already being manufactured and sold worldwide. CONCH will have close to the same margins as the parent corporation. It shares R&D expenses proportionally and it obtains Maniacs for sale at the same factory price that MNC divisions pay, so that its Cost-of-Goods-Sold (CoGS) is known. CONCH can reimburse MNC for any general services (SG&A) it needs that it cannot provide itself, perhaps paying a modest markup. Since the earnings margin on revenues of selling

Maniacs is 41 %, it should pay a royalty rate on earnings that is not much less [FC.3]. The amount CONCH would pay is then a bit less than its RAB share of the total earnings of MNC. That is, of course, similar to what MNC would realize if it had kept control of all worldwide operations.

The current IRS regulations do not distinguish settings where royalties are appropriate and where they are not. That flexibility allows a taxpayer to propose a royalty arrangement in situations where it is unlikely that royalty payments will achieve a fair return for the intellectual capital rights made available to its offshore subsidiary.

C.3 Royalty Contracts

License contracts do not have to follow any fixed rules. Specifics of license contracts vary greatly to account for the differences in expected benefits and assumed risks of the licensee versus the licensor. The specification of the IP made available, with all the attached conditions of use and scope, is termed the "box."

The literature lists over 100 considerations that influence the setting of royalty rates and any other payments [Razgaitis:03]. Those make up the "wheelbarrow." Contract considerations listed when selecting comparables for valuations apply here as well. They were described with the M4, the CUT-VM approach, in Chap. 5, Sect. 5.3.4 (M4.1).

License contracts can contain clauses to:

(a) Encourage the licensee to be fast, as having reduced royalty rates in the first 3 years.
(b) Assure the licensee's commitment by having an upfront lump-sum payment. The payment helps the licensor to pay debts incurred in creating the IP and getting it to a state needed for effective licensing, as obtaining patent protection.
(c) Increasing the motivation to move rapidly towards production by requiring a lump-sum payment up front, with terms that reduce near-term royalty rates.
(d) If the licensee has inadequate resources, the licensor may provide help or investments. Such assistance will increase the royalty rate or lead to partial ownership of the licensee's business.
(e) Encourage the licensee to sell more, by having lower royalty rates once sales exceed a certain level.
(f) Specify termination date, typically at time when patents expire or when no more sales are expected, allowing the licensee to clear out inventory without payment concerns.
(g) The licensor may also expect to profit from the licensee's effort. For instance, in software development, inadequacies in a prototype are only perceived during further development. Feedback from the developer can have a high value to the creator.

These terms in this wheelbarrow interact. When other financial considerations, as partial upfront lump-sum payments or co-investments, are included, the royalty payments may be deferred initially or the royalty rate will be applied to less than the full revenues.

In any arm's-length situation involving valuable IP, careful and specific legal contracts will be written up. Those will specify in detail the "box," namely the rights the licensor provides to the licensee, and the "wheel-barrow," the terms of payment that the licensee commits to. Once the license contract is signed an arm's-length licensor has lost control over the IP in the box as long as the licensee complies with the terms.

C.3.1 Exclusivity

Common licenses are exclusive to the licensee and have an indefinite life. If the licensor makes the license nonexclusive, the licensee is subject to a risk that the licensor will issue a license to a potential competitor as well. Licenses issued by governments and some universities are typically nonexclusive to avoid bias in selection. A nonexclusive license will be licensed at about half the royalty rate of an exclusive license, but if many companies create products, the licensor can still do well [Razgaitis:03]. The Stanford-UCSF license for the Cohen-Boyer patent on PCR DNA amplification, available to all requestors, brought in over $250M [Eisenberg:97]. In more commercial settings the licensee will insist that the box specifies a period where the license is exclusive and has a clause that compensates the initial licensee if another license is issued that would diminish its market.

Giving the licensee a nonexclusive or time-limited license allowing an alternate sale of the IP reduces the licensor's risk of the licensee failing and not developing and marketing a successful product. A contract can provide that if sales are less than expected, the license can be withdrawn or become nonexclusive. If the licensee is not competent, the licensor can try to locate an alternative.

C.3.2 Royalty Period and Income Generation

Royalties are commonly set for an indefinite period. It is hard for the licensor to judge when an arms-length licensee will derive significant revenue from sales of products based on the covered IP. While converting prototype software to a marketable product can be rapid, electronic gadgets take longer, and pharmaceuticals take many years before they are approved for marketing [Razgaitis:03]. A long delay increases risk and reduces the expected return for the licensor.

Royalty rates may be renegotiated when situations change. The ability to make changes must have been specified in the initial contract. Since future events are hard to specify, there may just be a general clause allowing renegotiations. Renegotiation can be requested when needed, since it is in both parties' interest to extract as much value from the IP as possible.

For instance, when a competitor enters the field, the IP becomes less valuable than it was originally. In that case, lowering the royalty rate allows the licensee to lower its prices and remain in business, and the licensor will continue to receive some income.

C.3.3 Intracompany Royalty Contracts

In a buy-in or platform transfer the contract terms (a) to (g) listed in the beginning of Sect. C.3 are not needed. The motivation of the licensor and licensee are identical. The financial effect is undistinguishable in the consolidated accounts. We summarize the conditions in for an intracompany IP transfer in the context of the CONCH buy-in.

1. There is no difference in resources, effort needed, timing of income, etc., among the parties. MNC and CONCH are still the same company, under the same management; there is just a split of revenues and earnings by region.
2. CONCH starts generating revenue as soon as the license arrangement is set. CONCH has no investment risk and MNC does not have to worry about delays in receiving a royalty stream.
3. The box of IP received is comprehensive. CONCH automatically obtains very broad and valuable intellectual capital from MNC. All of MNC's designers, engineers, marketing strategies, customers, and trademarks remain available. All MNC's stays located where they are, and continues to interact completely unaware of the sale of IP to an offshore holding company. CONCH is an invisible division of an ongoing business.
4. CONCH has the rights to all the IP needed to sell the MNC Maniacs and avoids the risk faced by an arm's-length licensee that additional licenses have to be negotiated for its product to be completed.
5. The issue of relative risk mitigation is absent. CONCH cannot fail in design, manufacturing, or marketing in any way that MNC would not. If CONCH fails in its offshore marketing, MNC would have failed similarly.
6. A license clause that specifies a limited term or a nonexclusive arrangement is meaningless in intracompany transactions. The license will continue as long as it makes sense to MNC. Any loss from competitors at CONCH are losses to MNC. Not granting exclusive rights allows MNC alone to sell globally to multinational customers, even when the revenue for offshore sales will flow to CONCH because of the rights sold to CONCH.
7. The reasons for basing royalty on revenue rather than on earnings are absent, since MNC is in complete control of all cost accounting and income allocation. There is no actual staff at CONCH that could introduce spending to hide earnings from MNC [Kopits:76]. Basing a royalty on earnings would increase annual payments to MNC by about another $1M [FC.4].
8. The lack of comparable data for transactions as the CONCH buy-in of MNC's intellectual capital makes it very hard to assess whether proposed royalty rates, terms, and periods are reasonable.

In practice, many multinational corporations did not initially make formal licensing arrangements with their subsidiary divisions, since any excess profits at the CFC flow back as dividends to the parent corporation [Contractor:81].

Contracts that allow renegotiation provide excessive flexibility for intracompany arrangements. Since there is licensor controls the licensee, any changes to the contract will, in fact, be arbitrary, even when the contracts are written as if they were made among parties at arm's length. When royalties for intracompany transfer are formalized to satisfy documentation requirements, conflicts arise.

Concerns about the emerging use of taxhavens required internal transfers to be documented. Many internal royalty licensing arrangements are only formalized when royalties for IP transfers to taxhavens are questioned.

C.3.4 Annual Royalty Payments

When the taxpayer elects to have the subsidiary make a sequence of royalty payments, the taxpayer has an incentive to overstate its projections of the sub's post buy-in sales. In contrast, when the taxpayer elects to have the sub make a lump-sum payment, we observe that the taxpayer has an incentive to understate the subsidiaries post buy-in sales [DyeGG:07].

Once payment by royalties is instituted, validation that the set royalty rate is reasonable given the current business relationships is required. This validation requires considerable efforts by the taxpayer, the taxpayers accountants, and the IRS. If it is determined that the difference in payments is <20 % the safe harbor clause for such tax returns comes into play. Since the computations are complex and include the uncertainties if any IP assessment, there are again opportunities for incremental tax avoidance, by staying each year just under the 20 % boundary.

C.4 Published Royalty Rates

In the commercial licensing world a rule-of-thumb is that royalties on earnings are around 25 % and royalties on revenue around 5 %. However, such a rule has no legal support [Smith:11]. These numbers implicitly assume that earnings margins for products having considerable IP contents are about 35 %, with 10 % allocated to routine earnings [GoldscheiderJM:02]. Surveys show that royalty rates of 5 % on revenue is the most common rate used, although the range starts at 0 % and goes as high as 50 % [Parr:07].

The common 5 % rate is appropriate for the basic case when the licensor holds IP that has never been "reduced to practice." However, so many factors are involved in setting royalty rates that surveys cannot tell the whole story [CavesCK:83]. For high-technology companies royalty rates on revenues for provided IP range from 5.2 to 7.2 % [Razgaitis:03].

Unusually low rates should be ignored for comparisons; they indicate that something else is going on. Very low rates may be charged to a casual, non-competing infringer of IP, just to show that the owner does defend its IP, as discussed in Chap. 3,

Sect. 3.1.1. Zero royalty rates are common when the IP is held by a membership association that promotes a common standard. Such instances must be eliminated when mean royalty rate is to be computed [Matsunaga:83].

C.4.1 Products Requiring Multiple Licenses

A licensee making complex products has to obtain IP rights from many sources. Hundreds of licenses are needed to allow marketing of multifunction electronic products, say a smartphone with its embedded software. The cost and delays in negotiating many licenses is high. Changing product designs to avoid a problematic licensor is costly as well [ChavezTW:98]. In those settings licensors must share the income among all the licenses, so that royalty rates for individual licenses become quite small. The fractions may not reflect the IPs contribution to the product's income [CavesCK:83].

An attractive solution is to use "paradigm licensing" where an intermediary organization manages a box all of IP rights needed for a common objective, say a wireless communication standard. Then all the diverse IP rights needed to implement the standard are obtained by the paradigm organization, typically initiated by promoters and potential users of the standard. For instance, licenses for 3G communication are managed by 4G Americas, created by 18 companies as Nokia, Ericsson, etc. [Seymour:12]. A new 3G product manufacturer can obtain all needed licenses there. Such a paradigm organization then distributes the royalty income among all the original IP owners. Members that invested initially in the research, development, and promotion of the standard may now have access to the IP at a reduced or zero royalty rate.

C.4.2 Governmental Constraints

To encourage indigenous development of IP, some countries limit the amount of royalty payments transferred out of the country [SAT:09]. In those cases a licensee receiving valuable IP may invest earnings in the licensor's name within the country. If royalties are part of the IP transfer arrangement, any data needed for valuation will be distorted.

C.4.3 Side Letters

Formal contracts made public can omit informal arrangements that are documented only as "side-letters." For instance, plans for dealing with patent suits may not appear in public documents since the concerns imply uncertainty about the validity of the IP; legal costs to deal with any such risks are high. Often conditions affecting valuations appear in such side-letters. Hiding side-letters have caused major valuation errors and even landed executives in jail [SchilitP:10].

C.4.4 *Royalties to Recover Sunk Costs*

Royalties are also used when an unforeseen opportunity to reuse IP arises. For instance, companies that mainly focused on US markets did not consider in their planning income from foreign sales. When offshore opportunities arose, they had no model to guide the setting of proper royalty rates. All prior R&D and marketing costs were already accounted for, and were considered "sunk costs." Any additional royalty income was viewed as pure profit. Royalty rates and conditions for offshore use of IP were negotiated based on what the licensee was able and willing to pay [Contractor:81]. The rise of globalization is reducing the parochial view, which just assessed a company's local market and costs, and granting foreign IP rights at low rates because of sunk costs.

C.4.5 *Alternate Bases for Royalty Rates*

We already presented the reasons why royalty rates are typically set as a percentage of product revenues. In multilevel supply chains revenues occur at each level, but may not always be documented. The fractional contribution of the IP to the product revenue is an issue as well. To a chip fabricator a chip design is crucial and will command at least a 20 % royalty on its chip revenues. If that fabricator also produces complete personal computers (PCs) with that chip, the royalty on its PC revenues are likely to be closer to 5 %.

C.5 Arm's-Length Versus Intracompany Royalties

Royalties are the primary means to reimburse inventors for intellectual property and rights to access intellectual capital. They can remove much of the uncertainty in making valuations when the level and timing of income cannot be predicted. Royalties provide indirection in the collection of future income, the fundamental basis for profiting from intellectual property.

In an arm's-length setting the conditions may vary greatly. However, much experience exists that allow licensing contract to be drawn up among the parties that are fair to the licensor and the licensee. Published resources summarizing royalty contracts are available and can be inspected for relevance and conditions that influenced the contractual royalty rate.

Outside of an arm's-length setting the principles that determine royalty rates are violated, as sketched in Fig. C.1. When companies transfer IP rights offshore to corporate divisions, that are under their control, all experience from arm's-length settings counts for nothing. The company has only split its platform of intangible capital into two parts. There are no independent parties that can negotiate fairly. Any contract drawn will be signed. Since there is a cohesive workforce, all past and

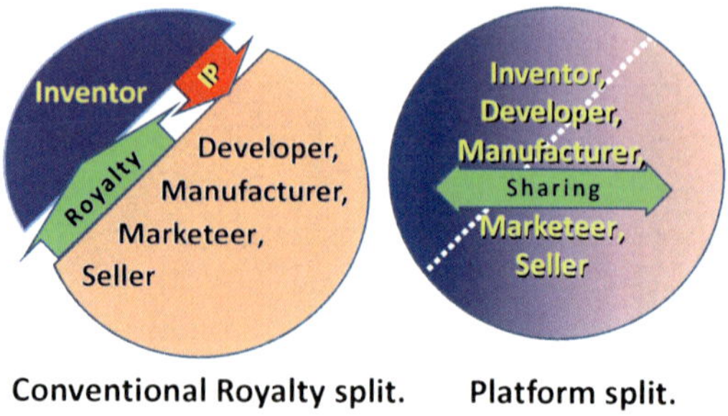

Fig. C.1 Settings for Royalty licensing

new information is shared. The implicit sharing of all intellectual capital at MNC's US operation cannot be captured in a royalty arrangement. For such cases a platform contribution transaction (PCT) is appropriate.

Use of published royalty rates to set intracompany royalty rates is based on counterfactual relationships. Sometimes tax authorities have had information on intracompany royalties and rates that do not appear in the public record. The settings may well match other, comparable, taxpayer cases. Such "secret" data have been used in countries as Australia to determine an appropriate royalty rate where the submitted rate appeared to be out-of-line [Markham:05]. In general, such an approach is not acceptable, since the taxpayer has no recourse.

C.5.1 Alternative Payments

Going back to fundamentals, and simply ensuring that the expected return from royalties is commensurate with alternate valuations of the IP being transferred, is a fair solution. It does require that future income be estimated, as had to be done when the M4, the CUT-VM, and M6, the PS-M, approaches in Chap. 5 only provided estimates of a fair royalty. An appropriate royalty would be close to the profit margin of MNC, 41 % [FA.1]. In general, costs at CONCH are similar to those at MNC; sales costs borne by MNC before the split are now shifted to MNC's offshore sales organizations in Europe (EMEA), Asia (PRJ), and Latin America (LSA).

MNC also commits itself to ongoing maintenance, paid for in part by cost-sharing payments made by CONCH. No arm's-length research organization would sell its results at cost or even for a modest markup; such an organization needs adequate earnings to continue to prosper. CONCH only took over the existing distribution structure. On the books CONCH is only responsible for its share of CoGS, SG&A, and R&D, as sketched in Fig. 7.4.

However, buy-in valuations use discounted values. Using a discount rate for the royalty income of 9 %, we find that to yield an amount equal to a lump sum of $800M, the royalty rate should be 34 % [FC.5]. To return the amount of the ATA's buy-in estimation, $50M, would require a royalty rate of only 2.0 % [FC.6]. That rate clearly does not make sense when MNC turns over nearly half of its income-producing potential to CONCH.

C.6 Summary

Royalties are in important means to allow creative individuals to get their concepts and inventions into the market place. They allow manufacturers to develop novel products without incurring excessive risks. Complex products require access to a wide variety of IP rights, including patents, that are not unique to any particular product. Bundling and paradigm licensing enable the development and later their sale and income from these products.

The use of royalties in situations where there is no reason for risk mitigation is inappropriate. The counterfactual setting in platform split transactions creates confusion, administrative and accounting overheads, and invites misuse.

Appendix D: Definitions and Glossary

The glossary extensively defines technical and financial terms that I have used here. Cross-references are set in bold italics. The definitions are specific to the context of this book. My hope is that consistent definitions will reduce the confusion now seen when intellectual capital and its effects on corporate and national economies are discussed. Because I expect it to be read by a variety of audiences, specialized experts will find some of them naïve. I added some of the obvious ones merely because they have been misused in some referenced diatribes. An important authority is the Oxford English Dictionary [OED:02]. An extensive glossary of terms used in tax avoidance can be found online [MurphyEa:09]. About 200 detailed definitions are found in [CordesEG:05]. Abbreviations are not listed if the full entry appears nearby.

10-K Annual report required for public stock companies since 1934, delivered to and available from the SEC and public sources (Chap. 8).

1040 The primary IRS form for reporting individual income tax due.

1120 The primary IRS form for reporting corporate income tax due, together with a Form 926.

Account Contents of documents or *books* used to keep track of tangible transactions and reporting the results on annual income statements and balance sheets, as shown in Tables A.1 and A.2 for a manufacturing company like *MNC* [FA.1].

Account balance sheet A report that shows all the assets in financial terms on the corporate books [F2.29]. An excess of assets over liabilities is the shareholders' equity [Vause:09].

Accounting and advising firm A business as modeled by ATA **in this book**, which provides financial and management advising services to its clients, typically corporations like MNC. Many are organized under the Swiss Vereinsgesetz and are members of WCOTA in the City of London. The major international players are referred to as the "big four" firms.

Accounting Principles Board (APB) Issued rules in proper accounting, now superseded by FASB. Affects data used for taxation, as APB 23, issued in 1972, re deferral of repatriation.

G. Wiederhold, *Valuing Intellectual Capital: Multinationals and Taxhavens*, Management for Professionals 23, DOI 10.1007/978-1-4614-6611-6,

Acquisition A company that is purchased by a parent company. Such an investment is an alternative to investing in R&D for organic growth. Acquired assets appear as new assets on the parent's book excess amounts paid become goodwill. Acquisitions may be paid for in cash or company stock. The choice made by the acquirer depends on the availability of cash versus the current stock market value of its shares, and on the seller's willingness to accept stock. Combining with a large company is often done as a merger.

Acquisition price method A valuation based on the purchase price of an acquired company, specified in [B.3.4 7(d)(1)(iii)], [B.1.2 #7(g)(5)]. It is the basis for the Purchase Price Valuation Method (Chap. 5, M8 PP-VM).

Active capital Funds generated by a business and needed for running it or for held for future acquisitions; a critical issue in applying Subpart F taxation rules.

AERR Actually Experienced Return Ratio, the NPV of total earnings or profits divided by the NPV of the investment that generated those earnings.

Affiliate Related or subsidiary division; a business not at arm's length.

AFR Applicable Federal Rate of tax.

After-tax profit A phrase used to distinguish earnings from profit. This book uses just the word profit for what is left after taxes are paid on earnings.

AG Aktiengesellschaft, a corporation in a German-speaking country, see GmbH.

AJCA American Jobs Creation Act of 2004, for an overview see [Clausing:04].

Alpha The percentage by which an instance of a margin beats the average. For a corporation, its margin minus the average of its peers in the same SIC classification. For a broad equity fund, alpha is the percentage by which it beats the S&P 500 return, and for a managed mutual fund the percentage by which it beats a hypothetical benchmark of equal risk, before its fees are considered [Fox:09] [JensenM:76]. It is not as stable a metric as beta. The margins are important when one is determining discount rates.

American Jobs Creation Act (AJCA) A law passed by Congress in October 2004, including the Homeland Investment Act (HIA) [AJCA:04]. The HIA allowed a one-time cash repatriation of dividends held offshore at an 85 % discount, so that instead of 35 % the tax rate became only 5.25 %. Companies that had inadequate records of their foreign holdings were limited to repatriating $500M. The total amount repatriated under the act was $362,000M [FD.1]. The HIA included some constraints on the use of the repatriated capital, as documented in IRC §965 (Chap. 2), but because money is fungible, they were not effective. Repatriation of IP rights held offshore was not considered (Chaps. 2 and 9).

Amortization An annual reduction of the value assigned on a balance sheet to assets such as capitalized research and development (R&D) expenses that have generated patents, designs, and software. The amortization can be linear over 15 years [AJCA:04]. Since 2004, goodwill is not amortized, but can be written off if its value has been impaired.

AMP Advertising, Marketing, and Promotion. AMP denotes the part of SG&A that can generate IP, typically embodied in a trademark.

AMT Alternative Minimum Tax, a recomputation of income tax liabilities to reduce tax avoidance [Sullivan:11] (Chap. 10).

Annual report A yearly report prepared by corporations to inform their shareholders. It will contain information delivered to the SEC in the corporate 10-K reports as well as informal statements by management, sometimes implying intellectual capital assets.

Anti-deferral rules Regulations that disallow accumulating income in offshore accounts. They typically distinguish active capital from passive income. In the USA they are referred to as Subpart F rules [B.2.10 (a)(3)(i)]. A blocker allows deferral of taxes otherwise due [IRS-F:09].

APA Advanced Pricing Agreement, negotiated multiyear agreement between a company and the IRS regarding transfer pricing.

APM Acquisition Price Method, the Purchase Price Valuation method (Chap. 5 M8, PP-VM).

Arm's length A condition where the parties in a business transaction are not related to each other. Corporate divisions are never at arm's length. Rules regarding such subsidiaries are given in the tax regulations [B.3.1 (b)].

Arm's-length comparison An approach to assess the value of an asset by comparing what the arm's-length prices were when similar assets were sold by a willing seller and purchased by an independent and willing buyer, without coercion [AviYonah:95].

Arm's-length lag An estimate of the lag parameters applicable for an arm's-length competitor who wants to replace an entrenched product. To recreate or match an existing product in the market, the gestation period and the effective lag will be less than the total period and total lag experienced by the original product producer. The re-creation cost and a lag were compared in Fig. 5.9. The estimate of the expected effort needed to recreate the product is based on the sum of the cost and time spent on the initial creation as affected by the lag, plus the cost and time spent to create additional versions, reduced by the efficiencies of re-creation, because there is an existing example and the objective is well understood [W:09]. The arm's-length lag creates a first-to-market advantage (Chap. 5, M3). An example of a successful re-creation was the Lotus 1-2-3 spreadsheet program, which replaced VisiCalc [ChristensenR:03].

Arm's-length price The price for an asset sold by a willing seller to an independent and willing purchaser [B.3.1 (b)]. A counterfactual argument when applied to intracompany transfer pricing [McDonald:08].

ASC Accounting Standards Codification, a hierarchical structure for rules issued by the SEC and the FASB to define GAAP, replaced SFAS in 2009. Income taxes are "topic 740."

Asset An item of value in a business; a tangible, including cash, or an intangible [B.3.1 (d) (6)]. Assets are listed on corporate balance sheets.

Asset-to-gross-income ratio A metric to judge how well investments perform. In 2008 for US manufacturers it was about 1.3. The return on investment ratio (ROI) is a related metric, but it implies a sale.

ATA Associated Tax Advisers, a fictional accounting and advising firm providing advice on taxation and related services to multinational companies, among them MNC (Chap. 2).

ATAT Abusive Tax Avoidance Transaction, IRS term for an action leading to extreme tax reductions.

ATRA American Taxpayer Relief Act, the 2013 fiscal cliff legislation, raising individual tax rates and leaving corporate taxes and credits unchanged

B Billion, used for large $ amounts. I use the short scale, where one billion is $1,000 million or $$10^9$, as is used in the USA. Most European countries use the long scale, where a billion is a million million (10^{12}), the same as a US trillion. The term "milliard" denotes €10^9 in the EU. The UK moved in 1974 from the long scale to the short scale, making it much easier to become a £ billionaire.

Balance sheet Account balance sheet (Appendix A).

BALRM Basic Arm's-Length Return Method—the CUT-VM or CP-VM valuation methods, informally known as the ballroom methods.

Bankruptcy Going out of business because of unresolvable financial losses. Creditors have first rights to what remains of a going concern, its salvage value; the shareholders come last.

BCD British Crown Dependency, as the Channel Islands and the Isle of Man.

BEA In finance, the Bureau of Economic Analysis, part of the US Department of Commerce. It produces US and regional GDP estimates and trade information.

Beneficial owners The actual owners of a corporation, not revealed in typical secrecy jurisdictions, as taxhavens.

Berry ratio The ratio of gross income to CoGS + SG&A. It measures profitability. Companies with more IP should have a higher Berry ratio (Chap. 5, M6).

Besloten Vennootschap (BV) Or, fully, *besloten vennootschap met beperkte aansprakelijkheid*, which translates into a "closely held company with limited liability"; as a closed corporation a BV is not listed on the stock market in The Netherlands, and for US law it is a foreign LLC [Laskey:00]. The minimum capital required is €18,000, but since 2006 no capital tax is levied. Under conditions defined as a "participation exemption" no taxes are due on major external sources of income [Pollock:12]. No audit is required unless the BV's gross Dutch-sourced income exceeds €12M or there are more than 50 employees [Romano:02]. A public corporation in The Netherlands is a *Naamloze Vennootschap* (NV) (Chaps. 2 and 6).

Beta The percentage sensitivity of an individual stock to basic market conditions. Available data are compiled for each industry sector [Barra:98], [BrealeyMA:06], [Fox:09], [Sharpe:85]. Beta is applied to the risk-adjusted rate, the sum of the equity risk premium and a risk-free base, typically set by Treasury bonds. The result is an appropriate discount rate.

BfS Bundesamt für Steuern, the German tax authority.

Black-Scholes A method of pricing options for a stock of known or assumed volatility given a number of simplifying assumptions, including normal distributions [Orrel:10].

Blocker Use of APB23, stating that accumulated offshore funds are intended for offshore use, so that repatriation to the US can be indefinitely deferred.

Board of directors In a corporation, a group of people responsible for the direction of a company, representing the actual owners, the shareholders of a company. The board must act in the owners' best interests. Some members of the board are the corporate executives who carry out the decisions. As a group they are responsible for the legal behavior of the company. Specifics follow state law. The UK also imposes some ethical rules.

Books Informal term for the corporate account balance sheet and its substantiating details. For book-tax conformity, see the congruency principle.

Book value The sum of corporate assets reported in an annual report.

Book-to-market ratio The inverse of the market/book ratio.

Box In licensing, a list of all included IP and constraints on the use of that IP. Traded against the wheelbarrow of payments and obligations.

British Crown Dependencies (BCD) The Channel Islands and the Isle of Man, countries that formally belong to the British monarch and have many links with the U.K. Queen Elizabeth II holds the title of Lord of Mann. The BCDs are not part of the U.K. and have their own governments. They determine their own tax laws, giving an advantage for UK and other foreign residents and businesses to manage their income. They are not regular members of the EU or the U.N., but some have representatives in those bodies.

British Overseas Territories (BOT) Independent countries that retain some connection to the UK, such as for Privy Court legal decisions. Many do not have the level of independence needed to become members of the UN. A number of them have become taxhavens, especially in the Caribbean (Chap. 6). Palm Island is my surrogate.

BTLA Buy-in Technology License Agreement, part of a cost-sharing agreement.

Bush tax cuts Temporary income tax reductions, part of the JGTRRA legislation of 2003, partially continued by the ATRA.

Business An organization that derives income from sales and services. Large businesses are often organized as C-corporations; smaller ones may be partnerships or S-corporations.

Business units Parts of a business with a specific function, product line, customer type, or sales region. Business units are the lowest level where separate books are kept. Those data are relevant if detailed information to allocate IP and income is needed. Major business units or groupings are organized as distinct divisions, often separately incorporated.

Buy-in An initial transfer payment to compensate the owner when an offshore corporation receives a tranche of rights to intellectual capital or platform of its parent. A buy-in is part of a broader cost-sharing agreement (Chap. 2).

Buyout A transfer payment to be paid by a US parent company if it needs to share IP acquired by an offshore division, often as the result of an acquisition of a foreign company. Taxes are reduced if the IP in the buyout is valued highly, reducing earnings.

BV Besloten Vennootschap, a Dutch corporate form, similar to a SàRL.

C-corporation A registered corporation with shareholders that are eligible to receive dividends, typically listed on a stock exchange.

CAAS Confidential Asset Accounting Services, MNC's CFI in Hilversum, The Netherlands, operated by ATA. Hans Brinker is the director (Chap. 6).

CAP Competitive Advantage Period, the interval for nonroutine earnings.

Capital Financial and equivalent assets shown on a company's books. Excludes intellectual capital unless it is explicitly included. Some jurisdictions annually collect taxes from capital holdings, typically at rate around 1 %. Sometimes the term "taxing capital" just means taxing earnings from capital investments [Bartlett:12B].

Capital gains The taxable earnings when assets are sold at a higher price than the purchase price [IRS-550:12]. The apparent gains are affected by inflation, especially if held for a long period. If a shareholder sells shares, the sale reduces the shareholder's ownership in the corporation; income from dividends does not (Chap. 8).

Capital gains tax rate Assets, such as corporate shares, that have been held for a specified holding period qualify as bona-fide investments, so that any gains upon sale qualify in the USA for a lower tax rate. The rates have been changed frequently [Eisenwein:06]. In 2008 the TIPRA legislation (the Bush tax cuts) set tax rates at 15 % for qualified capital gains for most US recipients. For couples earning <$17,000 that year the rate is 0 %. The rates are due to revert to 20 and 10 % in 2013. Since 1998 corporate stock has to be held for 1 year to qualify; other asset types have different holding periods [Paschall:00]. The reasons for reduced rates are questionable: There is no double taxation, investors' risk is reflected in expected profits, since inflation also raises corporate market values.

Capitalization Computing the current imputed cost of an asset by aggregating the expenses from each prior year, applying a capitalization rate for the prior years (Chap. 5, M7).

Capitalization rate The percentage applied each year to past investments to account for the past investment cost. The capitalization rate mirrors the discount rate, except that it is applied to past expenses, as R&D, rather than to future income. The capitalization rate for low-risk investments can be based on the actual WACC.

Capitalized R&D The value of R&D that can be shown on an account balance sheet. R&D expenses should be capitalized once it has been determined that the result will lead to a feasible product. All subsequent expenses are accumulated and grown annually by a capitalization rate at least equal to the WACC. This guidance is vague, and often R&D, especially software R&D, is not capitalized at all [Lev:01]. Figure 3.4 shows feasibility being established when product testing and QA commences. Prior R&D is considered Research in progress. MNC capitalized only $20M of its R&D in preparation for planning a derived product, the ManiMobile.

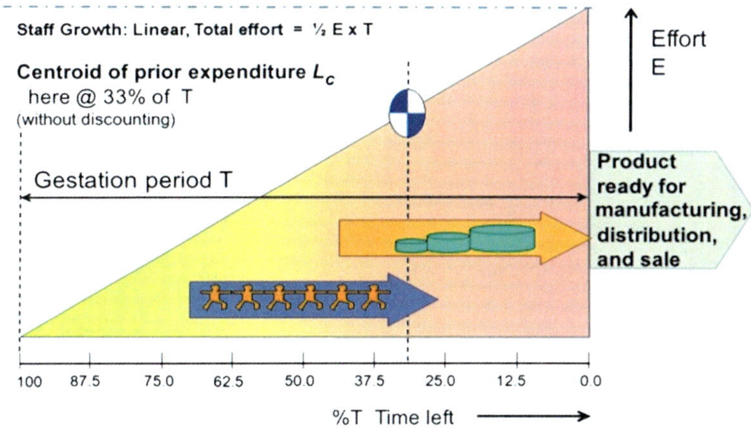

Fig. D.1 Centroid for the effective lag of a linearly growing development

Captive foreign company Controlled foreign company or holding.

Carried interest An option for declaring deferred earnings from financial holdings of a partnership to be considered as risky management fee income and taxed in the USA at the 15 % tax rate for capital gains [ToderB:07].

Cash or Cash equivalents Financial resources in a corporation that are available on short notice when needed for working capital or immediate investments.

Cash flow tax A consumption tax where the tax base is funds used for spending, namely the income after deducting all savings, investments, withdrawals, and investment income [BradfordS:77]. Purchasing consumer durables—homes, cars—is not an investment. Current US individual taxes allow many such deductions.

CCC A hypothetical computer chip manufacturer in California, fabricating the chips in Taiwan and delivering them to the MNC JB manufacturing CFC in Malaysia (Chap. 2).

CCCTB Common Consolidated Corporate Tax Base, a EU proposal for tax harmonization [BettendorfEa:09].

CEN Capital Export Neutrality, the setting of tax parameters and criteria so that investments yield the same benefits anywhere in the world [GordonH:02]. Related terms used are CIN for retained imports and CON for ownership [GrubertA:08].

Centroid A single value ◐ to represent the value Lc for an arbitrary function [FD.1]. Figure D.1 shows the centroid for a product development lag.

Certified Public Accountant (CPA) A financial professional who is licensed by the state after having attained a level of education equivalent to an MBA, passed an exam administered by a professional organization (AICPA), maintained expertise through ongoing education, and subscribed to published ethical standards [WhittingtonD:12]. There are more than 600,000 CPAs in the USA.

CFC Controlled foreign corporation or captive foreign corporation. Also Consumption of Fixed Capital, the annual consumption of tangible assets, a term not used here.

CFH Controlled foreign holding, a captive foreign holding corporation.

CFI Controlled financial intermediary, a captive financial intermediary business entity.

CFIUS Committee on Foreign Investment in the USA, an interagency committee of the US government that reviews the national security implications of foreign investments in US companies or operations.

CFR Code of Federal Regulations. The voluminous Title 26 regulations, established by the US Treasury in response to relevant laws (IRC), govern the operation of the IRS. The §-numbers match the ones in the IRC (Appendix B).

Channel Islands The bailiwicks of Jersey and Guernsey. These small islands in the English Channel, near France, are British Crown Dependencies, enabling their use as nearshore taxhavens. Guernsey includes the minor islands Sark, Alderney, and Brecqhou. They are not members of the EU and not full members of the United Nations.

Chapter C-corporation The formal designation of the common limited liability corporation, as presented in this book. They can list their shares on a stock exchange, allowing them to be traded in the open. Most US multinationals are C-corporations.

Chapter S-corporation A corporation that allocates and assigns its earnings and taxes directly to its owners and does not pay any taxes itself. Limits on size and activities are imposed.

Check-the-box subsidiary A CFC for which the option not to report detailed data has been taken on IRS form 8832 by making an entity classification election. Only the name and location of the subsidiary has to be reported. The parent entity incorporates the data for its subsidiaries in a consolidated report. The option was enabled by the Paperwork Reduction Act of 1995 [GerthMH:11]. The election has no meaning for tax authorities in other jurisdictions [Romano:02].

CHORD Example of a multinational corporation engaging in an inversion. Also **CHORD6**, the foreign-based holding division controlled by CHORD, and **CHORD64**, a US resident subsidiary of CHORD6, established to take over its parent, CHORD (Chap. 2).

Churning percentage The fraction of taxes returned to a taxpayer in the form of incentives. It was 9.0 % overall in the USA and 18.2 % for 11 OECD countries in 1995 [TanziS:00]. Certain industrial sectors, such as manufacturing, tend to be favored [IRS-ST:09].

CIP Coordinated issue paper.

CIT Corporate Income Tax. The income tax with provisions specifically applicable to C-corporations using IRS form 1120 and many attachments (Chap. 8).

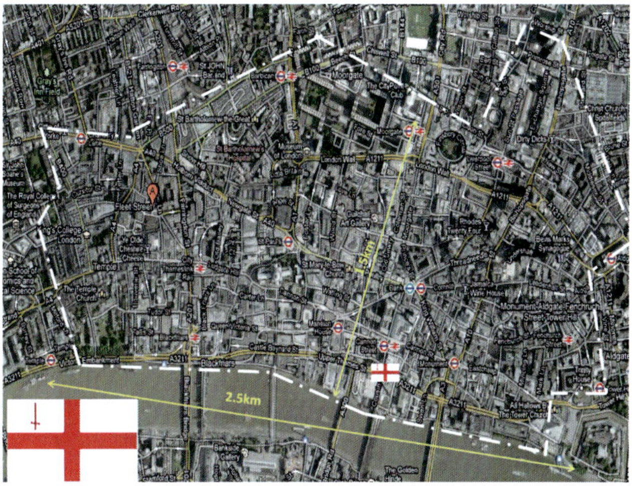

City The City of London Corporation, is an independent jurisdiction established in 1189 of 1.2 square miles (about 2.50 km along the Thames river and about 1.25 km north) within Greater London in the U.K. [Roberts:08]. The outline of "The City" and its flag is shown on page 365. In the middle ages it hosted the *kantor* of the Hanseatic League. It is the domicile of many banks, hedge funds, insurance brokers, and tax consulting firms (Chap. 8). Membership in a guild, such as WCOTA, allows businesses to participate in the City's governance. It is also the primary location for the ***Euromarket***.

Clawback A provision in a contract providing for a partial refund if expected events do not occur. Some clawback requirements for executive compensation were formalized in 2009 [Title 18 US Code, section 7243].

CMVM or CMM Comparable Margin Valuation Method, the CP-VM (Chap. 5, M5).

COCA Cost of Capital Allowance, used at times to offset inflation, as by using the CPI [Kleinbard:05].

CoGS Cost of Goods Sold, the expenses occurred in making and selling a product.

CoM Cost of Money, the interest rate for riskless investments.

Commissionaire An agent on commission who distributes a product but acts only as an intermediary and never takes formal ownership [DuhiggB:12]. No taxable transactions need to be reported at the location where the sale takes place. The sales can be advantageously booked in a low-tax jurisdiction.

Commodity profits Profits that are realizable by a company that does not have unique intellectual capital; a typical range is 2 % to 10 % [Dobuzinskis:10]. Getting to the top of that range requires some uniqueness (Chap. 1). Before taxation, these funds are referred to as routine earnings.

Comparable Uncontrolled Transaction-based method of valuation A valuation method based on comparables CUT-VM (Chap. 5, M4).

Comparables Transactions or acquisitions used as benchmarks to assess similar properties when the fair values should be determined, typically for intracompany transactions.

CONCH MNC's Controlled Offshore Nominal Capital Holding division, a CFH (Chap. 2).

Conduit taxhaven A jurisdiction that allows funds to flow among other jurisdictions without taxation and with little record-keeping. The facilities may be granted only to nonresidents who satisfy specified constraints (Chap. 6).

Conformance or Congruency principle The concept that books kept for commercial purposes must strictly match the books presented to the tax authorities [HanlonM:09]. Conformance is not required in the USA [Rossotti:05], [F7.4]. Book-tax conformity has also been called the authoritative principle. Congruency, the Massgeblichkeitsprinzip, has been a requirement in Germany since 1900.

Consolidated report A company with check-the-box subsidiary divisions will produce a consolidated annual report, and, if incorporated, a matching 10-K report for the SEC, where all activities and balances are aggregated, motivated in part by the PRA. The advantage is that everything is brought together and less paper is used. Owners of a foreign corporation that is included in a consolidated report are not required to file IRS form 5471. The disadvantages for the public of consolidated reporting are that transfers among divisions are not shown, and that the effects of transfer pricing among offshore divisions become obscure. UK regulations require a distinct report for the parent company, which can help in understanding the remaining offshore operations.

Consumption tax A tax levied on consumption, either at the time of spending as sales taxes or as a cash flow tax. A consumption tax (in contrast to an income tax) encourages investments for businesses and savings for individuals (Chap. 8).

Container A standard multimodal metal shipping box that has enabled low-cost worldwide shipping of volume goods. A standard unit (1 TEU) is 20′ long, 8′ wide, and 10′ high. Other lengths, such as 40′, are common (Chap. 6). Containers are easily transported by ship, train, or truck.

Contemporaneous valuation In the definition for the IRS, a valuation is to be delivered at the same time as the corporate income tax filing (Chaps. 5 and 7).

Contingent payments See royalty payments (Appendix C).

Control Ownership by a person or a group of more than 50 % of a corporation.

Control premium The excess of the share price over the amount a minority shareholder investor is willing to pay for a share. A plain shareholder considers only future capital gains and dividends, whereas a purchaser gaining a majority is willing to pay more per share because it enables him to exert control and better exploit the assets of the corporation.

Controlled financial intermediary (CFI) Organized to be similar to a CFH, but used primarily to facilitate transient asset transfer transactions, typically located in a conduit taxhaven. MNC's CFI is CAAS, located in Hilversum, The Netherlands (Chap. 6).

Controlled foreign corporation (CFC) or Captive foreign company A wholly or effectively owned and incorporated subsidiary division located in a different country from the owning, parent corporation [B.2.7 (h)(6)] (Chaps. 2 and 4). If US-owned it should file a form 5471. CFCs with actual operations are mostly located in semi-taxhaven jurisdictions. In this book we distinguish two special kinds of nonoperational CFCs: holding companies (CFHs) and financial intermediaries (CFIs). Information about a CFC may appear in a consolidated report as a check-the-box entity [B.1.1 §957, §958].

Controlled foreign holding corporation (CFH) an offshore division of a company, a CFC that is a shell company, used to hold assets such as capital and IP rights, but performing no actual productive business operations. A CFH will be located in some primary taxhaven. MNC's CFH is CONCH (Chaps. 2 and 6). Sometimes a CFH can be combined with a CFI.

Coordinated issue paper (CIP) An IRS publication going into depth on some contentious issue, typically preceding a change in regulations. A relevant CIP for this work was mandated in 2004 [IRS-TP:04]. The resulting report: *CSA Buy-in Adjustments*, introducing PCTs, was issued in September 2007 [IRS-CIP:07], [Stewart:11] (Chap. 8).

Copy exactly A process for managing offshore **manufac**turing initiated by Intel [McDonald:98]. Identical pilot manufacturing lines with many measuring devices are set up at the parent and the offshore site. Once the parent line produces products at satisfactory yields, the offshore line is started and run until it produces identical products at the same yield in the same way. Only then is quantity offshore production initiated (Chap. 2).

Corporation a legal entity owned by its shareholders, which garners income, distributes profits, and absorbs liability. A Chapter S-corporations is restricted. Once the number of its shareholders exceeds 500, a corporation must file annual reports to the SEC. Most multinationals are Chapter C-corporations, and they are the focus of this book. Corporations have right of personhood under US law. US states all have their own corporation laws, which differ significantly; companies can select domiciles that are beneficial to them, often Delaware or Nevada.

Cost of Goods Sold (CoGS) The cost of supplies used and manufacturing expenses attributed to a company's specific products, and the expenses of shipping to centers for retail distribution (Chap. 3). General costs are classified as SG&A expenses.

Cost of Money (CoM) The interest rate for riskless investments, as derived from Treasury bond rates. It became 3.25 % in 2010, but has typically been around 5 %. It was about 6 % when the CONCH buy-in occurred and became 4.5 % when MNC made the AJCA-motivated acquisition [IRS-PP:10]. Because businesses experience risk, their costs of money will be higher; see WACC. In tax cases the Federal rate can be invoked to provide a safe harbor.

Cost of ownership The total of the initial purchase cost of an asset plus the sum of all maintenance expenditures required to keep the asset productive.

Cost plus A reimbursement method based on net cost plus a reasonable routine profit, typically within a range of 4–12 %, depending on the uniqueness of the goods or services provided. Computations in this book use a 5 % markup here in the absence of any IP provided by the supplier [F5.18].

Cost-plus valuation method A method used to determine values of tangibles or commodities. It is used in this book to determine the profitability of MNC JB in Malaysia for contract manufacturing [B.1.2 #3(d)].

Cost sharing In transfer pricing *regulation*s, the payments by a foreign corporate division to maintain or obtain intellectual assets shared with the parent and any other division. The share is determined by the RAB. Defined for transfer pricing in [B R3 (b)], initially used for possession taxhavens.

Cost-sharing agreement (CSA) An agreement among partners to share costs of development of products and also share the benefits of selling them. Execution requires a CST or PCT.

Cost-sharing transaction (CST) In a CSA a buy-in payment is due from the participant that will gains benefits. The buy-in and ongoing costs are to be allocated according to a ratio of Reasonably Anticipated Benefits, or RAB. When one party contributes all, it becomes a Platform Contribution Transaction (PCT) [B.1.2 #7(i)].

Counterfactual A hypothetical used as a straw man [McAfee:83]. A legal fiction [Levin:12].

Country An independent, sovereign jurisdiction, formally defined as being eligible for U.N. membership. Not all primary taxhavens satisfy that definition, although they set their own laws and regulations.

CPA Certified Public Accountant, a licensed financial professional (Chap. 8).

CP Corporate Profits, a term used in some Federal Reserve Bank (FRED) publications.

CPI Consumer Price Index, a measure of inflation, for tax use [B.1.1 §1(f)(5)].

CP-VM or CPM Comparable Profits Valuation Method, an approach based on profits of comparable companies (Chap. 5, M5).

CPSVM or CPSM Comparable Profit-Split Valuation Method based on profits allocation relative to contribution among partners; see PS-M (Chap. 5, M6).

CRS Congressional Research Service, it provides analysis of laws being proposed.

CSA Cost-Sharing Agreement, an agreement to share product development costs and benefits, requiring a buy-in [B.3.4 7(a)] (Chaps. 2 and 4). An alternative is a *PCT* [IRS-TP:12].

CST Cost Sharing Transaction, an activity that shares intangible development costs (IDCs), such as ongoing R&D or an acquisition [B.3.4 (b)(1)(i)] (Chap. 5).

CUP Comparable Uncontrolled Price, a valuation where prices are compared, as when using an IFP for products or the PP-VM for acquisitions [King:10].

CUSP Comparable Uncontrolled Service Price, the IFP for services.

CUT Comparable Uncontrolled Transaction-based method of valuation.

Customs duties or tariffs Taxes on imports and exports, the primary source of US federal government income before income taxes were legalized. On importing goods that have a partial US origin, tariffs are levied on only the added value. Tax harmonization rules can allow imports to be completely free of tariffs if the added value is more than 35 %.

CwI Commensurate with Income, a principle that alternative methods in taxation should not distort the relationship of taxes paid to income to [B.2.5 (d)(2)(A)(ii)].

Decentering The process by which global firms have their actual headquarters in one *jurisdiction*, their tax *domicile* in another—often one without any employees—and their actual productive operations in yet other countries.

Deduction An adjustment in income taxation that removes an amount from taxable earnings.

Deferred Tax Taxes due, but not paid, on earnings while they are held in tax-havens because of a blocker. Deferral is formally permitted only for funds held for later investment.

Demosclerosis The inability of government to get rid of obsolete and ineffectual grants and tax expenditures in the face of lobbying by affected interests [Rauch:94].

Depreciation An annual reduction of allocation on the books of tangible assets such as buildings and machinery. On many assets, depreciation tax rules allow a faster reduction of asset on the books than the actual economic reduction in the asset value [Sullivan:11]. Accelerated depreciation is a tax expenditure. Depreciation does not apply to IP, but an annual diminution of IP value can be computed (Chap. 5, M2).

Derivative A loan, typically on an intangible tranche of an asset held by the other party, where the interest rate is replaced by a risk-sensitive increment, i.e., a very large beta.

Diatribe A dissertation or discourse directed against some person or work, a bitter and violent criticism, invective [OED:02]. Often written with a preconceived point of view, citing evidence from only one point of view. Many books about taxes are diatribes.

Dicta Statements made by a judge in a case that should not be used as a precedent.

Diluted stock price The price of a stock when one considers the effect of stock options.

Diminution The reduction in IP value due to replacement of IP by improvements and maintenance. Diminution provides a basis for a technically justified depreciation.

Discount rate The percentage each year that income is reduced to account for the loss of value of money, based on safe investments, such as US Treasury bonds, to adjust for inflation, plus the risk of loss and uncertainty (beta) (Chap. 5).

Distributor The wholesaler or seller of a product; can be a controlled foreign company, a domestic corporate division, a commissionaire, or an independent person or company. Product revenue is typically determined before any distributor markup. Distributors are responsible for taxes on their earnings.

Dividend Payment to shareholders out of the profits of a corporation. Dividend payments are often taxed at a lower dividend tax rate to compensate for double taxation [IRS-550:12].

Dividend tax rates Tax rates on dividends received from corporations by individuals and businesses. To reduce the effect of double taxation, that rate is commonly lower than the rate applied to ordinary earnings. Double taxation here refers to taxes by two distinct parties, the corporation paying the dividends and the shareholders receiving the dividends. Globally, dividend tax rates vary from

0 to 25 % after various adjustments.In 2008 the US TIPRA legislation (the Bush tax cuts) set dividend tax rates for long-term, qualified dividends paid to US individuals to 15 % and to 0 % for couples earning <$69,000 that year. Since 2003, stock dividends qualify if they are held at least 2 months. There is a further exclusion of $100 for an individual or $200 for a couple. Dividend tax rates are due to revert to the same rates as individual income taxes in 2013.Dividend payments to corporations receive a 70 % deduction so are taxed effectively at 30 %. The deduction is 100 % if the payments come from owned domestic divisions, so that no tax is due on domestic internal transfers (26 USC §243). When a foreign subsidiary (CFC) repatriates profits (possibly untaxed there) to its parent—its formal shareholder—those payments are also considered to be dividends, but taxed at the current tax rate for the receiving corporation, likely 35 %. Portions of foreign dividends attributed to US sources are not taxed [B.1.1 §245] (Chap. 8).

Division A part of a company, possibly organized as a distinct corporation, that maintains separate books, but is owned and controlled by a parent corporation. Below the level of the parent can be many levels of subsidiary divisions. Of concern in tax avoidance are offshore divisions, including operating CFCs, financial holding CFHs, and financial intermediaries, CFIs (Chap. 2). Some may be shell entities used just to transfer assets among corporate divisions in different countries. Small divisions need no longer be listed in consolidated corporate reports, but may be found in earlier 10-K reports [Simpson:05]. Business units without their own accounting exist at a lower level.

DoJ Department of Justice in the US federal government; it has a division dedicated to tax cases (Chap. 8).

Domicile The formal residence of an individual or the formal location of a business for tax purposes. For a corporation, the domicile is typically the place of incorporation. Tax authorities in various countries have different rules for allowing companies to claim a domicile versus their residency or their principal place of business. Corporations can select other jurisdictions as domiciles for their subsidiary divisions.

Double Irish A combination of two CFCs, one a CFH holding IP rights in a primary taxhaven and the other actually manufacturing products based on that IP, often located in Ireland or another semi-taxhaven (Chap. 6). When carefully implemented, the operation in the semi-taxhaven earns only routine income and is taxed on that portion, while the high-margin portion is in the primary taxhaven and not taxed. Any country with territorial taxation, not only Ireland, can host the manufacturing base; MNC uses Austria.

Double taxation Taxes paid more than once on the same income. The definition of the term varies and rarely indicates that taxes are actually paid twice on the same earnings amount. Typically the second tax paid by a person or corporation is applied to profits left after prior taxes have been deducted. Without a tax credit, earlier taxes paid are a deduction in computing subsequent taxable earnings [IRS-CT:02]. In general, a full tax credit for taxes paid to foreign governments is allowed. The term is used even when, because of incentives, no taxes were paid in the first jurisdiction.Double taxation is also used to describe taxes on an individual's dividend income or capital gains when those dividends or gains come from a company's profit after it has paid corporate taxes on its earnings (Chap. 8).

DPAD Domestic Production Activities Deduction; A tax incentive established by the AJCA for US manufacturers, significantly reducing corporate taxes; replacing FSCs.

DPR Dividend Payout Ratio: the fraction of earnings distributed as dividends versus the amount kept for investment that should lead to capital gains.

DtS Distribution to Sales, the point in time when sufficient product has been manufactured that sales can commence (Chap. 3). Different terms are used in various industry sectors. It occurs after RtP and a manufacturing delay. If the delay is long, product samples may be available earlier.

Due diligence reports Reports prepared for a corporate board of directors that support a proposed acquisition price or corporate merger. A report should assign values to all substantial tangible and intangible items being acquired, as well as detail all costs of integration, of staff, tools, and technology, changes in organization, and risks (Chaps. 4 and 5). These reports may be compiled rapidly and lack information that becomes available only after the acquisition is completed.

Dutch sandwich A triangular combination of three CFCs, a Double Irish combination and an intermediate CFI in a conduit taxhaven. The motivation is to minimize taxation in a semi-taxhaven while concealing the sources and amount of funds being shuffled (Chap. 6).

EAT Earnings After Taxes: the actual *profit*, the amount of income left after taxes are paid for paying *dividends* and future investment. Many items contributing to company growth, such as *R&D* and marketing, can be subtracted before taxable earnings are computed.

Earmark An amendment to a broader law, added by one or a few members of Congress, that provides incentive funds to a narrow sector or project.

Earnings Net income minus interest costs and other costs incurred to obtain needed capital. Excess capital held will garner interest income. Earnings after deductions represent the taxable income, because taxes are imposed on earnings (Chap. 2).

EBIT Earnings Before Interest and Taxes, equal to net income from operations, plus nonoperating income, such as income and costs from financial activities. Our simple model MNC has only income from operations, so that its EBIT equals earnings.

EBITDA Earnings Before Interest, Taxes, Depreciation, and Amortization, equal to the gross income minus operating expenses (SG&A) and nonoperating income. R&D expenses are ignored, as they are considered only relevant for future income. For *MNC* we ignore depreciation and amortization as cost elements, so that EBITDA equals EBIT.

Economic Life The period that a product remains useful to its owner. A product may no longer be produced, or may have become a commodity, but it can still be useful to the extent that its replacement and the attendant costs are not warranted. See IP life.

Effective tax rate (ETR) The tax rate paid on operating income, before reductions in earnings due to incentives and preferences, and after tax credits. The intent is to obtain the percentage of corporate taxes actually paid on earnings from local operations, methods and definitions differ [Ditmer:11]. Rates include the reduction of published statutory tax rates obtained by tax expenditures and also indirect benefits provided, such as reduced employment costs, investment costs, etc., offered by semi-taxhavens [KellerY:09]. Effective tax rates are an estimate, because the taxable basis is affected by deductions, which are selectable depending on intent. For instance, should all depreciation of assets be included, or only the effect of accelerated depreciation? Effective tax rates differ from jurisdiction to jurisdiction, but can also be aggregated in consolidated reports.

EGTRRA The Economic Growth and Tax Relief Reconciliation Act of 2001 [B.1.1 §1022(a)(1)], was due to expire in 2010, but was extended to 2012.

Elasticity The effect of the flexibility a taxpayer has to shift expenses and income into specific categories to avoid paying taxes. Differences in tax rates for various income categories, such as salaries versus dividends, and activities that provide tax credits and deductions increase elasticity.

EMU Economic and Monetary Union of the EU, or European Monetary Union, a subset of the EU countries, excluding the UK, Denmark, Sweden, and recent EU members. The currency is the euro (€). A number of countries, such as Latvia, Lithuania, Bulgaria, the Czech Republic, Hungary, Poland, and Romania, as well as French dependencies such as New Caledonia are scheduled to join. Some non-EU countries are members as well: Croatia, and most EU microstates (Chap. 9).

Encumbered IP IP that has lost part of its value as the result of a legal challenge (Chap. 3). IP, such as a trademark, is encumbered if it was used by others and not well defended [Weiler:95].

Entity classification election The election in US tax filings (by checking a box on IRS form 8832) whether to prepare distinct tax returns for controlled subsidiaries, both foreign and local. A subsidiary for which the option not to file is taken is referred to as a check-the-box corporation [B.1.1 §957, §958].

Erlang distribution A distribution curve useful for modeling product sales, shown in Fig. 3.6. [F3.3].

ETI Extraterritorial Income, earnings outside of the jurisdiction of a business's domicile.

ETR Effective Tax Rate, the rate actually paid.

EU European Union, a confederation of 27 countries joined in a political union, with open borders and few trade restrictions. Missing are Switzerland, Norway, and countries that were formerly part of Yugoslavia and the Soviet Union. European microstates have various types of limited membership: Andorra, the Channel Islands, Gibraltar, Iceland, the Isle of Man, Liechtenstein, Monaco, San Marino, and Vatican City.

Eurodollars Debt obligations traded internationally within the Euromarket [VatterW:96]. The value of Eurodollars in circulation was estimated as $2,500,000M in 1988, a dozen years after trading using Eurodollars was established [DufeyG:94]. Eurodollars are not issued by the US Federal Reserve Bank and are not backed by the US government or any other government. The backing of Eurodollars is primarily the assets held by financial subsidiaries in primary taxhavens. The existence of such virtual monetary instruments motivates a return to the gold standard [Paul:10].

Euromarket A market trading mainly in US-dollar-denominated debt obligations, Eurodollars [Clarke:99]. This currency is managed primarily out of the City of London, but not controlled by UK authorities, because it does not involve UK currency obligations [Helleiner:94], [Roberts:01]. Funds transferred in the Euromarket are largely invisible to tax authorities and policy makers [Kynaston:01] (Chap. 4).

Evasion Illegal nonpayment of taxes, subject to penalties.

European Union Code of Conduct on Business Transaction Rules accepted by the EU's Council of Economics and Finance Ministers in December 1997. It is a political document providing guidance for treatment of transactions within the EU (Chap. 6).

Excess capital Capital held beyond the amount needed for working capital and planned investments. If held for a long time, it is considered passive, and interest on it is deemed to be passive income. The allocation is based on statements by corporate management.

Exclusive rights A promise that the owner will not exploit the rights conveyed directly or issue licenses for the same IP to other parties (Chap. 4).

Exclusivity An assumption made in most economic analysis that an asset can be in only one place at a time, and hence can generate income in only one place at a time [Leamer:99]. Intangibles are nonexclusive.

Expanded income The income before deductions and exemptions are subtracted to arrive at the taxable income. For corporate taxes it is hard to decide what deductions to include and exclude.

Expatriation Moving a company legally to another country, an inversion (Chap. 2).

Expenses A general term covering the costs that can be attributed to making, distributing, and selling a product (CoGS), the general expenses for selling and general administration (SG&A) that cannot be attributed to specific products, and other spending, such as the cost of capital (Chap. 2).

Extraordinary profits Nonroutine profits or earnings due to trade secrets [Smith:1776].

Extraterritorial income (ETI) exclusion A deduction of a fraction of income due to foreign earnings from US taxation, established in 2000 and repealed by the AJCA legislation in 2004 [Misey:02]. Intangible property was excluded.

Fabless manufacturer A nominal manufacturing company, often found in the electronics industry, that focuses on the design and testing aspects of its products, plus dealing with customer contracts. It outsources the actual product manufacturing to independent service providers.

FairTax A proposal for a national sales tax. The assessment of fairness is in the eye of the beholder (Chap. 10).

FASB Financial Accounting Standards Board, a membership organization that sets and promulgates the SFAS and ASC rules in the USA that define GAAP [FASB:09]. Replaced APB in 1973, but important prior rules on deferral of repatriation remain [Cosper:12].

FATCA Foreign Accounts Tax Compliance Act, enacted 2010 as part of the HIRE Act; a law intended to reduce tax evasion by creating transparency and accountability in the offshore financial markets [Shulman:100C]. It tries to close a loophole in treating dividends.

FCTAX Federal Corporate income Tax, term used in the FRED; also referred to as CIT.

Federal Insurance Contributions Act (FICA) The legislation enabling payroll taxes.

Federal rate, or Applicable Federal Rate (AFR) Interest rates specified every month for short-term, mid-term, and long-term loans. These interest rates are then used as the basis for other computations, such as the safe harbor provision [B.1.2 2(a)(2)(iii)(B)(1)]. In January 2000, when CONCH was funded, the three rates were 5.88, 6.21, and 6.45 %. By January 2010 they had dropped to 0.43, 1.95, and 3.88 %.

FDI Foreign Direct Investment, financial transfers among entities in different countries, not offset by purchase; a component of the difference of GDP and GNP. It is sensitive to its tax treatment by source and receiver jurisdictions [FeenstraEa:10], [Leamer:99].

FDIC Federal Deposit Insurance Corporation. A US government fund that insures bank deposits, up to $100,000, but not investments in corporate shares or bonds.

FFBV The Dutch financial intermediary (CFI), Forest Finance BV, of Forest Labs (Chap. 2).

Fiat money Currency based on intangible assets, such as taxation rights and trust of the issuer. The opposite of specie, gold or silver. While still considered tangible, all modern currencies are fiat money [Paul:10].

FinCen Financial Crimes Enforcement Network of the US Treasury, established 1990.

FIPC Full IP Cost, namely Operating income/(Operating expenses + R&D cost), a metric for judging corporate performance.

Firm A business that focuses on services, primarily valued for its talented workforce.

First-to-market The advantage of having the first product in a certain market sector. Technically it can be quantified as due to the arms-length lag. Retaining that advantage depends on owning IP, having the ability to assert IP rights, and continually improving the product (Chap. 5). However, a competitor may decide to build a simpler and more attractive product, so MNC cannot relax with confidence while it is ahead of the game.

Flash title The temporary ownership of products made by a third party, where the nominal product manufacturer, here CCC, is assigned momentary title to the chips that it designed, but actually manufactured at a Taiwan chip foundry (an IFC) and delivered to the MNC JB assembly line for insertion into the MNC

Maniacs. Using a flash title defines the nexus of the sales transaction while minimizing inventory risk for CCC. The foundry interacts directly with MNC JB to assure a smooth supply chain.

Flat Tax Proposal for a simplified income tax, eliminating most deductions and applying the same tax rate to all taxpayers above a certain income level [Pozen:11].

Foreign tax credit A tax credit equal to the taxes paid in a prior jurisdiction for taxes to be paid in a second taxing jurisdiction, so that the final tax rate will not exceed the tax rate of the second jurisdiction. Initially granted to possession tax-havens [B.2.6 (a)(2)(A)(i), (a)(4)].

Forest Labs Forest Laboratories Inc. (FRX), a pharmaceutical company headquartered in New York City, with research operations (FLR) in St. Louis, MO, selling in the US, manufacturing in Ireland (FLI), collecting income in The Netherlands (FFBV), and keeping its capital and IP rights in Bermuda (FLH) [Drucker:10].

Foregone Profits Method or Foregone Income Method Alternative terms for the Income-based Valuation Method (Inc-VM), when estimating losses due to asset transfers (Chap. 5, M2).

Form 926 The IRS form for reporting a transfer of property to a foreign corporation, including CFCs. In Part III intangible property is to be listed. Other IRS forms are 1040 and 1120.

Form 5471 The IRS form for a US owners and officers of a CFC, reporting the owners of the business, its earnings, and profits. Includes its accounts and balance sheet [B.1.1 Title 2, §6038].

Formulary tax allocation Allocation of worldwide or US taxable income to regions or US states by an apportionment formula using actual regional sales or contributions (Chap. 5, M6).

FPJ Financial Privacy Jurisdiction, a corporate term for a *taxhaven*.

FRED Federal Reserve Economic Data, information provided by the St. Louis Federal Reserve Bank; complements information produced by the BEA, serving the executive branch, and the CRS, serving Congress.

Free-Trade Zone (FTZ) or Export Processing Zone A jurisdiction within a host country that has special rules for excise and income taxes. Countries typically levy no duties on material imported for manufacturing within the FTZ or on exports out of the host country. Other incentives are also common.

FSC Foreign Sales Corporation, a structure to give incentives to exports by US corporations, held to be illegal by the WTO and replaced by the DPAD.

FTC Foreign Tax Credit, the tax subtraction of foreign taxes paid from US taxes due. An FTC generator creates excess foreign tax credits offshore [Pollock:12].

FTZ Free-Trade Zone.

Fungible The concept that money can never be dedicated to a specific purpose [Clausing:05]. For instance, if a law, such as AJCA, specifies that repatriated funds should go to R&D, that assignment frees up other funds, which then can be used for shareholder dividends, executive compensation, or stock buybacks [DharmapalaFF:09].

G-7 Seven industrialized nations, the core of the OECD, see Fig. 9.7.

GAAP Generally Accepted Accounting Principles, rules as defined by the FASB in the USA and the IASB, based in the City of London, internationally.

GASB Government Accounting Standards Board, a private organization, since 1984 promoting standards for financial reporting by US government entities. Operates parallel to the FASB. Not relevant to MNC or taxation.

GCV Going Concern Value, the value of an enterprise in excess of the aggregate of identifiable IP components [SmithP:05, p. 20].

GDP Gross Domestic Product, the sum of all economic activity in a country.

Gestation period The interval from an initial investment in a technology, project, or product to the time when the result is available for production, covering the needed development and testing. A common metric is the lag, the effective delay determined by the centroid of the expenses, typically ranging from 0.55 to 0.25 of the total interval (Chap. 3).

Gibraltar A self-governing British Overseas Territory located at the southern end of Spain. It is a member of the EU via the UK, but not of the EMU. Some analysts consider it a taxhaven. The governmental Gibraltar Financial Centre facilitates operations in the offshore financial sector (Chap. 6).

GLAM Generic Legal Advice Memorandum issued by the IRS to its field agents [BlairM:06].

Globalization The process whereby companies become multinational and are able to benefit from having customers, capabilities, resources, and rules applied in many countries.

GmbH Gesellschaft mit beschränkter Haftung, a German LLC, more common there than an AG or C-corporation.

GNP Gross National Product, the GDP adjusted for foreign income and extracted earnings.

Going-concern value (GCV) An intangible that reflects the additional value of a company's tangibles and intangibles beyond their sum, due to a workforce in place that is familiar with corporate goals, resources, and ethics, having worked together in the past and presumably continuing in the future. It is recognized by investors when setting share prices, but, although significant, it is rarely valued as such on the books. Going concern value is lost in bankruptcy and may be reduced in major reorganizations (Chap. 3).

Gold standard Currency or money based on tangibles, such as specie, gold or silver, in contrast to fiat money.

Goodwill An intangible typically placed as an asset on the books when a company is acquired, to reflect unspecified items that justify the price paid beyond tangibles and identified intangibles. According to "IFRS 3" issued in 2004, it has an indefinite life and cannot be simply amortized, but parts can be written off if they are impaired. An annual check is required. Goodwill has no value as such if a company is sold, unless components such as trademarks and customer lists can be segregated and valued. The balance sheet for MNC shown in Table A.2 includes $140M of goodwill, an intangible created by accountants when MNC's acquisitions, which comprised considerable IP in their valuations over recognized R&D, were put on the books of MNC (Chap. 3).

Gordon's rule A simple formula to estimate the net present value of a perpetual income stream, using the current income, the expected growth percentage, and the discount rate [F5.11].

Grant A government payment or subsidy given to a group or an individual recipient for a specific purpose. Often untaxed, it is an alternative to a tax expenditure.

Greenfield investment Investing in starting new projects rather than growing through mergers and acquisitions. The ratio in The Netherlands is 40 % versus 60 % [deMooij:05].

Gross Domestic Product (GDP) The annual total of all recorded economic activity in a country. It is a useful basis for assessing changes in taxation over time. It is computed by aggregating consumption [BEA:06]. The actual or Nominal GDP (NGDP), if compared over a long time, is best adjusted for inflation to obtain the real GDP [JohnstonW:11]. For consistency with multiple sources, the NGDP is the basis for our estimates (Chap. 9).

Gross income The revenue due to product sales minus the Cost of Goods Sold (CoGS). The IRS term is *Gross profit* [B.3.5 (d)(2)]. The GAO uses *Gross receipts*. We assume that MNC has no other income-generating activities so that its gross income matches its operating income (Chap. 9).

Gross National Product (GNP) The GDP, adjusted for foreign income by adding capital gains and dividends from overseas investment and subtracting domestic income earned by foreign corporations and individuals. As a result of US overseas investments, the GNP tends to be about 3 % greater than the GDP, but this excess varies and can be negative, depending on the relative activity in the US and the global economy [D.8].When we analyze multinational activities, the GNP should be more relevant than the GDP. Two factors make the GNP less trustworthy than the **GDP**: the movement of Eurodollar funds, not attached to any nation country, is not well captured [Argy:06]; and the inadequate reporting and valuation of IP transfers means that export and import amounts of high-technology products depend on unreliable data.

Guild A traditional cooperative of similar businesses, organized to promote the interest of its members. The WCOTA is a guild of tax advisors that is part of the governance of the City of London.

H29 A type of holding company established in Luxembourg under a 1929 law, with minimal reporting requirements. The H29-based approach is being phased out as a result of EU pressures and replaced by *SàRL*s that are designated as *SOPARFI*s [Statec:10].

Harmful tax avoidance A polite term for extreme or aggressive tax avoidance or tax evasion [OECD:98] (Chap. 6). Harmful tax competition refers to taxhaven support practices.

Harmonization The process of making taxation rules, rates, and practices consistent among countries [Sharman:06] (Chap. 10).

HIA The Homeland Investment Act of 2004, legislation within the AJCA.

High-technology or High-tech company A modern business that derives much of its value from its intellectual capital. Many require little financial capital.

HIRE Hiring Incentives to Restore Employment legislation enacted 18 March 2010; a law to provide payroll tax breaks and incentives for businesses to hire unemployed workers [Pub.L. 111-147, 124 Stat. 71]; it included FATCA to deal with financial tax evasion.

HMRC Her Majesty's Revenue and Customs, the UK government tax authority.

HNWI High Net Worth Individual, a formal designation for multimillionaires used when discussing tax avoidance and evasion covering investors as well as professional stars. They may hold citizenship in multiple countries, but should have only one domicile.

Holding or Holding Company A subsidiary company that holds rights to assets such as shares, capital, or IP. They are typically set up in taxhavens. When fully owned by another company, as CONCH is it becomes a controlled foreign holding (CFH) company (Chap. 7).

Hollowing out The aspect of offshoring that moves also the experience and the resulting intellectual capital gained from actual manufacturing, to offshore countries (Chap. 9).

IAS International Accounting Standard or International Auditing Standard, set by the *IASB*.

IASB International Accounting Standards Board of 16 members, based in the City of London. They are responsible for the rules covering GAAP internationally. Members are selected by the trustees of a foundation based in Delaware, USA. Many members were associated with accounting and advising firms like ATA [IASB:10]. Issues IFRS standards.

IASC International Accounting Standards Committee, the foundation that oversees the IASB. Up to 2001 it issued 41 accounting standards (IAS). A focus now is international harmonization.

ICANN The Internet Corporation for Assigned Names and Numbers. It is the top-level authority for assigning Internet domain names, such as "Stanford.edu" or "Google.com."

IC-DISC Interest Charge-Domestic International Sales Corporation.

IDC Intangible Development Costs, such as ongoing R&D or acquisitions; similar to IGE.

IFC Independent Foreign Contractor, an arm's-length offshore contractor (Chap. 4).

IFP Independent Factory Price. A price established using public arm's-length transaction data (Chap. 5). A price from an IFC may not qualify depending on the source of the IP.

IFRS International Financial Reporting Standard, issued by the IASB.

IGE IP-generating expenses.

IIP-VM Identified IP Valuation method (Chap. 5, M3).

Impaired goodwill A term used to justify reducing goodwill on the books. Since 2004 goodwill is considered to have an indefinite life, so it can no longer just be amortized [Vause:09].

In-progress research and development (IPR&D) The portion of acquired research in progress that cannot be booked according to US GAAP rules, because it is an intangible property and transition to producing income cannot be assured (SFAS 2). The amount paid is often added to goodwill or considered part of a control premium (Chaps. 3 and 7). Changes in accounting rules are being considered [SlavinK:06].

Inc-VM or Income Valuation Method Income-based valuation (Chap. 5, M2).

Incentives Deductions or tax credits written into the tax law to encourage desirable actions or behaviors. The losses of tax revenue due to incentives are called tax expenditures.

Incentive stock options Options to purchase and hold stock after vesting to qualify for a capital gains tax rate when the shares are sold [B.1.2 §421, §422]. Stock options are viewed as a bonus, rather than as an augmentation of salary. The issuing corporation does not claim a deduction for the indirect pay gains received by the employee, but can put the cost on the books using an estimate, computed with the Black-Scholes formula (Chap. 5).

Income Shorthand for operating income, but not always used consistently (Appendix A).

Income method A principled valuation method based on the future income of the IP being valued [B.3.4 7(d)(ii)], [B.1.2 #7(g)(4)] (Chap. 5, M2 Inc-VM).

Income tax Tax paid on earnings, using form 1190 for US corporations and form 1040 for US individuals, substantiated by employer-provided W-2 and 1099 forms.

Independent foreign contractor (IFC) An independent service provider located offshore, or an independent company located offshore performing outsourced work. They provide an alternative to using a controlled foreign corporation (CFC).

Independent service provider (ISP) A company that provides outsourcing services, operating at arm's length (Chap. 4). An ISP may work for many customers. Flextronics is a prime example [Doebele:04]. If the ISP has its own intellectual capital, say in quality control in manufacturing, it can charge more than commodity rates to its customers.

Inflation-adjusted capital gains Capital gains reduced by a cumulative inflation adjustment as COCA because the investment was made in order to separate out the actual growth of value.

Inflation adjustments Reducing amounts for each year between the base year and the current year by the CPI. Commonly applied to economic data series, such as the GDP. To combine results from differed base year is arbitrary, they must be reduced to the NGDP.

Installment payments Payment of a determined lump sum over a set period at a specified interest rate. Used by CONCH to reimburse MNC for the value of the buy-in (Appendix C).

Intangible assets, or simply intangibles Literally, items that one cannot touch, used to denote items of value that are not tangibles or money (Chaps. 1 and 3).

Intangible Property (IP) Owned intangibles; intangible products of intellectual work; intellectual property. In a more narrow sense, ownership has to be protectable. Intangible property covers documented rights, such as licenses to derive income from the exploitation of tangibles, intangibles, and a committed workforce (Chap. 3). Identified IP is valued using the IIP-VM.

Integration of income tax Methods that combine corporate and individual income tax, using some mix of tax rates and concessions [BradfordS:77]. The objective is to avoid of double taxation. One approach is no corporate and full individual taxation [Hubbard:92] (Ch.10).

Intellectual assets Corporate assets created by employing intellectual capital, as know-how and intangible property. Rights to such assets can be transferred (Chap. 3).

Intellectual capital The know-how of the workforce and the intangible property that enable the creation of intangible assets. A concept in economics and valuation, but not shown on corporate accounting balance statements (Chap. 3).

Intellectual property Intangible property created through intellectual efforts. In practice identical to intangible property, but used where the focus is on the creative process rather than on documentable ownership, such as writing that has not been explicitly copyrighted (Chap. 3).

Interest Charge-Domestic International Sales Corporation (IC-DISC) An internal US corporate division permitted by law to hold up to $10M earnings from foreign sales (Chap. 4). Those earnings are considered a loan and incur modest interest charges. Transfers of earnings to the parent are considered dividends and taxed at the dividend rate of 15 %. The approach is mainly suitable for smaller corporations that don't have offshore taxhavens.

Internet A worldwide communication system allowing rapid and very low-cost sharing of information and IP (Chap. 6).

Interquartile mean and interquartile range Because results from economic predictions tend to vary a great deal, economists, to obtain more reliable results from multiple results, eliminate outliers. The basic method is sketched on the left-hand side of Fig. D.2. The upper 25 %, marked dark red, and the lower 25 %, marked light yellow, are taken to be nonrepresentative transactions and are ignored. The remainder defines Interquartile means and interquartile ranges, using values within the central 50 % of the result range, are applied, for instance, when comparing a proposed valuation of an intracompany transaction with a set of similar arm's-length transactions [R.1 (e)(2)(iii)].

The interquartile range (here 330–1,380), and its average value (925) becomes the interquartile mean. Proposed values in the interquartile range are deemed acceptable. If a proposed value lies outside of the interquartile range, it is replaced by the interquartile mean. As shown in this example, the interquartile range still encompasses much uncertainty, but conveys at least an order-of-magnitude estimate. The IRS recommends a more generous formula for the interquartile range [B.1.2 #1(e)(2)(iii)(C)].

Analyzing each of the 16 available comparables improves the results. Checking the facts, especially for the outliers, determines that the circumstances of seven

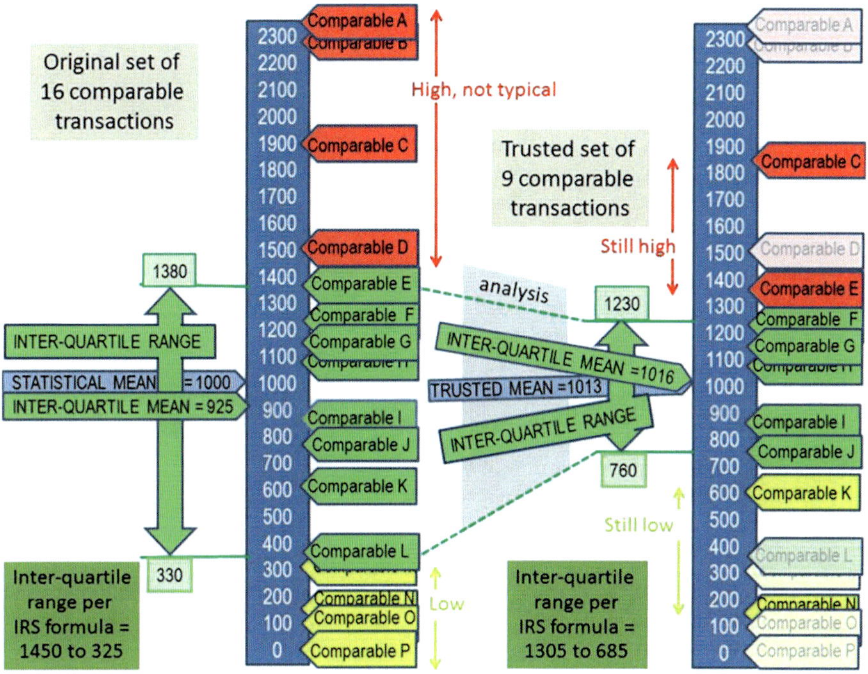

Fig. D.2 Use of Interquartile ranges to verify an arm's-length estimate

of those supposedly comparable transactions differed substantially. These seven are now colored much lighter on the right-hand side of Fig. D.2. By using only the remaining nine trustworthy comparables and recomputing the interquartile mean, we obtain a more reliable mean (1,013). If enough comparables are left, computing a new interquartile range with those nine trustworthy comparables generates a much tighter acceptable range (760–1,230) to assess whether proposed valuations can be considered to be at arm's length.

Intracompany transaction A transfer of assets among divisions within a company, so that it is not at arm's length and its fairness cannot be taken for granted (Chap. 4).

Inversion A process in which a company changes its domicile and rights to its assets to a foreign jurisdiction. The IRS also refers to that process as an expatriation (Chap. 9).

Investment An expenditure of funds expected to generate profits in the future. Can be spent on tangible or intangible assets.

IP Intangible property or Intellectual Property (Chap. 3).

IP-generating expenses (IGE) Expenses that contribute to the creation of intellectual property, such as R&D and marketing costs. Because the results are not counted as assets on the books, financially stressed companies often reduce such expenses, constraining future growth [Damodaran:02]. IGE are the base for the IDC amounts used for cost sharing.

IP life The length of time that IP, once created, remains productive for its owner. Explicit evidence is reuse of unique technology in subsequent products or product versions (Chap. 5). IP life terminates when the technology is commonly available or no longer protected.

IPR&D In-process research and development, R&D by an acquisition that is in progress, but not complete, and cannot yet be booked.

IP rights Authority to exploit IP or a tranche of IP for further development, product creation, or sale. A license to collect income from tangible property can be included in IP rights.

IR&D Internal Research and Development; expenses that cannot be booked according to US GAAP rules, because it is intangible property and transition to producing income is assured to be feasible (Chap. 3).

IRC Internal Revenue Code, the laws passed by the US Congress. Laws governing the IRS are collected as Title 26. They are substantially expanded by the matching regulations (CFR).

IRM **Internal Revenue Manual**, contains audit guidelines in Part 4, Section 61.

IRS Internal Revenue Service of the US Treasury, the US tax authority, also standing in for national taxing authorities in general, such as the BfS, HMRC, IT&C, ITD, and NLbd.

Isle of Man or Mann An island of about 500 km^2 in the Irish Sea, between Northern Ireland and Scotland. Mann is an independent British Crown Dependency and not a member of the EU, enabling its use as a taxhaven. Queen Elizabeth II holds the title Lord of Mann.

ISO Incentive Stock Option or International Organization for Standardization in Geneva.

ISP Independent Service Provider, an IFC focusing on services.

IT&C Irish Tax and Customs, or Cáin agus Custaim na hÉireann, the tax authority of Ireland.

ITD The Income Tax Department of the Government of India, India's tax authority.

International Trade (was Tax) and Investment Organization (ITIO) An initiative based in Barbados to coordinate taxhaven responses to external pressures.

IWWID A typical Worldwide Internet-oriented Distributor, used an example (Chap. 5).

JCT Joint Committee on *Taxation* of the US Congress. Issues many reports, as [JCT-18:12].

Jersey The primary Channel Island, a British Crown Dependency just off the coast of France.

JGTRRA The Jobs and Growth Tax Relief Reconciliation Act of 2003, a major tax legislation, which reduced tax rates across the board to 2008. It was extended to 2010 by TIPRA and in 2010 by the TRUIRJA to 2012. Also known as the "Bush tax cuts."

JITSIC Joint International Tax Shelter Information Center, a means for the USA, Canada, the UK, and Australia to share information on abusive tax schemes.

Jurisdiction A term denoting an area with specific laws and regulations, often a country, but also smaller governmental units such as provinces, cantons, states, municipalities, and free-trade zones. Some jurisdictions for taxation benefits can be as small as single buildings designated by a superior jurisdiction.

K-street Insider shorthand for lobbyists [Dwoskin:12]. Refers to K-street in Washington, DC.

Know-how The ability of the workforce to create products and intellectual assets beyond the documented public and private records. Corporate know-how grows over time as existing and added staff work together to recognize and solve problems.

Lag A metric to measure the effective investment delay, as shown in Fig. 3.4. The lag metric expresses the effect of the costs over the gestation period or lag period needed for product development or improvement when a single value, its centroid, is computed or estimated, as shown in Fig. 3.5. For short periods the effect of capitalization can be ignored.

Law A rule of conduct imposed by authority [OED:02]. In the USA, the authority is the Congress. The president of the USA can only veto or refuse to sign a law. Tax laws are to authored in the US House of Representatives. The execution of tax laws is determined by regulations; in the USA the Department of the Treasury has the authority to write tax regulations.

LB&I Large and International Business division of the IRS, up to 2010 called LSMB. A separate section for transfer pricing was established in 2011, with Sam Maruca as its head.

Leverage The factor by which an investment can control funds, often in the future and involving risks.

License A contract between an owner—the **licensor**—and a buyer—the **licensee**—that spells out the conditions for a transfer of rights to property, including intangible assets. Payments can be a lump sum, installments, royalties, or a combination. Many conditions can be specified, such as exclusivity, the box of IP covered, geographic region, customer industry sectors, the period of the agreement, actions when there is a failure to perform, and conditions allowing amendments and termination (Appendix G).

Life The period that an asset is useful; see also economic life, IP life. In certain situations, IRS regulations limit asset life to 20 years [B.3.5 (c)(3)(B)]. That rule does not apply to transfer pricing, although a 20-year limit would not alter reasonable valuation results greatly.

LIFFE London International Financial Futures and Options Exchange, established 1982 following the removal of foreign exchange controls in the UK, major trading base in the City of London.

Limited Liability Company (LLC) A Limited Liability Partnership (LLP) in the US tax code [B.1.2 §301.7701-3]. An LLC is an extension of an LP that conveys limited liability to its members. Members can be individuals, other LLPs, or corporations. Taxes on the income of an LLC and other partnerships are paid directly by the members. Some LLCs become akin to corporations, and may own other business entities, including CFCs.

Limited Liability Partnership (LLP) A non-publicly traded organization under state regulation, which protects the owners from most liabilities; recognized in the US tax code as a Limited Liability Company. An LLP is a relatively recent structure and combines the advantages of a limited partnership (LP), in not having to reveal detailed business data, with those of a corporation, which absolves the owning shareholders from liability for debts and any incurred legal obligations [Manesh:12].

Limited Partnership (LP) A legal business entity operating as a pass-through, whose partners share resources and contribute effort, but remain individually responsible for their actions. Tax obligations pass through to the partners. Partnerships are covered in the USA by diverse state laws, often following a model provided by the ULPA. Federal taxation is controlled by [B.L (Chapter 1(K)). The rules for LPs differ widely among offshore jurisdictions. To avoid liability, an LP can be set up as an LLP.

LLC Limited Liability Company.

LLP Limited Liability Partnership. For tax purposes we often use the more common term LLP to cover all forms of partnerships, including LLCs.

LMSB Large and Medium-Sized Business division, of the IRS, established 2000 to replace district-based management and improve its focus. Renamed in 2011 to L&IB.

Loophole Originally, a breach in a wall used to repel attackers with small-arms fire. Now used to criticize an aspect of a law or regulation that provides incentives for some worthy goal, when misused to avoid or evade either taxation or penalties. Its use depends on the speaker's point of view; often used in diatribes.

LP Limited Partnership, see also Limited Liability Partnership.

Lump sum An expression for an actual cash payment, often upfront, in exchange for some property or rights to property, typically used when a reimbursement also involves other forms of payment.

M&A Mergers and Acquisitions, the processes of combining companies.

Maintenance The effort made by the manufacturer to keep products up to date and marketable. Crucial for software and electronic products that have to adapt to changing expectations.

Make–sell rights Rights to make and sell copies of a product or product line that can be transferred broadly, allowing the exploitation of all extant IP of a company, typically restricted to a specific region. Their exact scope can differ. For IP that has to be maintained, the make–sell rights can include ongoing access to the creators of the original product (Chap. 5, M4).

Maniac and ManiMobile The products designed, manufactured, and distributed for sale by MNC. MNC was not aware that a 1951 computer built by Nicholas Metropolis at Los Alamos, NM, was also called MANIAC [Dyson:12].

Manufacturing Producing products for sale. The definition gets muddied when the actual production involves only mechanical copying of simple items such as CDs, or shipping copies over the Internet.

Manufacturing revenue Product revenue for a manufacturer.

Maquiladora Formally, a Mexican corporation established under 1989 and subsequent rules of SECOFI encouraging manufacturing by foreign owners. In general, a maquiladora is an offshore manufacturing facility established as a semi-taxhaven, allowing imports, assembly, and exports without taxation or customs duties. Suppliers to a maquiladora inherit most of the same privileges.

Margin A percentage ratio. A profit margin is commonly the fraction of corporate earnings or profits relative to revenues. A wide variety of margins are used to indicate corporate performance (Chap. 5, M5).

Marginal rate The tax rate that is applies to the last dollar due.

Market capitalization (market cap) or market value The value of a company as seen by the collective insight of its shareholders [B.3.4 7(d)(1)(iii)], [B.1.2 #7(g)(6)]. It is computed as the product of the number of shares issued and their price on a stock market. Having restricted shares and stock options complicates the market cap computation (Chap. 5, M1).

Market/book The ratio of a company's market capitalization to its assets listed on its books. In a company without intangibles, a ratio of more than one means that investors assign excess value to its shares. In companies with substantial intangibles, ratios of 2–5 are common. See Tobin's Q.

Marketing Efforts and expenditures to promote sales of products and services. For IP generation, distinctions are made between marketing to enhance the corporate brand name and trademark, promote specific products, or organize a time-specific campaign.

Markup An increment over the cost charged or paid for goods or services to provide nonroutine earnings to the vendor. A markup of 5 % is typical, reflecting routine earnings [F5.18]; the IRS has suggested that 7 % is acceptable for services [VidanoT:07].

Massgeblichkeitsprinzip The use of identical books for taxes and shareholder reporting. See congruency principle, defined in German law [EStG§5 exp. 1 P. 2]. It is being weakened somewhat by Germany's acceptance of European GAAP rules [KesslerE:10].

MC-VM or MCM Market capitalization-based method of valuation (Chap. 5, M1).

Mean A computation of an average to establish an expected value, as of royalty rates. There is the common arithmetic mean or average and the more reliable **interquartile mean**.

Merchanting The routine activities of distributing and selling products [dAroma:27, article I.5].

Merger A combination of two companies, often similar in size, but differing in assets and IP. With simple pooling of interest, no explicit valuation of either party is needed, as expected in an acquisition. To make a merger successful, much management effort will be needed. Often substantial write-downs are taken and jobs cut to eliminate redundancies. Mergers do not provide organic growth.

Misvaluation A valuation that is substantially wrong, likely because important assets were ignored. Valuations that differ from each other may not be misvaluations, but may vary just because they legitimately use alternative data and methods (Chap. 7).

MNC A model of a multinational corporation in the high-technology sector. It is used throughout this book to illustrate the importance of intellectual capital and its valuation. Over several years MNC moves into tax avoidance (Chap. 2). A spreadsheet covering its books for 25 years documents its actions [W:12].

MNC EMEA A CFC of our MNC in Graz, Austria having rights to sell products in Europe, the Middle East, and Africa, and performing some local product adaptations (Chap. 2).

MNC LSA A CFC of our MNC in Belize having rights to adapt and sell products in Central and South America, Latin language-speaking countries. It may share some adaptations with MNC EMEA for Spain and Portugal (Chap. 2).

MNC PFE A CFC of our MNC in Yokohama, Japan, having rights to sell products in the Pacific and Far East Asian region. MNC PFE adapts the MNC trademark and labels (Chap. 2).

MNC MY A CFC of our MNC in Mysore, India, set up for testing and developing software for Maniacs (Chap. 2).

MNC JB A CFC of our MNC in Johor Bahru, Malaysia manufacturing its Maniacs (Chap. 2).

MNC US Parent component of our MNC; a designation used only when the distinction of MNC's US operations from MNC as a whole is important (Chap. 2).

MNE Multi-National Enterprise, an alternate term for a multinational business such as MNC.

MobiIP A sample company, acquired by MNC for IP that may enable creation of ManiMobiles.

Model An abstraction of a real world situation, simplified to allow predictions to be computed.

Mobile assets Assets that are easily moved among jurisdictions, such as capital and intangibles, including rights to exploit tangible and intangible assets.

MRP Market Risk Premium, the additional percentage over the cost of money that accounts for the risk in holding shares versus cash or cash equivalents. The increment has been assessed globally at about 5.5 % [Fernandez:13].

Multinational corporation or multinational An international company with distinct controlled subsidiary divisions that have established domicile in more than one country and are able to transfer assets among those countries.

Mutual Agreement Procedure (MAP) A section in a tax treaty to match transfer pricing rules.

NAICS A code to identify sectors of industry, replacing the SIC code [PierceS:09].

NCP Net Cost Plus, Operating income/Operating expenses, a metric for judging corporate performance (Chap. 5, M6).

NDA Non-Disclosure Agreement, a contract promising not to reveal proprietary information obtained while working with company.

Nearshore taxhaven A taxhaven in a jurisdiction (as a state or Territory) within the same or a closely related country, as for the USA possessions such as Puerto Rico and for the UK the British Crown Dependencies.

Nearshoring Outsourcing work to a subsidiary (CFC) in a jurisdiction within a country that provides semi-taxhaven incentives not available throughout the country (Chap. 6).

Net income What is left of the operating income after research and development costs are deducted. Economists refer to that amount as EBIT. In realistic settings, depreciation and amortization should also be deducted, producing a sum defined as EBITDA. Terms involving income are not always used in this sense or consistently.

Net Present Value (NPV) The value of future income today. The NPV is computed as the sum of annual payments or income in future years, reduced each year by a discount rate that reflects a riskless financial stream and the degree of risk expected for a particular transaction [F3.4].

Net revenue What is left from gross revenue after accounting for discounts and promotional payments that do not appear as Cost of Goods Sold (CoGS). For simplicity we assume that MNC does not use such means to promote sales.

Nexus The location where sales formally take place, actual revenue is generated and where sales taxes are to be applied (Chap. 6). For tax avoidance a nexus will be located in a conduit taxhaven. The nexus is hard to define for mail order sales, Internet sales, and transactions using a flash title [GriffithS:09].

NGDP Nominal GDP, not inflation adjusted; used throughout this book.

NLbd Nederlandse belastingdienst, the Dutch tax authority (Chap. 6).

NOL Net Operating Loss, leading to negative earnings. Can be carried forward or back under certain conditions to offset earnings and reduce tax obligations in other years.

Nonexclusivity A property of intangible assets that can be used to generate income simultaneously in multiple places [Leamer:99].

Non-qualified stock options Options granted to employees as an additional benefit in addition to their salary. After a vesting period the employee can exercise the stock options, that is, convert them to actual shares by paying the strike price. The difference in value is taxable to the employee. Before vesting, the shares have an option value. The issuing corporation can take a tax deduction for the benefit the employee receives.

Nonroutine profits The earnings in excess of commodity earnings by a company having unique intellectual capital [B R5 (c)(3)(B)]; because we focus on tax avoidance, we will actually consider nonroutine earnings whenever we analyze multinational businesses (Chap. 1). Exploitation of natural resources, as in mining, can also generate nonroutine earnings, also referred as economic rent. To what extent academic analyses of rent are applicable to earnings based on intellectual capital is unclear.

Normal returns Routine earnings.

NOPA Notice of Proposed Adjustment, sent when IRS auditors determine that the amount of taxes paid does not match taxes actually due (Chap. 8).

NPV Net Present Value, the discounted sum of annual payments or income in future years.

NQSO Non-qualified stock option.

NSF National Science Foundation, the primary funder of basic and fundamental research in the USA; DARPA, part of the US Department of Defense, supports fundamental and applied research, other US government departments support research relevant to them.

NV Naamloze Venootschap, a Dutch public liability company, a public corporation.

OECD Organisation for Economic Co-operation and Development, sometimes referred to as a "club of capitalists."

Offshore financial center (OFC) A jurisdiction that combines financial services with taxhaven advantages, such as Macao, Bermuda, Liechtenstein, and Guernsey [Ramos:07]. OFCs serve mainly CFIs and are characterized by having a financial transaction activities disproportionate to their population [Zoromé:87]; at times used for a specific CFI or CFH.

Offshoring Outsourcing work to a contractor (IFC) or a subsidiary or affiliated division (CFC) in a foreign jurisdiction (Chap. 4).

OMB Office of Management and Budget, analyzes proposed laws and tax proposals in the executive branch of the US government.

OMC Open Method of Coordination, an EU initiative to limit harmful tax competition [Radaelli:03].

One-book country A jurisdiction where income reporting follows the congruency principle.

Ongoing business value The value of a business that would be lost if the business were to stop operating. An estimate of the ongoing business value is the difference between the market value and the salvage value of a business. There is no reliable accounting measure of a business's ongoing value.

Open-source software Software with no or minimal property-rights protection. It falls outside the focus of this book, although open-source software is often embedded in software over which property rights are asserted (Chap. 3) [W:11].

Operating expenses The overhead of running a business, primarily SG&A [B.3.1 (d)(3)]. Interest expenses, R&D expenses, and taxes are excluded (Table A.1).

Operating income The difference between gross income from operations and operating expenses (SG&A). The IRS term is *Operating profit* [B.3.1 (d)(3)]. The gross income of a company can be larger than operating income as a result of nonoperating income, such as income from asset sales and dividends or interest payments from long-term investments. MNC's only nonoperating income was the interest on the loan it extended to CONCH for the buy-in (Table A.2).

Option value The value of a purchase of an asset to obtain rights for an option to later commercialize or use the purchased asset. The risk that the rights will not be used affects its value (Chap. 5, M8).

Organic growth The growth that a company can expect through internal investments only. If growth is by acquisitions, it is not considered organic, although acquiring IP from external sources by spending net income is a valid alternative to obtaining IP by internal R&D. A corporate merger is unlikely to reflect organic growth.

Organisation for Economic Co-operation and Development (*OECD*) An organization founded in 1961 primarily to promote and guide global development. It is located in Paris and in 2010 had 34 members, all high-income economies. The USA is represented by an Ambassador to the OECD. The OECD is a successor to the 1948 European OEEC organization to help administer the Marshall Plan. It was concerned about taxhaven activities.

Outsourcing Contracting service and manufacturing activities to domestic and foreign firms or businesses. Domestic outsourcing excludes work given to corporate affiliate divisions [NorwoodEa:06].

Overhead costs The cost of supporting Selling, General, and Administrative (SG&A) expenses that cannot be associated directly with the cost of selling individual products (CoGS) and R&D. Accountants have flexibility in allocating selling costs [Vause:09]. The class typically includes ongoing marketing expenses, which also create IP, and are part of IGE.

Ownership A documented and enforceable right to an asset. Distinguishes intellectual property from intellectual assets and intellectual capital.

P/B ratio Share Price to *Book* ratio, see *market/book*. A measure of stock value.

p/e multiple Price to earnings multiple, a ratio used to assess stock prices (Chap. 5, M8).

P/R or P/S A metric for judging corporate performance. Ratio of Operating Profit to Revenues or Sales (Chap. 5, M5).

P&L statement Profit and Loss statement, based on the account balance sheet.

PAD Production Activities Deduction, a tax expenditure that provides a significant incentive for US manufacturers. More properly referred to as the Domestic PAD or DPAD.

Palm Island A surrogate primary taxhaven, levying no corporate income tax but benefiting from annual registration fees for the many companies legally domiciled in the island. The name does not refer to the former Prune Island in the Grenadines, renamed Palm Island in 1967 by Johnny "Coconut" Caldwell [Dey:89]. That island is too isolated to be an effective taxhaven.

Paperwork Reduction Act (PRA) A law passed in 1995 that gave the US Office of Management and Budget the authority to allow companies not to report details of their subsidiaries, but rather to consolidate the information by checking the box [PRA:95]. The preamble of the law mentions the benefits for small businesses, but the body includes all corporations [PRA:95]. By 2004 it became unnecessary to list subsidiaries that contribute <20 % or 15 % to the consolidated income on the 10-K statements required by the SEC [Deloitte:11].

Paradigm licensing The use of an intermediary organization that obtains all the IP needed to satisfy a public standard, so that potential producers have to deal with only a single entity for the full box of needed IP. The paradigm organization will distribute income to the original IP owners. Investors in the paradigm organization can contribute their IP and then pay no or small royalties. The paradigm organization may also promote that standard (Appendix C.4).

Partnership A business entity whose partners assume joint responsibilities. Partnerships are governed by state laws. A limited partnership (LP) absolves the partners from certain obligations incurred by the LP. There are many varieties, providing limited liability and tax benefits, such as carried interest, to their partners (LLPs). Partnerships are accorded a single specific status by IRS regulations, and have to file tax form 1065, but pass their tax obligations through to their owners.

Pass-throughs Business entities that pass their earnings through to their owners and are not taxed directly. Recognized forms are sole proprietorships, partnerships, LLPs, LLCs, and S-corporations [Sullivan:11]. They still submit income tax forms and can deduct interest on loans, etc., when computing their earnings.

Passive income Income from dividends, interest on excess capital held, or resales that do not require a significant effort or involvement by the recipient [L.10 (a)(3)(i)].

PBGC Pension Benefit Guarantee Corporation, a US federal corporation, insures employee retirement benefits when corporations go bankrupt.

PCT Platform Contribution Transaction, the exchange of rights to a tranche of a platform of existing intangibles provided by the controlling participant for further IP development and the payment by the recipient CFC [B.3.4 7(b)(1)(ii)]. It resolves the imbalance when a CSA is used for very unequal participants after 5 Jan 2009 (Appendix C).

Penalty Payment levied for evasion of laws or regulations [B.1.1 §6662-§7201].

Perpetuity Assumption of stable continuation, typically of discounted income or expenses, used to extrapolate current information into the future. Gordon's rule provides a convenient means of computing a net present value estimate into the future [F5.12]. Its use is also dangerous, because it is unlikely that current growth will continue forever. In general, long-term growth cannot be expected to exceed GDP growth.

Personhood Having the rights of an individual, in particular when applied to corporations [Harlan:1886]. There are exceptions, such as the right to own another corporation.

PFA Post Formation Acquisition, acquisitions that occur after a cost-sharing buy-in agreement.

Pigouvian or Pigovian taxation Taxation or subsidies to balance external social costs, as from pollution, imposed on businesses and enterprises [BovenbergdM:94].

Platform The shared intellectual capital provided by the primary participant in a Platform Contribution Transaction (PCT) [IRS-CIP:07]. Part of regulations issued in 2012 [B.3.4 7(c)].

PLI Profit Level Indicator, a metric to compare companies, as margins used in the CP-VM (Chap. 5, M5).

POOF A fictitious US Parent company that Offshores Oodles of Financial assets and subsequently declares bankruptcy, while it has substantial intangible assets in a CFH called **POOCH** that "Persists Offshore and Obscurely Conceals Holdings" (Chap. 6).

Pooling of interest Combining assets in a merger.

Possessions corporation A corporate division set up in a US possession, primarily Puerto Rico, that offered concessions similar to those of offshore semi-tax-haven*s*. When those concessions ended, many corporate divisions moved further offshore [B.2.1 (h)(5)(F)].

PPE Property, Plant, and Equipment, corporate tangibles other than cash or cash equivalents.

Purchase Price Valuation Method (PP-VM) A method use to derive the value of the IP of a company from the price paid when it was acquired (Chap. 5, M8).

PRA Paperwork Reduction Act [PRA:95].

Precautionary principle In rule making, the legitimacy to impose regulations that consider a possible but unproven risk (Chap. 10, R4).

Pretax profit A term often used to denote corporate earnings. The IRS just uses the term *profits*.

Price The amount paid for an asset, which should match its value. In this book all prices are given in US dollars ($), for major assets in millions (M).

Price-to-book ratio The ratio of the market value of a public company to its book value. For all US information technology companies it was 3.7 in 2011 [CampbellW:12]. The difference is largely due to the company's intellectual capital or ongoing business value.

Price to earnings multiple (p/e multiple) Ratio of the share price to earnings per share. It is a metric to assess whether the price for stock shares is reasonable, given a company's earnings. The typical range is from 5 (buy it!) to 50 (avoid it, unless you know something very nice that nobody else knows!). A p/e multiple of 10 is reasonable for a stable company, and 20 indicates a company that is seen as having potential for growth due to IP it holds, but that will also have a high risk [BodieKM:08]. MNC's p/e multiple at the time CONCH was being created was 12, but higher when adjusted for its margin [FD.4].

Primary taxhaven A country or jurisdiction that offers no or negligible taxation and few reporting requirements to companies registering there. For small countries, the setup and registration fees paid by many locally registered corporate divisions are a substantial part of the government's income. A primary taxhaven is not focused on growth of a broader economy. Typically, corporate divisions set up in a primary taxhaven have no employees. The OECD defined taxhavens in a mandated study; [OECD:98] (Chap. 6).

Privacy A poorly formulated right to prevent others from seeing records of one's activity. Corporate privacy can be pierced when there is evidence of fraud, but without access to records it is hard to show illegality. Information collected by government agencies, such as the IRS, are covered under USC, Title 5, Part 1, Chapter 5, Subchapter II, §552a.

Product line A sequence of models or versions of a product type, with periodic improvements to gain stable revenues over a long time (Chap. 3).

Profit The amount left and available to pay dividends or add to capital after all expenses, research costs, and taxes are subtracted from income; see accounting terms. Before taxes the company has earnings that can alternatively be used to grow the company. In corporate reports and in general business literature, the term pretax profit or just *profit* is often used for intermediate amounts as well, such as for earnings or even gross profit, where this book uses gross income [BermanKC:06]. The IRS and some other authors use the term *profits* for earnings, but for the company and its shareholders a profit is only what is left after taxes have been paid.

Pro forma An accounting statement that presents useful, but informal data, such as restatements of joint assets for years preceding a merger. We suggest that pro formas be used to report all intellectual assets of corporations, while standards for reliable reporting in corporate accounts are being developed (Chap. 10).

Profit-Split Method (PS-M) An analysis method that allocates earnings, as obtained from royalties, as part of a valuation [B.2.6(c)(2)], [B.1.2 #6] (Chap. 5, M6).

PSR Price-to-Sales Ratio, or in our terms market capitalization to revenue ratio. Stocks with a PSR <1.0 are candidates for overlooked values [FisherH:11].

Purchase Price Valuation Method A valuation of the intangibles obtained in an acquisition where the price is known or can be estimated (Chap. 5, M8 PP-VM).

QA Quality Assurance, a task in product development often carried out in a distinct division to ensure that products satisfy specifications and customer expectations, rather than just satisfying the developers [SlavinK:06]. MNC MY performs much of that function for MNC.

QBU Qualified Business Unit, an IRS term for a division of company.

Qualified intermediary (QI) A foreign financial institution that has signed an agreement with the US Treasury to share information [Harvey:12].

Qualified R&E (QRE) Research expenses that qualify for tax credit [B.2.8(d)(4)]. Credits will reduce taxes due for increasing corporate R&E spending. The credit is 20 % of expenses incurred, but only for Qualified R&E (QRE), costs exceeding an expected spending R&D base and growth over a prior period. Excluded is low-risk, routine, nonexperimental development or maintenance of products [Rashkin:07]. The 20 % credit on the qualifying costs can amount to more than half of the nominal US tax rate for corporations.

R&D Research and Development, expenses are part of IGE.

R&E Research and Experimentation, a classification of R&D efforts by the IRS eligible for tax credits, which excludes low-risk routine, nonexperimental development of products. They are mainly collected by large corporations, although pass-through entities are also eligible [SmithEa:12].

RAB Reasonably Anticipated Benefit.

Rate of return RoA, an alternative term for margin on earnings.

Reasonably anticipated benefits (RAB) The basis for allocating costs, such as the buy-in and ongoing R&D expenses in a CSA [B.2.7(h)(4)(B)] [B B1.2 #7(e)(1)] (Chap. 4, Sect. 4.2.3, Chap. 5, Sect. 5.5.3). Based on tranches of expected income or net profits in the future.

Regulations A collection of rules that define how laws are actually to be applied. Tax regulations are written by the US Treasury, with input from the public. The IRS tax regulations are about three times the volume of the law empowering the regulations, but in transfer pricing the regulations are more than 100 times as voluminous (Appendix B, Chap. 8).

Related person In legal tax terminology, a division of the same parent corporation; one can be the parent itself. Being related means that any joint transactions are not at arm's length.

Relevant territory In EMU parlance, an extraterritorial jurisdiction whose residents are exempt from taxation.

Remembrancer The lobbyist for the City of London; he sits behind the speaker in the UK House of Commons (Chap. 6).

Rent Economists' term for a portion of earnings covering nonroutine returns from active past investments, but not focusing on the exploitation of IP [deMooij:05].

Repatriation The movement of assets held in foreign accounts back to the parent corporation. The term primarily applies to capital held in a taxhaven subsidiary; the repatriation is considered to be payment of dividends out of earnings held in a CFH to the parent. Repatriation can be encouraged by applying penalties to passive funds or providing tax breaks, such as AJCA in 2004. Deferral of repatriation is enabled by APB23 blockers.

Research Activities not directly related to product creation. A finer distinction is (a) **Curiosity-driven research**, say Astronomy; (b) **Fundamental research**: motivated research, say experiments with materials; (c) **Applied research**, say, developing computing algorithms for a defined task, and (d) **Literature research**, often using the Internet. *Basic research* covers (a) and (b). Research in manufacturing companies tends to do little (b), but mainly coves (c) and (d). Expenses and funding sources differ for the three research types.

Research and Development (R&D) Activities that typically include all activities listed as research before a product is ready for manufacture. The two parts, R and D, are rarely rigidly segregated, as most corporate research has at least long-term product development objectives. For hardware development, computer simulation has become an essential tool, obviating costly early prototyping. Testing of prototypes is often included as well, even if carried out by distinct staff or outsourced. Development of product improvements is normally considered R&D as well. In this book we ignore curiosity-driven research, which is now mainly relegated to universities.

Research in progress (RiP) The product of a research and development process that has not reached a stage in which feasibility is shown. That definition is vague and depends on interpretation, so the creators, marketing personnel, management, and accountants can easily differ. A definition used in this book is the point where efforts should be capitalized. In acquisitions research in process is often booked as goodwill.

Residence The actual home address of a person following rules particular to a jurisdiction. The domicile for taxation can be elsewhere.

Residual Profit-Split Method (RPSM) The Profit-Split Method applied to shared investments or to value Platform Contributions [B.3.4 7(g)(1)(v)], [B.1.2 #7(g)(7)] or a CSA [B.2.6(c)(3)], [B.1.2 #6(3)] after routine contributions are eliminated [Chap. 5, M6].

Retained earnings Earnings kept for investments and not distributed as dividends.

Revenue Product revenue is income received by a manufacturer, commonly derived from product sales to a distributor of the products [B.3.1 (d)(1)]. The final sales revenue includes the markup covering all costs of sales borne by the distributors. Tax revenue is received by a jurisdiction.

Revenue agent The IRS official in charge of collecting taxes. For MNC it is Matthew.

Revenue neutrality Changes to tax laws and regulations that will not change the total government revenue collected. It is hard to predict, because taxpayers' behavior will change in reaction to rule changes.

Rightshoring Moving offshore activities to a suitable jurisdiction [HendelMT:08].

Ring fencing A governmental strategy that employs preferential rules and tax rates for foreigners and companies that are domiciled outside of a country versus rules and rates that it applies to its own residents. Ring fencing is used by semi- and conduit taxhavens, which rely on tax revenues from their local businesses but are willing to forgo tax revenues from companies based in other countries in return for fees and jobs (Chap. 6).

Risk The probability of loss. Because risk is typically expressed as a percentage, valuation of the assets subject to risk is essential to actually quantify the amount of risk for a business [WGM:06].

Risk-free interest rate The interest an investor can obtain without incurring risk, normally based on 30-day US Treasury bills or Treasury bonds for long-term investments during the analyzed period. Bond rates account for inflation, requiring no further adjustment.

Risk premium Also called *equity risk premium*, the increment over the risk-free interest rate experienced by investors in corporate stock shares [Fernandez:13]. Historically it is 8.1 % overall (1926–1999) [Ibbotson:04].

RO-VM Roll-Over Valuation Method, a valuation based on local experience.

RoA or ROCE Rate of Return on Capital Assets Employed, a metric for determining the profitability of a company (Chap. 5, M5). Not relevant for companies that depend on IP.

RoI Return on Investment, the ratio of the net benefit of investment when it is sold over the original cost of the investment. Can be corrected for like. Variations are RoA and **ROTC** (Return on Total Costs).

Rollover Benefits of IP transfer from earlier and possibly external investments.

Roll-Over Valuation Method (RO-VM) A valuation based on extrapolating the benefits achieved in the past from investments in R&D (Chap. 5, M7).

ROS Return on Sales, a less specific variant of the P/R margin.

ROSE A fictitious company set up to collect Royalties Offshore Still Emanating from POOCH after its parent company, POOF, declared bankruptcy [Shakespeare:1597] (Chap. 6).

Round tripping The practice of shifting assets, such as earnings, to a taxhaven that does not tax capital gains to avoid taxes, and then repatriating them as tax-free foreign investments (FDIs). Conduit intermediaries (CFI) are used to hide the origin of the FDIs [RauG:12].

Routine earnings or routine profit The earnings a company can realize from operations without use of IP [B R5 (c)(3)(A)]. In such a situation any competitor could step in, so the earnings margin must be low to keep one's market. Also referred to as commodity profit. For MNC we compute the margin of routine earnings over all earnings to be 4.7 % [FD.5] and for its competitors as 5.0 % [F5.17]. The margins vary by industry and can be as low as 3 %, but will not exceed 10 %.

Roux Rule An observation that software grows in every version by an amount equal to the size of the first working version [F5.22]. This rule gives guidance for prospective estimation of IP diminution [W:06]. It summarizes earlier expert observation on software growth.

RoW Rest of the World, a common designation for non-US or non-North American regions.

Royalty Payments for use of IP. Typically a royalty rate is a percentage of sales of products using that IP, as specified in a license contract. The description of the IP made available is referred to as the box, and the payments as the wheelbarrow [Razgaitis:03] (Appendix G).

RPSM Residual Profit-Split Method, applying the Profit-Split Valuation Method (PS-VM) to a residual, left after routine earnings have been subtracted (Chap. 5, M6).

RRA IRS Restructuring and Reform Act of 1998 [RothEa:98] (Chap. 8).

RtP Release to Production, the point in time that R&D and testing and QA are completed (Chap. 3). Different terms are used in various industry sectors.

Rule making The writing of regulations that expand on laws passed by Congress. For taxation, the US Treasury has the right of rule making. Because many tax laws only give guidance and intention, rule making has a great influence on the way the laws are applied.

S-corporation An organizational form for small businesses, available in the USA, which conveys limited liability. There are about 4.4 million S-corporations in the USA. An S-corporation submits income statements to the IRS (form 1120 S), but does not pay taxes itself. Most earnings not used for further investments are passed through to its owners to be taxed as their income, avoiding double taxation. Reasonable gains from investments made by the owners can be distributed as dividends to the owners. When this book discusses corporations in general, S-corporations are excluded, although they, like any individual, can also benefit from offshore *taxhaven*s.

SA Société Anonyme, the French designation for a publicly traded corporation.

Safe harbor A condition that, if satisfied, will avoid IRS challenges in an audit. Safe harbor provisions provide certainty for the taxpayer [ChapotonG:88]. For instance, the safe harbor interest rate for most intracompany loans is a rate between 100 and 130 % of the applicable federal rate [B.1.2 #2(a)(2)(iii)(B)(1)]. Safe harbor rates can be misused when arm's-length setting are used for comparables. Another safe harbor provision allows actual incomes to differ from estimates by up to 20 % [B.1.2 #4(f)(2)(ii)(C)].

Salvage value The value of an asset, or of an entire company when it is sold outside its ongoing operating business setting. In Table A.2 the salvage value for MNC is at most $190M, but it is uncertain whether those assets could be sold for that much (Chap. 5, M8).

Sarbanes-Oxley Act Federal legislation enacted in 2002 to improve and limit corporate accounting practices [B.1.2 Title 17 §210, §240, §249 and §274]. It is intended to ensure audit and advising separation and independence.

SàRL Société à Responsibilité Limitée, a corporate form in Luxembourg with limited and closed owner participation, redefined in 2006 to satisfy EU rules allowing access to tax treaties; a replacement for H29 corporations. Some local capital is required, about €12,000. A capital tax of 0.5 % is due annually or a one-time fee of €1,200 is to be paid [LowTax:11]. A SàRL designated as a SOPARFI focuses on offshore activities, other choices are available and registration can be done online <http://www.rcl.lu>.

SAT State Administration of Taxation of China. The law pertaining to corporations is the Enterprise Income Tax (EIT) law. As of 2009 it includes regulations on transfer pricing.

SBA and SBIR The US Small Business Administration; it administers Small Business Innovation Research (SBIR) programs to assist start-ups and small businesses selected by other government departments.

SECOFI The Mexican Secretariat of Commerce & Industrial Development, controls maquiladoras.

Securities and Exchange Commission (SEC) Oversees the financial reporting of public companies. It receives and makes available annual (10-K) and quarterly reports of all public companies [Edgar:10] (Chap. 3). The information is crucial for shareholders and potential investors [SEC:11].

Secrecy jurisdiction A taxhaven with an emphasis on the provision of privacy.

Sector A segment of industry or taxpayers, identified by a SIC or NAICS code.

Semi-taxhaven An offshore jurisdiction that offers incentives for corporations to invest and hire workers there (Chap. 6). Semi-taxhaven jurisdictions often employ ring fencing.

Service transaction A transaction in which no formal IP is transferred, but services are provided. Those services can be enabled by access to IP [Klein in Feinschreiber:01].

SFAS or FAS Statement of Financial Accounting Standards, replaced in 2009 by the ASC. The about 170 rules issued by the FASB define GAAP.

SG&A Selling, General, and Administrative overhead costs. A classification used to allocate all business costs that cannot be associated directly with the cost of selling individual products (CoGS), R&D, or financing. Accountants have flexibility in the allocation of selling costs [Vause:09]. The class typically includes ongoing marketing expenses, which also create IP, and are part of IGE.

Share A unit of ownership in a corporation. The total number of shares can be the count of shares actually issued to external shareholders, the count of issued shares plus shares committed to employees as stock options, or the total number of shares the corporation is authorized to issue, as set by its board of directors.

Acquisitions may require the number of authorized shares to be increased. Some share types are not eligible to receive dividends, but can be sold for capital gains. Other share types omit voting rights.

Shareholder An investor in a C-corporation, eligible to receive dividends proportional to the number of shares owned.

Shareholders' equity The amount shown on a corporate account balance sheet that represents the net book worth, assets over liabilities of a company. In Table A.2 the shareholders' book equity for MNC is $330M. But $140M of that is due to the asset labeled goodwill (Appendix A).

Shazam A case-specific legal advice process by the IRS to provide taxpayer-specific advice to its field agents [BlairM:06]. A GLAM provides general advice.

Shell or shell company A division of a company set up to hold assets but with no or nominal staff, operated by an accounting and advising firm often located in a jurisdiction that provides advantages not available to the owner in its actual domicile.

SIC code Standard Industry Classification, a coding system used to identify industrial sectors and products. The three leading digits define industrial sectors [B L1 (h)(5)(C)(i)(I)(e)]. An alternative is NAICS.

Small business In the USA, businesses with assets of $10M or less. Can be a sole proprietorship, a partnership, or a corporation. Unless it is a C-corporation it should have positive earnings for at least 3 of the last 5 years.

SME Small and medium-sized enterprises or businesses. For the US Small Business Administration the limit is 500 employees, but other organizations often have lower limits.

Software Technology Park (STP) or Special Economic Zone (SEZ) (India) Types of Free-Trade Zones.

Sole proprietorship A business entity having a single owner who receives all revenues and is liable for all expenses and taxes on earnings, in the USA by filing a 1040-schedule C form annually with the IRS. The owner also has to withhold payroll taxes for any employees. If the business is carried out under a "fictitious" name, it must be publicized or registered. Multiple owners can form a partnership or limited partnership.

SOPARFI SOciété de PARticipations FInancières, a closed holding corporation (SàRL) in Luxembourg oriented towards conduit transactions. Under defined conditions no taxes are due on major external sources of income such as dividends and capital gains.

SOX Sarbanes-Oxley Act. Sets laws and regulations for the SEC.

Special-purpose entity (SPE) A corporate division that maintains separate books, so that its assets will not show on a consolidated balance sheet (Chap. 5, M8) [Schwarcz:04]. There are many structural options in the USA and many more offshore: partnerships, trusts, charitable trusts in BOTs and BCDs, *Anstalts* in Liechtenstein, etc. [PalanMC:10].

Special-purpose vehicle (SPV) An alternative Special-purpose entity; the term may emphasize its size or its ability to move about and reduce risk [Basel:06].

SPF Société de Gestion de Patrimoine Familial, a closed corporation in Luxembourg, replacing the earlier H29 holding company type. A SPF does not have access to double taxation treaties. To satisfy EU constraints only money management is allowed, commercial activities are excluded, and external dividend income must be <5 %. No taxes are due other than an annual subscription tax of 0.25 % on capital. Alternatives are having a SÀRL, with an optional SOPARFI designation.

Spread The difference between the value of a stock when a stock option is purchased and the price of the stock when the option was granted.

Start-up An entrepreneur or a small company, with no or minimal income, not yet eligible for incorporation.

Statutory tax rate A tax rate published by the tax authorities. The statutory rate is reduced by deductions, exemptions, and tax credits, becoming an effective tax rate.

Stewardship expenses Expenses incurred by the parent in overseeing a CFC solely for its own benefit [B.1.1 §861-(8)(e)(4)].

Stock A term designating holdings of shares in a public corporation.

Stock options Rights granted to important employees to buy shares at a later exercise date, at a strike price. The employee is expected to stay with the company until the options are vested and the option can be exercised. Taxation differs for non-qualified stock options versus incentive stock options. A complexity is that stock options dilute the value of the stock when issued, but taxes are due only when the options are exercised.

Stop Tax Haven Abuse Act Legislation proposed in 2007, integrated in part into the 2010 International Tax Competitive Act (HR 5328) [BrownEa:12]. That bill died as well.

Strike price The price of a share on the day a stock option is granted, which will have to be paid when the stock option is exercised and exchanged for real shares.

Subchapter C-corporation Chapter C-corporation or just corporation.

Subchapter S-corporation S-corporation.

Subpart F taxation Reference to the US tax law as of 1966, which specifies that taxes must be paid on passive foreign income, kept in foreign accounts [B.2.10 (a)(3)(i)]. A more general term is anti-deferral rules. Deferral means failure to repatriate earnings by invoking APB23.

Subsidiary A company owned by another company. If more than 50 % of a company is owned by another company, it is deemed to be controlled by the owner. Some jurisdictions have rules about foreign ownership requiring, say, a >50 % of local ownership. Even then subsidiaries can be controlled in practice by the foreign owner, through arrangements with the local owners. Local owners may be passive investors. I use the term divisions to indicate subsidiaries that are both controlled and well integrated into MNC. Subsidiaries of a corporation may also be found in 10-K reports or other sources [Hoovers:10].

Subsidy A payment or grant by a government to individuals or businesses to achieve some balance or incentivize desirable behaviors; an alternative to tax expenditures. Subsidies may be ongoing until revoked.

Sunk costs Expenses (IGEs) that have already been accounted for and spent. Because IP does not wear out, when an opportunity arises to use the IP for other products in a new location, sunk costs may be disregarded in setting prices. It is better to reduce prices and increase sales in all markets.

Supernormal returns Nonroutine earnings.

Talent acquisition The purchase of a company that is motivated primarily for its creative workforce, without obtaining other significant assets.

Tangible Formally, able to be touched or identified. In accounting, all items can be listed as an identifiable asset on the books of a company under GAAP, including cash on hand and expected income and expenses, as well as real estate and equipment owned.

Tariff Duty or tax levied on imports and exports (Chap. 8)

Tax Payment to generate revenues for a jurisdiction for services provided, applied as a tax rate on an entity's taxable income.

Tax authority The department of a country's government concerned with collecting taxes, such as the IRS in the USA, the BfS in Germany, HMRC in the UK, the IT&C in Ireland, the ITD in India, NLbd in The Netherlands, and the SAT in China.

Tax avoidance Reducing taxes within legal bounds [HallR:07].

Tax breaks An informal term for concessions leading to lower taxation and adding to a jurisdiction's tax expenditures.

Tax competition The effort by countries to gain national advantage by providing ever-increasing tax breaks and similar incentives to taxpayers [JanebaS:03].

Tax credit A reduction of taxes due. For a US corporation, a tax credit is three times as valuable as a tax exemption or deduction [FD.6]. In international taxation, the foreign tax credit.

Tax evasion "A polite way of describing cheating" [HallR:07].

Tax exemption Earnings in a category that is not subject to taxes or that can be deducted, increasing profits by the tax rate.

Tax expenditures Concessions, credits, exemptions, deductions, and preferences for specific types of costs, activities, and industries [Bickley:11]. Their total was about $1,000B for the USA in 2010; an amount between $100B to $200B applies to corporations (Appendix E).

Tax haven See taxhaven.

Tax Information Exchange Agreement (TIEA) An initiative of the OECD, coordinated by the ITIO in Barbados; quite "ineffective" [PalanMC:10]. Applies mainly to criminal cases.

Tax harmonization Making taxation rules similar within a region such as the EU, to avoid tax competition [BettendorfEa:09].

Tax rate A percentage to be applied to taxable income. It can vary, depending on the level of income and many other considerations, such as double taxation.

Tax shield A measure that keeps income from being taxed, a tax deduction.

Tax sparing Credits for outbound foreign investment. Not directly offered by the USA.

Tax treaty or convention A document defining the tax treatment in two countries of individuals and businesses that are active in both jurisdictions. A principal objective is to avoid unfair double taxation. US tax treaties are based on a 43-page common model, adapted to specific circumstances [IRS-MTC:06].

Taxable income Earnings on which taxes are levied. The taxable income from a business is reduced by applicable deductions [B L1 (a)(2)(A)].

Taxation Imposition of payments by a jurisdiction. Taxes are typically a percentage, the tax rate, applied to earnings, and as such they reduce profits. Taxes may also be levied on other categories of income, on sales or purchases of goods, and annually on capital held.

Taxhaven A jurisdiction providing tax advantages to companies settling there [PalanMC:10]. Chapter 6 recognizes four flavors, which differ greatly, but cooperate. Primary taxhavens are jurisdictions that primarily support shell companies. The OECD definition is given in Chap. 6. Conduit taxhavens support financial tax avoidance transactions. Semi-taxhavens encourage local operations. Possession taxhavens are semi-taxhavens located in US territories. Nearshore taxhavens is the global term. Because *taxhaven* is a concept used throughout this work, I spell taxhaven as one word (Chap. 6).

Taxpayer Advocate Service (TAS) Independent office within the IRS to observe and analyze problems and make recommendations, TAS delivers two reports to Congress annually.

Territorial taxation Taxes levied only on income within a jurisdiction, rather than worldwide. Taxes on income from passive use of capital are typically still taxed worldwide, because capital can move rapidly among jurisdictions (Chap. 8). It encourages use of the Double Irish strategy (Chap. 8).

TIEA Tax Information Exchange Agreement, part of a tax treaty, specifically with a taxhaven.

TIGTA Treasury Inspector General for Tax Administration of the IRS.

TIPRA The Tax Increase Prevention and Reconciliation Act of 2008. It extended JGTRRA and reduced dividend and capital gains rates for some taxpayers to 2010; next came TRUIRJA.

TLA Technology licensing agreement, the box part of a CSA.

TNC Transnational corporation, I use the term multinational corporation.

TNMM The Transactional Net Margin Method for valuations, based on earnings margins, a type of CP-CM, best used for routine returns. A preferred method per OECD guidelines [King:10].

Tobin's Q A metric to locate stocks that have fewer assets on the books than are reflected in their share prices. Identifies excess intangible assets (Chap. 5, M8).

TPC Tax Policy Center of the Urban Institute and the Brookings Institution. Publishes much taxation data in spreadsheet form.

TRA'86 The Tax Reform Act of 1986, HR 3838. The last major revision of the US tax code (IRC) signed by president Reagan 22 Oct 1986. More than 15,000 changes have modified the tax code since that time [Birnbaum:06].

Trademark An icon or a name of a business or a product, which conveys value (or issues) to the observer. A well-maintained trademark is a valuable corporate intangible asset (Chap. 3).

Tranche A fractional amount or slice of rights to an asset. For a buy-in the tranche is computed on the basis of the RAB derived from the expected total earnings (Chap. 3).

Transaction A business event where assets are exchanged. To be fair, the assets should be valued at arm's length (Chap. 4). For a transaction tax, see UTT.

Transaction method A valuation based on transaction information for an acquisition, such as PP-VM (Chap. 5, M8).

Transfer The move of an asset, making it available to another party. IP can be transferred with little or no loss to the original owner or licensor.

Transfer pricing The setting of fair prices for assets transferred among divisions of a company.

Treasury bonds Debt instruments issued by the US Treasury. Their interest rates form the basis for risk-free investment estimates. They are issued for various intervals, which can be used to match discount rates. The rates of Treasury bonds should cover inflation.

TRUIRJA The complex Tax Relief, Unemployment Insurance Reauthorization and Job Creation Act of 2010, which extended the provisions of TIPRA to 2013.

Type of asset A categorization of an asset. A distinction is that assets may be tangible or intangible (Chap. 3).

UBIT Unrelated Business Income Tax, taxes on income not derived from the business purpose of a company, and not eligible for business tax incentives.

UK The United Kingdom, it comprises England, Northern Ireland, Scotland and Wales, but not the British Crown Dependencies (BCDs). Great Britain excludes Northern Ireland.

ULPA The Uniform Limited Partnership Act, a model statue for US state laws that govern business partnerships, LPs or LPPs. Since 1976 it has been frequently updated to deal with the increasing variety and capabilities of partnership arrangements, such as LLCs.

USA The United States of America. The book follows modern conventions and uses *US* as the corresponding adjective.

USC United States Code, the laws of the USA. They are organized into 50 Titles. Title 26 is the Internal Revenue Code (IRC), governing the IRS. The largest part is Chap. 1, Income taxes. Title 15 governs Commerce and Trade, with a Chap. 2 delegated to the SEC.

UTP Uncertain Tax Position, a statement on corporate books about possible tax liabilities, requiring a contingency reserve to be placed on corporate books.

UTT Universal Transaction Tax, a proposal that one tax on all financial and business interactions can replace all other taxes [Lawley:05]. Requires global agreement (Chap. 8).

VA Veterans' Administration, the part of the Department of Defense providing educational and health care services to US military veterans. A number of their benefits interact with *IRS regulations*.

Value The financial measure of the future contribution of benefits to the owner by an asset, simple for a known income [Fernandez:13]. Intangible assets are hard to value (Chap. 5).

Valuation The process of assigning a value to an asset (Chap. 5).

Valuation methods Methods for valuation. Chapter 5 presents the use of the CP-VM, CUT-VM, IIP-VM, Inc-VM, MC-VM, PS-M, RO-VM, and PP-VM for valuing intellectual capital and IP. Other methods can typically be mapped onto these eight methods (Chap. 5).

Value-added tax (VAT) A sales tax levied at the same percentage on every transfer of parts or material needed for making a product. The prior amount of tax paid is subtracted, up to the end consumer. Border tax adjustments apply on transfer out of one taxing jurisdiction to another [DiamondZ:08] (Chap. 10).

Vereinsgesetz A law governing clubs in German-speaking countries, such as Switzerland. The members of a club can be individuals or companies. Members of a club share resources and information, without being liable for each other's actions and statements (Chap. 2).

Version One of series of products in a product line. The term is used primarily in software, with major and minor version. Alternate terms are **generation**, **model**, and **release**.

WACC The Weighted Average Cost of Capital.

WCOTA The Worshipful Company of Tax Advisers, a City of London guild founded in 1995, incorporated by Royal Charter in 2009. Its motto is *Veritas Caritas Comitas* (Truth Charity Fellowship), as shown on its coat of arms [Woolf:10]. WCOTA membership allows member companies, such as ATA, to vote in City elections based on their number of employees.

Weighted average return on assets (WARA) The financial benefits from corporate assets, the result of a computation that lists and sums proportionally all identified assets and their expected financial benefits. It is useful in planning, but because corporate earnings convolute the benefits of many assets, it is difficult to trace the benefits of individual assets and their IP back to their sources. The WARA should be larger than the WACC to ensure profitability.

Weighted average risk-adjusted return on assets (WARRA) An improved WARA, the result of a computation that lists and sums all identified assets, their expected financial benefits with their risk factors, as used in discount and capitalization computations. It is useful to assess the benefits of financial tranches with defined risks, but like the WARA, hard to assess in practice because it is impossible to tease out the effect of separate assets from corporate earnings. The WARRA provides insight to balance investments and risks when compared with the weighted cost of corporate capital.

Weighted average cost of corporate capital (WACC) Obtained by multiplying each type of capital cost in a company by its proportional weight and then taking their sum [FD.7]. a basis for setting discount and capitalization rates. Businesses obtain capital from loans and investors. Loan costs are based on the riskless Cost of Money (CoM) plus a risk premium. Investors look toward sharing future profits and also consider the a risk, and typically provide money at less cost, hoping for *capital gains* [Fernandez:13]. Businesses discount cash flows at WACC to determine the Net Present Value of a project. Businesses that are stable and successful will have a WACC of <10 % [LeonardS:05]. Rates of 20–25 % have been used for offshore operations of high-technology companies [Veritas:09].

Welfare A measure in economics to capture the benefits to a country, often just the expected percentage returned from local investment. Used to assess foreign investment (FDI).

Wheelbarrow In licensing, all the specifications, such as the base for royalty computations, the royalty rates, any adjustment intervals, and lump-sum payments to pay for a box of IP.

Working capital Funds needed for day-to-day operation, such as wages and materials for products that will bring in revenue soon after they are sold. In high-technology companies, it can be a substantial component of the tangible assets on their books.

Worldwide taxation Taxes levied on the worldwide income of a company headquartered in a jurisdiction with foreign taxes paid being credited (FTC).

Workforce, workforce in place, or assembled workforce In valuations of intangibles, the value of the team of employees available for the creation of IP [SmithP:05]. It is part of the going-concern value of a company and has a higher value than simply the cost of hiring an equal number of new employees at the same experience level. It should be valued distinctly and not as part of goodwill [Arellano:08]. If a team is fully disbanded and was listed in the corporate balance sheet, its value can be written off.

Write-down or write-off Removal from the books of corporate assets that are deemed to have lost their value. Goodwill is often written off rapidly. Write-downs reduce earnings and profits when taken.

WTO World Trade Organization, an international organization trying to assure fairness in international trade, often defined as tariff-free trade. The WTO was founded in 1993; about 150 countries were members by 2010.

Yield The fraction of salable items produced in a *manufacturing* line. It is a prime metric for the quality of operations for semiconductor manufacturers.—New terms will be invented as business and finance become more complex.—

Appendix E: Tax Expenditures

Tax expenditures are incentives given through the tax code that allow taxes to be less for deserving taxpayers than for taxpayers who are not eligible for special considerations [JCT:11]. These concessions forego tax revenues and are an alternative to subsidies [SurreyMcD:85]. The term covers a variety of special rules in the tax code that reduce taxes and taxable income [HallS:99]. Alternative terms are tax credits, deductions, exemptions, incentives, tax subsidies, deferral, economic stimuli, etc., depending on the objectives of the writers. A less charitable term used is "loopholes," but the application of that term depends on the viewpoint of the observer. A congressional definition is

> *Tax expenditures are revenue losses resulting from federal tax provisions that grant special tax relief designed to encourage certain kinds of behavior by taxpayers or to aid taxpayers in special circumstances* [Bickley:11].

Some tax expenditures are motivated by fairness, as avoiding double taxation, and others to encourage desirable actions, as facilitating equal access to buildings by disabled individuals. Those incentives are often subject to change, confusing businesses as well as the tax authorities [Slemrod:99]. Some tax expenditures merely shift taxable categories or defer payments, as allowances for accelerated depreciation. Some are justified by an expectation that they will stimulate business and increase future tax revenues.

For major US corporations the statutory rate is 35 %, but as discussed in Chap. 9, the effective rate is much less because of credits and deductions allowed in situations specified in the US tax code. To help readers to understand commonly debated issues of corporate tax concessions this appendix lists some of the tax expenditures that affect multinational corporations. This book considers systemic issues of corporate taxation and does not present opinions on the social and behavioral objectives of tax expenditures, as excessive churning.

Listed tax expenditures on the books were expected to reduce US tax revenues in 2011 by $1,100B [BowlesS:10]. Nearly 100 tax expenditures are temporary and

G. Wiederhold, *Valuing Intellectual Capital: Multinationals and Taxhavens*, Management for Professionals 23, DOI 10.1007/978-1-4614-6611-6,

were due to expire, reducing their cost by $244B in 2011 and by $444B by 2016 [GAO:08]. Many temporary tax expenditures are repeatedly renewed. While some do go away, every year Congress approves new incentives using the tax laws, and the president signs them [Toder:11].

Another $16B is spent on specific "earmarks," one-time payments that do not affect the tax code [BowlesS:10]. There are also subsidies paid directly to deserving entities. Many proposals for changing taxation address these payments as well. We ignore such expenses in this book.

E.1 Cost

Since 1974 tax expenditures are listed as part of the US annual budget. There are many questions on what items should be included in that list [HallS:99]. The cost is often reported as percentages of US tax revenues; however, revenues vary with economic conditions. The variations are even greater for corporate taxes, since corporations are more severely affected by changes in economic climate. For instance, in Fig. 9.1 we only selected the good years to make a valid comparison with the model MNC, which was not affected by the 2008 recession.

Data tend to be late. The 2012 US budget projects costs for 2012 of 173 tax expenditures to be $1,083 billion (B) based on 2010 data [OMB:12A]. The 2010 totals were $1,112B, of which $124B or 13 %, were attributed to corporations [F E.1]. A Congressional study, based on 2004 data, estimates the amount to be about 23 % of US tax revenues, which would scale the total to $547B by 2011 [Hungerford:11]. A report by a presidential committee, focusing on tax expenditures for corporate and noncorporate businesses, estimated the costs to amount to $1,326B, of which $414B can be assigned to corporations [VolckerEa:10]. A deficit reduction study identified 12 corporate taxation changes amounting to $196B [F E.2].

Data supplied by the IRS uses different baselines than Congress, which is one reason that results do not match [CBO:08], [Kocieniewski:10]. Many tax expenditures apply to individuals, including pass-through receipts of small businesses, as well as to corporations. Corporate tax revenues are about 1/5th of the revenues received from individuals [F E.3]. Not surprisingly, it appears that corporations benefit relatively more from tax expenditures than individuals.

The most contentious issue is considering any specific deduction to be an acceptable business expense versus a tax expenditure. Once a deduction has been labeled as a tax expenditure, it is still unclear what the effect will be if it is repealed. Just using the current amounts is unreliable. There are many ways that corporations can restructure themselves and that accountants can book income in response to a change in taxation. Estimating the direct effect of any change to government revenues is already hard. The trustworthiness of estimates is gone when indirect effects of regulations are also to be assessed.

E.2 Alternatives

Only a few of the major tax expenditures are specific to corporations. Of the 25 major categories only 15 % of the amounts can be assigned to corporations [F E.4].

Tax expenditures fall into three major categories:

1. Credits, amounts subtracted from taxes computed by applying a tax rate to earnings, the taxable income.
2. Deductions and exemptions, amounts deducted or omitted from the computation of taxable income.
3. Zero or lowered tax rates to be applied to certain types of incomes, as dividends and capital gains, before they are added into the taxable income. They are treated as credits.

E.2.1 Credits and Lowered Tax Rates

Credits and lowered tax rates reduce the taxes that would otherwise by due. The primary credits relevant to multinational corporations are the foreign tax credit and R&E credit for increasing research expenditures. There are other credits for domestic manufacturing and specific activities, such as software development. Other credits are specific for increasing employment, but those have a minor effect on the total amounts of corporate taxes [Sullivan:10M]. For some industrial sectors the effects on corporate taxes are substantial.

An example is a tax credit available to purchasers of heavy hybrid trucks [IRS-QV:11]. This law gives tax concessions to a few profitable businesses and has cost the US government about $200M annually for several years [CBO:08]. The additional costs to the IRS of drafting the regulations, considering the interaction with other regulations like the Clean Air Act, designing forms, administering and auditing the credits—and the cost to the taxpayer to comply—are not taken into account when the incentives are legislated.

E.2.2 Deductions from Taxable Income

Estimates of actual taxes paid are commonly based on a corporation's taxable income. A plethora of deductions and exemptions is taken by taxpayers from operational income and earnings before the taxable income is computed. Common business deductions are grouped as Selling, General, and Administrative expenses (SG&A). A deduction or exemption not available to all businesses is likely a tax expenditure [ChapotonG:88]. A deduction or exemption only reduces the taxable amount, so that for corporations at most 35 % of the amount deducted will be gained.

Many deductions were abolished or reset in the 1986 tax code update, but about 400 deductions were kept [RostenkowskiEa:86]. Subsequent to 1986 thousands of minor amendments have crept into the tax code "causing it to collapse under its own weight" [Bartlett:12B].

Many new deductions were included in the AJCA of 2004. Some of those were amazingly specific, as a deduction for bow-and-arrow manufacturing, an industry threatened by imports, not cowboys. Each new deduction seems modest and reasonable, and not worth fighting about. It is their totality and their interactions that have created a veritable jungle. The concern about US job losses around 2008 has introduced several new types of deductions.

Data on deductions is available to the IRS, but making decisions about which deductions are tax expenditures is not its role. Congress and reformers have to decide which are unnecessary and candidates to be eliminated and which are fundamental to business operations and should be retained. The choices are not obvious [Sullivan:11L].

Some tax expenditures are intended to counteract double taxation, as the benefits accorded to retirement savings plans. Others were put into place to benefit the US economy. Individuals and businesses now depend on these benefits and just eliminating them is unacceptable to the beneficiaries [Slemrod:99].

E.3 Established Tax Expenditures

There are a number of well-established deductions that can be considered tax expenditures. Many apply to individuals as well as corporations. They amount to about 2/3 of all tax expenditures [Hungerford:11]. The estimate for 2011 was about $700B, but any reported value will greatly depend on a designation of deductions and credits as tax expenditures.

These established tax expenditures are based on current laws and regulations [OMB:11b]. Congress can still, and will, change or limit them. The financial effects of changing any of them are hard to foresee, since in response, corporate behavior would change rapidly, even before they take effect. Table E.1 focuses on some long-standing tax expenditures that benefit corporations. They are arranged by estimates of magnitude. The table also lists some potential tax expenditures that are not now used by the US government, but employed in other countries. Table E.1 also shows the prime motivations for the incentive, but in practice many more factors are involved [Schmidt:12]. The focus is still on corporate tax benefits.

The number of tax expenditures that apply to corporations is much greater than those that apply primarily to individuals, often addressing specific industrial sectors. Corporate tax specialists can spend the required time to deal with the documentation for tax expenditures that benefit their specific industry. Because many such segment-specific expenditures only amount to a few $100M per year they are easily ignored when budgets are reviewed [Hungerford:11].

Table E.1 Permanent tax expenditures, focusing on corporations

Established tax expenditures	Motivation
Exclusion of medical insurance premiums	Encourage provision of health insurance
Exclusion of payments into employee IRA plans	Encourage employee retirement savings
Deductibility of Interest payments†	Reduce an expense for growing business
Mortgage Interest Deduction	Purchase, rather than lease facilities
Accelerated inventory depreciation schedules†	Encourage investment in capital goods
Domestic manufacturing credit §199†	Encourage investment in US manufacturing
Application to Software	Encourage US software producers
Application to filming offshore	Encourage US movie producers
Exemption for reinvested foreign earnings and	Encourage investment in foreign markets and
Deferral of taxation of foreign earnings†	Allow holding of funds for foreign investment
Interest-charge Domestic Sales Corporations	Shelter small business foreign income
Expensing of R&D costs	Encourage investment in intangibles
Deductibility of investments	Encourage domestic and foreign growth
Carried Interest (Fees for capital management)	Income taxed as capital gains to offset risk
Deduction for domestic oil and gas production	Energy independence
Credits for providing employee health care	Reduce cost of care obligations
ADA compliance costs	Equal access for disabled people
Considerations for Veterans (minor example)†	Transfer defense obligation to business
And about another 1,000	All for specific worthy causes
Total US corporate tax reduction	Between $300 and $150 billion
No taxation of capital held	US tradition
Credits for outgoing direct foreign investment	Not directly offered by US tax laws
No taxation among domestic subsidiaries	Promote integration of complex enterprises
No sales or VAT taxes on intracompany sales	Do not interfere with business internals

Five of the entries, marked† in Table E.1, are described in more detail in this section. Only one set is specific to multinational corporations. All these tax expenditures will be affected if corporate taxation is significantly reduced or abolished.

E.3.1 Deductibility of Interest Payments

The most visible tax expenditure is the deduction of interest payments by individuals for real estate mortgages, estimated to amount to nearly $100B in 2010 [F E.5]. Up to the 2008 recession the deduction had been growing steadily as house prices have increased, more individuals acquired second homes, and downpayment requirements have been lowered [Saxton:99]. Other interest payments for personal loans are not deductible by individuals, so that homeowners take out home-equity loans when they need money.

Corporations, however, can already deduct all interest payments as business expenses [BurnhamO:05]. Interest expenses incurred as part of doing business are an important item for small businesses as well as for corporations. The deductibility of interest makes financing from banks and bonds excessively attractive [VolckerEa:10].

For MNC interest payments were about 3 %, as shown in Table A.1, reducing its taxable income by 1 %. Loans and bond amounts vary greatly among businesses. For traditional industries that have high capital needs, the effect will be much greater. As companies mature they are able to reduce their loans, reducing the importance of that tax deduction.

E.3.2 Borrowing Versus Selling Shares

Balancing sources for needed financial capital becomes a game of "cat and mouse" [Schlunk:00]. The deductibility of interest costs incurred in obtaining capital from loans or bonds also conveys an advantage to financial institutions versus shareholders who only share after-tax profits, while shareholders bear greater risks, since if a corporation fails, the lenders get paid off first. In extreme cases, losses from financial activities of large manufacturing corporations can reduce the US taxable earnings base to zero or less; then any foreign tax credits remaining have to be paid by the IRS to the corporation [Kocieniewski:11G].

If corporate taxation is substantially reduced or completely abolished, corporations will reassess the balance of corporate financing. The tax rate affects the leverage that debt financing provides [MackieMason:90]. Low interest rates, as experienced in 2011, also reduce that leverage, making debt less attractive relative to issuing stock.

E.3.3 Changing Deductibility of Interest

That deduction is so fundamental that it is not considered a tax expenditure by most experts. For instance, it would affect the trading of corporate bonds. The deduction of interest is included as an item to be scrapped in more radical proposals for changing taxation [BurnhamO:05]. Scrapping the interest deduction would be a major change. A less ambitious proposal is to reduce the deduction to 90 % of the interest paid on loans over $5M; that change would reduce that specific tax expenditure already by $7 billion annually [VolckerEa:10].

E.3.4 Accelerated Depreciation of Inventory

Companies must invest in facilities and equipment. Several tax expenditures provide incentives as "accelerated depreciation" and even "instant expensing" of productive investments. Early deduction of investments for equipment with long-term benefits reduces loan costs and interest payments. However, deductions in future years are reduced, so that future taxes will be larger.

Accelerated depreciation is important for companies that make tangible products, as MNC's Maniacs. Some companies also hold substantial inventory between the point of manufacture and the final sale. Holding that inventory consumes working capital. Inventory levels depend on how effectively products are distributed. Companies differ greatly in those respects, so that estimates of the effect of changing these rules on tax revenues are unreliable [BowlesS:10].

For modern companies that focus on short supply chains the importance of inventory accounting methods has diminished [Waters:10]. The embedded software component of a Maniac is only integrated into the product at the final step of MNC's distribution process, and never a part of MNC's inventory. Those intangibles do become a part of the product value in the inventories of the selling companies, but then the use rights are restricted and the IP is not valued distinctly.

E.3.5 Domestic Manufacturing Credit

In 2004 legislation, "Section 199," was enacted which reduces the tax rate applied to domestic manufacturing activities by all eligible businesses to 32 % [B.1.2 §199]. The rules are complex to assure that all businesses having manufacturing activities can benefit, including pass-through entities.

The §199 credit replaces earlier US incentives specific for foreign sales, which were held to be illegal under the fair trading rules of the World Trade Organization (WTO). Reducing certain corporate taxes equally is not considered unfair. It includes many specific provisions; subsections give further preferences to software writers and film producers. The estimated gain in tax revenues, if the current form of the §199 credit were repealed, increases over the years 2012–2016 from \$5.3B to \$16.7B [ElmendorfEa:11].

E.3.6 Exemption for Funds Stated to Be for Foreign Reinvestment

The USA does not provide tax credits to US corporations for investing offshore as available in some countries, as Japan [Miyatake:09]. Instead, US laws exempts foreign earnings of US corporations held for foreign reinvestment. Specifically, earnings and accumulated capital identified by corporate management as intended for future offshore investments, is not taxed. Since such a "blocker" statement only states the current intent, management can change its mind, as it did when the AJCA tax holiday arrived, as shown in Fig. 9.2. Interest-Charge Domestic Sales Corporations (IC-DISC) provide similar concessions for small businesses [DesaiH:00].

This exemption covers excess capital held in taxhavens, available for repatriation when there is a tax holiday, as was provided by the AJCA legislation in 2004. The effect of the accumulation was shown in Fig. 9.8. The estimate of the revenue lost due to those two provisions is over \$17B annually [F E.6].

E.3.7 Example of a Minor Tax Expenditure

To illustrate the trade-offs that occur when Congress chooses tax incentives instead of a direct subsidy for a worthwhile goal, we show a minor tax expenditures passed while this book was being written.

A business tax incentive to encourage businesses to hire veterans was passed and signed into law 10 November 2011 [B1.1 112-569(261)(E)]. Helping returning veterans addresses a crucial societal problem that everyone agrees must be solved [PearS:11]. The expectations is that 10 % of US veterans and up to 0.7 % of US businesses will participate [F E.7].

See Example E.1

We see that the implementation of even a small tax expenditure presents some pragmatic issues. An alternate approach to provide the intended benefit to veterans would be to let them, or their employers, file claims with the VA for the amount due. Then all businesses, profitable or not, actually employing veterans could benefit. By interacting directly with the proper agency, fraud would be more difficult. However, an approach that provides a subsidy will increase government spending explicitly and was not politically acceptable.

Example E.1 Estimated Benefits and Costs of a Minor Tax Expenditure

The "VOW to Hire Heroes Act of 2011" provides tax credits to employers who hire unemployed and disabled US veterans. Records of veterans are maintained by the US Veteran's Administration (VA). However, the 60 % of US businesses that do not pay taxes now will not benefit from provisions that reduce their taxes, although their owners might. Several costs are incurred:

C1. The IRS must write regulations for the law. The interaction with all other corporate tax regulations must be checked and codified. For instance, provisions of the law that interact with current tax incentives in US possession taxhavens have to be codified [B1.1 112-569(261)(E)(f)]. Congressional staff and lobbyists will become involved.
C2. Tax forms for business will become yet another increment more complex.
C3. Tax forms for businesses will have to be redesigned.
C4. Companies must update their taxation software.
C5. All businesses will now have to check an entry on their new income tax forms.
C6. To assure that privacy of tax data is maintained joint procedures have to be set up and responsible VA personnel must be trained and validated
C7. IRS audits will require verification of eligibility with the VA.

An estimate of the administrative cost of this law imposed on businesses and the IRS is well over 15 % of the possible tax credits received by profitable businesses hiring veterans [F E.8].

E.4 Temporary Tax Expenditures

Table E.2 lists tax expenditures that are intended to be temporary, with estimates for 2011 [F E.9]. While temporary, many have been frequently extended. Their renegotiation provides motivations for corporations to lobby, interact with, and support legislators [Sullivan:11].

Table E.2 Major temporary tax expenditures for corporations

Tax expenditure	Motivation	Amount $M
Shelter Active Financing Income (Subpart F)	Protect offshore investment capital	32,200
Reduced Tax Rates on Capital Gains	Reduce taxation for investors	11,300
Credit for Research & Experimentation (R&E)	Encourage investment in R&D	8,300
Reduced Tax Rates on Dividends	Reduce double taxation	5,000
Extraterritorial CFC Transactions untaxed	Flexibility for multinationals	4,200
Section §179 expensing, versus depreciation	Encourage investment	3,200
Depreciation of leasehold and restaurant equip.	Encourage investment	1,300
Empowerment and Community Renewal Zone	Help disadvantaged regions	1,000
Generalized System of Preferences	Help developing countries	900
Dividends of Mutual Funds	Encourage savings	500
Tax Incentives for Diesel Fuel Production	Energy independence	400
Depreciation on Indian Reservations	Help disadvantaged regions	400
New Markets Tax Credit §45D(e)(2)	Help disadvantaged regions	400
Brownfield Expensing §198	Remediation of blighted property	300
Expensing of Refinery Property	Encourage domestic refining	280
Contributions of Computers to Schools	Aid education	200
Credit for Maintaining Railroad Tracks	Maintain transport infrastructure	200
Deduction for Production in Puerto Rico	Help disadvantaged regions	200
Dispositions of Electric Transmission Property	Restructuring of energy services	200
Hybrid Heavy Truck Credit	Help industry with environment	200
Andean Trade Preference Initiative	Help disadvantaged regions	200
Alternative-Fuel Vehicle Refueling Property	Create infrastructure for clean air	100
Credit for Business Solar Energy Property	Help industry with environment	100
Contributions of Food Inventory	Help agriculture and the poor	100
Depreciation Period for Motor Trucks	Maintain transport infrastructure	100
Expensing of Film and TV Productions	Help innovative industry	100
Rum Excise Tax Revenue to Puerto Rico et al.	Help disadvantaged regions	100
Tax Incentives for Investment in DC	Help disadvantaged regions	100
Other temporary tax provisions that benefit corporations		262
Federal Unemployment Tax (FUTA) Surtax	Offset high unemployment payouts	(1,500)
Total 2011 effect of extending temporary tax provisions		$69,042M

The motivations for providing the temporary tax expenditures listed in Table E.2 is that they need not be as persistent as the ones shown in Table E.1, although most cover many years. Governmental analyses and serious tax proposals list effects over many future years, as their effects change [CBO:08]. Dividends and capital gains were covered in Chap. 8, Sect. 8.6. Only one example, the credit for research and experimentation, is covered in this section. All amounts are estimates of annual costs, in $B. Since they are temporary and have many conditions, they are often, and better reported over 10-year intervals. But that type of reporting lessens the impact.

E.4.1 Credits for Research and Experimentation (R&E)

A substantial tax expenditure is support for research by US businesses. The R&E credit reduces taxes by a fraction of amounts spent on research, including experimentation prior to development [B.1.1 §41]. It allowed US businesses to reduce their taxes in 2004 by $9.3B [Rashkin:07]. The intention of the R&E credits is to help grow innovative research, create IP, and in time generate manufacturing jobs. Quite complex regulations are in place to prevent that maintenance costs booked as R&D are qualified to be eligible for R&E credit [Chaback:08]. Most R&E credits go to C-corporations [SmithEa:12]. For taxation it does not matter if the funding for the research comes from domestic operating income in the USA or from repatriated earnings of offshore operations. CONCH shares R&D costs incurred at MNC in California. Those cost-sharing payments assure that rights to the IP that has been shifted offshore will stay offshore.

The R&E credits indeed support US research activities [Sougiannis:94]. However, the rights to exploit the results of that research are partially held offshore [Kocieniewski:11V]. Those rights will keep earnings in MNC's taxhaven operation, CONCH, free of taxes. To provide businesses with the certainty they need to plan long-term investments in research and innovation, the White House had proposed making the R&E tax credit permanent, providing a tax cut of $74.5 billion over 10 years to businesses that invest in the USA [Greeley:12]. The 2012 FBTCCA legislation extended it for 2 years.

E.5 Summary

Tax expenditures have a major impact on tax revenues. They appear in various guises when changes in taxation are discussed. In terms of US tax revenues, corporate tax incentives are less important than those provided to individuals. For the corporations they are quite important. Many are intended to assure that the USA remains competitive with foreign countries [Atkinson:12]. Since multinational corporations are very agile in avoiding taxes, the potential effect of limiting corporate tax avoidance using tax incentives can be large, but will also be very difficult to implement. Domestic corporations remain at a disadvantage.

A new tax expenditure is seen by many observers as a benefit, while spending an equivalent amount for the same objective is seen as wasteful spending [BurmanGT:08]. Reducing someone's taxes is always applauded, even if the obligations of all taxpayers increase by some immeasurable amount. The trade-off is not simple [Toder:00]. Tax expenditures keep growing.

Short-range effects of cancelling tax expenditures can be quantified in terms of data from the current year. The actual effect of any substantial change reaches far into the future, and any estimation depends on many assumptions. Often rapid economic growth is forecast in response to tax reductions [LafferM:10]. Deeper analyses of long-term effects showed about a 30 % offsetting increase in tax revenue due to economic growth triggered by a corporate tax reduction [MankiwW:05]. Reducing taxes on labor cost has only half that effect in their model. A problem is that such analyses depend on the traditional view that economic output requires substantial investments in financial capital and ignores the effect of intellectual capital. It appears that if financial capital is less relevant, the offset of tax reductions will be less. Due to the recognized absence of data on intangibles those factors are not included.

During the 2012 election cycle dozens of proposals have been floated that affect tax expenditures. Every proposal wants to eliminate loopholes and promises great benefits, but the details made available are sparse [Sullivan:11]. Being specific is bound to upset directly affected communities and voters.

Appendix F: Formulas

This appendix presents all the formulas used throughout the book with their justification. For lengthy calculations the formulas shown here only illustrate the principles. The base data are documented and computed in a single multi-worksheet spreadsheet file used throughout this book. Having a consistent source enables the presentation of consistent results. Base data include a 25-year model of MNC, with annual data on its business activities. The primary data were chosen to match as well as possible reasonable business situations. MNC follows the "conformity principle"; its shareholder and tax data match. Data that complement the model come from trustworthy external sources, cited with the formulas that use them.

The spreadsheet is accessible on the Internet [W:12]. The first worksheet of that file lists all the formulas used in this appendix, with pointers to the worksheets used to compute them, and important values that were extracted from the worksheet.

Financial results shown in this appendix are typically rounded to millions ($M) with one decimal place. In the book itself they are mainly presented as whole $M. In chapters where national revenues and economics are introduced, US style billions ($B) are used as well. Percentages are similarly rounded. Because of rounding, totals can differ in the last digit position. I try to avoid showing more digits than can be trusted.

Any variable names, in italics, are local to the specific formula entry. Where business or technical terms are used, we follow the definitions given in Appendix D, the Glossary.

F.0 Preface Formula

F0.1 It was reported that in 2008 US-based multinational companies employed 21.1 million workers, 8 % less than 10 years earlier [Ensinger:11]. The total number of employed people in the USA in 2009 was 150.4 million, making multinational employment 14 % of the US total [JohnstonW:11], [SSN:11].

G. Wiederhold, *Valuing Intellectual Capital: Multinationals and Taxhavens*, Management for Professionals 23, DOI 10.1007/978-1-4614-6611-6,

The 21.1 million is of the same magnitude as the US employment in goods-producing industries in 2008, 21.3 million [BLS:11]. The non-farm goods-producing sector shrunk since 2008, and was down to 17.8 million in 2010.The GAO estimated that 80 % of large US companies operate internationally. Note that many multinational corporations, as financial institutions, do provide services, accounting for a substantial part of USA, as well as for offshore, employment. For high-technology companies the distinction of having manufacturing versus financial operations is not rigid, so that entries in statistical summaries rarely match precisely.

F.1 Chapter 1, International Corporations and Taxes Formulas

F1.1 We used summarized data compiled covering nearly 13,000 profitable firms in most industry sectors, with information about spending for intangibles [HandL:03]. Companies were segregated into seven categories (0–6), based on their relative intangible spending. Since categories 0–2 show overall net losses, we ignore categories 0 and 1 and combine categories 2 and 3 as being representative of businesses with little IP, a total of 12,989 companies. Both R&D and advertising spending in these categories is negligible, indicating that these companies represent commodity manufacturing. Their ratio of earnings before taxes to gross income is 2 %.

Taking category 3 with its 6,364 entries by itself, also with negligible R&D and advertising spending, shows a ratio of earnings before taxes to gross income of 10 %.

We then look at companies which invest in R&D and advertising. The 2,865 companies in categories 5 and 6 spend 7 % of their net income on R&D and 5 % of their net income on advertising. The ratio of earnings before taxes to gross income in categories 5 and 6 is 25 %. Category 6 by itself, comprising only 556 companies, with R&D spending of 8 % and advertising spending of 6 % of their net income also shows a 25 % margin of earnings over income. The data also support Fig. 6.4 and calculations in Chap. 9.

F1.2 Annual reports of specific high-tech companies can show earnings to net income ratios as high as 80 %. For instance, eBay showed in its 10-K reports an average of 76.6 % between 2006 and 2008 [Edgar:10].

F1.3 In the 10th year of its existence, MNC had revenues of $565.5M. Of that amount over 50 % was due to foreign earnings. But MNC had transferred over 68 % of the IP, primarily generated in the USA, to its taxhaven division CONCH, so that it has to pay only $64.2M in taxes. The details are available in an online file [W:12, MNCdata]. Due to various credits for domestic manufacturing and research efforts, MNC's domestic tax rate was 21.8 %, less than the rate of 23.8 % for manufacturers, but more than the 18.8 % rate for computer product manufacturers reported by the IRS [IRS-ST:09].

F1.4 Paying 2.3 % on earnings leaves 97.7 %. Paying 35 % on earnings leaves 65 %. Profits reduce by (97.7 − 65)/97.7 = 33.5 %.

F.2 Chapter 2, Growth of a Multinational Company Formulas

F2.1 We assume that Maniacs are sold for $1,000 to a customer. The seller has a 40 % margin (Table A.1) so that MNC's independent offshore distributors were getting only $1,000/1.4=$715 per Maniac delivered to the sellers. MNC gave the distributors 20 % for their activities leaving $572, and also paid 4 % for having them approved and relabeling them to satisfy demands of the EU and other countries where Maniacs were sold, another $22 per Maniac. The price that MNC in the USA received for each Maniac shipped to Austria was then $550, or 55 % of the assumed selling price.

F2.2 Double taxation of corporate divisional earnings transferred from an offshore subsidiary can occur in two ways: (other conditions are detailed in Chap. 8, Sect. 8.6.1).

a. The taxes paid to the foreign country are credited against US taxes due. This is the common case when there is a tax treaty among countries; the USA has tax treaties with most countries where MNC might consider setting up operations. Then the total taxation is based on the US statutory tax rate of 35 % [IRS-CT:02].
b. The taxes paid earlier to the foreign country are considered to be expenses, and only deducted to reduce earnings for US taxation. Then the result becomes [LeveyW:07]

$$total\_tax\_rate = local\_rate + (1\text{-}local\_rate) \times US\_rate.$$

Belize has a 25 % rate for corporate taxes, reducing MNC's taxable earnings there to 75 % of actual earnings. For MNC's taxable earnings in Belize the combined rate becomes 25 % + 75 % × 35 % = 51.25 %.See Chaps. 8 and 10 and the Glossary for double taxation of corporate shareholders.

F2.3 Assuming that EMEA sales of Maniacs are 24 % of total, or $131.5M, revenue by the distributor in Austria amounted to $93.9M. Of that revenue $72.1M is remitted to MNC, leaving $21.8M. Just like MNC, it has a 25 % CoGS, 11 % SG&A, and a 9 % cost-of-capital overhead, leaving it with taxable earnings of 9.6 % of the Maniac sales price. Austria collects its 25 % taxes on that income, amounting to 2.4 % of the Maniac sales price. The Austrian government collected the Euro equivalent of $3.2M annually.

F2.4 MNC invested $6M to start CONCH and also loaned CONCH $50M to enable it to purchase a tranche of MNC's IP rights. The details of the ATA valuation appear in Chap. 7 [F7.8]. ATA used a method limited to selected IP which ATA identified at MNC. ATA excluded the value of having an ongoing operation and an experienced workforce. Those intellectual resources create steady improvements in the Maniac product line. The result for all of MNC, $119M, was then multiplied by the Reasonably Anticipated Benefits (RAB) tranche, which was based on relative sales outside of North America, 42 %, so that CONCH had to pay 42 % × $119M = $50M for the rights to 42 % of MNC's income. For more detail check out [F5.5] and [F7.20].

F2.5 MNC's income the year of the buy-in was $250M. CONCH received 42 %, $105M, that year and had to pay various operational costs from that income, including the purchase of Maniacs shipped from Malaysia. Those amounted to $25M. Sharing the costs of the research at MNC and the taxes on the transfer required an additional $37M leaving $68M [F2.6]. That amount equates to an unusually attractive p/e multiple of 1.2 [F5.43]. Some of those earnings are returned to MNC to pay back the loan that MNC's management arranged to pay for the buy-in [F4.8].

The profit ratio outside North America is a bit higher, and CONCH has an earnings share of $(68/154M) or 44 %, higher than the sales share used by ATA in [F2.4].

F2.6 The 5-year loan of $50M was taken out by MNC US. The annual cost of all debts at MNC at the time of the buy-in was only $9.5M [FA.1]. Those amount to just 2.1 % of its book value. That small ratio qualifies MNC to borrow money at a low interest rate; based on its good standing MNC had to pay only an 8 % interest rate, and payments were due quarterly, amounting to $12.23M annually.

F2.7 Even though the cost-sharing payments pay for research at the parent, which are just booked as nontaxable expenses, the cost-share payments to the USA from foreign earnings are taxable income to the parent [Dye:08]. To pay for the $26M share needed the first year, an additional 35 % for taxes must be transferred, making it a total of $36M, leaving $105M – $36M = $69M of MNC's income. Such expenses could be deducted by CONCH, but since CONCH is situated in a taxhaven, there is no benefit there. CONCH can charge those expenses to its contributors, MNC EME, MNC PSA, and MNC LSA, allowing those MNC divisions to reduce their taxes.

F2.8 Being a high-tech operation, MNC aims to spend 20 % of its net income on R&D; see Table A.1. Later, when its sales and, hence its income, rise rapidly, that high ratio cannot be sustained. Our model limits hiring of R&D staff and the resulting expenses to 12 % growth per year, so that in some years the R&D to net income ratio is as low as 10 %.

F2.9 As the fraction of foreign sales increased from 42 to 58 %, the actual share of income going to CONCH keeps increasing. For year 26 the ratio is 55.9 %/42 % = 1.33. The fraction is 45 % when in 2004 the AJCA legislation makes it cheap for MNC to acquire more US companies.

F2.10 The main motivation of MNC to acquire the companies was to obtain experienced personnel and IP to help MNC grow. MNC had 538 employees at the time. ATA performed an independent analysis. In valuing the components of the $300M initial acquisitions for tax purposes, ATA identified $30M as tangibles shown on the books: buildings, machinery, and cash on hand minus liabilities. ATA also determined that $28M was a control premium, an excess paid on top of the market value of acquired public companies. The research that was in progress, valued at $25M, could not be placed as IP on the books and was written off. ATA counted 150 employees in the USA. Based on public records the estimated cost to hire and train an equal number of employees is $100,000 each; their value is $15M [DelMonte:10].

Of the $202M remaining, ATA determined that $50M was identified as beneficial transferable IP for MNC, so that the accountants assigned $152M to goodwill kept at MNC.

The share to be paid by CONCH was based on the RAB of 42 % of sales at the time of those acquisitions requiring a payment of $21.5M and reimbursement of taxes at 35 % or $7.5M, so that CONCH had to pay a total *IP_cost* of <$29M for its share of the benefits of those initial acquisitions.

$$IP\_cost = \$(300 - 30 - 28 - 25 - 15 - 152)M \times 42\ \% \times \left(1 + 35\ \%\right) = \$28.4M.$$

F2.11 The value of MNC, as viewed by its shareholders at the time of the first round of acquisitions, was $1,850M based on 18.5 million shares outstanding at $100 each. To obtain capital for its initial acquisition MNC sold 1.5 million shares at that price, adding $150M to its cash balance. It also took out a loan of $70M at 8 % interest. Those funds, together with cash on hand, were used to pay for the initial round of acquisitions and the start-up of CONCH. These actions overlapped. The dilution of the stock caused the share value to drop slightly, but it soon recovered, and was again $100 per share at the end of the year, making the market cap again 20 million × $100 = $2,000M. See [F5.1].

F2.12 The AJCA for repatriated dividends reduced the US tax rate by 85 %, so that a base rate of 35 % became 35 % × (1 – 85 %) = 5.25 % [AJCA:04].

F2.13 The funds available at CONCH by 2004 were $475M from retained earnings including $49M from interest it had collected on that amount. Since MNC management could expect $84M more earnings at CONCH the next year, it could commit $500M since all payments and the taxes on the repatriation did not come due immediately [W:12, MNC taxes]. There was no dilution of MNC's shares now. It was just a transfer of passive capital held to an active investment, so that the shareholders viewed the acquisitions favorably, and the stock price and hence the market value of MNC increased.

F2.14 Because of the AJCA, MNC decided to have CONCH accounts pay the entire amount, $500M. The AJCA legislation reduced the US tax rate for repatriated funds to 5.25 % [F2.12], so that only taxes of $475M × 5.25 % = $24.9M were due. By staying under $500M the repatriation satisfied the AJCA safe-haven limit [AJCA:04]. If a company were to repatriate more than $500M it had to document how the offshore funds were obtained. By staying under that limit there was no requirement to document how the funds were accumulated in CONCH.

F2.15 At the regular corporate tax rate $475M × 35 % = $166M taxes would have been due. The total amount of acquisitions and taxes would also have exceeded the funds available at CONCH at that time.

F2.16 Only high-value personnel were kept, 200/350=57 % [F2.17]; the remainder of the staff was redundant and let go.

F2.17 The acquisitions at the time of the AJCA were valued similarly to the initial acquisitions. But now CONCH paid for all of the acquisitions. These acquisitions, amounting to \$475M, were all US companies. ATA identified \$41M as tangibles, \$50M as a control premium, and \$40M as research in process to be written off. MNC had about 1,000 employees at the time. Of the 350 employees acquired, the 200 senior and R&D staff were valued at \$27.4M, and \$106.7M were identified as IP. The remainder of the acquisition price, \$210M, was posted as goodwill.

F2.18 Both sets of acquisitions totaled \$300M and \$475M, or \$775M [F2.10] [F2.13]. CONCH paid for the IP it obtained \$29M + \$500M, a total of \$529M. Earlier CONCH paid the buy-in of \$50M for the initial rights [F2.4]. That required a payment of taxes at 35 %, \$17.5M, or a total of \$67.5M for the initial rights. The total paid by CONCH amounts to \$596.5M.

F2.19 CONCH obtained IP rights valued per ATA

$$\$(475-41-50-40-27-210)M=\$106.7M.$$

Given the RAB during that time, 45.2 %, CONCH would have had to pay \$39.1M plus \$2.1M in taxes for its share alone, a total of \$41.2M. The share of IP held at CONCH keeps increasing, from 62 % during the acquisitions to 75 % another 15 years later, giving CONCH rights to yet more of MNC's earnings.

F2.20 In the AJCA motivated acquisitions, CONCH paid for the full share of the IP rights. Once all the acquisitions are finalized, CONCH owns

$$\$119M+\$50M+\$106.7M=\$275.7M worth\ of\ IP rights,$$

while having paid

$$\$50M+\$21.5M+\$106.7M=\$177.1M\ or\ 64\,\%.$$

Since overseas sales grow, after the AJCA acquisitions are completed, the share of MNC's nonroutine earnings allocated to its offshore accounts increases to 69.1 %.

F2.21 To look into the future we use results determined in later chapters. The year of the AJCA acquisitions, 8 years after the buy-in, the CONCH RAB, based on net income, is 48.2 %, leaving a US income share of 51.8 %. Subsequently CONCH owns 66.9 % of MNC's IP, so that the MNC's US share becomes only 33.1 % of the nonroutine income; 18.7 % of MNC's US income or \$45.8M are untaxed. At 35 % tax the loss to the US Treasury is \$16.0M. This fraction rises rapidly, so that 3 years later the annual tax loss is \$21M.

F2.22 Due to the AJCA motivated acquisitions CONCH's share has increased from a sales-based RAB of 45 % [F2.9] to 62 % [F2.19], an additional 17.8 % of net income, and will increase further as the sales-based RAB tranche increases from 45 % to nearly 58 % in the 20 years after those acquisitions, averaging 51.5 % over the future. With the 17.8 % increment the share of nonroutine profits due to CONCH of MNC's net income grows from 62 to 75 %, giving CONCH the rights to nearly half of the earnings from US sales.

F2.23 The IP rights purchase by CONCH leaves 38 % of earnings for the US, reducing for MNC's taxable earnings in the USA to 26 %. The consolidated reports will just report the total, 100 % of the net income, and the low aggregate tax rate, 35 % × 26 % = 9 %. Even on MNC's US-sourced income, those taxes only amount to a 13.7 % tax rate.

F2.24 Commodity income for businesses similar to MNC is 5 % [F5.17]. Taxes on 5 % on income would be equal to 35 % × 5 % = 1.75 %.

F2.25 Lexapro estimates are derived from a Business Week article [Drucker:10] and Forest Labs' 10-K reports [Edgar:10]. Some typical business factors are used to relate the data. FFBV pays $5 for the actual product to FLI and $12 for FLI's IP license fees to Bermuda as CoGS. A cost-plus markup of 5 % [F5.19] is levied by FLI, representing Irish earnings, which are then taxed at 12.5 % there, amounting to $0.11 per unit on income. The US operation had collected $12 for its overhead (SG&A), and will receive $7 for R&D support from offshore; on that latter amount US taxes are due, a bit over $2 before tax credits [F5.27], leaving $5 for Forest Labs' St. Louis, MO, research group. The license fee and remaining profits are collected at FLH in Bermuda. ATA divisions get a 3.2 % cut on the $76 net income for its services in Bermuda and The Netherlands, $2.40 per unit.

F2.26 The Irish subsidiary routine manufacturing operation generates only routine income, since all nonroutine income goes to Bermuda. It gets a markup of 5 % [F5.19] for all of its costs: manufacturing ($5), license fee ($12), and on the reimbursement of FRX's consultant services for its operation of FFBV ($2.40) [F2.25]. Those amounts are then taxed by the Irish Tax & Customs (IT&C) at 12.5 %, yielding

$$(\$5+\$12+\$2.40)\times 5\,\%\times 12.5\,\% = \$0.12\,per\ unit.$$

Paying the bills for their Dutch operation from Ireland helps keep FFBV below the radar of the Dutch tax authority (NLbd). US taxes at the statutory rate would be $2.38 [F2.27]. The IRS subtracts the $0.12 Irish taxes paid leaving $2.26 per unit as foreign tax credits, *ftc*.

Forest Labs is also eligible for US research credits, as described in Appendix E. Those R&E credits reduce the US statutory tax rate for Forest Labs from 35 to 19 %. Left is a US tax of $1.09 per unit. Forest Labs worldwide taxes become $(1.09 + 0.12) = $1.21 per unit, amounting to 2.43 % of Forest's revenue.

F2.27 Forest Labs profits on its gross sales after foreign tax amounts to

$$gross\_sales - SG\&A\ cost\_per\_pill\text{-}ATA\_fees - US\ tax + ftc$$

or

$$\$76 - \$12 - \$5 - \$2.40 - \$2.38 + \$0.12 = \$54.$$

Its margin is then \$54/\$76 = 71 %, excluding R&E research tax credits.

F2.28 A generic drug with the same flow and costs as Lexapro, no expenses going to ATA, proportional SG&A, half of the R&D cost, and paying expected US corporate taxes, but earning a 12.5 % generous commodity profit margin, and would cost

$$\$11+\$3.79+\$5.00+\$0.03+\$1.87+\$2.53+\$3.54+\$1.17+\$3.00 \approx \$32$$

at the counter, about a third of the price of the drug under patent protection.

F2.29 In year 11 after the buy-in MNC should pay taxes on \$98M at a 35 % tax rate which amounts to 10.8 % on its earnings. But MNC will be able to reduce its taxes even more by also taking advantage of other tax expenditures, such as the R&E credit.

F.3 Chapter 3, The Value of Intellectual Capital Formulas

F3.1 For each product in Table 3.1 several estimates are used: the length of the creation period C, the number of creative people involved P, average effort spent percentages E, the cost of manufacturing the first prototype F, successive product units S, and the expected sales volume V. The effort fraction E and the effective lag L are based on the type of industry, as sketched in Fig. 3.5 [W:08]. For initial development the lag fraction L_c can range from 0.27 to 0.42 of the development period [F3.2]. The period for the Maniac 1000 to be ready for production was 4 years; some of the R&D occurred before MNC was founded. Assuming a centroid at $L_c = 0.30$, suitable for a fast start-up, the effective lag becomes $L = 1.2$ years. For successive development, we apply lag fractions L_c between 0.38 and 0.45, to the development periods. Those estimates are typical numbers in industry, but can be refined for a particular industry.For each of the eight types of products the cost of initial creation I is

$$I = P \times C \times E \times \$100{,}000.$$

A modest interest rate of 12 %, without compounding was used, so that
the initial investment $M = I \times L \times 12$;
the cost per unit is $U = (I + F + M)/V + S$.

The sales price P accounts for all the business overheads and the profit margin. P was set at double the cost U with some rounding: $P \approx 2 \times U$. The sales price also covers the cost of distribution. Here is where businesses have the most flexibility.

$$\text{The sales revenue becomes } R = P \times V.$$

The IP content in each unit sold, used for ranking the entries, is $C = I/R$.

F3.2 The centroid represents a distribution $h(x)$ as a single value x_c. Its position is at $x_c = \Sigma(h \times x) / \Sigma h$,

Table F.1 MNC organic income based on an *Erlang(12)* distribution

Year	0.5	1.5	2.5	3.5	4.5	5.5	6.5	7.5	8.5	9.5	10.5
$M	375	620	866	1,059	1,161	1,161	1,076	933	764	595	444
year	11.5	12.5	13.5	14.5	15.5	16.5	17.5	18.5	Remainder		Total
$M	318	220	148	96	61	38	23	14	365		10,004

where h is the ordinate of a function and x is the abscissa.

This function is used to compute L_c from known data for [F3.1]. An example of a centroid estimation is shown in the Glossary, Appendix D.

F3.3 Sales distribution of a product without replacement versions can be modeled by an Erlang distribution [ChatfieldG:73]. The Erlang curve is an asymmetrical version of the normal distribution used to describe customers' purchasing behavior [Moore:91]. Just like the normal distribution, the Erlang distribution has as parameters the mean, or rather its inverse, the average amount or frequency of sales λ, and the standard deviation σ of the data being modeled. A specific Erlang distribution has a parameter $m = (1/\lambda\sigma)^2$. *Erlang*(1) is identical to a negative exponential, and *Erlang*(∞) represents constant sales levels.

The Erlang distribution is computed as

$$freq(t) = \frac{(\lambda m)^m t^{m-1}}{(m-1)!} e^{-m\lambda t} \quad \text{for } t \geq 0$$

Figure 3.6 shows Erlang curves for a total sales volume of 50 million. For technology product sales distributions the value of m will range in practice from 2 to 20 [W:83]. Detailed tables of the Erlang functions are available [Leijon:02].

Shown in Table F.1 is the *Erlang*(12) distribution applied to revenues amounting to $10,000M total used for MNC. The entries represent the average annual value, interpolated to the middle of the year. The total sales after year 19, when sales become <1 % of the highest rate, amount to <$18M. That distribution determines a sales lag of 5.06 years, computed using [F3.2]. It takes about 5 years for the average sales rate to be realized, or over 6 years for an investor to maximize gains [F10.28].

Since the cost of the goods sold (CoGS) and the cost of doing business in the various regions do not differ significantly, we assume that the operating income and MNC's costs of doing business (SG&A) follow the same pattern worldwide.

F3.4 As an approximation of the NPV of that income we use the lag 5 years and an annual discount rate of 12 %. A quick estimate of the return is $(100 - 12)^5 = 53$ %. A more precise calculation would apply discounting, and use the sum of the discounted results for each year. Such calculations are shown in [F5.11].

Table F.2 Alternatives for setting benefit ratios

MNC to CONCH ratios at the buy-in date		Total world	North America US	Canada	Total	CFC's Amount	Ratio (%)
MNC net income	$M	100.0	Combined		56.00	44.00	44
MNC sales	$M	250.0	Combined		145.00	105.00	42
MNC customers	Million	100	54	Included	54	46.00	46
Customer spending	$M	580.7	267.2	Included	267.2	313.48	54
GDP	$M	58,070,000	14,430,000	1,335,000	15,765,000	42,305.000	73
Population	Million	6,500	305	33	338	6,162	95

F.4 Chapter 4, Transfer Pricing and Rights Transfer Formulas

F4.1 The Reasonably Anticipated Benefit (RAB) tranche for CONCH, MNC's controlled holding company is:

$$CONCH\ share = (worldwide - (US + Canada))\,/\,worldwide.$$

The RAB can be based on revenues, net income, actual or potential customers, or GDP. The numbers shown in Table F.2 are for the year of the initial IP transfer from MNC to CONCH.

The first ratio uses net income rather than earnings since R&D costs are investments into the future and do not reflect the current ratio of the shared benefits. Such investments should be weighed separately, but that complexity is needed for MNC, since CONCH reimburses MNC in the USA proportionally for R&D expenses. If substantial capital costs are part of ongoing operations, those costs should be subtracted from the net income, but capital obtained for future investment is not to be considered.

The first three ratios will increase over time as MNC's product sales increase outside of North America. The last three ratios depend on the economic growth in those areas. MNC expects the current CONCH net income ratio to rise to the proportion of customer spending, 54 %. That is a conservative estimate and does not account for a disproportional growth of GDP in the worldwide regions ceded to CONCH.

F4.2 Figure 2.9 showed a value for MNC at the time of the buy-in of \$2,000M. MNC's balance sheet in Table A.2 shows tangible assets of \$310M. At an RAB based on net income, 44 % (Table 4.1), CONCH should pay the approximate buy-in amount of

$$\$(2{,}000 - 310)M \times 44\ \% \approx \$744M.$$

Using the RAB based on sales, 42 %, the amount becomes

$$\$(2{,}000 - 310)M \times 42\ \% \approx \$710M.$$

The difference is \$(744–710)M/\$744M ≈ 4.55 %.

F4.3 Maintenance costs M increase each year y as assets age. We use the total prior cost each year as a new base, so that each year $M_{(y+1)} = (\textit{purchase cost} + \Sigma^Y M) \times \textit{maintenance rate}$.

F4.4 Lifetime maintenance cost $L = \Sigma^{life} M$ (the red, center bars in Fig. 4.3).

F4.5 Cost of Ownership O = *purchase price* (the blue, left bars) + L [F4.4].

F4.6 Lifetime maintenance cost ratio $R = L/O$ [F4.4], [F4.5].

F4.7 Simple annual depreciation = *Purchase cost/life* (the green, right bars in Fig. 4.3).

F4.8 "*Our estimate for the depreciation rate of physical capital is 0.059 and that for R&D capital is 0.12*" [NadiriP:96]. The interesting observations from the paper are:

(a) The US manufacturing industry now only spends 5 % annually on IP reinvestment, i.e., maintenance.
(b) Spending 13.75 % would keep the value of the IP investment constant according to an analysis based on [NadiriP:96]'s equations [WTGS:09].

For intangible assets with indefinite life, the global maintenance cost at 13.75 % reduces the initial value of an asset to 10 % after 15.85 years, simplified to 16 years in subsequent estimates.

F4.9 Applying a discount rate of 15 % over the annual remaining values to an asset life of 16 years [F4.8] allows the setting of a discounted life expectation to a 10 % level. Solving for a life t in

$$(1-13.75\,\%)^t \times (1-15\,\%)^t = 10.00\,\%$$

gives t = 7.4166 or 7 years and 5 months. We simplify the discounted result to 7.5 years.

This estimate is used later as a lower bound on IP life when no other trustworthy data are available. A problem, however, is that because it is based on a computation using discounting, its use will underestimate results that use an NPV calculation [F5.11].

F4.10 M&C deducts in Spain €4,000 + €1,000 – €400, and at 43 % pays €1,978 less tax. M&C in Gibraltar deducts €400, and at 10 % pays €40 less tax, so that M&C overall gains €2,018. The unequal split is not justified, since Miguel and Carlos are equal partners. The price of repair parts which were never purchased is irrelevant. In an equal split M&C would deduct in Spain €2,500 and at 43 % pays €1,075 less tax. M&C in Gibraltar deducts the other €2,500, and at 10 % pays €250 less tax, so that M&C overall gains only €1,325. Such shifting of costs is hard to detect by tax authorities.

F4.11 MNC's acquisition of Pat-inc at \$4.0M for its patent portfolio is a business expense that can be deducted from its taxes. The \$1.0M employee severance costs are also a business expense. MNC only booked 20 % of the price as goodwill for the patents. The remainder, \$3.2M, was written off as "impaired" goodwill, leaving just the \$0.8M on its books as goodwill for those patents.

CONCH pays only for its 42 % RAB share of the IP placed on the books and the employee severance costs, 42 % × \$(80 % × 4.0 +1.0)M = \$0.756M. MNC's net cost is now \$(5.000 – 0.756)M = \$4.244M. After the 35 % tax deduction \$2.759M remains. CONCH paid \$0.756M/\$(2.759 + 0.756)M = 21.5 % of the final costs for its share, even though it will share 42 % of earnings from those patents after Pat-inc is acquired.

A more extreme case was MNC's acquisition of Wf-inc, acquired solely for its workforce, described earlier in the chapter. No tangibles were acquired. All booked assets of Wf-inc were written off. CONCH had to pay nothing, but gained access to valuable intellectual capital, which will create new IP and products.

F.5 Chapter 5, Valuation Methods for IP Formulas

F5.1 The simple market cap value of MNC is due to 18.5 million issued shares valued in the market at \$100 each = \$1,850M.

F5.2 Outstanding stock options to MNC directors and employees as incentives amount to another five million shares. If all the stock options were already vested and exercised now, the number of outstanding shares would increase from 20 to 25 million.

Those option shares dilute the value of the shares in the market by 5M/25M = 20 %. But MNC's shareholders were aware of the benefits of retaining crucial personnel and the later income and were still willing to pay \$95 per share. When options are exercised, the holders of those options will have to pay for them at the strike price, the share price when they were granted, an average of \$60 per share. We simplify the computation by assuming all options were issued 4 months earlier and will be exercised 2 years hence. When all the options are exercised MNC gains \$300M tangible income.

The current value of that \$300M is the NPV (\$300M at 15 % for 2.33 years) = \$217M [F5.11]. The correct market value is the sum of the current value of the 20M outstanding shares and the option shares:

$$18.5\ million \times \$95 + \$217M = \$1{,}974M.$$

F5.3 The current value of the workforce covered by stock options is now assessed using the current stock value, \$95, minus the current value of the payments when the stock options are exercised [F5.2]:

$$5\ million \times \$95 - \$217M = \$258M.$$

This value was already of interest when assessing IP contributions in Chap. 3.

F5.4 MNC paid \$300M to acquire smaller companies, wisely using a 50/50 balance of cash and equity. It used \$150M from cash on hand and loans and 1.5M shares, which had recovered to \$100. Its market capitalization became *20 million × \$100 = \$2,000M without considering the stock options, or*

20 million × \$100 + \$217M = \$2,217M with the effect of the stock options.

The price included ~10 % tangibles, so that MNC gained about \$270M of intangibles.

F5.5 To compute the intangibles for an MC-VM we start with the market cap and subtract the tangibles. The events around the time of the buy-in affected the intangibles. We just estimate the values at two times, prior and after the buy-in period. Table A.2 shows MNC's balance statement after the acquisitions.

Prior to granting stock options, making the acquisitions, and the buy-in, the intangibles are simply the market cap [F5.1] minus the tangibles (including cash) shown on MNC's books. Those tangibles were \$(30 + 20 + 40 + 200)M = \$290M.

The value of the intangibles are then estimated to be \$(1,850 – 290)M = \$1,560M.

Tobin's Q, a measure of excess intangibles, is \$1,850M/\$350M = 5.3 [F5.40g].

Subsequently MNC spent \$300M on acquisitions; \$30M were tangibles on their books. MNC used \$150M in cash for acquisition and \$50M for CONCH. MNC took out a loan of \$50M, but since the cash stayed within the company, the books still show \$100M cash.

The tangibles shown now on MNC's books are \$220M [FA.4]. Now also \$90M of the \$270M of intangibles obtained are visible in the books. The acquisitions seemed wise and the share price held steady. The market cap, with stock options, became \$2,217M [F5.4].

CONCH's assets are consolidated within MNC's reports. Most of the \$50M loan is balanced out by funds held at CONCH until the buy-in is completed. Soon MNC will receive interest payments on that loan. Only \$6M [F2.4] was spent to get CONCH started; MNC US received restricted shares documenting its ownership.

The total intangible portion of the market cap after all these events is

$$\$2,217M - \$(220-6)M = \$1,786M.$$

The substantial changes to intangibles, from retaining the workforce [F5.3] and acquisitions, is ignored in MNC's books [F5.3]. Tobin's Q also considers outstanding loans, and all assets on the books increases to \$(2,217 – 50) M/\$450M = 4.7, since cash on hand was converted to intangibles [F5.40g].

F5.6 The number of companies in SIC code 7372, Prepackaged Software, went down after the 2001 Internet stock market bubble, as shown in Fig. 5.2 and Table F.3 [Compustat:04]. These numbers are mainly of interest to understand the differences between reporting averages and the total of stock values.

F5.7 The Veritas case dealt with a 1999 buy-in valuation of an Irish subsidiary of a US software company. The taxpayer submitted documents supporting a buy-in payment of \$166M based on a single CUT-VM valuation.

Table F.3 Software company counts during Internet bubble

No. of companies reporting/month	1999	2000	2001	2002	2003	2004	2005
Min in year	413	503	503	459	403	368	330
Max in year	475	536	537	501	462	402	379
Rise/drop in 2 year intervals	30 % rise		Peak			18 % drop	

After going through a lengthy exam process the case wound up in the US Tax court, finally decided in 2009 [Morgan:10]. The judicial case documents showed that one IRS expert submitted a market cap-based buy-in valuation for a buy-in of \$2,500M and another expert submitted an income-based valuation of \$1,675M [Veritas:09]. Errors in the IRS experts' computations of these valuations were brought to the attention of the judge. The significance of those errors could not be resolved in court [Birnkrant:10]. The taxpayer's estimate, based on the taxpayer's single valuation was deemed best and accepted with some corrections [F5.68]. The final settlement also involved a \$9.6M trademark adjustment to be added to the buy-in.

In July 2005 Veritas was sold to another US software company for \$13,200M [Johnson:05V]. Veritas had little cash on hand and was subject to some lawsuits, which would warrant a lower price. Now the buy-in, if it would not be settled in court, would become a cost-sharing payment for the IP in Ireland. Let's assume that 25 % of its value was in tangibles and its trademark. Veritas' income grew by 36 % from 2002, the date of the court case, to 2005, when it was acquired. This estimate yields a value for the IP of Veritas of

$$\$13,200M \times ((1-25\%)/(1+36\%)) = \$7,262M.$$

At the 26 % RAB used in the court for the valuation of the buy-in of the IP, the Irish share becomes

$$\$7,262M \times 26\ \% \approx \$1,860M.$$

This result was in the range of the two estimates of the IRS experts: the market-based estimate was 32 % above this value and the income-based valuation was 11 % below.

The taxpayer's submission is only 8.9 % of the realistic PP-VM valuation enabled by the 2005 sale. The information about this sale of Veritas and the price actually paid was ignored by all parties and not presented to the judge. The purchaser likely had access to low-taxed AJCA funds and was willing to pay a control premium [F2.10]. The actual price paid in 2005 by an arm's-length buyer, expecting to make a profit from its purchase, valued Veritas in the range of the two estimates produced by the IRS experts.

As a cross-check we obtain Veritas' market capitalization in 2005, \$12,000M [Edgar:10]. That is 9 % less than the amount that Veritas was actually sold for, perhaps because of the pending shareholder and an SEC suits. It appears

Table F.4 Alternative Market Capitalization-based valuations

MNC results	Prior	Prior + stock options	Prior + acquisitions	Prior + both; stock price back	Prior + both + CONCH
Total market cap	1,850.0M	1,757.5M	2,000.0M	2,216.8M	2,216.8M
Tangibles	220.0M	436.8M	100.0M	286.8M	280.8M
Intangibles	1,630.0M	1,230.8M	1,900.0M	1,930.0M	1,906.0M
CONCH at 44 %	717.2M	581.1M	836.0M	849.M	838.6M

Table F.5 Expected future incomes and their present values

End of year	1	2	3	4	5	6	7	8	9	10
Earnings	250.0	265.0	280.4	296.4	313.6	332.2	352.6	375.2	400.2	428.2
NPV	233.1	214.9	197.7	181.8	167.2	154.0	141.4	129.5	118.3	107.8
End of year	11	12	13	14	15	16	17	18	19	20
Earnings	425.2	443.8	462.4	481.0	499.6	518.2	536.8	555.4	574.0	592.6
NPV	98.01	88.95	80.59	72.90	65.84	59.39	53.49	48.13	43.25	38.83
End of year	21	22	23	24	25	26	Total years 1–20		Total years 1–26	
Earnings	611.2	629.8	648.4	667.0	685.6	704.2	$8,341.4M		$12,287.6M	
NPV	34.82	31.20	27.93	24.99	22.33	19.95	$2,295.0M		$2,456.3M	

that Veritas' stockholders had a reasonable understanding of the company's prospects. No such information had been provided to the court. As was typical for the 2005 time frame, their assessment exceeded that of a valuation based on expected income, the most principled approach for IP valuation.

F5.8 Final results for the MC-VM are shown in Table F.4.

Since first and last columns are obtained at a relatively stable point in MNC's growth we take those for further analyses.

F5.9 MNC's margin of income at the time of the buy-in is the earnings $154M over the operating income of $250M or 62 %.

F5.10 Projecting sales is difficult. For our model MNC we start with the income estimates as of the buy-in date. Nearly all revenues are from the current Maniac 2000 product; some repair parts for Maniac 1000 may still be sold. The new acquisitions made at that time do not generate much revenue, but since they were paid for with loans and shares, they do not contribute much to costs either. For the income-based method, M2, Inc-VM, we must project MNC's revenues, and then compute the value of that income at the present time, when the buy-in occurred.

The Net Present Value (NPV) of a future income is the sum of periodic incomes times a discount rate appropriate to the interval from today to when the income occurs. For a fixed discount rate d the NPV of earnings e in a given period y years into the future is $v = e/(1 + d)^y$.

The total NPV is the sum of all v's.

The values for MNC are shown in Table F.5. We assume that the acquisitions did not generate independent revenue stream, but just enabled a steady, super-linear growth of operating income. The discount rate d is again 15 % [F4.9]. Ongoing maintenance assures that growth is extended over the life of just a single product, as shown in Fig. 3.6. The growth of MNC's income is based on ongoing Erlang-based assumptions for organic growth of operating income, as shown in Fig. 3.6. The NPV rows of Table F.5 are computed according to [F5.11f].

Table F5 that at the end of year 10, the operating income of $428.2M adds only $107.8M to the current NPV. The years from 21 to 26 add only $161M to the NPV.

F5.11 The discount rate to be used is derived from the interest rate that an alternative secure investment could yield, with a correction for risk. Any high-tech company is risky. Appropriate discount rates vary from 12 to 25 %; new start-up ventures have yet higher rates [SlavinK:06]. For risky investments the discount rate will be around 20 % and the effect will be even greater. The value of past investments is computed similarly, using a capitalization rate, as shown in [F5.48].

MNC was well established by the time it started offshore operations, so that a discount rate of 15 % was used in the model [F4.9]. Income promised a year later is then valued at only 87 %, and the effect increases exponentially for subsequent years [F5.10].

The effect of discounting is great, as already seen in [F3.4]. This section provides examples to illustrate the importance of discounting for readers not familiar with the concept. Given a discount rate of d percent, the net present value (NPV) NPV of an annual income ey arriving throughout the year for y years is

$$NPV = \Sigma^{y} e_{y} \,/\left(1+d\right)^{(y-0.5)}$$

Using the midyear convention (y – 0.5) and applying a 15 % discount rate:

(a) To a one-time $250M income after 1 year, and get just $233M or 93 %;
(b) To a one-time $250M income after 10 years, and get just $66M or 25 %;
(c) To a one-time $250M income after 20 years, and get just $16M or 6 %;
(d) To a steady $250M income over 20 years, and get just $1,678M instead of the undiscounted total income of $5,000M, or 31 % [W:12];
(e) To a steady $250M income in over 32 years, and get just $1,761M instead of the total $8,000M, or 22 %. That is only $83M more than obtained from the initial 20 years.
(f) Discounting the annual amounts to the Erlang(12) [F3.3] sales curve growing from $250M to nearly $1,000M annually, as shown in Fig. 3.2, yields a total income of $10,000M over the first 20 years, but its NPV = $2,473M or 25 % of the income.

Example (f) shows that the NPV of a realistic income, one that first grows and then goes down in the future, is less than the NPV from an equal-sized steady income, twice the amount from the steady income shown in Example (d), where $10,000M or $500/year would yield $3,358M, because the bulk of the income arrives later.

F5.12 A handy formula to estimate the net present value (NPV) of a long future income stream is "Gordon's rule" [GordonG:97]. For long-range projections reliable income data are rarely available. Gordon's rule estimates the NPV of perpetual earnings e (continuing forever), growing annually by g % and discounted at d % to be

NPVG = net_annual_income/(discount_rate – growth_rate) = e/(d – g)

For a fixed income the growth rate g is zero. The Gordon estimate is fairly good for values of d and g below 20 %.

For instance case (e) of [F5.11], where the rule estimates from its starting point, NPVG = $250/15 % = $1,667M, instead of $1,761M for 32 years [F5.11e]

However, it is wise to use any trustworthy income projections that are available. If estimates are available for, say the next 5 years, then those years can be used as shown in Table F.5. Beyond that 5th year Gordon's rule can be used, with the last growth rate of 5.8 % per year from year 5 to 6 and again a 15 % discount rate. The Gordon result itself is discounted for year 6. The result is $995M for the 5 prior years and $1672M, or $2,667M total, versus the $2,456M from the detailed summation of Table F.5.

Because in the detailed projection MNC did not sustain the earlier growth rate, the NPV of the modeled income is nearly 9 % less than the NPV of the 5-year projected income plus the Gordon estimate NPVG for the beyond that beyond.

Although its results can be very useful, Gordon's rule depends on stable long-term growth rates. No prediction can deal with future external events, as the AJCA tax reduction. Its use was criticized in court since perpetual growth cannot be assumed [Veritas:09].

F5.13 Table F.6 shows the actual income for MNC, with the benefits of the acquisitions. The NPV computation is omitted for the current year 1. It does not make sense to show an annual NPV contribution reduced to a time that is earlier than data it is computed from. To illustrate the modest effect of errors far out we show the implied NPV value of the actual results. While MNC's actual income over 26 years was 44 % greater, its implied NPV is only 20 % more than the estimated NPV.

F5.14 ATA used a benefit ratio of 42 % based on sales [F4.1]. Given that the RAB based on earnings of CONCH increases from 44 to 54 %, the expected income to be allocated to CONCH over the next 20 years becomes of $4,150M. The NPV over the 20 years becomes $1,089M. That amount changes little at the 15 % discount rate if a period longer than 20 years were used [F5.11e].

F5.15 Distribution is the major function not requiring IP. Distribution alone does not require in-house IP, and hence distributors only have routine IP. There are companies acting as distributors for other US manufacturers of products similar to those produced by MNC who operate at arm's length from their suppliers. A hypothetical search finds nine such companies, making profits from 0.7 to 11.3 % of sales, with a mean of 5.1 %. We use the interquartile mean [FD.3] instead and obtain 5.0 % as shown in Table F.7.

Table F.6 Actual incomes versus projected incomes and NPVs

End of year	1	2	3	4	5	6	7	8
Earnings $	250.0	265.0	280.4	296.4	313.6	332.2	352.6	375.2
End of year	9	10	11	12	13	14	15	16
Earnings $	400.2	428.2	459.4	494.2	533.0	576.0	623.8	676.6
End of year	17	18	19	20	21	22	23	24
Earnings $	734.8	798.8	868.8	945.4	1,028.8	1,119.4	1,217.6	1,323.6

End of year	25	26	Total years 1-20	Total years 1-26
Earnings $	1,438.0	1,561.0	$10,004.6M	$17,693.0M
Equivalent NPV at buy-in time of actuals for illustration *a*			$2,472.6M	$2,779.8M
Projected earnings [from Table F.5]			$8,341.4M	$12,287.6M
NPV based on projected earnings *p* [from Table F.5]			$2,140.1M	$2,290.5M
Difference estimated/actual NPV *d=a−p*			$332.5M	$489.3M
Actual versus projected incomes *d/p*			≈ 13%	≈ 20%

Table F.7 Earnings of arm's-length distributors, arranged by earnings/sales

Distributor	D1	D2	D3	D4	D5	D6	D7	D8	D9
Earnings margin	0.70 %	2.30 %	3.10 %	4.70 %	4.90 %	5.50 %	6.70 %	7.10 %	11.30 %
Quartile	1	1	iq	iq	iq	iq	iq	4	4

The mean earnings of all distributors D1…D9 = 5.1 %. The interquartile covers D3…D7, and their mean = 5.0 % [FD.3] with Table F.18.

F5.16 An alternative is to analyze the distribution function of MNC separately. We model a hypothetical situation, where MNC slices off its distribution function and appoints an independent, arm's-length distributor. There is a loss of efficiency, so that both MNC and the distributor carry 66 % of the SG&A costs of MNC operating by itself. That distributor earns 4.9 % for its services, and the amputated MNC earns slightly less on its revenues, namely 39 % instead of just over 41 % shown on the books [FC.3]. While MNC does not earn much from doing its own distribution, it does have better control.

F5.17 Modeling routine income, the income garnered by a company which produces similar commodity products, can be estimated by analyzing some companies that do not have significant IP. Commodity profits are driven down by competition. Information for most industries can be found in public documents. Another source for commodity profits is found in reports from offshore fabricators and semiconductor foundries, who, while they produce high-quality products for many brands, do not add the IP needed for nonroutine profits. We analyze a commodity company, without any IP, but making products similar to MNC, in the abstract. Such a company will have similar tangibles, but sales at a lower price. By keeping its operational parameters, except its product prices and research costs, identical to MNC, we find that its earnings margin is 7.8 %. The distribution-only function of such a company should have a lower margin; we allocate 4.4 % for the distribution effort. The average of this range of values is 6.1 %.

F5.18 The routine income is created by productive resources which are commonly available. We take the value of MNC's plant and machinery, \$40M + \$50M, from Table A.2, to represent productive resources. We use the post-buy-in value of the IP, \$1,816M, as estimated by the shareholders to represent the unique intellectual capital [F5.5]. The remaining tangibles contribute to both routine and nonroutine income. The margin of routine income is then

$$\$(40+50)M \,/\, \$(1{,}816+40+50)M = 4.7\,\%.$$

F5.19 We have four computed estimates of routine income margins [F5.15], [F5.16], [F5.17], [F5.18]. We also have a range from the literature, 2–8 %, giving a mean of 5 % [Rosenberg:10]. The average, rounded, of {5.0 + 4.9 + 5.0 + 4.6 + 5.1} is also ≈ 5 %. Those 5 % must be applied to the MNC's revenue of \$375M [F2.27] [MiseyS:07]. That amount is \$18.7M. The nonroutine income margin for MNC = Total MNC income margin – the routine margin becomes about 41–5 % ≈ 36 % [F5.16].

F5.20 Applying the 36 % to the projected NPV results [F5.13] gives an NPV of the nonroutine income of MNC \$2,295 × 36 %/41 % ≈ \$2,012M. The amount to be used for the buy-in payment by CONCH to MNC using the Inc-VM becomes \$1,089M × 36 %/41 % ≈ \$955M.

Table F.8 Maniac earnings

Actual (incl. AJCA acquisitions)			Projected	
Earnings over 20 years	MNC overall	CONCH	MNC overall	CONCH
Total	\$10,004.6	\$5,247.4	\$8,341.4	\$4,150.5
NPV @15 %, applied midyear	\$2,472.6	\$1,218.5	\$2,295.0	\$1,089.4
Nonroutine earnings	\$2,168.0	\$1,068.4	\$2,012.3	\$955.2

Table F.9 Maniac releases and IP retention

Maniac release (version × 1000)	1000	2000	3000	4000	5000	6000	7000
Release interval, months		21	32	21	40	47	13
Life in the market, y, m	1, 9	4, 5	6, 2	9, 5	13, 5	14, 6	Unknown
Relative SW contribution *Rel_SW_cont*		50.0 %	61.0 %	73.5 %	80.0 %	89.0 %	95.0 %
SW IP diminution		100.0 %	43.4 %	13.4 %	7.2 %	3.8 %	2.3 %
Total IP left from Maniac 1000		100.0 %	60.7 %	33.2 %	23.6 %	12.9 %	9.6 %

F5.21 For the Identified IP (IIP-VM) method we consider the life of the IP and its diminutions as it ages. The development interval for new Maniacs varies greatly; the average is 2.5 years. Minor updates are made by shipping software via the Internet, so that no new or updated Maniac hardware needs to be released.

F5.22 The metric of effort during product line development are the expenses spent on R&D for each improved release in MNC's Maniac product line. As time passes the software effort dominates, since hardware improvements are due to purchasing greatly improved chips. Those chips do not contain MNC's IP and are competitively priced.

The IP of the original Maniac 1000 release is retained in the Maniac product line in the market until the 10 % cutoff point is reached, computed to occur during the sale interval for the Maniac 6000, after Maniacs have been on the market for 13 years and 10 months.

F5.23 We assume that hardware and software efforts for the initial Maniac 1000 release were equally balanced. We also assume that after the initial design, hardware changes little. The MNC product is, of course, updated by using better and higher performance parts, but such updates do not represent MNC's IP. The importance of the hardware effort diminished linearly over time, becoming about 22 % at the end of Maniac 5000 sales. The Maniac 6000 actually had a software problem, so the hardware contribution was only 9 % there, recovering to 12.5 % during the life of the Maniac 7000. Over time the hardware components for the Maniacs become more and more commodity products, but the unique architecture of the Maniac retains its value.

We estimate that the software component contribution Rel_SW_cont embedded in the product grows from 37.5 % to about 98 %. The software component growth follows the "Roux rule" with a 7.5 % annual adjustment for deleted code [F5.24]. The software diminution, *SWdim*, is

$$SW\,\mathrm{dim} = 1/version\_no - 7.5\,\% \times \mathrm{int}erval\_size \times \mathrm{Re}l\_SW\_cont.$$

The total Maniac product diminution (Maniacdim) is

$$Maniacdim = (1 - relative\_SW\_contribution) + SWdim.$$

We see that M3, the Identified IP Valuation Method, allows making distinction of the distinct investments in IP creation and maintenance that cannot be captured by broad-based methods.

F5.24 The Roux rule allows making estimates of software growth when no data on the effort spent are available. It states that each new major version of a software product grows by the size of the first working version [Roux:97]. The Roux rule summarizes observations by several software researchers [W:07]. Software growth is used as a surrogate for the effort spent, and as such, reduces the relevance of the prior software code [Zeidman:11]. Without accounting for code deletion, the IP ratio IPf from Maniac 1000 is then simply

$$IPf = (1 / version\_no) \text{ or here} \approx (1{,}000 / Maniac\_release\_number).$$

There is an additional effort to compensate for deleted code. During ongoing software development and maintenance some original code will be deleted. A typical annual code deletion rate is 5 %, but the rate tends to be greater for embedded software, so for the Maniacs we will assume a high annual rate of 7.5 % [W:06].

Combining the Roux rule and the effect of code deletion has the effect that, for instance, Version 2.0 only benefits from 43 % of the Version 1.0 software. The problems leading to the rapid replacement of the Maniac 6000 by the Maniac 7000 are solely due to software, and we assume that 30 % of the code was deleted during that cleanup, a maximum for code stability [Bernstein:03]. The 10 % cutoff limit is just reached before year 8.

F5.25 For valuation at later Maniac release times, we apply the Roux rule similarly to the software version that is current at the actual buy-in point. The growth of new code from software Version 3.0 (size = 3 × size(V1.0)) to Version V4.0 (size = 4 × size(V1.0)), so that relative software size is then 3/4 = 75 %. After Version V7.0 the release interval is based on the prior experience, averaging 42 months. We assume that we can look further into the future at this time, as shown in Table F.10. For Table F.10 the same deletion rates used for a diminution from V1.0 are applied [F5.24]. Figure 5.7 applies the Roux rule and the deletion rates to MNC's software release.

The rate of IP diminution is much lower for mature software than that for novel software. Figure 5.5 shows the effect using MNC's actual release intervals [F5.22]. Even though there was a drastic 30 % code deletion from Version V6.0 to Version V7.0, only by Version V8.0, released 18 years later, is the IP contributed at Version 3.0 reduced to <10 %.

To obtain an estimate for IP life we use as the cutoff point where only 10 % of the IP available at the valuation time remains. A linear interpolation for the case shown in Fig. 5.7 gives a life based on actual, retrospective data of over 16½ years. The computed actuals are shown in Table 5.7.

F5.26 For a true forward-looking estimation we have no future release dates. We are forced to predict based on the experience we have. The average release

Table F.10 Maniac releases after buy-in date and IP retention

SW version sequence	V1.0	V2.0	V3.0	V4.0	V5.0
Relative size to V 1.0	base	200%	300%	400%	500%
Roux diminution relative to V 3.0		prior	100%	86%	69%
Development interval, months *		32	4 prior 17	40	47
Years, months after valuation		prior	1, 5	4, 3	8, 2
Code from version 3 left		prior	100%	79.4%	43.7%

SW version sequence	V6.0	V7.0	Inter-polation to 10% IP	V8.0
Relative size to V 1.0	600%	700%		800%
Roux diminution relative to V 3.0	58%	49%		42.9%
Development interval, months	13	67		42
Years, months after valuation	9, 3	14, 10	16 , 6	18, 4
Code from version 3 left	23.5%	13.1%	10.0%	6.0%

* The transfer of IP rights to CONCH occurred while Version 3 of the Maniac software was being developed

interval of the two prior Maniacs is just over 2 years and 2 months. The MNC engineers predict that the Maniac currently in development, the Maniac 3000, will come out on a similar schedule. A discussion with the engineers tells us that 26 months is a reasonable schedule.

For a prediction, the expected release intervals can be kept constant or allowed to increase gradually. The atypical situation, a product failure, shown with Maniac 6000 and inherited by Version V6.0 of the software, can never be predicted. More frequent releases reduce the risk and can avoid problems which MNC encountered in Version V6.0: "30 % is the max one can change in a version release" [Bernstein:03]. In the prior version MNC violated that rule.

Computing the prediction of the software at the buy-in date is identical to the one shown in Table F.9; it just omits the diminution prior to the valuation point [F5.25].

Figure 5.7 also compares the prediction with the actuals from our known model. It shows that our estimate is conservative for the software which is released with the Maniac 3000, but overall optimistic. The 10 % level is not reached until estimated Version 10.0, but that point is reached already in <15½ years.

F5.27 The average release interval for Maniacs is 2.86 years, and an appropriate centroid is 0.42, giving an effective lag of 1.2 years [W:08]. See Fig. 3.3 [F3.2].

F5.28 The lag precedes the diminution of the initial IP value due to the introduction of new IP in successive years and delays the effect of diminution, shown in Fig. 5.12. The predicted life and lag together are 15.5 +1.2 = 16.7

years [F5.26], [F5.27]. The income at CONCH from the Maniacs over that period is $3,161M. When the annual incomes are reduced by the annual diminution year, $1,207M remains.

The supporting calculations here were done on an annual basis and disregard when events should be placed within the year. In commercial practice they would be done on a quarterly basis, giving smoother results.

F5.29 MNC started 1½ year before it released the Maniac 1000, its first product. The time to market is about half the time for a typical product, because the founders benefitted from research at their prior employer. The CONCH buy-in occurred while the Maniac 3000 was on the market, an interval of 6 years since the release of the Maniac 1000. We can compute an estimate of an arm's-length lag two ways:

(i) Take the sum of the effective lags encountered, each computed by each interval period times their centroid, as shown in Fig. 3.4. The appropriate centroid for MNC's start-up phase is 0.27 and for its subsequent efforts is 0.42. The arm's-length effective lag becomes $(1.5 \times 0.27) + (6 \times 0.42) = 2.9$ years.

(ii) Use the general period ratio of 0.41 shown in Fig. D.1, and multiply it by the prior period (the initial interval plus the sum of the subsequent development intervals). The result is $(6.0 + 1.5) \times 0.41 = 3.1$ years [W:09].

We will use the average, 3.0 years, for an arm's-length lag. Even then MNC, and hence CONCH, has a head start, because in a few months CONCH will obtain the rights to the Maniac 4000. A true arm's-length competitor will not know what its features are.

F5.30 If we replace the version lag of 1.2 years with the arm's-length lag of 3.0 years the diminution curve is shifted nearly 2 years into the future. Life and lag together now are $15.5 + 3.0 = 18.5$ years [F5.25] [F5.29]. The projected income at CONCH from the Maniacs over that period is $3,723M. For the first 3 years the income is not diminished, since a purchaser of the existing IP can sell Maniacs immediately, gaining the benefits of the prior 3-year R&D spending. When the annual incomes are reduced by the effect of lag and diminution for each year, $1,559M remains.

F5.31 The discounted income of the $1,559M [F5.30] at the arm's-length lag is $667M, which is the most reasonable result for the technical contribution using the IIP-VM. The increase is a technical measure of the "first-to-market-advantage," $117M or 21 % over the simpler estimate.

F5.32 For completeness we also compute the incomes for a life based on the global and discounted IP life estimate of 7.42 years [F4.8]. We obtain for the 1.2-year version lag a period of 8.62 years and an income of $1,247M, diminished to $742M. For the 3-year arm's-length lag the total period becomes 10.4 years, the income at CONCH $1,617M, diminished to $1,047M. Discounting as before, at a 15 % rate, provides the NPV values,

$464M for the 1.2-year lag and $591M for the arm's-length lag. However, now discounting has been applied twice, since the 7.42-year estimate was already based on a discounted IP life. A lower discount rate, say a riskless discount rate of 10 % for the ongoing maintenance, may be appropriate, but it is wise to avoid yet more complexity.

F5.33 The results from [F5.31] and [F5.32] provide a range of reasonable predicted values, an important input to test the sensitivity of computations when making estimates into the future. At a 15 % discount rate their NPVs range from $464M to $670M, or a range of

$$\$(670-464)M \,/\, \$(Average\_of\_4\_results)M = 36\,\%$$

Or

18 % above or below the mean.

Their average is $567M. Without the outliers the average is $570M.

F5.34 The differences between the discounted actuals in the last row of Table 5.7 and the corresponding estimates from Table 5.6 are minimal, 2.7 and 0.9 %, even though actual events shifted release dates and hence changed actual IP growth.

F5.35 Recomputing the diminished income for the IIP-VM over the estimated total life and arm's-length lag yields an income due to the transferred IP to $1,559M and a net present value of $665M [F5.32]. At that time an arm's-length competitor still has a product which is 3 years behind the state reached by MNC's Maniac development. The financial benefit of MNC staying ahead is ignored. We add the current RAB share [F4.2] of the critical workforce value of $258M [F5.3]. The sum is $665M + 0.44 × $258M = $778M.

It is unlikely that any IIP-VM valuation could identify and value all the detailed intangibles needed for a comprehensive aggregation. It would require a level of detail and specific projections which are never available. Some triage is needed to select the intangibles that must be valued, approximate other groupings, and ignore minor ones.

F5.36 In a survey where common licenses averaged 5 %, exclusive licenses averaged 7 %, or 43 % more [F7.14]. The author also stated that reported intra-company royalty rates are meaningless because of manipulation for tax reasons [Parr:07].

F5.37 An appropriate royalty on revenues for the IP ceded to CONCH, using comparables extracted from [Parr:07], yields a rate of 20 %.

F5.38 In the CUT-VM royalty rates are compared. A reasonable royalty rate on a make–sell license for distributed products which contain both hardware IP and software IP becomes (25 %+35 %)/2 = 30 % on earnings. MNC's revenues exceed its earnings by $(375 – 250)M = $125M (Table A.2), making the royalty on revenue 19.97 %.

CONCH also takes over MNC's existing distribution network. A typical value for an independent, existing network with its customer lists and existing contracts, would command a royalty of 2–7 % on revenues. Those were created by SG&A costs, and are incremental to the IP benefits. We use the 5 % estimated earlier [F5.19]. The total royalty becomes nearly 25 %.

F5.39 We still want to obtain a transfer price estimate for the CUT-VM applied to the buy-in. We use the CONCH revenue for 15 years by multiplying the MNC revenue [F5.9] by the CONCH RAB [F5.13]. Those amounts are multiplied each year by the royalty rate. Because of the absence of risk in a royalty arrangement, we chose a discount rate of 10 % to obtain the net present value (NPV). At the 20th year we apply the Gordon perpetuity [F5.12] at the 10 % discount rate and the 4.6 % growth rate at that time.

The NPV becomes \$778.9M [F5.10]. No RAB allocation is needed because the royalty is applied to the CONCH income.

F5.40 To obtain the indicators for CP-VM comparisons we use the values from Table A.1, MNC's income accounts, and obtain candidate metrics for CP-VM assessment. The use of such ratios for recognizing interstate tax avoidance has even been patented [CookC:10]. The patent lists several of the margins and likely sources for the needed data.For public companies all of the data needed to compute these indicators are available in public documents. The sample calculation applies to MNC's books (Appendix A).

(a) Rate of return on Assets (RoA) is \$154M/\$450M ≈ 34.3 %. However, financial assets are not relevant to MNC. Only capitalized R&D (\$90M) and goodwill (\$140M) obtained in acquisitions appear as intangible assets [FA.4]. If those were ignored as well, the RoA would be an unreasonably high 70.1 %.
(b) Operating profit to Revenues (P/R), \$250M/\$375M ≈ 67 %.
(c) Berry ratio, \$284M/\$(92 + 34)M ≈ 2.26.
(d) Net Cost Plus (NCP), \$250M/\$(92 +34)M ≈ 1.99.
(e) Full IP Cost (FIPC), \$250M/\$(85 % × 86 + 92 + 34)M ≈ 1.26.
(f) Obtaining the p/e multiple requires share price and volume information in corporate annual and 10-K reports. MNC's simple market cap was \$1,850M, so its p/e multiple is \$(1,850/154)M ≈ 12.01.
(g) Initially Tobin's Q, based on all booked assets, is

$$Q = \$(1{,}850 - 50)M \,/\, \$350M \approx 5.3,$$

but becomes less once acquired R&D and goodwill appear on the books.

F5.41 A Berry ratio is used in Table 5.9. The value appropriate to CONCH is computed by using the market caps of six hypothetical companies which operate similar businesses and produce similar products as MNC. The interquartile computation rejects C1 and C6 based on extreme values of the ratio m as shown in Fig. D.3. The mean im of the 4 other companies becomes 2.35. That Berry ratio is used to validate CONCH operations.

The computation can be repeated with other parameters, each contributing additional insight to the value of MNC. Given that most of the companies used in the interquartile computations are substantially smaller, we should expect that the SG&A overhead should be relatively less at MNC and MNC's profitability should be greater. Since CONCH is in practice not an independent operation, further adjustments might be appropriate.

F5.42 Combining the MNC's initial market cap valuation of $1,630M [F5.8] and MNC's earnings $154.2M [FA.1] yields an intangible price to earnings, ip/e of = 10.57.

F5.43 Table 5.10 uses the same six hypothetical uncontrolled companies that were used for Table 5.9. Their market capitalizations are also reduced now to provide an IP only valuation for CONCH. This time C2 and C4 are rejected as being outside of the interquartile range, and the average ip/e of the four companies within the range is 10.3.

F5.44 If CONCH would have the same ip/e multiple as its peers, based on its earnings, its value would be 10.3 × 42 % × $154M ≈ $667M. The indirection of the CP-VM computation provides little accuracy, but is a useful general indication of value.

F5.45 The CoGS of MNC was $92M in the accounting sheet of Table A.2, but 25 % of that cost is material and supplies used at MNC MY for manufacturing, leaving $69M as the actual MNC contribution for the base to be split for the PS-M.

F5.46 The total MNC contributions to be removed to obtain the residual used to split IP contributions between the US parent and CONCH are shown in Table F.11.

F5.47 The royalty on CONCH income to pay for the intangibles provided by MNC is 36 % after 5 % for the distribution on MNC revenue was deducted [F5.19]. The 36 % includes 9 % for the management and capital costs. CONCH will reimburse its share of that cost, leaving a 27.1 % royalty to be paid. We use 9 % for the contract manufacturing margin [FC.5]. MNC pays a fair transfer price (the IFP) for the Maniacs brought into and sold in the USA.

F5.48 We compute the capitalized R&D going back to the start of MNC's life [F5.11]. Since not all R&D survives we apply the diminution due to ongoing development and maintenance in hardware and software, computed to reduce earlier investments [F5.25]. The diminution is interpolated to pro-

Table F.11 MNC routine revenue contribution

Contribution to MNC revenue		$M
Distribution at 5 %	[F5.18]	19
Manufacturing net of materials	[F5.34]	69
Management	[F2.27]	34
Research and Development	[F2.27]	Excluded
Capital cost	[F2.27]	9
Total revenue contributions		$131M

Table F.12 Capitalization of prior MNC R&D costs

Relative year	−5	−4	−3	−2	−1	0	Totals: organic, with acq's	
R&D spending	13.8	17.3	34.6	51.8	69.1	86.4	$273.0M	$393.0M
Diminution	41 %	56 %	66 %	81 %	96 %	100 %	←Going back	
Diminished R&D	5.6	9.7	22.9	35.3	42.1	86.4	$233.0M	$353.1M
Capitalized R&D	16.7	23.8	45.9	69.2	89.5	95.4	$340.4M	$473.0M
Conch share @44 % with distribution							$149.8M	$215.4M

Table F.13 Capitalization of IWWID prior R&D costs

Relative year		−1	0	totals
R&D spending	$M	15.0	35.0	$50.0M
Diminution	(1–30 %)	70 %	100 %	←Going back
Diminished R&D	$M	10.5	35.0	$45.5M
Capitalized R&D	$M	14.1	38.7	$52.8M

vide the annual diminution for 6 years, as shown in Table F.12 and then applied to the R&D spending.

The remaining R&D investments can then be capitalized. R&D is considered high risk, so again we use a high capitalization rate of 22 % [F5.23]. The value for MNC's R&D investment at the buy-in time becomes $340.4M. Applying the 44 % RAB for CONCH leaves $149.8M for the full share. With the acquisitions the CONCH share is $215.4M.

F5.49 IWWID had spent $75M over 2 years developing its Internet technology. Those expenses will be capitalized similarly to R&D investments. Without a known diminution we use a standard reduction of R&D of 30 % per year; the result is shown in Table F.13.

IWWID replaces the 7 % distribution share, but leads to increased sales outside the USA, and those revenue benefit MNC in the USA as well. The selling price (the IFP) of the Maniacs distributed by IWWID is the same, so that the same total margin of 41.1 % applies (Table A.1). The total R&D margin is unchanged as well and stays at 25 %.

F5.50 IWWID's research innovations increase sales, benefiting both IWWID and MNC in the USA; the prices charged to the customer remain the same, so that the margins on revenue are the same. MNC contributed $215.4M and IWWID, $52.8M. The nonroutine part of the margin was 41 % − 5 % = 36 %. To account for its additional contribution IWWID sales deserve a margin of (36 % × $(215.4 + $52.8)M/$215.4M) ≈ 45 %. However, since the margins are fixed, we estimate that the royalty that IWWID should pay MNC for the nonroutine rights to sell Maniacs should be adjusted from the base rate 27.1 % [F5.47]. The adjustment makes the rate 27.1 % × 36 %/45 % ≈ 21.7 %, or 26.7 % total after a 5 % routine cost-plus markup. In practice, all actual payments should be readjusted.

F5.51 CONCH continues to receive income and will pay MNC according to the set royalty rate revenue of 27.1 % as long the cost-sharing arrangement remains in force [F5.47]. While this rate is high, one has to consider that CONCH is actually just an agent for MNC outside the USA and owes its entire value and existence to its parent.

To estimate the value of the royalty payments at the 27.1 % rate, we again use only the expected income. Beyond 26 years the remainder is estimated using Gordon's rule. The future growth is based on last year's RAB and income growth and a discount rate of 8 %, based on MNCs Weighted Average Cost of Capital (WACC) [Fernandez:13]. The total income after the buy-in is estimated to be $2,971M; the discounted NPV is $804M.

F5.52 The Roll-over Valuation Method (RO-VM) depends on having a leverage factor *m* for research investments. An annual rate of return (RoA) between 20 and 35 % equates over a 7½ year life to a leverage factor of 1.5–2.6, with an average of 2.0.

F5.53 The capitalizations of R&D expenses used in the roll-over method (RO-VM) and those in the profit-split methods (PS-M) to allocate MNC's contribution are similar [F5.48]. For the roll-over method the R&D was capitalized from the start of MNC. Since not all R&D survives, a loss factor is applied annually reducing the prior investments. For a prospective valuation we do not know the fraction of loss in the future, and simply apply a survival factor 2/3 to the IP capitalization. Such a high loss rate is appropriate for research where feasibility has not yet been proven. Estimates in the literature have used 4/5 [Damodaran:00]. The result, based on a 2/3 survival factor, is in Table 5.12. The surviving R&D spending becomes <10 % of the total after 5 years into the past. At that level it can again be ignored, so that the R&D aggregation is limited to 6 years.

F5.54 For MNC the research expenses were 23 % of the 5-year prior years' revenues, namely 23 % of ~$(375, 620, 866, 1,059, 1,161)M. The spending becomes less significant as the IP ages in subsequent years, ~$(86, 97, 108, 121, 136)M, as shown on the top line of Table 5.12. R&D is risky, so we use a published capitalization rate of 22 % with a midyear adjustment [Veritas:09]. Actually, early investments would warrant a higher rate, and later R&D spending a lower rate [SlavinK:06]. For a more mature company such a variable adjustment should be considered, since eventually many expenses booked as R&D mainly contribute to IP maintenance.

F5.55 The computation used here keeps the capitalization rate simply fixed. Applying the capitalization rate to the organic, technical R&D investment during the initial 6-years yields a past research cost of $187.7M.

During the last year 50 % of the intellectual capital acquired, $135M, is to be added assuming that half of the acquisition was R&D, making the total $323M. The R&D investments can be capitalized every subsequent year, and, although reduced by the loss factor [F5.53], keep increasing, representing a component of the value of MNC.

F5.56 To gain reliability in the estimate of the R&D capitalization, the computation is performed three times, using the planned R&D spending for 1 and 2 years after the buy-in. The investments in later acquisitions are ignored. Only the two additional results and the 3-year total, \$709.7M, are shown in Table 5.13.

F5.57 For the computation of the income we ignore the delay between completion of research and product availability. Since we don't have any actual data, we use here the income expectations by management. Not using actual data here violates the principle of the RO-VM approach since the computation of the leverage factor m should be based on actual experience, which we don't have.

To compute the aggregate income data over a long time span more data are required than our MNC model has. We proceed with what we have. For the earnings we use the organic revenues as of the start of MNC, and reduce the revenues by the earnings margin of 41 % in effect at the time of the buy-in. These earnings already account for ongoing R&D expenses, since that spending is needed to sustain the earnings. In practice it will be hard to maintain a 41 % earnings margin. We also ignore taxes here, being aware that MNC has initiated an effective tax avoidance strategy for CONCH. For the period we used the life obtained earlier, 7.5 years [F4.9].

F5.58 The leverage factor m becomes \$4,899/\$710 = 6.9. The nonroutine discounted earnings in Table 5.12 average nearly 7× the capitalized research costs, expenses which generate those earnings shown in Table 5.13. This is a very attractive ratio, explained by the high margins that MNC enjoys. As companies become more mature, we'd expect the earnings margin and hence the RO-VM estimate of the leverage factor to reduce.

F5.59 The expected value of earnings is then V = m × C = 6.9 × \$187.7M = \$1,295M and is, of course, close to the actual result at the buy-in date used here, \$1,465M. This income stream is equivalent to what shareholders expect. Multiplying this amount by the 44 % RAB for CONCH leaves \$570M for its roll-over valuation.

F5.60 The effect of R&D on actual income is delayed by the development lag (1.2 years [F5.27]) and the sales lag (about 5 years [F3.3]). The RO-VM leverage factor m predicts earnings of 6.9 × \$86.5M ≈ \$597M after 6.2 years beyond the buy-in.

At the fixed R&D ratio the nonroutine income at that time is only \$459.6M [F5.10]. It appears that early R&D expenses had not yet paid off in the income interval used to compute the leverage factor. We will encounter that effect when comparing the result from the RO-VM valuation with the results of other valuations in Table 5.13.

However, at that time the actual modeled nonroutine income had grown to \$630.6M. The assets of the acquisition being valued should, of course, be ignored here. At the time of creating a contemporaneous valuation report, they may already appear on the books and create income, and that has to be checked.

The actual results include the effect of acquisitions, which replaced some organic R&D spending, and create income faster. Balancing the predicted organic result and the actual result, we obtain an average of \$(459.6, 630.6)M ≈ \$545.1M. The simple point prediction, while in mid range, is only adequate for a general guess.

F5.61 Following Fig. 5.12 the capitalization on the books allowed by GAAP at MNC can start 1.4 years prior to the completion of the software. The reduced R&D expenses eligible for capitalization during that time are \$114M, which become \$118M at the 22 % capitalization rate, or 63 % of the \$188M [F5.45] total capitalization. Starting the R&D capitalization depends on a decision to consider the product creation feasible. R&D staff rarely communicate such information to corporate accountants. Capitalization only starts if there is some benefit, while expensing reduces taxes. There may actually be loss if the company is receiving R&E credits.

F5.62 We only sketch the computation of the option value MIPov of the MobiIP acquisition. Given that the decision to actually develop, manufacture, and sell ManiMobiles is made a year later, and that actual sales start after 2 years, the expected sales curve starts 3 years out. The positive value itself is computed the same way as the primary benefit, starting at the assumed decision point, minus the price of the MobiIP acquisition.

The option benefits only accrue if the decision is to go ahead, so they must be multiplied by the probability p_{build} of making that positive decision. The Net Present Value (NPV) discounts all alternatives to bring all results back to the acquisition date.

$$MIPov = -price(MobiIP) + p_{build} \times NPV(G) + (1 - p_{build}) \times NPV(N)$$

where

$$G = (income - \cos ts)\, from\, ManiMobile$$

and

$$N = salvage\_value(MobiIP).$$

The carrying costs of the investment on MobiIP over the additional period to the decision point are incorporated into the NPV [BarIlanS:96]. A p_{build} of 60 % and a delay of 3 years reduce MNC's RO-VM expected leverage of investment from 6.9 [F5.58] to 3.3 for MobiIP, which makes the acquisition still quite worthwhile. We assume that there were no alternate, better investments and that the salvage value of MobiIP is zero. Any costs of abandoning MobiIP, as personnel separation charges, are ignored as well.

F5.63 For the \$300M acquisitions around the time of the buy-in, the value of the IP obtained by MNC was 90 % of \$300M = \$270M. At the 42 % RAB for CONCH used by ATA the cost-sharing payment that is due to MNC for those acquisitions is 42 % of \$270M ≈ \$113M.

A more relevant result is obtained by considering the future offshore income that the acquisitions will bring, since the main focus is on the market outside of the USA, where mobile technology has a higher penetration. We use the RAB based on sales foreseen over the next 2 years, 44.8 %, and obtain a valuation of $121M.

A corresponding calculation for the second round of acquisitions produces $202M.

F5.64 Table Ch5.13 summarizes the data of seven valuations. The simple statistical average is $783.0M, with a range of $385.2M, or 49 %, while the standard deviation is $121.4M, or 16 % of the mean. The range is uncomfortably large. Much of that is due to the low estimate produced by the M7, RO-VM method. That method is based on MNC's past experience, high R&D expenses that have not yet returned as much income. If we remove extreme values, namely the two that are more than 1.0 standard deviation from the mean, we get a range of $223.3M or 29 %, which is quite acceptable for methods based on very different principles.

Economists prefer to select trustworthy values by using the interquartile range, described in Appendix D. The conventional interquartile of the three central values is $799.6M. The IRS method gives a mean of $789.5M [F5.65]. Since all are estimates in a similar range, we will, at times, just use the common interquartile mean, namely $800M.

F5.65 The highest interquartile value is $839.0M for the MC-VM and the lowest is $778.9M for the CUT-VM, a range of $60.1M or 7.5 %. The IRS sanctioned interquartile computation uses the average of the results at the breakpoints ($864.6M, $723.0M) and produces a mean of $789.5M. Using the IRS specified formulas, the interquartile range is [B.1.2 #1(e)(2)(iii)(C)]

$$\$864.6M - \$723M = \$60.1M$$

Or

$$\$60.1M \,/\, \$789.5M = 17.9\% \textit{ of the IRS mean}$$

After removing outliers, both the statistical and the interquartile range are quite tight for greatly varying methods and data derivations. The tight range of the results shown was not foreseen during the creation of the MNC valuation model. I was surprised that they were so close. Using the same data from a consistent underlying model helps of course.

F5.66 The ATA proposed fraction for the buy-in is 6.25 % of the interquartile mean of the seven methods evaluated for the buy-in, and 8.8 % of the very low RO-VM valuation.

F5.67 The ATA proposed fraction of the initial cost-shared acquisition versus the result produced in Sect. 5.2.8 (M8) is $21.0M/$121M = 17.4 %. ATA also used a PP-VM approach, but assigned much of the intellectual capital obtained to goodwill. That goodwill that was not allocated to the offshore division, CONCH.

F5.68 The two expert economists hired by the IRS estimated the buy-in values in this case at $2,500M based on the MC-VM and at $1,675M based on an Inc-VM [F5.7]. A problem was that by using Gordon's formula it appeared that they claimed "intangibles as if they have a perpetual useful life" [OatesO:11]. They were challenged by the taxpayer's lawyers and experts, and the IRS lost the case [Veritas:09]. The taxpayer had proposed $166M, only 7.95 % of the mean of the two IRS expert's valuations [Morgan:10]. The final settlement also involved a $9.6M trademark adjustment to be added to the buy-in. Complexities included that at the time Veritas also had a shareholder and an SEC suit pending.

Other information, from an arms-length transaction, came to light later, but could not affect the extremely low valuation outcome set in the court case [F5.7].

F.6 Chapter 6, Taxhaven Formulas

F6.1 A former IRS commissioner showed that 23 % of corporate 1996 earnings escaped taxation by not appearing on the books [Rossotti:05]. More recently the total earnings of US resident companies from 2005 to 2010 are provided by the US Department of Commerce [BEA:11]. The data lack detail, and do not distinguish earnings from tangible versus intangible products. To provide a generally applicable historical overview we exclude the recession years (2008–2009) and use $1,550B annually as being typical.

For Fig. 6.4, $1,250B is used as typical domestic earnings and $300B as the typical foreign earnings, after subtracting $100B foreign expenses [DesaiH:04]. For instance, in 2006 20 % of US worldwide income, over $300B was kept out of the USA as being deferred shown as line *b*) in Table F.14 [Barthold:11]. Other sources for Table F.14 are *a*) [BEA:11], *c*) [CBO:08] and [CBO:11], *d*) [IRS-ST:09].

The totals of domestic and foreign earnings are greater than the total corporate earnings because of payments to foreign suppliers and governments. Some of those expenses are foreign income taxes that will be cred-

Table F.14 Taxes paid by corporations

Amounts in $B		2005	2006	2007	2008	2009	2010
Corp. Earnings	*a*	1,501.100	1,572.300	1,510.700	1,262.800	1,258.000	1,624.800
Domestic		1,261.600	1,315.500	1,159.800	851.500	905.700	1,241.000
Foreign		384.100	434.400	510.600	571.800	480.600	568.500
Moved abroad	*b*	300.000	314.500	351.400	399.200	455.400	524.500
Total US Taxes	*c*	1,998.326	2,093.110	2,011.105	1,681.091	1,674.701	2,163.000
Corp. Taxes		420.455	427.182	370.000	364.000	356.000	334.000
On Foreign	*d*	10.000	10.000	10.000	10.000	10.000	10.000

ited, and as such lower the taxes much more than deductions for common business costs, as described in Appendix E.

A 2003 US treasury study showed that \$293B of the domestic earnings, or 30 %, was designated as belonging to taxhavens and untaxed [Shropshire:09]. That process is accelerating, given the growth of the economy and the increased use of taxhavens, amounting to 5.6 × earnings between 2000 and 2010 for 30 big companies [CoyD:11]. Some of the increase can be ascribed to the growth of the US economy and GDP. However, that calculation, 19 % annually, leads to an estimate over the 2005–2010 span of \$662B per year if applied to all foreign deferrals. Our calculation, used for Table F.14, considers only half of that growth. In combination we use a modest estimate of \$400B.

Only a small fraction of corporate foreign earnings is taxed. The amount of foreign corporate taxes is based on the 0.4 % foreign corporate income recognized by the IRS, which at the same tax rate as effective for domestic corporations would yield about \$5B in tax revenues, or \$7.5B if taxed at the full US statutory rate. Since multinational corporations contributed only \$16B in taxes in 2007, we use \$10B as a generous contribution from foreign earnings [Tichon:09]. A much larger number, \$50B, has been proposed with data from 1973 to 2000 using stylized rules and statutory tax rates to determine what a company should pay annually, namely \$20B directly and \$30B assuming that there is no long-term deferral [DesaiH:04]. That analysis did recognize that there has been a recent sharp reduction in corporate foreign taxes received. CONCH paid relatively much because of its cost-sharing obligations.

F6.2 Estimated corporate tax collections for 2011 and 2012 were \$333B and \$354B [CBO:08]. Actual collection, because of the recession and many incentives, was only \$194B in 2011, with an expectation for 2012 now of \$333BM [OMB:11b]. Beyond that date estimates are uncertain, because in 2012 taxation is under active discussion in the US Congress. For the span 2005–2010, discounting the recession years 2008 and 2009, we obtain an average of \$370B. The corporate tax collected is much lower than our estimate based on prior years. Corporate tax collections were much less as the 2008 recession took hold, and have not recovered as much as other tax revenues. Given the data from [F6.1] taxes on domestic earnings are, now in billions, \$370B − \$10B = \$360B, leaving \$490B. That reduction is likely due to the general trend of reduced corporate tax reduction, shown in Fig. 9.3. Those are, at least in part, due to increased government incentives for US companies. These include a combination of credits for domestic manufacturing and for R&D expenses, increased deductions due to expensing of investments and inventory treatment, and growing use of taxhavens.

F6.3 Available for investments in taxhavens by US multinational corporations every year is about \$400B + \$300B − \$10B = \$690B [F6.1], [F6.2].Any active investments in relevant projects should be subtracted, but given the growth of funds in taxhavens, that seems like a modest fraction. Already in

2001 the amount of sheltering was documented to be about $150B annually, and was rapidly rising, as shown in Fig. 9.8 [Shropshire:09].

F6.4 From [F6.1] we can derive that the uncollected potential US federal taxes at an average corporate rate of 33 % [Cray:09] amounts to $(140 + 95)B = $235B. Other estimates yield numbers of a loss of $174B and $292B. Given the growth of the GDP one would have expected $502B of corporate income taxes, or $(502 – 370)B ≈ $132B more than in 2000.

F6.5 Additional data and validations for Fig. 6.4 come from a variety of sources. US investment available in 1992 was $300B. US-source income of $293B was sent offshore for tax year 2003; 68.4 %, or ~$200.5B, flowed to foreign corporations through both Qualified Intermediaries and US Withholding Agents, with only 1.4 % or $3B withheld tor taxation [Shropshire:09].

Average 2006–2010 US corporate taxes were $370B [IRS-SC:12], of which about $30B was for miscellaneous other taxes, leaving $340B. US corporate income was $1,550B [F6.1]. The split of US corporate dividends and investment is based on [FeldsteinHH:95]; the fraction of dividends would be less for high-tech industries. At the US statutory rate corporate income taxes from US sources would be $(1,250–300)B × 35 % = $332B.

F6.6 Worldwide shipping has about $500B annual revenues, and Greek companies control nearly 16 %. At the Greek 35 % corporate tax rate, Greek ship owners manage to avoid about $28B in taxes, an amount equal to about 55 % of the annual Greek deficit of $51B in 2009, by registering their vessels in Liechtenstein and similar taxhavens [Marisec:10].

F6.7 Forest Labs' Irish operation FLI has a $5 cost per unit and pays $12 to FLH in Bermuda. The markup of 5 % generates $0.85 earnings per unit and, at the Irish 12.5 % annual tax rate, generates $0.11 tax revenue per unit, or $5.7M on the equivalent of 54M units sold. On the income booked at FFBV Amsterdam of $64 per unit the taxable amounts in Europe would be $0.40 per unit or $21.6M total. European Union rules and Irish territorial taxation avoid collecting those taxes.

F6.8 In 2009 Ireland spent 0.3 % of its GDP on job training, a rate 7.5 × the US rate [Bennett:11U]. Based on a GDP of $227B, that spending amounts to over $600M. That is over 16 % of Ireland's corporate 2010 tax revenues of $3,900M actual receipts.

F6.9 There were 26,342 foreign affiliates of 2,270 US multinational companies in 2006, or 11.6 average per company [Jackson:10]. Foreign companies had 10,941 affiliates in the USA. The number varies greatly. Enron alone had 3,500 domestic and foreign subsidiary entities at the time of its bankruptcy in December 2001. Its foreign subsidiaries booked 83 % of the corporate losses. Enron paid taxes only 1 year between 1996 and 2001, at a rate of 0.063 % of its revenues. The many subsidiaries and Special Purpose Entities (SPFs) of Enron are too complex to understand by any single individual [Schwarcz:04].

F6.10 A low effective tax rate is the primary hint that a country is a taxhaven, especially if nondomestic corporations are not taxed, but others, including natural persons, are taxed [KesslerE:06]. Additional metrics to validate taxhavens shown in Table 6.1 are:

(A) A large fraction of aggregate net income of CFCs of US companies
(B) A large number of corporations compared to its population
(C) An unusually high revenues or profit per employee
(D) A large amount of booked assets per employee
(E) A large amount of funds flowing through the country relative to its GDP.

The information on taxhaven criteria A and F is from [MarkleS:09], using [BEA:09]. Criterion D is used by [Sullivan:11]. The revenue generated per employee of MNC worldwide is \$0.215M; in comparison, by criterion D, Singapore overall is not a taxhaven. MNC has no employees in Palm Island; if the effort of ATA employees on MNC accounts there are counted, the value of criterion D would be extremely high. Most of MNC's offshore employees are at the MNC JB factory in Malaysia; their individual earnings would match Singapore's.

About 70 countries are candidates for becoming prime taxhavens [Savodnik:13]. Recent data are found in [Hines:10H] and [Shaxson:11].

F6.11 The GDP of Greater London is \$414B and its population is about 7.8 million. The City of London's share is 14 % or \$58B while its population is about 5,000 [Roberts:08].

F6.12 The cost of moving a 20' long "T1" shipping container from Singapore to Trieste is about \$1700. It can hold, with allowance for packing, nearly 900 Maniacs, yielding a shipping cost of \$2 per Maniac [Marisec:06].

F.7 Chapter 7, Taxation of MNC Formulas

F7.1 We use values computed by ATA, \$50M [F2.10], and the statistical average of seven computed valuations, \$783M [F5.64] as the benchmarks, so that the ATA estimate is 50/783 = 6.4 % of the mean.

F7.2 The full range of the seven valuations was \$385M, or 385/783 ≈ 49 % [F5.64]. Refinements can remove the outliers and narrow the range [F5.65]. Other parameters are shown in Table 5.13.

F7.3 The price proposed by ATA for CONCH was \$50M. The known first-year net earnings after taxes on all remittances to the USA and the loan repayment for CONCH are \$57.7M. Using that valuation, the p/e multiple for CONCH is only 1.24, indicating an unreasonable price by business expectations. Textbooks indicate that a very desirable investment might have a p/e of 5 or below, 10 being average [BodieKM:08]. When investors expect growing earnings, an acceptable p/e multiple will yet be higher.

F7.4 Removing the outliers leaves the three results M1, M3, and M4 for an interquartile range of \$60.1M, which is 7.5 % of the conventional interquartile mean of \$799.6M. The results produced by the IRS methods give an interquartile mean of \$842M and a 21 % range. We can see how easily conformance between incomes reported to shareholders and the tax authorities is lost [F9.36]. For approximate results we can use a rounded average of \$800M [F5.64].

F7.5 The ATA estimate of \$50M is only 6.25 % of the reliable interquartile mean. It is also only 8.8 % of the lowest of the seven valuations made in Chap. 5, the M7, RO-VM [F5.65].

F7.6 On a \$800M buy-in from CONCH, MNC would expect to pay \$279.9M in taxes. The savings in taxes alone due to the low valuation the first year are \$262.4M. Taxes are also due on the income from the loan repayment and interest paid by CONCH. There were also \$6M expenses in setting up this operation; the combined tax saving is \$234.6M. The long-range effect is that, from this transaction alone, CONCH accumulates over the next 20 years about \$8,300M for future offshore investments.

F7.7 ATA used the IIP-VM approach, but it allocated much intellectual capital to goodwill and did not assign any goodwill to CONCH. Because of that ATA just assessed \$50M/\$783M = 6.4 % of the fair value [F7.1] to the buy-in in Chap. 5. Even if only the technical IP is counted, at \$667M [F5.26], the ATA estimate covers only 7.5 %. Discrepancies D1, D2, and D3 in Table 7.2 are caused by this misallocation.

F7.8 Discrepancy D1 in the ATA valuation occurs because the IP box is incomplete. Just covering the identifiable technical IP, and leaving out the value of all the other intellectual capital contributing to CONCH income, is most obvious. The estimate on line D1a in Table 7.2 is based on the ratio of the technical portion of the IIP-VM at \$667M [F5.26] versus the Inc-VM at \$955M [F5.20]. That ratio reduces the buy-in valuation by 30 %. Staying within the IIP-VM approach and just omitting the value of the senior manpower lose \$258M for all of MNC [F5.3]. The omission amounts to \$144M for CONCH or 15 % of the valuation.

F7.9 Discrepancy D2 happens because ATA went by the accounting books and ignored the research in progress when estimating the IP being made available to CONCH. Since CONCH benefits from that effort, it should not be left out. Omitting valuable research, a motivation for the acquisition, reduces the buy-in valuation by 22 %.

F7.10 Discrepancy D3 is due to improper setting of IP diminution and life. ATA set the life of the IP embodied in the Maniacs' life equal to their sales' life, rather than the life of the underlying IP. ATA then used a linear diminution of IP over that life, based on conventions used for amortization. We see in Fig. 7.1 that the initial diminution rates match approximately but then diverge. The effect reduces the valuation by 35 % using the IIP-VM valuation as the base. The life of IP can be based on, or validated by, information obtained in interviews with MNC engineers. However, working engineers are not trained in IP valuation, and will consider anything that can be replaced as being obsolete. They can also be presented with counterfactuals, as

"How long would the software be valuable if there is no further maintenance?"

"... pre-existing product intangibles would "wither on the vine" within 2 to 4 years without ongoing R&D." [Veritas:09]

The response to such a hypothetical question is not a valid basis for a valuation [AF:04]. Any software business manager knows that maintenance is essential [Glass:03]. During the interviews, the engineers were not asked to consider the actual situation at CONCH, which will continue to benefit from improved Maniacs being continually developed at MNC. Interviewed engineers also failed to consider that an initial steep diminution is not appropriate for ongoing development and IP maintenance, as shown in Fig. 5.7.

F7.11 Discrepancies D4a, b are due to estimating the lag based on recent experience with product model gestation intervals. Currently the software only undergoes maintenance and can be rapidly refreshed. That current lag in Maniac development causes an estimated reduction in the valuation of $91M, reducing the valuation to $870M or ~90 % of the Inc-VM [F2.20]. This correction still does not represent a true arm's-length correction, as summarized in Table 5.6, where an independent company tries to make a competing product. The increased lag causes a shift of the diminution to be applied to the income over the remaining life.

The average release interval for Maniac is 2.86 years, giving an effective lag of 1.2 years [F5.27]. But at the time of the buy-in less information was known. Past intervals had averaged out to 28 months, but were now about 36 months. Changing the lag from 12 to 32 months, but applying a 37 % centroid appropriate for a growing mature company (Fig. 3.5) instead of the simplistic 50 %, leaves 89 % of the Inc-VM estimate. Discounting that effect increases the relative loss to 17 % because early income is more affected by the lag. Figure 5.7 showed the effect of life and lag combined.

In a comprehensive valuation the effect of a poor estimate of the diminution curve interacts with the expected income distribution. If such a valuation purports to assess an arm's-length situation, the "arm's-length lag" should be estimated [F5.29].

F7.12 Discrepancy D4c is due to a simplistic estimate of the centroid position. Incorporated in the effects described is a mitigating effect. The simplistic linear diminution yields a lag centroid position at 0.5 of the gestation period. The actual diminution of Maniac hardware and software produces a centroid at 0.41 of the gestation period, decreasing the computed result by 22 % [W:08]. Since the effect of a misestimated centroid is incorporated in the result of [F7.11], it will not be a factor in [F7.19].

F7.13 Discrepancy D5 is due to an excessive discount rate. Assuming that the risks which CONCH incurs in this transaction are those of a high-technology company, ATA applied a high discount rate of 20.47 % [Veritas:09]. Later ATA used a low 8 % for an interest rate [F7.18].

However, CONCH is actually a continuation of existing operations. In the IIP-VM valuation we applied a more realistic discount ratio to the income at CONCH, namely 15 %. This rate difference can be applied to a steady income stream, yielding a reduction in the IIP-VM valuation of 80 %. If the high rate is applied to the expected, but unlagged, incomes, the reduction becomes 71 %. If applied to the NPV of these incomes, the reduction becomes 79 %. A later section in Chap. 7 analyzes the effect of excessive assignment of risk, when the payments by CONCH to MNC are based on royalties. For simplicity we use the 80 % for a steady stream as being representative in our estimates.

F7.14 Discrepancy D6 is due to assessing a meaningless "nonexclusive license" clause. Since the licensing contract issued to CONCH specified that the rights were not exclusive, ATA applied a 3 %/7 % = 43 % reduction to the CONCH IP share, using general numbers for arm's-length licenses from the public literature [Razgaitis:03]. However, there would never be a benefit to MNC in licensing competitors since all of CONCH's earnings flow to MNC. MNC has no intent to set up offshore distributors outside of CONCH.

The reason for MNC's management putting a nonexclusive clause into the licensing contract is because CONCH has no actual personnel on Palm Island. MNC needs the freedom to negotiate contracts with all purchasers, including US-based headquarters of multinationals, that would be receiving Maniacs directly offshore. CONCH will still receive all income from offshore deliveries. The contract clause actually enhances the benefits flowing offshore rather than reducing them.

F7.15 Discrepancy D7 occurs because the RAB (Reasonably Anticipated Benefit) ratio used is based on revenue. When ATA assessed the share for CONCH, it used 42 % based on the current sales ratio, following the prior contracts which MNC had made with its distributing CFCs, which were based on royalties applied to sales. Using the sales fraction favors CONCH. All alternatives shown in Table 4.1 would have made the fraction larger and increased the amount which MNC would have received in the USA.

Conceptually CONCH should pay according to its share of net income, initially 44 %. But sales revenue was used, at 42 %, as is common in arm's-length settings to avoid accounting trickery by the licensee. There is no reason, when all parties are within the MNC umbrella, to use a revenue base. The difference reduces the buy-in by another 5 %.

F7.16 Discrepancy D8 is because the benefit ratio is not updated. ATA kept the fraction of benefits, the RAB ratio, fixed into the future. It used the RAB based on sales as of the valuation date, 42 % [F5.8]. Over the 20 years of Maniac sales the RAB was expected to increase to 54 %. We estimate a correction based on the 15 % discounted income. Applying a corrected RAB ratio shows that the fixed RAB generates only 86 % of the expected discounted benefits into the future.

F7.17 Discrepancy D9 is due to the true loan being set according to a buy-in value that is much too low. The interest cost of a \$50M loan over 5 years at 8 % paid quarterly, i.e., 20 periods at 2 %, using the "CumInt" spreadsheet function, is

$$Cost = \$(CumInt(2\ \%, 20, -50))M = \$11.157M.$$

If the full value of the IP, \$783M [F7.1], would have to be paid, the loan would have to be proportionally bigger. In this hypothetical situation the full interest costs for the start-up loan to CONCH would be \$182.3M over the initial 5 years. The net cost would be less, \$159M, because corporate interest payments are deductible from earnings. Not paying for the full value of the buy-in alone reduces the buy-in to 83 % of what it would otherwise be.

F7.18 Discrepancy D10 is due to an inappropriate low interest rate for the loan taken out to start CONCH. The rate charged by MNC to CONCH was 8 %, which fell within the safe harbor criteria of being between the Federal rates of 6.45 % and 1.3 × 6.45 % = 8.4 %, and may be hard to challenge [B.1.2 #2(a)(2)(iii)(B)(1)]. That safe harbor rate was established to put limits on financial manipulations, where high interest rates can lower taxes, but that safe harbor can be cited here, inappropriately, for MNC's offshoring plans.

Allowing CONCH to be funded by MNC at the interest rate which MNC experiences, rather than at an arm's-length interest rate a new venture would be charged, reduces the cost to MNC and reduces the buy-in valuation substantially.

An external banker would have to regard a CONCH-like entity operating at arm's length a fairly risky proposition. A loan to a venture with just a nonexclusive license to MNC's IP and no rights of access to the workforce warrants a much higher interest rate. Just applying a reasonable 18 % cost-of-money rate at CONCH has the effect of reducing the buy-in to 98 %. But an acceptable interest rate should actually be applied to the full amount, determined in [F7.16]. The combination reduces the effect of the buy-in to 49 %. We will not use that number in [F5.19], since in practice the entire CONCH licensing transaction now becomes unreasonable.

F7.19 The product of the relevant reductions due to the Discrepancies from [F7.8] to [F7.18] is 10.0 % or 4.0 % depending if low or high reduction factors are used. All of these numbers are rough approximations, since they compare a model based on consistent data with a counterfactual and impossible situation. In general, having many unidirectional adjustments within the accuracy bounds of economic projections has a huge effect. This is no magic, after all 10 misvaluations to the low side of just 20 % reduce a 100 % entry to $(100\ \% - (1 - 20\ \%)^{10}) = 10.7\ \%$.

Each of the ten items in Table 7.2 is indeed difficult to value reliably. There is "great potential for differing interpretations of both facts and the law, and significant procedural latitude" [LeveyW:07].

F7.20 ATA's actual calculation for the CONCH share of the buy-in was as follows: ignore workforce, and raise the amount of goodwill, leaving only the technical IP, \$600M. Then do a linear diminution, and ignore lag, obtaining \$119M for all of MNC intangibles. That is already much less than the market cap minus tangibles shown in MNC's balance sheet. Then use the past RAB on sales, setting the buy-in prices at \$50M. That amount is 6 % of the \$830M average interquartile valuation obtained in Chap. 5.

F7.21 At the US federal tax rate of 35 % MNC would have paid in the buy-in year on its \$250M earnings, about \$87.5M. With 44 % of net income now being accumulated at CONCH, only \$55M tax is due on the remaining US earnings. That year MNC receives three quarterly installments for the amortization and the interest on the loan of \$50M MNC took out to set up CONCH, another \$9.2M. The loan to CONCH is a business expense, reducing MNC's taxable income by \$50.0M. The net effect of the loan reduces taxes to be paid by 35 % × \$(50.0 – 9.2)M = \$14.3M. Now the total taxes due that year by MNC are \$39.7M. This computation just show the effect of the IP movement to CONCH and ignores other gains and losses which MNC incurs, for instance due to cost sharing of R&D and acquisitions. The buy-in installments only last 5 years. After those 5 years the federal taxes paid are reduced to about \$29M annually, plus increases due to growth of US income.

As more IP generation is supported from funds collected at CONCH, the US share of taxes on nonroutine profits keeps getting smaller. Of course, changes in taxes being paid year to year are common, and reflect normal variations in business. Relating changes in US income to an export of IP is not obvious to accountants who do not see the transfers of IP on corporate books.

F7.22 The federal taxes which would be due if the full value of the IP buy-in, \$817M, were to be paid by CONCH, again over 5 years with an 8 % interest rate, would be \$52M in the first year after the deduction from taxable income for the investment, and \$69M in the next 4 years. The deductions would create an unreasonably high loss that year as well, although such losses can be carried forward. Without the deductions the total tax bill for MNC would then be over \$122M. In practice, a different business strategy would be devised. In any case, MNC might not be able to borrow the entire amount needed to set up CONCH. There would also be less motivation to move IP to an offshore taxhaven without the immediate tax avoidance it allows.

F7.23 For a 5-year period the amortization and interest payments on a loan for the full valuation amount would become \$193M annually at the 8 % interest rate. The first year's payment skips the first quarter and is only \$145M. The annual payments would be \$243M at the 18 % interest rate. Those amounts exceed the earnings at CONCH by a factor of two. Of course, the repayments could be repaid from the loan itself, making it all a sham transaction [Schlunk:00]. Sham "round-tripping" transactions are disallowed, but become hard to track when multiple active business operations are involved [DesaiFH:01].

F7.24 A schedule to the pay the loan off at an 8 % rate takes 14 years, using all the income. No capital would be accumulated and CONCH could not even pay its cost share and could not participate in the AJCA acquisitions. Its IP rights would diminish, further reducing its earnings. At an 18 % rate the debt accumulates faster than it is being paid off, a familiar story for people having credit card balances.

F7.25 A loan based on IIP-VM of $781M amounts to 35 % of MNC's market cap of $2117M. CONCH would need a loan of that size just to pay MNC for the value of the IP rights it received. Even relative to the bottom range of the interquartiles the valuation is still 32.6 %. Any repayment terms would have to change drastically to allow CONCH to build up the capital needed for repayment.

F7.26 In a documented case that went to court, the relationships were similar [F5.7]. Veritas' advisors valued the buy-in of IP to its Irish subsidiary at $166M, using an RAB for Ireland being somewhat over 40 % [Veritas:09]. That RAB was later reduced to 26 %. The IRS challenged the buy-in amount and employed two experts in succession valuing the buy-in at $2,500M and $1,675M [OatesO:11]. Given their average, the challenged buy-in amounted to ~8 % of the IRS estimates [F5.7]. Only $545M taxes were paid [Davis:09].

F7.27 The initial round of acquisitions by MNC cost $300; the IP component was $270M [F5.63]. They were paid half in stock, half in cash. CONCH only has to cost share the part paid as cash. While the acquisition round started earlier, 60 % of the acquisitions closed after the buy-in and became part of the cost-share obligation. The payment was next year, when the income ratio of CONCH was 44.5 %. CONCH paid

$$\$270M\ /\ 2 \times 60\ \% \times 44.5\% = \$36.1M.$$

CONCH also transferred the US tax due by MNC making the total amount repatriated $55.5M, of which $19.4M are taxes computed at 35 %. CONCH has now received IP rights from initial the acquisitions valued at $270M × 44.5 % = $120M.

F7.28 The earnings at CONCH for the first 5 years are shown in Table F.15. It assumes a risk-free interest rate of 3.75. %.

F7.29 For the first round of acquisitions ATA started with the total acquisition price of $300M. ATA then deducted $30M for the tangibles which remain in the USA. The accountants had booked $150M of the acquisitions as goodwill, leaving $120M. From the remaining intangibles ATA subtracted $30M for a control premium, $25M for research in process which could not be booked, and $15M for the workforce in place, using replacement cost estimates of $100K for each of the 150 total employees. $50M was left, and at the 42 % RAB the CONCH share became $21M.

F7.30 MNC had issued stock worth also $150M to pay for half of the initial acquisitions. If CONCH would be truly an arm's-length operation, it would have had to pay its RAB share, $66M, for that stock. Because there is actually joint ownership, that stock issue was not charged to CONCH. CONCH

Table F.15 Earnings retained at CONCH

Year relative to buy-in	1	2	3	4	5	Totals	
Income from operations	110.0M	118.0M	126.3M	135.1M	145.6M	634M	
Loan repayment	(9.2M)	(12.2M)	(12.2M)	(12.2M)	(12.2M)	(58M)	
R&D Cost-share payment	(38.0M)	(43.1M)	(48.8M)	(55.3M)	(62.7M)	(248M)	
Acquisition share & tax		(55.5M)				[F7.27]	
Service reimbursements	(4.7)	(11.3)	(12.0)	(12.7)	(13.4)	(54.1)	
Retained earnings	67.5M	18.5M	77.2M	80.2M	83.1M	327M	
Interest on aggregate	2.5M	3.3M	6.3M	9.6M	13.1M	11.4M	34.4M
Available for investment next year		$70M	$92M	$175M	$265M	$361M	$373M

received all of the benefits while paying only half. Counterfactual assumptions, as arm's-length relationships, are selectively misused.

F7.31 A market cap-based valuation would be based on the $272M, the sum of the market value of the acquired companies. MNC paid actually $300M, or a $28M control premium. Of those costs, $28M were tangibles that could not be shared by CONCH, leaving $242M. CONCH benefits from all other intellectual capital. The CONCH share according to the current RAB (44.8 %) then becomes $112.8M.

F7.32 At the end of a 5-year period CONCH has $373M capital in hand [F7.28], but MNC expects another $302M in earnings to be collected in its offshore accounts over the next 3 years, as well as $49M in interest. Those $675M should be invested more profitably than in 3.75 % Euromarket bonds [Roberts:01]. Since investing in bonds does not count as an active investment, it also risks being threatened with US taxation of passive holdings, although many US enterprises are deferring much larger amounts [DevereuxH:03].

F7.33 The uncapitalized spending on research by MNC, cost-shared by CONCH, was $548M for the first 5 years after the buy-in and $1,058M over the 8-year period that includes the AJCA-motivated acquisitions. MNC's spending on research was already limited by the rate at which competent developers could be hired and integrated.

F7.34 The acquisitions were stretched out over a 2-year period. During that period the capital held in CONCH accounts became negative during several quarters, but MNC had enough working capital to bridge those gaps, and ongoing income at CONCH rapidly replenished those accounts. The amounts totaled $475M and at 5.25 % tax an amount of $475 × (1 − 5.25 %) = $501M, was required, close to MNC's directors' plans to spend $500M.

F7.35 During the AJCA tax holiday MNC's accounting quarters did not match the US government's. During quarters where there was a deficit CONCH paid interest to MNC. In the fourth quarter of the third year no more acquisition payments were due. The quarterly surplus of nearly $39M left a negative balance of just $0.8M in the last quarter.

F7.36 ATA started with the acquisition price of $475M. It then deducted $41M for the tangibles, which remained in the USA. The accountants had booked $210 of the acquisitions as goodwill, leaving $244M. From the remaining intangibles it subtracted $50M for a control premium, $40 for research in process, which could not be booked, and $27M for the workforce in place, using replacement cost estimates of $140K for each of the 200 acquired employees. $107M was left, and now the entire amount was assigned to CONCH, giving CONCH the rights to all of the acquired IP.

F7.37 The initial acquisitions, at the time of the buy-in, were paid with cash and stock. Since not all the intellectual capital acquired was put on the books, the shareholders' equity was diluted by more than 8 % [F7.29]. However, MNC shareholders reacted positively, so that MNC share price stayed high.

F7.38 Using the same intangible deductions used by ATA in the cost-sharing valuation for CONCH, MNC can now put 77 % for the acquisition costs on its books [F7.36].

F7.39 Much cash out of MNC's consolidated accounts was being spent for the acquisitions made in response to the AJCA legislation. Again, not all of the intellectual capital paid for was put on the books. In this round the shareholders' equity was diluted by about 7 %. Paying greatly reduced taxes on the repatriated capital meant that acquisitions were a good deal, and only a few observers noted that consolidated capital had gone down a lot, and actually reached levels equivalent to a lean start-up. MNC still looked healthy.

F7.40 CONCH paid only $50M to MNC following the ATA valuation [F7.20], but it received rights to an income stream valued between at about $800M [F5.64]. The offshore accounts at CONCH have received a gift of $700M minus an obligation to cost-share R&D expenses at MNC. MNC's R&D has a high leverage [F5.58], and can exploit that gift using the rights to the intellectual capital of its parent, MNC.

F7.41 Immediately after the buy-in, CONCH participated in the acquisitions. The acquisitions added a market value of $272M to MNC, without the control premium [F7.29]. That increase amounts to 14.76 % over MNC's prior market value of $1,850M [F2.11]. The market value allocable to CONCH at that time was $678M, and should also increase similarly by $101M to $787M. That's quite a bargain for a $21M investment [F7.28]. Such a deal would, of course, not be available to an arm's-length client.

Estimating changes in market value based on corporate actions is very unreliable, since the shareholders have to be convinced of effective execution corporate plans. In an acquisition much depends on the integration of the acquired resources with the existing MNC operation. We projected that MNC was able to manage a successful integration.

F7.42 If shareholders expect that the \$28M control premium [F7.29] paid is an intangible that would indeed yield commensurate benefits then the value of final intangibles at CONCH also increases from \$839M [F5.8] to \$851M.

F7.43 CONCH pays nearly \$100M annually for its share in MNC research [F7.33]. Initially all those funds flow to the US R&D accounts. There they are eligible for US R&E credits, as presented in Appendix E. Expenses incurred by foreign workers are not eligible. As the operation in India grows, funds for the research in India can flow directly, via MNC's CAAS intermediary, to MNC MY in India, and avoid being taxed. The ability to transfer funds extraterritorially fairly invisibly among offshore divisions is more beneficial than the US tax credits which reimburse at most 20 % of R&D expense. Within a few years the ratio of the US R&D cost and the staff in India is 3 to 1.

The ability to pay offshore workers without repatriation and taxation encourages growth offshore versus growth at the parent company. Offshore investment also reduces the passive capital held offshore, holdings that are potentially subject to US tax penalties. We did not model that benefit further, but it is implicit in the data shown in Chaps. 9 and 10.

F7.44 R&D expenses at MNC had risen as fast as is possible to grow organically. In the 5 years after the initial acquisitions they grew from \$97M annually to \$166M annually. When the American Jobs Creation Act (AJCA) was passed in 2004, providing an 85 % dividend reduction, a repatriation of nearly \$500M of funds held in CONCH was initiated, an amount 3 × current US R&D expenses. MNC used the funds to purchase \$475M worth of other US companies. MNC had to pay taxes only at a rate of 35 % × (1 − 85 %) = 5.25 %. MNC transferred from CONCH \$475M/(1 − 5.25 %) = \$501M and paid \$26M taxes.

Growth at that rate by acquiring companies is risky and will engender some waste. There is no assurance that customers will be ready to buy more products. Most US companies spent the windfall from the AJCA tax holiday instead on dividends to shareholders and buybacks of outstanding shares, strategies that do not contribute to corporate growth [DharmapalaFF:09].

F7.45 The benefits that CONCH obtained by obtaining IP rights that were misvalued amounted to \$780M in the initial buy-in, \$85.7M in the first set of acquisitions, and \$95.7M from the AJCA acquisitions, a total of \$961M. The relative misvaluations of the acquisitions were less than those in the buy-in, because the public purchase prices provided a base, even though the M7, the purchase-price valuation method, was not used. All that financial leverage is now offshore, as are the corresponding rights to MNC's intellectual capital.

F7.46 Total purchases were \$475M [F7.32]. The amount of tangibles included in the acquisitions amounted to \$41M, leaving \$434M of intangible assets.

F7.47 Acquired product lines valued at \$20M were written off. Those product lines were not part of the motivation for the acquisitions, and hence were not included in setting the price which MNC offered. Since they could be valued in the acquired companies, they were used, inappropriately, to reduce the value of the IP made available to CONCH.

F7.48 During major acquisitions general costs rise. There will be redundant staff and operations in multiple locations. Existing personnel has to take on unfamiliar management roles. MNC's management ran a tight ship and integrated the new resources rapidly. Most acquisitions were local California companies making it easy to move staff. MNC was soon back to its comfortable level of 12 % SG&A based on its gross income [FA.1].

F7.49 MNC added 350 employees in the two rounds of acquisitions. When the AJCA acquisitions were completed, 182 employees, 52 %, were redundant and let go [F2.16].

F7.50 Following ATA's calculation, the ratio of offshore sales to total MNC sales went from 42 to 58 % [F2.22]. Because the actual net income ratio of CONCH to MNC at the time of the AJCA was 46.6 %, adding that increment gives CONCH the right to book 70.1 % of MNC's nonroutine earnings once all of the AJCA round of acquisitions is paid for. At that time the sales-based RAB of CONCH is 49.3 %. MNC's taxable income is based on the remainder, 29.9 % of its nonroutine income, plus its routine income.

MNC's total earnings are $600.5M, so that the US taxable amount becomes $200M. US taxes on that amount at the rate for US manufacturers [F1.2] become $43.7M, or 7.3 % of MNC's worldwide taxable earnings. CONCH accounts are also used to pay taxes now on funds repatriated from CONCH as part of its cost-sharing payments. That is a transfer of $219M, and adds $47.8M in taxes. MNC's total tax rate then becomes 15.2 %.

F7.51 MNC's offshore capital holdings continue to grow. Without further spending on active investments they would reach $1,353M in the 5 years beyond the AJCA acquisitions and will continue to grow as sketched in Fig. 7.3. Such an accumulation of offshore capital is not wise and would identify MNC as being more of a financial than a manufacturing business.

F7.52 The computation has not yet considered other factors that reduce MNC's effective tax rate. MNC, like all US corporations, also deducts many expenses from is gross revenues before arriving at its taxable income. For instance, US companies deduct depreciation, reducing earnings by about 3 % average. That amount would appear in MNC's SG&A posting. An alternate way, not affected by bookkeeping, is to look at taxes versus actual revenues, as done in the Forest Labs' example of Fig. 2.10. We obtain a rate of 5.8 % on MNC revenues and 4.1 % on final consumer sales revenues.

F7.53 For the graph in Fig. 7.4 we used the 68 % of rights held by CONCH during the AJCA acquisitions [F7.50]. The left side of the graph depicts income allocations that do not count into earnings. The tax share for the repatriated R&D cost-sharing obligations comes out of that column.

F.8 Chapter 8, US Taxation Formulas

The results here use data that come from public sources. Most are found on the IRS websites, shown in the references such as [IRS-ED:10]. When IRS or other government sources have authors associated with them, they are listed under the author's name, such as [ChapotonG:88].

F8.1 The IRS 2008 budget request was $11,100M and for 2011 the budget was $12,100M. The requested amount for 2012 was $13,300M, but the US House of Representatives only approved $11,500M and the Senate made the amount $11,700M [RubinZ:11]. The loss of tax revenues due to reduced enforcement is estimated as $4,000M.

F8.2 Estimates of uncollected taxes are $2,680 per household are based on a sample, with a total quoted as $345,000M or 16 % of 2008 revenues [Blake:10]. The focus was on self-employed individuals; it appears that corporate taxes were not sampled.

F8.3 The data shown in Table 8.1 primarily come from historical data on budgets supplied by the Office of Management and Budget [OMB:11a]. Percentages reported in the sources are based on collected revenues, but I show the percentages of tax revenues relative to the total federal US government spending, as reported by the Congressional Budget Office [CBO:11]. The majority of the business taxes collected by the IRS are corporate taxes, about $228.5B of the $304.3B in 2008 [IRS-SC:12]. Many books provide useful background on taxation [SlemrodB:08].

F8.4 The IRS publishes data on its organization and staffing [IRS-ED:10], [IRS-EF:09], [Shulman:10R]. A major reorganization took place in 2000 [Rossotti:05]. Complementary sources for the data shown here and in Fig. 8.1 are various IRS online publications and books directed towards individual taxpayers and small businesses [Daily:02], [HedemannSP:10]. The most obvious task of the IRS is the actual processing of incoming tax forms and payments; that part is highly automated. The IRS employs much seasonal personnel [IRS-ED:10]. About 56 % of individual forms are filed electronically and move directly to the operations side of the IRS, keeping costs low [Olson:11]. Responding to congressional requests and making changes to the already complex tax regulations and forms takes much effort and always have a high priority [Rossotti:05].

F8.5 The story was reported in the business press [Kocieniewski:11G]. Data are found in General Electric's annual report [Immelt:11]. Offshore capital holdings grew from $14B to $79B.

F8.6 By not paying taxes on offshore income our model multinational, MNC, gained annually

$$annual\_actual\_tax\_rate \times CONCH\_earnings = 26\,\% \times \$135M = \$35M.$$

Being a mid-size business MNC has a 2 % chance of being audited [Zerbe:10]. Its offshore subsidiaries do not submit distinct forms, because

Table F.16 Double taxation of foreign earnings

Flavors of Double taxation, foreign country to other company or division				
Full	Sequential	Credited	Hidden incentives	Exempt
$T_F + T_H$	$T_S + (1 - T_S) \times T_H$	$T_C + (T_H - T_C)$	$T_H - T_S + (T_S - I_S)$	T_I, no T_G
10 + 35 = 45 %	25 + 0.75 × 35 = 51.25 %	33 + (35–33) = 35 %	35 – 25 + (25–20) = 15 %	12.5 %

MNC treats them as being consolidated, using the "check-the-box" selection. Once selected, it takes a variety of expertise at the IRS to cover all possible issues in complex offshore transactions [Shiner:12].

F8.7 After the Astra Zeneca (AZ) case with the IRS was settled, AZ paid $1.1B to the IRS and returned $2.3B to its capital account [Wright:11]. It appears that AZ placed on its books a contingency reserve of $(1.1 + 2.3)B = $3.4B for the expected but uncertain tax liability. AZ had to pay only ($1.1B/$3.4B) = 32.35 % of the tax obligations it expected. Typically booked contingencies are less than the possible tax obligations, since companies expect some fractional success, while putting excessive tax obligations on the books would depress their balance sheet and share prices. Recent treasury rules require reporting of "Uncertain Tax Positions" [Harvey:12]. We don't know what AZ's internal decisions were.

F8.8 There is a variety of double taxation flavors among jurisdictions. For Table F.16 we assume that the US corporate tax rate is T_H = 35 %, that the company is incorporated in a state which levies no income tax, and that the taxes in different foreign jurisdictions are T_F = 10 %, T_S = 25 %, and T_C = 33 %. A fourth case is an emerging economy, which has a formal rate of T_S = 25 %, but offers incentives to certain investors worth I_S = 20 %. Finally, in a tax union, we assume tax rates T_I = 12.5 % and T_G = 24 %, and let the business make a choice of domicile [vandenDool:12]. The results are transcribed to Table 8.2.

Some countries, as Japan, apply the "Full double taxation" flavor to countries that have a corporate tax rate of <25 %, unless exempted by a tax treaty [Miyatake:09].

F8.9 Belize taxes are 25 %, so that taxes on earnings in Belize are 0.25 + (1 – 0.25) × 35= 51.25 % [F8.8, sequential flavor]. However, Belize taxes only its local income, just 4 % for MNC; MNC's rate becomes just 4 % × 0.25 or 1 % × total MNC LSA earnings [BarlettS:00]. MNC's total tax rate on LSA earnings is then still 1 % + (1 – 0.01) × 35 % = 35.65 %.

F8.10 Double taxation of dividends affects individual income taxes. While we don't cover those in general, the benefits provided to shareholders affect business tax strategies, especially if the owners or directors of the company have large shareholdings.

The majority of US individual taxpayers earned <$139,000 per year, the breakpoint for the 25 % personal income tax in 2011. The IRS reported that

Table F.17 Double taxation of dividends

Double taxation of US dividends distributed to domestic entities (2003–2012), as		
Individuals, at full and actual average corporate rate		Corporate recipients
$T_H + (1 - T_H) \times T_D - \$100$	$T_E + (1 - T_E) \times T_D - \$100$	$T_E + 70\ \% \times T_{E2}$ [F8.12]
35 % + (1 − 35 %) × 20 %	25.3 % + (1 − 25.3 %) × 20 %	25.3 % + 0.7 × 25.3 %
≈ 48.0 %	≈ 40.3 %	= 43.1 %

21 % of taxpayers earned more than $75,000 per year, 12 % earned more than $100,000 per year, and only 2.8 % earned more than $200,000 per year The US tax brackets, with the Earned Income Tax Credit (EITC), are as of 2013 −10, 0, 10, 15, 25, 28, 33, 35, and 39.6 %. The rate of 39.6 % was reintroduced for 2013 for joint incomes above $450,000 [Henchman:13]. A blended income rate for the top three brackets, based on estimates of relative income from 2008 IRS data, is 36.8 %.

Individual recipients in the USA were paying taxes on dividends at a reduced rate of 15 % established for qualified dividends and capital gains [BurnhamO:05]. The Fiscal cliff legislation added a 20 % rate for taxpayers with joint incomes above $250,000. In addition, a $3.8 % tax is a healthcare levy (Obamacare) on incomes above $223,050, which we ignore in our analysis, since it does not affect corporate taxation directly. The base rates are now 20, 15, and 0 %.

Then, after the $T_H = 35\ \%$ corporate tax it appears that for an individual in the 20 % dividend bracket the duplicate taxation on corporate earnings becomes 48.0 %, as shown in Table F.17.

However, few companies pay tax at the 35 % rate. In Table F.17 we also show the result assuming that a US company pays taxes at a rate of T_E = 25.3 % [F8.11]. It distributes some of its profits to its individual shareholders in the form of dividends. US resident individuals in the top dividend bracket are subject to a rate of 20 %, starting in 2013. The examples in Table 8.3 also use the average corporate tax rate of 25.3 % and the individual dividend tax rates of 0 or 20 %; the 0 % rate applies to individuals in income tax brackets of 15 % or below. About 20 % of individual income tax filers declare some dividend income [IRS-SI:12]. While not a one-to-one match, 21 % of individual filers showed an annual taxable income above $75,000 [IRS-SI:12]. The final column shows the effective rate for domestic arm's-length dividend payments at the effective rate.

When arguments about double taxation are made, the full statutory rates tend to be used, greatly increasing the apparent effects of double taxation [Gigot:12]. An identical computation can be used for specific companies as well as for industry sectors, using available IRS data by industrial sectors and subsectors [IRS-SC:11].

F8.11 In the years 2006–2008, US corporations had, after deductions, an average total taxable income of $1,092B. The taxes on that amount at 35 % would have been \$382B. Because of various tax credits, part of the tax expenditures presented in Appendix E, they only paid \$277B, or 25.3 % (T_E) on their income. Other documents compute 20.2 % for manufacturing companies [IRS-SC:12].

F8.12 If the recipient owner is another arm's-length corporation, then a 70 % deduction applies, making the final rate 43.1 %, if its rate, T_{E2}, is also 25.3 %, as shown in Table 8.3.

F8.13 US corporations had a taxable income of \$1,092B [F8.11]. If they can reduce their effective tax rates by just 1 %, they will gain about \$11B.

F8.14 Total US government outlays in 2008 were \$2,931B, while revenues were \$2,521B. Most of the amounts go to mandatory programs and interest, leaving \$880B in discretionary funding. Subtracting security funding (DoD, Homeland Security, and War on Terror) leaves \$382B for all other government departments. The US Treasury received \$12B. For 2013 the budget request is \$13,381M, of which \$12,070M is for the IRS, an increase of 1.8 %. Additional funds depend on budget caps and congressional actions.

F.9 Chapter 9, Effect on the National Economy Formulas

F9.1 Using data around MNC's AJCA-motivated acquisition the earnings of MNC were \$314M [F5.10, year 5]. The total earnings of all US corporations averaged \$1,550,000M [F6.1]. The fraction of MNC is then just 0.02 % of the US total. The composition of MNC's earnings is also much simpler, since all of MNC's income is from product sales and none from financial services.

F9.2 Figure 9.1 is based on Fig. 7.4 for MNC [F7.53] and Fig. 6.4 for all US corporations [F6.5].

F9.3 Many companies are small and cannot be compared with MNC. There are over 25 million companies in the USA with a wide range of sizes [GAO:05]. MNC is a fairly large company by several metrics. In 2007 there were just 6,327 businesses with more than 1,000 employees each. Their employees represented 42.3 % of the employed workforce [UScensus:08]. MNC is representative of that important fraction.Alternative common metrics are:

(a) From a sales-based point of view, a large company is one that has at least \$50M gross income. Out of about 25 million companies in the USA there are 42,376 companies in the USA with revenues more than \$50M [SpringerEa:11]. Some large companies may be missed if they don't pay tax.

(b) Based on the value of assets owned, a large company is one that has more than \$250M in assets on its books [GAO:05]. This metric focuses on traditional industries, which have many tangibles, as railroads; those are less likely to be truly multinational, but it also includes financial institutions, who can have their holdings anywhere.

(c) From a taxation point of view, a large company is one paying more than $1M annually in taxes. We expect that companies in group (a) would have earnings at 7.5 % of revenue and a net federal tax rate of 20 % so that they'd pay at least $1M annually in taxes. Paying less draws scrutiny [Drucker:08].
(d) From an employment point of view, businesses with fewer than 20 employees are classified as being small [F9.6].

IRS derived data show that, in a sample of 7,364 large companies by metrics (a), (b), and (c), the average tax on gross receipts was 7.85 % [GAO:05]. That puts MNC pretty much into the average given the scale.

F9.4 Out of 27,281,452 firms 21,351,320 or 78 % had no employees, and 5,294,970 or 19 % had 1–19 employees [UScensus:08]. That left just 635,162 firms or 2.3 % in the medium to large category. The annual payroll of the other 97.7 % small firms was only 14.6 % of the total US payroll. Only a very small fraction of the small companies are start-ups that are likely to grow; most are quite stable businesses as local stores and services [HurstP:11].

F9.5 In a 2005 sample covering about 1.9 million US corporations, 14,132 were large by metrics (a) and (b). Of the large corporations sampled 36 % paid less than $1M in taxes and 12 % paid less than $0.1M. Those are then excluded from metric (c) in [F9.3] [GAO:08].

F9.6 In 2006, after the AJCA-motivated acquisitions, MNC paid taxes at a rate of 11.84 % on its worldwide earnings, or 6.4 % on its estimated gross receipts, while its peers paid 7.85 % of their gross receipts [F9.3]. Except for R&D cost-sharing receipts, a necessary business expense, MNC paid taxes only on the amounts it repatriated for interest and for the early acquisitions, an average of 9.1 % on its offshore income over the year prior to the AJCA acquisitions.

In our model MNC did not take advantage of any means other than tax-havens to reduce its taxes. MNC could likely have lowered its tax rate further with research (R&E) credits and many other provisions in the tax regulations [Appendix E]. Figure 9.2 shows that MNC's behavior matched that of other US multinational corporations. The MNC trend data were created independently.

F9.7 According to a report submitted to Congress, US corporations overall receive about 20 % of their revenues from exports [Jackson:10]. The report includes detailed breakdowns. Tangible exports are much more visible to tax authorities than intangibles; for instance, shipping documents can provide evidence [BernardJS:06]. We have no information on missed or undervalued intangibles [F9.6]. Analyses based on export data, even when they purport to include intangibles, are distorted. Such data can lead to a statement that the global "Income distribution effects of nonexclusive intangibles are likely small in comparison with the transfer of physical capital" [Leamer:99]. The growth of capital in taxhavens that do not receive tangible goods invalidates that observation.

F9.8 All US corporations spent $233,920M on R&D in 2008. Another $50,000M is spent by foreign corporations for R&D in the USA. [Bogoslaw:10]. The US rate is 1 % of US corporate revenues, and about 13 % of earnings. The rate by industrial sector varies widely, but it does not change as rapidly as earnings do in economic downturns. Worldwide corporate data cite 1.3 and 7.7 % R&D spending but should not be directly compared. MNC, being a growing high-technology company spent 23 % of revenues initially [FA.1], reducing it soon to 13 %, and then to about 12 % as it grew [F2.8].

F9.9 Data on asset ratios are again from the IRS statistics office [IRS-SC:12].

F9.10 Data on expected p/e multiples are given throughout the business literature and were used for the M6, PS-VM valuation [F5.43].

F9.11 Data on multinational corporations were published in a broad summary [LynchEa:11].

F9.12 The fraction of multinationals was verified by adjusting the result of [F9.7] with employee counts provided by [LynchEa:11]. The average multinational corporation is larger than the average US corporation.

F9.13 and F9.14 Repatriating and taxing offshore capital could have a significant effect on the US federal deficit and debt. A study of 30 high-technology companies showed that they had increased their foreign capital holdings by nearly $430B or 21 % [KangN:12]. That rate implies that now they alone are holding nearly $2,500B offshore. The increase from 2010 to 2011 is about 99 % of the federal deficit in 2008. The stimulus funding increases the annual deficit, but the total holdings amount to over 90 % of the sum of the 2009 and 2010 deficits. Some of the information used came from [GAO:08], [Shropshire:09].

F9.15 MNC spent between 17.8 and 6.2 % in the interval from the buy-in to the AJCA date on R&D and acquisitions that provided IP, averaging 12.4 %. Forest labs spent between 13.8 and 25.9 % of revenues between 2007 and 2010, averaging 19 %.

F9.16–F9.19 The comparisons are based on [F9.8], [F5.28], and data from Forest Laboratories' 10-K SEC submission [Edgar:10].

F9.20 In 2004, the most recent year for which data were available, US multinational corporations paid about $16B of US tax on approximately $700B of foreign active earnings, an effective tax rate of about 2.3 % [Gibbs:09].

F9.21 Given the earnings ratio of MNC versus its multinational peers MNC would shelter $690B [F6.3] × 0.02 % [F9.1] = $141M annually. The growth of MNC's offshore holdings before the AJCA acquisitions averaged $202M annually, as plotted in Fig. 7.3.

F9.22 The cost-sharing payments by CONCH were substantial, averaging $97M in the years used in Fig. 9.1. US taxes were levied on them. Those data are not known for multinational corporations in general, since they are intra-company reimbursements. All R&D expenditures by offshore affiliates of US companies amounted to $35,019M in 2007 [Jackson:10]. Those data cannot be directly related to cost-sharing payments by multinational companies for R&D performed by their US parents.

F9.23 Figure 9.4 shows the growth of pass-through entities (LLPs, LLCs, S-corporations), which avoid double taxation by passing earnings directly through their owners. About 31 million noncorporate businesses paid taxes [MackEa:05]. Some of them are quite large and have become indistinguishable from real, C-corporations [Sullivan:11L].
Between 1990 and 2001 the GDP grew by 181 %.

(a) By 2001 corporations contributed $270B to tax revenues. In 1990 their contribution was $280B. If contributions would have grown following the growth of the GDP, except for recession effects, one would expect that they would have contributed $510B annually by 2001. Their contribution became $240B less than this expectation.
(b) By 2001 pass-through businesses contributed $690B to tax revenues. In 1990 their contribution was $230M. If they would have grown at the rate of the GDP, one would expect that pass-throughs would contribute $420M by 2001. The increase of $190M explains much of the reduction in tax revenues from C-corporations.

After accounting for that shift C-corporations still contributed $240B – $190M = $50B less in 2001 than expected. There are many possible reasons.

F9.24 Analyzing the factors that explain the reduction in corporate spending versus the rate of growth of the GDP did not lead to a clear conclusion. It is likely that taxhavens were involved, but large pass-through entities can use taxhavens even more effectively than corporations, because their reporting requirements are less. Any C-corporation that converts to an LLC will certainly continue its ownership of taxhavens.

F9.25 The growth of spending between 1950 and 2010 above the tax revenue base in Fig. 9.6 shows how tax receipts have not kept up with spending.

F9.26 Appendix E, on tax expenditures, expands on loophole removal. The $85B annual estimate is taken from a proposal of a 2012 political candidate expecting a $850B savings over 10 years from a "flat tax." There will indeed be a transition period and then a behavioral adjustment to any major tax change. The effects of any change will vary over time, and only if there are no other ways to avoid taxes will the full effect be realized.

F9.27, F9.29, and F9.30 The estimates of tax rates are computed in [W:12] from data extracted from the 2007 records provided by the IRS [IRS-ST-12]. The reason to use 2007 records is that by 2008 the US was experiencing a recession. In 2012 some data for 2009 appeared. Since lags of corporate responses differ when economic activities contract, misleading conclusions can be drawn by simple comparisons. For instance, research appears to expand relative to earnings in a recession, when it may actually be reduced slowly.

F9.28 Companies increasing their research expenditures may receive tax credits, as described in Appendix E, Tax Expenditures. We can estimate, based on MNC's growth in research spending, that it would not have qualified for the maximum R&E credit of 20 % on its taxable income, but only for about

2.6 % in the 5 years between its acquisitions. That would still amount to \$6.6M over that period. Since R&E incentives are mainly a domestic issue, we did not include benefits from R&E tax exemptions in our model.

F9.31 and F9.32 These data are based primarily on [BEA:09], [Shropshire:09], [Wunder:09] and the MNC model. The start points of each trend line have been adjusted relative to their endpoint by applying the growth of the GDP at the midyear [SaniskiEa:12]. The counts of individual and corporate taxpayers have been adjusted by the square root of the GDP growth to compensate for an equal mix of GDP and actual corporate growth.

F9.33 US regional GDP data, used for comparison with offshore capital, came from [BEA:11]. There are many estimates of the amounts and growth of offshore US capital; we used Morgan Stanley's [Davidoff:11]. The ability to invest in US dollars, but book dividends in Eurodollars, make it difficult to have reliable estimates of the amounts available for potential repatriation. Some companies arguing for repatriation have provided corporate estimates [Chambers:10].

F9.34 The computation used the top 25 tax expenditures projected for 2004 to 2008 [Burman:03]. I used their annual average and classified them as being wholly or in part (20 %) beneficial to corporations. The total was just under \$72B. Some tax expenditures are temporary, such as the benefits for operating in possession taxhavens (Chap. 6, Sect. 6.5). Those expenditures amount to about 7 %, but growth of the economy increases the amount in later years. Other estimates assign about \$100B to corporate tax expenditures (Appendix E).

F9.35 Some illustrations to show the magnitude of offshore corporate holdings are shown here. It is always hard to envisage many millions of dollars; stacking them up to match the Empire State building does not help. I compare them here with some related US government expenditures.

(a) US federal taxes on CISCO's 2010 offshore holdings of \$30,000M, if repatriated and taxed at 35 %, would yield about \$10,500M to the US Treasury [Chambers:10].Immelt:11

The total of NSF and DARPA's 2009 funding is \$(6,490 + 3,361)M = \$9,851M. \$10,500M/\$9,851M = 106.6 % [OMB:12B and prior years].

(b) GE's offshore holdings are \$84,000M. If those funds were repatriated and taxed at 35 %, it would yield \$29,400M to the US Treasury [Immelt:11].Chambers:10

The US Department of Education administers a budget of \$63,700M in FY 2010 discretionary appropriations, excluding funding provided under the American Recovery and Reinvestment Act of 2009. Out of that amount, 45 % is allocated to Pell grants to support students, or P = \$28,654M. A student gets an annual maximum stipend of S = \$5,550. With a repatriation of GE's offshore that P/S = 5,163,000 students could be supported for a year, leaving over \$1M for administrators. GE would still receive the after-tax income.

F9.36 Employment estimates are based on [BronfenbrennerL:04], [Ensinger:11], [Grove:10], and [Jackson:10]. They use different bases, making numbers hard to compare. The mismatch in job estimates is based on older data: 4,663 jobs lost [US Labor Department, 1Q04] versus 50,000 jobs gained [Indian NAS&S Cos, Fy04/4]. Figure 10.6 provides a comparison [Sullivan:11L], based on BEA data ending in 2007, avoiding the distortions due to the recession.

F9.37 Lack of conformance of corporate reports and income tax data creates yet more uncertainty in all data. Already in 1996 reported corporate book income was $650B, while corporate income reported to the IRS was $500B [Rossotti:05].

F.10 Chapter 10, Recommendations Formulas

F10.1 Revenues of US-based corporations in 2008 were about $8,594B or 60 % of the US GDP. This amount excludes their overseas sales. Foreign-based corporations add another $2,518B [IRS-ST:09]. The spending is mainly by US consumers and the US government. Published GDP estimates only count corporate investments in order to avoid double counting of consumer and government spending.

F10.2 The AJCA bill is 423 pages long, but only 9 pages dealt with the actual repatriation of offshore capital. Another 23 pages dealt with related matters, as penalties for misuse of the repatriated funds. Tobacco quotas and excise taxes on bows and arrows took 13 pages. The remaining 88 % of the pages were not related to taxation [AJCA:04].

F10.3 A global estimate for IP maintenance is 13.75 % per year on its prior investment [F4.8]. For software the rule is 15 % [W:06]. This means that for a high-tech company as MNC, spending $86M of its annual revenue on R&D and having $473M in capitalized R&D is actually spending $66M, or $66M/$86M = 77 % on routine organic IP maintenance, which is a cost associated with maintaining a product line rather than novel research.

F10.4 MNC's RAB fraction was set initially based on 42 % of offshore sales [F2.4]. By the time the acquisitions motivated by the AJCA were completed, the offshore sales fraction was 49 % [F7.50]. At that time MNC had about 1,000 employees and its capital investment offshore amounted to about 20 % [F2.17]. The AJCA transfer increased the IP rights held at CONCH to 62 % [F2.22]. Before the AJCA transfer CONCH held $473M [F2.13], whereas capital held in the USA was limited to working capital, varying around $100M [FA.1].

F10.5 Receiving income from royalty payments takes place over many years. In arm's-length arrangements royalty rates tend to be fixed over time since the timing of the sales by a licensee cannot be predicted. Surveys from arm's-length arrangements are available [Parr:07]. For a company splitting itself, including its entire intellectual capital platform into a US and an offshore component, the benefits occur immediately. The margins would be identical, but can be adjusted for differences in expenses. IP that generates high margins also deserves high royalties. The 1:3 relationship is a gross estimate, validated by some actual instances; Appendix C provides more details.

F10.6 The percentage of R&E credits for 2008–2010 for all US industries averaged 3.5 % of taxable earnings. It varies greatly according to fluctuations in the economy, since increased spending on R&D changes less than corporate profitability in a downturn. The R&E benefits go primarily to manufacturing companies; financial enterprises are specifically excluded. For the manufacturing sector the benefits are about 3 × as great as the corporate economy overall. Since recent information on R&E benefits is not yet available, we used that multiplier and estimate the percentage for manufacturers as 10.84 %.

F10.7 Corporate taxes as a fraction of tax revenues vary with the economy; the average over 2008–2010 was 9.7 %. These data are from the IRS statistical website [IRS-SC:12]. Unfortunately, the last comprehensive data available in early 2012 were from 2009, giving data for the tax year 2008, in the middle of the recession. Earlier data report US corporate tax collected to be about 12 % of US tax revenues [Wolf:05]. Figure 10.6 extrapolates the trend.

F10.8 The rate of taxes paid on earnings by businesses varies depending on their industrial sector. An overall estimate yields 27.9 %. Because many, mainly smaller corporations, have switched their structure to become pass-through entities, the rates change in ways that are hard to analyze. For all C-corporations the rate reported by the IRS is 27.5 %. The average US tax rate including worldwide income from multinationals is 20.2 % in 2011; due to the recession it was much less in 2008 (14.7 %), although still 17.5 % for the manufacturing sector. Other sources estimate 27.9 % [Ditmer:11]. In prior years all corporations paid overall 26.5 % (2007) and 23.4 % (2008). It is clear that the 35 % statutory rate is not relevant for quantifying effects of changes to corporate taxation.

F10.9 US multinationals pay a slightly higher rate on their domestic-only income, 29 % [GriffithK:04] and [HassettM:11]. Domestic-only corporations pay 23 %, while the rate for all corporations is 27.5 % [MarkleS:09]. Those rates differ greatly by industry segment and on the state of the US economy.

F10.10 In our model the comparison is simple. After the AJCA acquisitions MNC earnings were $318.2M, and $111.4M taxes would be due on the full amount. But MNC had sheltered by then 69.1 % offshore at CONCH, so that only $34.4M were due, leaving a profit $283.8M. If taxation is abolished, after tax profits would be reduced by those $34.4M. MNC's profits would increase by 10.8 %, leaving more money in the USA for investments. But, like many multinationals, MNC holds much capital offshore.

F10.11 For estimates involving individual taxation we use a blended income tax rate of 36.8 % and the top rate for of dividends and capital gains of 20 % [F8.10]. Applying this rate to dividend income means that high earners will pay (36.8 % – 20 %)/20 % = 84.1 % more taxes on their dividend income. For individuals now in the 10 % bracket or below, the relative increase will be larger, but those individuals receive little income from dividends [AltshulerHT:10].

F10.12 Shareholders with incomes over $450,000, in the 39.6 % bracket, can be compensated for their increased taxes by increasing dividend payouts by

$$((1-20\%)/(1-39.6\%))-1=32.5\,\%,$$

For shareholders with incomes above $250,000, applying the blended marginal tax rate [F8.10], the compensation needed on dividend payouts becomes 36.8 %. Increasing dividend payouts by 26.6 % would restore their after-tax dividend income.

F10.13 Buffet and Burlington Northern data are obtained from [Edgar:10], as cited by [Buffett:11]. This, mainly domestic company, paid $1,250M in dividends that year. Recommendation R20 the double taxation of dividends paid to individual shareholders in all corporations is eliminated. Multinational corporations can still decide to defer paying dividends and hence avoid taxation of dividends, but when shares are sold by US residents, taxes on capital gains income received are due, and taxed identically under the R20 recommendation. Dividends and capital gains paid to investors offshore can still escape taxation. For US citizens any undeclared income is tax evasion, a problem that exists now and is not changed by changes to corporate taxation.

F10.14 Since GE reported a net tax loss in the USA in 2011, it would not benefit that year from abolishing corporate taxation. However, GE has considerable offshore capital available for repatriation; see [Chittum:11], [Stahl:11]. The amount needed to increase dividends to compensate shareholders fully for full taxation is nearly $1,400M. However, this amount is <1.5 % of GE's $92,000M offshore holdings in 2010 [Immelt:11].

F10.15 Retirement funds held at least 22.6 % of corporate stock in 2004 [Auerbach:05]. They are becoming more aggressive to assure adequate returns [Farrell:12].

F10.16 The required dividend payout rate increase for retirees is complex. We just use a graph provided in an argument for cutting taxes [Rubin:12]. For the typical retired taxpayer in the mid-income effective 20 % tax bracket, the increase in dividends needed is 6.25 %.

F10.17 The IRS assessed businesses $205B in 2009 [IRS-ST:12] and prior reports. The amounts for 2010 and 2011 were estimated to be about $191B and $194B [OMB:11a]. However, about half of that income is passed through to the owners of S-corporations and LLCs. That could mean that the actual loss by abolishing corporate taxation could be just half that amount. The flexibility that taxpayers have makes using half a risky estimate. The average annual income for the many pass-through entities is just $116,000. Their size varies greatly though. Taxes on that income are collected from either wages or dividends paid. Dividend payouts are currently attractive, because they enable tax avoidance, but will be captured under recommendation R20 [F10.19]. We assume that only half of the pass-through income will be covered, and use 75 % to be the fraction of the tax revenue loss. At that fraction, abolishing corporate taxation causes the Treasury to lose $143.25B. The 2013 legislation did not change corporate taxation and renewed several tax expenditures [ATRA:13].

F10.18 Fully taxing dividends increases US Treasury revenues by $31.2B per year based on scaled data from 2007 to 2009, extrapolated for 2010, once the statutory tax rate is increased from 20 % to the 36.8 % blended rate [F10.17] [IRS-SI:12] and prior reports, [HallR:07]. Little adjustment should be needed. I just reduce the estimate by 2.5 % to $30.4B to account for some taxpayers moving their dividends to Palm islands.

F10.19 Tax rates for capital gains vary widely worldwide [Paschall:00]. The majority of US dividend payouts will be subject to 20 % on capital gains. Recommendation 20 will tax capital gains at the full personal rate, so that the statutory rate increases for individuals from 20 % to effectively 36.8 % [F8.10]. Fully taxing capital gains would increase US Treasury revenues by $99B per year based on scaled data from 2007 to 2009, and extrapolated for 2010 [IRS-SC:11], [HallR:07].

In Table 10.1, I only post 70 % of that amount, since individuals will change behavior when faced with higher capital gains tax rates, as when dealing in real estate, making the estimate ~$69B [DowdMM:12]. Actual measured changes in behavior in response to tax rate changes have been modest [KravitzB:05]. Using a 2013 base and moving from 20 % to a blended rate of 36.8 % yield amounts from $39M to $93M using historical data and the same 70 % behavior factor. We expect that data, not yet available, from 2012 may indicate high capital gains payouts due to the uncertainty of the fiscal cliff resolution. The New Year's 2013 legislation did not resolve all issues [ATRA:13].

Capital assets can be revalued at death, effectively eliminating capital gains taxation, reducing posted tax revenues by $51B in 2011 [OMB:11b]. Abolishing corporate taxation will not change the death rate. Gains when selling homes are excluded, now up to a $5M limit, reducing tax revenues by another $27B in 2011 [OMB:11b]. Any broader tax reform will certainly have to deal with these issues.

The total estimated offset in US tax revenues due to taxation of dividends and capital gains increases is then $99.5B [F10.18]. All these estimates are quite conservative, so that Table 10.1 can be viewed with confidence.

An independent estimate is $87.3B for a combination of dividends and capital gains increases, with full taxation of dividends and capital gains tax rates raised to 28 %, matching earlier US tax rates [AltshulerHT:10]. The $99.5B estimate used in Table 10.1 with a full reset of capital gains is 114 % of that amount. If the capital gains fraction of the $83.35B estimate scales with the tax rate, then the estimated offset would be $123.7B, and my $99.5B estimate be only 80 % of that amount.

F10.20 We assume that once dividends are taxed higher, while corporations are not taxed at all, there will be pressure from individuals and institutions to increase dividend payouts. Experience of corporate behavior from past changes is sketchy. Increases in dividend taxation, while corporate taxes were not changed, reduced dividend payouts in the past, likely because it became wiser to invest [Gigot:12]. Abolishing corporate taxation already increases funds for investment. After abolishing corporate taxation companies that paid dividends in the past should increase the payouts to their shareholders in the range from by 25 to 30 % to keep the recipients after-tax income level [F10.12]. A specific corporate rate estimate can consider their current tax rate. Overall, the cost will be about $26B, or 18.2 % of the abolished taxes.

F10.21 An increased payout of about $26B will be also taxed, yielding $9.6B. Corporations will still have over $117B, or over 80 % of the gain from abolishing taxes, left for investments.

F10.22 A prediction of secondary effects of the additional funds available to corporations is based on a thorough analysis of the effect of military contracts on regional economies [NakamuraS:11]. Receiving a DoD contract means that government funds, derived from tax revenues, are injected in a region. They will be used to produce goods. Workers have to be hired and supplies have to be purchased. The result was a multiplicative effect of 1.5. When a company receives a substantial tax break, equal to 80 % of its former taxes [F10.20], a similar reaction can be expected.

A difference is that the military contractor has a guaranteed customer. A company with money to invest has to make sure that its products are attractive and will spend on advertising as well as in manufacturing. DoD purchasing restrictions mean that many components have be obtained from vetted suppliers, reducing the regional impact. For the recommended federal tax abolition the region that will benefit is all of the USA, although some base materials may be sourced offshore. By abolishing corporate taxation US businesses gains $116B [F5.21]. The 50 % secondary effect of the enabled spending on the US economy would be $58.3B. Abolishing taxes is permanent, so that the additional tax revenues from corporate spending will be at least $20.4B annually. That amount is just 14.2 % of the $143.2B tax reduction.

F10.23 The total effect of Recommendation R20, using [F10.17] to [F10.22], is that $61.5B or 32.2 % of the change of the $191B business tax receipts [F9.25], due to abolishing corporate taxes, is compensated. The loss, applied to total tax receipts, is 2.3 %.

F10.24 The estimate of 25 % tax preparation overhead is based on the 1993 estimate of $50B by [HallR:07] and the $191B amount of corporate taxes paid in 2002 [F10.11]. It is obviously very rough. The source costs were accumulated in 1993 using data back to 1985 to make a point for the flat tax. While only a small fraction of tax revenues comes from corporations, they spend a much greater effort on documenting their income and costs, since tax avoidance is so important to their profits. Given all these unknowns it is easiest to stick with the simple estimate.

F10.25 The IRS budget is approximate \$11B, of which \$5.5B is for enforcement [GAO:12]. The fraction on auditing corporations is likely disproportionate to the amount of taxes collected from corporations. An older source of data estimated IRS audit cost to be \$1B in 1993 [HallR:07]. In either case the cost incurred by the IRS in dealing with corporate taxes is at least of 1 % of corporate tax revenues collected. The intensity of audits changes over time, but costs per audit certainly increased since then. How the IRS will reallocate resources in the future cannot be predicted.

F10.26 In 2009 about 140.5 million individual tax returns were filed; of those 25.5 million (~18.1 %) reported income from qualified dividends, 20.3 million (~14.5 %) reported capital gains or losses, while 22.1 million (~15.7 %) had business income to report (1040 Schedule C). Since these groups will overlap substantially, we assume that 80 % of tax returns report neither dividend income nor qualified capital gains [IRS-SI:12].

F10.27 The amount of corporate stock owned by charitable organizations in 2004 is about 4 % of outstanding stock values [Auerbach:05].

F10.28 The development lag for the first Maniac was 1.2 years, following earlier research before MNC was founded [F3.1]. The sales lag was 5.1 years [F3.3]. The period an investor would have to hold an investment in MNC to maximize capital gains is over 6 years.

F10.29 The statutory worldwide corporate tax rate cited for 63 countries [Worldwide:12], excluding the USA, was computed as

$$(\Sigma rate \times GDP) / \Sigma GDP = 26.4\%$$

Those countries comprised 68 % of the worldwide GDP [Worldbank:10]; the US share is an additional 23 %. Data collected around 2006 for 28 major countries, comprising about 48 % of the worldwide GDP, gave a GDP-weighted corporate tax rate of 33.7 %; the US share of world GDP was 28 %. The summation in the source documents and in [Wolf:05] presents just the averages, favoring small countries over large ones. The effect is seen in Fig. 10.6 where the differences are plotted.

F10.30 In 2012 the US population was 311,591,917 and the world population was 7,026,475,425, making the US fraction 4.43 % [UScensus:10]. The fraction of undocumented immigrants in the USA is estimated to be 10 % of the US population [HoefnerRB:11].

F.A Appendix A, MNC's Annual Report Formulas

FA.1 MNC's income sheet assembles data from a variety of typical business sources, such as product revenue of \$375M [F5.9] and operating income of \$250M [F2.2]. Table A.1 also shows the 40 % markup expected for its independent distributors, giving the expected customer sales price. MNC publishes the expected sales prices (the IFP for Maniacs), making it hard for a distributor to charge more. MNC's earnings amount to 41 % of revenues, its "earnings margin," which matches that of high-tech product manufacturers, but is much higher than average margins in the entire electronics sector.

The cost of capital, over $9M, is derived from obligations related to the assets shown in Table A.2. It includes MNC's mortgage payments, funds needed for rent, the interest on debts incurred for working capital. Deducted are interest payments for capital held in short-term accounts. MNC pays currently no dividends to shareholders, so that capital obtained from selling shares is effectively free.

MNC paid taxes in the USA at the 35 % US statutory rate. Its peers paid only 27 % on their earnings because of various US tax credits available for corporations. We ignore this advantage now.

The taxes paid by MNC were $154M – $100M =$54M, amounting to 54/154 = 35 % in its earnings or 54/375 = 14 % on its revenues. The subsequent restructuring allowed MNC to move earnings out of the USA, eventually lowering its tax rate on its foreign revenues to 2.71 % 7 years later, after the AJCA acquisitions, or 4.9 % on its total revenues [FA.2].

We estimate that worldwide taxes on offshore reduce to 2.44 % in another 7 years. Forest Labs is ahead in that game, paying <3 % on its revenues, even though all sales were in the USA.

Our organic growth model is not reliable regarding revenues due to acquisitions, so that any long-range projections are estimates. In any case, taxes are not based on revenues, so these numbers are mainly useful for rough comparisons, as found in the literature. Revenues data are easier to access and more reliable than internal corporate data, such as earnings.

The values for Forest Labs are based on [Drucker:10], as used in [F2.24], [F2.25], and [F2.27] and were further elaborated with data from its 10-K reports [W:12, ForestEtAl].

FA.2 With a p/e multiple of 10 MNC would have a market value of about 10 × $154M ≈ $1,500M.

FA.3 Ignoring goodwill, the books show $310M in tangible value and capitalized R&D, giving a market-to-book ratio of nearly 5, a ratio that is typical for a high-technology company, as exemplified by SAP (Table 3.4). The additional value is due to income expectations from exploiting the company's intellectual capital.

FA.4 MNC's balance sheet, shown as Table A.2, gives a picture of MNC just after CONCH was created and the initial acquisitions were put on the books. It shows total tangible assets of $220M and tangible liabilities of $120M. On that basis the remaining shareholder's equity would be $100M. But the books already show $90M of capitalized R&D and $140M of goodwill, left over from $300M spent on earlier acquisitions and not yet written off or amortized. The total assets on the books are then $450M, and the shareholders' equity is $330M. The cost of capital is derived from the obligations shown in Table A.1.

FA.5 The market value of Forest Laboratories, according to its 10-K report, filed with the SEC, was $14,961M, while its book value was $6,106M, giving a market-to-book ratio of 2.4.

The problem was that the intellectual capital of Forest Laboratories is mainly due to the licenses to patents held by arm's-length pharmaceutical companies. When their patents run out, generic companies can produce medications at about $31 per unit [F2.28] rather than $76, as shown in Table A.1.

F.B Appendix B, Tax Laws and Regulations Formula

FB.1 In 2007 the IRS issued updated, but temporary, transfer pricing regulations [B.2.R.4 7T(g)]. In general, they tried to deal more appropriately with modern business approaches and focus on fundamentals. A parent company which contributes to a new split-off CFC is said to perform a Platform Contribution Transaction (PCT) [IRS-CIP:07]. The regulations expanded on many important concepts [B.1.2 #7T(g)]. However, there were many objections to their implementation from several sides, and they were not fully moved into practice [Stewart:11]. Since the regulations covered new terrain, they include many examples. About 62 % of the words and 71 % of the volume were devoted to those examples.

F.C Appendix C, Royalties Formulas

FC.1 Based on a 1–5 ratio of simple costs, a fair allocation to the licensor would appear to be 16.67 % of earnings. But the licensor spent the money earlier and had a higher risk. For the valuation of CONCH using M7, the Roll-over method, we showed a total R&D spending over 5 years preceding the buy-in of $273M. The capitalized value at a 33.3 % annual loss and a 22 % capitalization rate [F5.48] became $340M, or 125 % of the simple aggregated cost. The effect is that in this simple case the license contract should specify a 25 % rate of earnings. The income does not get discounted here, since it is paid as it is received.

FC.2 Converting a royalty rate based on earnings to one based on revenues means reducing the rate by the earnings margin.

FC.3 In an intracompany platform split, relative costs are irrelevant. The new CFC had no prior cost and only pays cost-sharing payments subsequently. MNC's margin of earnings on revenues was a bit over 41 %. Unless costs are allocated very differently that would be the base for a royalty rate to be paid by CONCH.

FC.4 CONCH actually has lower selling costs than MNC, so that its earnings are 44 % of MNC's while its revenues are 42 %.

FC.5 In a situation where the development costs and risks are borne by the licensee receiving the IP, 25 %, is a common royalty fraction on earnings. Given a margin on revenues of 41 %, as encountered at MNC, subtracting 6 % for the routine earnings that a manufacturer might make without having IP yields 35 % nonroutine profit due to the IP. The royalty rate on income then becomes 25 % of 35 % = 8.8 % on revenues. Having proprietary manufacturing IP can raise the royalty further. A PS-M method can be used for allocation.

FC.6 Using a discount rate for the royalty income of 9 %, we find that to yield an amount equal to the lump sum of $800M, the royalty rate should be 34.2 %.

FC.7 A royalty rate of only 2.0 % would return the values of the buy-in estimated by ATA, namely $50M [F7.7].

F.D Appendix D, Definitions and Glossary Formulas

FD.1 In 2004 companies repatriated $362B, of which $312B, more than 85 %, was in response to the reduced AJCA tax rate, requiring only $16B in taxes [CoyD:11], [DavisRKM:11]. Since much of the funds were used for acquisitions, it was even referred to as the "year of the mergers" [Schaefer:04].

FD.2 The position of a centroid L_c can be computed for n samples of height h at a distance d from an endpoint over an interval by

$$L_c = \left(\Sigma^l \left(h_i \times d_i\right), i = 1\ to\ n\right) / (\Sigma^l h_i, i = 1\ to\ n).$$

FD.3 The interquartile mean and range shown in Fig. D.2 present a simple case, where the total number of comparables is divisible by 4. The formula recommended by the IRS computes the range by including the means of the underlined value pairs (m, n), being at the boundaries of the lower and upper quartiles [B.1.2 #1(e)(2)(iii)(C)]. The computation the IRS specifies is shown in Table F.18 for counts below 20.

Some textbooks and formulas provided by spreadsheets use minor variations. When there are enough comparables, the results barely differ.

FD.4 Price to earnings ratio in general: the p/e multiple is a quick measure to assess expected benefits for a share of stock. The earnings are expressed per share of stock. If the routine growth of earnings for a company is 1 % annually and a discount rate of 12 % is used, then a p/e multiple of about 9 reflects an expected $9.00 NPV income in perpetuity for a $1.00 share [F5.12]. A lower p/e multiple indicates that the shares are undervalued. Current earnings would be less in a company which invests substantially in R&D and is expected to have a high, 7 %, growth rate; then a p/e multiple as high as 20 is acceptable.

The price to earnings multiple for MNC used to measure MNC's business performance is based on MNC's market capitalization and earnings prior to taxes. However, shareholders also judge the companies on after-tax profits, the basis for any dividends they receive. At the time of the buy-in, MNC had 18.5 million shares outstanding, which were valued in the market at $100 each.

If earnings are used, before taxes for full taxation are deducted, the p/e multiple

Table F.18 IRS interquartile range computations

Number of comparables k	1	2	3	4	5–7	8	9–11	12	13–15	16	17–19
Top of interquartile range	1	2	3	3,4	$k-1$	6,7	$k-2$	9,10	$k-3$	12,13	$k-4$
Bottom of interquartile range	1	1	1	1, 2	2	2, 3	3	3, 4	4	4, 5	5

Earnings-based p/e multiple was ($100 × 18.5 million)/$154M = 12.0 [F5.40(f)].

However, investors who understand MNC's intellectual capital, as expressed by Tobin's Q initial value of 5.3, would be motivated to invest even that high p/e multiple. Knowledgeable investors may also be aware of the plans to reduce taxes by using tax incentives and shelter income in a CFH, when MNC management engaged ATA, who had previously created a similar structure for MNC's chip supplier, CCC (Chap. 2, Sect. 2.5.2).

FD.5 Routine earnings are those that a company can obtain without any unique competence. Examples are provided in Chap. 5, M2, the income-based method and support by [F5.15] to [F5.19]. The margins vary by industry and can be as low as 3 %, but will not exceed 10 % [HandL:03].

FD.6 A tax credit is fully deducted from taxes; an exemption reduces taxable income. A tax credit hence, for corporations, at the marginal rate applicable after all deductions are taken, is worth 1/35 % = 2.86 ≈ 3 × as much.

FD.7 The Weighted Cost of Corporate Capital or WACC is obtained by multiplying the two sources of corporate capital, sale of shares and loans, by their proportional weight and then taking their sum

$$WACC = E/(E+D)\times Re + D/(E+D)\times Rd \times (1-Tc)$$

where E = market value of the firm's equity, Re = cost of equity, D = market value of the firm's debt, Rd = cost of debt, and Tc = corporate tax rate.

F.E Appendix E, Tax Expenditures Formulas

FE.1 To assemble data on tax expenditures a variety of sources are available [OMB:11b]. Such data are never fully factual, because they try to compute what would happen if a current tax expenditure were repealed or reduced by changes in regulations. The delays in effects and the responses that taxpayers make are also uncertain. Incomes that depend on intellectual property have few base data. In general, taxpayers will respond quickly to changes, even delaying their tax form submission dates if necessary. Even government data, which should be trustworthy, are inconsistent. The 2012 US budget projections depend on estimates created in 2010, and do not take into account many recent incentives passed by Congress [OMB:12A]. Data used in current congressional arguments go back to 2004 [Hungerford:11].

FE.2 Often tax expenditures are presented as percentages of tax revenues. Since corporate earnings vary greatly with the state of the economy, such presentations have to be carefully looked at before they can be extrapolated. Variations are due to effects of recessions, foreign investments, increased use of taxhavens, interest rates, foreign exchange rates, and changes in business classifications. Where choices are possible, avoiding taxes is a motivation. Where we present numbers, averages of the most trustworthy results were taken, after adjustment by GDP growth to 2011.

FE.3 We used 2011 projections to minimize the effect of the recession, but at the same time have up-to-date estimates. Use of averages of earlier data to span the recession is not realistic, since corporate tax collections dropped steadily after 1999, as seen in Fig. 9.4. Individual tax revenues used were $899B with corporate tax revenues at $191B, giving a ratio of 4.7 in income tax receipts [OMB:11A]. Payroll taxes collected for Social Security and Medicare were ignored.

FE.4 Some tax expenditures are only for corporation, some are only for individuals, and some are for both. Some significant corporate tax credits, as $5.7B for building low-income housing, actually benefit individuals [Sullivan:11]. We followed [VolckerEa:10] in assigning 15 % of tax revenues to corporations.

FE.5 While business pay mortgages for real estate as well, those interest deductions are subsumed under the general ability by businesses to deduct all interest payments. US individual income taxes in 2008 brought in $1,146B [Table 8.1]. The deduction for mortgage interest reduced individual taxes by average of about 4 %, or $44.5B, but is expected to increase greatly [OMB:11b]. Like most tax expenditures, the numbers vary with the economic standing of the taxpayers; an estimate for 2000 reported already $48B that year, and an earlier estimate was $65.5B [Saxton:99]. A more recent estimate for 2012 of the cost of tax expenditures to government revenues is about $79.7B [Bartlett:12B]. Because of the uncertainties it became unwise to populate Table F.1.

FE.6 Several provisions enacted in US tax laws to encourage US corporations to grow offshore interact with each other. Subsequently they raised concern because they allowed financially motivated tax evasion. I summarize three such provisions.

P1. A primary objective for not taxing offshore income is that foreign income should be available for continued further investment without having to flow through the US tax system, similar to US investments that are deductible from earnings. The amount kept available offshore will vary greatly with business decisions. Estimates of that amount for all US businesses vary between $1,000B [Wunder:09] and $1,375B [Drucker RM:11].

P2. In order to achieve the first objective (P1) capital has to be held offshore to be ready for deferred investments. Here the amount of capital held has grown well beyond what could be needed for Objective P1. It is well over $1,000B [Sullivan:11]. All that is required to allow deferral is a statement from management that they are holding the funds for future offshore active investment in their business [Immelt:11]. It is clear from the response to the 2004 AJCA tax holiday that such statements were not credible, since a large fraction of capital held offshore was repatriated when taxes were lowered. Lobbying for another tax holiday in 2011 shows that such statements are still not credible [Chambers:10]. An alternative would be to force all foreign holdings to be repatriated, gaining tax revenues of about $8B annually [Hungerford:11] or $45B now [VolckerEa:10], and then to provide equivalent incentives for foreign investment. That approach is used by Japan, but the USA has never directly supported Foreign Direct Investment (FDI) [Miyatake:09].

P3. Interest from passive funds held offshore is taxable under the "subpart F" regulations [B.2.10 (a)(3)(i)]. Excessive amounts held for P2 fall into this category, and are estimated to cost $4.6B in lost taxes [CBO:08]. Not all funds held offshore are visible to US agencies. Offshore funds can be held in anonymous accounts and not be reported. Noncorporate entities held by individuals take advantage of keeping capital untaxed offshore as well. Such holdings are then part of outright tax evasion, a topic we have not dealt within this book. That amount is likely much larger, but unknowable [Shaxson:11].The total estimate of the annual revenue lost, using averages of published data after adjustment by GDP ratios to 2011, is over $17B, but this amount seems quite unreliable.

FE.7 The estimate for the cost and benefits of the "VOW to Hire Heroes" legislation is based on likely costs over benefits for the two provisions in the new laws, covering unemployed and wounded veterans. The current government estimate is that 100,000 vets will participate; I assume optimistically that 10 % of the potential 1.850 million veterans or 185,000 will benefit for 5 years. I also assume that 10 % of those are eligible for the higher wounded veterans benefit.

FE.8 Taxpayer costs are based on dealing with the forms at $1 per business over 5 years plus $20 for the paperwork when actually hiring a veteran, using the stated 1 h estimate for the cost of filling in the current form VET-100 over 5 years. IRS costs are estimated based on spending $5M initially to write the regulations for the two new laws, and interacting with lobbyists and Congress, plus $5M annually to process the tax returns, including auditing some of the returns to assure that the beneficiaries are truly eligible veterans.

Businesses will need upgraded software, as they do every year. I allocate $1,000 to the 1 % of the businesses that do write and maintain their own software and $2,000 to each of the 100 software companies that provide the packages used by most businesses. The total costs become $401M. I obtain $2,960M in total benefits over 5 years, using the averages of the tax credits businesses are eligible to receive for the two groups. The ratio of overhead costs over business benefits is 15.8 %.

FE.9 Temporary tax expenditures are mainly estimated by taking the 2011 corporate tax expenditures from [CBO:08]. The annual amounts varied quite a bit. When 2011 estimates were missing or unusual, we took the average of the 2009–2013 totals reported in the reference [CBO:08].

References[1]

[AbramitzkyB:04]Ran Abramitzky and Fabio Braggion: Malthusian and Neo-Malthusian Theories; *Oxford Encyclopedia of Economic History*, Oxford University Press, 2004.

[ADLittle:85]A.D.Little Inc: Development of a Methodology for Estimating the Taxpayer Paperwork Burden; Internal Revenue Service, Jun.1988.

[AF:04]The Appraisal Foundation: Uniform Standards of Professional Appraisal Practice; Standard 9, 2004 Edition.

[Aiken:09]Alex Aiken: Measure of Software Similarity Software; MOSS Software, 2009, http://www.similix.com.

[AJCA:04]U.S. Congress: American Jobs Creation Act; H.R.4520, Title VIII, Subtitle A, Section 422 (a), IRC §965(a)(1), 2004.

[AlcockBG:09]Alistair Alcock, John Birds, and Steve Gale: *Alcock, Bird and Gale on the Companies Act 2006*; Jordans, 2009.

[Alderman:10]Liz Alderman: "In Ireland, Low Corporate Taxes Go Untouched"; *New York Times*, 25 Nov.2010.

[AlmDM:04]James Alm, John Deskins, and Michael McKee: "Tax Evasion and Entrepreneurship: The Effect of Income Reporting Policies on Evasion"; *97th Annual Conference of the National Tax Association*, Minneapolis MN, Nov.2004.

[Almeida:04]Aloisio Almeida: Tax Havens: An Analysis of the OECD Work with Policy Recommendations; Ford School of Public Policy, Apr.2004.

[Alter:11]Jonathan Alter: "Coming Lobbyist Brawl May (Really) Fix Our Taxes"; *Bloomberg Businessweek*, 5 Aug.2011.

[AltshulerACK:08]Rosanne Altshuler, Alan J. Auerbach, Michael Cooper, and Mathew Knittel: Understanding U.S. Corporate Tax Losses; NBER Tax Policy and the Economy Conference, Washington DC, 6.Oct.2008.

[AltshulerHT:10]Rosanne Altshuler, Benjamin Harris, and Eric Toder: "Capital Income Taxation and Progressivity in a Global Economy"; *Virginia Tax Review*, Vol.30, Fall 2010, pp.355-388.

[Amadi:02]Confidence W. Amadi: Double Taxation of Dividends: A Clarification; BQuest, West Georgia University 2002, http://www.westga.edu/~bquest/2002/double.htm.

[1]This list includes all the references cited in this book. Some were used in the supporting spreadsheets. Many more were perused before and during the writing of this book and are listed on the author's website. For general information, I selected some recent publications, trusting they will be easy to locate and will cite earlier work. As is common in tax matters, opinions abound. Be aware that references to <webpages> on the Internet tend to be volatile. Refereed sources are *italicized*.

G. Wiederhold, *Valuing Intellectual Capital: Multinationals and Taxhavens*, Management for Professionals 23, DOI 10.1007/978-1-4614-6611-6,

[AmdahlBB:64]Gene M. Amdahl, Gerrit A. Blaauw, and Frederick P. Brooks jr.: "Archi-tecture of the System/360"; *IBM Journal of R&D*, Vol.8 no.2, Apr.1964, pp.87-101.

[AmirLS:03]Eli Amir, Baruch Lev and Theodore Sougiannis: "Do financial analysts get intangibles?"; *European Accounting Review*, Vol.12 no. 4, 2003, pp.635-659.

[Anderson:09]Eric Anderson: Take the Money and Run, Sovereign Wealth Funds and the Demise of American Prosperity; Praeger Security International, 2009.

[Anderson10]David Anderson: Remodeling Pre/Post Conflict Development Assistance for Weak and Failing States; Entrepreneurship and Expeditionary Economics, Kauffman, Command and General Staff College Foundation, 2010.

[Andriessen:03]Daniel Andriessen: Making Sense of Intellectual Capital: Designing a Method for the Valuation of Intangibles; Butterworth-Heinemann, Dec. 2003.

[AngusNSW:10]Barbara Angus, Tom Neubig, Eric Solomon, and Mark Weinberger: "The U.S. International Tax System at a Crossroads"; *Tax Analysts*, E&Y, 2010.

[AP:11]AP: "Western Union to Pay $220M More in Internal Revenue Service Settlement"; Associated Press, *Bloomberg Businessweek*, 15 Dec.2011.

[Arellano:08]Sergio Arellano: Exit Strategies; Internal Revenue Service, 2002, http://www.irs.gov/businesses/article/0,,id=179270,00.html.

[Argy:06]Victor Argy: The Postware International Money Crisis: An Analysis; Taylor and Francis, 1981, reprinted 2006 by Routledge.

[ASCAP:10]The American Society of Composers, Authors and Publishers: Customer licensees; ASCAP, 2010, http://www.ascap.com/licensing/licensingfaq.html.

[AsprayMV:06]William Aspray, Fred Mayadas, and Moshe Y.Vardi (editors): Globalization and Offshoring of Software; A Report of the ACM Job Migration Task Force, ACM, 2006.

[Atkinson:11]Robert D. Atkinson: U.S. Corporate Tax Reform: Groupthink or Rational Debate?; The Information Technology & Innovation Foundation (ITIF), Washington DC, Jul.2011, http://www2.itif.org/files/2011-corporate-tax-reform.pdfl.

[Atkinson:12]Robert D. Atkinson: Enough is Enough: Confronting Chinese Innovation Mercantilism; The Information Technology & Innovation Foundation, Washington DC (ITIF) report, 28 Feb.2012, http://www.itif.org/2012-enough-is-enough.pdfl.

[ATRA:13]U.S. Congress: American Taxpayer Relief Act; HR-8, 3 Jan 2013.

[Audretsch:95]David B. Audretsch: "Firm Profitability, Growth, And Innovation"; Review of Industrial Organization, Vol.10 no.5, 1995, pp.579-588.

[Auerbach:99]Alan J. Auerbach: "Measuring the Impact of Tax Reform"; in [Slemrod:99], pp.353-361.

[Auerbach:05]Alan Auerbach: Who Bears the Corporate Tax, A Review of What We Know; NBER's Tax Policy and the Economy conference, Sep.2005.

[Auerbach:06]Alan Auerbach: Why Have Corporate Tax Revenues Declined -- Another Look; CESifo workshop, The Future of Capital Income Taxation, Venice, Jul. 17–18, 2006, updated Dec.2006.

[AuerbachF:02]Alan J. Auerbach and Martin Feldstein (eds.): Handbook of Public Economics, Elseviers/North-Holland, 2002.

[Aujean:01]Michel Aujean (chair): Company Taxation in the Internal Market; Commission of the EC, 23 Oct.2001.

[Austin:08]David Austin: Effects of Gasoline Prices on Driving Behaviour and Vehicle Markets; Congressional Budget Office, Congress of the United States, Jan.2008.

[AviYonah:95]Reuven S. Avi-Yonah: "The Rise and Fall of Arm's Length: A Study in the Evolution of U.S. International Taxation"; *Virginia Tax Review*, Vol.15, 1995, p.89.

[AviYonah:02]Reuven S. Avi-Yonah: "For Haven's Sake: Reflections on Inversion Transactions"; Univ.of Michigan Law School, *Tax Notes*, Vol.95 no.12, 17 Jun.2002.

[AviYonah:12]Reuven S. Avi-Yonah: Statement to Congress; University of Michigan School of Law, Permanent Subcommittee on Investigations, U.S. Congress, 20 Sep.2012.

[Babcock:68]Henry A. Babcock: Appraisal Principles and Procedures; American Society of Appraisers, 1968; 5th edition 1994.

[Baker:05]Raymond W. Baker: Capitalism's Achilles Heel, Dirty Money and How to Renew the Free Market System; Wiley, 2005.

[Baker:07]Leroy Baker: Halliburton Feels Democrat Wrath After Dubai Move; Tax-News.com, 15 Mar.2007.

[Baranson:78]Jack Baranson: Technology and the Multinationals; Lexington Books, 1978.

[BarIlanS:96]Avner Bar-Ilan and William C. Strange: "Investment Lags"; *American Economic Review*, American Economic Association, Vol. 86 No.3,1996, pp. 610-622.

[BarlettS:00]Donald L. Barlett and James B. Steel: The Great American Tax Dodge, How Spiraling Fraud and Avoidance Are Killing Fairness, Destroying the Income Tax, and Costing You; Little, Brown, and Co., 2000.

[Barra:98]BARRA: *United States Equity* Version 3 (E3); MSCI, BARRA, Berkeley, CA, 1998.

[Barthold:11]Thomas A. Barthold: Response to Lloyd Doggett, containing revenue estimates for a new repatriation under IRC 965; Joint Committee on Taxation, Congress of the United States, 15 Apr.2011.

[Bartlett:12B]Bruce Bartlett: The Benefit and the Burden, Tax Reform, Why We Need It and What It Will Take; Simon and Schuster, 2012.

[Bartlett:12T]Bruce Bartlett: "How to Avoid Reinventing the Wheel on Tax Reform"; New York Times, 24 and 31Jan.2012.

[Basel:06]Basel Committee on Bank Supervision: International Convergence of Capital Measurement and Capital Standards; Bank for International Settlements, Jun.2006.

[Basili:90]Victor Basili: "Viewing Maintenance as Reuse-Oriented Software Development"; IEEE Software, Vol.7 no.1, Jan.1990, pp.19-25.

[Basse:11]Søren Hetland Basse: Science History and The Future; Royal Danish Library reg.1992, translated and updated 11 Feb.2011, <unifiedscience.blogspot.com/>.

[Baum:10]Caroline Baum: "The Good Old Bad Days"; Bloomberg Businessweek; 6 Sep.2010, pp.4-5.

[Baxandall:12]Phineas Baxandall: Rogues Gallery of Major Corporate Legal Settlements; U.S. Public Interest Research Group (PIRG), 17 Apr.2012.

[Baz:09]Aureliano Gonzales Baz: Manufacturing in Mexico: The Mexican In-Bond (Maquila) Program; Banco Nacional de Comercio Exterior, 2009, http://www.bancomext-mtl.com/invest/vox128.htm.

[BEA:06]BEA: A Guide to the National Income and Product Accounts of the United States; Bureau of Economic Analysis, U.S. Department of Commerce, undated, retrieved 2006, http://www.bea.gov/national/nipaguid.pdfl.

[BEA:09]BEA: U.S. Direct Investment Abroad: Financial and Operating Data for U.S. Multinational Companies; Bureau of Economic Analysis, U.S. Department of Commerce, retrieved 2009, http://www.bea.gov/international/di1usdop.htm.

[BEA:11]BEA: Economic Recovery Widespread Across States in 2010; Bureau of Economic Analysis, U.S. Department of Commerce, 7 Jun.2011.

[Becker:02]Brian C. Becker: "Cost-Sharing Buy-Ins"; Chapter A in [Feinschreiber:01]: 2002 supplement.

[BeckerEM:09]Sascha O. Becker, Karolina Ekholm, and Marc-Andreas Muendler: Offshoring and the Onshore Composition of Tasks and Skills; IAW Discussion Papers 55, Institut für Angewandte Wirtschaftsforschung (IAW), 2009.

[Bell:11]Kevin A. Bell: Transfer Pricing: "Internal Revenue Service to Elevate Transfer Pricing Function, Move Directly Under Deputy Commissioner"; BNA Daily Tax Report, 16 Dec.2011.

[Bennett:11]Alison Bennett: "Tax Regulations: 'Mayo' Ruling Raises Bar for Challenges To Tax Regulations, Practitioners Say"; BNA Daily Tax Report, 14 Feb.2011.

[Bennett:11U]Drake Bennett: "Do the Unemployed Get a Second Act"; Bloomberg Businessweek, 14 Sep.2011.

[BermanKC:06]Karen Berman and Joe Knight, with John Case: *Financial Intelligence: A Manager's Guide to Knowing What the Numbers Really Mean*; Harvard Business School Press, 2006.

[BernardJS:06]Andrew Bernard, J. Jensen and Peter Schott: "Transfer Pricing by U.S.–Based Multinational Firms"; NBER working paper 12493, Aug.2006.

[Bernasek:10E]Anna Bernasek: The Economics of Integrity; Harper Studio, 2010.

[Bernasek:10T]Anna Bernasek: "Should Tax Bills Be Public Information?"; New York Times, 13 Feb.2010.

[Bernstein:03]Philip Bernstein: Remark at NLM/NSF planning meeting, Bethesda, MD, 3 Feb.2003.

[BettendorfEa:09]Leon Bettendorf, Michael P. Devereux, Albert van der Horst, Simon Loretz and Ruud A. de Mooij: Corporate tax harmonization in the European Union; CPB Document 133, Netherlands Bureau for Economic Policy Analysis, Nov.2009.

[Bickley:11]James M. Bickley: Tax Reform: An Overview of Proposals in the 112th Congress; Congressional Research Service, R41591, 20 Apr.2011.

[BierceEa:11]William B. Bierce et al.: 'Startup America', A Vision for American Entrepreneurs, What Role Global American Entrepreneurship?; Outsourcing-Law.com, Bierce & Kennerson, 11 Feb.2011.

[Bingham:12]Amy Bingham: "Robin Hood Activists Look to Make Fairy Tale a Reality"; ABC News, 19 Jun.2012.

[Birnbaum:06]Jeffrey H. Birnbaum: "Taxing Lessons, 20 Years in the Making"; The Washington Post, 22 Oct.2006.

[Birnkrant:10]Henry Birnkrant: "The Service's Approach to Transfer Pricing Takes a Drubbing from the Tax Court In Veritas"; Journal of Taxation, Vol.112 no.4, 2010, p.197.

[Bishop:08]Keith Paul Bishop: "Silver Standard"; Los Angeles Lawyer, Nov.2008, pp.32-42.

[Black:96]Fischer Black: "Noise"; *Journal of Finance*, Jul.1986.

[BlairM:06]David B. Blair and Dwight N. Mersereau: "Chief Counsel revamps case-specific advice procedures to match LMSB's new enforcement paradigms"; The Tax Executive, Jul.-Aug.2006.

[Blake:10]Rich Blake: "Smaller Fish to Fry–Internal Revenue Service Targets Self-Employed"; ABC News, 9 Apr.2010.

[Blessing:09]Peter H. Blessing: Testimony, Hearing on Banking Secrecy Practices and Wealthy American Taxpayers; The Subcommittee on Select Revenue Measures of the House Committee on Ways & Means, 111th Cong. Feb.2009, <http://waysandmeans.house.gov/media/pdf/111/pbless.pdf>.

[Bloomberg:12]Bloomberg View: "The Silliness of Soak-the-Rich Schemes"; *Bloomberg Businessweek*, 23 Mar 2012.

[BlouinKR:12]Jennifer Blouin, Linda Krull, and Leslie Robinson: Where in the world are 'permanently reinvested' earnings?; SSRN 2154662, Sept. 2012.

[BLS:11]Establishment Data Historical Employment (employees on nonfarm payrolls 1961 to April 2010, http://www.bls.gov/data/.

[BlumenthalS:06]Marsha Blumenthal and Joel B. Slemrod: "The Compliance Cost of Taxing Foreign Income its Magnitude, Determinants, and Policy Implications"; in [Slemrod:96].

[BodieKM:08]Zvi Bodie, Alex Kane, and Alan J Marcus: Investments, 8th edition; McGraw-Hill/Irwin, 2008.

[Bogoslaw:10]David Bogoslaw: "Tough Times Spur Shifts in Corporate R&D Spending"; Bloomberg Business Week, 9 Aug.2010.

[Bohr:18]Niels Bohr: 'It's hard to make predictions, especially about the future'; quoting a Danish expression in 1918.

[BoortzL:06]Neil Boortz and John Linder: The Fair Tax Book; Regan Books, HarperCollins Publishers, 2006.

[BorstellH:09]Thomas Borstell and John Hobster: 2009 Global transfer Pricing Survey, Tax Authority Insights, Perspectives, Interpretations, and Regulatory Changes; Ernst & Young, Sep.2009, 180 pp.

[Boskin:10]Michael J. Boskin: "Time to Junk the Corporate Tax"; Wall Street Journal, 6 May 2010.

[BoultonLS:00] Richard Boulton, Barry Libert, and Steve Samek: Cracking the Value Code; Arthur Andersen. Harper Business, 2000.

[BovenbergdM:94]A. Lans Bovenberg and Ruud A. de Mooij: "Environmental Levies and Distortionary Taxation"; The American Economic Review, 1994, Vol.84 no.4 pp.1085-1089.

[BowlesS:10]Erskine Bowles and Alan Simpson (co-chairs): The Moment of Truth; plan by The National Commission on Fiscal Responsibility and Reform, The White House, 9 Dec.2010, 66pp.

[BradfordS:77]David F. Bradford and William E. Simon: Blueprints for Basic Tax Reform; Office of Tax Analysis, US Dep. of the Treasury, 17 Jan.1977.

[BradfordEa:91]David Bradford (ed): NBER Book Series Tax Policy and the Economy; NBER, Vol.5, 1991, http://www.nber.org/booksbyseries/TPE.html.

[BrealeyMA:06]Richard A. Brealey, Stewart V. Meyers, and Franklin Allen: Principles of Corporate Finance, 8th edition; Mc GrawHill, 2006.

[Brennan:10]Thomas J. Brennan: "What Happens After a Holiday?: Long-Term Effects of the Repatriation Provision of the AJCA"; Northwestern Journal of Law and Social Policy, Spring 2010.

[Brittain:05]William Brittain-Catlin: *Offshore – The Dark Side of the Global Economy*; Farrar, Strauss and Giroux, 2005.

[BronfenbrennerL:04]Kate Bronfenbrenner and Stephanie Luce: The Changing Nature of Corporate Global Restructuring: The Impact of Production Shifts on Jobs in the US, China, and Around the Globe; Cornell Univ., Oct.2004, http://www.news.cornell.edu/releases/Oct04/jobs.outsourcing.rpt.04.pdfl.

[Brooks:95]Frederick Brooks: *The Mythical Man-Month, Essays in Software Engineering*; Addison-Wesley, 1975, reprinted 1995.

[Brooks:12]Sheena Brooks: "France Blacklists SKN as Offshore Tax Haven"; *The St.Kitts Nevis Observer*, 1 May 2012; http://www.panamalaw.org/nevis_llc_and_nevis_bank_account.html.

[BrooksKW:02]Bryant Brooks, Russell Kwiat, and Robert Weissler: Approaches to Valuing Cost Sharing Buy-Ins; Internal Revenue Service APA Program Training, 20 Aug.2002, http://www.irs.gov/pub/irs-apa/study_guide_exhibit_g.pdfl.

[Browne:12]James Browne: The 50p income tax rate; Institute for Fiscal studies, March 2012, http://www.ifs.org.uk/budgets/budget2012/budget2012jamesbrowne.pdfl.

[BrownEa:12]Jim Brown et al.: Report on the Mangement and Control Provision of the 'International Tax Competiveness Act of 2011'; New York State Bar Association, Tax Section, Rep. no.1232, 31 Jan.2011.

[Browning: 07]Lynnley Browning: "Gimme Tax Shelter"; *New York Times*, 4 Feb.2007.

[Browning:10]Lynnley Browning: "I.R.S. Shifts to Combat Tax Evasion"; *New York Times*, 4 Aug.2010.

[Browning:11]Lynnley Browning: "Insight: Microsoft's use of low-tax havens drives tax bill to 7 percent of profit"; *Reuters / Huffington Post Business*, 28 Jul. 2011.

[Buffett:11]Warren Buffett: "Stop Coddling the Super-Rich"; *New York Times*, 14 Aug.2011.

[Burman:99]Leonard E. Burman: The Labyrinth of Capital Gains Policy: a Guide for the Perplexed; The Brookins Institution, 1999.

[Burman:03]Leonard E. Burman: "Is the Tax Expenditure Concept Still Relevant?"; *National Tax Journal*, Sep.2003.

[Burman:11]Leonard E. Burman: Tax Reform Options: Marginal Rates on High-Income Taxpayers, Capital Gains, and Dividends; Statement before the Senate Committee on Finance, 14 Sep.2011.

[BurmanGT:08]Leonard E. Burman, Christopher Geissler, and Eric J. Toder: "How Big Are Total Individual Income Tax Expenditures, and Who Benefits from Them?"; *American Economic Review*, Vol.98 no.2, May 2008, pp.79-83.

[BurnhamO:05]Paul Burnham and Larry Ozanne: Taxing Capital Income, Effective Rates and Approches to Reform; Congressional Budget Office, Congress of the United States, Oct.2005.

[Burns:12]Alexander Burns: Romney Endorses Ryan Plan; *Politico*, 20 March 2012.

[Bush:05]George W. Bush, President's Advisory Panel on Federal Tax Reform: Simple, Fair, and Pro-Growth: Proposals to Fix America's Tax System; 1 Nov.2005, Doc 2005–22112, 2005 TNT 211–14.

[Byrne:12]Janet Byrne (ed.): "The Occupy Handbook"; Back Bay Books, 2012.

[ByrnesL:03]Nanette Byrnes and Louis Lavelle: "The Corporate Tax Game"; *Business Week*, 31 Mar.2003.

[Cairncross:97]Frances Cairncross: *The Death of Distance*; Orion, 1997.

[Camp:11]David Camp: Tax Reform Act of 2011; Ways and Means Discussion Draft, House of Representatives, 26 Oct.2011.

[CampbellW:12]Matthew Campbell and Zijing Wu: "Why Europe's Tech Firms Love New York"; *Bloomberg Businessweek*, 9 Apr.2012.

[Canale:09]David Canale et al.: Global Transfer Pricing Survey Findings – Tax Authority Insights; Ernst & Young, Thought Center Podcast, 2 Oct.2009.

[Cantley:03]Beckett G. Cantley: "Corporate Inversions: Will the REPO Act Keep Corporations from Moving to Bermuda?"; *Houston Business and Tax Law Journal*, Vol.3, 2003.

[Carney:13]Tim Carney: How corporate tax credits got into the 'cliff' deal; *Tax Notes*. 2 Jan. 2013.

[Carroll:32]Mitchell B. Carroll: Taxation of Foreign and National Enterprises; League of Nations Doc. C73M38.1932.II.A, 1932.

[Carson:08]Ron Carson: "Intellectual Property Audit and Management"; Chapter 33B in [ParrS:05], *2008 Cumulative Supplement*, Wiley 2008.

[Castle:11]Stephen Castle: "Europeans Introduce Corporate Tax Plan"; *New York Times*, 10 Mar.2011.

[CavenaughEa:04]John Cavenaugh, Jerry Mander, et al.: Alternatives to Economic Globalization, A Better World Is Possible; Report of the International Forum on Globalization, 2nd edition, Berrett-Koehler, 2004.

[Caves:07]Richard E. Caves: *Multinational Enterprise and Economic Analysis*, 3rd edition; Cambridge University Press, 2007.

[CavesCK:83]Richard E. Caves, Harold Crookell, and J. Peter Killing: "The Imperfect Market for Technology Licenses"; *Oxford Bulletin of Economics and Statistics*, 1983, pp.249-268.

[CBO:05]CBO: Corporate Income Tax Rates: International Comparison; Congressional Budget Office, Congress of the United States, Nov.2005.

[CBO:08]CBO: Revenues, Outlays, Deficits, Surpluses and Debt Held by the Public, 1968 to 2007; Congressional Budget Office, US Congress, Sep.2008, http://www.cbo.gov/budget/data/historical.pdfl.

[CBO:11]CBO: The Budget and Economic Outlook: Fiscal Years 2011–2021; Congressional Budget Office, Congress of the United States, Jan.2011, http://www.cbo.gov/ftpdocs/120xx/doc12039/01-26_fy2011outlook.pdfl.

[CBO:12]CBO: Comparing the Compensation of Federal and Private-Sector Employees, Congress of the United States, Jan.2012, http://www.cbo.gov/ftpdocs/126xx/doc12696/01-30-FedPay.pdfl.

[CCH:09]CCH Editorial Staff: *Internal Revenue Code*; 2 volumes, CCH Wolters Kluwer, Winter 2009.

[CCH:10]CCH Editorial Staff: *Income Tax Regulations, Including Proposed Regulations*; 7 volumes, CCH Wolters Kluwer, Winter 2010.

[Censky:11]Annalyn Censky: "Boost spending on equipment, create more jobs"; *CNN*Money, 12 Sep.2011.

[Chaback:07]Patricia Chaback: Industry Directive #1 on Research and Experimentation (R&E) Credit Claims; Internal Revenue Service, 4 Apr.2007.

[Chaback:08]Patricia Chaback: Tier 1, IRC 482 Cost-sharing Arrangements with Buy-in Payments; Internal Revenue Service IOE, Apr.2008

[Chamberlain:06]Andrew Chamberlain: Twenty Years Later: The Tax Reform Act of 1986; Tax Foundation, The Tax Policy Blog, 23 Oct.2006.

[Chambers:10]John Chambers: U.S. Jobs, Innovation, Growth and Investment; Cisco Blog, 5 Nov.2010.

[ChapotonG:88]O. Donaldson Chapoton and Lawrence B. Gibbs: *A Study of Intercompany Pricing*; Claitor's Publishing; Discussion Draft, U.S. Treasury Department, 18 Oct.1988. Also referred to as the '1988 White Paper'.

[ChatfieldG:73]C. Chatfield and G.J. Goodhardt: "A Consumer Purchasing Model with Erlang Interpurchase Times"; *Journal of the American Statistical Association*, Vol.68, Dec.1973, pp.828-835.

[ChavezTW:98]Andrea Chávez, Catherine Tornabene, and Gio Wiederhold: "Software Component Licensing Issues: A Primer"; *IEEE Software*, Vol.15 no.5, Sept-Oct 1998, pp.47-52.

[Chittum:11]Ryan Chittum: "GE Flubs a Pushback Against New York Times"; Columbia Journalism Review, 31 Mar.2011.

[ChoiH:04]E. Kwan Choi and James Harrington (eds.): *Handbook of International Trade*, two volumes; Basil Blackwell, 2004, 2005.

[ChoiSW:97]Song-Yong Choi, Dale O. Stahl, and Andrew Whinston: *The Economics of Electronic Commerce*; Macmillan, 1997.

[ChristensenCN:01]K. Christensen, R. Cline, and T. Neubig: "Total corporate taxation: 'Hidden'"; *National Tax Journal*, Sep.2001, Vol.54 no.3, pp.495-506.

[ChristensenR:03]Clayton M. Christensen and Michael E. Raynor: The Innovator's Solution: Creating and Sustaining Successful Growth; Harvard Business School, 2003.

[Christians:09]Allison Christians: "Sovereignty, Taxation, and Social Contract"; *Minnesota Journal of International Law*, Vol. 18, August 2009, p.99.

[Churchill:26]Winston Churchill: "Double Income Tax" and "Tax Avoidance"; Hansard of the House of Commons, Vol.194, 26 Apr.1926, p.1705 and Vol.205, 11 Apr.1927, pp.85-87.

[Ciesielski:12]Jack T. Ciesielski: Statement to Congress; Permanent Subcommittee on Investigations, U.S. Congress, 20 Sep.2012.

[Clark:10]Sue Clark: Letter of response to Martin Hearson, ActionAid UK; SABMiller plc, 11 Nov.2010, http://www.actionaid.org.uk/doc_lib/sabmiller_right_of_reply_and_response1.pdfl.

[Clarke:99]William Clarke: *How the City of London Works*; Sweet and Maxwell, 1999.

[Clausing:03]Kimberly Clausing: "Tax Motivated Transfer Pricing and U.S. Intrafirm Trade Prices"; *Journal of Public Economics*, 2003, pp.2207-2223.

[Clausing:04]Kimberly Clausing: The American Jobs Creation Act of 2004, Creating Jobs for Accountants and Lawyers; Urban-Brookings Tax Policy Center, Dec.2004.

[Clausing:05]Kimberly Clausing: The Role of U.S. Tax Policy in Offshoring; Working paper, Dept.of Economics, Reed College, Jun.2005.

[Clausing:06]Kimberly Clausing: "International Tax Avoidance and U.S. International Trade"; *National Tax Journal*, Jun.2006.

[Clausing:09]Kimberly A. Clausing: Multinational Firm Tax Avoidance and Tax Policy; *National Tax Journal*, Vol.62 no.4, Dec 2009, pp.703-725.

[ClevengerP:04]Novella Clevenger and Ken Pfannestiel: "Double Taxation of Dividends: Is the question resolved?"; *New Accountant*, REN Publishing, 2004.

[Clinton:11]Hillary Clinton: Remarks preceding President Hu's State visit to the U.S.; U.S. Department of State, 14 Jan.2011.

[CMSR:11] Centre for International Cooperation and Development: Corporate income tax; Slovenia, document ACT-2, 2011, www.cmsr.si/en/.

[Coglianese:11]Cary Coglianese: Federal Agency Use of Electronic Media in the Rulemaking Process; Final Report to the Adminstrative Conference of the United States, Dec.2011.

[Coglianese:12]Cary Coglianese (ed.): *Regulatory Breakdown: The Crisis of Confidence in U.S. Regulation*; University of Pennsylvania Press, 2012.

[CohanA:12]William D. Cohan and Jonathan Alter: "A Fair and Balanced Plan for Eliminating the Corporate Income Tax"; *Bloomberg Businessweek*, 25 Jun.2012.

[Cohn:12]Michael Cohn: IRS Commissioner Shulman Addresses Tax Delays; Accounting Today, 22 Mar. 2012.

[CohnC:11]Peter Cohn and Mathew Caminiti: "The Multinational Advantage"; *Bloomberg Businessweek*, 20 and 24 Jan.2011.

[Collins:11D]Chuck Collins: Stop Corporate Tax Dodging: Talking Points and Background Information; Institute for Policy Studies, 23 Mar.2011.

[Collins:11I]Lauren Collins: "House Perfect, is the IKEA concept comfy or creepy?"; *New Yorker*, 3 Oct.2011.

[CollinsS:99]Julie H. Collins and Douglas B. Shackelford: Corporate Domicile and Average Effective Tax Rates; in [Slemrod:99].

[Compustat:04]Compustat: Financial Results of Companies in SIC Code 7372 for 1999 to 2002; Nov.2004.

[Conard:12]Edward Conard: Unintended Consequences: Why Everything You've Been Told About the Economy Is Wrong; Portfolio, 2012.

[Contractor:81]Farok J. Contractor: *International Technology Licensing*; Lexington Books, 1981.

[Contractor:01]Farok J. Contractor (ed.): *Valuation of Intangible Assets in Global Operations*; Quorum, 2001.

[CookC:10]Nancy Cook and Eric Cook: System and method for analyzing tax avoidance; US patent 7,716, granted 11 May 2010.

[CordesEG:05]Joseph J. Cordes, Robert D. Ebel, and Jane G. Gravelle: *Encyclopedia of Taxation and Tax Policy*, 2nd edition; Urban Institute Press, Oct.2005.

[Cornford:04]Andrew Cornford: Enron and Internationally Agreed Principles for Corporate Governance and the Financial Sector; G-24 Discussion paper 30, UNCTAD, Jun.2004.

[Cosper:12]Susan M. Cosper: Statement to Congress; Permanent Subcommittee on Investigations, U.S. Congress, 20 Sep.2012.

[CowenT:11]Tyler Cowen and Alex Tabarrok: *Modern Principles, Macroeconomics*, 2nd edition; Worth Publishers, 2011.

[CoyD:11]Peter Coy and Jesse Drucker: "Apple, Google May Profit on a Tax Holiday"; *Bloomberg Businessweek*, 17 Mar.2011.

[Cray:09]Charlie Cray: Obama's Tax Haven reform: Chump Change; CorpWatch, 15 June 2009.

[CremerG:00]Helmuth Cremer and Fahrouz Gahvari: "Tax Evasion, Fiscal Competition, and Economic Integration"; *European Economic Review*, Vol.44, pp.1633-1657.

[CroninHKLP:11]Doug Cronin, Mike Heimert, Robert Kirschenbaum, Charles Larson, and Irving Plotkin: "'Useful Life' Determination in the Context of Intangibles Transfer Pricing Valuation Theoretical / Heuristic Framework for Analysis (i.e., Not Driven by Regulations)"; NABE Transfer Pricing Symposium, Jul. 2011.

[Crowell:37]Chester Theodore Crowell: "Our Tax Jungle"; *Harper's Magazine*, Nov.1937.

[Cusack:11]Bob Cusack: Gang of Six Collapses: Winners and Losers; The Hill, 22 May 2011.

[Cusumano:04]Michael A. Cusumano: The Business of Software; Free Press, 2004.

[Dagan:00]Tsilly Dagan: "The Tax Treaties Myth"; *NYU Journal of International Law and Politics*, Vol.32, Oct.2000, pp.939-996. <http://papers.ssrn.com/sol3/papers.cfm?abstract_id=379181>.

[Daily:02]Frederick W. Daily III: *Stand Up to the IRS*; Nolo, 2002.

[Dalio:09]Ray Dalio: A Template for Understanding What Is Going On; in *Insghts Into the Global Financial Crisis*, CFA institute, Research Foundation, 2009, pp.94-109.

[Daly:11]Spencer Daly: "Secrecy in Limbo: What the Most Recent Settlement with the IRS Means for UBS and the Rest of the Swiss Banking Industry"; *Journal of International Business & Law*, no.108, Hofstra University, 30 Mar.2011, pp.133-152.

[Damodaran:99]Aswath Damodaran: Research and Development Expenses: Implications for Profitabilty Measurement and Valuation; Stern School of Business, NYU working paper no.FIN-99-024, 1999.

[Damodaran:00]Aswath Damodaran: "An Updated Amazon Valuation"; working spreadsheet at <http://pages.stern.nyu.edu/~adamodar/amazon2000-1.xls>, 2000.

[Damodaran:02]Aswath Damodaran: The Dark Side of Valuation; Valuing Old Tech, New Tech, and New Economy Companies; Prentice-Hall, 2002.

[Damodaran:05]Aswath Damodaran: "The Value of Control: Implications for Control Premia, Minority Discounts and Voting Share Differentials"; S-DRP-05-02, Stern School of Business, Jul.2005.

[Damodaran:06]Aswath Damodaran: *Damodaran on Valuation*, 2nd edition; New York: John Wiley and Sons, 2006.

[DarbyL:07]Joseph B. Darby IIII and Kelsey Lemaster: "Double Irish More than Doubles the Tax Savings"; *Practical US/International Tax Strategies, WorldTrade Executive*, Vol.11 no.9, 15 May 2007.

[dAroma:27]Pasquale d'Aroma, chair Committee of Technical Experts on Double Taxation and Tax Evasion: Double Taxation and Tax Evasion; League of Nations report G.261 M85, 1927. II. Geneva, Apr.1927, scanned and re-typeset by Michel J. McIntyre, 8 Feb.2004 at the University of Michigan.

[DauchyN:09]Estelle Dauchy and Tom Neubig: "President Obama's Business Tax Proposals: Industry Effects"; *Tax Notes*, 19 Oct.2009, p 314.

[Daum:01]Juergen Daum: The New DASB rules for reporting in Intangible Asset – The U.S. Versus the European way; The *new* New Economy Analyst Report, 10 Nov.2001.

[Davidoff:11]Steven M. Davidoff: DealBook: "The Benefits of Incorporating Abroad in an Age of Globalization"; New York Times, 20 Dec.2011.

[Davis:09]Manny Davis: Symantec Wins Tax Case – Not Responsible for IRS Back Taxes; BackTaxHelp.com, 11 Dec.2009, retrieved 11 Oct.2011.

[DavisRKM:11]Benjamin Davis, Elizabeth Ridlington, Gary Kalman, and Jeffrey Musto: "Tax Shell Game: How Much Did Offshore Tax Havens Cost You in 2010?"; U.S. Public Research Interest Group, 18 Apr.2011, http://www.uspirg.org/reports/usp/tax-shell-game-how-much-did-offshore-tax-havens-cost-you-2010.

[delaVega:1668]Joseph Penso de la Vega: *Confusión de Confusiones*; 1668; Wiley, 1996.

[DelMonte:10]James Del Monte: IT Employer Information, Cost of Hiring/Turnover (CoH); JDA Professional Services, 2010, http://www.jdapsi.com/Client/articles/coh.

[Deloitte:10]Deloitte: Uncertain Tax Positions and the IRS Transparency Initiative, No Holds Barred; Deloite Development LLC, 10 May 2010.

[Deloitte:11]Deloitte: SEC Compliance Checklist – General; Deloitte TAX, Jan.2011.

[deMatteis:99]Bob deMatteis: From Patent to Profit: Secrets and Strategies for the Successful Inventor, 3rd edition; Berkeley Publishing, 1999.

[deMooij:05]Ruud Aloysius de Mooij: "Will Corporate Income Taxation Survive?"; *De Economist*, Springer Verlag, Vol.153 no.3, Dec.2005, pp.277-301.

[deMooijN:08]Ruud de Mooij and Gaëtan Nicodème: "Corporate tax policy and incorporation in the EU"; *International Tax and Public Finance*, Springer, Vol.15 no.4, Aug.2008, pp.478-498.

[DengL:06]Z. Deng and Baruch Lev: "In-process R&D, to Capitalize or Expense?"; *The Journal of Engineering and Technology Management*, Mar.2006, pp.18-32.

[Derman:11]Emanual Derman: *Models.Behaving.Badly*; Free Press, Simon and Schuster, 2011.

[Desai:09]Mihir A. Desai: Securing Jobs or the New Protecionsim: Taxing the Overseas Activities of Multinational Firms; Harvard University working paper 09-107, 2009.

[DesaiD:07]Mihir A. Desai and Dhammika Dharmapala: Taxes and Portofolio Choice: Evidence from JGTRRA's Treatment of International Dividends; NBER working paper 13,281, Jul.2007, <http://papers.ssrn.com/sol3/papers.cfm?abstract_id=1000680>.

[DesaiFH:01]Mihir A. Desai, C. Fritz Foley, and James R. Hines jr.: "Repatriation Taxes and Dividend Distortions"; *National Tax Journal*, Vol.54 no.4, Sep.2001, pp.829-851.

[DesaiFH:04F]Mihir A. Desai, C. Fritz Foley, and James R. Hines jr.: "The Costs of Shared Ownership: Evidence From International Joint Ventures"; *Journal of Financial Economics* 73 no.2, Aug.2004, pp.323-374.

[DesaiFH:04R]Mihir A. Desai, C. Fritz Foley, and James R. Hines jr.: *Economic Effects of Regional Tax Havens*; NBER working paper 10806, SSRN no.601108, Sep.2004.

[DesaiFH:05D]Mihir A. Desai, C. Fritz Foley, and James R. Hines jr.: "The Demand for Tax Haven Operations"; *Journal of Public Economics*, Vol.90, Elseviers, Feb.2006, pp.513-531; SSRN No. 593546, March.2005.

[DesaiFH:05E]Mihir A. Desai, C. Fritz Foley, and James R. Hines jr.: "Do Tax Havens Divert Economic Activity?"; *Economics Letters*, Vol.90, Elseviers 2006, p.219-224.

[DesaiFH:06A]Mihir A. Desai, C. Fritz Foley, and James R. Hines jr.: "Taxation and Multinational Activity; New Evidence, New Interpretations"; *Survey of Current Business*, Vol.82 no.6 Feb.2006, pp.16-22.

[DesaiFH:06E] Mihir A. Desai, C. Fritz Foley, and James R. Hines jr.: "The Demand for Tax Haven Operations"; Journal of Public Economics, Vol.90, Elseviers, Feb.2006, pp.513–531.

[DesaiFH:07]Mihir A. Desai, C. Fritz Foley and James R. Hines jr.: "Economic Effects of Dorgan, Levin, & Feingold, Deficit Reduction. Senate Bill 110, Subtitle B, Section 212.R 25 Jan.2007.

[DesaiH:00]Mihir A. Desai and James R. Hines Jr.: "The Uneasy Marriage of Export Incentives and the Income tax"; *Tax Policy and the Economy*, Vol.15, MIT press; National Bureau of Economic Research, NBER working paper 8009, Nov.2000.

[DesaiH:04]Mihir A. Desai and James R. Hines jr.: "Old Rules and New Realities: Corporate Tax Policy in a Global Setting"; *National Tax Journal*, Vol.57 no.4, Dec.2004, pp.937-960.

[Devasabai:09]Kris Devasabai: "Cayman registration fees to rise"; Hedge Funds Review News, 15 Dec 2009.

[DevereuxH:03]Michael P. Devereux and R. Glenn Hubbard: "Taxing Multinationals"; *International Tax and Public Finance*, Springer Verlag, Vol.10 no.4, Aug.2003, pp.469-487.

[DevereuxK:09]Michael Devereux and Christian Keuschnigg: Distorting the Arm's-length principle; Oxford University Centre for Business Taxation, working paper 09/10, Jul.2009.

[DevereuxL:11]Michael Devereux and Simon Lorentz: How would EU corporate tax reform affect US investment in Europe; National Bureau of Economic Research, NBER working paper 17576, Oct.2011.

[Dey:89]Richard Morris Dey: *I*n the Way of Adventure: The Story of John Caldwell and Palm Island; Offshore Press, 1989, 35pp.

[Dharan:02]Bata G. Dharan: Enron's Accounting Issues – What We Can Learn to Prevent Future Enrons; Testimony prepared to US House Energy and Commerce Committee's Hearings on Enron's Accounting, Feb.2002.

[DharmapalaFF:09]Dhammika Dharmapala, C. Fritz Foley, and Kirstin J. Forbes: 'Watch what I do, Not what I say': The unintended Consequences of the Homeland Investment Act; NBER working paper 15023, Jun.2009.

[DharmapalaH:06]Dhammika Dharmapala and James R. Hines jr.: Which Countries Became Tax Havens?; National Bureau of Economic Research, 2006; revised May 2009.

[DiamondZ:08]John W. Diamond and George R. Zodrow (eds): *Fundamental Tax Reform: Issues, Choices and Implications*; MIT Press, 2008. Foreword by James Baker III.

[DickinsNW:05]Denise Dickins, Thomas G. Noland, and Kenneth M. Washer: "Primer on Partnership-Compensation Models"; *The CPA Journal*, Aug.2005.

[Ditmer:11]Philip Dittmer: "U.S. Corporations Suffer High Effective Tax Rates by International Standards"; Tax Foundation Special Report no.195, Sep.2011.

[Dobuzinskis:10]Alex Dobuzinskis: Flextronics Sees Pressure on Operating Margins; Reuters, 8 Sep.2010.

[Doebele:04]Justin Doebele: "Flex Forward: Flextronics' Michael Marks says that outsourcing can only get much, much bigger"; *Chief Executive*, 1 Jul.2004.

[Doernberg:08]Richard L. Doernberg: *International Taxation in a Nutshell*, 8th edition; Thomson Westlaw, 2008, 612pp.

[Dohmen:09]Joep Dohmen: "Multinationals betalen vrijwel geen belasting"; *NRC Handelsblad*, 25 Nov.2009, http://www.nrc.nl/economie/article1855259.ece/Multinationals_betalen_vrijwel_geen_belasting.

[Doggart:02] Caroline Doggart: Tax Havens and Their Use; Economist Intelligence Unit, 2002.

[DonadioP:11]Rachel Donadio and Elisabetta Povoedo: "Italy Tries Raising the Social Stigma on Tax Evaders"; *New York Times*, 24 Dec.2011.

[Dorgan:07]Dorgan et al.: US Senate Deficit Reduction Bill of 2007, Senate Bill 681, Subtitle B, S. 212, 110th Congress, 1st Sess., 2007.

[DoT:07]Department of the Treasury: Treasury Conference on Business Taxation and Global Competitiveness; background paper, 23 Jul.2007, 54pp.

[DowdMM:12]Tim Dowd, Robert McClelland, and Athiphat Muthiacharoen: New Evidence on the Tax Elasticity of Capital Gains; Joint Committee on Taxation. June 2012, JCX 56–12, 49pp.

[Drucker:08]Jesse Drucker: "Corporate Tax Reporting Draws GAO Scrutiny"; *Wall Street Journal*, 13 Aug.2008.

[Drucker:10]Jesse Drucker: "Globe-trotting Profits, U.S. Companies Dodge $60 Billion in Taxes with Global Odyssey"; *Bloomberg Businessweek*, 14 May 2010.

[Drucker:10A]Jesse Drucker: "Tax 'Shenanigans' Turn U.S. Sales to Foreign Income with Billions Offshore"; *Bloomberg Businessweek*, 20 Jul. 2010.

[Drucker:10B]Jesse Drucker: "The Tax Haven That's Saving Google Billions"; *Bloomberg Businessweek*, 21 Oct.2010.

[Drucker:10C]Jesse Drucker: "Dodging Repatriation Tax Lets U.S. Companies Bring Home Cash"; *Bloomberg Businessweek*, 28 Dec.2010.

[Drucker:11P]Jesse Drucker: "Puerto Rico Tax Break Shifts to Cayman Islands"; *Bloomberg Businessweek*, 20 Dec.2011.

[DruckerRM:11]Jesse Drucker, Richard Rubin, and Ryan Mac: "The Trillion-Dollar Tax Holiday"; *Bloomberg Businessweek*, 3 Oct.2011, pp.66-67.

[Drum:11]Kevin Drum: Chart of the Day, Corporate Taxation in America; Mother Jones, 17 Nov.2011.

[DufeyG:94]Gunter Dufey and Ian H. Giddy: *The International Money Market*, 2nd ed; Prentice Hall, 1934.

[DuhiggB:12]Charles Duhigg and Keith Bradsher: How the U.S. Lost Out On iPhone Work, Apple's Experience Shows Why Jobs Are Flowing to China; *New York Times*, 22 Jan.2012.

[DuhiggK:12]Charles Duhigg and David Kocieniewski: "How Apple Sidesteps Billions in Taxes"; *New York Times*, 28 Apr.2012.

[Dumagan:95]Jesus C. Dumagan: Examining the Cost-Effectiveness of the Research and Experimentation Tax Credit; Office of Business and Industrial Analysis, US Department of Commerce, Jun.1995.

[DuPont:79]E.I. DuPont de Nemours & Co. v. United States, 608 F.2d 445 (Ct. Cl.1979).

[DurstC:03]Michael C. Durst and Robert E. Culbertson: Clearing Away the Sand: Retrospective Methods and Prospective Documentation in Transfer Pricing Today; Tax Law Review, Vol.37, NYU School of Law, Fall 2003.

[Dwoskin:12I]Elisabeth Dwoskin: "The Incrementalist"; Bloomberg Businessweek, 11 Jun.2012.

[Dye:08]Ronald A. Dye: Cost-sharing Agreements, a Tax Saving Device for Multi-nationals; *Kellogg Insight*, Northwestern University. Apr.2008, <http://insight.kellogg.northwestern.edu/index.php/Kellogg/article/cost_sharing_agreements>.

[DyeGG:07]Ronald A. Dye, Rajiv Gokhale, and Timothy Guimond: Valuation Issues Related to Buy-in Payments in Cost-Sharing Agreements; Oct.2007, Columbia University, http://www4.gsb.columbia.edu/filemgr?file_id=72157.

[Dyson:12]George Dyson: *Turing's Cathedral, The Origins of the Digital Universe*; Pantheon, 2012.

[Economist:11F]Economist (ed.): "The Craze for Flat Taxes"; *The Economist*, 29 Oct.2011.

[Economist:11L]Economist (ed.): "Money and Politics"; *The Economist*, 1 Oct.2011.

[Economist:11M]Economist (ed.): "Exports to Mars, Official statistics probably exaggerate global current- account imbalances"; *The Economist*, 12 Nov 2011, p.90.

[Economist:11S]Economist (ed.): "Unsettling Wall Street"; *The Economist*, 3 Dec.2011.

[Economist:11T]Economist (ed.): "Marginal Revolutionaries"; *The Economist*, 31 Dec.2011.

[Economist:12A]Economist (ed.): "Over-regulated America, The home of laissez-faire is being suffocated by excessive and badly written regulation"; *The Economist*, 18 Feb.2012.

[Economist:13] Economist: Tax havens, The missing $20 trillion, How to stop companies and people dodging tax, in Delaware as well as Grand Caymans; Economist special report, 16 Feb.2013.

[EdenK:05]Lorraine Eden and Robert T. Kudrle: "Tax Havens: Renegade States in the International Tax Regime"; *Law & Policy*, Vol.27 no 1, Jan.2005.

[Edgar:10]U.S. Securities and Exchange Commission: Company Search; Edgar Access to Corporate Report Submissions, http://www.sec.gov/edgar/searchedgar/webusers.html, updated 11 Feb.2010.

[Edwards:03] Chris Edwards: The U.S. Corporate Tax and the Global Economy; Tax and Budget Bulletin, The Cato Institute, Sept.2003, no.18.

[EikelenboomDG:11]Siem Eikelenboom and Gaby de Groot: “Nederland in Trek bij Multinationals”; *Het Financieele Dagblad*, 12 Sep.2011; and subsequent articles.

[Eisenberg:97]Rebecca S. Eisenberg (chair): *Intellectual Property Rights and Research Tools in Molecular Biology*; National Academy Press, 1997.

[Elliott:12]Amy Elliott: International Practice Networks Differ from Issue Practice Groups, Danilack Says; *BNA Daily Tax Report*, 4 Oct.2012.

[ElmendorfEa:11]Douglas W. Elmendorf (director) et al.: Reducing the Deficit: Spending and Revenue Options; Congressional Budget Office, Congress of the United States, Mar.2011, pp.182–183. http://www.cbo.gov/ftpdocs/120xx/doc12085/03-10-ReducingTheDeficit.pdf.

[Ensinger:11]Dustin Ensinger: Multinational Corporations Creating Jobs…Overseas; *Economy in Crisis*, 4 Nov.2010, <http://economyincrisis.org>.

[EntinM:12]Stephen Entin and Will McBride: Simulating the Economic Effects of Romney's Tax Plan; Tax Foundation Fiscal Fact No.330, 3 Oct.2012.

[Eisenwein:06]Gregg A. Esenwein: Individual Capital Gains Income: Legislative History; Congressional Research Service, 19 May 2006, <assets.opencrs.com/rpts/98-473_20060518.pdf>.

[EU:08]Council of the European Union: Proposal for a Council Directive amending Directive 2003/48/EC on taxation of savings income in the form of interest payments; 23 Nov.2008.

[Farrell:12]Maureen Farrell: “Calpers: We're getting even more activist”; *CNN*Money, 2 May 2012.

[FarrellKS:05]Diana Farrell, Noshir Kaka, and Sascha Stürze: “Ensuring India's offshoring future”; *McKinsey Quarterly*, Sep.2005.

[FASB:85]Financial Accounting Standards Board: Accounting for the Costs of Computer Software to be Sold, Leased, or Otherwise Marketed; Financial Accounting Foundation, FAS 86, 1985.

[FASB:04]Financial Accounting Standards Board: Disclosures about Intangible Assets, Removal of Project on Recognition of Unrecognized Intangibles; Financial Accounting Foundation, 21 May 2004.

[FASB:05] Financial Accounting Standards Board: Practical Accommodation to the Application of Grant Date as Defined in FASB Statement No. 123(R); FAS 123(R)-2, Financial Accounting Foundation, 18 Oct.2005.

[FASB:09]Financial Accounting Standards Board: Accounting Standards Codification, version 3; Financial Accounting Foundation, 2009.

[FeenstraEa:10]Robert C. Feenstra et al.: Report on the Sate of Available Data for the Study of International Trade and Foreign Direct Investment; National Bureau of Economic Research, Working paper 16254, Aug.2010.

[FeenstraMRS:09]Robert C. Feenstra, Benjamin Mandel, Marshall B. Reinsdorf, and Matthew Slaughter: Effects of Trade Gains and Tariff Changes on the Measurement of U.S. Productivity Growth; NBER working paper no.15592, Dec.2009.

[Feinschreiber:01]Robert Feinschreiber: *Transfer Pricing Handbook*, 3rd edition; Transfer Pricing Consortium, John Wiley Publishers, Apr.2001.

[FeldsteinHH:95]Martin Feldstein, James R. Hines Jr. and R. Glenn Hubbard (eds.): *Taxing Multinational Corporations*; University of Chicago Press, 1995.

[FeldsteinS:78]Martin Feldstein and Joel Slemrod: “Inflation and the Excess Taxation of Capital Gains on Corporate Stock”; *National Tax Journal*, Vol.31, 1978, pp.107–118.

[Felt:76]Mark Felt: Discussion with Bob Woodward; *All the President's Men*, Warner Brothers, 1976.

[Fernandez:13]Pablo Fernandez: *Valuation and Common Sense*; IESE Business School, Spain, SSRN eLibrary, 2013 http://ssrn.com/abstract=2209089.

[Fifield:11]Anna Fifield: “Buffet calls for tax rises for the rich”; *Financial Times*, 15 Aug.2011.

[Finfacts:10] Finfacts Ireland: US Multinationals Profit from Tax Havens; retrieved 2010, Finfacts Reports, http://www.finfacts.com/irelandeconomy/usmultinationalprofitsireland.htm>.

[FisherH:11]Ken Fisher and Lara Hoffman: Markets Never Forget (But People do); Wiley. 2012

[FishmanW:01]Raymond Fishman and ShangYu Wei: Tax rates and Tax Evasion: Evidence from ‘Missing Imports' in China; National Bureau of Economic Research (NBER), working paper 8551, Oct.2001.

[FlignorO:06]Paul Flignor and David Orozco: Intangible Asset & Intellectual Property Valuation: A Mutidisciplinary Perspective; ipthought.com, Kellogg School of Business, June 2006.

[Folbre:11]Nancy Folbre: Tax Havens and Treasure Hunts; *New York Times*, 4 Apr.2011.

[Fornito:05]Roberto Fornito: Haftung im Verein; Müller-Eckstein Rechtsanwälte, Staad, Switzerland, 2005.

[Fox:09]Justin Fox: *The Myth of the Rational Market*; Harper Business, 2009.

[Frank:11]Robert Frank: "Are Taxes Causing the Rich to Renounce Their Citizenship?"; The Wealth Report, *Wall Street Journal*, 13 Jun.2011.

[FreemanAB:09]Nick J. Freeman, George Abonyi, and Atipol Bhanich Sipapol: Globalization of Production and the Competitiveness of Small and Medium-sized Enterprises in Asia and the Pacific: Trends and Prospects; UN Studies in Trade and Investment no.65, ST/ESCAP/2540, 2009.

[Friedman: 86]Milton Friedman: "On the 1986 Tax Reform"; Wall Street Journal: 7 Jul.1986.

[FurmanB:08]Jason Furman and Jason Bordoff: *Path to Prosperity*; Hamilton Project Ideas on Income Security, Education, and Taxes, Brookings Institution Press, 2008.

[Gabriel:11]Trip Gabriel: "Gingrich Strikes Economic Themes in Hitting Romney"; *New York Times*, 27 Dec.2011.

[GAO:03]GAO: IRS and TIGTA Should Evaluate Their Processing of Employee Misconduct under Section 1203; Government Accountability Office, report GAO-03-394, 14 Feb.2003.

[GAO:04]GAO, International Taxation: Tax Haven Companies were More Likely to Have a Cost Advantage in Federal Contracting; U.S. General Accounting Office report GAO-04-856, Jun.2004, 27pp.

[GAO:05]GAO: Tax Compliance: Better Compliance Data and Long-term Goals Would Support a More Strategic IRS Approach to Reducing the Tax Gap; Government Accountability Office, report GAO-05-753, 12 Jul.2005.

[GAO:07]GAO: Tax Administration: Additional Time Needed to Complete Offshore Tax Evasion Examinations; Government Accountability Office, report GAO-07-237, Mar.2007.

[GAO:08]GAO: Comparison of the Reported Tax Liabilities of Foreign- and U.S.-Controlled Corporations, 1998–2005; Government Accountability Office, report GAO-08-957, July 2008.

[GAO:09]GAO, International Taxation: Large U.S. Corporations and Federal Contractors with Subsidiaries in Jurisdictions Listed as Tax Havens or Financial Privacy Jurisdictions; U.S. Government Accountability Office, report GAO-09-157, Dec.2008, 63pp.

[GAO:12]GAO: Internal Revenue Service, Interim Results of 2012 Tax Filing Season and Summary of the Fiscal Year 2013 Budget Request; US Government Accountability Office, report GAO-12-566, 20 Mar.2012, 33pp.

[GardnerR:98]William Gardner and Joseph Rosenbaum: "Intellectual Property: Database Protection and Access to Information"; Science, Vol.281 no. 5378, 7 Aug.1998, pp.786-787.

[Garofalo:12]Pat Garofalo: CEOs of Tax Dodging Corporations Want to Cut Their Own Taxes Too; Nation of Change, 15 May 2012.

[GaukeEa:10]David Gauke et al.: Corporate Tax Reform: Delivering a More Comprehensive System; HM Revenue and Customs, 20 Oct. 2010.

[George:11]J. Russell George: Management and Performance Challenges Facing the Internal Revenue Service for Fiscal 2012; Inspector General for Tax Administration, 14 Oct.2011.

[GerthMH:11]Jeff Gerth, Megan Murphy, and Vanessa Houlder: "Corporations Couldn't Wait to 'Check the Box' on Huge Tax Break"; ProPublica, *Nation of Change*, 27 Sept.2011.

[Gibbs:09]Robert Gibbs: Leveling the Playing Field: Curbing Tax Havens and Removing Tax Incentives for Shifting Jobs Overseas; The White House, 4 May 2009.

[Gideon:05]Kenneth W. Gideon: The Comprehensive Business Income Tax; presentation slides, Skadden et al., 13 May 2005, <govinfo.library.unt.edu/taxreformpanel/meetings/…/gideon_052005.ppt>.

[Gigot:12]Paul Gigot: "Obama's Dividend Assault"; *Wall Street Journal*, 22 Feb.2012.

[Gladstone:1898]William Gladstone: "Notes from a Diary"; 1898, p.140: 'To be engaged in opposing wrong affords but a slender guarantee of being right'.

[Gladwell:07]Malcom Gladwell: "Open Secrets"; *New Yorker*, 8 Jan.2007; also in *What the Dog Saw*; Little Brown and Company, 2009.

[Gladwell:11]Malcom Gladwell: "The Creation Myth"; *New Yorker*; 16 May 2011.

[Glass:03]Robert L. Glass: *Facts and Fallacies of Software Engineering*; Addison Wesley, 2003.

[Gleckman:02]Howard Gleckman: "Sealing off the Bermuda Triangle?"; *Business Week*, 1 Jul.2002.

[Gleckman:11]Howard Gleckman: Gingrich's Tax Plan: Big Tax Cuts, Big Deficits; Tax Policy Center and Brookings Institution, 12 Dec 2011.

[Gleeson:94]William Gleeson: "Anderson near to £1m per partner"; *The Independent*, 12 Jun.1994.

[GoldscheiderJM:02]Robert Goldscheider, John Jarosz, and Carla Mullhern: "Use of the Twenty-Five Percent Rule in Valuing Intellectual Property"; *Les Nouvelles*, LES, Dec.2002.

[Gooch:00]Lawrence Gooch: "In-Process R&D"; Chapter 9 in *Handbook of Advanced Business Valuation*, p.176, McGraw-Hill, 2000.

[Goodman:67]George J.W. Goodman (Adam Smith): *The Money Game*; Random House, 1967, 1976.

[Goolsbee:04]Austan Goolsbee: "The Impact of Corporate Income Tax: Evidence from State Organizational Form"; *Journal of Public Economics*, Vol.88 no.112004, pp.2283-2299.

[Gordon:86]Roger H. Gordon: "Taxation of Investment and Saving in the World Economy"; *American Economic Review*, Vol.76, 1986, pp.1086-1102.

[GordonG:97]Joseph R. Gordon and Myron J. Gordon: "Finite Horizon Expected Growth Model"; *Financial Analysts Journal*, Vol.53 no.3, May/Jun.1997, pp.52-61.

[GordonH:02]Roger H. Gordon and James R. Hines jr.: "International Taxation"; in [AuerbachF:02], 2002, pp.1395-1995.

[GordonL:00]Roger H. Gordon and Young Lee: Do Taxes Affect Corporate Debt Policy? Evidence from U.S. Corporate Tax Return Data; *Journal of Public Economics*, Vol. 82, Nov.2001, pp.195-224.

[Gore:08]Al Gore: *The Assault on Reason*; Bloomsbury Publishing, 2008.

[GoreR:98]Al Gore and Robert E. Rubin: Reinventing Service at the IRS; GPO report 1998.

[Gowri:98]Aditi Gowri: "Speech and Spending: Corporate Political Speech Rights Under the First Amendments"; *Journal of Business Ethics*, Vol.17 no.16, Dec.1998, pp.1835-1860.

[GPO:12]US Budget Summary Tables; Government Printing Office, 2009–2012.

[GravelleS:06]Jane Gravelle and Kent A. Smetters: "Does the Open Economy Assumption Really Mean That Labor Bears the Burden of a Capital Income Tax?"; *Advances in Economic Analysis & Policy*, Vol.6 no.1, 2006.

[Greeley:12]Brendan Greeley: "Obama Spoils for an Election Year Tax Fight"; *Bloomberg Businessweek*, 27 Feb.2012, pp.34-36.

[Green:12]Peter S. Green: "Plenty of Love, But where is the Action?"; *Bloomberg Businessweek*, 17 Sep.2012.

[Gregory:12] Dolores W. Gregory: IRS Withdrawing 2007 Issue Paper on Cost Sharing Buy-Ins; BNA Daily Tax Report, Jan.20, 2012.

[GregoryS:11] Neil Gregory and Susan Symons: Paying Taxes 2011, The global picture; The Word Bank Group and Price Waterhouse Coopers, PWC, 2011.

[GriffithK:04]Rachel Griffith and Alexander Klemm: What has been the tax competition experience of the past 20 years?; Institute for Fiscal Studies, IFS working paper W04/05, 2004.

[GriffithS:09]Cara Griffith and Stephanie Stewart: "Drop shipments and flash title: establishing sales tax nexus in complex commercial transactions"; *The Tax Adiser*, Vol.40 no.9 American Institute of CPAs, 22 Sep.2009.

[Grimes:11]Seamus Grimes: Can China become an Innovation Hub?; East Asian Bureau of Economic Research, http://www.eastasiaforum.org/2011/07/22/can-china-become-an-innovation-hub/, 22 Jul.2011.

[GrimesC:09]Seamus Grimes and Patrick Collins: "The Contribution of the Overseas ICT sector to expanding R&D investment in Ireland"; *Irish Geography*, Routledge, Vol.42 no.1, 1 Mar.2009, pp.45-67.

[Grove:10]Andy Grove: "How to Make an American Job"; *Bloomberg Businessweek*, 5 Jul. 2010, pp.48-53.

[GrubertA:08]Harry Grubert and Rosanne Altshuler: "Corporate Taxes in the World Economy: Reforming the Taxation of Cross-Border Income"; in [DiamondZ:08], pp.319-354.

[Gu:01]Ferdinand A. Gu: "Free cash flow, debt-monitoring and managers' LIFO/FIFO policy choice"; *Journal of Corporate Finance*,Volume 7, Issue 4, Dec.2001, pp.475–492.

[GuptaS:07]Amar Gupta and Satwik Seshasai: "The 24-Hour Knowledge Factory, Using Internet technology to leverage spatial and temporal separations"; *ACM Transactions on Internet Technology*, Vol.7 no.3, Aug.2007, article 14.

[GuptaWS:09]Amar Gupta, Gio Wiederhold, David Branson Smith, and Devin Sreecharanai: Outsourcing from the Perspectives of International Protocols, Law, Intellectual Property, and Taxation; Arizona Legal Studies Discussion Paper 09-18, 7 Jan.2009, <http://ssrn.com/abstract=1324242>.

[Guru:12]GuruFocus: Market Valuations; http://www.gurufocus.com/stock-market-valuations.php, accessed May 2012.

[Haass:13]Richard Haass: *Foreign Policy Begins at Home*; Basic Books, 2013.

[HackerL12]Jacob S. Hacker and Nate Loewentheil: *Prosperity Economics, Building an Economy for all*; Yale University, 2012.

[HackerP:10]Jacob S. Hacker and Paul Pierson: *Winner-Take-All Politics*: *How Washington Made the Rich Richer-and Turned Its Back on the Middle Class*; Simon & Schuster, 2010.

[Hall:01] Bronwyn H. Hall: Tax Incentives for innovation in the United States; Asesoria Industrial ZABALA-Spain, report Inno-00-93 the EU, 15 Jan.2001.

[HallR:07]Robert E. Hall and Alvin Rabushka: *The Flat Tax*, *Silver Anniversary Edition*; Hoover Institution Press Publication 423, Stanford CA, 2007.

[HallS:99]Joshua Hall and Jim Saxton: Tax Expenditures, A review and Analysis; Joint Economic Committee, United States Congress, Aug.1999.

[Halperin:11]Daniel Halperin: "Is Income Tax Exemption for Charities a Subsidy?"; *Tax Law Review*, Vol.64 no.3, Spring 2011, pp.283-312.

[Hampton:96]Mark Hampton: The Offshore Interface: Tax Havens in the Global Economy; Macmillan, 1996.

[Hand:35]Judge Learned Hand: *Gregory v. Helvering*; 69 F.2d 809, 810 (2d Cir.1934), aff'd, 293 U.S. 465, 55 S.Ct. 266, 79 L.Ed. 596, 1935; *Yale Law Review*, Vol.167, 1947.

[HandL:03]John Hand and Baruch Lev (eds.): *Intangible Assets*, *Values*, *Measures. and Risks*; Oxford University Press, 2003.

[HanlonM:09]Michelle Hanlon and Edward L. Maydew: "Book-Tax Conformity"; *National Tax Journal*, Vol.62, 2009, p.127.

[Harlan:1886]John Marshall Harlan: *Santa Clara County v. Southern Pacific Railroad*; US Supreme Court, Session 228, 394, 1886.

[Harrison:03]Bonnie Harrison: "Intangible Assets"; Chapter 10 in Weygandt, Kieso and Warfield: *Fundamentals of Intermediate Accounting*, Wiley 2003.

[Harvey:12]J. Richard Harvey: FATCA and Schedule UTP, Are these unilateral US actions doomed unless adopted by other countries?; Villanova Public Law and Legal Theory Working paper series, No. 2012–2005, Mar.2012.

[HassettB:07]Kevin A. Hassett and Alex Brill: Revenue-Maximizing Corporate Income Taxes: The Laffer Curve in OECD Countries; AEI working paper 137, Washington, DC, 31 Jul.2007, http://www.aei.org/paper/26577.

[HassettM:10]Kevin A. Hassett and Aparna Mathur: Spatial Tax Competition and Domestic Wages; American Enterprise Institute for Policy Research (AEI), working paper, 1 Dec.2010.

[HassettM:11]Kevin A. Hassett and Aparna Mathur: "Report Card on Effective Corporate Tax Rates: United States Gets an F"; *Tax Policy Outlook 2011*, no.1, American Enterprise Institute for Policy Research (AEI), Feb.2011.

[Hawkes:08]Alex Hawkes: "Isle of Man urged to rebrand"; *Accountancy Age*, 18 Jun 2008, http://www.accountancyage.com/aa/news/1747208/isle-man-urged-rebrand.

[HedemannSP:10]Janice M. Hedemann, Michael Sebastiani, and Andre Palmer: Calendar Year Tax Return Projections for the United States and IRS Campuses, CY2010-2017; Internal Revenue Service Office of Research, Document 6186, Oct.2010.

[Helleiner:94]Eric Helleiner: *States and the Reemergence of Global Finance*; Cornell University Press, 1994.

[Helman:10]Christopher Helman: "What the Top U.S. Companies Pay in Taxes"; *Forbes Magazine*, 1 Apr.2010.

[Henchman:11]Joseph Henchman: Rethinking U.S. Taxation of Overseas Operations: Subpart F, Territoriality, and the Exception for Active Royalties; The Tax Foundation, 22 Nov.2011.

[Henchman:13]Joseph Henchman: Detail of the Fiscal Cliff Deal; The Tax Foundation, 1 Jan.2013.

[HenchmanD:13]Joseph Henchman and Scott Drenkard: North Carolina Tax Reform Options: A Guide to Fair, Simple, Pro-Growth Reform; Carolina Business Coalition and the Tax Foundation, Jan.2013.

[HendelMT:08]Anja Hendel, Wolfgang Messner, and Frank Thun (eds.): *Rightshore! - Successfully Industrialize SAP® Projects Offshore*; Springer Verlag, 2008, 292 pp.

[Heymann:10]Jody Heymann: *Profit at the Bottom of the Ladder*; Harvard Business Press, 2010.

[Hines:05C]James R. Hines, jr.: Corporate Taxation and International Competition?; Ross School of Business paper 1026, University of Michigan, Jul.2005, <http://ssrn.com/abstract=891233>.

[Hines:05D]James R. Hines, jr.: "Do Tax Havens Flourish?"; in James M. Poterba (ed.): *Tax Policy and the Economy*, Vol.19, NBER, MIT Press, 2005.

[Hines:10H]James R. Hines Jr.: "Treasure Islands"; *Journal of Economic Perspectives*, Vol.24 no.4, Fall 2010, pp.103-126.

[HinesS:09]James R Hines, jr. and Lawrence H. Summers: "How Globalization Affects Tax Design"; *in* Jeffrey R. Brown and James M. Poterba (eds.): *Tax Policy and the Economy*, Vol.23, University of Chicago Press, 2009, pp.123-157.

[HirscheyW:85]Mark Hirschey and Jerry J. Weygandt: "Amortization Policy for Advertising and Research and Development Expenditures"; *Journal of Accounting Research*, Vol.23 no.1, Spring 1985, pp.326-335.

[Hirst:02]Clayton Hirst: "Silicon fen 'needs £2bn' to stop business exodus"; *The Independent*, 21 Sep.2002.

[HirtleHK:09]Peter B. Hirtle, Emily Hudson, and Andrew T. Kenyon: Copyright and Cultural Institutions; Cornell University Library, 2009, <http://ecommons.cornell.edu/handle/1813/14142>.

[Hitchner:06]James R. Hitchner (ed.): *Financial Valuation: Applications and Models*, 2nd edition; Wiley, 2006.

[HMT:10]Her Majesties Treasury: Corporation Tax Reform: Delivering a More Competitive System; HMT Newsroom Release 64/10, 29 Nov.2010.

[Hochschild:81]Jennifer L. Hochschild: *What's Fair: American Beliefs about Distributive Justice*; Harvard University Press, 1981.

[Hodge:12]Scott A. Hodge: The Countdown is Over. We're #1; Fiscal Facts, the Tax Foundation, 1 Apr.2012.

[HoefnerRB:11]Michael Hoefner, Nancy Rytina, and Bryan C. Baker: Estimates of the Unauthorzed Immigrant Population Residing in the United States: January 2010; Population Estimates, DHS, Feb.2011.

[HoggEa:08]Andrew Hogg et al.: Death and Taxes, the true toll of tax dodging; Christian Aid, London UK, 2008, http://www.christianaid.org.uk/images/deathandtaxes.pdfl.

[Hoovers:10]Hoovers: Company Information: Need it? We've got it; retrieved 2010 http://www.hoovers.com/.

[Houlder:10B]Vanessa Houlder: "OECD Hails tax haven crackdown "; *Financial Times*, 19 Jan.2010.

[Houlder:10C]Vanessa Houlder: "Tax haven drive will mean greater scrutiny"; *Financial Times*, 20 Mar.2010.

[Houlder:11]Vanessa Houlder: "Secrecy Under Scrutiny: Pressure for transparency persists as havens yield billions for G20 treasuries"; *Financial Times*, 12 Jan.2011.

[HoulderMG:11]Vanessa Houlder, Megan Murphy, and Jeff Gerth: "Did Barclay's Help U.S. Banks Get Undeserved Foreign Tax Credits?"; *Financial Times*, 25 Sep.2011.

[HousemanR:09]Susan N. Houseman and Kenneth R Ryder, jr (eds.): *Measurement Issues Arising from the Growth in Globalization*; Conference papers, National Academy of Public Administration, 6 Nov.2009, 16 papers, 421 pp.

[Howard:01]Philip K. Howard: *The Collapse of the Common Good*; updated version of: *The Lost Art of Drawing the Line*; Random House, 2001.

[HsiehMG:03]Ping-Hung Hsieh, C.S. Mishra, and D.H. Gobeli: "The Return on R&D versus Capital Expenditures in Pharmaceutical and Chemical Industries"; *IEEE Transactions on and Engineering Management*, May 2003, Vol.50 no.2, pp.141– 150.

[Hubbard:92]Glenn Hubbard: *Integration of the Individual and Corporate Tax Systems: Taxing Business Income Once*; US Treasury report, 1992.

[Hulten:06]Charles Hulten: Intangible Capital and Economic Growth; NBER working paper 11948, Jan.2006, <papers.nber.org/tmp/16760-w11948.pdfl>.

[Hummels:07]David Hummels: "Transportation Costs and International Trade in the Second Era of Globalization"; *Journal of Economic Perspectives*, Vol.21 no.3, Summer 2007, pp.131-154.

[Hungerford:11]Thomas L. Hungerford: Tax Expenditures and the Federal Budget; Congressional Research Service, RL34622, 1 Jun.2011.

[Hunt:12]Al Hunt: "A Budget Band-Aid on Corporate Taxes"; *Bloomberg Businessweek*, 20 Feb.2012, p.10.

[Huntsman:11]Jon Huntsman: 'Time to Compete', An American Jobs Plan; Gov. Huntsman, 31 Aug.2011.

[HurstP:11]Erik Hurst and Benjamin Wild Pugsley: "What Do Small Businesses Do?"; Brookings Papers on Economic Activity, Conference, Aug.2011.

[IASB:10]International Accounting Standards Board: Who we are and what we do; IFRS Foundation, Mar.2010.

[IATI:12]IATI: The Israeli Success Story; Israel Advanced Technology Industries, 2012, http://www.iati.co.il/high-tech-in-israel/the-israeli-success-story.

[Ibbotson:04]Ibbotson Associates: *Stocks, Bonds, Bills, and Inflation*; 2004 Yearbook, Wiley.

[Idris:03]Kamil Idris: Intellectual Property: A Power Tool for Economic Growth – Overview, 2nd edition; World Intellectual Property Organization, Jun.2003.

[ILO:11]International Labour Organization: Key Indicators of the Labour Market, 7th Edition; ILO Publications, Geneva, Switzerland, 2011.

[Immelt:11]Jeffrey H. Immelt: Growth Starts Here, GE 2010 Annual Report; General Electric Corporation, 25 Feb.2011.

[ImmeltEa:11]Jeffrey Immelt, chair, The Jobs Council: Taking Action, Building Confidence; Interim Report to the President, The President's Council on Jobs and Competitiveness, 10 Oct.2011, 52 pp., http://www.jobs-council.com/2011/10/10/jobs-council-releases-taking-action-building-confidence-interim-report-to-the-president/.

[Interbrand:07]Interbrand: "The 100 Top Brands"; *Business Week*, 6 Aug.2007.

[IRS-1040:12]IRS: Instructions for Form 1040, U.S. Individual Income Tax Return; Dep. of the Treasury, IRS, http://www.irs.gov/pub/irs-pdf/i1040.pdf, 2011.

[IRS-1120:11]IRS: Instructions for Form 1120, U.S. Corporations Income Tax Return; Dep. of the Treasury, IRS, http://www.irs.gov/pub/irs-pdf/i1120.pdf, 2011.

[IRS-199:12]IRS: Guidance for Examiners on I.R.C. § 199 Benefits and Burdens of Ownership Analysis in Contract Manufacturing Arrangements; Dep. of the Treasury, IRS, http://www.irs.gov/businesses/article/0,,id=253819,00.html, 2012.

[IRS-550:12]IRS: Investment Income and Expenses; Internal Revenue Service Publication 550, http://www.irs.gov/publications/p550/, 2012.

[IRS-901:11]IRS: U.S. Tax Treaties; Publication 901; IRS, 2011 http://www.irs.gov/publications/p901/index.html.

[IRS-CIP:07]IRS: Coordinated Issue Paper – Sec. 482 CSA Buy-in Adjustments (CIP); Internal Revenue Service LMSB, 04-0907-6227, to be effective Sep.2007, http://www.irs.gov/businesses/article/0,,id=174320,00.html, see [IRS-TP:12], 29 Aug.2005.

[IRS-CSA:08]IRS: Checklist for Cost Sharing Arrangments; Internal Revenue Manual, 27 May 2008, http://www.irs.gov/Businesses/Checklist-for-Cost-Sharing-Arrangements, Aug.2012.

[IRS-CT:02]IRS: Corporation Income Tax Brackets and Rates, 1909–2002; Internal Revenue Service, http://www.irs.gov/pub/irs-soi/02corate.pdfl, 2002.

[IRS-ED:10]IRS: IRS Employee Data; Internal Revenue Service, <jobs.irs.gov/mn-attorney.html>, retrieved Dec.2010.

[IRS-EF:09]IRS: Fiscal Year 2008 Enforcement Results; Internal Revenue Service, http://www.irs.gov/pub/irs-news/2008_enforcement.pdf, 2009.

[IRS-F:09]IRS: Transaction of Interest – Subpart F Income Partnership Blocker; IRS Notice 2009–7, 29 Jan.2009.

[IRS-FR:93]IRS: The Final Regulations: A Review of Comparability under the 1993 482 regulations; Internal Revenue Service http://www.irs.gov/pub/irs-apa/comparable_selection_data.pdfl.

[IRS-MTC:06]IRS: United States Model Tax Convention of November 15, 2006; Internal Revenue Service, http://www.irs.gov/pub/irs-trty/model006.pdfl, 15 Nov.2006.

[IRS-PP:10]IRS: Prompt Payment Act Interest Rate; Treasury Direct, updated semi-an-nually in the Federal Register, http://www.treasurydirect.gov/govt/rates/tcir/tcir_opdprmt2.htm, 2010.

[IRS-PS:96]IRS: Internal Revenue Service Simplification of Entity Classification Rules; (317) 630-7660, PS-43-95, 9 May 1996.

[IRS-QV:11]IRS: Qualified Alternative Fuel Motor Vehicles and Heavy Hybrid Vehicles; Internal Revenue Service, Businenss Topic, 10 Jan.2011.

[IRS-SC:12]IRS: SOI Tax Stats – Corporation Source Book; IRS Statistics Office, for 2009 and prior years, http://www.irs.gov/taxstats/article/0,,id=165716,00.html, 26 Apr.2012.

[IRS-SI:12]IRS: SOI Tax Stats – Individual Income Tax Returns; IRS Statistics Office, for 2009 and prior years, http://www.irs.gov/taxstats/indtaxstats/article/0,,id=134951,00.html, 3 Aug.2012.

[IRS-ST:09]IRS: Tax Stats – Corporation Complete Report; IRS Statistics Office (SOI), http://www.irs.gov/taxstats/bustaxstats/article/0,,id=112834,00.html, 2009.

[IRS-ST:12]IRS: Statistics of Income - 2009, Corporation Income Tax; IRS Statistics Office (SOI), http://www.irs.gov/pub/irs-soi/09coccr.pdf, 11 June 2012.

[IRS-TG:07]IRS: Reducing the Federal Tax Gap, A Report on Improving Voluntary Compliance; Department of the Treasury, http://www.irs.gov/pub/irs-ews/, 2 Aug.2007.

[IRS-TG:12]IRS: Official IRS Local Travel Guide; Internal Revenue Manual, Part 1, Chapter 32, Section 1, 7 Feb.2012.

[IRS-TI:11] IRS tax information for corporations: FASB Interpretation No. 48, Accounting for Uncertainty in Income Taxes; IRS, 17 March 2011.

[IRS-TP:94]IRS: Regulations on Transfer Pricing, Methods to Determine Taxable Income In Connection with a Transfer of Intangible Property; U.S. Internal Revenue Service: Title 26 §1.482-4, 8 Jul.1994; amended 4 Aug.2006, 30 Jan 2012.

[IRS-TP:04]IRS: Studies into Transfer Pricing Rules, Income Tax Treaties, and Corporate Expatriation, amendments to IRC §482; Pub.L.108-357, 2004, see [IRS-CIP:07].

[IRS-TP:12]Regulations on Transfer Pricing, Methods to Determine Taxable Income In Connection with a Cost Sharing Arrangement; U.S. Internal Revenue Service T.D. 9568, 19 Mar.2012, implements part of [IRS-CIP:07].

[IRS-TS:06]IRS: Final Report on Treatment of Services under Section 482--9T; Internal Revenue Service, Aug.2006, 189pp.

[IRS-WT:06]IRS: Withholding of Tax on Non-resident Aliens and Foreign Entities; Internal Revenue Service Publication no.515, 2006, updated annually.

[Jackson:10]James K. Jackson: Outsourcing and Insourcing Jobs in the U.S. Economy: Evidence based on Foreign Investment; Congressional Research Service, Report for Congress, Cornell University, 15 Apr.2010.

[JanebaS:03]Eckhard Janeba and Michael Smart: "Is Targeted Tax Competition Less Harmful than its Remedies?"; *International Tax and Public Finance*, Vol.10, 2003, pp.259-280.

[Jayson:10] Seth Jayson: Here's How Flextronics International May be Failing You; The Motley Fool, 30 Nov 2010.

[JCT:03]Joint Committee on Taxation: Report of the Joint Committee on Taxation Relating to the Internal Revenue Service as Required by the IRS Reform and Restructuring Act of 1998; JCT report JCX- 53–03, 20 May 2003, 174pp.

[JCT:06]Joint Committee on Taxation: The Impact of International Tax Reform: Background and Selected Issues Relating to U.S. International Tax Rules and the Competitiveness of U.S Businesses; JCT report JCX-22-06, 21 Jun.2006.

[JCT:10]Joint Committee on Taxation: Present Law and Background Related to Possible Income Shifting and Transfer Pricing; JCT report, JCX-37-10, 20 Jul. 2010.

[JCT:11]JCT: Tax Incentives for Research, Experimentation, and Innovation; Joint Committee on Taxation JCX-15-11, 28 Feb.2011 and JCX-45-11, 16 Sep.2011.

[JCT-12:12]JCT: Selected Issues Relating to Choice of Business Entity; Joint Committee on Taxation, 27 Jul.2012, JCX 66–12, 88 pp.

[JCT-18:12]JCT: Overview of the Federal Tax System as in Effect for 2012; Joint Committee on Taxation, 24 Feb.2012, JCX 66–18, 32pp.

[JefferySO:88]David Jeffery, Brian Sturgeon, and Michael O'Brien: *Tolley's Tax Investigations*; Tolley Publishing, 1988.

[JensenM:11]Mathew H. Jensen and Aparna Mathur: "Corporate Tax Burdens on Labor: Theory and Empirical Evidence"; *Tax Notes*, 6 Jun.2011.

[Johnson:05S]Calvin H. Johnson: Tales from the Skunk Works: The Basis-Shift or Defective Redemption Shelter; Tax Analysts, special report, 2005.

[Johnson:05V]Erinn R. Johnson: "A $13.5 billion merger between Symantec Corp. and VERITAS Software Corp"; *Black Enterprise*, 2005.

[Johnson:07]Calvin H. Johnson: "Replace the Corporate Tax with a Market Capitalization Tax"; *Tax Notes*, Vol.117, 10 Dec.2007, pp.1082-1087.

[Johnston:03]David Cay Johnston: *Perfectly Legal*; Portofolio Publishers, 2003, Penguin 2005.

[Johnston:12]David Cay Johnston: "Congress' Potential Faulty Tax Logic"; *National Memo*, 3 Mar.2012.

[JohnstonW:11]Louis Johnston and Samuel H. Williamson: What Was the U.S. GDP Then?; Measuring Worth, 2011, http://www.measuringworth.org/usgdp/.

[JollyK:12]David Jolly and Brian Knowlton: "5 European Nations Agree to Help U.S. Crack Down on Tax Evasion"; *New York Times*, 8 Feb 2012.

[Jones:96]Capers Jones: Applied Software Measurement: Assuring Productivity and Quality; McGraw-Hill, 1996.

[Jovanovich:02]Juan Martin Jovanovich: *Customs Valuation and Transfer Pricing: Is It Possible to Harmonize Customs and Tax Rules?*; Kluwer, Series on International Taxation, 2002.

[Jussawalla:92]Meheroo Jussawalla: *The Economics of Intellectual Property in a World Without Frontiers*; Praeger/Greenwood, 1993.

[Kahn:12]Jeremy Kahn: "Malta Lures Hedge Funds with 300 Days of Sunshine"; *Bloomberg Markets Magazine*, 10 Jan.2012.

[Kaiser:09]Robert G. Kaiser: So Damn Much Mone: The Triumph of Lobbying and the Corrosion of American Government; Knopf, 2009.

[KangN:12]Samuel S. Kang and Tuan S. Ngo: "Top U.S. Tech Companies' Tax Avoidance Can Be Mitigated, Report Says"; *Tax Notes Today*, Tax analysts. 18 Apr.2012.

[Kao:07]John Kao: Innovation Nation, How America Is Losing Its Innovation Edge, Why It Matters, and What We Can Do to Get It Back; Free Press, 2007.

[KaplanN:04]Robert S. Kaplan and David P. Norton: *Strategy Maps: Converting Intangible Assets into Tangible Outcomes*; Harvard Business School Press, 2004.

[Kaplow:99]Lois Kaplow: "Tax complexity and enforcement"; in [Slemrod:99], 1999, pp.381-396.

[KarC:09]Dev Kar and Devon Cartwright-Smith: Illicit Financial Flows from Developing Countries: 2002–2006; Executive Report, 2009, Global Fin. Integrity, Center for International Policy, http://www.gfip.org.

[Keating:10]David Keating: A Taxing Trend: The Rise in Complexity, Forms, and Paperwork Burdens; National Taxpayers Union, NTU Policy Paper 127, 15 Apr.2010.

[KellerY:09]Wolfgang Keller and Stephen R. Yeaple: "Multinational Enterprises, International Trade, and Productivity Growth, Firm-level Evidence from the United States"; *The Review of Economics and Statistics*, MIT Press, Vol.91 no.4, pp.821-831.

[Kennedy:06]Justice Anthony Kennedy: *Garcetti v. Ceballos*; Supreme Court of the United States, 547 U.S. 410; 2006.

[Kennedy:07]Justice Anthony Kennedy: Microsoft Corp. v. AT&T Corp.; Supreme Court of the United States, 550 U.S. 437. 30 Apr.2007.

[KesslerE:06]Wolfgang Kessler and Rolf Eicke: "Closer to Haven? New German Tax Planning Opportunities"; *Tax Notes International*, Vol.42 no.6, 8 May 2006.

[KesslerE:10]Wolfgang Kessler and Rolf Eicke: "The New German GAAP – the Gap Between Commercial and Tax Accounting"; *Tax Notes International*, Vol.59 no.7, 16 Aug.2010.

[Khimm:11]Suzy Khimm: Bipartisanship lives! And it will likely cost taxpayers money; Ezra Klein's blog, Washingon Post, 5 Oct 2011.

[KingEa:07]Steve King, Dan Burton, John Culberson, John Linder, Jeff Miller, Thomas Tancredo, and David Weldon: Proposing an amendment to the Constitution of the United States to repeal the sixteenth article of amendment; H.R. Resolution 16, 110th US Congress, 17 Jan 2007, <http://www.house.gov/list/press/ia05_king/pr_050202eliminateirs.html> originally submitted 2 Feb.2005.

[King:10]Eizabeth King: Transfer Pricing and Corporate Taxation: Problems, Practical Implications and Proposed Solutions; Springer Verlag, 2010.

[Kleinbard:05]Edward Kleinbard: The Business Enterprise Tax [BEIT]; presented to The President's Advisory Panel on Tax Reform, USC, May 2005.

[Kleinbard:07]Edward Kleinbard: Rehabilitating the Business Income Tax; Hamilton Project, Brookings Institution, Jun.2007.

[Kleinbard:12]Edward Kleinbard: "Stateless Income"; *Florida Tax Review*, Vol.9, 2011, p.699.

[Kocieniewski:10]David Kocieniewski: "I.R.S. plans to uncover Companies' Tax Strategies"; *New York Times*, 24 Aug.2010.

[Kocieniewski:11B]David Kocieniewski: "U.S. Business Has High Tax rates, But Pays Less"; *New York Times*, 2 May 2011.

[Kocieniewski:11G]David Kocieniewski: "G.E.'s Strategies Let It Avoid Taxes Altogether"; New York Times, 24 Mar.2011.

[Kocieniewski:11V]David Kocieniewski: "Rich Tax Breaks Bolster Makers of Video Games"; New York Times, 10 Sep.2011.

[KonvisserS:11] Joshua Konvisser and Sanjeev Sachdeva: Indian Outsourcing, End of the Offshore Tax 'Vacation'?; Pillsbury Client alert, 7 March 2011.

[Kopits:76]G. Kopits: "Intra-firm Royalties Crossing Frontiers and Transfer-Pricing Behavior"; *The Economic Journal*, Dec.1976, pp.791-803.

[Kornhauser:05]Marjorie E. Kornhauser: "Doing the Full Monty: Will Publicizing of Tax Information Increase Compliance?"; *Canadian Journal of Law & Jurisprudence*, Vol.18, 2005, p.95.

[Kornhauser:07]Marjorie E. Kornhauser: "A Tax Morale Approach to Compliance: Recommendations for the IRS"; *Florida Tax Review*, Vol.8 no.6, 2007, p.599, http://www.irs.gov/advocate/article/0,,id=177301,00.html.

[Kovacs:05]László Kovács: "Tax harmonisation versus tax competition in Europe"; *Tax harmonisation and legal uncertainty in Central and Eastern Europe*, Austrian Chamber of Professional Accountants and Tax Advisors, Vienna, 20 Oct.2005.

[KravitzB:05]Troy Kravitz and Leonard E. Burman: "Capital Gains Tax Rates, Stock Markets, and Growth"; *Tax Facts*, Tax Analysts, Jul.2005.

[Kroll:06]Karen M. Kroll: "IRS seeks Truth in Veritas Deal"; *CFO magazine*, 20 Sep.2006.

[Kroon:00]Andries Kroon: "The Netherlands and Netherlands Antilles in International Tax Planning"; in [Ogley:00], 2000, pp.32-46.

[Krouse:12]Sarah Krouse: "Budget day scramble for estate agents and lawyers"; *Financial News*, DowJones, 23 Mar.2012.

[Kynaston:01]David Kynaston: *The City of London, A Club No More, 1945–2000*; Chatto & Windus, Random House, 2001.

[LafferM:10]Arthur B. Laffer and Stephen Moore: *Return to Prosperity*; Threshold Publications, Simon & Schuster, 2010.

[LaMonica:05]Martin LaMonica: "Open source reshaping services market"; CNET News, 10 Jan.2005.

[Larson:11]Charles Larson: Panel Statement at National Association for Business Economics 2011 Transfer Pricing Symposium in Arlington, VA; *Tax Analysts*, 27 Jul. 2011.

[Laskey:00]Frederick A. Laskey: Letter Ruling 00–11: Massachusetts Tax Treatment of a Netherlands BV, Department of Revenue, Commonwealth of Massachusetts; 29 Aug.2000.

[LauLW:05]Gloria T. Lau, Kincho H. Law, and Gio Wiederhold: "Analyzing Government Regulations Using Structural and Domain Information"; *IEEE Computer*, Vol.38 no.12, Dec.2005, pp.70-76.

[Laurie:04]R. Laurie: "IP Valuation: Magic or Myth?"; in *Intellectual Property Issues in M&A Transactions*, Apr.2004.

[Lawley:05]Duard Lawley: *Common Sense Tax Reform*; AuthorHouse, 2005.

[LB&I:10]IRS: Large Business and International Division at-a-Glance; Internal Revenue Service, U.S. Dept. of the Treasury, 1 Oct 2010, http://www.irs.gov/irs/article/0,,id=96387,00.html.

[Leamer:99]Edward E. Leamer: "What do we know About the Impact of Offshore Investment on the U.S. Economy?"; in [Slemrod:99], 1999.

[Leijon:02]H. Leijon (ed.): Extract from the table of the Erlang loss formula; International Telecommunications Union, PLANITU Doc-18-E, 2002.

[LenterSS:03]David Lenter, Joel Slemrod, and Douglas Shakelford: "Public Disclosure of Corporate Tax Return Information: Accounting, Economics, and Legal Perspectives"; *National Tax Journal*, Mar.2010, pp.1733-1759.

[Lentz:89]Karen Panetta Lentz: "Hardware is petrified software"; in Manoj Franklin: *Computer Architecture and Organization: From Software to Hardware*; Prentice-Hall, 2010.

[Lessig:11]Lawrence Lessig: *Republic, Lost*; Twelve, Hachette Book Group, 2011.

[LeuzTW:06]Christian Leuz, Alexander Triantis, and Tracy Wang: "Why Do Firms Go Dark? Causes and Economic Consequences of Voluntary SEC Deregistrations"; American Finance Association, Boston, 2006.

[Lev:01]Baruch Lev: *Intangibles, Management, Measurement and Reporting*, with comments by conference participants; Brookings Institution Press, 2001.

[LeveyW:07]Marc M. Levey and Steven C. Wrappe: *Transfer Pricing, Rules, Compliance and Controversy*, 2nd edition; CCH, Wolters Kluwer Pub., 2007.

[LeveyWC:06]Marc M. Levey, Steven C. Wrappe, and Kerwin Chung: *Transfer Pricing Rules and Compliance Handbook*; CCH, Wolters Kluwer, 2006.

[LevinEa:11]Carl Levin et al.: Repatriating Offshore Funds: 2004 Tax Windfall for Select Multinationals; United States Senate Permanent Subcommittee on Investigations, 11 Oct.2011.

[Levin:12]Carl Levin: Statement; Permanent Subcommittee on Investigations, U.S. Congress, 20 Sep.2012.

[Levinson:08]Daniel R. Levinson: Medicare Payment for Irinotecan; Dept. of Health and Human Services, Office of the Inspector general, OEI-03-08-00310. Aug.2008.

[LevN:04]B. Lev and D. Nissim: "Taxable Income, Future Earnings, and Equity Values"; *The Accounting Review*, Oct.2004, pp.1039-1074.

[LevS:96]Baruch Lev and Theodore Sougiannis: "The Capitalization. Amortization, and Value-Relevance of R&D"; *Journal of Accounting and Economics*, 1996, pp.107-128.

[LevS:99]Baruch Lev and T. Sougiannis: "Penetrating the Book-to-Market Black Box: The R&D Effect"; *Journal of Business, Finance and Accounting*, April/May 1999, pp.419-449.

[Lewis:11]Michael Lewis: *Boomerang: Travels in the New Third World*; W. W. Norton, 2011.

[LientzS:80]B.P. Lientz and E.B. Swanson: *Software Maintenance Management*; Addison-Wesley, 1980.

[LII:92]Legal Information Institute: Constitution, US code (IRC) and Federal regulations (CFR), Supreme Court Cases, etc.; Cornell Law School, since 1992, continuously updated, see Appendix B.

[Lindsay:09]Brink Lindsay: *Paul Krugman's Nostalgianomics*; Cato Institute, Washington DC, 2009, SSRN#1464854 http://www.cato.org/pubs/wtpapers/Nostalgianomics.pdfl.

[LocherB:02]Peter Locher and Ernst Blumenstein: *System des Schweizerischen Steuerrechts*, 6th edition; Schulthess, 2002.

[Lohman:02]Judith Lohman: Stanley Works Reincorporation Proposal; OLR Research Report, Office of Legislative Affairs, State of Connecticut, 002-R-063, 19 Jul.2002.

[Lohr:06]Steve. Lohr: "Study Plays Down Export of Computer Jobs"; *New York Times*, 23 Feb.2006. p.C11.

[LonzoOscar:47]Loyd George and Rollin Sullivan: I'm My Own Grandpa; song written by Dwight Latham and Moe Jaffe, 1947.

[LowTax:11]Lowtax: Global Tax & Business Portal; BSiMedia, Hastings, East Sussex, UK, 2011, accessed Feb.2011 http://www.lowtax.net/.

[Lynch:11]David J Lynch: "Too many Modest Proposals"; in [LynchEa:11].

[LynchEa:11]David J Lynch, et al.: "Cracking the code"; *Bloomberg Business Insider*, Spring 2011, *Bloomberg Businessweek*, 11 Apr.2011, pp.B1-B20.

[MackEa:05]Connie Mack III, chair, et al.: Simple, Fair, and Pro-Growth: Proposals to Fix America's Tax System; Report of the President's Advisory Panel on Federal Tax Reform; Nov.2005.

[MackieMason:90]Jeffrey K. Mackie-Mason: "Do Taxes Affect Corporate Financing Decisions?"; *The Journal of Finance*, Vol.45 no.5., Dec.1990, pp.1471-1493.

[Makhlouf:02]Gabriel Makhlouf: List of Uncooperative Tax Havens; Committee on Fiscal Affairs, OECD, Paris, France, 19 Apr.2002.

[Manesh:12]Mohsen Manesh: "Contractual Freedom under Delaware Alternative Entity Law: Evidence from Publicly Traded LPs and LLCs"; University of Oregon School of Law, to appear in *Journal of Corporation Law*, 2012.

[Mankiw:12]H. Gregory Mankiw: "A Better Tax System (Instructions Included)"; *New York Times*, Economic View, 22 Jan.2012.

[MankiwW:05]N. Gregory Mankiw and Matthew Weinzierl: Dynamic Scoring: A Back-of-the Envelope Guide; Harvard University, 12 Dec.2005.

[Marisec:06]Marisec: *International Shipping, Carrier of World Trade*; Maritime International Secretariat Services Ltd, London, 2006, http://www.marisec.org/worldtradeflyer.pdfl.

[Marisec:10]Marisec: *Shipping and World Trade*; Maritime International Secretariat Services Ltd, London, 2010, http://www.marisec.org/top-20-largest-shipping-flags.php.htm.

[Markham:05]Michelle Markham: *The Transfer Pricing of Intangibles*; Wolters-Kluwer, 2005.

[MarkleS:09]Kevin S. Markle and Douglas A. Shakelford: Do Multinationals or Domestic Firms Face Higher Effective Tax Rates; University of North Carolina, Jun.2009.

[MarrH:11]Chuck Marr and Brian Highsmith: Tax Holiday for Overseas Corporate Profits would Increase Deficits, Fail to Boost the Economy, and Ultimately Shift More Investment and Jobs Overseas; Center on Budget and Policy Priorities, 23 Jun.2011.

[Martin:11]Roger L. Martin: *Fixing the Game*; Harvard Business Review Press, 2011.

[Maruca:11]Samuel Maruca: "Strategic Case Selection Key Aspect of Transfer Pricing Practice"; *BNA Daily Tax Report*, 29 Jul. 2011, reported by [Schuster:11].

[Matsunaga:83]Yoshio *Matsunaga*: "Determining Reasonable Royalty Rates"; Les Nouvelles, Journal of the *Licensing* Executives *Society*, Dec.1983, pp.216–219.

[MauldinA:08]Tiffany Mauldin and Edward Abahoonie: "More likely than not: A comparison of FIN 48 and the tax penalty standard"; *The Tax Executive*, Mar.2008.

[Mazarov:12]Michael Mazarov: 'Digital Goods and Services Fairness Act' Would Impair Funding for Education, Health care, and Other State and Local Services; Center for Budget and Policy Priorities. 29 May 2012.

[McAfee:83]R.Preston McAfee: "American Economic Growth and the Voyage of Columbus"; *American Economic Review*, Vol.73, 1983.

[McDonald:98]Chris McDonald: "The Evolution of Intel's Copy Exactly! Technology Transfer Method"; *Intel Technology Journal*, Q4 1998.

[McDonald:08]Michael McDonald: Income Shifting from Transfer Pricing: Further Evidence from Tax Return Data; US Department of the Treasury, Office of Tax Analysis, OTA Technical working paper 2, Jul.2008.

[McIntyre:08]Robert S. McIntyre: Time to Stop Subsidizing Wall Street, Eliminate Loopholes for Capital Gains and Dividends; Citizens for Tax Justice, 1 Oct.2012.

[McIntyreGWP:11]Robert S. McIntyre, Matthew Garner, Rebecca J. Wilkins, and Richard Phillips: Corporate Tax Dodgers, 2008–2011; Citizens for Tax Justice & Institute on Taxation and Economic Policy, Nov.2011.

[McKenney:12]Michael E. McKenney: Final Audit Report ROTER; Treasury Inspector General for Tax Administration (TIGTA), 7 Aug.2012 http://www.tigta.gov.

[McKinsey:03] McKinsey: "Fighting Complexity in IT"; McKinsey Quarterly, April 2003.

[McNair:03]Carol J. McNair: *The Profit Potential: Taking High Performance to the Bottom Line*; Wiley, 2003.

[MeyerK:04]David Meyer and Martin Kenny: "Economic action does not take place in a vacuum: Understanding Cisco's acquisition and development strategy"; *Journal of Industry and Innovation*, Dec.2004.

[Mihaly:93]Stephen A. Mihaly: "United States: How to Escape the Wrath of Thrasbulus' Sword and Establish Reasonable Royalty Rates in Intercompany Licensing of Intangibles Under the 'Best Method Rule'of the New Section 482 Regulations"; *Bulletin for International Fiscal Documentation*, Vol.47 no.309, Jun.1993.

[Miles:05] Miles: "Intermediary Dutch Holding Company Qualifies for Parent/Subsidiary Directive Relief"; Tax Planning International Review, Vol. 32, 2005, pp.16, 17.

[Milsted:12]Carl Milsted jr.: The Limits to the Laffer Curve; National Debt Solutions, 2012, http://www.nationaldebtsolutions.org/.

[Misey:02]Robert J. Misey, jr.: "An International Tax Review": *The U.S.-based Multinationals, Annual Checkup*; CCH Wolters-Kluwer, Dec.2002.

[MiseyS:07]Robert J. Misey jr. and Michael S. Schadewald: *Practical Guide to U.S. Taxation of International Transactions*, 6th edition; CCH Wolters-Kluwer, 2007.

[Mitchell:11]Rick Mitchell: "At G-20, Sarkozy names Switzerland, Liechtenstein among 11 Tax Havens"; *BNA Daily Tax Report*; 7 Nov.2011.

[Miyatake:09]Toshia Miyatake: "Japan's Foreign Subsidiaries' Dividend Exclusion"; *Proceedings from the 2009 Sho Sato Conference on Tax Law, Social Policy, and the Economy*, Mar.2009.

[Moore:91]Geoffrey A. Moore: *Crossing the Chasm*; Harper Business, 1991.

[Morgan:10]R. William Morgan: Testimony before the Committee on Ways and Means; Joint Committee on Taxation (JCT), 22 Jul.2010.

[Morgenthau:09] Robert M. Morgenthau: Cayman Islands hold $1, 900B; Charlie Rose Interview, 8 Apr.2009.

[MoskRC:12]Matthew Mosk, Brian Ross, and Megan Chuchmach: Romney Parks Millions in Cayman Islands; ABC News Nightline, 18 Jan.2012.

[MS:11]M.S.: "Foreign Aid, Why Ron Paul is wrong"; *The Economist*, 16 Nov.2011.

[MurphyCK:05]Richard Murphy, John Christenson, and Jenny Kimmis: Tax us if you can; Tax Justice Network, Sep.2005, 78pp.

[MurphyEa:09]Richard Murphy et al.: The language of Tax; Mapping the Fault Lines, Tax Justice Network, Nov.2009, http://www.secrecyjurisdictions.com/PDFL/Glossary.pdfl.

[Murthy:11]N.R. Narayana Murthy: Infosys Annual Report; 2010–2011, Infosys corporation and its subsidiaries, 2011.

[Musher:00]Steven A. Musher: Cost-sharing of Ongoing Research and Development ('R&D') on Acquired Technology; IRS Field Advice, released 7 Jan.2000.

[NadiriP:96]Ishaq M. Nadiri and Ingmar R. Prucha: "Estimation of the Depreciation Rate of Physical and R&D Capital in the U.S. Total Manufacturing Sector"; *Economic Inquiry*, Vol. XXXIV, Jan.1996, pp.43-56.

[Nakamura:99]Leonard Nakamura: "Intangibles: What put the New in the New Economy"; *Federal Reserve Bank of Philadelphia Business Review*, Jul.1999.

[Nakamura:08]Leonard Nakamura: "Intangible Assets and National Income Accounting"; Federal Reserve Bank of Philadelphia working paper 08–23, 16 Oct.2001, SSRN#1285048.

[NakamuraS:11]Emi Nakamura and Jón Steinsson: Fiscal Stimulus in a Monetary Union: Evidence from U.S. Regions; NBER Working paper no.17391, Sep.2011, SSRN#1931161.

[Nakaso:12]Dan Nakaso: "U.S. tax shelter appears secure"; *San Jose Mercury News*, 25 Dec. 2012, p.1,5.

[NAM:04]R&D Credit Coalition: America's Future: R&D; National Association of Manufacturers; 2004.

[NDT:11]Nevada Department of Taxation: "Federal Income Tax"; *Nevada Tax Notes*, no.174, Apr.2011.

[NicolaidisH:01]Kalypso Nicolaidis and Robert Howse (eds.): The Federal Vision: Legitimacy and Levels of Governance in the United States and the European Union; Oxford University Press, 2001.

[Nolan:10]Deborah Nolan: A new chapter in achieving certainty through alternative dispute resolution; Tax Administration Without Borders, Ernst & Young, Issue 5, Oct.2010.

[NorwoodEa:06]Janet L. Norwood (chair): Off-shoring, How Big Is It?; National Academy of Public Administration (NAPA), Oct.2006, 274pp.

[OatesO:03]Mark A. Oates and James O'Brien: "For Settlement Purposes Only"; Transfer Pricing, *Taxation of Global Transactions*, CCH Wolters Kluwer, Summer 2003, pp.31-34.

[OatesO:09]Mark A. Oates and James O'Brien: "The Arm's-length Standard: Why it Matters"; Transfer Pricing, *International Tax Journal*, CCH Wolters Kluwer, Jul.2009.

[OatesO:11]Mark A. Oates and James O'Brien: "Lux et Veritas: IRS's Actions Speak Loader Than its Words"; Transfer Pricing, *International Tax Journal*, CCH Wolters, Jan.2011.

[Obama:12]Barak Obama: Startup America Legislative Agenda; 24 Jan 2012, http://www.whitehouse.gov/sites/default/files/uploads/startup_america_legislative_agenda.pdfl.

[OBrienC: 90]James O'Brien and Robert J. Cunningham: "Protecting Against the Disclosure of Trade Secrets to Independent Experts and Third-Party Fact Witnesses During an Internal Revenue Service Audit"; *Tax Executive*, Vol.42, Mar.1990, pp.99-108.

[OBrienEa:98]James M. O'Brien, et al.: *U.S. Corporations Doing Business Abroad*; Baker McKenzie, Tax Advisors Planning, Vol.28, Research Institute of America, (RIA) Checkpoint, 1 Jan.1, 1998, 376 pp.

[OBrienO:99]James M. O'Brien and Mark A. Oates: "Caveat Expert: Let the Expert Witness Beware"; *Taxes*, CCH Wolters Kluwer, Vol.77 no.11, Jul.1999.

[OBrienO:02]James M. O'Brien and Mark A. Oates: "Common Sense and the Art of Transfer Pricing"; Transfer Pricing, *Taxation of Global Transaction*, CCH Wolters, Winter 2002, pp.33-34, 63–64.

[OConnor:08]Kevin J. OConnor: Statement before the Senate Committee on Homeland Security and Governmental Affairs, Hearing on Tax Haven Financial Institutions: Their Formation and Administration of Offshore Entities and Accounts for Use by U.S. Clients, 17 Jul.2008.

[OECD:86]OECD Committee on Fiscal Affairs: Double Taxation Convention and the use of Conduit Companies; OECD, Paris, 1986.

[OECD:98]OECD Committee on Fiscal Affairs: Harmful Tax Competition, An Emerging Global Issue; Organisation for Economic Co-operation and Development (OECD), Paris, Apr.1998.

[OECD:06]OECD, CTPA: Transactional Profit Methods – Responses to the OECD Invitation to Comment; Centre for Tax Policy and Administration, 6 Sep.2006. http://www.oecd.org/dataoecd/17/12/37421921.pdf.

[OED:02]Oxford English Dictionary, 2nd Edition, updated: Oxford University Press, 2002.

[OGara:10]Patrick O'Gara: UK Tax Residence of Offshore Companies: Laerstate BV v. HMRC; Baker & McKenzie, Jun.2010, http://www.bakermckenzie.com/RRUKTaxResidenceOfOffshoreCompanies/.

[Ogley:00]Adrian Ogley (ed.): *Tolley's Tax Havens*, 3rd edition; Tolley Publishing, 2000.

[Olson:11]Nina E. Olson: National Taxpayer Advocate: 2011 Report to Congress; Taxpayer Advocate Service, Internal Revenue Service, 31 Dec.2011, http://www.irs.gov/pub/irs-utl/irs_tas_arc2011_exec_summary.pdfl.

[OMB:11A]OMB Fiscal Year 2012, Historical Tables, Budget of the U.S. Governments; Office of Management and Budget (OMB), 14 Feb.2011, <budget.gov>.

[OMB:11B]OMB's 2012 Mid-Session Review, Budget of the U.S. Government; Office of Management and Budget (OMB), 1 Sep.2011, <budget.gov>.

[OMB:12A]Fiscal Year 2012, Analytical Perspectives, Budget of the U.S. Government; Office of Management and Budget (OMB), <budget.gov>.

[OMB:12B]Fiscal Year 2013, Budget of the U.S. Government; Office of Management and Budget (OMB), <budget.gov>.

[OPA:10]Online-Publishers Association: Improving Ad Performance Online, the Impact of Advertising on Content Sites; Apr.2010, http://www.online-publishers.org/.

[Orrel:10]David Orrel: *Economyths: Ten Ways Economics Gets It Wrong*; Wiley, 2010.

[Orszag:07]Peter R. Orszag: Taxation of Carried Intrest; Congressional Budget Office (CBO) 11 Jul.2007.

[OsterB:02]Christopher Oster and Ken Brown: "AIG, A Complex Industry, A Very Complex Company"; *Wall Street Journal*, 23 Jan.2002.

[OTP:07]Office of Tax Policy: Approaches to Improve the Competiveness of the U.S. Business Tax System for the 21st Century; U.S. Department of the Treasury, 20 Dec.2007.

[PackmanC:11]Andrew Packman and Augusto Lopez Claros: Paying Taxes 2012, The Global Picture; Price Waterhouse Coopers and the World Bank, 2011, http://www.pwc.com/payingtaxes.

[Palan:06]Ronen Palan: *The Offshore World: Souvereign Markets, Virtual Places, and Nomad Millionaires*; Cornell University Press, 2006.

[PalanMC:10]Ronen Palan, Richard Murphy, and Christian Chavagneux: Tax Havens: How Globalization Really Works; Cornell Studies in Money, 2010, http://www.cornellpress.edu.

[PalettaMcK:11]Damian Paletta and John D. McKinnon: "Treasury Weighs New Tax Scheme"; *Wall Street Journal*, 10 Sep.2011.

[Palmer:10]Griff Palmer: "Decision Could Allow Anonymous Political Contributions by Business"; *New York Times*, 27 Feb.2010.

[Palmisano:06]Samuel J. Palmisano (CEO): 2005 Annual Report; IBM Corporation, Feb.2006.

[Parr:07]Russell Parr: Royalty Rates for Licensing Intellectual Property; Wiley, 2007.

[ParrS:05]Russell L. Parr and Gordon V. Smith: *Intellectual Property; Valuation, Exploitation, and Infringement Damages*, 4th edition; Wiley; Adobe E-book, May 2005.

[Paschall:00]C. Thomas Paschall: "U.S. Capital Gains Taxes: Arbitrary Holding Periods, Debatable Tax Rates"; *USC Law Revue*, Vol.73, 2000, pp.843-878, http://www-bcf.usc.edu/~usclrev/pdfl/073404.pdf.

[Paul:10]Ron Paul: *The Case for Gold, A Minority Report of the U.S. Gold Commission*; Laissez Faire books, 2010, reprint of a 1983 report.

[Paul:12]Ron Paul: Plan to Restore America; Ron Paul Presidential Campaign Committee, 2012.

[Payne:93]James L. Payne: *Costly Returns; The Burdens of the U.S. Tax System*; ICS press, Jan.1993.

[Pearlstein:11]Steven Pearlstein: Charlie Rose Interview: Facebook, Steve Jobs; at 40 min, Audio Books, Audible.com, 10 Jan.2011.

[PearS:11]Robert Pear and Jennifer Steinhauer: "Senate Approves Two Pieces of Jobs Bill"; *New York Times*, 10 Nov.2011.

[Pearson:06]Thomas C. Person: "Preparing Multinational Companies for Tranfer Pricing Audits of Intangibles"; *International Law & Management Revirew*, BYU, Vol.2, pp.159-200, 2006.

[Philips:12]Matthew Philips: "Time to Head Home for Some Manufacturers"; *Bloomberg Business Week*, 6 Feb 2012.

[PierceS:09]Justin R. Pierce and Peter K. Schott: A Concordance Between Ten-Digit U.S. Harmonized System Codes and SIC/NAICS Product Classes and Industries; Center for Economic Studies, U.S. Bureau of the Census, Nov.2009.

[Pigoski:97]Thomas M. Pigoski: Practical Software Maintenance - Best Practices for Managing Your Software Investment; IEEE Computer Society Press, 1997.

[PiotrowskaV:08]Joanna Piotrowska and Werner Vanborren: The corporate income tax rate-revenue paradox: Evidence in the EU; Taxation Papers 12, Directorate General Taxation and Customs Union, European Commission, revised Oct.2008.

[Pollock:12]Lisa Pollock: "Tax arbitrage 101"; *Financial Times*, 25 May 2012.

[Posner:77]Richard A. Posner: Economic Analysis of Law; Little, Brown, 1977.

[Pozen:11]Robert C. Pozen: Gingrich's Flawed Social Security and Income Tax Proposals; Brookings Opinions, 27 Dec.2011.

[PRA:95]U.S. Congress: Paperwork Reduction Act of 1995; S.244, Title 44, Chapter 35, 'Coordination of Federal Information Policy', 4 Jan.2004.

[PrattRS:96]Shannon P. Pratt, Robert F. Reilly, and Robert P. Schweihs: *Valuing a Business, The Analysis and Appraisal of Closely Held Companies*, 3rd edition; Irwin Professional Publications, 1996.

[Protalinski:12] Emil Protalinski: Last Facebook pre-IPO Valuation is Biggest yet: $102.8 billion; ZDNet, 30 Mar.2012.

[PrzysuskiL:05]Martin Przysuski and Srini Lalapet: "A Comprehensive Look at the Berry Ratio in Transfer Pricing"; *Tax Notes International*, Tax Analysts, Vol.40 no.8, 21 Nov.2005, p.759.

[PSoI:03]Permanent Subcommittee on Investigations: U.S. Tax Shelter Industry: The Role of Accountants, Lawyers, and Financial Professionals, Four KPMG Case Studies, FLIP, OPIS, BLIPS, and SC2; Report on Hearings held 18&20 Nov.2003, U.S. Senate Homeland Security and Governmental Affairs Committee, on the 'Role of Professional Firms in the U.S. Tax Shelter Industry'; US Senate S402-21, 130 pp.

[Quiggin:98]John Quiggin: "Individual and Household Willingness to Pay for Public Goods"; *American Journal of Agricultural Economics*, Vol.80 no.1, Feb 199), pp.58-64.

[Quinlan:02]Andrew Quinlan: Fiscal Protectionism and the Need for Territorial Taxation; CF&P Press Release, Center for Freedom and Prosperity, Washington, 12 Mar.2002.

[Radaelli:03]Claudio M. Radaelli: The Code of Conduct Against Harmful Tax Competion: Open Method of Coordination In Disguise; *Public Administration,* Vol.81, no.3, 2003.

[Rahn:09]Richard W. Rahn: "In Defense of Tax Havens"; *Wall Street Journal*, 17 Mar.2009.

[RamelliEa:12]Rudolph Ramelli et al.: Comments and Recommendations for Guidance to the Transfer Pricing of Related Party Guarantees; American Bar Association, letter to Commissioner Shulman, 13 Sep. 2012, 93 pp.

[Ramos:07]Joanne Ramos: "A survey of offshore finance"; *The Economist*, 22 Feb.2007.

[Rashkin:07]Michael Rashkin: Practical Guide to Research and Development Tax Incentives: Federal, State, and Foreign, 2nd edition; CCH Wolters Kluwer Publications, 2007.

[Rasmus:06]Jack Rasmus: the War at Home: the Corporate Offensive from Ronald Reagan to George W. Bush; Kyklos Productions, 2006.

[RauG:12]Aswath Rau and Pallabi Ghosal: "Entering the Tiger's Den: Foreign Investment in India Through Mauritius or Singapore"; *Singapore Law Gazette*, Feb.2012.

[Rauch:94]Jonathan Rauch: *Government's End*: *Why Washington Stopped Working*; Public Affairs, Perseus Publishing, 1994.

[Razgaitis:03]Richard Razgaitis: *Valuation and Pricing of Technology-Based Intellectual Property*; Wiley, 2003.

[RazinS:90]Assaf Razin and Joel Slemrod, eds.: *Taxation in the Global Economy*; NBER, University of Chicago Press, 1990.

[Reich:11]Robert B. Reich: *Aftershock*, *The Next Economy & America's Future*; First Vintage Books, 2010, updated 2011.

[Reich:12]Robert Reich: *Beyond Outrage*: *What Has Gone Wrong with Our Economy and Our Democracy*, *and How to Fix Them*; Knopf, Random House digital, May 2012, 87 pp.

[ReillyS:98]Robert F. Reilly and Robert P. Schweihs: *Valuing Intangible Assets*; McGraw-Hill, 1998.

[ReinhartR:09]Carmen M. Reinhart and Kenneth S. Rogoff: *This Time Is Different*, *Eight Centuries of Financial Folly*; Princeton University Press, 2009.

[ReinhartR:10]Carmen M. Reinhart and Kenneth S. Rogoff: "Growth in a Time of Debt"; Harvard University Economics Dept. report 51, for the *American Economic Review Papers and Proceedings*, 7 Jan.2011.

[ResslerM:11]Peter Ressler and Monika Mitchell: Conversations with Wall Street: The Inside Story of the Financial Armageddon & How to prevent the Next One; Fast Pencil Premiere, Nov.2011.

[RhoadesL:12]Rufus von Thulen Rhoades and Marshall J. Langer: *International Taxation and Tax Treaties*; Mathew Bender Co, Lexis Nexis, 2012.

[Ricardo:1817]David Ricardo: *The Principles of Political Economy and Taxation*; 1817; Kindle edition, 2010.

[RICS:04]The Royal Institution of Chartered Surveyors: The Value of Intellectual Property, Intangible Assets and Goodwill, 26 Oct.2004, http://www.rics.org.uk/Property/Propertyappraisalandvaluation/iprvaluation.htm.

[RicuperoEa:00]Rubens Ricupero (Sec.Gen.) et al.: Tax Inventives and Foreign Direct Investment: A Global Survey; United Nations Conference on Trade and Development, ASIT Advisory Studies, no.16, 2000.

[RileyV:12]Michael Riley and Aslee Vance: "It's not Paranoia If They're Stealing Your Secrets"; *Bloomberg Businessweek*,19 Mar.2012, pp.76-84.

[RistucciaEa:11]Henry Ristuccia et al.: Effective Integration, Enhanced Decision Making, The Risk Intelligent Tax Executive; Risk Intelligence Series, no.17, Deloitte Development LLC, 2011.

[Rittel:10]Claudia Isabel Rittel: "Bitter Losses"; *Development and Cooperation Magazine*, Deutsche Stiftung für Entwicklungsländer, Deutsche Gesellschaft für Internationale Zusammenarbeit, 7 Aug.2010, http://www.inwent.org/ez/articles/178169/index.en.shtml.

[Roberts:01]Richard Roberts: Take your Partners; Palgrave, 2001.

[Roberts:08]Richard Roberts: *The City, A Guide to London's Global Financial Center*; The Economist, Bloomberg Press, 2008.

[Roberts:11]Justice John Roberts: FCC et al. v. AT&T Inc. et al.; Supreme Court of the United States, 562 U.S., 1 Mar.2011.

[Romano:02]Carlo Romano: *Advance Tax Rulings and Principles of Law: Towards a European Tax Rulings System*; International Bureau of Fiscal Documentation (IBFD), Amsterdam, 2002.

[Romano:11]Andrew Romano: "Maneuver allows Career Lawyer to Wield Power in the Tax Division"; *Main Justice*, 18 Mar.2011.

[Rosenbaum:95]David E. Rosenbaum: Chairman Proposes Redefining Tax Code; *New York Times*, 7 Jun.1995.

[Rosenberg:98]Barr Rosenberg: United States Equity Version 3; BARRA, Berkeley, CA, 1998.

[Rosenberg:10]Dave Rosenberg: "Oracle-Sun versus commodity hardware"; *Cnet News*, 31 Jan.2010.

[Rosenthal:12]Steven Rosenthal: France Collects a Financial Non-trnsaction Tasx; Tax Policy Center, 8 Aug.2012.

[Rossotti:05]Charles O. Rossotti: *Many Unhappy Returns*; Harvard Business School Press, 2005.

[RostenkowskiEa:86]Dan Rostenkowski et al.: Tax Reform Act of 1986, Conference report, HR 3838; 22 Nov.1985.

[RothEa:98]William V. Roth, jr. (chairman): IRS Restucturing and Reform Act of 1998, Conference Report; US Congress, to accompany Bill H.R. 2676, Apr.1998.

[Roux:97]David Roux: Statement about software growth; Silver Lake Partners, 1997.

[Rubin:12]Richard Rubin: "Romney Tax Cut Proposal Relies on Rapid Growth Paired with Missing Details"; *Bloomberg Businessweek*, 24 Feb.2012.

[RubinZ:11]Richard Rubin and Andrew Zajac: "IRS Warns Busy Signals, Weaker Enforcement Will Follow Cuts"; *Bloomberg Businessweek*, 17 Oct.2011.

[Sachs:05]Jeffrey Sachs: *The End of Poverty: Economic Possibilities for Our Time*; Penguin Press, 2005.

[Sahadi:11]Jeanne Sahadi: "Corporate Tax Reform: Talk Grows Louder"; *CNN*Money, 15 Jan 2011.

[Saitto:10]Serena Saitto: "U.S. tech firms shop abroad to avoid taxes"; *Bloomberg Businessweek*, 6 Sep.2010, pp.31-32.

[Sakey:12]Matt Sakey: Assemblageddon; *Digital Manufacturing Report*, 1 Feb.2012.

[SalantG:11]Jonathan Salant, Greg Giroux: "Playing the Tax Break Game"; in [LynchEa:11].

[SaniskiEa:12]Daniel Saniski et al.: GDP, United States; Data360, retrieved Apr.2012, http://www.data360.org/dsg.aspx?Data_Set_Group_Id=230.

[SanJuan:11]Eric A. San Juan: From Tax Collector to Fiscal Automaton: Demographic History of Federal Income Tax Administration, 1913–2011; Volume 2 of [Olson:11].

[SAT:09]SAT: China Transfer Pricing Regulations; China State Administration of Taxation, Circular Guoshuifa 2009 no.2, 8 Jan.2009; English text available at KPMG http://www.kpmg.com/cn/en/whatwedo/tax/global-transfer-pricing-services/pages/china-transfer-pricing-regulations.aspx.

[SaterianoB:11]Adam Sateriano and Peter Burrows: "Apple's Supply-Chain Secret: Hoard Lasers"; *Bloomberg Businessweek*, 7 Nov.2011, pp.35-37.

[Savodnik:13]Peter Savodnik: "Gimme Shelter"; *Blomberg Businessweek*, 21 Jan.2013, pp.66-67.

[Saxton:99]Jim Saxton: Tax Expenditures: A Review and Analysis; Joint Economic Committee, United States Congress, Aug.1999.

[Schaefer:04]Bernie Schaeffer: Dynamic Market Opportunities; PRNnewswire, 17 Dec.2004.

[Schapiro:09]Mary L. Schapiro: Address to Practising Law Institute's 'SEC Speaks in 2009' Program; U.S. Securities and Exchange Commission, Ronald Reagan International Trade Center, 6 Feb.2009.

[Scheier:11]Bruce Scheier: Do Corporations have a Right to Privacy?; Scheier on Security, 20 Jan.2011. http://www.schneier.com/blog/archives/2011/01/do_corporations.html.

[SchilitP:10]Howard Mark Schilit and Jeremy Perler: *How to Detect Accounting Gimmicks & Fraud in Financial Reports*, 3rd ed.; McGraw-Hill, 2010.

[Schlunk:00]Herwig J. Schlunk: "The Zen of Corporate Capital Structure Neutrality"; *Michigan Law Review*, Vol.99 no.2, Nov.2000, pp.410-451.

[Schlunk:06]Herwig J. Schlunk: "A Minimalist Approach to Corporate Income Taxation"; SMU *Law Review*, Vol.59 no.2, Spring2006, pp.785-834.

[Schmidt:12]Robert Schmidt: "Meet the Man Who Is Defending the 1%"; *Bloomberg Businessweek*, 20 Feb.2012, p.32.

[Schuster:11] Steve Schuster: "Samuel Maruca: Strategic Case Selection Key Aspect of Transfer Pricing Practice; BNA Daily Tax Report, 29 July 2011.

[Schwarcz:04]Steven L. Schwarcz: "Rethinking the Discourse Paradigm in a World of Complexity"; *University of Illinois Law Review*, Vol.2004 no.1, University of Illinois School of Law, 2004, pp.1-37.

[SEC:03]U.S. Securities and Exchange Commission: Strengthening the Commission's Requirements Regarding Auditor Independence; SEC, 27 Mar.2003, http://www.sec.gov/rules/final/33-8183.htm.

[SEC:11]U.S. Securities and Exchange Commission: Financial Reporting Manual; U.S. Securities and Exchange Commission, Division of Corporate Finance, 1 July 2011, Reference 17 CFR part 211.

[SeshasaiG:09]Satwik Seshasai and Amar Gupta: "The 24-hour Knowledge Factory"; *ACM Transactions on Internet Technology*, Aug.2009.

[Seymour:12]Jim Seymour et al.: 4G Mobile Broadband Evolution; 4Gamericas, Jan.2012. <4gamericas.org>.

[Shakespeare:1597]William Shakespeare: *Romeo and Juliet*; first quarto edition, 1597.

[Sharman:06]Jason C. Sharman: *Havens in a Storm*: *The Struggle for Global Tax Regulation*; Cornell University Press, 2006.

[Sharpe:85]William F. Sharpe: *Investments*; Prentice-Hall, 1985.

[Shaviro:11]Daniel Shaviro: "The Rising Tax-Electivity of U.S. Corporate Residence"; Tax Law Review, Vol.64 no.3, Spring 2011, p.333.

[Shaw:06]Helen Shaw: "Must Reading for IRS agents"; *CFO magazine*, 31 May 2006.

[Shaxson:11]Nicholas Shaxson: *Treasure Islands, Tax Havens and the Men Who Stole the World*; The Bodley Head, London, 2011.

[Shay:12]Stephen E. Shay: Testimony to Congress; Permanent Subcommittee on Investigations, U.S. Congress, 20 Sep.2012.

[Sheppard:04]Hale E. Sheppard: "Reduced Tax Rates on Foreign Dividends Under JGTRRA: Ambiguities and Opportunities"; *Journal of International Taxation*, Jul.2004, pp. 14, 16–17.

[ShimSD:10]Jae K. Shim, Joel G. Siegel, and Nick Dauber: 2009-2010, *Corporate Controller's Handbook of Financial Management*; CCH-Wolters, 2010.

[Shiner:12]Keegan Shiner: The Corporate Tax Evasion Task Force; Community Tax Relief, 21 Mar.2012.

[Shropshire:09]Philip Shropshire: A Combination of Legislative Actions and Increased IRS Capability and Capacity are Required to Reduce the Multi-Billion U.S. International Tax Gap; Treasury Inspector General for Tax Administration, 2009-IE-R001, 27 Jan.2009.

[Shulman:08]Douglas H. Shulman: Written Testimony of Douglas Shulman, Commissioner of Internal Revenue, before the Senate Committee on Homeland Security and Governmental Affairs' Perma-nent Subcommittee on Investigations Hearing on Tax Haven Financial Institutions: Their Formation and Administration of Offshore Entities and Accounts for Use by U.S. Clients, 17 Jul.2008.

[Shulman:10C]Douglas H. Shulman: Prepared Remarks of Commissioner of Internal Revenue to New York State Bar Association Taxation Section Annual Meeting in New York City; IRS, 26 Jan.2010,

[Shulman:10D]Douglas H. Shulman: Prepared Remarks of Commissioner of Internal Revenue before the OECD/BIAC; 8 Jun.2010, Washington DC, http://www.oecd.org/document/16/0,3746,en_2649_33749_45425296_1_1_1_1,00.html.

[Shulman:10R]Douglas H. Shulman: IRS Realigns and Renames Large Business Division, Enhances Focus on International Tax Administration; IRS IR-2010-08, 4 Aug.2010.

[Simms:11] James Simms: "Japan Needs to Muffle That Hollow Sound", Wall Street Journal, 9 Dec.2011.

[Simpson:02] Glenn R. Simpson: "Enjoy, A New Twist in Tax Avoidance: Firms Send Best Ideas Abroad"; Wall Street Journal, 24 June 2002.

[Simpson:05] Glenn R. Simpson: "Irish Subsidiary Lets Microsoft Slash Taxes in U.S. and Europe"; The Wall Street Journal, 7 Nov.2005, p. A1.

[SlavinK:06] Nathan S. Slavin and Abu Ryan Khan: "In-Process R&D in Business Acquisitions More Disclosure Needed for Transparency and Comparability"; The CPA Journal, August, 2006.

[Slemrod:94]Joel B. Slemrod: "On the High-Income Laffer Curve"; J. Slemrod (ed.), *Tax Progressivity and Income Inequality*, Cambridge University Press, 1994, pp.177-210.

[Slemrod:95]Joel B. Slemrod: "Professional Opinions About Tax Policy, 1994 and 1934"; *National Tax Journal*, Mar.1995, Vol.85 no.2, pp.121-147; also in [Slemrod:99].

[Slemrod:96]Joel B. Slemrod (ed.): *The Taxation of Multinational Corporations*; Kluwer Academic Publishers, 1996.

[Slemrod:99]Joel B. Slemrod (ed.): *Tax Policy in the Real World*; Cambridge University Press, 1999.

[SlemrodB:08]Joel B. Slemrod and Jon Bakija: *Taxing Ourselves, A Citizen's Guide to the Debate over Taxes*, 4th edition; MIT Press, first edition 1999.

[SlemrodW:09]Joel Slemrod, and John D. Wilson: "Tax Competition with Parasitic Tax Havens"; *Journal of Public Economics*, Vol.93 no.11-12, 2009, pp.1261-1270.

[Smith:1759]Adam Smith: *The Theory of Moral Sentiments*; 1756, reprinted by Uplifting Publications, Amazon Kindle edition, 2010.

[Smith:1776]Adam Smith: *The Wealth of Nations*; 1776, Amazon Kindle edition, 2009.

[Smith:97]Gordon V. Smith: Trademark Valuations, 3rd; Wiley, 1997.

[Smith:11]Judge William E. Smith: Uniloc v. Microsoft; United States District Court for the District of Rhode Island in Case No. 03-CV-0440, 4 Jan.2011.

[SmithEa:12]Patrick Smith, Jason Johns, David Wong, Mary Lee, Chris Bard, and Hoon Lee: The Research Credit and Deduction for Passthrough Entities; *The Tax Adviser*, AICPA, 1 May 2012.

[SmithP:00]Gordon Smith and Russell Parr; *Valuation of Intellectual Property and Intangible Assets*; 3rd edition; Wiley, 2000.

[SmithP:05]Gordon Smith and Russell Parr: *Intellectual Property*, 4th edition; Wiley 2005.

[Sougiannis:94]Theodore Sougiannis: "The Accounting Based Valuation of Corporate R&D"; *Accounting Review*, Vol.69 no.1, Jan.1994, pp.44-68.

[Spolsky:04]Joel Spolsky: *Joel on Software*; Apress, 2004.

[SpringerEa:11]Pamela Springer et al.: Manta, Where small business grows; retrieved 2011. http://www.manta.com/coms2/page_about_manta.

[SSA:11]SSA: Social Security History; http://www.ssa.gov/history/briefhistory3.html, and <.../BudgetTreatment.html>, retrieved Oct 2011.

[SSN:11]SSA: Wage Statistics for 2010; Social Security Online, Social Security Administration, retrieved 30 Oct.2011, http://www.ssa.gov/cgi-bin/netcomp.cgi?year=2010.

[Stahl:11]Leslie Stahl: A look at the world's new corporate tax havens; CBS News, 60 Minutes, 25 Mar.2011; http://www.youtube.com/watch?v=MxgezC4KhXQ.

[Stapleton:12]Michael Stapleton: Why Ireland? Investing and Setting up a Business in Ireland; IDA Ireland, Sep.2012.

[Statec:10]Statec: Portrait économique et social du Luxembourg; Government of Luxembourg, Statistics Department, Nov.2010, http://www.statistiques.public.lu/.

[Steele:10]Jacien Steele: CFO Insights: Taxing board discussions? A framework for action; Deloitte Development LLC, 2010.

[Stern:11]Andy Stern: "China's Superior Economic Model"; *Wall Street Journal*, 1 Dec.2011.

[Stewart:11]David Stewart: "IRS to Take a 'Fresh Look' at Cost Sharing Case Inventory, Transfer Pricing Director Says"; *Tax Notes*, 28 Jul.2011.

[Stewart:12]James B. Stewart: "Tax me if you Can"; *New Yorker*, 19 Mar.2012, pp.46-53.

[Stiglitz:06]Joseph Stiglitz: *Making Globalization Work*; W.W. Norton, 2006.

[Stobbs:00]Gregory Stobbs: *Software Patents*, 2nd edition; Aspen Publishers, 2000.

[StolowyJ:01]Hervé Stolowy and Anne Jeny-Cazavan: "International accounting disharmony: the case of intangibles"; *Accounting, Auditing & Accountability Journal*, MCB UP Ltd., 2001, Vol.14 no.4, pp.477–497.

[Stossel:12]John Stossel: *No, They Can't, Why Government Fails-But Individuals Succeed*; Threshold Editions, Simon and Schuster Digital Sales Inc, 2012.

[Studt:07]Tim Studt: "R&D Outsourcing Becomes More Strategic"; *R&D Magazine*, Jun.2007, pp.26-29, http://www.rdmag.com;guidance/references.

[Styron:07]W. Joey Styron: "Transfer Pricing and Tax Planning"; *CPA Journal*, Vol.77 no.11, 2007 pp.40-45.

[Sullivan:04]Martin A. Sullivan: "Data Show Dramatic Shift of Profits to Tax Havens"; *Tax Analysts*, 2004.

[Sullivan:06]Martin A. Sullivan: "Drug Firms Move Profits to Save Billions"; *Tax Notes*, TaxAnalysts, 7 Aug.2006.

[Sullivan:09]Martin A. Sullivan: "Economic Analysis: So 1980s: The Return of Nickel-and-Dime Tax Policy"; *Tax Notes*, Vol.151 no.6, 6 Aug.2009.

[Sullivan:10M]Martin A. Sullivan: Multinationals and Jobs; *Tax Notes*, 8 Feb.2010.

[Sullivan:10P] Martin A. Sullivan: "Pharmaceutical Companies Keep Profits Abroad"; Tax Notes, Mar.2010.

[Sullivan:11]Martin A. Sullivan: *Corporate Tax Reform: Taxing Profits in the 21st Century*; Apress, 2011.

[Sullivan:11L]Martin A. Sullivan: What the Debt Limit Debacle Teaches Us About Tax Reform; Tax.com, 18 Jul.2011.

[SullivanZS:09]William F. Sullivan, Thomas A. Zaccaro, and Adam D. Schneir: "The SEC's View of Auditor Independence"; *Bloomberg Law Reports -- Risk and Compliance*, Vol.2 no.1, 2009.

[Summers:08]Lawrence Summers: "A Strategy to Promote Healthy Globalization"; *Financial Times*, 4 May 2008.

[Surowiecki:04]James Surowiecki: *The Wisdom of Crowds*; First Anchor Books, Random House, 2004.

[SurreyMcD:85]Stanley S. Surrey and Paul R. McDaniel: *Tax Expenditures*; Harvard University Press, 1985.

[Sveiby:97]Karl-Erik Sveiby: *The New Organizational Wealth*; Berrett-Koehler Publishers, 1997.

[Swenson:01]Deborah L. Swenson: "Tax Reforms and Evidence of Transfer Pricing"; *National Tax Journal*, Vol.54 no.1, Mar.2001, pp.7-25.

[SwensonS:11]C. David Swenson and Gary B. Stone: Transfer Pricing Perspectives; Thought Leadership Journal, Price Waterhouse Coopers, PWC, 2011.

[Taleb:07]Nassim Nicholas Taleb: *The Black Swan: The Impact of the Highly Improbable*; Encounter Books, Random House, 2007.

[TambeH:10]Prasanna B. Tambe and Lorin M. Hitt: "How Offshoring Affects Workers"; *Communications of the ACM*, Vol.53 no.10, Oct.2010, pp.62-70.

[Tang:93]Roger Tang: Transfer Pricing in the 1990's: Tax and Management Perspectives"; Quorum, 1993.

[Tanzi:11]Vito Tanzi: *Government versus Markets: the Changing Economic Role of the State*; Cambridge University Press, May 2011.

[TanziS:00]Vito Tanzi and Ludger Schuknecht: *Public Spending in the 20th Century: A Global Perspective*; Cambridge University Press, 2000.

[TaylorFC:06]Paul Taylor, Cary Funk, and Peyton Craighill: A Barometer of Modern Morals; Pew Research Center, Washington DC, 28 Mar.2006.

[TempleWest:12]Patrick Temple-West: IRS forms SWAT Team Crack Down on Tax Dodgers; *Accounting Today*, 20 Mar.2012.

[Terr:10]Leonard B. Terr (chair): Handling Federal Tax Controversies in the United States; North American Tax Practice Group, Baker & McKenzie, 2010.

[Thomas:11]Library of Congress: THOMAS; The official source for legislative information; <http://thomas.loc.gov/home/thomas.php>, accessed 2011.

[Thomas:12]Ken Thomas: "Who's the Rich Guy?"; Associated Press, *Miami Herald*, 10 Apr.2012.

[Thompson:12]Derek Thompson: How We Pay Taxes: 11 Charts; *The Atlantic*, 16 April 2012.

[Thomson:12]Ainsly Thomson: "U.S. Firms Face British Grilling on Tax Practoces"; *The Wall Street Journal*, 12 Nov. 2012.

[Tichon:09]Nicole Tichon: "Tax Shell Game: The Taxpayer Cost of Offshore Corporate Havens"; U.S. Public Interest Research Group, Apr.2009, http://www.uspirg.org/news-releases/tax-and-budget/tax-and-budget-news/washington-d.c.-taxpayers-footing-a-100-billion-bill-for-tax-dodgers.

[Tobin:69]James Tobin: "A general equilibrium approach to monetary theory"; Journal of Money Credit and Banking, Vol. 1 no.1, 1969, pp.15-29.

[Toder:00]Eric J. Toder: "Tax Cuts or Spending—Does it Make a Difference?"; *National Tax Journal*, Vol.53 no.3, part 1, Sep.2000, pp.361-372.

[Toder:11]Eric Toder: Closing Loopholes Won't be Simple; *New York Times*, 2 Feb.2011.

[ToderB:07]Eric J. Toder and Lily Batchelder: "Business Taxation"; Chapter II-12, *The Tax Policy Briefing Book*, Urban-Brookings Tax Policy Center, Dec.2004.

[Toombs:13]Zach Toombs: "Passage of tax deal hangs in the Balance"; *New York Times*, 2 Jan.2013.

[TownsendJ:99]John A. Townsend and Lawrence R. Jones, jr.: DHL - A Strategy Lesson in Transfer Pricing Controversy; Townsend & Jones Newsletter, Jan.1999.

[Trivedi:12]Shamik Trivedi: "DeNard Describes Impending LB&I Domestic Realignment"; *Tax Notes Today*, 4 Oct.2012.

[Trumbull:11]Mark Trumbull: "Deficit Super Committee Fails: Who's to Blame"; *Christian Science Monitor*, 21 Nov.2011.

[TTB:11]TTB: About TTB; The Alcohol and Tobacco Tax and Trade Bureau of the U.S. Treasury, http://www.tbd.gov/about, 2011.

[TuerffEa:08]T. Timothy Tuerff, Daniel Shaviro, Douglas A. Shackelford, Timothy M. McDonald, and Michael Mundaca: "Panel Session 4: Alternatives for Taxation of Foreign Source Income"; *Taxes—The Tax Magazine*, CCH Wolters Kluwer, Jun.2008, pp.71-86.

[Tyson:11]Laura d'Andrea Tyson: "The Logic of Cutting Corporate Taxes"; *New York Times*, 8 Apr.2011.

[Tzu:340BCE]Sun Tzu: *The Art of War*, translated by Samuel B. Griffith; Oxford University Press, 1983.

[UScensus:08]U.S. Census Bureau: Statistics about Business Size (including Small Business); US Department of Commerce, 2008, retrieved April 2010, http://www.census.gov/econ/smallbus.html.

[UScensus:10]U.S. Census Bureau: Facts about the Census 2010 Residence rule; US Department of Commerce, 2010.

[USCoC:11]U.S. Chamber of Commerce: Jobs Agenda, Intellectual Property; http://www.uschamber.com/ip, 2011.

[UStreasury:07]U.S. Treasury: *Report to Congress on Earnings Stripping, Transfer Pricing and U.S. Income Tax Treaties*; Treasury Department, Office of Tax Analysis, Nov.2007.

[UStreasury:11]U.S. Treasury Department: Investing in U.S. Competetiveness: The Benefits of Enhancing the Research and Experimentation (R&E) Tax Credit; Treasury Department, Office of Tax Policy, 25 Mar.2011.

[Vance:10]Ashlee Vance: "Suit Over Faulty Computers Highlights Dell's Decline'; *New York Times*, 28 Jun.2010.

[vandenDool:12]Pim van den Dool: "NS ontwijkt belasting via Ierland"; *Nieuwe Rotterdamse Krant*, 1 Sep.2012.

[vanDijkWM:06]Michiel van Dijk, Francis Weyzig, and Richard Murphy: *The Netherlands: A Tax Haven*?; Stichting Onderzoek Multinationale Ondernemingen (SOMO), Amsterdam, Nov.2006, <bit.ly/aC2zuB>.

[vanHiltenEa:10]Dirk van Hilten, Richard Fletcher, Antonio Russo, Clive Jia-A-Joen, Margreet G. Nijhof, and Pawel Wrblewki: Maximizing Tax Benefits from Intangible Property Development and Ownership; Baker McKenzie, The Netherlands, 10 Mar.2010, http://www.bakermckenzie.com/files/Uploads/Documents/Amterdam/Ahead of Tax/ pn_amsterdam_aheadoftax_maximizingtaxbenefits_russovarious_mar10.pdfl.

[VatterW:96]Harold G. Vatter and John F. Walker (eds.): *History of the U.S. Economy since World War II*; Sharpe, 1996.

[Vaud:09]Canton de Vaud: Economic Promotion; Office for Economic Affairs, retrieved 2009, http://www.dev.ch/.

[Vause:09]Bob Vause: *Guide to Analysing Companies*, 5th edition; Bloomberg Press, 2009.

[VBM:04]editor (VBM): The Value of Intellectual Capital, Do intangible assets yield a return above the cost of capital?; Value Based Management, Bilthoven, The Netherlands, http://www.valuebasedmanagement.net/faq_do_intangible_assets_create_value.html, retrieved 2004.

[Veritas:09]US Tax Court: "Veritas Software and Subsidiaries v. Commissioner of Internal Revenue; 133 T.C. no.14, Docket no.12075-06, filed 10 Dec.2009"; *Tax Management Transfer Pricing Report*, Vol.18 no 15, 2009, pp.890-925.

[VidanoT:07]Thomas A. Vidano and Carol B. Tan: Request for comments on Temp. Treas. Reg. § 1.482-9T(b)(4)(i); IRS, Office of Associate Chief Counsel (International), 2007, finalized Jan 2012.

[Vigueras:08] Juan Hdez. Vigueras: Andorra: A Tax Haven as Solid as Liechtenstein and Switzerland; Tax Justice Network, May 2008.

[Violino:09]Bob Violino: "Time to Reboot"; *Communications of the ACM*, Vol.52 no.4, Apr.2009, p.19.

[VolckerEa:10]Paul A. Volcker (chair), Austan Goolsbee, et al.: The Report on Tax Reform Options, Simplification, Compliance, and Corporate Taxation; The President's Economic Recovery Advisory Board (PERAB), Aug.2010.

[W:83]Gio Wiederhold: *Database Design*, 2nd edition; McGraw-Hill, 1983; republished in the ACM Digital Library, 2002.

[W:95]Gio Wiederhold: "Modeling and Software Maintenance"; in Michael P. Papazoglou (ed.): OOER'95: *Object-Oriented and Entity Relationship Modelling*; LNCS 1021, Springer Verlag, Dec.1995, pp.1-20.

[W:06]Gio Wiederhold: "What is Your Software Worth?"; *Communications of the ACM*, Vol.49 no.9, Sep.2006, pp. 65–75.

[W:07]Gio Wiederhold: What is Your Software Worth?; full study report, updated 11 Apr.2007, at <http://infolab.stanford.edu/pub/gio/inprogress.html#worth>.

[W:08]Gio Wiederhold: "Determining Software Investment Lag"; *Journal of Universal Computer Science* (JUCS), Springer Verlag, Vol.14 no.22, 2008.

[W:09]Gio Wiederhold: CS 207, The Economics of Software; Stanford University, Fall 2009, 2010, 2011, <cs.stanford.edu/wiki/cs207/>.

[W:11]Gio Wiederhold: "Follow the IP: How Does Industry pay Programmer's Salaries When the Required Intellectual Property Is Offshored?"; *Communications of the ACM*, Vol.54 no.1, Jan.2011, pp.65-74.

[W:12]Gio Wiederhold: Spreadsheet to accompany *Valuation of Intellectiual Capital*; <infolab.stanford.edu/pub/gio/VIC/MNC.pdf> and <infolab.stanford.edu/pub/gio/VIC/MNC.xlsx>.

[Wald:98]Matthew L. Wald: "F.A.A. Inspectors Are Divided Over Safety Violations by ValuJet"; *New York Times*, 1 Mar.1998.

[Walker:06]David M. Walker: Tax Compliance, Challenges to Corporate Tax Enforement; US Government Accountability Office report GAO-06-851T, 7 Jul.2006, 26pp.

[Walsh:11]Rep. Joe Walsh: Capital Gains Inflation Act of 2011; US Congress, H.R. 2935, 15 Sep.2011.

[Wamoff:12]Steve Wamoff: Policy Options to Raise Revenue; Citizens for Tax Justice, 8 Mar.2012.

[Waters:10]C. Donald J. Waters: Global Logistics: *New Directions in Supply Chain Management*, 6th edition; Kogan Page, 2010.

[Wayne:12]Leslie Wayne: How Delaware Thrives as a Corporate Tax Haven; *New York Times*, 30 Jun.2012.

[Weiler:95]Dave G. Weiler: More on Trademark Royalties; AUS, Mt.Laurel NJ, 1995, http://www.ausinc.com/news/More_on_Trademark.pdf.

[Wessel:11]David Wessel: "U.S. Firms Shift Hiring Abroad"; *Wall Street Journal*, 19 Apr.2011.

[Wessner:08]Charles W. Wessner (ed.): An Assessment of the Small Business Innovation Research (SBIR) Program; NRC, NAS, 2008.

[Weyzig:12] Francis Weyzig; "Tax Treaty Shopping: Structural Determinants of Foreign Direct Investment Routed through The Netherlands"; Journal of International Tax and Public Finance, 2012.

[WGM:06]Gio Wiederhold, Amar Gupta, and Rajat Mittal: "The Value of Outsourced Software"; in M. Josef and B. Meyer (eds.): *Software Engineering Approaches for Offshore and Outsourced Develop-ment (SEAFOOD)*, Springer Verlag Lecture Notes in Computer Science, 2007, pp.141-151.

[WGN:10]Gio Wiederhold, Amar Gupta, and Erich Neuhold: "Offshoring and Transfer of Intellectual Property"; *Information Resources Management Journal (IRMJ)*; Vol.23 no.1, Jan.-Mar.2010, pp.74-93.

[WhittingtonD:12]O. Ray Whittington and Patrick R. Delaney: *CPA Exam Reciew 2012*; Wiley, 2012.

[WilliamsF:06]Jonathan Williams and Patrick Fleenor: Options for Reforming the U.S. Corporate Income Tax; Fiscal Facts no.58, the Tax Foundation, 8 May 2006.

[Wills:11]John Wills: The Competitive Advantage Period as a Measure of Economic Life; Bureau of National Affairs (BNA), Tax Management Transfer Pricing Report Analysis, 1 Dec.2011.

[Wilson:89]James Q. Wilson: Bureaucracy; Basic Books, 1989.

[Wilson:07]Fred Wilson: Failure rates in early-stage venture deals; Union Square Ventures Fund, 29 Nov.2007.

[WilsonB:01]D. Mark Wilson and William Beach: The Economic Impact of President Bush's Tax Relief Plan; The Heritage Foundation Center for Data Analysis, Report #01-01, 27 Apr.2001.

[Wipfel:09]Hildegard Wipfel: International Taxes on Financial Transactions; The International Alliance of Catholic Development Agencies (CIDSE), Austria, Nov.2009.

[Wolf:05]Martin Wolf: *Why Globalization Works*; Yale Nota Bene, Yale University Press, 2005.

[Wolverson:11]Roya Wolverson: Outsourcing Jobs and Taxes; Renewing America, Council on Foreign Relations, 11 Feb.2011.

[Woodall:11]Robert Woodall: H.R. 25, the FairTax Proposal; U.S Congress, 6 Jan.2011.

[Woodbury:1845]Charles G. Woodbury: Davoll et al. v. Brown; US Circuit Court, I.56.

[Woolf:10]Nicholas Woolf: Royal Charter Presentation for Tax Advisers Livery Company; The Worshipful Company of Tax Advisers, 14 May 2010, http://www.taxadvisers.org.uk/allnews/article.4.

[Worldbank:10]World Bank: Data on Country GDP; 2010.

[Worldwide:12]Worldwide-tax: Key Data on World Taxes; http://www.worldwide-tax.com, accessed 24 Mar.2012.

[Wright:11]Tamu N. Wright: Transfer Pricing: "AstraZeneca Announces Plan to Pay IRS $1.1 Billion to Settle Transfer Pricing Issues"; *BNA Daily Tax Report*, 30 Mar.2011.

[WTB:00]OTPR: World Tax Database; Office of Tax Policy Research, Uni. of Michigan, 2000, http://www.bus.umich.edu/otpr/otpr/default.asp.

[WTGS:09]Gio Wiederhold, Shirley Tessler, Amar Gupta, and David Branson Smith: "The Valuation of Technology-Based Intellectual Property in Offshoring Decisions"; *Communications of the Association for Information Systems* (*CAIS*), Vol.24 no.31, Jan.2009.

[Wunder:09]Haroldene Wunder: "The Scope and Distribution of Permanent Reinvested Earnings"; *Tax Notes*, 6 Oct.2009.

[Wydick:08]Bruce Wydick: *Games in Economic Development*; Cambridge University Press, 2008.

[Yablon:10]Jeffrey L. Yablon: Avoidance, Evasion, and Planning; Tax Analysts, Sep.2010.

[Yamamura:12]K. Yamamura: Changing corporate tax rules; Sacramento Bee, 15 Oct.2012.

[YoungV:11]Christobal Young and Charles Varner: Millionaire Migration and State Taxation of Top Incomes: Evidence from a Natural Experiment; *National Tax Journal*, Jun.2011, Vol.64 no.2 pt 1, pp.255–284.

[Zeidman:11]Bob Zeidman: The Software IP Detective's Handbook, Measurement, Comparison, and Infringe-ment Detection; Prentice Hall, Pearson Publishing, 2011.

[Zerbe:10]Dean Zerbe: IRS Audits Small Biz More, Big Guys Less; Expert View, FORBES.com, 11 Apr.2010.

[Zoromé:87]Ahmed Zoromé: Concept of Offshore Financial Centers: In Search of an Operational Definition; International Monetary Fund (IMF), Working Paper/07/87, 1987, http://www.imf.org/external/pubs/ft/wp/2007/wp0787.pdfl.

Author and Book Background

Gio Wiederhold is professor emeritus of Computer Science at Stanford University. He holds a PhD from the University of California, San Francisco, and an honorary D.Sc. from the National University of Ireland, Galway. He has been elected as a fellow of the ACM, the IEEE, and the ACMI.

Gio was born in Italy and lived in Germany and The Netherlands. He emigrated to the USA in 1958. His first 16 working years were spent in industry as a programmer, software designer, manager, and division director. He became a professor at Stanford in 1976, advising PhD students in several departments, integrating concepts from multiple disciplines. His students now have responsible positions in finance, academia, and industry. He currently teaches two courses at Stanford: Business on the Internet and Software Economics.

Breaks from Stanford include tours as visiting professor at IIT Kanpur in India, at EPFL in Switzerland, representing UNDP at projects in Asia, as a researcher at IBM Germany, and as a program manager at DARPA of the US Department of Defense, initiating the Intelligent Integration of Information (I3) program. I3 supported initiatives like the Digital Library, leading to several significant Internet applications and companies, including Google.

Gio has been consulting on technical and business issues since 1963 in government, academia, and industry, including several multinationals in finance, computing, and pharmaceuticals. Related travel has allowed him to understand the torturous global paths from innovation to the generation of income needed to sustain industrial enterprises. The first brush with taxation occurred in 1971, advising the Luxembourg operation of a US bank.

Gio has authored and coauthored over 400 books, papers, and reports, covering a wide variety of scientific and business domains. His first book was published by Springer, a 1971 monograph on *Databases for Healthcare*. His 1977 book, *Database Design*, published by McGraw Hill, became a standard in quantitative database courses at colleges and universities.

G. Wiederhold, *Valuing Intellectual Capital: Multinationals and Taxhavens*, Management for Professionals 23, DOI 10.1007/978-1-4614-6611-6,

The writing of a book on *Valuing Intellectual Capital* was motivated by a need to bring clarity to the three-way interaction of technology, modern business models, and the economic underpinnings of taxation—all essential domains when dealing with the export of intellectual property (IP). Intellectual resources play a crucial role in industrial growth. The intellectual capital maintained by corporations drives their current and future value.

The need for a comprehensive exposition of IP flow in high-technology enterprises became clear during a *Rebooting Computer Science* meeting organized by Peter Denning [Violino:09]. It was not possible to convey the issues and conflicts arising when assigning rights to IP in global and offshore commerce to my colleagues, all important contributors to its creation. Simple statements can only present simple concepts, which then are used to propose simplistic solutions. A major objective for this book was to provide recommendations to assure that taxation processes involving IP are transparent and fair. An unexpected result is Recommendation R20: abolish corporate taxation. It derives from the insight gained while writing this book and analyzing the handling of intellectual capital. It appears that globally taxation of corporations cannot be fair under any reasonable scenario.

Gio's web page is at http://infolab.stanford.edu/people/gio.html.

Index

G. Wiederhold, *Valuing Intellectual Capital: Multinationals and Taxhavens*, Management for Professionals 23, DOI 10.1007/978-1-4614-6611-6,

D

G

J

Q

R

T

Printed by Publishers' Graphics LLC